1 MONTH OF
FREE
READING

at

www.ForgottenBooks.com

By purchasing this book you are eligible for one month membership to ForgottenBooks.com, giving you unlimited access to our entire collection of over 1,000,000 titles via our web site and mobile apps.

To claim your free month visit:
www.forgottenbooks.com/free918758

ISBN 978-0-265-97984-6
PIBN 10918758

This book is a reproduction of an important historical work. Forgotten Books uses state-of-the-art technology to digitally reconstruct the work, preserving the original format whilst repairing imperfections present in the aged copy. In rare cases, an imperfection in the original, such as a blemish or missing page, may be replicated in our edition. We do, however, repair the vast majority of imperfections successfully; any imperfections that remain are intentionally left to preserve the state of such historical works.

ACTS OF A LOCAL NATURE,

PASSED AT THE FIRST SESSION OF THE

THIRTY-FOURTH GENERAL ASSEMBLY

OF THE

STATE OF OHIO;

Begun and held in the City of Columbus,

DECEMBER 7, 1835.

IN THE THIRTY-FOURTH YEAR OF SAID STATE.

VOL. XXXIV.

PRINTED BY AUTHORITY.

Columbus:

JAMES B. GARDINER, PRINTER TO THE STATE.

1836.

LAWS OF A LOCAL NATURE.

To amend an act, passed March 7, 1835, entitled "An act to amend an act, to incorporate the village of Cleveland."

Sec. 1. *Be it enacted by the General Assembly of the State of Ohio,* That the committee created by virtue of the act, passed March, 7th, 1835, are hereby authorized to assess upon the property in said village, any sum of money expended by the trustees thereof, in grading and improving the streets in said village, by virtue of an act for that purpose, passed February 18, 1834, over and above the sum originally assessed and collected therefor, which new assessment, shall be made upon the same principle as the original assessment, according to the supposed benefit accruing to the property assessed.

Sec. 2. The committee, on the completion of the assessment roll, shall file it in the office of the recorder of said village, where it shall remain at least five days for examination, notice of which shall be given in one or more newspapers printed in said village: after which time, the committee may correct any errors that may have been discovered, and may also correct any inequalities in the assessment, by adding to, or deducting from the amount first assessed, after which, they shall file the amended roll with said recorder.

Sec. 3. The sums so assessed shall be added to the sums assessed by the committee, for damages under the act of March 7, 1835, and shall be a lien upon the property assessed, and shall be collected by the marshal, together with the sums assessed for damages, within four months after receiving the duplicate, as provided by the act of February 18, 1834, and in case of delinquency, the like interest and penalty shall be chargeable, as provided in said act.

Sec. 4. All persons claiming to be injured by the improvements, so as aforesaid made in said village, who shall omit to present their claims to the said committee, shall be deemed to have waived the same.

WM. SAWYER,
Speaker of the House of Representatives.
ELIJAH VANCE,
Speaker of the Senate.

December 17th, 1835.

AN ACT

To incorporate the members of the Methodist Episcopal Church of Cadiz, in Harrison county.

Sec. 1. *Be it enacted by the General Assembly of the State of Ohio,* That Edmund Tipton, William Tingley; John Davis, William Boyce, Isaac Meek, Philip Trine and others, their associates, members of the Methodist Episcopal Church of Cadiz, in Harrison county, for the time being, and their successors, be, and the same are hereby created a corporation and body politic, by the name and style of the "Methodist Episcopal Church of Cadiz," and as such, shall remain and have perpetual succession.

Sec. 2. That the members of said corporation shall convene on the first Monday of May next, and on the first Monday of May annually thereafter, ten days public notice having first been given, and elect nine trustees from their own body; who shall continue in office for one year, and until their successors shall have been chosen; a majority of whom shall form a quorum for the transaction of all the business of the corporation; they shall have power to fill all vacancies which may occur, from time to time, in their body, by death, resignation, or otherwise; and the person or persons chosen to fill such vacancies, shall continue in office until the next stated annual election, and until their successors be chosen.

Sec. 3. That said corporation shall be capable of receiving, acquiring, and holding, either by gift, grant, devise, or purchase, any estate, real or personal, for the sole use of said corporation: *Provided,* That the annual income of all such property, shall not exceed the sum of two thousand dollars; and all the estate so acquired, holden and possessed, by the said corporation, as well as all the estate acquired, holden and possessed, by the Methodist Episcopal Church, in the town of Cadiz, in said county, at the time said corporation may commence its corporate powers, the trustees thereof are hereby authorized and empowered to sell, lease, or otherwise invest; and the proceeds, rents, issues and profits thereof, to receive and dispose of, for the sole use and benefit of said corporation: *Provided,* That nothing in this act contained, shall be construed to authorize the corporation hereby created, to divert any real estate in Cadiz, which may have heretofore been conveyed or donated to, and in trust for the Methodist Episcopal Church, from the purposes and uses expressed in such deed or donation; and it shall be the duty of the trustees, at the annual meeting, on the first Monday of May, in each year, to make out for the inspection of the said corporation, an exhibit, containing a full and fair account of the receipts and disbursements of the preceding year.

Sec. 4. That said corporation, by its name aforesaid, shall be capable of suing and being sued, defending and being defended, pleading and being impleaded, in all courts having competent jurisdiction.

Sec. 5. That Matthew Simpson, Edmund Tipton, Robert M'Kee, James Poulson, William Tingley, Philip Trine, John Davis, Elijah Laisure and George White, shall be, and they are hereby constituted trustees of said corporation, to continue in office, from and after the passage of this act, until the first Monday of May, one thousand eight hundred and thirty-six, and until their successors shall be chosen.

Sec. 6. . Any future Legislature shall have power to alter, amend or repeal this act: *Provided,* Such modification, or repeal shall not affect the title to any real or personal estate, acquired or conveyed under its provisions, or divert the same to any other purpose than originally intended.

WM. SAWYER,
Speaker of the House of Representatives.
ELIJAH VANCE,
Speaker of the Senate.

December 18, 1835.

AN ACT

To change the name of John Pond to that of John M'Neal.

Sec. 1. *Be it enacted by the General Assembly of the State of Ohio,* That the name of John Pond, of the county of Clinton, be, and the same is hereby changed to that of John M'Neal: *Provided,* That nothing herein contained, shall operate or be construed to defeat or affect any right or interest acquired or vested in him by the name of John Pond.

WM. SAWYER,
Speaker of the House of Representatives.
ELIJAH VANCE,
Speaker of the Senate.

December 18, 1835.

AN ACT

To lay out and establish a State road, from East Liberty, in Logan county, to Kenton, in Hardin county.

Sec. 1. *Be it enacted bo the General Assembly of the State of Ohio,* That Job Garwood and Abner Snoddy, of Logan county, and John G. Marks, of Hardin county, are hereby appointed commissioners, and William Scott, Esq. of the county of Hardin, surveyor, to lay out and establish a State road; commencing at East Liberty, in Logan county; thence on the nearest and best route, to the town of Kenton, in Hardin county.

Sec. 2. That the said commissioners are hereby authorized to receive, and appropriate on snid road, all such subscriptions and donations as may be made, for opening and improving the same.

Sec. 3. That the commissioners, and surveyor, as aforesaid, shall, in all respects, be governed by the laws in force, defining the mode of laying out and establishing State roads; and should either of the commissioners or surveyor die, or remove out of the county, or refuse to serve, the county commissioners, of their proper county, are authorized to fill such vacancies as often as the same may occur.

WM. SAWYER,
Speaker of the House of Representatives.
ELIJAH VANCE,
Speaker of the Senate.

December 19, 1835.

AN ACT

An act to incorporate the Universal School of Massillon.

Sec. 1. *Be it enacted by the General Assembly of the State of Ohio,* That Alexander M'Cully, Benjamin Lemoin, Samuel Pease, Osee Welch, and John Everhard, with their associates and successors, shall be, and are hereby created a body politic and corporate, by the name and style of the Universal School of Massillon; with perpetual succession, and by that name shall be capable in law and equity, to receive, purchase, possess and enjoy to them and their successors, any estate, real or personal, and the same to sell, dispose of, and convey; to sue and be sued, to plead and be impleaded, to answer and be answered, to defend and be defended in any court of competent jurisdiction; and also, to have and use a common seal, and the same to break, alter, change or renew at pleasure; and also, to make, ordain and execute such by-laws, ordinances, resolves and regulations, as they may deem necessary and convenient for the government of said corporation, not incompatible with the constitution and laws of the United States, and of this State.

Sec. 2. That any three of the above named persons shall have power to call a meeting, either annual or special, by giving ten days previous notice thereof, by advertisements set up at three of the most public places in the town of Massillon; that the annual meeting of the trustees shall be held on the first Monday of April, of each succeeding year, at which time they shall elect by ballot five trustees, one treasurer, and one secretary, who shall serve for term of one year, and until their successors be chosen; and in case an election should be neglected to be held on that day, the society, for that cause, shall not be dissolved, but it shall be lawful to hold an election at such other time as the by-laws shall direct.

Sec. 3. That the funds of said society shall not be applied or invested for any other than for literary and scientific purposes; the purchase of a lot and building for the use of the society, the purchase of books, maps, charts, newspapers, pamphlets, periodical publications, and the necessary expenses of the institution.

Sec. 4. That this act may be amended or altered by any future Legislature of this State, as they may judge proper.

WM. SAWYER,
Speaker pro tem. of the House of Representatives.
ELIJAH VANCE,
Speaker of the Senate.

December 30th, 1835.

AN ACT

To lay out and establish a State road in the counties of Mercer and Shelby.

Sec. 1. *Be it enacted by the General Assembly of the State of Ohio,* That John Simeson, and Jonas Richardson, of Mercer county; and William N. Flinn, of Shelby county, be, and they are hereby appointed commissioners, to lay out and establish a State road, commencing at some suitable point at or near Nine Mile creek, in Shelby county, and running a north-westwardly direction to section 35, range 2, township 7, in Mercer county; and from thence in a weswardly direction, to intersect the Huntington road at the State line near Fort Recovery, in Mercer county.

Sec. 2. That in case either of the commissioners die, refuse to serve, or remove out of the county, his place shall be supplied by the commissioners of the county where the vacancy shall happen, as often as it may occur.

Sec. 3. That the commissioners shall be govered in all respects by the law now in force defining the mode of laying out and establishing state roads, passed March 14th, 1831, and the expense of laying out and establishing said road shall be paid, as pointed out in said act.

WM. SAWYER,
Speaker of the House of Representatives.
ELIJAH VANCE,
Speaker of the Senate.

December 30, 1835.

AN ACT

To repeal the first clause in the proviso of the seventh section of the act entitled "An act to incorporate the Cleves Bridge and Cleves and Cincinnati Turnpike Company.

Sec. 1. *Be it enacted by the General Assembly of the State of Ohio,* That the first clause in the proviso of the seventh section of the act, entitled "An act to incorporate the Cleves Bridge and Cleves and Cincinnati Turnpike Company," passed January 26th, 1832, which grants to public mails the privilege of passing said bridge, free from toll, be, and the same is hereby repealed.

WM. SAWYER,
Speaker of the House of Representatives.
ELIJAH VANCE,
Speaker of the Senate.

December 30, 1835.

AN ACT

To incorporate the Associate Reformed Church of Piqua, in the county of Miami.

Sec. 1. *Be it enacted by the General Assembly of the State of Ohio,* That John Wiley, Samuel Townsley, and John Hamilton, and their associates, together with such other persons as may hereafter be associated with them, be, and they are hereby created and declared a body corporate and politic, by the name of the Associate Reformed Church of Piqua: and as such shall remain and have perpetual succession; and by their corporate name may contract and be contracted with, sue and be sued, in any court of competent jurisdiction, in all manner of actions, causes, and complaints whatsoever; and may have a common seal, which they may change, alter, or renew at pleasure.

Sec. 2. That the said corporation, by the name and style aforesaid, shall be capable in law of holding property, real, personal, or mixed, either by purchase, gift, grant, devise, or legacy, which may become the property of the said corporation: *Provided*, That the annual income of all such property shall not exceed the sum of two thousand dollars: *And provided, also*, That all such property shall be considered as held in trust, under the management, and at the disposal of said corporation, for the purpose of promoting the interests of said society or congregation; defraying the expenses incident to their mode of worship, and maintaining institutions of charity or education, that may be therewith connected: *Provided, moreover*, That when any money or other property shall be given, granted, bequeathed, or devised to said congregation, for any particular use or purpose, it shall be faithfully applied to such use or purpose; and that the property and other concerns of the corporation shall be under the management and control of trustees to be appointed agreeably to the directions of the congregation.

Sec. 3. That the second Wednesday of April, in the year one thousand eight hundred and thirty-six, and on the second Wednesday in April, in each and every year thereafter, between the hours of twelve, M. and three, P. M. there shall be elected by said congregation, three trustees, and such other officers as the society may deem necessary; who shall hold their offices for one year, and until their successors shall be elected: *Provided*, That in case of any failure to elect officers as aforesaid, the trustees may call a meeting at such time and place as they may think proper, for the purpose of electing such officers.

Sec. 4. That the persons named in the first section of this act, be, and they are hereby appointed trustees until the first election, and until others are elected in their places.

Sec. 5. That the trustees, or any two of them, shall have power to call a meeting of the corporation, either for the election of officers, or for the transaction of other business of the society, by giving, or causing to be given to the society, immediately after public worship, ten days previous notice of said meeting, or by causing notifications thereof to be put up in three or more public places within the limits of said congregations, at least fifteen days before said meeting.

Sec. 6. That any meeting of the congregation, duly assembled, may adopt and establish such by-laws and ordinances, as may be deemed proper and necessary for the good government of said corporation: *Provided*, That such by-laws and ordinances shall be compatible with the constitutions and laws of the United States and of this State.

Sec. 7. That process against said corporation shall be by summons; which shall be served by leaving an attested copy with one or more of the trustees; and such service shall be deemed sufficient in law to bind said corporation.

Sec. 8. That any future Legislature shall have power to modify or re-peal this act: *Provided,* That such modification or repeal shall not affect the title to any real or personal estate, acquired or conveyed, under its provisions, or divert the same to any other purpose than originally in-tended.

WM. SAWYER,
Speaker of the House of Representatives.
ELIJAH VANCE,
Speaker of the Senate.

December 30, 1835.

AN ACT

To incorporate the Mechanic's Union of Springfield.

Sec. 1. *Be it enacted by the General Assembly of the State of Ohio,* That Jacob W. Kills, John Hooper, Samson Hubbell, John M. Gallagher, of the county of Clark, and their associates, together with such other per-sons as may hereafter be associated with them, are hereby created a body politic and corporate, by the name of "The Mechanic's Union of Spring-field," with perpetual succession; and by their corporate name they are hereby empowered to make contracts, and may sue and be sued, answer and be answered unto, in any court of law or equity in this State; they may have a common seal, which they may alter or destroy at pleas-ure; and they are also empowered to make such by-laws and regulations for their good government, as they may think fitting: *Provided,* The same be not incompatible with the Constitution or laws of the United States, or of this State.

Sec. 2. Said association may hold any personal or real estate, by pur-chase, gift, bequest or devise: *Provided,* The annual income of such real estate shall not exceed three thousand dollars: *And provided, also,* That the funds of said association shall be used for none other than literary, sci-entific, and benevolent purposes.

Sec. 3. Any future Legislature may alter, amend, or repeal this act: *Provided,* That such alteration, amendment or repeal, shall not affect the title to any real or personal estate belonging to said association at the time thereof, nor to any transferred or conveyed by said association previ-ous thereto.

WM. SAWYER,
Speaker of the House of Representatives.
ELIJAH VANCE,
Speaker of the Senate.

December 30, 1835.
2—L

AN ACT

To authorize the town council of the town of Urbana to borrow money.

Sec. 1. *Be it enacted by the General Assembly of the State of Ohio,* That the town council of the town of Urbana, be, and they are hereby authorized, to borrow for the use of said town, a sum of money not exceeding five thousand dollars, at a rate of interest not exceeding seven per centum, per annum, and pledge the revenue of said town for the redemption of the same.

WM. SAWYER,
Speaker of the House of Representatives.
ELIJAH VANCE,
Speaker of the Senate.

December 30th, 1835.

AN ACT

To incorporate the First Presbyterian Church in the town of Dover, in the county of Tuscarawas.

Sec. 1. *Be it enacted by the General Assembly of the State of Ohio,* That Thomas Stevenson, John Emerson, Wright Warner, and Smith A. Towner, and their associates for the time being, be, and they are hereby created a body corporate and politic, by the name of "The First Presbyterian Church of Dover," and as such shall remain and have perpetual succession.

Sec. 2. That the said corporation shall be capable in law by the name aforesaid, of suing and being sued, pleading and being impleaded in any action or suit, in any court having competent jurisdiction; and they may have a common seal, which they may alter, change or renew at pleasure.

Sec. 3. That the said corporation, by the name and style aforesaid, shall be capable in law and equity of having, receiving, acquiring and holding either by gift, grant, devise or purchase, any estate, real, or personal or mixed, for the use of said corporation, and of transferring the same at pleasure: *Provided,* That the annual income of all such property shall not exceed two thousand dollars.

Sec. 4. That there shall be a meeting of the corporation on the second Monday in June, one thousand eight hundred and thirty-six, and on that day, annually thereafter, at the usual place of holding public worship for said society, and such meeting shall have power to adjourn from time to time; at which meeting there shall be chosen by ballot, three trustees who, for the time being, shall have power to manage the concerns of said corporation; a majority of whom shall be a quorum to do business; and the said meeting may elect any other officers the corporation may think proper: *Provided,* That in case of failure to hold such meeting, the trustees shall have power to appoint such other day for an election as they may deem proper; and the said officers shall hold their offices until their successors are duly elected.

Sec. 5. That any regular meeting of the corporation may ordain and establish such by-laws and regulations for the government of its officers and members, and for the general benefit of the corporation as they may think proper: *Provided*, They be consistent with this act, and the constitution and laws of this State and of the United States; and which by-laws or regulations they may amend, alter or repeal at any annual meeting.

Sec. 6. That the trustees may call a special meeting of the corporation at any time, by giving at least ten days' previous notice; either by publishing immediately at the close of public worship, or in the newspaper, or by putting up written notices in three of the most public places in the village.

Sec. 7. That in all meetings, each male member in communion of the church, and each owner or renter of a pew or part of a pew, shall be entitled to vote, and a majority of the votes shall determine all elections.

Sec. 8. That original process against the corporation shall be by summons, which shall be served by leaving an attested copy with any one of the trustees, at least twelve days previous to the return day thereof; and such service shall be deemed sufficient in law, to bind the corporation.

Sec. 9. That Thomas Stevenson, John Emerson and Wright Warner, be, and they are hereby constituted trustees of said corporation, with full power to act as such, until the first annual meeting, or until their successors are elected.

Sec. 10. That any future Legislature to amend, modify or repeal this act.

WM. SAWYER,
Speaker of the House of Representatives.
ELIJAH VANCE,
Speaker of the Senate.

January 1st, 1836.

AN ACT

To incorporate the Methodist Episcopal Church and Society of Canton, Stark county.

Sec. 1. *Be it enacted by the General Assembly of the State of Ohio,* That Thomas S. Bonfield, Newberry Kline, William Dunbar, George N. Webb, and Peter Toffler, and their associates, members of the Methodist Episcopal Church in Canton, together with such other persons as may be hereafter associated with them, be, and they are hereby created a body politic and corporate, by the name of "The Methodist Episcopal Church and Society in Canton," and as such, shall remain and have perpetual succession; and by their corporate name, may contract and be contracted with; may sue and be sued; answer and be answered; defend and be defended; plead and be impleaded, in any court of competent jurisdiction, in all manner of actions, causes and complaints whatsoever; and may have a common seal, which they may change or alter at pleasure.

Sec. 2. That said corporation shall be capable in law and equity, in their corporate name, aforesaid, of having, receiving acquiring and holding, by purchase, gift, grant, devise, or legacy, any estate, real, personal or mixed, for the use of said corporation: *Provided,* That the annual income of all such property, shall not exceed the sum of two thousand dollars; and that all the property of whatever kind, shall be considered as held in trust, under the management and at the disposal of said corporation, for the purpose of promoting the interest of said society, and maintaining any institutions of charity, and particularly a female seminary intended to be connected therewith: *And provided also,* That where money, or other property, shall be given, granted, devised or bequeathed, for the purposes of education, or any other purpose, it shall be faithfully applied to the purpose for which it may be intended.

Sec. 3. That, for the better managing of the affairs of said society, and promoting the interest thereof, there shall be elected on the first Monday of May, one thousand eight hundred and thirty-six, and on the first Monday in May, in each succeeding year thereafter, five trustees, and such other officers as the corporation may deem necessary, who shall hold their offices for one year, and until their successors shall be elected: *Provided,* That, if from any cause, an election of officers should not be made on the day appointed for the annual election, the society may elect their officers at any meeting of the corporation duly assembled.

Sec. 4. That Thomas S. Bonfield, Newberry Kline, William Dunbar, George N. Webb and Peter Toffler, named in the first section of this act, be, and they are hereby appointed trustees until the first annual election, and until others are elected in their place.

Sec. 5. That all elections of the corporation shall be by ballot, and the person or persons having a majority of the votes for any office, shall be considered duly elected; each member shall have one vote; and all matters of the corporation shall be determined by a majority of the members present at any meeting of the society, duly assembled.

Sec. 6. That the trustees, a majority of whom shall be a quorum for the transaction of business, shall, under the direction of the society, have the management and control of the property and other concerns of the corporation, and they, or a majority of them, shall also have power to call a meeting of the society, either for the election of officers, or for the transaction of any other business of the society, by giving at least ten days notice thereof, by causing notice thereof to be set up in three of the most public places within the limits of said society.

Sec. 7. That any meeting of the society, duly assembled, may adopt and establish such by-laws and ordinances as may be deemed proper and necessary for the good government of said corporation: *Provided,* That such by-laws and ordinances shall be compatible with the constitution and laws of the United States, and of this State.

Sec. 8. That original process against the corporation, shall be served by leaving an attested copy with one or more of the trustees, at least ten days before the return day thereof; and such service shall be deemed sufficient to bind the corporation.

Sec. 9. That any future Legislature shall have power to modify or repeal this act: *Provided,* That such modification or repeal, shall not affect the title to any estate, real or personal, acquired or conveyed under its provisions.

WM. SAWYER,
Speaker of the House of Representatives.
ELIJAH VANCE,
Speaker of the Senate.

January 1st, 1836.

AN ACT

To lay out and establish a State Road, in the counties of Wood, Henry, and Williams.

Sec. 1. *Be it enacted by the General Assembly of the State of Ohio,* That Guy Neering, of Wood county, John Patrick, of Henry county, and Sidney S. Sprague, of Williams county, be, and they are hereby appointed commissioners, to lay out and establish a state road; commencing at the town of Miltonville, in the county of Wood; thence on the nearest and best route to Gillead, in said county of Wood; and from thence to Defiance, in the county of Williams.

Sec. 2. That in the event of the death of either of the commissioners, or should either of them refuse to serve, or remove out of the county, his place shall be supplied by the commissioners of the county where the vacancy shall happen, as often as it may occur.

Sec. 3. That the commissioners shall be governed, in all respects, by the law now in force, defining the mode of laying out and establishing state roads, passed March 14th, 1831; and the expense of laying out and establishing said road shall be paid as pointed out in said act.

WM. SAWYER,
Speaker of the House of Representatives.
ELIJAH VANCE,
Speaker of the Senate.

January 1st, 1836.

AN ACT

Supplementary to the act, entitled, "An act directing the manner of leasing the lands granted by Congress for the use of Schools within the Virginia Military District," passed February 26th, 1816.

Sec. 1. *Be it enacted by the General Assembly of the State of Ohio,* That it shall be the duty of the register of the Virginia Military District, forthwith to appoint two disinterested persons, who shall proceed on oath or affirmation, to revalue the lands granted by Congress for the use of schools within the district aforesaid, in such manner as is required by the provisions of the sixth section of the act to which this is supplementary.

Sec. 2. That each of the persons so appointed to re-value the lands aforesaid, shall receive for his services, the sum of two dollars per day, for every day he may be necessarily employed in the performance of the duties of his appointment; to be paid out of the Virginia Military School Fund, upon the certificate of the register of said lands.

WM. SAWYER,
Speaker of the House of Representatives.
ELIJAH VANCE,
Speaker of the Senate.

January 1st, 1836.

AN ACT

To change part of Perry street, in the town of Dayton.

WHEREAS, it is made known to the General Assembly, that those persons whose real estate is appropriated, in order to the change of a street as made in the following act, have received all damages they claim, by reason of said change, and are desirous that the same should be made: Therefore,

Sec. 1. *Be it enacted by the General Assembly of the State of Ohio,* That the following change be, and the same is hereby made in Perry street, in the town of Dayton, and county of Montgomery, that is to say: commencing at the north-west corner of a stable, built by George Newcom, on the east line of said Perry street, seventeen feet northwardly of the point where the northern boundary of an alley, from St. Clair street, to Perry street, intersects the said Perry street, and a corresponding point on the western boundary of Perry street; thence to run north fifteen degrees and thirty minutes west, parallel with Wilkinson street, to the southern boundary of First street; and that so much of Perry street, as is now located northwardly of the said beginning points, be, and the same is hereby vacated.

WM. SAWYER,
Speaker of the House of Representatives.
ELIJAH VANCE,
Speaker of the Senate.

January 1st, 1836.

AN ACT

To incorporate the Evangelical Lutheran Church of Liverpool, in the county of Medina.

Sec. 1. *Be it enacted by the General Assembly of the State of Ohio,* That G. W. E. Melzger, Charles Gaier, Jacob Roth, Jacob Keller, and their associates, together with such persons as may hereafter become associated with them, be, and they are hereby created a body politic and corporate, with perpetual succession, by the name and style of "The Evangelical Lutheran Church of Liverpool;" and by such name, shall be capable in law of contracting and being contracted with, of suing and being sued, of pleading and being impleaded, in all courts and other tribunals of competent jurisdiction; and shall have power to make and use a common seal, and the same to alter at pleasure; and to acquire and enjoy, control, rent, sell, or dispose of, any property, real, personal, or mixed: *Provided,* The annual income thereof shall not exceed two thousand dollars: *And provided, also,* That said property shall be applied to objects incident to the support of public worship, and the ordinances of said church, together with such institutions of learning and charity, as may be connected therewith, and to no other purpose.

Sec. 2.   There shall be a meeting of the members connected with the said church and society, annually, on Easter Monday; at which time, not less than three, nor more than seven trustees shall be elected, and such other officers as the said members may deem necessary; and if at any time the election should not be held on the day above specified, the corporation shall not thereby be dissolved, but the officers previously chosen shall serve until their successors are elected; and such election may be held at any time, ten days public notice having been given of the time and place of holding such election.

Sec. 3.   That said corporation shall have power to adopt and enforce such by-laws and regulations, as may be deemed proper and necessary for its government, and the efficient management of its concerns: *Provided,* That such laws and regulations shall be compatible with the constitution and laws of this State, and of the United States.

Sec. 4.   That original process against the corporation shall be served by leaving an attested copy with one or more of the trustees, and such service shall be sufficient to bind the corporation.

Sec. 5.   Any future Legislature may alter or repeal this act, but such alteration or repeal shall not affect the title to any property acquired or transferred under its provisions.

WM. SAWYER,
Speaker of the House of Representatives.
ELIJAH VANCE,
Speaker of the Senate.

January 1st, 1836.

AN ACT

To amend the act, entitled, "An act to incorporate the town of Canton, in the county of Stark;" passed January 30, 1832.

Sec. 1.   *Be it enacted by the General Assembly of the State of Ohio,* That the president, recorder, and trustees, of the town of Canton, in the county of Stark, for the purpose of enabling them to pay the amount of stock, by them subscribed, in the books of the Nimishillen and Sandy Navigation Company, pursuant to the second section of an act, entitled, "An act to amend an act, entitled, an act to incorporate the Nimishillen and Sandy Navigation Company," passed March 9th, 1835, be, and they are hereby empowered and authorized, to borrow the sum of ten thousand dollars; and for the payment of the sum, together with interest, to pledge the property, resources, faith, and integrity, of said town of Canton.

WM. SAWYER,
Speaker of the House of Representatives.
ELIJAH VANCE,
Speaker of the Senate.

January 1st, 1836.

AN ACT

To change the name of Prosper Coulton.

Sec. 1. *Be it enacted by the General Assembly of the State of Ohio,* That the name of Prosper Coulton, of the county of Portage, be, and the same is hereby changed to that of Lyman Prosper Coulton; by which name he shall be hereafter known: *Provided,* That nothing herein contained, shall operate or be construed to defeat or affect any right or interest acquired or vested in him by the name of Prosper Coulton.

WM. SAWYER,
Speaker of the House of Representatives.
ELIJAH VANCE,
Speaker of the Senate.

January 1st, 1836.

AN ACT

To provide for the sale of section sixteen, in Fox township, in the county of Carroll.

Sec. 1. *Be it enacted by the General Assembly of the State of Ohio,* That the auditor of the county of Carroll shall cause the assessor of said county, between the first day of March and the first day of July, one thousand eight hundred and thirty-six, to make a true valuation in money, of section sixteen, range four, in township thirteen, in said county, taking into consideration all the local advantages thereof; and such assessor shall enter in a book, to be procured for that purpose, the value of each quarter section, half quarter section, or other division separately, as the case may require; giving the value, and a proper and suitable description of each quarter section, half quarter section, or other division; and such assessor shall also note whether the same is improved or unimproved, and shall return the valuation so made to the auditor of said county, who shall preserve the same in his office, and make a true copy thereof, and forward such copy to the Auditor of State.

Sec. 2. The Auditor of State, and the Auditor of the aforesaid county of Carroll, shall be governed, in the sale of said section, by the provisions of the act to provide for the sale of section sixteen, granted by Congress, for the use of schools, passed January the twenty-ninth, one thousand eight hundred and twenty-seven.

WM. SAWYER,
Speaker of the House of Representatives.

ELIJAH VANCE,
Speaker of the Senate.

January 1st, 1836.

AN ACT

To incorporate the Ashtabula county Mutual Fire Insurance Company.

Sec. 1. *Be it enacted by the General Assembly of the State of Ohio,* That Joshua R. Giddings, Lynds Jone, Samuel Hendry, Peck Clark, James M. Bloss, Horace Wilder, Henry Keyes, Ashbel Dart, Lemuel Moffit, Roger W. Griswold, Joseph L. B. Barber, Samuel Kannady, Abner Kellogg, Ansel Udell and Alvin Bagley, and all other persons who may hereafter become members of said company, in the manner hereinafter prescribed, be, and they are hereby incorporated and made a body politic, by the name of the Ashtabula County Mutual Fire Insurance Company, for the purpose of insuring their respective dwelling houses, stores, offices, shops, and other buildings, household furniture and merchandize, against loss or damage by fire, whether the same shall happen by accident, lightning, or by any other means, excepting that of design in the insured, by the invasion of an enemy or insurrection of the citizens of this State, or of any of the United States; and by that name, may sue and be sued, plead and be impleaded, appear, prosecute and defend, in any court of competent jurisdiction in this State or elsewhere; may have and use a common seal; may purchase and hold such real and personal estate as may be necessary to effect the object of their association, and the same may sell and convey at pleasure; may make, establish and put in execution, such by-laws, ordinances and resolutions, not being contrary to the laws of this State or of the United States, as may be necessary or convenient for their regulation and government, and for the management of their affairs, and do and execute all such acts and things as may be necessary to carry into full effect the purposes intended by this grant.

Sec. 2. That all and every person and persons who shall at any time become interested in said company, by insuring therein, and also their respective heirs, executors, administrators and assigns, continuing to be insured therein as hereinafter provided, shall be deemed and taken to be members thereof for and during the term specified in their respective policies, and no longer, and shall at all times be concluded and bound by the provisions of this act.

Sec. 3. That there shall be a meeting of said company, at Jefferson, in the county of Ashtabula, on the third Tuesday of October, annually, or

3—L

on such other day as the said company may hereafter determine, notice of which shall be given by the secretary, or on his failure, by the president, or either of the directors, stating the time and place of said meeting, by publication, three weeks successively, in one or more newspapers printed in said county, the last of which publications shall be at least six days previous to the time of holding said meeting; at which meeting shall be chosen by a major vote of the members present, a board of directors, consisting of not more than nine, nor less than five members, who shall continue in office until others shall have been chosen, and accepted the trust in their stead; all vacancies happening in said board, may be filled by the remaining members, to continue until the next annual meeting; and a majority of the whole number shall constitute a quorum for the transaction of business; special meetings of the company may be called by order of the directors, or in such other manner as the by-laws may prescribe.

Sec. 4. That the board of directors shall superintend the concerns of said company, and shall have the management of the funds and property thereof, and of all matters and things thereto relating, and not otherwise provided for by said company; they shall have power from time to time, to appoint a president, a secretary, treasurer, and such other officers, agents and assistants, as to them may seem necessary, and prescribe their duties, fix their compensation, take such security from them as they may deem necessary for the faithful performance of their respective duties, and them to remove at pleasure; they shall determine the rules of insurance, the sum to be insured on any building, and the sum to be deposited for the insurance thereof: they shall order and direct the making and issuing of all policies of insurance, the providing of books, stationery and other things needful for the office of said company, and for the carrying on the affairs thereof, and may draw upon the treasurer for the payment of all losses which may have happened, and for expenses incurred in transacting the business of said company; and shall keep a record of their proceedings; and any dissenter disagreeing with the majority of the board at any meeting, may enter his dissent, with his reasons therefor, on record.

Sec. 5. That any person who shall become a member of said company by effecting insurance therein, shall, before he receives his policy, deposit his promissory note for such a sum of money as shall be determined by the directors, a part, not exceeding five per cent. of which said note shall be immediately paid, for the purpose of discharging the incidental expenses of the company, and the remainder of said deposite note shall be payable in part, or the whole, at any time when the directors shall deem the same requisite for the payment of losses or other expenses; and at the expiration of [the] term of insurance, the said note, or such part of the same as shall remain unpaid, after deducting all losses and expenses accruing during said term, be relinquished and given up to the signer thereof.

Sec. 6. That any member of said company shall be, and hereby is bound and obliged to pay his, her or their proportion of all losses and expenses happening or accruing in or to said company, and all buildings insured by and with said company, together with the right, title and interest of the insured to the lands on which they stand, shall be pledged to said company, and the said company shall have a lien thereon against the insured, during the continuance of his, her, or their policies.

Sec. 7. That in case of any loss or damage by fire happening to any member, upon property insured in and with said company, the said member or members shall give notice thereof, in writing, to the directors, or some one of them, or to the secretary of said company, within thirty days from the time such loss or damage may have happened; and the directors, upon a view of the same, or in such other way as they may deem proper, shall ascertain and determine the amount of said loss or damage; and if the party suffering is not satisfied with the determination of the directors, the question may be submitted to referees, or the said party may bring an action against said company for the loss or damage at the next court of common pleas holden in said county of Ashtabula thereafter, unless said court shall be holden within sixty days after said determination; but if holden within that time, then at the next term of said court holden in said county thereafter; and if, upon trial of said action, a greater sum shall be recovered than the amount determined upon by the directors, the party suffering shall have judgment therefor against said company, with interest thereon from the time said loss or damage happened, and costs of suit; but if no more be recovered than the amount determined upon by said directors, the said party shall become non-suited, and the said company shall recover their costs: *Provided, however,* That the judgment last mentioned, shall in no case affect the claim of said suffering party to the amount of loss or damage, as determined by the directors aforesaid: *And provided, also,* That execution shall not issue on any judgment against said company until after the expiration of three months from the rendition thereof.

Sec. 8. That the directoes shall, after receiving notice of any loss or damage by fire, sustained by any member, and ascertaining the same, or after the rendition of any judgment as aforesaid, against said company for such loss or damage, settle and determine the sums to be paid by the several members thereof, as their respective proportions of such loss, and publish the same in such manner as they shall see fit, or as the by-laws shall prescribe; and the sum to be paid by such member shall always be in proportion to the original amount of his deposite note or notes, and shall be paid to the treasurer within thirty days next after the publication of said notice; and if any member shall, for the space of thirty days after the publication of said notice, neglect or refuse to pay the sum assessed upon him, her or them, as his, her or their proportion of any loss or damage as aforesaid, in such case the directors may sue for and recover the whole amount of his, her or their deposite note or notes, with costs of suit; and the money thus collected shall remain in the treasury of said company, subject to the payment of such losses as have or may thereafter accrue, and the balance, if any remaining, shall be returned to the party from whom it was collected, on demand, after thirty days from the expiration of the term for which the insurance was made.

Sec. 9. That if it ever shall so happen that the whole amount of deposite notes shall be insufficient to pay the loss occasioned by any one fire or fires, in such case, sufferers insured by said company shall receive, towards making good their respective losses, a proportionate dividend of the whole amount of said notes, according to the sums by them respectively insured, and in addition thereto, a sum to be assessed on all the members of said company, not exceeding fifty cents on every hundred dollars by them respectively insured; and the said members shall never be required to pay for any loss occasioned by fire, at any one time more than fifty cents on each hundred dollars insurance in said company, in addition to the amount of his, her, or their deposite note, nor more than that amount for any such loss, after his, her, or their said note shall have been paid in and expended; but any member, upon the payment of the whole of his, her, or their deposite notes, and surrender of his, her, or their policy, before any subsequent loss or expense has occurred, may be discharged from said company.

Sec. 10. That the said company may make insurance for any term not exceeding ten years; and any policy of insurance, issued by said company, signed by the president and countersigned by the secretary, shall be deemed valid and binding on said company, in all cases where the insurance has a title in fee simple, unincumbered, to the building or buildings insured, and to the land covered by the same; but if the insured have a less estate therein, or if the premises be incumbered, the policy shall be void, unless the true title of the insured, and the incumbrances of the premises, be expressed therein, and in the application therefor.

Sec. 11. That the directors shall settle and pay all losses, within three months after they shall have been notified as aforesaid, but no allowance is to be made, in estimating damages in any case, for gilding, historical or landscape painting, stucco or carved work.

Sec. 12. That when any house or building shall be alienated, by sale or otherwise, the policy shall thereupon be void, and be surrendered to the directors of said company to be cancelled; and upon such surrender, the insured shall be entitled to receive his, her, or their deposite note or notes upon the payment of his, her, or their proportion of all the losses and expenses, that have accrued prior to such surrender: *Provided, however,* That the grantee or alienee, having the policy assigned to him, her, or them, may have his, her, or their right thereto, ratified and confirmed to him, her, or them, for his, her, or their own proper use and benefit, upon application to the directors, and with their consent, within thirty days next after such alienation, on giving proper security to the satisfaction of said directors, for such proportion of the deposite or premium note as shall remain unpaid; and by such ratification and confirmation, the party causing the same shall be entitled to all the rights and privileges, and subject to all the liabilities to which the original party insured was entitled and subjected to under this act.

Sec. 13. That if any alteration shall be made in any house or other building by the proprietor thereof, after insurance has been made thereon with said company, whereby it may be exposed to greater risk or hazard from fire, than it was at the time it was insured, then, and in any such case, the insurance made upon such house or other building, or upon household furniture, merchandize, or other property insured in said house or other building, shall be void, unless an additional premium and deposite, after such alteration, be settled with and paid to said directors; but no alterations or repairs in buildings, not increasing such risk or hazard, shall, in anywise, affect insurance previously made thereon.

Sec. 14. That in case any building or buildings, situated upon leased lands, and insured by said company, be destroyed by fire, in such case the directors may retain the amount of the premium note given for insurance thereof, until the time for which insurance was made, shall have expired; and at the expiration thereof, the insured shall have the right to demand and receive such part of said retained sum or sums, as has not been expended in losses and assessments.

Sec. 15. That if insurance on any house or other building, or on any property insured under the provisions of this act, shall be, and subsist in said company, and in any other office, or from and by any other person or persons at the same time, the insurance made in and by said company, shall be deemed and become void, unless such double insurance subsists with the consent of the directors of said company, signified by endorsement on the back of the policy, signed by the president and secretary.

Sec. 16. That Joshua R. Giddings, Roger W. Griswold, Ashbel Dart, James M. Bloss, or either two of them, may call the first meeting of the members of said company, by advertisement in either of the newspapers printed in said county, giving at least ten days notice of the time and place, and design of said meeting, for the purpose of choosing the first board of directors, of making and establishing by-laws, and of transacting any business necessary and proper to carry into effect the provisions of this act: *Provided, however,* That no policy shall be issued by said company until applications shall be made for insurance on twenty-five thousand dollars at least.

Sec. 17. That each and every of the directors of said company shall, before he enters upon the duties of his office, give bond to the treasurer of the county of Ashtabula, in the sum of five thousand dollars, with good and sufficient security, to the satisfaction of said treasurer, conditioned for the faithful discharge of the duties of his office, agreeably to the regulations, requirements and instructions of this act, and on the complaint of any person who has been injured by the misconduct of any director, it shall be the duty of said treasurer to cause said bond to be put in suit, on receiving security to indemnify the said county against costs, and to certify to the court who is prosecutor in such cause; and the said court may, on motion of the defendant or defendants in said cause, order the prosecutor to find sureties to indemnify the defendants for their costs, should he fail to prosecute or recover thereon; and if the defendant or defendants shall plead performance to the conditions of said bond, the prosecutor may reply as many breaches respecting his interest as he shall think fit; and the jury, on the trial of such issues as shall be put to them, shall assess damages for such breaches as the prosecutor shall prove, and the court shall enter up judgment for the whole penalty of the bond, and issue execution in favor of the prosecutor, for such a sum as the jury shall have found for damages and the costs; and the judgment shall remain for the benefit of such person or persons as may, by *scire facias* thereon, show that they have been injured by any breaches of the condition of said bond; and if the presecutor shall fail to recover in such suit, the court shall award costs to the defendants, and issue execution therefor against such prosecutor.

Sec. 18. That any future Legislature shall have authority to alter or repeal this act: *Provided*, That if said company shall not go into operation by the first day of January, one thousand eight hundred and thirty-seven, this act shall be null and void.

WM. SAWYER,
Speaker of the House of Representatives.
ELIJAH VANCE,
Speaker of the Senate.

January 2, 1836.

AN ACT

To authorize the Urbana and Champaign Mutual Insurance Company, to increase their capital stock.

Sec. 1. *Be it enacted by the General Assembly of the State of Ohio*, That the capital stock of the Urbana and Champaign Mutual Insurance Company, may be increased to an amount not exceeding an additional sum of fifty thousand dollars, to be divided into shares of fifty dollars each; and the additional shares shall be subscribed and paid for in such manner and on such terms as the board of directors for the time may prescribe; which stock shall be subject to all the regulations and restrictions provided for in the act establishing said company.

WM. SAWYER,
Speaker of the House of Representatives.
ELIJAH VANCE,
Speaker of the Senate.

January 2, 1836.

AN ACT

To lay out and establish a graded State road from Zanesville, in the county of Muskingum, to Frew's Mill, in the county of Coshocton.

Sec. 1. *Be it enacted by the General Assembly of the State of Ohio*, That Joseph Sharp, of the county of Muskingum, and Charles Barrow, of the county of Coshocton, be, and they are hereby appointed commissioners, and George Smith, of the county of Muskingum, surveyor, to lay out and establish a graded state road; commencing at Zanesville, in Muskingum county; thence up the east bank of the Muskingum river, to Samuel Beaver's, in Washington township; thence to John Johnston's, in Madison township; thence to John G. Pigman's, in Coshocton county; thence to intersect the graded state road leading from Norwich to the town of Coshocton, near Frew's mill, on Wills creek, in Coshocton county.

Sec. 2. That said road shall in no case exceed an angle of five degrees with the horizon; and the commissioners shall in all respects be governed by the act defining the mode of laying out and establishing State roads, passed March 14th, 1831.

Sec. 2. That should either of the commissioners or surveyor die, remove out of the county, or refuse to serve, the commissioners of the county in which such vacancy shall happen, shall forthwith, on being notified of the same, appoint some suitable person to fill such vacancy, as often as the same may occur; and in case of any disagreement between the said commissioners, the surveyor shall act as umpire.

WM. SAWYER,
Speaker of the House of Representatives.
ELIJAH VANCE,
Speaker of the Senate.

January 2d, 1836.

AN ACT

To lay out and establish a State road in the counties of Allen and Putnam.

Sec. 1. Be it enacted by the General Assembly of the State of Ohio, That Richard Matheany and John Tam, of Allen county, and William Clevinger, of Putnam county, be, and they are hereby appointed commissioners, to lay out and establish a state road, commencing at the town of Wapaukonnetta, in Allen county; thence on the nearest and best route, to Kalida, in Putnam county.

Sec. 2. That in case either of the commissioners die, refuse to serve, or remove out of the county, his place shall be supplied by the commissioners of the county, where the vacancy shall happen, as often as it may occur.

Sec. 3. That the commissioners shall be governed, in all respects, by the law now in force, defining the mode of laying out and establishing state roads, passed March 14th, 1831; and the expense of laying out and establishing said road shall be paid as pointed out in said act.

WM. SAWYER,
Speaker of the House of Representatives.
ELIJAH VANCE,
Speaker of the Senate.

January 2d, 1836.

AN ACT

To incorporate the Predestinarian Old School Regular Baptist Church, called Elk creek, adjoining the town of Trenton, Butler county, Ohio.

Sec. 1. Be it enacted by the General Assembly of the State of Ohio, That Stephen Gard, Joseph Kelly, Samuel M. Potter, Samuel Landis, Robert Busenbark, Ellis Miller, David Burley, Thomas Shinn and David Long, and their associates, and such others as may hereafter become associated with them, be, and they are hereby created a body corporate and politic, to be known by the name, style and title of the "Predestinarian Old School Regular Baptist Church, in the county of Butler," with perpetual succession; and by their corporate name, may contract and be contracted with, sue and be sued, answer and be answered unto, plead and be impleaded, defend and be defended, in all courts of law and equity in the State of Ohio, or elsewhere; they may have a common seal, which they may break, alter and renew at pleasure; and shall be capable of holding property, real, personal, or mixed, either by purchase, gift, grant, devise or legacy; and may sell, alien, and dispose of and convey the same: *Provided*, That the annual income of said property shall not exceed the sum of two thousand dollars.

Sec. 2. There shall be elected on the first Monday of May, annually, by the members of said church, three trustees, a treasurer and clerk, who shall hold their offices respectively for the term of one year, and until their successors shall be duly elected; but if, by negligence or casualty, the election should not be held on the day appointed in this act for the annual election, said corporation shall not thereby be dissolved; but an election may be holden at any meeting of the members of said church, duly notified and assembled for that purpose.

Sec. 3. All such property as may be holden by said church, shall be under the control and management of the trustees; a majority of whom shall have power to make any contract in behalf of said church, which may become necessary to carry into effect the objects of said corporation, and to manage all pecuniary and prudential concerns which appertain to the interests and welfare of said church: *Provided*, They shall not have power to sell or alienate any real estate belonging to said corporation, unless directed so to do by a resolution of the church, passed at a regular meeting for business.

Sec. 4. The property and funds which now belong or may hereafter belong to said church, shall be appropriated exclusively to the support of public worship, in such manner and form as said church from time to time may deem proper and advisable: *Provided*, Said church, as a body, shall not appropriate any part of said property or funds in any other way than for the benefit of a Predestinarian Old School Regular Baptist Church, known and designated by articles of faith laid down, agreed to, and adopted by said church, on the fourth day of July, in the year eighteen hundred and thirty-five; and the property so held by said church shall be the property of the members of said corporation, for the purposes aforesaid, or such a part or portion of the members of said corporation as shall continue to adhere to the said articles of faith and practice hereinbefore referred to.

Sec. 5. The corporation shall have power to make such by-laws, rules and regulations as may be deemed proper for the regulation and good government of said church: *Provided*, The same be not inconsistent to the constitution and laws of the United States and of the State of Ohio: *And provided, also*, That said by-laws, rules and regulations shall be agreed to by a meeting of said corporation specially held for that purpose, of which meeting the members shall be duly notified.

Sec. 6. Any future Legislature shall have power to alter, amend, or repeal this act: *Provided*, That such alteration, amendment or repeal, shall

not affect the title to any property acquired or conveyed under its provisions.

Sec. 7. That Ellis Miller, David Burley and Aaron Ball, be, and they
are hereby appointed trustees until the first annual election is held, and
until others are elected.

WM. SAWYER,
Speaker of the House of Representatives.
ELIJAH VANCE,
Speaker of the Senate.

January 4th, 1836.

AN ACT

For the relief of Jacob Hammer.

Sec. 1. *Be it enacted by the General Assembly of the State of Ohio,*
That Jacob Hammer shall be allowed, until the first day of January, in
the year one thousand eight hundred and thirty-seven, to complete the
payments due on in-lot No. 183; purchased of the register of the Virginia
Military School lands, on the twenty-fourth day of October, one thousand
eight hundred and twenty-eight, in the town of Mansfield, in Richland
county.

WM. SAWYER,
Speaker of the House of Representatives.
ELIJAH VANCE,
Speaker of the Senate.

January 4, 1836.

AN ACT

To incorporate the "Young Men's Mercantile Library Association of Cincinnati."

Sec. 1. *Be it enacted by the General Assembly of the State of Ohio,*
That Moses Ranney, Elbridge Lawrence, William N. Green, Isaac D.
Wheeler, Samuel A. Spencer, Robert Brown, Roland G. Mitchell, Charles
G. Springer, William R. Smith, and their associates, who have associated
together in a library association, be, and they are hereby created a body
corporate and politic, with perpetual succession, by the name and style of
the "Young Men's Mercantile Library Association" of the city of Cincinnati; and by that name shall be competent to contract and be contracted
with, to sue and be sued, plead and be impleaded, answer and be answered
unto, defend and be defended, in all courts and places, and in all matters
whatsoever, with full powers to acquire, hold, possess, use, occupy and
enjoy, by gift, grant, devise or otherwise, and the same to sell, convey
and dispose of, all such real estate and other property as may be necessary and convenient for the support and the transaction of business of said
association, or which may be conveyed to the same for security or in

4—L

payment of any debt which may become due and owing to said associa-tion, or in satisfaction of any judgment at law, or any decree of a court of equity in its favor; and may make, have and use a common seal, and the same break, alter and renew at pleasure:. *Provided*, That the proper-ty, funds and revenues of said association, shall not be used for any other than the purposes of a Mercantile Library Association.

Sec. 2. That the real and personal estate, property, funds, revenues, and other concerns of said association, and the administration of its affairs, shall be under the exclusive direction, management and control of a board of seven directors, who shall be chosen on the first Tuesday of January, annually, at such time of the day, and at such place in the city of Cincin-nati, as the directors for the time being shall appoint; which directors shall be members of said association, and shall hold their office for one year, and until their successors shall be chosen; they shall fill all vacancies in their board during the term for which they shall be elected; shall appoint a li-brarian, and such other agents, as they shall deem fit and expedient; shall have power to make all by-laws, rules and regulations, for the good gov-ernment of said association, annex reasonable pecuniary fines as a penalty for the breach thereof, and otherwise do all such other acts as appertain to their office: *Provided*, That no such by-laws, rules and regulations shall in any wise be contrary to the constitution and laws of this State, or of the United States: *Provided, also,* That any future Legislature shall have pow-er to alter, amend, or repeal this act.

Sec. 3. That this act shall be taken and received in all courts, and by all judges, magistrates and other public officers, as a public act; and all printed copies of the same, which shall be printed by or under the author-ity of the General Assembly, shall be admitted as good evidence thereof, without any other proof whatever.

WM. SAWYER,
Speaker of the House of Representatives.
ELIJAH VANCE,
Speaker of the Senate.

January 5, 1836.

AN ACT

To authorize the Commissioners of Stark county to borrow money for the purpose therein specified.

Sec. 1. *Be it enacted by the General Assembly of the State of Ohio,* That the board of commissioners of Stark county, be, and they are hereby authorized and empowered to borrow, on the credit of the county, any sum not exceeding eight thousand dollars, for the purpose of erecting a poor house in said county.

WM. SAWYER,
Speaker of the House of Representatives.
ELIJAH VANCE,
Speaker of the Senate.

January 5, 1836.

AN ACT

To amend "An act to incorporate the Woodward High School, of the city of Cincinnati," passed Jan. 15th, 1831.

Sec. 1. *Be it enacted by the General Assembly of the State of Ohio,* That the trustees incorporated by the act to which this is amendment, and their successors in office, shall have power to establish a college department, be governed and managed by said trustees, and their successors in office, to be called "The Woodward College of Cincinnati."

Sec. 2. That the said trustees and their successors in office, shall have power to confer all such degrees as are usually conferred in colleges, and universities: *Provided,* That they shall not establish a medical, law, or theological department, or confer degrees in medicine, law, or divinity.

Sec. 3. That the said trustees and their successors in office shall be authorized to appropriate such part of the funds of the institution as to them shall appear proper, to defray the expense of educating in said college, that class of students, described in the second section of the act to which this is amendatory: *Provided,* That nothing herein contained shall be so construed as to discharge said trustees, or their successors in office, from a strict and faithful performance of all the duties and responsibilities which are imposed upon them, by the provisions of the act, to which this is an amendment, or to divert the funds of the institution from the uses and purposes to which they were originally intended. Any future Legislature shall have power to amend or repeal this act.

WM. SAWYER,
Speaker of the House of Representatives.

ELIJAH VANCE,
Speaker of the Senate.

January 7, 1836.

AN ACT

To lay out and establish a State road in the counties of Geauga and Trumbull.

Sec. 1. *Be it enacted by the General Assembly of the State of Ohio,* That Robert Moody, and Robert Blair, of Geauga county, and Ephraim Brown, of Trumbull county, are hereby appointed commissioners; and George E. White, of Geauga county, surveyor; to lay out and establish a State road, commencing at the public square, in the village of Painesville, in Geauga county, running thence by the way of Concord, to Leroy, thence on the most direct and eligible route, to intersect the Warren and Ashtabula turnpike road, in the township of Bloomfield, in Trumbull county.

Sec. 2. That in case either of the commissioners or surveyor aforesaid should die, refuse to serve, or remove out of the county, the commissioners of the county where such vacanny may happen, shall fill the same as often as it may occur.

Sec. 3. That the commissioners shall in all respects be governed by the law now in force defining the mode of laying out and establishing state roads, passed March 14th, 1831.

WM. SAWYER,
Speaker of the House of Representatives.
ELIJAH VANCE,
Speaker of the Senate.

January 7, 1836.

AN ACT

To incorporate the First Congregational Society in Rome, in Ashtabula county.

Sec. 1. *Be it enacted by the General Assembly of the State of Ohio,* That David Walkley, Daniel Hall, Erastus Chester, Charles Crowell, Levi Crosby, Samuel Ackley, Ammiel Coffin, Noah Newton, Samuel O. Ackley, Joseph D. Hall, Lemuel L. Chester, Elijah Crosby, Ichabod Hulbert, and Eliel Crosby, and their associates, together with such other persons as may hereafter be associated with them, be, and they are hereby created a body corporate and politic, by the name of the First Congregational Society in Rome; and as such shall remain, and have perpetual succession; and by their corporate name may contract, and be contracted with, sue and be sued, answer and be answered, plead and be impleaded, defend and be defended, in any court of competent jurisdiction, in all manner of actions, causes, and complaints whatsoever; and may have a common seal, which they may change or alter at pleasure.

Sec. 2. That the said corporation, by the name and style aforesaid, shall be capable in law of holding property, real, personal or mixed, either by purchase, gift, grant, devise, or legacy, which may become the property of the corporation: *Provided,* That the annual income of such property, exclusive of a house for public worship, and payment of a preacher shall not exceed six hundred dollars: *And provided, also,* That all such property shall be held in trust, under the management and at the disposal of such corporation, for the purpose of promoting the interests of the society: defraying the expenses incident to the maintenance of any institution of charity or education, that may be therewith connected: *Provided, moreover,* That when money, or other property shall be given, granted, devised or bequeathed to said society, for any particular use or purpose, it shall be faithfully applied to such use or purpose; the property and other concerns of the corporation shall be under the management and control of trustees, to be appropriated agreeable to the direction of the society; a majority of the trustees shall be a quorum, for the transaction of business.

Sec. 3. That on the second Monday in April, one thousand eight hundred and thirty-six, there shall be elected by ballot, three trustees, one treasurer, and a clerk: *Provided,* That on the first election, the first trustee chosen shall hold his office for one year, the second for two years, and the third for three years; and (at) all subsequent elections, the first chosen for trustee shall hold his office for the term of three years; and all officers of this society shall hold their offices until their successors are elected.

Sec. 4. That all elections of the corporation shall be by ballot, and the persons having the greatest number of votes shall be considered duly elected; and all matters of the corporation shall be determined by a majority of the members present at any meeting of the society, duly assembled.

Sec. 5. That the trustees, or a majority of them, shall have power to call a meeting of the society, either for the transaction of business, or the election of officers, by giving or causing to be given ten days previous notice of said meeting, immediately after public worship of the society, or causing notifications thereof to be put up in three or more public places, within the limits of the society, one of which shall be at the place of public worship, at least sixteen days previous to such meeting.

Sec. 6. That any meeting of the corporation duly assembled, may adopt and establish such by-laws and ordinances as may be deemed proper and necessary for the good government of the corporation: *Provided,* That such by-laws and ordinances be compatible with the laws of the United States, and of this State.

Sec. 7. That original process against the corporation shall be by summons, which shall be served by leaving an attested copy with one or more of the trustees; and such service shall be deemed sufficient in law to bind the corporation.

Sec. 8. That David Walkley, Daniel Hall, and Erastus Chester, named in the first section of this act, be, and they are hereby appointed trustees; Charles Crowell is hereby appointed clerk; and Levi Crosby treasurer of said society; to hold their offices until their successors are chosen.

Sec. 9. That any future Legislature shall have power to modify or repeal this act: *Provided,* such modification or repeal shall not affect the title to any real or personal estate, acquired or conveyed under its provisions, or divert the same to any other use than originally intended.

WM. SAWYER,
Speaker of the House of Representatives.
ELIJAH VANCE,
Speaker of the Senate.

January 7th, 1836.

AN ACT

To divorce Susan Jennings from her husband, David Jennings.

Sec. 1. *Be it enacted by the General Assembly of the State of Ohio,* That the marriage contract, heretofore solemnized, between Susan Jennings, of Belmont county, and David Jennings, her husband, be, and the same is hereby dissolved; and that they, and each of them be, and they are hereby released and absolved from all obligations arising from the same.

Sec. 2. That from and after the passage of this act, the said Susan

Jennings shall have the exclusive guardianship of her minor children, being her issue in said marriage.

WM. SAWYER,
Speaker of the House of Representatives.
ELIJAH VANCE,
Speaker of the Senate.

January 7th, 1836.

AN ACT

To incorporate the Conneaut and Beaver Rail Road Company.

Sec. 1. *Be it enacted by the General Assembly of the State of Ohio,* That Henry Keyes, Ashbel Dart, Robert Lyon, Greenleaf Fifield, Josiah Brown, James M. Bloss, George G. Gillett, Jonathan Tuttle, Selah Whiting, of the county of Ashtabula; John Kinsman, Ambrose Hart, Tensand R. De Wolf, of Trumbull county; be, and they are hereby appointed commissioners, under the direction of a majority of whom, subscriptions may be received to the capital stock of the Conneaut and Beaver Rail road company, hereby incorporated: and they, or a majority of them, may cause books to be opened at such times and places as they may direct, and for the purpose of receiving subscriptions to the capital stock of said company, after giving notice of the time and place of opening the same, by publication in a newspaper printed nearest the place of opening the books, for at least thirty days; and that upon the first opening of said books, they shall be kept open for at least ten days in succession, from ten o'clock, A. M. until two o'clock, P. M.; and if, at the expiration of that period, such a subscription to the capital stock of said company, as is necessary to its incorporation, shall not have been obtained, then said commissioners, or a majority of them, may cause said books, by giving notice as aforesaid, to be opened from time to time, after the expiration of said ten days, and for the space of three years thereafter; and if any of said commissioners shall die, resign, or refuse to act, during the continuance of the duties devolved upon them by this act, another or others may be appointed in his or their stead, by the remaining commissioners, or a majority of them.

Sec. 2. That the capital stock of the Conneaut and Beaver Rail road company, shall be five hundred thousand dollars, and shall be divided into shares of fifty dollars each; which shares shall be subscribed for by individuals only; and it shall and may be lawful for the said corporation to commence the construction of the said Rail road or way, and enjoy all the powers and privileges conferred by this act, as soon as the sum of twenty thousand dollars shall be subscribed to said stock.

Sec. 3. That all persons who shall become stockholders pursuant to this act, shall be, and they are hereby created, a body corporate, and shall be, and remain a corporation forever, under the name of the Conneaut and Beaver Rail road company; and by that name, shall be capable in law of purchasing, holding, selling, leasing, and conveying estates, real, personal and mixed, so far as the same shall be necessary for the purposes hereinafter mentioned, and no further; and shall have perpetual succession; and by said corporate name, may contract and be contracted with; sue and be sued; and may have and use a common seal, which they shall have power to alter or renew at their pleasure; and shall have, enjoy, and may exercise, all the powers, rights and privileges which corporate bodies may lawfully do, for the purposes mentioned in this act.

Sec. 4. That upon all subscriptions, there shall be paid at the time of subscribing, to the said commissioners, or their agents, appointed to receive such subscriptions, the sum of five dollars on every share subscribed; and the residue thereof shall be paid in such instalments, and at such times, as may be required by the president and directors of said company: *Provided*, No payment other than the first, shall be demanded, until at least thirty days' public notice of such demand shall have been given by said president and directors, in some newspaper of general circulation in the State of Ohio; and if any stockholder shall fail or neglect to pay any instalment or part of said subscription thus demanded, for the space of sixty days next after the time the same shall be due and payable, the said president and directors, upon giving at least thirty days' previous notice thereof, in manner aforesaid, may, and they are hereby authorized to sell at public vendue, so many of the shares of the said delinquent stockholder or stockholders, as shall be necessary to pay such instalment and the expenses of advertising and sale, and transfer the shares so sold to the purchasers; and the residue of the money arising from such sale, after paying such instalment and expense, shall be paid to said stockholder on demand.

Sec. 5. That at the expiration of ten days for which the books are first opened, if four hundred shares of said capital stock shall have been subscribed, or if not, as soon thereafter as the same shall be subscribed, if within three years after the first opening of the books, the said commissioners or a majority of them, shall call a general meeting of the stockholders, at such time and place as they may appoint, and shall give at least sixty days' previous notice thereof; and at such meeting the said commissioners shall lay the subscription books before the stockholders then and there present; and thereupon the said stockholders, or a majority of them, shall elect thirteen directors by ballot, a majority of whom shall be competent to manage the affairs of said company; they shall have the power of electing a president of said company, from among the directors, and of allowing him such compensation as they may deem proper; and in said election, and on all other occasions wherein a vote of the stockholders of said company is to be taken, each stockholder shall be allowed one vote for every share owned by him or her; and every stockholder may depute any stockholder to vote and act for him or her, as his, her or their proxy; and the commissioners aforesaid, or any three of them, shall be judges of the first election of said directors.

Sec. 6. That to continue the succession of the president and directors of said company, thirteen directors shall be chosen annually, on the third Monday of October, in every year, in the borough of Conneaut, or at such other place on the line of said road as a majority of the directors shall appoint; and if any vacancy shall occur, by death, resignation, or otherwise, of any president or director, before the year for which he was elected shall expire, a person to fill such vacant place for the residue of the year, may be appointed by the president and directors of said company, or a majority of them; and that the president and directors of said company shall hold and exercise their offices until a new election of president and directors; and that all elections which are by this act, or the by-laws of the company, to be made, on a particular day, or at a particular time, if not made on such day or time, may be made at any time within thirty days thereafter.

Sec. 7. That a general meeting of the stockholders shall be held annually, at the time and place appointed for the election of directors of said company; that meetings may be called at any time during the interval between the said annual meetings, by the said president and directors, or a majority of them, or by the stockholders owning at least one-fourth of the stock subscribed, upon giving at least thirty days' public notice of the time and place of holding the same, as provided in the first section of this act; and when any such meetings are called by the stockholders, such notice shall specify the particular object of the call; and if, at any such called meeting, a majority, in value, of the stockholders of said company are not present, in person or by proxy, such meeting shall be adjourned from day to day, without transacting any business, for any time not exceeding three days; and if, within said three days, stockholders holding a majority, in value, of the stock subscribed, do not thus attend, such meeting shall be dissolved.

Sec. 8. That at the regular annual meetings of the stockholders of said company, it shall be the duty of the president and directors in office for the previous year, to exhibit a full, clear and distinct statement of the affairs of the company; that at any called meeting of the stockholders, a majority of those present, in person, or by proxy, may require similar statements from the president and directors, whose duty it shall be to furnish them when thus required; and that at all general meetings of the stockholders, a majority, in value, of all the stockholders of said company, may remove from office any president, or any of the directors of said company, and may appoint others in their stead.

Sec. 9. That any president and directors of said company, before he acts as such, shall take an oath or affirmation, as the case may be, that he will well and truly discharge the duties of said office to the best of his skill and ability.

Sec. 10. That the said president and directors, or a majority of them, may appoint all such officers, engineers, agents, or servants, whatsoever, as they may deem necessary for the transaction of the business of the company, and may remove any of them at their pleasure; that they, or a majority of them, shall have power to determine, by contract, the compensation of all engineers, officers, agents or servants, in the employ of said company, and to determine by their by-laws, the manner of adjusting and settling all accounts against the said company; and also the manner and evidence of transfers of stock in said company; and they, or a majority of them, shall have power to pass all by-laws, which they may deem necessary or proper for exercising all the powers vested in the company hereby incorporated, and for carrying the objects of this act into effect: *Provided*, That such by-laws shall be approved by a majority of the stockholders at their annual or any regularly called meeting, and shall not be contrary to the laws of this State or of the United States.

Sec. 11. That the said corporation shall be, and they are hereby, vested with the right to construct a double or single rail road or way, from Conneaut Harbor, in the county of Ashtabula, through Kinsman, in the county of Trumbull, to the line dividing the States of Ohio and Pennsylvania, in the townships of Vernon, Hartford, Brookfield, or Hubbard, in Trumbull county; to transport, take and carry, property and persons upon the same; by the power and force of steam, of animals, or of any mechanical or other power, or of any combination of them, which the said corporation may choose to employ.

Sec. 12. That the president and directors of said company shall be, and are hereby invested with all the rights and powers necessary for the location, construction and repair of said road, not exceeding one hundred feet wide, with as many sets of tracks as the said president and directors may deem necessary; and that they may cause to be made, contract with others for making said rail road, or any part of it; and they, or their agents, or those with whom they may contract for making any part of the same, may enter upon and use and excavate any land which may be wanted for the site of said road, or for any other purpose necessary and useful in the construction, or in the repairs of said road, or its works; and that they may build bridges, fix scales and weights, lay rails, take and use any earth, timber, gravel, stone, or other materials, which may be wanted for the construction or repair of any part of said road, or of its works; and may make and construct all works whatsoever, which may be necessary in the construction or repairs of said road.

Sec. 13. That the president and directors of said company, or a majority of them, or any persons authorized by them, or a majority of them, may agree with the owner or owners of any lands, earth, timber, gravel, stone, or other materials, or any improvements which may be wanted for the construction or repair of said road, or any of their works, for the purchase, use or occupation of the same: and if they cannot agree, and if the owner or owners, or any of them, be a married woman under age, insane person, or out of the county in which the property wanted may lie, when such lands and materials are wanted, application may be made to any justice of the peace of such county, who shall thereupon issue his warrant, under his hand and seal, directed to the sheriff of said county, or to some disinterested person, if the sheriff shall be interested, requiring him to summon a jury of twelve men, inhabitants of said county, not related, or in anywise interested, to meet on the land, or near to the other property or materials to be valued, on a day named in said warrant, not less than ten, nor more than twenty days after the issuing of the same; and if at the said time and place any of said persons summoned do not attend, the said sheriff or summoner, shall immediately summon as many persons as may be necessary, with the persons in attendance, to furnish a pannel of twelve jurors in attendance; and from them each party, or its, his, her or their agent, if either be not present, in person or by agent, the sheriff or summoner, for him, her, it or them, may strike off three jurors, and the remaining six shall act as a jury of inquest of damages: and before they act as such, the said sheriff or summoner, shall administer to each of them an

4—L

oath or affirmation, as the case may be, that they will faithfully and impartially value the damages which the owner or owners will sustain by the use or occupation of the same required by said company, and the jury estimating the damages, if for the ground occupied by said road, shall take into the estimate the benefits resulting to said owner or owners, by reason of said road passing through or upon the land of such owner or owners, towards the extinguishment of such claim for damages; and the said jury shall reduce their inquisition to writing, and shall sign and seal the same, and it shall then be returned to the clerk of the court of common pleas for said county, and by such clerk filed in his office, and shall be confirmed by the said court at its next session, if no sufficient cause to the contrary be shown; and when confirmed, shall be recorded by said clerk, at the expense of said company; but if set aside, the court may direct another inquisition to be taken in the manner above described; and such inquisition shall describe the property taken, or the bounds of the land condemned; and such valuation, when paid or tendered to the owner or owners of said property, or his, her, or their legal representatives, shall entitle said company to the full right of such personal property, and to the use and occupation of such landed property thus valued, as fully as if it had been conveyed by the owner or owners of the same; and the valuation, if not received when tendered, may at any time thereafter be received from the company without cost, by the owner or owners, his, her, or their legal representative or representatives; and that such sheriff or summoner and juries, shall be entitled to demand and receive from the said company, the same fees as are allowed for like services in cases of fixing the valuation of real estate, previous to sale under execution.

Sec. 14. That whenever in the construction of such road, it shall be necessary to cross or intersect any established road or way, it shall be the duty of the said president and directors of said company, so to construct the said rail-road across such established road or way, as not to impede the passage or transportation of persons or property along the same; or when it shall be necessary to pass through the land of any individual, it shall also be their duty to provide for such individual proper wagon ways across said road, from one part of his land to another.

Sec. 15. That if said company should neglect to provide proper waggon ways across said road, as required by the fourteenth section of this act, it shall be lawful for any individual to sue said company, and to be entitled to such damages as a jury may think him or her entitled to, for such neglect on the part of said company.

Sec. 16. That if it shall be necessary for such company, in the selection of the route or construction of the road by them to be laid out and constructed, or any part of it, to connect the same with or to use any turnpike road or bridge, made or erected by any company or persons incorporated, or authorized by any law of this State; it shall be lawful for the said president and directors, and they are hereby authorized to contract and agree with any such other corporation or persons, for the right to use such road or bridge, and for the transfer of any of the corporate or other rights or privileges of such corporation or persons, to the said company hereby incorporated; and every such other incorporation, or persons incorporated by, or acting under the laws of this State, is, and are hereby authorized to make such an agreement, contract or transfer, by and through the agency of the person authorized by their respective acts of incorporation, to exercise their corporate powers, or by such persons as by any law of this State, are intrusted with the management and direction of said turnpike, road or bridge, or of any of the rights and priviliges aforesaid; and any contract, agreement, or transfer, made in pursuance of the power and authority hereby granted, when executed by the several parties under their respective corporate seals, or otherwise legally authenticated, shall vest in the company hereby incorporated, all such road, part of road, rights and privileges, and the right to use and enjoy the same as fully to all intents and purposes, as they now are or might be used and exercised by the said corporation, or persons in whom they are now vested.

Sec. 17. That the said president and directors, shall have power to purchase, with the funds of the company, and place on any rail-road constructed by them under this act, all machines, wagons, vehicles or carriages of any description whatsoever, which they may deem necessary or proper, for the purposes of transportation on said road; and that they may demand and receive for tolls upon, and the transportation of persons, goods, produce, merchandize or property of any kind whatsoever, transported by them, along said rail-road any sum not exceeding the following rates on all goods, merchandize or other property of any description whatsoever transported by them, a sum not exceeding one and one half cents per mile for tolls, and five cents on a ton per mile for transportation on all goods, produce, merchandize or property of any description whatsoever, transportated by them or their agents, and for the transportation of passengers, not exceeding three cents per mile for each passenger: and it shall be lawful for any other company, or any person or persons whatsoever, to transport in proper cars or carriages, any person or persons, merchandize, produce or property of any description whatsoever, along said road, or any part thereof, subject to such rules and regulations as the said president and directors may prescribe under the provisions of this act; and the said road, with all their works, improvements and profits, and all machinery used on said road for transportation, are hereby vested in said company, incorporated by this act, and their successors forever; and the shares of the capital stock for said company, shall be deemed and considered personal property, transferable by assignment, agreeably to the by-laws of said company.

Sec. 18. That the said president and directors shall, semi-annually, declare and make such dividend as they may deem proper, of all the nett . profits arising from the resources of said company, deducting the necessary current and probable contingent expenses; and shall divide the same amongst the stockholders of said company, in proportion to their respective shares.

Sec. 19. That if any person or persons shall wilfully, by any means whatsoever, injure, impair or destroy any part of said rail-road, constructed by said company under this act, or any of the works, buildings or machinery of said company, such person or persons, so offending, shall each of them, for every such offence, forfeit and pay to the said company, a sum not exceeding three fold the damages, which may be recovered in the name of the company, by an action of debt in the court of common pleas, for the county wherein the offence shall be committed, and shall also be subject to an indictment in said court; and upon conviction of such offence, shall be punished by fine and imprisonment, at the discretion of the court.

Sec. 20. That if said rail-road shall not be commenced in three years and finished in ten years from the passage of this act, then this act shall be null and void: *Provided*, That the State shall have the power at any time after the expiration of thirty-five years from the passage of this act, to purchase and hold the same for the use of the State by paying to said corporation therefor, the amount expended by said corporation in locating and constructing the same, together with fifteen per centum thereon, of which cost, an accurate account shall be kept, and submitted to the General Assembly, duly attested by the oath of the officers of said company, if the General Assembly shall require it.

WM. SAWYER,
Speaker of the House of Representatives.
ELIJAH VANCE,
Speaker of the Senate.

January 11th, 1836.

AN ACT

To incorporate the Waterville Bridge Company.

Sec. 1. *Be it enacted by the General Assembly of the State of Ohio,* That John Pray, Theophilus Short, Phineas P. Bates, Lyman Dudly, Henry Reed, Ira Wilder, Parris Pray, of Wood county, and their associates, be, and they are hereby created, a body corporate and politic, by the name and style of "The Waterville Bridge Company;" and as such, shall remain and have perpetual succession; and, by their corporate name, may contract and be contracted with, sue and be sued, answer and be answered, plead and be impleaded, defend and be defended, in any court of competent jurisdiction; and may have a common seal, which they may change or alter at pleasure.

Sec. 2. That the said corporation be, and they are hereby authorized, to erect a free bridge across the Maumee river, at Waterville: *Provided,* The said company shall own the land on both banks of said river where said bridge shall be erected, or shall obtain in writing, from the owner or owners of the land on both sides of the river, where said bridge may be built, their consent to the building of said bridge; unless said banks on both sides be a public highway.

Sec. 3. That the said company, in the erection of said bridge, shall in no wise injure or obstruct the navigation of said river.

Sec. 4. That if said company shall erect and complete said bridge in a substantial manner, of proper width, and being in other respects of sufficient strength and dimensions, so as to admit of the safe passage of passengers, teams and carriages, of the usual dimensions, within three years from the passage of this act, they shall, from the time of completing said bridge, enjoy all the privileges secured to them by this act.

Sec. 5. That if any person or persons shall wilfully remove, or in any way spoil, injure or destroy, any materials, or any thing belonging to said bridge, either in the building of said bridge, or for repairs thereof, such person or persons shall forfeit and pay to said corporation treble the amount of damages sustained by means of such offence or injury, to be sued for and recovered with cost of suit, in action of debt, in any court having competent jurisdiction, by the treasurer of said corporation, or any person thereunto by said company authorized.

Sec. 6. That the said company shall have power to adopt such by-laws, rules and regulations, for the government of the same, as they may deem expedient.

WM. SAWYER,
Speaker of the House of Representatives.
ELIJAH VANCE,
Speaker of the Senate.

January 11, 1836.

AN ACT

For the relief of John W. Davis.

WHEREAS, it is represented to the General Assembly, that John W. Davis, of the county of Perry, in the State of Ohio, together with John B. Allen, and David Adams, entered into a recognizance, and became bound for the appearance of one Billings Allen, to the court of common pleas of said county, to answer to a criminal charge: *And whereas,* It is further represented, that the said recognizance became forfeited by the absconding of said Billings Allen, and that a judgment, by default, has been had in said court, against the said Billings Allen, John B. Allen, and David Adams; and that proceeding in *scire facias* is now pending in said court, to charge the said John W. Davis with the amount of said recognizance; and which recognizance is said to be excessive: Therefore,

Sec. 1. *Be it enacted by the General Assembly of the State of Ohio,* That the court of common pleas of said Perry county, be, and they are hereby authorized, on the trial of this cause against the said John W. Davis, to examine into the facts and circumstances; and should they be of opinion that the amount of said recognizance was excessive, or that any circumstance in said cause require a mitigation of the amount of said recognizance, as to the said John W. Davis, the said court are hereby authorized to adjudge such sum only, as to said court shall appear just and reasonable, without taking into consideration the amount of the said recognizance.

WM. SAWYER,
Speaker of the House of Representatives.
ELIJAH VANCE,
Speaker of the Senate.

January 12, 1836.

AN ACT

To lay out and establish a graded State Road in Coshocton, Knox, and Licking counties.

Sec. 1. *Be it enacted by the General Assembly of the State of Ohio,* That F. W. Thornhill, of Coshocton county, Andrew McCammet, of Knox county, and Peter Kirkpatrick, of Licking county, are hereby appointed commissioners, and William Anderson, of the county of Licking, surveyor, to lay out and establish a graded state road, commencing at the termination of the graded road from Coshocton to East Union, in Coshocton county; thence the nearest and best route to Bladensburg, in Knox county; thence to Martinsburg, in said county; t' ence to Utica, in Licking county; and thence the nighest and best route to Johnstown, in said county.

Sec. 2. That the said commissioners are hereby authorized to receive and appropriate on said road, all such subscriptions and donations as may be made, for opening and improving the same.

Sec. 3. That the commissioners, and surveyor aforesaid, shall, in all respects, be governed by the laws in force, defining the mode of laying out and establishing graded State roads; and should either of the commissioners or surveyor die, or remove out of the county, or refuse to serve, the county commissioners of their proper county, are hereby authorized to fill such vacancy, as often as the same may occur.

WM. SAWYER,
Speaker of the House of Representatives.
ELIJAH VANCE,
Speaker of the Senate.

January 12, 1836.

AN ACT

To authorize the County Commissioners of the county of Hardin, to purchase, for the use of the county of Hardin, lands therein named.

WHEREAS, by a resolution of the General Assembly of the State of Ohio, passed February 12th, A. D. 1829, the Governor of the State of Ohio was authorized to reserve a tract of land, in the counties of Allen, Putnam, and Hardin, not exceeding one section in each county, out of the lands selected for canal purposes, for the benefit of the seats of justice for said counties, under the direction of the Governor of the State of Ohio: *And whereas,* The fractional section, No. 31, in township No. 4, S. in range 11, supposed to contain two hundred and two acres, more or less, lying in said county of Hardin, was selected for the purposes aforesaid: *And whereas,* By an act, entitled, "An act to organize said county, and establish the seat of justice for the same," passed 9th January, 1833, the commissioners appointed to select a seat of justice for said county, selected a site for the seat of justice, a short distance from said fractional section 31, township N. 4, S. and range 11: *And whereas,* The county of Hardin is desirous to purchase the same, for the benefit of the seat of justice of said county, at the minimum price: Therefore,

Sec. 1. *Be it enacted by the General Assembly of the State of Ohio,* That the county commissioners of the county of Hardin, be and they are hereby authorized, to purchase, at the minimum price, for the use and benefit of the county seat of Hardin county, the whole of the fraction numbered thirty-one, in township No. 4, S. and range eleven, lying in the county of Hardin aforesaid, which now remains unsold.

Sec. 2. That the town director of the town of Kenton, the county seat of said county, be and is hereby constituted and appointed to superintend, under the direction of the commissioners of said county, all the arrangement in all things in relation to the purchase and sale of said land, in the same manner and with the same powers as is by law conferred on town directors.

WM. SAWYER,
Speaker of the House of Representatives.
ELIJAH VANCE,
Speaker of the Senate.

January 12, 1836.

AN ACT

To incorporate the town of Clinton, in the county of Huron.

Sec. 1. *Be it enacted by the General Assembly of the State of Ohio,* That so much of the township of Fitchville, in the county of Huron, as is comprised within the following limits, to wit: Beginning at a point where the Wooster road crosses the north and south section road in said township, and running thence north to a line running due east and west, intersecting the north corner of the burial ground on Husted Moe's land; thence east to a line running north and south, parallel to the north and south section line in said township, intersecting a stake and stone, east of Samuel Palmer's log barn; thence south to a line running due east and west, intersecting a point at high water mark, on the south and west side of the bend of the Vermillion river, south of Randall Palmer's dwelling house; and thence west to a line running north and south, parallel to the north and south section line in said township, and six rods west of Joseph Washburn's new dwelling house, be, and the same is hereby created a town corporate, and shall henceforth be known and distinguished by the name of the town of Clinton.

Sec. 2. That for the good order and government of said town, it shall be lawful for the white male inhabitants who have resided within the aforesaid limits of said town for the space of three months next preceding the second Tuesday of April next, and who have the qualifications of electors of members of the General Assembly, to meet at the usual place of holding elections in said township of Fitchville, on the said second Tuesday of April next, and on the first Tuesday of April annually thereafter, at such place as the town council may direct, which shall be determined by notices of the time and place, posted up in three of the most public places in said town, at least ten days before the election; which notice shall be signed by the mayor and recorder, and then and there proceed by ballot to elect, by a plurality of votes, one mayor, one recorder, and five trustees, who shall be either householders or freeholders, residing within the limits of said town, and who shall hold their respective offices for one year, and until their successors are elected and qualified; such mayor, recorder and trustees being so elected and qualified, shall constitute a town council, any five of whom shall constitute a quorum for the transaction of business.

Sec. 3. That at the first election to be holden under this act, there shall be chosen *viva voce*, by the electors present, three judges and a clerk of said election, who shall each take an oath or affirmation faithfully to discharge the duties required of them by this act; and at all subsequent elections, the trustees, or any two of them, shall be judges, and the recorder clerk; and at all elections held under the provisions of this act, the polls shall be opened between the hours of one and two, and closed at four o'clock, P. M. of said day; and at the close of the polls the votes shall be counted, and a true statement thereof proclaimed by one of the judges, to the electors present; and the clerk shall make a true record thereof, who shall notify the persons elected to their respective offices, of their election within five days; and the persons so elected and notified, shall, within five days thereafter, take an oath or affirmation to support the constitution of the United States, and of the State of Ohio, and an oath of office; any person elected as aforesaid, neglecting or refusing to qualify as aforesaid, shall forfeit and pay into the treasury of said town, the sum of five dollars, to be recovered by an action of debt, before the mayor of said town; and the recorder shall, in the name of said town, demand, receive, or sue for such forfeiture, and pay over the same when collected to the treasurer, taking his receipt therefor: *Provided*, That no person shall be compelled to serve in any office in said corporation two years in succession.

Sec. 4. That the mayor, recorder and trustees of said town shall be a body corporate and politic, with perpetual succession, to be known and distinguished by the name of the Town Council of Clinton; and they and their successors in office shall be authorized to use a common seal, and the same to alter at pleasure; to receive, purchase, acquire, hold and convey any estate, real, personal or mixed, and to manage and dispose of the same in such manner as they, or a majority of them may deem proper; they shall be capable in the name aforesaid of suing and being sued, pleading and being impleaded, answering and being answered, in any suit or action in any court of law or equity in this State; and when any suit or action shall be commenced against said corporation, the first process shall be by summons, a copy of which shall be left with the mayor, or in his absence, at his usual place of abode, at least five days before the return day thereof.

Sec. 5. That it shall be the duty of the mayor, and in his absence or disability to serve, the recorder, to preside at all meetings of the town council; it shall also be the duty of the recorder to attend to all such meetings, and keep an accurate record of their proceedings, to be recorded in a book provided for that purpose; it shall moreover be the duty of the recorder to attend all elections under the provisions of this act; but in case of his absence or disability to serve as such, the trustees shall have power to appoint one of their number clerk of said election, *pro tempore*.

Sec. 6. That the town council shall have power to fill all vacancies which may occur in their body by death, resignation, or otherwise, from among the electors in said town, whose appointment shall continue until the next annual election, and until their successors are elected and qualified; and whenever it may happen that neither the mayor or recorder is present at any meeting of said town council, the trustees shall have power to appoint one of their number to perform the duties of such mayor or recorder, or both, as the case may be, which appointment shall be *pro tempore*; and that the mayor, or a majority of the trustees shall have power to call a meeting of the town council whenever in his or their opinion the public good of said corporation shall require it.

Sec. 7. That the mayor, recorder, and trustees, or a majority of them, whereof the mayor or recorder shall always be one, or in their absence, one of the trustees appointed to fill their vacancy, shall have power and authority to make, ordain and publish all such by-laws and ordinances, consistent with the constitution of the United States, and of this State, as they may deem necessary and expedient for the regulation, interest, safety, health, cleanliness and convenience of said town, and the same to alter or repeal at pleasure; they shall have power to appoint a treasurer, town marshal, and such other subordinate officers as they may deem necessary; to prescribe their duties, and to require of them such security as they may deem necessary for the faithful performance of their duties; to remove them at pleasure; to fix and establish the fees of the officers of said corporation not established by this act, except the trustees, who shall receive no fees; said town council shall also have power to affix to the violation of the by-laws and ordinances of said corporation, such reasonable fines and forfeitures, as they may deem proper, and provide for the collection and disposition of the same; they shall have power to lay out and regulate the lots, streets, lanes, alleys, and public ground; to lay out and determine the width of the side walks, and regulate the same; they shall also have power to remove or cause to be removed all nuisances and obstructions, and do all things which a corporation of a similar nature can do, to secure the health, peace and good order of the inhabitants of said town.

Sec. 8. That for the purpose of more effectually enabling the town council to carry into effect the provisions of this act, they are hereby authorized and empowered to assess for corporation purposes an amount of tax on all property within said town, made taxable by the laws of this State, for State and county purposes, not exceeding in any one year one par cent. on the value thereof, which value shall be ascertained by an assessor to be appointed by said town council for that purpose; they shall also have power to equalize any injudicious assessments thus made, on complaint of the owner or owners, his, her, or their agent so aggrieved.

6—I.

Sec. 9. That it shall be the duty of the town council to make out or cause to be made out by the recorder, a duplicate of taxes, charging each individual therein, an amount of tax in proportion to the property of such individual assessed as aforesaid within said town; which duplicate shall be signed by the mayor and recorder, and delivered to the marshal or such other person as shall be appointed collector, whose duty it shall be to collect the same within such time and in such manner as the by-laws shall direct; and the collector shall have power to sell both personal and real estate for the non-payment of taxes within said town, and shall be governed therein by the same laws and regulations as the collectors of State and county taxes; and in case of the sale of any real estate, the recorder shall have power to make and execute deeds therefor, in the same manner that county auditors are by law empowered to do for lands sold by the county treasurer; and the said collector shall, within ten days after collecting said taxes, pay the same over to the treasurer of said corporation, taking his receipt therefor; and who shall receive for his fees such sum as the town council may direct, not exceeding six per cent. on all moneys so by him collected, and paid over; said fees to be paid by the treasurer, on the order of the recorder.

Sec. 10. That the said town council shall have power to require every able bodied male person above the age of twenty-one, and under sixty years, who may have resided twelve months within said town, to perform annually two days work on the streets, alleys, or public ground of said town, under the direction of the marshal or such other person as may be appointed to superintend the improvement of such streets, alleys, or public grounds, in addition to the labor required under the present laws regulating roads or highways; and upon refusal or neglect to perform such work under the proper officers, the delinquent shall be liable to the same penalties as are provided by law against persons refusing to perform the two days labor required in the last named act, to be recovered in the name of the treasurer for the use of said corporation.

Sec. 11. That the by-laws and ordinances of said town, shall be posted up in two or more of the most public places within said town, at least ten days before the taking effect thereof, and the certificate of the recorder upon the town record shall be considered sufficient evidence of the same having been done.

Sec. 12. That the town council shall, at the expiration of each year, cause to be made out and posted up in one or more of the most public places in said town, an exhibit of the receipts and expenditures of the preceding year; which statement shall be certified by the recorder of said town.

Sec. 13. That the mayor of said corporation shall be a conservator of the peace throughout said town, and shall have within the same all the powers and jurisdiction of a justice of the peace in all matters, civil or criminal, arising under the laws of this State, to all intents and purposes whatever; he shall give bond and security as is required by law of justices of the peace, and the said mayor shall perform all the duties required of him by the by-laws and ordinances of said corporation; and appeals may be taken in all cases from the decisions of said mayor, in the same manner as from the decisions of justices of the peace; he shall keep a docket, wherein he shall keep a fair record of all matters of difference tried before him, and shall be allowed and receive the same fees that justices of the peace are or may be entitled to in similar cases.

Sec. 14. That the marshal shall be the principal ministerial officer of said town, and shall have the same powers as constables have by law; and his jurisdiction in criminal cases shall be co-extensive with the county of Huron; he shall execute the process of the mayor, and receive the same fees for his services that constables are allowed in similar cases.

Sec. 15. That said corporation shall be allowed the use of the jail of the county of Huron, for the imprisonment of such persons as may be liable to imprisonment under the by-laws and ordinances of said corporation; and all persons so imprisoned, shall be under the charge of the sheriff of the county of Huron, as in other cases.

Sec. 16. That the mayor, recorder, trustees and other officers of said corporation shall, on demand, deliver to to their successors in office all such books and papers as appertain in any wise to their office.

Sec. 17. That any future Legislature shall have power to alter, amend or repeal this act: *Provided*, That such alteration, amendment, or repeal shall not divert the property of said corporation from the purpose expressed in this act.

WM. SAWYER,
Speaker of the House of Representatives.
ELIJAH VANCE,
Speaker of the Senate.

January 12, 1836.

AN ACT

To incorporate the Presbyterian Church of Monroesville, in the county of Jefferson.

Sec. 1. *Be it enacted by the General Assembly of the State of Ohio,* That Abram Croxton, Aaron Aten, Joseph L. Hosack, Joseph F. Williams, John Halderman, Thomas Creighton, Joseph Barclay and Samuel Clark, and their associates, together with such other persons as may hereafter be associated with them, be, and they are hereby created and declared a body corporate and politic, by the name of "The Presbyterian Church of Monroesville;" and as such shall remain and have perpetual succession; and by their corporate name, may contract and be contracted with; sue and be sued; answer and be answered; plead and be impleaded; defend and be defended, in any court of competent jurisdiction; and may have a common seal, which they may break or renew at pleasure.

Sec. 2. That the said corporation, by the name and style aforesaid, shall be capable in law of holding property, real, personal or mixed, either by purchase, gift, grant, devise, or legacy, which may become the property of the corporation: *Provided*, That the annual income of all such property, shall not exceed the sum of two thousand dollars: *And provided also,* That all such property shall be considered as held in trust, under the management and at the disposal of said corporation, for the promoting of the interest and well being of said church, defraying the expenses incident to their mode of worship, and maintaing any institutions of charity or education that may be therewith connected: *Provided, moreover*, That when any money or other property already or which hereafter shall be given, granted, bequeathed, devised, or pledged to said church for any particular use or purpose, it shall be faithfully applied to such use or purpose.

Sec. 3. That the management and control of the property and other concerns of the corporation shall be vested in three trustees, to be annually elected by the corporation upon the first Saturday after Christmas day; or if there be a failure to elect upon that day, then, upon any other day that the trustees for the time being shall designate: *Provided*, That said corporation may, at any time, by ordinance, increase or decrease the number of trustees; or they may invest their ruling elders with said office and duties as herein provided, either by themselves, or in concert with the annually chosen trustees.

Sec. 4. That Aaron Aten, John Haldeman, and Samuel Clark, be, and they are hereby appointed trustees until the first annual election, and until their successors are chosen.

Sec. 5. That the trustees or a majority of them shall have power to call a meeting of the corporation for the election of officers, or for any other business pertaining to said church and society, by causing to be published upon a day of public worship, ten days' previous notice of said meeting, or causing a notice thereof to be put up in three or more places within the vicinity of the place of worship, at least fifteen days previous.

Sec. 6. That any meeting of the corporation, duly assembled, may adopt and establish such by-laws and ordinances as may be deemed proper and necessary for the good government of said corporation: *Provided*, That such by-laws and ordinances shall be compatible with the constitution and laws of the United States, and of this State.

Sec. 7. That original process against the corporation, shall be by summons, which shall be served by leaving an attested copy with one or more of the trustees or elders of said corporation or church, and such service shall be valid to bind said corporation.

Sec. 8. That any future Legislature shall have power to alter, amend, or repeal this act.

WM. SAWYER,
Speaker of the House of Representatives.
ELIJAH VANCE,
Speaker of the Senate.

January 12th, 1836.

AN ACT

To authorise the Recorder of Knox county to transcribe a part of the records of said county.

Sec. 1. *Be it enacted by the General Assembly of the State of Ohio,* That the recorder of Knox county, under the direction of the commissioners of said county, be, and he is hereby authorized to transcribe books B. & C. being part of the land records of said county; and such transcripts and certified copies thereof, shall be received in all courts of justice in this State and elsewhere, as *prima facie* evidence of the original records; and such original records shall be carefully preserved in the recorder's office.

Sec. 2 That said recorder, for the performance of the duties required by the first section of this act, shall be entitled to receive such fees as the county commissioners in said county may direct.

WM. SAWYER,
Speaker of the House of Representatives.
ELIJAH VANCE,
Speaker of the Senate.

January 13th, 1836.

AN ACT

To incorporate the German Reformed Church of Dayton, in the county of Montgomery.

Sec. 1. *Be it enacted by the General Assembly of the State of Ohio,* That Frederick Boyer, Peter Bear, and Valentine Winters, and their associates, be, and they are hereby created and declared a body corporate and politic, by the name of "The German Reformed Church of Dayton, in the county of Montgomery," and as such shall remain and have pepetual succession; and by their corporate name, may contract and be contracted with; sue and be sued; answer and be answered unto; plead and be impleaded; defend and be defended, in any court of competent jurisdiction, in all manner of actions, causes and complaints whatsoever; and may have a common seal, which they may change, alter or renew at pleasure; and shall have power to make such by-laws, rules and regulations, for the government of said church, or corporation, as they may deem necessary and expedient: *Provided,* That such by-laws, rules and regulations be not inconsistent with the constitution and laws of the United States and of this State.

Sec. 2. That the said corporation, by the name and style aforesaid, shall be capable in law, of holding property, real, personal, or mixed, either by purchase, gift, grant, devise or legacy, which may become the property of said corporation: *Provided,* That the annual income of all such property, shall not exceed the sum of two thousand dollars: *And provided, also,* That all such property shall be considered as held in trust, under the management, and at the disposal of said corporation, for the purpose of erecting a house or houses for religious worship, a grave yard, parsonage or house of public instruction, and to be used for no other purpose whatever, except such further sums as the trustees of said corporation may from time to time, think absolutely necessary to defray the expense of public worship in said church.

Sec. 3. That Frederick Boyer, Peter Bear, and Valentine Winters, be, and they are hereby appointed trustees of said corporation, to serve until other trustees are elected in conformity with such by-laws, rules and regulations, as may be made for the government of said corporation.

Sec. 4. That any future Legislature may alter, amend, or repeal this act: *Provided*, Such alteration or repeal, shall not affect the title to any property acquired or transferred under this act.

WM. SAWYER,
Speaker of the House of Representatives.
ELIJAH VANCE,
Speaker of the Senate.

January 13th, 1836.

AN ACT

To incorporate the First Cumberland Presbyterian Church in Belmont county, by the name and style of the Shilo Congregation.

Sec. 1. *Be it enacted by the General Assembly of the State of Ohio*, That Cephas Hathaway, Ephraim Day, Thomas A. Welsh, Reuben Falkner and Jesse Lewellen, and their associates, for the time being, be, and they are hereby created a body corporate and politic, to be known by the name and style of the "Shilo Congregation;" and as such shall remain and have perpetual succession, subject, however, to such alterations and regulations as the Legislature may, from time to time, think proper to make.

Sec. 2. That the said corporation shall be capable in law, by the name aforesaid, of suing and being sued, pleading and being impleaded, in any action or suit, in any court having competent jurisdiction; and they may have a common seal, which they may alter, change or renew at pleasure.

Sec. 3. That the said corporation, by the name and style aforesaid, shall be capable in law and equity, of having, receiving, acquiring and holding, either by gift, grant, devise or purchase, any estate, real, personal, or mixed, for the use of said corporation, and of transferring the same at pleasure: *Provided*, That the annual income of all such property shall not exceed two thousand dollars.

Sec. 4. That there shall be a meeting of the corporation on the first Monday in June, one thousand eight hundred and thirty-six, and on that day annually thereafter, at the usual place of holding public worship for said society; and such meeting shall have power to adjourn from time to time; at which meeting there shall be chosen by ballot, three trustees, and such other officers as the society may deem necessary, who shall have power to manage the concerns of said corporation; a majority of whom shall be a quorum to do business: *Provided*, That in case of failure to hold such meeting, the trustees shall have power to appoint such other day for an election as they may deem proper; and the said officers shall serve until others are duly elected.

Sec. 5. That at any regular meeting, the society may establish such by-laws and regulations for the government of its members, and the general benefit of the corporation, as they may think proper: *Provided*, That such by-laws and ordinances shall be compatible with the constitution and laws of the United States, and of this State; and which by-laws or regulations they may amend, alter or repeal, at any annual meeting.

Sec· 6.   That the trustees may call a special meeting of the corporation at any time, by giving at least five days previous notice; either by publishing immediately at the close of public worship, or by putting up written notices in five of the most public places within the bounds of said congregation.

Sec. 7.   That in all meetings of said society, each male member in communion with the church, and each pew holder, shall be entitled to vote, and a majority of votes shall determine all elections.

Sec. 8.   That original process against said corporation shall be by summons, which shall be served by leaving an attested copy thereof with any two of the trustees or elders, at least fifteen days before the return day of said writ; and such service shall be deemed sufficient in law to bind said corporation.

Sec. 9.   That Reuben Falkner, Jesse Lewellen, Cephas Hathaway, Ephraim Day and Thomas A. Welsh, be, and they are hereby constituted trustees of said corporation, with full power to act as such, until the first annual meeting, or until their successors are duly elected.

Sec. 10.   That any future Legislature may modify, amend or repeal this act: *Provided*, That such modification or repeal shall not affect the title to any personal or real estate, acquired or conveyed under its provisions, or divert the same to any other purpose than originally intended.

WM. SAWYER,
Speaker of the House of Representatives.
ELIJAH VANCE,
Speaker of the Senate.

January 13th, 1836.

AN ACT

To incorporate the First Methodist Society of Sandusky, in the county of Huron.

Sec. 1.   *Be it enacted by the General Assembly of the State of Ohio,* That John Beatty, David Hamilton, John H. Williams, Roswell J. Jennings, Daniel Lawton, J. W. Hollister, and their associates, together with such other persons as may be hereafter associated with them, be, and they are hereby created a body politic and corporate, by the name and style of the "First Methodist Society of Sandusky City;" and as such, shall be and remain, and have perpetual succession; and by their corporate name, may contract and be contracted with, sue and be sued, answer and be answered, plead and be impleaded, defend and be defended, in any court of competent jurisdiction, in all manner of actions, causes and complaints whatsoever; and may have a common seal, which they may change or alter at pleasure.

Sec. 2.   That the said corporation shall be capable in law and equity, in their corporate name aforesaid, of having, receiving, acquiring, and holding by purchase, gift, grant, devise or legacy, any estate, real, personal or mixed, for the use of said corporation: *Provided*, That the annual income of all such property shall not exceed the sum of two thousand dollars; and that all the property of whatever kind shall be considered as held in trust, under the management and at the disposal of said corporation, for the purpose of promoting the interest of said society, defraying the expenses incident to their mode of worship, and maintaining any institutions of charity or education that may be connected therewith: *And provided, also,* That when money or other property shall be given, granted, devised, or bequeathed, for any particular use or purpose, it shall be faithfully applied to such use or purpose, and no other.

Sec. 3. That for the better managing of the affairs of said society, and promoting the interests thereof, there shall be elected on the first Monday in June next, and on the first Monday in January in each succeeding year thereafter, five trustees, and such other officers as the corporation may deem necessary, who shall hold their offices for one year, and until their successors shall be elected: *Provided,* That if, from any cause, an election of officers should not be made on the day appointed for the annual election, the society may elect their officers at any meeting of the corporation duly assembled.

Sec. 4. That the five first named persons mentioned in the first section of this act, be, and they are hereby appointed trustees, until the first annual election, and until others are appointed.

Sec. 5. That all elections of the corporation shall be by ballot; and the person or persons having a majority of the votes given, for any office, shall be considered duly elected; each male member, or other person owning a pew or part of a pew in the church of said corporation, shall be entitled to one vote; and all matters of the corporation shall be determined by a majority of members present at any meeting of the society duly assembled.

Sec. 6. That the trustees, or a majority of them, shall be a quorum for the transaction of business; and shall, under the direction of the society, have the management and control of the property and other concerns of the corporation; and they, or a majority of them, shall also have power to call a meeting of the society, either for the election of officers or for the transaction of any other business of the society, by giving to said society immediately after public worship, at least ten days notice of said meeting, or causing notification thereof to be put up in three public places within the limits of said society, one of which shall be at the usual place of holding public worship.

Sec. 7. That at any meeting of the society duly assembled, they may adopt and establish such by-laws and ordinances as may be deemed proper and necessary for the good government of said corporation: *Provided,* That such by-laws and ordinances be not inconsistent with the constitution and laws of this State or of the United States.

Sec. 8. That original process against said corporation shall be served by leaving an attested copy with one or more of the trustees, at least five days before the return day thereof; and such service shall be deemed sufficient to bind said corporation.

Sec. 9. That any future legislature shall have power to amend or repeal this act: *Provided,* That such amendment or repeal, shall not affect the title to any estate, real or personal, acquired or conveyed, under its provisions.

WM. SAWYER,
Speaker of the House of Representatives.
ELIJAH VANCE,
Speaker of the Senate.

January 13th, 1836.

AN ACT

To incorporate the Utility Fire Engine and Hose Company, No. 1, of the town of Springfield.

Sec. 1. *Be it enacted by the General Assembly of the State of Ohio,* That Charles Cavilier, Edward H. Cumming, Henry Williamson, Pierson Spinning, Samuel Clark, and their associates, and those who may hereafter be associated with them, are hereby made a body politic and corporate, under the name of the Utility Fire Engine and Hose Company, No. 1, of the town of Springfield, in the county of Clark, with perpetual succession: and by such name, and their corporate capacity, they may make contracts, may sue and be sued, answer and be answered unto, in all courts of this State, having cognizance; may hold property, personal or real, whether by purchase, gift, bequest, or devise; and may make and establish by-laws for their government, not incompatible with the constitution of the United States, or of this State.

Sec. 2. The annual income of said company shall not exceed two thousand dollars, nor shall their funds be used for any other purpose than to make said company efficient in the extinguishment of fires.

Sec. 3. Any future Legislature may alter, amend, or repeal this act: *Provided,* Such alteration, amendment or repeal shall not affect the title to any property, real or personal, belonging to said company, nor to any which they may have conveyed or transferred. This act shall be taken in all courts of Justice and elsewhere in this state as a public act.

WM. SAWYER,
Speaker of the House of Representatives.
ELIJAH VANCE,
Speaker of the Senate.

January 13th, 1836.

AN ACT

To incorporate the Independent Fire Engine Company, No. 2, of the town of Springfield.

Sec. 1. *Be it enacted by the General Assembly of the State of Ohio,* That Jacob Peterman, John Hooper, Jacob W. Kills, Williams Kills and their associates, and those who may hereafter be associated with them,

7—L

are hereby made a body politic and corporate, by the name of the Independent Fire Engine Company, No. 2, of the town of Springfield, in the county of Clark, with perpetual succession; and by such name, and in their corporate capacity, they are empowered to make contracts, to prosecute and defend suits in all courts of this State and elsewhere, having cognizance; to hold property, real or personal, whether by purchase, gift, bequest, or devise, and to make such by-laws. for their government, not incompatible with the laws or constitution of the United States, or of this State, as they may deem proper.

Sec. 2. The annual income of said company shall not exceed two thousand dollars, nor shall the funds of the same be used for any other purpose than to make the said company efficient in the extinguishment of fires.

Sec. 3. Any future Legislature may alter, amend, or repeal this act; *Provided,* Such alterations, amendment or repeal shall not affect the title to any real or personal estate, held or conveyed by said company.

Sec. 4. This act shall be received in all courts of justice, and elsewhere, as a public act.

WM. SAWYER,
Speaker of the House of Representatives.
ELIJAH VANCE,
Speaker of the Senate.

January 13th, 1836.

AN ACT

To lay out and establish a State Road in the counties of Putnam and Hancock.

Sec. 1. *Be it enacted by the General Assembly of the State of Ohio,* That Jacob Foster, of Hancock county, and Daniel W. Gray and John Stout, of Putnam county, be, and they are hereby appointed commissioners, to lay out and establish a state road, commencing at some suitable point, where the Bucyrus and Van Wert state road intersects Cherry Ridge, in Putnam county; thence on the nearest and best route to Clavenger's Mill; thence to Rileysville, in said county; thence in an easterly direction, to Mount Blanchard, in Hancock county.

Sec. 2. That the commissioners aforesaid, shall be governed, in all respects, by the law now in force, defining the mode of laying out and establishing state roads, passed March 14th, 1831.

Sec. 3. That should a vacancy happen in any of the foregoing appointments, by death, removal or otherwise, the commissioners of the county, in which the vacancy occurs, shall forthwith fill such vacancies, on being notified of the same.

WM. SAWYER,
Speaker of the House of Representatives.
ELIJAH VANCE,
Speaker of the Senate.

January 13th, 1836.

AN ACT

To incorporate the Wardens and Vestrymen of Grace Church, in Sandusky City, in the County of Huron.

Sec. 1. *Be it enacted by the General Assembly of the State of Ohio,* That John G. Camp, Abner Root, James Hollister, John N. Sloan, James H. Bell, Ogden Mallary, Zenus W. Barker, Eleutheros Cook, and their associates, together with such persons as may hereafter become associated with them, members of the Parish of Grace Church, in Sandusky City, be, and they are hereby created a body politic and corporate, with perpetual succession, by the name and style of the "Parish of Grace Church in Sandusky City," and by such name shall be capable in law, of contracting and being contracted with; of suing and being sued; of answering and being answered; of pleading and being impleaded; of defending and being defended, in all courts having competent jurisdiction; and may use a common seal, with power to alter the same at pleasure; and with power to acquire, hold and enjoy, to sell, rent, convey and dispose of property, real, personal or mixed: *Provided,* That the annual income of all such property shall not exceed the sum of two thousand dollars: *Provided also,* That said property shall be applied to the building of houses of public worship, procuring a parsonage, and to other objects incident to the support of public worship in said parish and the ordinances of said church, together with such institutions of learning and charity as may be connected therewith, and to no other purpose.

Sec. 2. That there shall be a meeting of the male members of said parish on Easter Monday of each and every year, at which time they shall elect two wardens, five or more vestrymen, a treasurer and a secretary, and such other officers as they may deem necessary; and may also transact any other business within the scope of the power granted in this act: *Provided,* That if at any time an election of officers should not be had on the day above appointed, the corporation shall not thereby be dissolved; but the officers previously chosen shall serve until their successors are elected; and such election may be held at any meeting duly notified and assembled for that purpose.

Sec. 3. That said corporation shall have power to adopt, establish and enforce such by-laws, ordinances, rules and regulations as may be deemed proper and necessary for its government, and the efficient management of its concerns; and shall have all other powers usually incident to such a corporation and necessary to its existence: *Provided* That such by-laws, ordinances, rules and regulations shall be consistent with the constitution and laws of this State and of the United States

Sec. 4. That any future Legislature may alter or repeal this act: *Provided,* That such alteration or repeal shall not divert the title to any estate acquired or conveyed under its provisions.

WM. SAWYER,
Speaker of the House of Representatives.
ELIJAH VANCE,
Speaker of the Senate.

January 15th, 1836.

52

AN ACT

To lay out and establish a State road from Wilmington, in Clinton county, to Burlington, in said county; thence to Belbrook, in the county of Green; thence to Dayton, in the county of Montgomery.

Sec. 1. *Be it enacted by the General Assembly of the State of Ohio,* That Caleb Lucas, of Clinton county; David W. Brown, of Green county, and John Shelby, of Montgomery county, be, and they are hereby appointed commissioners, and David Wickersham, of Clinton county, surveyor, to lay out and establish a state road; commencing at Wilmington, in Clinton county; thence on the nearest and best route to Burlington, in the county aforesaid; thence to Bellbrook, in the county of Green; thence to Dayton, in Montgomery county.

Sec. 2. That said commissioners shall, in all respects, be governed, and the expenses of laying out and establishing said road be paid, according to the provisions of the act entitled "An act defining the mode of laying out and establishing state roads," passed March 14th, 1831, except in the appointment of surveyor, which is provided for in the first section of this act.

Sec. 3. That should a vacancy occur in any of the foregoing appointments, by death, removal, or otherwise, the county commissioners of the county in which such vacancy happens, shall fill the same by the appointment of some suitable person, without delay, on being duly notified of the fact, by any one concerned.

WM. SAWYER,
Speaker of the House of Representatives.
ELIJAH VANCE,
Speaker of the Senate.

January 15, 1836.

AN ACT

Further to amend "An act to amend the several acts regulating the township of Cincinnati."

Sec. 1. *Be it enacted by the General Assembly of the State of Ohio,* That the trustees of the township of Cincinnati shall, previous to entering on the duties of their office, (respectively) give bonds with two responsible securities, each to be approved of by the city council of Cincinnati, payable to the city of Cincinnati, in the sum of ten thousand dollars, conditioned for faithfully disbursing and paying over all moneys which may come into their hands for the use of said township, which bond shall be lodged with the clerk of the said council; and if the said bonds, or either of them shall become forfeited, the said clerk by order of the said council, is hereby authorized to sue for and collect the same for the use of the said township, or any other person or party entitled to the same.

Sec. 2. That the first act of the said trustees on entering upon the duties of their office, shall be to choose from among themselves a president, who shall be their receiving and disbursing officer; who shall neither draw for nor disburse any moneys but under the authority and sign manual of the other two trustees; and the said president shall pay away no moneys without taking receipts for the same, which receipts shall be the only vouchers admitted for the expenditure of such public money as may come to his hand.

Sec. 3. That the trustees of Cincinnati township, in the first week in March of each year, shall exhibit to the said city council of Cincinnati, a plain and intelligible statement of their accounts for the past year; the state of the funds of said township, at the time of their entering on the duties of their office; and at the time of making the statement hereby required, the amount of all moneys by them disbursed, the time when, to whom, and the purposes for which expended, and shall produce such vouchers as shall be satisfactory to the said council; and if the said city council shall deem the statement a just and fair one, they shall certify to the same; and the said annual statement so certified by the said city council, shall be published as soon thereafter as possible, at least two weeks previous to the spring election, in one or more of the newspapers printed in the city of Cincinnati.

Sec. 4. That the office, books and accounts shall at all times be open to the inspection of the said city council; and it is hereby made the duty of the said city council, at all times, at the request made in writing of any three tax payers of said township, to institute an inquiry, by a committee of their own body, or otherwise, into the transactions of the said township trustees, and into their books and accounts; and if any defalcation shall appear, to order their clerk to bring suit forthwith on the bond given by said trustees.

Sec. 5. That so much of the third section of the act to which this is an amendment, as conflicts with, or is contrary to the provisions of this act, be, and the same is hereby repealed.

WM. SAWYER,
Speaker of the House of Representatives.
ELIJAH VANCE,
Speaker of the Senate..

January 15, 1836.

AN ACT

*To incorporate the Protestant Episcopal Church and Society of Bellevue, in Huron county.

Sec. 1. *Be it enacted by the General Assembly of the State of Ohio,* That James H. Bell, Lyman Harkness, Josiah Hollister, Frederick Chapman, Pike H. Lattimer, John K. Campbell, James Durbin, and Amos Ameden, and their associates, together with such persons as may hereafter become associated with them, members of the Protestant Episcopal Church and Society of Bellevue, in Huron county, be, and they are hereby created a body politic and corporate, with perpetual succession, by the name and style of the "Protestant Episcopal Church and Society of Bellevue," in Huron county; and by that name shall be capable in law of contracting and being contracted with, of suing and being sued, of answering and being answered, of pleading and being impleaded, of defending and being defended, in all courts having competent jurisdiction; and may use a common seal, which they may alter at pleasure; with capacity to acquire, hold and enjoy, to sell, rent, convey and dispose of property, real, personal, or mixed: *Provided*, That the annual income of all such property shall not exceed the sum of two thousand dollars: *And Provided, also*, That said property shall be applied to the building of houses of public worship, procuring a parsonage, and to other objects incident to the support of public worship in said church and society, and the ordinances of the same, together with such institutions of learning and charity, as may be connected therewith, and to no other purpose.

Sec. 2. That there shall be a meeting of the male members of said church and society, on Easter Monday, of each and every year, at which time they shall elect two wardens, three or more vestrymen, a treasurer, and secretary, and such other officers as they may deem necessary, and may also transact any other business of said church and society, not inconsistent with the limitations and restrictions of this act: *Provided*, That if at any time an election of officers should not be held on the day above appointed, the corporation shall not thereby be dissolved; but the officers previously chosen shall serve until their successors are elected: and said election may be held at any meeting duly notified and assembled for that purpose.

Sec. 3. That said corporation shall have power to adopt, establish, and enforce such by-laws, ordinances, rules and regulations, as may be deemed proper and necessary for its government, and the efficient management of its concerns: *Provided*, That such by-laws, ordinances, rules, and regulations shall be consistent with the constitution and laws of the United States, and of this State.

Sec. 4. That mesne process against the corporation shall be served by leaving an attested copy with one of the wardens, or vestrymen, at least ten days before the return day thereof, and such service shall be deemed sufficient to bind the corporation.

Sec. 5. That any future Legislature shall have power to modify or repeal this act: *Provided*, That such modification or repeal shall not affect the title of any estate, real or personal, acquired or conveyed under its provisions.

WM. SAWYER,
Speaker of the House of Representatives.
ELIJAH VANCE,
Speaker of the Senate.

January 15, 1836.

AN ACT

To lay out and establish a State road in the counties of Union and Hardin.

Sec. 1. *Be it enacted by the General Assembly of the State of Ohio*, That James K. Smith, and John Johnson, of Union county, and Cyrus

Dilley, of Hardin county, be, and they are hereby appointed commissioners to lay out and establish a state road, commencing at Marysville, in Union county; thence through Summerville, in Union county, to Kenton, in
Hardin county.

Sec. 2. That in case either of the commissioners die, refuse to serve
or remove out of the county, his place shall be supplied by the commissioners of the county, where the vacancy shall happen, as often as it may
occur.

Sec. 3. That the commissioners shall be governed, in all respects, by
the law now in force, defining the mode of laying out and establishing state
roads, passed March 14th, 1831, and the expense of laying out and establishing said road shall be paid as pointed out in said act.

WM. SAWYER,
Speaker of the House of Repeesentatives.

ELIJAH VANCE,
Speaker of the Senate.

January 15th, 1836.

AN ACT

To amend an act passed February 18th, 1834, entitled "An act to incorporate the First Congregational Society of Wellington, in the county of Lorain."

Sec. 1. *Be it enacted by the General Assembly of the State of Ohio,*
That the annual meeting of the members of the First Congregational So-
ciety of Wellington, in the county of Lorain, shall be held on the first
Monday in January, in each and every year.

Sec. 2. That so much of the fourth section of the act to which this is
an amendment, as relates to the time of holding the annual meeting of the
members of said society, be, and the same is hereby repealed.

WM. SAWYER,
Speaker of the House of Representatives.

ELIJAH VANCE,
Speaker of the Senate.

January 15, 1836.

AN ACT

To lay out and establish a State road in the counties of Crawford and Seneca.

Sec. 1. *Be it enacted by the General Assembly of the State of Ohio,*
That William Bland, of Crawford county, and Charles W. Foster, and
Jacob Woolf, of Seneca county, be, and they are hereby appointed commissioners to lay out and establish a state road; commencing at the state
road from Upper Sandusky to Fort Findlay, where said road crosses the
east line of section 16, in Crawford township, in Crawford county; thence

by way of Springville, in Seneca county, to Rome, in said county of Seneca.

Sec. 2. That in case either of the commissioners should die, refuse to serve, or move out of the county, the commissioners of the county shall fill such vacancy as often as it may occur.

Sec. 3. That the commissioners shall be governed in all respects by the law now in force defining the mode of laying out and establishing state roads, passed March 14th, 1831; and the expense of laying out and establishing said road, shall be paid as pointed out in said act.

WM. SAWYER,
Speaker of the House of Representatives.
ELIJAH VANCE,
Speaker of the Senate.

January 16th, 1836.

AN ACT

To amend the "Act to incorporate the town of Carrollton," in the county of Carroll.

Sec. 1. *Be it enacted by the General Assembly of the State of Ohio,* That the *proviso* in the *fifth section* of the "Act to incorporate the town of Carrollton, in the county of Carroll," be, and the same is hereby repealed.

WM. SAWYER,
Speaker of the House of Representatives.
ELIJAH VANCE,
Speaker of the Senate.

January 18th, 1836.

AN ACT

To extend the Corporation Limits of the town of Jefferson, in the county of Madison.

Sec. 1. *Be it enacted by the General Assembly of the State of Ohio,* That the territory comprised in the following boundaries, shall, from the passage of this act, be included in the corporation limits of the town of Jefferson; beginning at the south east corner of the town plat of Jefferson; thence north, eighty-two and a half degrees east, to Little Darby creek, crossing the creek to the east bank; thence up said creek bank, to the mouth of Jones' mill race; thence up said mill race until it strikes the town plat of Jefferson; thence north, to the north east corner of said town plat; thence with said plat, south eighty-two and a half degrees west, to intersect a line running south, seven and a half degrees east, to strike the north east corner of David Mortimer's town plat; thence south, eighty-two and a half degrees west, with said town plat, to the north west corner; thence south seven and a half degrees east, to the south west corner; thence north eighty-two and a half degrees east, with said plat to the south east corner of said plat; thence south seven and half degrees east, so far that a line run ning north eighty-two and a half degrees, east, will include the town plat of Jefferson, to the place of beginning.

WM. SAWYER,
Speaker of the House of Representatives.
ELIJAH VANCE,
Speaker of the Senate.

January 16th, 1836.

AN ACT

To lay out and establish a State road from Sidney, in Shelby county, to St. Mary's, in Mercer county.

Sec. 1. *Be it enacted by the General Assembly of the State of Ohio,* That Richard Hathaway, of Shelby county, Shadrach Montgomery, of Allen county, and Picket Doute, of Mercer county, be and they are hereby appointed commissioners to lay out and establish a state road, commencing at Sidney, in Shelby county; thence to Hopewell; thence to Brown, Matthews & Co's. steam mill, in Allen county; and thence the nearest and best way to St. Mary's, in Mercer county.

Sec. 2. That the commissioners aforesaid shall be governed in all respects by the law now in force, defining the mode of laying out and establishing state roads, passed March 14th, 1831.

Sec. 3. That should a vacancy occur in any of the foregoing appointments, by death, removal, or otherwise, the commissioners of the county in which such vacancy occurs, shall forthwith fill such vacancy on being notified of the same, as often as it shall occur.

Sec. 4. That the state road, heretofore laid out and established, from Sidney to St. Mary's, is hereby vacated.

WM. SAWYER,
Speaker of the House of Representatives.
ELIJAH VANCE,
Speaker of the Senate.

January 18th, 1836.

AN ACT

To lay out and establish a State road from Cadiz, in Harrison county, to the National Road at or near St. Clairsville, in Belmont county.

Sec. 1. *Be it enacted by the General Assembly of the State of Ohio,* That Samuel McDowel, sen., and John Gruber, of Harrison county, and Crawford Welsh, of Belmont county, be, and they are hereby appointed commissioners, and John Auld, jr. of Harrison county, surveyor, to lay out and establish a state road; commencing at the town of Cadiz, running

8—L

thence through New Athens, in said Harrison county, to the national road, at, or near St. Clairsville, in said county of Belmont.

Sec. 2. That the grade of said road shall not exceed an angle of five degrees with the horizon.

Sec. 3. That the said road commissioners shall, in all respects, be governed by, and the expenses of laying out and establishing said road be paid, according to the provisions of the act entitled "An act defining the mode of laying out and establishing state roads," passed March 14th, 1831, except in the appointment of surveyor, which is provided for in the first section of this act.

Sec. 4. That should a vacancy occur in any of the foregoing appointments, by death, removal, refusal to serve, or otherwise, the county commissioners of the county in which such vacancy happens, shall fill the same as often as it may occur, by the appointment of some suitable person without delay.

WM. SAWYER,
Speaker of the House of Representatives.
ELIJAH VANCE,
Speaker of the Senate.

January 18th, 1836.

AN ACT

To lay out and establish a graded State road in Knox and Richland counties.

Sec. 1. *Be it enacted by the General Assembly of the State of Ohio,* That William Bevans, of the county of Knox, and Joshua Cannon and Jesse Edgington, of the county of Richland, are hereby appointed commissioners, and Thomas G. Plummer, of the county of Knox, surveyor, to lay out and establish a graded state road, commencing at Danville, in Knox county; from thence the nearest and best route to Loudonville, in Richland county; from thence the nearest and best route to Haysville, in said county; from thence to Sherrick's mill, in said county; thence north, along and with the division line of the section, to the north-east corner of Jaquas' meadow; thence to the south end of Tilton's lane; thence along and with the said lane to the east line of section thirty-five, in township twenty three, range sixteen; thence north, along and with the line to the Ashland and Elyria road; from thence, a north-east direction to the county line, at New Albany.

Sec. 2. That the said commissioners are hereby authorized to receive and appropriate on said road, all such subscriptions and donations as may be made for opening and improving the same.

Sec. 3. That the commissioners and surveyor aforesaid, shall in all respects be governed by the law now in force, defining the mode of laying out and establishing graded state roads; and should any of the commissioners or surveyor die, or remove out of the county, or refuse to serve, the county commissioners of their proper county are hereby authorized to fill such vacancy as often as the same may occur.

WM. SAWYER,
Speaker of the House of Representatives.
ELIJAH VANCE,
Speaker of the Senate.

January 18th, 1836.

AN ACT

To incorporate the Richmond Water Company.

Sec. 1. *Be it enacted by the General Assembly of the State of Ohio,* That John W. Okley, E. Shepherd, Geo. E. K. Day, John Barr, Ol. A. Crary, and their associates for the time being, their successors and assigns, be, and they are hereby created a body politic, for the purpose of supplying the village of Richmond, in the county of Geauga, with good and wholesome water, from a certain spring, on lot No. 4, in the township of Painesville, in the county aforesaid, known as the Jackman Spring, by the name of "The Richmond Water Company;" and by that name shall be, and are hereby made capable in law, of suing and being sued, pleading and being impleaded, in courts of record, or any other place whatever; may have a common seal, and the same may alter or renew, at pleasure; and shall be capable of taking, holding, and acquiring any estate, real, personal, or mixed: *Provided,* That such real estate shall be necessary for effecting the objects of this corporation.

Sec. 2. That the capital stock of said company shall be ten thousand dollars; the said stock to be divided into shares of fifty dollars each, and shall be deemed personal property, and may be transferred in such manner as the company, by their by-laws, shall direct.

Sec. 3. That the control and direction of the operations of said company, shall be in a board of three directors, to be chosen annually, at such times and in such manner as shall be directed by the by-laws of said company; and the first election shall be holden at some convenient and proper place in said village, at such time as may be designated by any three members of said company, by giving at least fifteen days' notice in some newspaper, published in said county; the said board of directors shall have power to appoint such agents as they may deem necessary, and to make and ordain all necessary by-laws, rules and regulations, not inconsistent with the laws of this state, for the government and control of said company, its operations and interests, not incompatible with the constitution and laws of the United States, or of this state, and to call in the capital stock of said company, in such instalments as they may deem proper.

Sec. 4. That said company shall have the sole and exclusive right of conveying water from the said spring to the said village of Richmond; and it shall be lawful for said company to enter into and upon the lands and tenements of any person, and to make and construct in, over, or through the same, such cisterns, reservoirs, aqueducts, pipes, and water courses, as

may be necessary to effect the purposes of this incorporation, doing no unnecessary damage to such lands and tenements: *Provided*, That the aforesaid company shall be the sole and *bona fide* owners of the aforesaid Jackman Springs: *Provided, also*, That said company shall pay the proprietors of all such lands and tenements such compensation, for any and all such damages as shall be assessed, by three disinterested persons, to be appointed by the court of common pleas of said county of Geauga.

Sec. 5. That the said company shall have power, by and with the consent of a majority of the electors, residing within said village of Richmond, or the proper authority thereof; and are hereby authorized to enter upon, dig, and excavate the streets, alleys, and public squares of said county and village, in suitable places, for the erecting and maintaining such suitable cisterns, reservoirs, aqueducts, pipes and water courses, as may be necessary for effecting the objects of this corporation: *Provided*, The same be done with as little detriment and destruction to the public convenience, as the nature of said works will admit, and are left in good repair, and condition.

Sec. 6. That if any person or persons shall, wilfully or maliciously, break down, injure or impair, any of the machinery, engines, works or devices of said company whatsoever, the person so offending, shall forfeit and pay to the said company double the amount of damages sustained by such injury, to be collected by action of debt, in any court having cognizance thereof.

Sec. 7. That the said company shall have power to lease, sell, contract, and receive pay, for all the water to be sold as aforesaid, brought into said village, at such a price as may be agreed upon by the parties to such contracts: *Provided*, That the cisterns, reservoirs, and outlets of such water, shall always be free and open for the purpose of extinguishing fires in said village, without any charge therefor: *And provided, further*, That the funds of said company shall at no time be used for banking purposes.

Sec. 8. That this act shall be deemed a public act.

Sec. 9. That any future Legislature shall have power to alter this act: *Provided*, That the property and stock of said company shall not be thereby divested, nor diverted to any other purpose than the objects herein expressed.

WM. SAWYER,
Speaker of the House of Representatives.
ELIJAH VANCE,
Speaker of the Senate.

January 19, 1836.

AN ACT

For the relief of Enoch Rush.

WHEREAS, It is represented to this General Assembly, that Enoch Rush did, on the 18th day of June, 1824, purchase of Quintus A. Atkins, agent on the part of the state of Ohio, a certain tract of land, for the sum of three hundred and fifteen dollars forty-nine cents: *And whereas*, It is further represented that the said Enoch Rush did, at the time of such purchase, pay to said agent the sum of one hundred and seventy-five dollars for the use of the state, in part payment for said lot of land, which was subsequently forfeited to the state, for non-payment of the balance of the purchase money: *And whereas*, The same lot of land was again sold by the agent of the state for a like sum of three hundred and fifteen dollars forty-nine cents; the whole amount of which last mentioned sum, has been paid to the use of the state, the state thereby sustaining no loss: *And whereas*, The said Enoch Rush did, by the payment of one hundred and seventy-five dollars, as above stated, and the subsequent forfeiture of the said lot of land to the state, sustain the loss of the last mentioned sum: Therefore,

Sec. 1. *Be it enacted by the General Assembly of the State of Ohio,* That the sum of one hundred and seventy-five dollars be, and the same is hereby appropriated to the benefit of Enoch Rush; which sum shall be paid to said Rush, or his legal representatives, out of any money in the treasury not otherwise appropriated, on the order of the Auditor of State: *Provided,* That the expenses necessarily incurred in consequence of the last sale, shall be deducted out of the sum hereby granted to the said Rush.

WM. SAWYER,
Speaker of the House of Representatives.
ELIJAH VANCE,
Speaker of the Senate.

January 19, 1836.

AN ACT

For the relief of Simpson McFadden, and others.

WHEREAS, The General Assembly of the State of Ohio, now in session, have been duly advised, that Jacob Simpson, late of Carroll county, who departed this life some time in the month of May, one thousand eight hundred and thirty-five, died intestate, and was seized at the time of his death of certain real and personal estate, lying and being in the county of Carroll, and that he left no widow or heirs entitled to inherit or claim any portion of said real or personal estate, which, therefore, has, or may escheat to the state: *And whereas*, This General Assembly is further satisfactorily advised, that Simpson McFadden, of the county of Carroll, John Stanley, of Mercer county, Pennsylvania, and Rebecca Stanley, intermarried with James Dawson, of Washington county, Pennsylvania, were the relations and kindred of the wife of the said Jacob Simpson, formerly Jane Stanley, (who departed this life prior to the decease of the said Jacob,) and were raised in the family of the said Jacob and Jane, and were promised by the said Jacob, during his lifetime, that in consideration of the love and affection which he bore them as the kindred of his wife, and inmates and children of their family, he would secure and leave to them at his decease, all his estate; and that immediately before his death he expressed his desire and determination to do so by his will, but was prevented from making such a will by a sudden dispensation of Providence: Therefore,

Sec. 1. *Be it enacted by the General Assembly of the State of Ohio,* That all the right and claim which the State of Ohio has, or may have, in or to any real or personal estate of the said Jacob Simpson, deceased, within the county of Carroll, or elsewhere, which has or may escheat to the state by reason that the said Jacob Simpson left no heirs entitled to receive the same, be, and the same is hereby transferred and vested in the said Simpson McFadden, John Stanley, and Rebecca Stanley, now intermarried with the said James Dawson, as tenants in common; and the said Simpson McFadden, John Stanley, James Dawson, and Rebecca his wife, are hereby authorized to take possession of said real and personal estate, and hold the same as tenants in common, against all persons whomsoever, except the legal heirs, (should there be any,) or the creditors of the said Jacob Simpson.

Sec. 2. Should any lawful heirs of the said Jacob Simpson hereafter appear and establish their title to the said real and personal estate of the said Jacob Simpson, in the possession of the said Simpson McFadden, John Stanley, and James Dawson and Rebecca his wife, their heirs and assigns, they and each of them, so in possession, shall be entitled as occupying claimants to the benefit of the act of this state, entitled, "An act for the relief of occupying claimants of land," as fully by virtue of this act, as if they could show a plain and connected title in law or equity, derived from the records of some public office.

WM. SAWYER,
Speaker of the House of Representatives.
ELIJAH VANCE,
Speaker of the Senate.

January 19, 1836.

AN ACT

To incorporate the Wellsville and Fairport Rail Road Company.

Sec. 1. *Be it enacted by the General Assembly of the State of Ohio,* That Albert G. Richardson, Geo. Wells, J. A. Riddle, Henry Cope, Wm. D. Peter, Geo. Sloane, Geo. Fries, Isaac Craig, Jos. J. Brooks, John Street, and Isaac Wilson, of the county of Columbiana; Robert Price and Horace Stevens, of the county of Trumbull; Alva Day, of the county of Portage; Charles C. Paine, Henry Phelps, Roderic W. Skinner. Lemuel G. Storrs, Peleg P. Sanford, John H. Matthews, Reuben Hitchcock, Thomas Richmond, Edward Paine, jr. and John P. Converse, of the county of Geauga; together with such other persons as may thereafter become associated with them, in the manner hereinafter prescribed, their successors and assigns, be, and they are hereby created a body corporate and politic, by the name of

"The Wellsville and Fairport Rail Road Company;" and by that name, shall be, and are hereby made capable in law to have, hold, purchase, receive and possess, enjoy, and retain to them, and their successors, all such lands, tenements, and hereditaments, with their appurtenances, as shall be necessary, or in anywise convenient for the transaction of their business, and such as may, in good faith, be conveyed to them by way of security, or in payment of debts, and the same to sell, grant, rent, or in any manner dispose of; to contract and be contracted with, to sue and be sued, implead and be impleaded, answer and be answered, defend and be defended in courts of record, or in any other place whatever; and also to make, have, and use a common seal, and the same to alter, break, or renew at pleasure; and they shall be, and are hereby invested with all the powers and privileges which are by law incident to corporations of a similar nature, and which are necessary to carry into effect the objects of this association; and if either of the persons named in this section shall die, or refuse or neglect to exercise the powers and discharge the duties hereby created, it shall be the duty of the remaining persons herein before named, or a majority of them, to appoint some suitable person or persons to fill such vacancy or vacancies, so often as the same shall occur.

Sec. 2. That the said corporation are hereby empowered to cause such examinations and surveys to be made between Wellsville, on the Ohio river, in the county of Columbiana, and Fairport, at the mouth of Grand river, in the county of Geauga, as shall be necessary to ascertain the most advantageous route whereon to construct a rail road, and shall cause an estimate to be made of the probable cost thereof, for each mile separately; and the said corporation shall be, and they are hereby invested with the right to construct a rail road, with one or more rail ways, or tracks, from the Ohio river, in the town of Wellsville aforesaid, to Fairport, at the mouth of Grand river, on the east side thereof, with the right of constructing a branch through the village of Richmond, on the west side of said Grand river, crossing said river at some point within the township of Painesville, in the said county of Geauga, where it shall be deemed expedient, passing through the town of Painesville, and through the towns of Hanover and Salem, in Columbiana county: *Provided*, The cost of such road per mile, in passing through those points, shall not exceed to the corporation per mile, the average cost per mile originally estimated for building the whole road; which cost shall be estimated by a board appointed by said corporation to survey, grade and lay down said road, immediately after the first survey of the line of said road; but if the cost of constructing said road through these points, should exceed to the corporation, per mile, more than the average cost of the whole road per mile, then the said corporation may construct the same on such route as they may deem best for the interest of the public, and of such corporation; and the said corporation shall have the right to take, transport or carry persons and property upon said road, when constructed, by the force of steam, animal, mechanical or other power, or any combination of them, which the said corporation may choose to employ.

Sec. 3. That the capital stock of said corporation shall be one million dollars, and shall be divided into shares of fifty dollars each; and five dollars on each share shall be paid at the time of subscribing.

Sec. 4. That the above named persons, or a majority of them, or the survivors of them, are authorized to open books for receiving subscriptions to the capital stock of such company, and shall prescribe the form of such subscription; which books shall be opened within one year from the passing of this act, in the counties of Geauga and Columbiana, at such other place or places as they may deem expedient, giving twenty days notice in some newspaper printed in each of said counties of Columbiana, Trumbull, Portage and Geauga, and in such other place or places as may be thought advisable, of the time and place, or times and places of opening said books: *Provided, however,* That if the publisher of any newspaper, printed in either of said counties, shall neglect or refuse to print such notice, then the required notice shall be published, by affixing the same to the door of the court house in said county, at least twenty days previous to the opening of said books; and said books shall be kept open for receiving subscriptions to said capital stock, at least ten days.

Sec. 5. That as soon as said stock, or fifty thousand dollars thereof, shall have been subscribed, the above named persons, or the same number thereof as shall have given the notice above required, shall give the like notice for a meeting of the stockholders to choose directors, at some time at least twenty days thereafter, at some place within the said counties of Columbiana, Trumbull, Portage or Geauga; and if, at such time and place, the holders of one half or more of said capital stock shall attend, either in person or by lawful proxy, they shall proceed to choose from the stockholders, by ballot, twelve directors, each share of capital stock entitling the owner to one vote; and at such election, the persons named in the first section of this act, or those appointed by its provisions to fill vacancies which may have occurred, or any three of them, if no more be present, shall be inspectors of such election, and shall certify in writing, signed by them or a majority of them, what persons are elected directors; and if two or more have an equal number of votes, said inspectors shall determine by lot which of them shall be director or directors, to complete the number required, and shall certify the same in like manner; and said inspectors shall appoint the time and place of holding the first meeting of directors, at which meeting seven shall form a board competent to transact all business of the company, and thereafter a new election of directors shall be made annually, at such time and place as the stockholders at their first meeting shall appoint; and if the stockholders shall, at their first meeting, fail to appoint the day of such election, then it shall be holden in the succeeding year, on the same day of the same month on which said first election was holden, unless the same should be the first day of the week, in which case it shall be holden on the next day succeeding; and if no election be made on the day appointed, said company shall not be dissolved, but such election may be made at any time appointed by the by-laws of said company; and directors chosen at any election shall remain directors until others are chosen; and directors chosen at any election shall, as soon thereafter as may be, choose of their number one person to be president of said company; and from time to time may choose such other officers, as by their by-laws they may designate as necessary: *Provided,* That no person shall be a director of such company, who is not a citizen of the State of Ohio.

Sec. 6. That the directors may require payment of subscriptions to the capital stock, at such times and in such proportions, and on such conditions as they shall deem fit, under penalty of forfeiture of all previous payments thereon or otherwise, provided they shall never require the payment to be made at any place out of the counties through which said road shall pass; and such directors shall, at least thirty days previous to the appointed time of such required payment, give notice thereof in the manner provided in the fourth section of this act, for giving notice of the opening of the books of subscription for the stock of said company.

Sec. 7. That the directors of said company shall have power at any time, to open books for receiving subscription to the capital stock of said company, observing the time and manner of giving notices prescribed in the fourth section of this act; and also to make from time time all needful rules, regulations and by-laws, touching the business of said company, and to determine the number of tracks or rail-ways upon said road, and the width thereof, and the description of carriages which may be used thereon; to regulate the time and manner in which passengers and goods shall be transported thereon, and the manner of collecting tolls for such transportation, and to fix penalties for the breach of any such rule, regulation, or by-law, and to direct the mode and condition of transferring the stock of said company; and penalties provided for by said by-laws may be sued for by any person or persons authorized thereto, in the name of said company, and recovered in an action of debt, before any court having jurisdiction of the amount; and said company may erect and maintain toll-houses, and such other buildings and fixtures, for the accommodation of those using said road, and of themselves, as they may deem in any way necessary for their interest or convenience.

Sec. 8. That said company shall have a right to enter upon any lands, to survey and lay down said road not exceeding one hundred feet in width, and to take any materials necessary for the construction of said road; and whenever any lands or materials shall be taken for the construction of said road, and the same shall not be given or granted to said company, and the owners thereof do not agree with said company as to the compensation to be paid therefor, the person or persons claiming compensation as aforesaid, or if the owner or owners thereof are minors, insane persons, or married women, then the guardian or guardians of said minor or minors, and insane persons, and the husbands of such married women, may select for themselves an arbitrator, and the said company shall select one arbitrator, and the two thus selected shall take to themselves a third, who shall be sworn and paid as arbitrators in other cases; and the three, or a majority of them, shall award as arbitrators between the parties, and render copies of their award to each of the parties in writing, from which award either party may appeal to the court of common pleas for the county in which such lands or materials may have been situate; and in all cases where compensation shall, in any manner, be claimed for lands, it shall be the duty of the arbitrators and the court to estimate any advantage which the location and construction of said road may be to the claimant for such compensation; and the value of such advantage, if any, shall be set off against the compensation so claimed of said company; and appeals in such cases shall, when taken, be in all respects proceeded in as appeals in other cases to said court, and be brought into said court by filing the award with the clerk of said court, whose duty it

9—L

shall be to enter the same on the docket of said court, setting down the claimant or claimants as plaintiffs, and said company as defendant; and when the valuation, so ascertained, shall be paid or tendered by said company, said company shall have the same right to retain, own, hold and possess said materials, and the use and occupancy of said lands, for the purposes of said road, as fully and absolutely as if the same had been granted and conveyed to said company by deed.

Sec. 9.   That the said company may construct the said rail road across or upon any public road, highway, stream of water or water course, if the same shall be necessary; but the said company shall, within a reasonable time restore such road, highway, stream of water or water course, to its former state, or in such manner as not to impair the usefulness of such road, highway, water or water course, to the owner or the public; when it shall be necessary to pass through the lands of any individual or corporation, it shall be the duty of said company to provide for such individual or corporation, proper wagon ways across said road.

Sec. 10.   That any rail way company now, or yet to be chartered by law of this State, shall have power to join and unite with the road hereby incorporated, at any point which the directors of such company may think advisable, on such terms as the directors of said companies may respectively agree; and (in) case of disagreement, then upon such terms as the supreme court may, in chancery, determine; and it shall be lawful for the company hereby incorporated, to lease for a term of years, or to purchase in fee simple, from the Painesville and Grand river rail road company, or from the Painesville and Fairport rail road company, the roads which may have been commenced or constructed under their respective charters; and by such leases or purchases, the company hereby incorporated shall be invested with all the rights and privileges to make and maintain a rail road from the village of Painesville that either of the companies so leasing or selling, may, at the time of such sale, be invested with.

Sec. 11.   That said company may demand and receive for tolls upon, and the transportation of persons, goods, produce, merchandize or property of any kind whatsoever transported by them along said rail-way, any sum not exceeding the following rates: on all goods, merchandize or property of any description whatsoever transported by them, a sum not exceeding one and one-half cents per mile for toll, and five cents on a ton per mile for transportation on all goods, produce, merchandize, or property of any description whatsoever transported by them or their agents: and for the transportation of passengers not exceeding three cents per mile for each passenger.

Sec. 12.   That all persons paying the toll aforesaid, may, with suitable and proper carriages, travel upon the said Rail-road, always subject, however, to such rules and regulations, as said company are authorized to make by the seventh section of this act.

Sec. 13.   That if proceedings be not had under this act within three years from the taking effect thereof, and if said road be not completed within ten years thereafter, then the same to be void and of non effect.

Sec. 14.   That so soon as the amount of tolls accruing and received for the use of said road, or any part thereof, according to the provisions of this act, shall exceed five per cent. on the amount of capital stock paid in, after deducting therefrom the expenses and liabilities of said company, the directors of said company shall make a dividend of such nett profits among the stockholders, in proportion to their respective shares; and no contingent or accumulating fund, exceeding one per cent. of the profits of said company, shall remain undivided more than six months.

Sec. 15. That if any person or persons, shall wilfully obstruct, or in any way spoil, injure, or destroy said road, or either of its branches, or any thing belonging or incident thereto, or any materials to be used in the construction thereof, or any buildings, fixtures, or carriages, erected or constructed for the use or convenience thereof, such person or persons shall each be liable, for every such offence, to treble the damages sustained thereby, to be recovered by action of debt, in any court having jurisdiction of that amount.

Sec. 16. If the Legislature of this state shall after the expiration of thirty-five years from the passage of this act, make provision by law for the re-payment to said company of the amount expended by them in the construction of said rail-road, together with all moneys expended by them for permanent fixtures for the use of said rail-road, with an advance of fifteen per cent. thereon, then said road, with all fixtures and appurtenances, shall vest in, and become the property of the state of Ohio: *Provided, however*, That the sum so to be received by said company, together with the tolls received by them, shall not be less than the amount expended by them, and six per cent. per annum nett income thereon.

Sec. 17. Whenever the dividends of said company shall exceed the rate of six per cent. per annum, the Legislature of this State may impose such reasonable taxes on the amount of such dividends, as may be received from other Rail-road companies.

WM. SAWYER,
Speaker of the House of Representatives.
ELIJAH VANCE,
Speaker of the Senate.

January 21st 1836.

AN ACT

To incorporate the Franklin Canal Company.

Sec. 1. *Be it enacted by the General Assembly of the State of Ohio*, That Henry Dixson, James Holloway, Samuel Townsend, Joseph L. Dixson, Holland Green, Jonathan Fawcett, Simeon Kerns, C. Frederick Best, and Brinton Darlington, their associates and successors, be, and they are hereby constituted and made a body politic and corporate, and shall be and remain a corporation forever, under the name of "The Franklin Canal Company;" and by that name may contract and be contracted with, sue and be sued, plead and be impleaded, answer and be answered unto, in all courts having competent jurisdiction; and may have a common seal, and the same alter and renew at pleasure; and shall be, and hereby are invested with all the powers and privileges which are necessary to carry into effect the objects of this association.

Sec. 2. That the said corporation be, and they are hereby authorized to locate, make, construct, and forever maintain a slack water navigation or navigable canal, with all necessary locks, towing paths, basins, aqueducts, culverts, waste-weirs, dams, wharves, embankments, toll houses, and other necessary appendages; to commence in or near the town of Franklin Square, in Columbiana county; from thence to pass down the middle fork of Little Beaver, until it shall intersect the Sandy and Beaver canal at some suitable point north-west of New Lisbon, in said Columbiana county.

Sec. 3. That for the purpose of assuring to said corporation all the lands, real estate, waters and materials, requisite for most economically constructing and maintaining said navigation or canal, and the waters connected therewith and incident and necessary to the navigation of the same: whenever the said lands, waters and materials shall not be obtained by voluntary donation or fair purchase, it shall be lawful for said corporation, by any of their officers, and by each and every agent, superintendent or engineer by them employed, to enter upon, take possession of and use all such lands and real estate as shall be necessary for the purposes aforesaid; and also to enter upon and take all necessary materials for the construction of said navigation or canal, adjoining or near said canal or navigation, on whose lands soever the same may be, doing thereby no unnecessary damage, they satisfying and paying all damages which may be occasioned thereby, to any person or persons, corporation or corporations, in the manner hereinafter provided.

Sec. 4. That said corporation be, and hereby are authorized and empowered to purchase and hold to them and their successors forever, real and personal estate, to any amount necessary for constructing, maintaining, and repairing said navigation or canal as aforesaid; and may receive, hold, and take all voluntary grants and donations of land and real estate, which shall be made to aid the objects of said corporation.

Sec. 5. That a toll be, and hereby is granted and established for the sole benefit of said corporation forever; and it shall be lawful for said corporation, from time to time, to fix, regulate and receive the tolls and charges by them to be received for the transportation of property or persons, on the said navigation or canal, authorized by this act: *Provided*, That the tolls and charges thus fixed, regulated and received by said corporation shall at no time exceed the highest rate of tolls and duties, together with the charges of freight, to which property of a similar kind is subjected, as the costs of transportation on the Ohio canal during the same period of time.

Sec. 6. That the president and directors of said corporation shall have power, from time to time, to make and ordain such by-laws, rules and regulations, as may be necessary, touching the premises, not inconsistent with the constitution and laws of the United States, and of this State; especially to fix upon and determine the size and form of boats, rafts, and all other vessels that shall be used for the purpose of navigating said slack water navigation or canal; to determine the time and manner of their passing the locks, and what commodities shall not be transported during a want of water, should such an event happen, and also to regulate the mode of transferring the stock of said corporation: and the penalties imposed by said by-laws, rules and regulations, may be sued for and recovered by the treasurer of said corporation, or by any other person thereunto by said corporation authorized, to their own use and benefit, before any court having competent jurisdiction; the amount of which penalties shall be assessed by the court, and shall in no case exceed the sum of ten dollars; and said corporation shall cause said by-laws, to the breach of which penalties are affixed, to be printed, and a copy thereof to be placed in some conspicuous situation at each toll house; and if any person or persons shall wilfully or maliciously mar, deface, or pull down any copy so set up, said corporation may sue for and recover, to their own use, a sum not exceeding ten dollars, nor less than five dollars, of any such person or persons: *Provided*, That nothing contained in this section shall be so construed as to prevent boats and other vessels employed in navigating the Sandy and Beaver canal, from passing on said navigation or canal.

Sec. 7. That if any person or persons shall wilfully obstruct the water or navigation, remove or in any way spoil, injure or destroy said navigation or canal, or any part thereof, or any thing belonging thereto, or any materials to be used in the construction or repairs thereof, such person or persons shall forfeit and pay to said corporation double the amount of damages sustained by means of such offence or injury; to be sued for and recovered with costs of suit, in action of debt, in any court having competent jurisdiction, by the treasurer of said corporation, or by any person thereunto by said company authorized.

Sec. 8. That whenever any lands, waters, or materials shall be taken and appropriated by said corporation for the location or construction of said canal or slack water navigation, or any work appertaining thereto, and the same shall not be given or granted to said corporation, and the proprietor or proprietors do not agree with the said corporation as to the amount of damages or compensation which ought to be allowed and paid therefor, and shall not mutually agree upon some person or persons to appraise the same, the damages shall be estimated and assessed by three commissioners, to be appointed by the court of common pleas for the county in which the damages complained of are sustained, in manner following: whenever said corporation shall have located said slack water navi! gation or canal, or any part thereof, and shall have put the same under contract, or shall have used any water or materials for the construction thereof, any person or persons, corporation or corporations injured thereby, may at any time within twelve months thereafter, file his, her or their claim for damages, in writing, particularly describing the premises, with some one of the said commissioners, or with the clerk of the court of common pleas for the county in which the damages complained of are sustained; and said commissioners, or any two of them, having been first duly sworn to a faithful and impartial discharge of their duties, within a reasonable time thereafter, (they themselves having had notice from the claimants in case the claim is lodged with the clerk of the court of common pleas, that such claim has been filed,) having given previous notice to all parties interested, of the time and of the claims to be examined, by publishing an advertisement thereof three successive weeks, in some newspaper printed in said county, or in general circulation therein, in case none should be printed in the county, shall meet and pass over the premises so used or appropriated by said corporation for the purposes aforesaid; and after hearing the parties in interest, or such of them as desire to be heard, shall, according to the best of their skill and judgment, estimate all such damages they shall think any person or persons, corporation or corporations, have sustained or will sustain by the opening of said canal or slack water navigation, through his or her or their lands, or by the construction of any towing paths, basins, wharves, or other appendages, or for any materials used in the construction thereof, over and above the benefit and advantage, which said commissioners shall adjudge may accrue to such person or persons, corporation or corporations, from opening said navigation or canal; and the said commissioners, or any two of them, shall make a report in writing, and as soon as may be file the same with the clerk of the court of common pleas for said county, and the same may be made the rule of said court at the next succeeding or any subsequent term thereof, and said court may affirm the report when so filed, or proceed therein as in cases of appeal from justices of the peace, as the justice of the case may require; and the report of said commissioners, when affirmed and recorded, shall forever be a bar to any action commenced or to be commenced for damages against said corporation on account of the injury for which such damages were awarded; and if the party filing a claim for damages as aforesaid, shall fail to obtain damages in his favor, such party shall be liable for all costs arising from such application, and the court may enter judgment and issue execution therefor, as in other cases; and on all judgments against said corporation for damages assessed as aforesaid, or for the costs thereof, execution may issue, and may be levied on the goods and chattels, lands and tenements of said corporation; and said commissioners shall be allowed three dollars a day each for their services, under the provisions of this act, to be paid by said corporation, except as hereinbefore provided: all persons and corporations conceiving themselves aggieved by the company, under the provisions of the third section of this act, who shall omit to present their claims, as aforesaid, for adjustment, within the said term of twelve months, shall be deemed to have waived all right to demand damages therefor of said company.

Sec. 9. That in all cases where any bridges across the said middle fork of the Little Beaver, are so located, that said navigation or canal cannot be laid out and made, without interfering therewith, it shall lawful for said corporation to cause such bridges to be so altered as that said navigation or canal may be laid out and constructed: *Provided,* That said corporation shall cause such bridges thus altered to be put in as good repair, without delay, as the old ones were at the time of removing them, at their own cost and expense.

Sec. 10. That the said corporation shall be, and is hereby authorized to raise sufficient funds for the accomplishment of the objects aforesaid; and for that purpose, the persons named in the first section of this act, or a majority of them, shall be commissioners, whose duty it shall be, so soon after the taking effect of this act, as a majority of them shall judge proper, to cause books to be opened at such times and places as they shall think fit. under the management of such persons as they shall appoint, for receiv-

ing subscriptions to the capital stock of said company, each share to be of
the amount of fifty dollars, and each subscriber to be a member of said corporation for all purposes; and thirty days previous notice shall be given in
one or more newspapers of general circulation in the neighborhood, of the
the times and places of opening said books; and the said commissioners, or
a majority of them, may prescribe the form of said subscription; and whenever the sum of five thousand dollars, or a greater part of the stock of said
company shall have been subscribed, it shall be the duty of said commissioners, or a majority of them, to call a meeting of the stockholders, by
causing notice to be published in one or more newspapers in general circulation in the respective places in which the books shall have been opened and stock subscribed, at least twenty days previous thereto, of the time
and place of such meeting, which shall be at some convenient town,
or place near the route of the contemplated canal; at which meeting the
stockholders who shall attend for that purpose, either in person or by lawful proxy, shall elect, by ballot, seven directors, who shall hold their offices
until the expiration of one year, and until others shall be chosen in their
places; and the said commissioners shall be inspectors of the first election
of directors of the said corporation, and shall certify under their hands the
names of those duly elected, and shall deliver over to them the said certificates and subscription books; and at said election, and at all other elections or voting, of any description, every member shall have a right to vote
by himself or proxy, duly authorized in writing, and each share shall entitle the holder to one vote; and that the management of the concerns of the
said corporation shall be entrusted to seven directors, to be elected annually by the stockholders by ballot; and that the directors first chosen, and
such directors as shall thereafter be chosen at any subsequent election,
shall immediately thereafter meet and elect one of their number, who shall
be president thereof, until another election, and also, elect a treasurer and
secretary, who may be removed at the pleasure of the said president and
directors, and others elected in their places; and that a majority of said
directors shall constitute a board for every purpose within the provisions
of this act: *Provided, however,* In case it should at any time happen that
the election of directors shall not be held on any day when, pursuant to this
act, it ought to be held, the said corporation shall not, for that cause, be
deemed to be dissolved, but such election may be held at any other time
directed by the by-laws of said corporation.

Sec. 11. That the books of subscription shall remain open as long as
the president and directors shall see fit, not less than six days; and each
subscriber shall be bound to pay, from time to time, such instalments on his
stock as the said president and directors may lawfully require, they giving
at least thirty days previous notice of the time and place of making the
payments required, in some newspaper having circulation in the county
where said canal is located; but no assessment shall ever be made, so
as to render any subscriber liable to pay more than fifty dollars for a
share.

Sec. 12. That if any subscriber shall neglect to pay his subscription,
or any part thereof, for the space of thirty days after he is required so to
do, by the said president and directors, notice having been given as required by this act, the treasurer of said corporation, or other officer duly

authorized for that purpose, may make sale of such share or shares at public auction to the highest bidder, giving at least thirty days notice thereof, in some newspaper in general circulation at the place of sale; and the same shall be transferred by the treasurer in the manner hereinafter provided, to the purchaser; and such delinquent subscriber shall be held accountable to the corporation for the balance, if his share or shares shall be sold for less than the amount remaining due thereon, and shall be entitled to the overplus, if the same shall be sold for more than the amount so remaining due, after deducting the costs of sale.

Sec. 13. That for and in consideration of the expenses the said company will be at, in constructing said navigation or canal, and in keeping the same in repair, the navigation or canal, together with all tolls and rents and profits arising therefrom, shall be, and the same are hereby vested in said corporation; *Provided,* That the state shall have the power, at any time after the expiration of twenty-five years from the passage of this act, to purchase and hold the same for the use of said state, by paying to the said corporation therefor, the amount expended by them in locating and constructing the same, together with fifteen per centum thereon.

Scc. 14. That the said corporation shall be entitled to the benefit of all laws which are, or shall be in force, for the collection of tolls, or for the protection of any canals constructed by this state; and in any suit instituted against the said corporation, the service of legal process on the president, any one of the directors, or on the treasurer or secretary of said corporation, shall be deemed and held in all courts and places, a sufficient and valid service on the said corporation.

Sec. 15. That this act shall be deemed a public act.

WM. SAWYER,
Speaker of the House of Representatives.

ELIJAH VANCE,
Speaker of the Senate,

January, 21st, 1836.

AN ACT

To render valid certain leases of section sixteen, in Montgomery township, Richland county.

WHEREAS, It is represented, that in the year 1820, the trustees of original surveyed township, number twenty-two, in the sixteenth range, in said county, now known as Montgomery, executed leases of section sixteen, in said township, but omitted to acknowledge the same, according to law; and also, that the lessees and their assigns have executed subseqent leases, but have also neglected to make the legal acknowledgment:

Sec. 1. *Be it enacted by the General Assembly of the State of Ohio,* That all such original and subsequent leases shall be as valid in law, as if the same had been duly acknowledged and recorded; and they shall be entitled to record, in the same manner, as if they had been duly acknowledged, at the time of execution: *Provided,* They be offered for record within one year from the passage of this act: And *Provided, further,* That no rights, which have accrued to third persons, by reason of said omissions, shall be, in any way, invalidated in this act.

WM. SAWYER,
Speaker of the House of Representatives.

. ELIJAH VANCE,
Speaker of the Senate.

January 21, 1836.

AN ACT

To incorporate the town of Milford, in the county of Clermont.

Sec. 1. *Be it enacted by the Genera l Assembly of the State of Ohio,* That so much of the township of Miami, in the county of .Clermont, as is recorded in the plat of the town of Milford, together with such plats as have been or may hereafter be recorded as an addition or additions thereto, and any or all tracts or parcels of land, lying between such original plat and any of such additional original plats, and westward of said plats to Matthias Kugler's mill race, be, and the same is hereby created into and constituted a town corporate, by the name of the Town of Milford.

Sec. 2. That for the order and good government of said town, and inhabitants thereof, it shall be lawful for the white male householders thereof, who have resided therein for the space of three months next preceding the day of election, having the qualification of electors of members of the General Assembly, to meet at some convenient place, in the said town of Milford on the second Saturday of March next, and on the second Saturday of March annually thereafter; and then and there proceed, by a plurality of votes, to elect by ballot, one mayor, one recorder, and five trustees, who shall be householders in said town, who shall hold their offices until the next annual election, and until their successors are elected and qualified; and such mayor, recorder and trustees, being so elected and qualified, shall constitute the town council of said town, any five of whom shall constitute a quorum for the transaction of business pertaining to their duties.

Sec. 3. That at the first election to be holden under this act, there shall be chosen, *viva voce,* by the electors present, two judges, and a clerk of said election, who shall each take an oath or affirmation, faithfully to discharge the duties required of them by this act; and at all subsequent elections, the trustees, or any two of them, shall be judges, and the recorder, or in his absence some other person, to be appointed by the judges, shall be clerk: the polls shall be opened between the hours of ten and eleven o'clock in the forenoon, and close at three o'clock in the afternoon of said day; and, at the close of the polls, the vo'es shall be counted, and a true statement thereof proclaimed to the voters present, by one of the judges, and the clerk shall make a true copy thereof; and within five days thereafter, he shall give notice to the persons so elected, of their election; and it shall be the duty of the town council, at least ten days before each

10—L

and every annual election, to give notice of the same by setting up advertisements at three of the most public places in said town.

Sec. 4. That the mayor, and in case of his absence, the recorder, shall
preside at all meetings of the town council; and the recorder shall attend
all meetings of the town council, and make a fair and accurate record of
all their proceedings.

Sec. 5. That the town council shall have power to fill all vacancies
which may happen in said board, from the householders, who are qualified
electors of said town, who shall hold their appointment until the next annual election, and until their successors are elected and qualified; and in the
absence of the mayor and recorder from any meeting of the town council,
the trustees shall have power to appoint any two of their number, to perform the duties of mayor and recorder, for the time being.

Sec. 6. That the mayor, recorder, and trustees of said town, shall be a
body corporate and politic, with perpetual succession, to be known and distinguished by the name and style of The Town Council of the town of
Milford; and shall be capable in law, by their corporate name, to acquire
property, real, personal and mixed, for the use of said town; and may sell
and convey the same at pleasure: they may have a common seal, which
they may break, alter, or renew at pleasure: they may sue and be sued,
plead and be impleaded, defend and be defended, in all manner of actions,
and in all courts of law and equity: and whenever any suit shall be commenced against said corporation, the process shall be served by copy,
which shall be left with the recorder, or at his usual place of residence, at
least ten days before the return day thereof.

Sec. 7. That each member of said town council, before entering upon
the duties of his office, shall take an oath, or affirmation, to support the
constitution of the United States, and the constitution of this State, and
also an oath of office.

Sec. 8. That the town council shall have power to make, ordain, and
establish by-laws, rules and regulations, for the government of said town,
and to alter or repeal the same at pleasure; to provide for the appointment of a treasurer, town marshal, and such other subordinate officers,
as they may think necessary; to prescribe their duties, and determine the
period of their appointments; and to fix the fees they shall be entitled to
for their services; and the treasurer, marshal, and other officers, shall, before entering upon their duties, take an oath of office, and shall respectively give bonds, with security, in such sums as shall be determined by the
town council, payable to the State of Ohio, conditioned for the faithful
performance of their respective duties: the town council shall also have
power to fix reasonable fines and penalties for any violations of the laws
and ordinances of the corporation, to provide for the collection and disposition of the same: *Provided*, Such by-laws or ordinances, rules and regulations, be not inconsistent with the constitution and laws of the United
States, or of this State: *And provided, also*, That no by-law, ordinance,
rule, or regulation, shall take effect, or be in force, until the same shall
have been posted up for two weeks, in one or more of the most public
places in said corporation; and the time of such posting up, shall be entered on the minutes of the board by the recorder, and shall be *prima facie*
evidence that such notice has been given.

Sec. 9. That the town council shall, at the expiration of each and every year, cause to be made out and posted up as aforesaid, the receipts and expenditures of the preceding year.

Sec. 10. That the town council shall have power to regulate and improve the streets, lanes and alleys, and determine the width of the side walks in said town: they shall have power to remove all nuisances and obstructions from the streets and commons of said town, and to do all things which similar corporations have power to do.

Sec. 11. That for the purpose of more effectually enabling said town council to carry into effect the provisions of this act, they are hereby authorized and empowered to levy a tax on all the real and personal property, subject on the grand levy to taxation, within the limits of said town, upon the appraisement made and returned upon said grand levy: *Provided*, That said tax, so levied by said town council, shall not, in any one year, exceed one half of one per centum, on the aggregate amount of all such taxable property within the limits of said town; and the said town council shall, annually, between the first day of April and first day of July, determine the amount of tax to be assessed and collected for the current year.

Sec. 12. That it shall be the duty of the recorder of said corporation, to make out duplicates of taxes, charging each individual, within said corporation, an amount of tax in proportion to the aggregate value of the taxable property belonging to such individual within the limits of said corporation, as the same appears upon the books of the auditor of said county of Clermont; and the said recorder shall have power of inspecting the books of said auditor. and to take any minutes or transcripts therefrom, as may be necessary to aid him in the discharge of the duties hereby enjoined upon him, free of expense; when said recorder shall have made out said duplicates as aforesaid, he shall deliver one of such duplicates to the marshal of said town, or to such other person as may be appointed collector, whose duty it shall be to collect the taxes charged thereon, in the same manner, and under the same regulations, as are provided by law for the collection of State and county taxes: and the said marshal, or collector, shall, immediately after collecting said taxes, pay the same over to the treasurer of said corporation, and take his receipt therefor; and the said marshal, or collector, shall have the same power to sell both real and personal property, as is given, by law, to county treasurers; and, when necessary, the recorder shall have power to make deeds for real estate, so sold, in the same manner that county auditors are, by law, empowered to do, for lands sold by the county treasurer; and the marshal, or collector, shall receive such fees for his services, as the town council may direct, not exceeding six per cent. on all moneys so by him collected, to be paid by the treasurer, on the order of the recorder.

Sec. 13. That the said town council shall have power to appropriate any money remaining in the corporation treasury, to the improvement of the streets, alleys, and side walks of said town, whenever they may deem it necessary; and to make any other improvement which may conduce to the health and comfort of said town.

Sec. 14. That the mayor of said town shall be a conservator of the peace, within the limits of said corporation; and shall have, therein, all the powers and jurisdiction of a justice of the peace, in all cases, civil or criminal, arising under the laws of this State; he shall perform all the duties enjoined upon him by the laws ond ordinances of the corporation; and appeals may be taken from the decision of the said mayor, in all cases where, by law, appeals are allowed from the decisions of justices of the peace, and in the same manner.

Sec. 15. That the marshal shall be the principal ministerial officer in said corporation, and shall have the same power as constables have, by law; and his authority, in the execution of criminal process, shall be co-extensive with the limits of said county of Clermont; and he shall receive, for his services, such fees as are allowed, by law, to constables in similar cases, for like services.

Sec. 16. That the mayor shall receive for his services, such fees as are allowed, by law, to justices of the peace, for similar services, in like cases; and the recorder shall receive such fees for his services, as shall be fixed by the by-laws and ordinances of the corporation.

Sec. 17. That if no election shall be held by the electors of said town on the second Saturday of March next, it shall be lawful for any ten householders of said town, to call a meeting of the electors, by giving ten days notice thereof, in writing, to be posted up in one or more of the most public places in said town; which notice shall state the time, place, and object of said meeting, and shall be signed by the said householders; and if a majority of the qualified electors of said town, shall attend at the time and place specified in said notice, it shall be lawful for them to proceed to the election of officers, in the same manner as hereinbefore provided for; and the officers, so elected, shall hold their offices until the second Saturday of March following, and until their successors are elected and qualified.

Sec. 18. That said corporation shall be allowed the use of the county jail, for the imprisonment of such persons as may be liable to impirisonment under the laws and ordinances of said town; and all persons so imprisoned shall be under the charge of the sheriff, or jailor, as in other cases.

Sec. 19. That any future legislature shall have power to alter, amend, or repeal this act.

WM. SAWYER,
Speaker of the House of Representatives,
ELIJAH VANCE,
Speaker of the Senate.

January 23, 1836.

AN ACT

To incorporate the Coolville Toll Bridge Company.

Sec. 1. *Be it enacted by the General Assembly of the State of Ohio,* That Alferd Hobby, E. A. Gibbs, John W. Lottridge, Simeon Cooly, Jacob Humphrey, A. S. Bestow and W. Lewis, of Troy township, in Athens county, and their associates, be, and they are hereby created a body corporate and politic, by the name and style of "The Coolville Toll Bridge Company," and as such shall remain and have perpetual succession; and, by their corporate name, may contract and be contracted with, sue and be sued, answer and be answered, plead and be impleaded, defend and be defended, in any court of competent jurisdiction; and may have a common seal, which they may change or alter at pleasure.

Sec. 2. That the said corporation be, and they are hereby authorized, to erect a toll bridge across the Hockhocking river, at, or near Coolville: *Provided*, The said company shall own the land on both banks of the said river where said bridge shall be erected, or shall obtain in writing, from the owner or owners of the land on both sides of the river, where said bridge may be built, their consent to the building of said bridge; unless said banks on both sides be a public highway.

Sec. 3. That the said company, in the erection of said bridge, shall in no wise injure or obstruct the navigation of said river.

Sec. 4. That if said company shall erect and complete said bridge in a substantial manner, of proper width, and being in other respects of sufficient strength and dimensions, so as to admit of the safe passage of passengers, teams and carriages, of the usual dimensions, within four years from the passage of this act, they shall, from the time of completing said bridge, enjoy all the privileges secured to them by this act.

Sec. 5. That after the completion of said bridge, as aforesaid, the proprietors thereof are hereby authorized to demand and receive, from passengers who may cross said bridge, the following rates of toll, to wit: for each foot passenger, two cents; for each horse, mule or ass, three cents; for each horse and rider, four cents; for each wagon, four wheeled carriage, sled, sleigh or cart, drawn by one horse, ox, mule or ass, eight cents; for every horse, mule or ass in addition, three cents; for each head of neat cattle, one cent; for each head of hogs or sheep, one half cent: *Provided*, That all troops of the United States or of this State, with their artillery, baggage and stores, all persons going to, or returning from public worship, and all teachers and children going to, and returning from school all funeral processions, and persons having the qualifications of an elector going to and returning from elections, and all persons necessarily going to and returning from military trainings, shall pass on said bridge free of toll.

Sec. 6. That the proprietors of said bridge shall, previous to receiving any tolls, set up and keep in a conspicuous place, over or near the gate, to be erected on said bridge, a board on which shall be painted or printed, in a plain and legible manner, the rates of toll allowed by this act.

Sec. 7. That if the proprietors of said bridge shall demand and receive any higher or greater toll than is by this act allowed, they shall be subject to the like fines and penalties, which are or may be provided in the case of ferries; and any future Legislature may regulate the rates of toll to be taken at said bridge.

Sec. 8. That the said company shall have power to adopt such by-laws, rules and regulations, for the government of the same, as they may deem expedient, not inconsistent with the constitution and laws of the United States or of this State.

WM. SAWYER,
Speaker of the House of Representatives.
ELIJAH VANCE,
Speaker of the Senate.

January 26, 1836.

AN ACT

To incorporate the Presbyterian Church of Bealsville, in Monroe county.

Sec. 1. *Be it enacted by the General Assembly of the State of Ohio,* That John Nelson, William Cox, Jacob W. Watts, Thomas Griffith, and John Rodgers, and their associates for the time being, be, and they are hereby created a body corporate and politic, to be known by the name and style of the "Presbyterian Church of Bealsville," and as such shall remain and have perpetual succession, subject, however, to such alterations and regulations as the Legislature may, from time to time, think proper to make.

Sec. 2. That the said corporation, by the name and style aforesaid, shall be capable in law and equity, of having, receiving, acquiring and holding, either by gift, grant, devise or purchase, any estate, real, personal, or mixed, for the use of said corporation, and of transferring the same at pleasure: *Provided,* That the annual income of all such property shall not exceed two thousand dollars.

Sec. 3. That the said corporation shall be capable in law and equity, by the name aforesaid, of suing and being sued, pleading and being impleaded, in any action or suit, in any court having competent jurisdiction; and they may have a common seal, which they may alter, change break, or renew at pleasure.

Sec. 4. That the said corporation shall on the second Monday of April annually, elect five trustees, a treasurer, and such other officers as the church may deem necessary; who shall hold their for offices for one year, and until their successors shall be elected: *Provided.* That if, from any cause, the aforesaid officers shall not be elected on the day appointed for the annual election, the church may elect its officers at any meeting of the corporation duly assembled.

Sec. 5. That all the elections of said corporation shall be by ballot; and the person or persons having a plurality of votes given for any office, shall be considered duly elected; and each and every male member of such church or society, of twenty-one years of age and upwards, shall have equal suffrage; and all the temporal concerns of said church shall be determined by a majority of the members present, at any meeting of the corporation duly assembled.

Sec. 6. That all meetings ofthe corporation, either for the election of officers or for other purposes, shall be called by the trustees, or a majority of them, who shall cause public notice of the time and place, and purpose, of such meeting, to be given at least ten days previous to any such meeting.

Sec. 7. That the trustees, or a majority of them, shall have power and authority to make all contracts on behalf of the church, and to manage all pecuniary and prudential matters, pertaining to the good order, interest and welfare of the corporation; and to make such rules, regulations and by-laws, consistent with the constitution of the United States, and of this State, as they may deem advisable, from time to time, for their own government, and that of the corporation: *Provided, always,* That they make no by-laws, or pass any order for the imposition of any tax on the corporation.

Sec. 8. That the treasurer give bond with security, to the trustees and their successors in office, in such sum as they shall deem sufficient, conditioned for the faithful performance of those duties that may appertain to his office by the regulations and by-laws of the corporation.

Sec. 9. That original process against the said corporation shall be by summons, which shall be served by leaving an attested copy thereof with the treasurer of the corporation, five days before the return day mentioned therein; and such service shall be deemed sufficient in law to bind said corporation.

Sec. 10. That John Nelson, William Cox, Jacob W. Watts, Thomas Griffith, and John Rodgers, be appointed trustees until the first annual election, and until others are elected in their place.

Sec. 11. That any future Legislature may modify, amend, or repeal this act: *Provided*, Such modification, amendment, or repeal, shall not affect the title to any estate, real, or personal, acquired or conveyed under its provisions, or divert the same to any other purpose than originally intended.

WM. SAWYER,
Speaker of the House of Representatives.

ELIJAH VANCE,
Speaker of the Senate.

January 26th, 1836.

AN ACT

To incorporate the First Congregational Society of La Grange, in the county of Lorain.

Sec. 1. *Be it enacted by the General Assembly of the State of Ohio,* That Nathan P. Johnson, William Dixon, Marquis D. Kellogg, Calvin Wilcox, Sylvester Merriam, and their associates, together with such other persons as may hereafter be associated with them, be, and they are hereby created and declared a body corporate and politic, by the name of "The First Congregational Society of La Grange;" and as such shall remain and have perpetual succession; and by their corporate name may contract and be contracted with, sue and be sued, answer and be answered unto, plead and be impleaded, defend and be defended, in any court of competent jurisdiction, in all manner of actions, causes and complaints whatsoever; and may have a common seal, which they may change, alter, or renew at pleasure.

Sec. 2. That the said corporation, by the name and style aforesaid, shall be capable in law of holding property, real, personal or mixed, either by purchase, gift, grant, devise, or legacy, which may become the property of said corporation, to any amount not exceeding two thousand dollars: *Provided,* That all such property shall be considered as held in trust, under the management and at the disposal of said corporation, for the purpose of promoting the interests of said society or congregation; defraying the expenses incident to their mode of worship, and maintaining or supporting any institutions of charity or education, connected therewith: *Provided, further,*

That when any money or other property shall be given, granted, bequeathed or devised to said congregation, for any particular use or purpose, it
shall be faithfully applied to such use or purpose; and that the property
and other concerns of the corporation shall be under the management and
control of trustees, to be appointed agreeably to the directions of the congregation.

Sec. 3. That on the second Tuesday in February, in the year one
thousand eight hundred and thirty-six, and on the second Tuesday of February, in each and every year thereafter, the members of said society
shall elect three trustees, and such other officers as they may deem necessary; who shall hold their offices for one year, and until their successors
shall be elected: *Provided*, That in any case of failure to elect officers as
aforesaid, the trustees may call a meeting at such time and place as they
may think proper, for the purpose of electing such officers.

Sec. 4. That the three first named persons, in the first section of this
act, be, and they are hereby appointed trustees until the first election, and
until others are elected in their places.

Sec. 5. That the trustees or any two of them shall have power to
call a meeting of the corporation, either for the election of officers, or for
the transaction of other business of the society, by giving, or causing to be
given to the society, immediately after public worship, ten days' previous
notice, or by causing notifications thereof to be put up in three or more
public places within the limits of said congregation, at least fifteen days
before said meeting.

Sec. 6. That any meeting of the congregation, duly assembled, may adopt
and establish such by-laws and ordinances as may be deemed proper and
necessary for the good government of said corporation: *Provided*, That
such by-laws and ordinances shall not be incompatible with the constitutions and laws of this State, and of the United States.

Sec. 7. That original process against said corporation shall be by summons, which shall be served by leaving an attested copy with one or more
of the trustees, at least ten days before the return day of said writ; and
such service shall be deemed sufficient in law to bind said corporation.

Sec. 8. That any future Legislature shall have power to modify or
repeal this act: *Provided*, That such modification or repeal shall not affect the title to any real or personal estate, acquired or conveyed under
its provisions; or divert the same to any other purpose than originally
intended.

WM. SAWYER,
Speaker of the House of Representatives.
ELIJAH VANCE,
Speaker of the Senate.

January 15th, 1836.

AN ACT

To revise and amend the act, entitled "An act to incorporate the First Presbyterian and Congregational Society, in Unionville.

WHEREAS, an act to incorporate the First Presbyterian and Congregational
Society of Unionville, was passed by the General Assembly, on the first

day of March, A. D. 1834, and the day appointed for holding the first meeting to elect the officers for said society, was the second Monday of May, in the same year: *And whereas*, said society did not meet and elect officers as therein provided: Therefore,

Sec. 1. *Be it enacted by the General Assembly of the State of Ohio*, That all owners or part owners of any pew in the house of public worship of said society, and all male contributors to the erection of such house, with other male members of the society, may, and are hereby authorized to meet on the fourth Monday in June, in the year of our Lord, one thousand eight hundred and thirty-six, and elect the officers required by said act of incorporation, and shall thereafter hold their annual elections on the day provided by the act to which this is an amendment, and shall thereafter have and enjoy all the privileges granted by said act of incorporation: *Provided*, That if said society fail to meet on the day appointed, then such meeting may be held on any day thereafter, by the trustees mentioned in the act to which this is an amendment, giving ten days notice in writing, posted up in three public places within the limits of said society.

Sec. 2. That the said corporation shall be capable in law or equity, of holding property, real, personal or mixed, either by purchase, gift, grant, devise, or legacy: *Provided*, That the annual income thereof, shall not exceed the sum of two thousand dollars; and that so much of the act to which this is an amendment, as is inconsistent with this act, be, and the same is hereby repealed.

Sec. 3. That any future legislature may alter, amend, or repeal this act, or the act hereby amended and revised.

WM. SAWYER,
Speaker of the House of Representatives.
ELIJAH VANCE,
Speaker of the Senate.

January 26, 1836.

AN ACT

To give immediate effect to the act to incorporate the town of Worthington.

WHEREAS, an inadvertency occurred in the form and date of the above recited act, delaying the operation thereof, contrary to the evident intention of the Legislature, from March last, until the first of March next; the same not being ascertained until after the election thus made of the corporation officers, according to the provisions of said act: *And whereas*, the citizens of said town are anxious to go into measures, during the present winter, for the better protection of the property in said town, against destruction by fire: Therefore,

Sec. 1. *Be it enacted by the General Assembly of the State of Ohio*, That the act aforesaid shall take effect from and after the passage hereof; and that the officers elected for the corporation, by the electors of said town, on the first Monday of March last, be, and they are hereby authori-

11—L

zed to procced, after being duly qualified, to the discharge of the duties of their respective offices, until the annual election, in March next, and their successors, duly elected and qualified.

WM. SAWYER,
Speaker of the House of Representatives.
ELIJAH VANCE,
Speaker of the Senate.

January 26, 1836.

AN ACT

To incorporate the Lutheran and German Reformed Church and Society of New Rumley, in the county of Harrison.

Sec. 1. *Be it enacted by the General Assembly of the State of Ohio,* That Peter Nap, John Kenouf, and Frederick Kimuel, and their associates, together with such other persons as may hereafter be associated with them, be, and they are hereby created and declared, a body corporate and politic, by the name and style of The Lutheran and German Reformed Church and Society of New Rumley; and, as such, shall remain, and have perpetual succession; and by their corporate name, may contract and be contracted with, sue and be sued, answer and be answered unto, plead and be impleaded, defend and be defended, in any court of competent jurisdiction, in all manner of actions whatsoever; and may have a common seal, which they may change, alter, or renew at pleasure.

Sec. 2. That the said corporation, by the name and style aforesaid, shall be capable in law of holding property, real, personal or mixed, either by purchase, gift, grant, devise, or legacy, which may become the property of said corporation: *Provided,* That the annual income of all such property shall not exceed the sum of two thousand dollars: *And provided also,* That all such property shall be considered as held in trust, under the management, and at the disposal of said corporation, for the purpose of promoting the interests of said church and society, and defraying the expenses incident to their mode of worship, and maintaining any institutions of charity or education that may be therewith connected: *And provided further,* That when any money, or other property, shall be given, granted, or devised, to said society, for any particular use or purpose, it shall be faithfully applied to such use or purpose; and that the property and other concerns of the corporation shall be under the management and control of trustees, to be appointed agreeably to the provisions of this act.

Sec. 3. That there shall be a meeting of the members of said church and society, on Whitsuntide Monday annually; at which time, there shall be elected three trustees, and such other officers as the said members shall deem necessary, who shall hold their offices one year, and until their successors are chosen; and if, at any time, the election should not be held on the day above specified, the corporation shall not thereby be dissolved, but the officers previously chosen, shall serve until their successors are elected; and such election may be held at any time, ten days public notice having been given of the time and place of holding such election.

Sec. 4. That the persons named in the first section of this act, be, and they are hereby appointed trustees, until the first election, and until others are elected in their places.

Sec. 5. That any meeting of the society, duly assembled, may adopt and establish such by-laws and regulations, as may be deemed proper and necessary for the good government of said corporation: *Provided*, Such by-laws and regulations be not incompatible with the constitution and laws of the United States, and of this State.

Sec. 6. That original process against the corporation, shall be served by leaving an attested copy with one or more of the trustees, and such service shall be sufficient to bind the corporation.

Sec. 7 Any future legislature may alter, amend, or repeal this act; but such alteration or repeal shall not affect the title to any property, acquired or transferred under its provisions.

WM. SAWYER,
Speaker of the House of Representatives.
ELIJAH VANCE,
Speaker of the Senate.

January 26, 1836.

AN ACT

To incorporate the Bellville Library Company, in the county of Richland.

Sec. 1. *Be it enacted by the General Assembly of the State of Ohio,* That Hugh Newell, Joseph Hildreth, Isaac Heath, James Doughty, John Moody, Elijah Clark, and Benjamin Jackson, and their associates, together with such other persons as may hereafter be associated with them, be, and they are hereby created a body politic and corporate, by the name of the Bellville Library Company, with perpetual succession; and by their corporate name may sue and be sued, plead and be impleaded, in all courts of law and equity, in this State and elsewhere; may have a common seal, and the same may alter at pleasure; shall be capable of holding personal and real estate, by purchase, gift, or devise, and may sell, dispose of, and convey the same: they shall have power to form and ratify a constitution, and adopt by-laws for the government of said corporation, and the arrangement and regulation of its fiscal concerns, the admission of its members and the appointment of its officers, together with all power necessary to the corporate existence and the proper and efficient management of its concerns: *Provided*, The funds of said company shall be applied to no other object than that of supporting a library, in the village of Bellville: *Provided*, That any future Legislature may have power to alter, amend or repeal this act.

WM. SAWYER,
Speaker of the House of Representatives.
ELIJAH VANCE,
Speaker of the Senate.

January 27th, 1836.

AN ACT

To incorporate the town of Defiance, in the county of Williams.

Sec. 1. *Be it enacted by the General Assembly of the State of Ohio,* That so much of the township of Defiance, in the county of Williams, as is comprised within the following limits, to wit: All the recorded town plat of Defiance, with all the fractional parts of lots lying between the town plat and the Auglaize river on the east, and the Maumee river on the north, to low water mark, be, and the same is hereby created a town corporate, and shall henceforth be known and distinguished by the name of the town of Defiance.

Sec. 2. That for the good order and government of said town, it shall be lawful for the white male inhabitants who have resided within the aforesaid limits of said town for the space of three months next preceding the second Tuesday of April next, and who have the qualifications of electors of members of the General Assembly, to meet at the usual place of holding elections, on the second Tuesday of April next, and on the first Tuesday of April annually thereafter, at such place as the town council may direct, which shall be determined by notices of the time and place, posted up in three of the most public places in said town, at least ten days before the election; which notice shall be signed by the mayor and recorder, and then and there proceed by ballot to elect, by a plurality of votes, one mayor, one recorder, and five trustees, who shall be either householders or freeholders, residing within the limits of said town, and who shall hold their respective offices for one year, and until their successors are elected and qualified; such mayor, recorder and trustees being so elected and qualified, shall constitute a town council, any five of whom shall constitute a quorum for the transaction of business.

Sec. 3. That at the first election to be holden under this act, there shall be chosen *viva voce,* by the electors present, three judges and a clerk of said election, who shall each take an oath or affirmation faithfully to discharge the duties required of them by this act; and at all subsequent elections, the trustees, or any two of them, shall be judges, and the recorder clerk; and at all elections held under the provisions of this act, the polls shall be opened between the hours of one and two, and closed at four o'clock, P. M. of said day; and at the close of the polls the votes shall be counted, and a true statement thereof proclaimed by one of the judges, to the electors present; and the clerk shall make a true record thereof, who shall notify the persons elected to their respective offices, of their election within five days; and the persons so elected and notified, shall, within five days thereafter, take an oath or affirmation to support the constitution of the United States, and of the State of Ohio, and an oath of office; any person elected as aforesaid, neglecting or refusing to qualify as aforesaid, shall forfeit and pay into the treasury of said town, the sum of five dollars, to be recovered by an action of debt, before the mayor of said town; and the recorder shall, in the name of said town, demand, receive, or sue for such forfeiture, and pay over the same when collected to the treasurer, taking his receipt therefor: *Provided,* That no person shall be compelled to serve in any office in said corporation two years in succession.

Sec. 4. That the mayor, recorder and trustees of said town shall be a body politic, and corporate with perpetual succession, to be known and distinguished by the name of the Town Council of Defiance; and they and their successors in office shall be authorized to use a common seal, and the same to alter at pleasure; to receive, purchase, acquire, hold and convey any estate, real, personal or mixed, and to manage and dispose of the same in such manner as they, or a majority of them may deem proper; they shall be capable in the name aforesaid of suing and being sued, pleading and being impleaded, answering and being answered, in any suit or action in any court of law or equity in this State; and when any suit or action shall be commenced against said corporation, the first process shall be by summons, a copy of which shall be left with the mayor, or in his absence, at his usual place of abode, at least five days before the return day thereof.

Sec. 5. That it shall be the duty of the mayor, and in his absence or disability to serve, the recorder, to preside at all meetings of the town council; it shall also be the duty of the recorder to attend to all such meetings, and keep an accurate record of their proceedings, to be recorded in a book provided for that purpose; it shall moreover be the duty of the recorder to attend all elections under the provisions of this act; but in case of his absence or disability to serve as such, the trustees shall have power to appoint one of their number clerk of said election, pro tempore.

Sec. 6. That the town council shall have power to fill all vacancies which may occur in their body by death, resignation, or otherwise, from among the electors in said town, whose appointment shall continue until the next annual election, and until their successors are elected and qualified; and whenever it may happen that neither the mayor or recorder is present at any meeting of said town council, the trustees shall have power to appoint one of their number to perform the duties of such mayor or recorder, or both, as the case may be, which appointment shall be pro tempore; and that the mayor, or a majority of the trustees shall have power to call a meeting of the town council whenever in his or their opinion the public good of said corporation shall require it.

Sec. 7. That the mayor, recorder, and trustees, or a majority of them, whereof the mayor or recorder shall always be one, or in their absence, one of the trustees appointed to fill their vacancy, shall have power and authority to make, ordain and publish all such by-laws and ordinances, consistent with the constitution and laws of the United States, and of this State, as they may deem necessary and expedient for the regulation, interest, safety, health, cleanliness and convenience of said town, and the same to alter or repeal at pleasure; they shall have power to appoint a treasurer, town marshal, and such other subordinate officers as they may deem necessary; to prescribe their duties, and to require of them such security as they may deem necessary for the faithful performance of their duties; to remove them at pleasure; to fix and establish the fees of the officers of said corporation not established by this act, except the trustees, who shall receive no fees; said town council shall also have power to affix to the violation of the by-laws and ordinances of said corporation, such reasonable fines and forfeitures, as they may deem proper, and provide for the collection and disposition of the same; they shall have power to lay out and regulate the lots, streets, lanes, alleys, and public ground; to lay out and determine the width of the side walks, and regulate the same; they shall also have power to remove or cause to be removed all nuisances and obstructions, and do all things which a corporation of a similar nature can do, to secure the health, peace and good order of the inhabitants of said town.

Sec. 8. That for the purpose of more effectually enabling the town council to carry into effect the provisions of this act, they are hereby authorized and empowered to assess for corporation purposes an amount of tax on all property within said town, made taxable by the laws of this State, for State and county purposes, not exceeding in any one year one per cent. on the value thereof, which value shall be ascertained by an assessor to be appointed by said town council for that purpose; they shall also have power to equalize any injudicious assessments thus made, on complaint of the owner or owners, his, her, or their agent so aggrieved.

Sec. 9. That it shall be the duty of the town council to make out or cause to be made out by the recorder, a duplicate of taxes, charging each individual therein, an amount of tax in proportion to the property of such individual assessed as aforesaid, within said town; which duplicate shall be signed by the mayor and recorder, and delivered to the marshal or such other person as shall be appointed collector, whose duty it shall be to collect the same within such time and in such manner as the by-laws shall direct; and the said collector shall have power to sell both real and personal estate for the non-payment of taxes within said town, and shall be governed therein by the same laws and regulations as the collectors of State and county taxes; and in case of the sale of any real estate, the recorder shall have power to make and execute deeds therefor, in the same manner that county auditors are by law empowered to do for lands sold by the county treasurer; and the said collector shall, within ten days after collecting said taxes, pay the same over to the treasurer of said corporation, taking his receipt therefor; and who shall receive for his fees such sum as the town council may direct, not exceeding six per cent. on all moneys so by him collected, and paid over; said fees to be paid by the treasurer, on the order of the recorder.

Sec. 10. That the by-laws and ordinances of said town, shall be posted up in two or more of the most public places within said town, at least ten days before the taking effect thereof, and the certificate of the recorder upon the town record shall be considered sufficient evidence of the same having been done.

Sec. 11. That the town council shall, at the expiration of each year, cause to be made out and posted up in one or more of the most public places in said town, an exhibit of the receipts and expenditures of the preceding (year;) which statement shall be certified by the recorder of said town.

Sec. 12. That the mayor of said corporation shall be a conservator of the peace throughout said town, and shall have within the same all the powers and jurisdiction of a justice of the peace in all matters, civil or criminal, arising under the laws of this State, to all intents and purposes whatever; he shall give bond and security as is required by law of justices of the peace; and the said mayor shall perform all the duties required of him by the by-laws and ordinances of said corporation; and appeals may be taken in all cases from the decisions of said mayor, in the same manner as from the decisions of justices of the peace; he shall keep a docket, wherein he shall keep a fair record of all matters of difference tried before him, and shall be allowed and receive the same fees that justices of the peace are or may be entitled to in similar cases.

Sec. 13. That the marshal shall be the principal ministerial officer of said town, and shall have the same powers as constables have by law; and his jurisdiction in criminal cases shall be co-extensive with the county of Williams; he shall execute the process of the mayor, and receive the same fees for his services that constables are allowed in similar cases.

Sec. 14. That said corporation shall be allowed the use of the county jail of the county of Williams, for the imprisonment of such persons as may be liable to imprisonment under the by-laws and ordinances of said corporation; and all persons so imprisoned, shall be under the charge of the sheriff of the county of Williams, as in other cases.

Sec. 15. That the mayor, recorder, trustees and other officers of said corporation shall, on demand, deliver to to their successors in office all such books and papers as appertain in any wise to their office.

Sec. 16. That any future Legislature shall have power to alter, amend or repeal this act: *Provided,* That such alteration, amendment, or repeal shall not divert the property of said corporation from the purpose expressed in this act.

WM. SAWYER,
Speaker of the House of Representatives.
ELIJAH VANCE,
Speaker of the Senate.

January 27, 1836.

AN ACT

To provide for the erection of certain bridges in the county of Coshocton.

Sec. 1. *Be it enacted by the General Assembly of the State of Ohio,* That the county commissioners of Coshocton county are hereby authorized to cause to be constructed a bridge across the Walhonding river, opposite to the end of Hill street, in the addition to the town of Roscoe; and another bridge across the Tuscarawas river, at or near the place where the former bridge stood.

Sec. 2. Said bridges shall have double tracks, and shall be constructed in such manner as said commissioners shall direct; the contract or contracts for their construction shall be made by said commissioners, and the work shall be done under their superintendence; or some other suitable person or persons appointed by said commissioners for that purpose; and no money shall be paid to the contractor, except upon the certificate of said commissioners that work to twenty-five per cent more than that amount has been done according to contract.

Sec. 3. Said commissioners are hereby authorized to borrow any sum of money not exceeding twenty thousand dollars, at a rate of interest not exceeding seven per cent. per annum, which they may deem necessary for the purpose aforesaid, and to execute therefor any instrument or assurance which may be necessary to secure the payment of the interest thereon, and the principal at such times as may be agreed upon: said commissioners are also hereby authorized and reqired to levy such annual tax as may be necessary to pay the interest upon said debt, and finally the principal at such time or times as may be specified in the contract.

Sec. 4. Said bridges shall forever be free to all the inhabitants of said county of Coshocton: such tolls may be required from non-residents who may cross the same, as shall be prescribed by the said commissioners: *Provided,* That said tolls for crossing each bridge, shall never exceed those allowed in like cases for crossing the upper bridge at the town of Zanesville: *And provided, also,* That said commissioners may make said bridge free to all persons, whenever they shall deem it expedient to do so.

WM. SAWYER,
Speaker of the House of Representatives.
ELIJAH VANCE,
Speaker of the Senate.

January 27th, 1836.

AN ACT

To authorize the Town Council of the town of Newark, to borrow money.

Sec. 1. *Be it enacted by the General Assembly of the State of Ohio,* That the Town Council of the town of Newark, and their successors in office, be, and they are hereby authorized to borrow, on the credit of the corporation of the town of Newark, in the county of Licking, a sum of money not exceeding ten thousand dollars; which money, when borrowed, under the provisions of this act, shall be applied to the improvement of said town, under the direction of the town council.

Sec. 2. That the annual revenue of said town, is hereby pledged for the redemption of any loan which may be made under the provisions of this act.

WM. SAWYER,
Speaker of the House of Representatives.
ELIJAH VANCE,
Speaker of the Senate.

January 27, 1836.

AN ACT

To increase the capital stock of the Fairport Aqueduct Company

Sec. 1. *Be it enacted by the General Assembly of the State of Ohio,* That the stockholders of the Fairport Aqueduct Company, may at any time hereafter augment the capital stock of said company to ten thousand dollars; to be divided into shares of twenty-five dollars each, whenever, at a special meeting of such stockholders convened for that purpose, of which at least ten days previous notice shall have been given by publication in some newspaper printed in the county of Geauga, two thirds of all the votes shall be given therefor, under such regulations, conditions, and restrictions as they shall at such meeting judge proper; and the stock subscribed by virtue hereof shall be subject to all the by-laws, rules and regulations of said company.

WM. SAWYER,
Speaker of the House of Representatives.
ELIJAH VANCE,
Speaker of the Senate.

January 29, 1836.

AN ACT

To lay out and establish a graded State road in the counties of Carroll and Stark.

Sec. 1. *Be it enacted by the General Assembly of the State of Ohio,* That Charles Fawcett, of the county of Carroll, and John Augustine, of the county of Stark, be, and they are hereby appointed commissioners, and Daniel Black of Carroll county, surveyor, to lay out and establish a graded state road; commencing on the graded state road, from Cadiz to Congress Furnace, where the county line between the counties of Harrison and Carroll crosses the same; thence through Leesburgh, on the nearest and best route to Waynesburg, Stark county; thence the nearest and best route to Osnaburg, in said county of Stark.

Sec. 2. That said road shall in no case exceed an angle of five degrees with the horizon.

Sec. 3. That the commissioners aforesaid shall, in all respects be governed by the laws in force, defining the mode of laying out and establishing state roads; and should either of said commissioners die, remove out of the county, or refuse to serve, the commissioners of the county in which such vacancy may occur are hereby authorized to fill the same.

WM. SAWYER,
Speaker of the House of Representatives.
ELIJAH VANCE,
Speaker of the Senate.

January 29, 1836.

AN ACT

To amend an act to incorporate the Massillon Rolling Mill Company.

Sec. 1. *Be it enacted by the General Assembly of the State of Ohio,* That said company is hereby authorized at any time agreed upon by said

12—L

company, to increase their capital stock to any amount not exceeding six hundred thousand dollars; and that it may be lawful for said stockholders, at any time agreed upon by said company, to increase the number of shares of said stock, not to exceed six thousand, of one huhdred dollars each.

Sec. 2. That so much of the act entitled "An act to incorporate the Massillon Rolling Mill Company," passed March 3, 1834, as is contrary to the provisions of this act, be, and the same is hereby repealed.

WM. SAWYER,
Speaker of the House of Representatives.

ELIJAH VANCE,
Speaker of the Senate.

January 29, 1836.

AN ACT

To declare the river of St. Mary's further a public highway.

Sec. 1. *Be it enacted by the General Assembly of the State of Ohio,* That St. Mary's river, from the town of St. Mary's to the Steam Mill owned by Cummings & Co., or a point opposite said mill, shall be, and the same is hereby declared a public highway.

Sec. 2. That if any person shall fell, or put, or cause to be felled or put, any tree, log, timber, rack, or brush, or other obstruction, into said river, within the bounds mentioned in the first section of this act, and neglect to remove the same, every person so offending shall forfeit and pay for every such offence the sum of five dollars, to be recovered by action of debt, before any justice of the peace having jurisdiction, in the name of the State of Ohio, upon the application of any elector of the township where the offence was committed; and when collected, shall be paid into the township treasury, and applied by the trustees of said township in improving the roads thereof: *Provided,* That nothing herein contained shall be so construed as to prevent any person owning lands on said stream from erecting a mill dam or mill dams, or other persons from rafting logs or timber on said stream.

Sec. 3. That all persons offending against the provisions of this act, shall be liable for all damage done to private property, in consequence of such offence, to be recovered in any court of competent jurisdiction, cr before any justice of the peace having jurisdiction thereof.

WM. SAWYER,
Speaker of the House of Repeesentatives.

ELIJAH VANCE,
Speaker of the Senate.

January 29, 1836.

AN ACT

To authorize the Commissioners of Cuyahoga county to levy taxes for building and repairing bridges in said county.

Sec. 1. *Be it enacted by the General Assembly of the State of Ohio,* That the county commissioners of the county of Cuyahoga, be, and they are hereby authorized to levy a tax annually, upon the taxable property of said county, not exceeding one and a half mill upon the dollar, which shall be collected in the same manner and at the same time that State and county taxes are, for the time being, collected and paid into the treasury of said county, and shall be appropriated exclusively to the erection and repair of bridges within said county, at the discretion of said commissioners.

WM. SAWYER,
Speaker of the House of Representatives.
ELIJAH VANCE,
Speaker of the Senate.

January 29, 1836.

AN ACT

Providing for the sale of Section Sixteen, in the township of Adams, in the county of Seneca.

' Sec. 1. *Be it enacted by the General Assembly of the State of Ohio,* That it shall be the duty of the assessor of Seneca county, on or before the first day of April next to provide himself with a suitable book for that purpose, and proceed to take the votes of all the white male inhabitants over the age of twenty-one years, residing in the bounds of original surveyed township number three, north, of range sixteen, in the county of Seneca, aforesaid, who have resided therein for twelve months next preceding the first day of April aforesaid, whether such white male inhabitants be, or be not citizens of the United States; and it shall further be the duty of said assessor, between the first day of April and the twenty-fifth day of May next, to call upon all the white male inhabitants residing in the township aforesaid, and request every such inhabitant to give his vote for or against a sale of the school land aforesaid, by signing his name under the head of the proper columns; and if such inhabitant be unable to write, the assessor aforesaid, shall write the name of such inhabitant, to which he shall affix his mark of approbation; which said vote taken as aforesaid, shall be entered in said book by said assessor, in form following, to wit: The votes of the white male inhabitants over the age of twenty-one years, residing within the bounds of said original surveyed township, (there being twenty of said inhabitants within the same,) for and against the sale of the said section sixteen; it being the tract granted by Congress for the use of schools in said original surveyed township.

Names of those who voted   Names of those who voted
     in favor of a sale.   against the sale.

Which said list of votes so taken as aforesaid, the assessor shall deliver to the county auditor of Seneca county, forthwith, after having taken the same as aforesaid; and if it shall appear from said list, that a majority of the white male inhabitants aforesaid, have voted in favor of a sale, then a sale of said school section may be made in the manner hereinafter provided.

Sec. 2. That Asa Crocket, Ira Phelps, and Samuel Whiteman, of the county of Seneca, be, and they are hereby appointed commissioners, whose duty it shall be to view and appraise said school section sixteen, so soon as the assessor shall have performed the duties required of him by the first section of this act, they having first taken an oath or affirmation, before some person competent to administer the same, faithfully and impartially to appraise said land.

Sec. 3. That should either of the commissioners die, or refuse to perform the duties required by this act, or remove out of said county of Seneca, then the county commissioners of said county shall fill such vacancy so often as it may occur.

Sec. 4. That the commissioners appointed by virtue of this act are hereby authorized, if they deem it expedient, to take to their assistance the surveyor of Seneca county, who, under their direction, shall make such surveys, divisions and maps thereof as may be necessary, for the performance of the duties required of them by this act; and said commissioners and surveyor shall each receive for his services one dollar and fifty cents for each day he may be employed in said service, to be paid out of the county treasury of said county of Seneca, which shall be refunded to said treasury in manner hereinafter provided.

Sec. 5. That so soon as said school section sixteen has been surveyed under the direction of said commissioners, and maps thereof made as provided in the fourth section of this act, the said commissioners shall cause to be delivered to the auditor of Seneca county, such surveys and divisions and maps thereof, and the separate appraisement of such lot laid off in said school section, if the same shall have been divided into lots, and otherwise the appraisement of the entire section so made under the requirements of this act; and it shall be the duty of such auditor, after having given thirty days previous notice thereof by advertisement in some newspaper printed in Seneca county, and if no newspaper be published in said county, or if the publisher of any newspaper in said county shall refuse to publish the same, then the notice shall be given by affixing such notice on the door of the court house in said county, and in five other public places in said county, three of which shall be in said township of Adams, thirty days previous to such sale; and the affidavit of one or more of such commissioners, certifying the manner, time, and places of publishing such notices, shall be conclusive evidence of such fact, to offer such section, or such lots laid off in such section separately for sale, between the hours of ten o'clock A. M. and of five o'clock P. M. on the day designated in such notice, and shall sell the same, and each of the same to the highest bidder: *Provided,* That neither said section, nor any part of said section, shall be sold for less than its appraised value, and that one-fourth of the money bid for the same shall be paid at the time of sale; and the remaining three-fourths of the money so bid, shall be payable in three equal annual instalments, payable annually, and successively after the day of said sale, with interest at the rate of six per cent. per annum, on all moneys unpaid, to be computed from said day of sale; and said commissioners may continue said sale, by adjournment, from day to day, for three successive days, if any portion of such section shall remain unsold; and if at the expiration of said three days, any portion of such land shall remain unsold, the sale thereof may be adjourned for a time not exceeding three months, and said commissioners shall in like manner proceed, giving like notice of each succeeding sale, until the whole be sold.

Sec. 6. That on the sale of said lands so made as aforesaid, the auditor of said county shall take a bond from each purchaser, with at least one sufficient surety, conditioned for the payment to the treasurer of Seneca county of all the money due for said lands, or for any part thereof, with the interest thereon to become due or accruing, to be applied to the use of schools in said township of Adams; and said auditor, on the final payment of said bond according to the condition thereof, shall make and execute a deed of said bond to the purchaser or purchasers thereof, in fee simple; and said purchase money, when received, shall be deposited in the common school fund, for the benefit of said township: *Provided,* That if any person or persons who shall purchase any part of said section sixteen, under the provisions of this act, shall be desirous of completing payment for the same, within a less time than that required by the obligation of the board aforesaid, he or they shall be allowed to complete payment for the same at any time, and shall be entitled to receive a deed in fee simple for said land, in the manner herein prescribed.

Sec. 7. That the auditor of said county shall be entitled to receive for all conveyances he may be required to make by virtue of this act, twelve and a half cents for each hundred words contained therein, and in like proportion for any smaller number; and that the asessor be entitled to receive for his services performed under the provisions of this act, the sum of one dollar and fifty cents for each day he may be necessarily employed in said service.

Sec. 8. That the treasurer of said county shall, out of the first moneys that may come to his hands of the interest of said purchase money or moneys, pay the said assessor, commissioners, surveyor, and auditor, the fees and compensation herein before specified, to be paid to said commissioners, surveyor, and auditor, as well as all necessary fees and expenses for acknowledging said deeds, and for publishing the advertisements, made necessary by the requirements of this act.

WM. SAWYER,
Speaker of the House of Representatives.
ELIJAH VANCE,
Speaker of the Senate.

January 29, 1836.

AN ACT

To repeal the first clause in the proviso of the 7th section of the act entitled, "An act to incorporate the Whitewater Bridge Company."

Sec. 1. *Be it enacted by the General Assembly of the State of Ohio,* That

the first clause in the proviso of the 7th section of the act entitled, "An act to incorporate the Whitewater Bridge Company," passed January 31st, 1826, which grants to public mails the privilege of passing said bridge free from toll, be, and the same is hereby repealed.

WM. SAWYER,
Speaker of the House of Representatives.
ELIJAH VANCE,
Speaker of the Senate.

January 29, 1836.

AN ACT

To amend and carry into effect, an act entitled "An act to incorporate the town of Lewisburg, in Preble county," passed February 9th, 1830, and also, to revive and carry into effect, "An act to amend the aforesaid act," passed December 22d, 1834.

Sec. 1. *Be it enacted by the General Assembly of the State of Ohio,* That there shall be an election held in the town of Lewisburg, in the county of Preble, Ohio, on the third Monday of March next, and on the third Monday of March annually, thereafter, at the usual place of holding elections in the town of Lewisburg, aforesaid; or, in case the said elections, or any of them, should not, by omission, accident, or any other cause, be held on the days and times fixed above for holding said elections, then said elections shall be held at such times as the qualified voters of said corporation, or any twelve of them, shall appoint; notice of the time and place of which elections shall be posted up in three public places in said town, at least ten days previous to such elections; which elections shall be held agreeably to the provisions of the act entitled "An act to incorporate the town of Lewisburg," passed February 9th, 1830, to which this is an amendment, and shall be governed in all things by said act.

Sec. 2. That the acts to which this is an amendment, are hereby declared to be completely, and to all intents and purposes, in force as fully as if there had been an election held on the third Monday of March last, as in said acts provided.

WM. SAWYER,
Speaker of the House of Representatives.
ELIJAH VANCE,
Speaker of the Senate.

January 29th, 1836.

AN ACT

To lay out and establish a State Road from Freeport, in Harrison county, to Eastport, in Tuscarawas county.

Sec. 1. *Be it enacted by the General Assembly of the State of Ohio,*

That Richard Price, of Harrison county, and Samuel Shane, of Tuscarawas county, be, and they are hereby appointed commissioners, and John Auld, jr., of Harrison county, surveyor, to lay out and establish a State road from the town of Freeport, in Harrison county, to William Shotwell's mill; thence to or near Norris's mill, in said Harrison county; thence by the way of S. Shane's mill, and the town of Waterford, to Eastport, in Tuscarawas county.

Sec. 2. That the grade of said road shall not exceed an angle of five degrees with the horizon.

Sec. 3. That said road commissioners shall, in all respects, be governed by, and the expenses of laying out and establishing said road be paid, according to the provisions of the act entitled "An act defining the mode of laying out and establishing State roads," passed March 14th, 1831, except in the appointment of surveyor, which is provided for in the first section of this act.

Sec. 4. That should a vacancy at any time occur, in the foregoing appointments, by death, removal, refusal to serve, or otherwise, the county commissioners of the county in which such vacancy may happen, shall fill the same, as often as any such vacancy may occur, by the appointment of some suitable person without delay.

WM. SAWYER,
Speaker of the House of Representatives.
ELIJAH VANCE,
Speaker of the Senate.

February 4, 1836.

AN ACT

To incorporate the First Congregational Society of Concord, in the county of Geauga.

Sec. 1. *Be it enacted by the General Assembly of the State of Ohio,* That William Merrel, Hiram Wescot, John Murray, Francis M. Leonard, Robert Murray, and Orson Wilson, and their associates, together with such other persons as shall hereafter associate with them, be, and they are hereby created a body politic and corporate, by the name of "The First Congregational Society of Concord;" and as such shall remain and have perpetual succession; and by their corporate name, may contract and be contracted with, sue and be sued, plead and be impleaded, answer and be answered unto, defend and be defended, in all manner of actions whatsoever, in any court of competent jurisdiction; and may have a common seal, which they may change or alter at pleasure.

Sec. 2. That the said corporation shall be capable in law and equity, in their corporate name aforesaid, of having, receiving, acquiring, and holding by purchase, gift, grant, devise, or legacy, any estate, real, personal, or mixed, for the use of said corporation: *Provided,* That the annual income of all such property shall not exceed the sum of one thousand dollars; and that all such property, of whatever kind, shall be considered as held in trust, for promoting the interests of said society, defraying the expenses incident to their mode of worship, and maintaining any institutions of charity or education: *And provided also*, That when any money or other property shall be given, granted, devised, or bequeathed, for any particular use or purpose, it shall be faithfully applied to that purpose.

Sec. 3. That for the better management of the affairs of said society, there shall be elected, on the first Monday of June, one thousand eight hundred and thirty-six, and on the first Monday in January in each succeeding year thereafter, three trustees, and such other officers as the corporation may deem necessary; who shall hold their offices for one year: *Provided*, That the officers elected at the first election under this act. shall only continue in office until the first annual election, under this act; and also, if, from any cause, an election of officers should not be holden on the first Monday in June, as mentioned in this section, on the day appointed for the annual election, then an election may be holden on any other day, by any member of said society giving ten days' notice in writing, posted up in three public places in said society.

Sec. 4. That the trustees, a majority of whom shall be a quorum for the transaction of business, shall, under the direction of the society, have the management and control of the property and other concerns of the corporation; and they, or a majority of them, shall also have power to call a meeting of the society for the transaction of any business whatever, relating to said society, by giving ten days notice, immediately after public worship, or by posting up notices in three public places in the bounds of said society, ten days previous to the time of holding such meeting.

Sec. 5. That any meeting of the society, duly assembled, may adopt and establish such by-laws and ordinances as may be deemed proper and necessary to the good government of said corporation.

Sec. 6. That original process against said corporation shall be served by leaving an attested copy with one or more of the trustees; and such service shall be deemed sufficient to bind said corporation.

Sec. 7. That any future legislature shall have power to alter, amend, or repeal this ac: *Provided*, That such modification or repeal shall not affect the title to any estate, real or personal, acquired or conveyed under its provisions.

WM. SAWYER,
Speaker of the House of Representatives.
ELIJAH VANCE,
Speaker of the Senate.

February 4th, 1836.

AN ACT

To incorporate the First Presbyterian Church of Lancaster, in the county of Fairfield.

Sec. 1. *Be it enacted by the General Assembly of the State of Ohio*, That Samuel F. Maccracken, Frederick A. Foster, William J. Reese, David Ewing, Joseph Work, Jr. William V. Thorne, and their associates that now are or may hereafter be associated with them, be, and they are hereby created a body politic and corporate, by the name and style of "The First Presbyterian Church, of Lancaster;" and as such shall have perpetual succession, and be capable in law, to sue and be sued, plead and be impleaded, answer and be answered, defend and be defended, in any court of law or equity; and may have a common seal, which they may alter, change, or renew at pleasure.

Sec. 2. That said corporation, by the name aforesaid, shall be capable in law and equity to have, receive, acquire and hold, either by gift, grant, devise, or purchase, any estate, real, personal and mixed, and may lease mortgage, sell and convey the same: *Provided*, That the annual income of all such property shall not exceed two thousand dollars.

Sec. 3. That there shall be elected, by ballot, on the first Monday in May, annually, three trustees, who shall have the entire control and management of the property and financial concerns of the corporation; they shall have power to appoint a clerk and treasurer, to fill all vacancies that may happen in their own body, until the next annual election thereafter, and make such written by-laws, rules and regulations, as may be necessary for the prudent and efficient management of its pecuniary affairs: *Provided*, The same be not inconsistent with the laws of the United States, and of this State.

Sec. 4. That at all elections, held under the provisions of this act, each pew-holder above the age of twenty-one years, shall be entitled to vote; and a plurality of votes shall in all instances be deemed sufficient to elect; and the officers so elected shall hold their offices until their successors shall have been duly elected: *Provided*, That a failure to hold an election shall not be a forfeiture of the rights and privileges herein granted.

Sec. 5. That (at) all meetings of the corporation, in their corporate capacity, either for the election of officers, or other purposes, shall be called by the trustees, who shall cause notice of the time and place of such meeting to be given, in any manner they may deem most suitable.

Sec. 6. That original process against the corporation shall be by summons, which shall be served by leaving an attested copy thereof, with any two of the trustees, at least ten days before the return day therein mentioned.

Sec. 7. That Samuel F. Maccracken, Frederick A. Foster, and William J. Reese, be and they are hereby appointed trustees of said corporation, until the first annual election, and until others are elected in their places.

Sec. 8. That any future Legislature may alter or repeal this act: *Provided*, That such alteration or repeal shall not affect the title of any property acquired or conveyed under its provisions, and that all contracts heretofore entered upon by the trustees, shall be binding upon the corporation.

WM. SAWYER,
Speaker of the House of Representatives.
ELIJAH VANCE,
Speaker of the Senate.

February 4, 1836.

13—L

AN ACT

To incorporate the Cheviot Presbyterian Church, in the county of Hamilton.

Sec. 1. *Be it enacted by the General Assembly of the State of Ohio,* That Helmes Bogart, William M. Orr, John Gilmore, James Biddle, and Thomas Reeves, their associates, and such other persons as may be hereafter associated with them, are hereby declared a body corporate and politic, with the name and style of "The Presbyterian Church of Cheviot;" with perpetual succession, and capacity of contracting and being contracted with, of suing and being sued, answering and being answered, pleading and being impleaded, defending and being defended, in all courts of law and equity; and may have a common seal, which they may break, alter or renew at pleasure.

Sec. 2. That the said Church shall be capable in law, in their corporate capacity aforesaid, of having, receiving, acquiring, and holding either by gift, grant, devise, or purchase, any estate, real, personal, or mixed, which may be necessary for a convenient meeting house or place of public worship, a grave yard, and dwelling for their preacher, and to defray the expenses incident to their mode of worship; and may also lease, mortgage, sell and convey the same; and all property of whatsoever kind, shall be held in trust, under the management and at the disposal of the trustees, for the uses and purposes aforeraid: *Provided,* That the annual income of all such property shall not exceed the sum of two thousand dollars: *And provided also,* That when money or property shall be given, granted, devised, or bequeathed, for purposes of charity, education, or any other purpose, it shall be faithfully applied to the purpose for which it may be intended.

Sec. 3. There shall be elected on the first Saturday in May next, and on the first Saturday in May in each and every year thereafter, by the members of said corporation, five trustees, a treasurer, and a clerk, who shall hold their offices one year, and until their successor shall be duly elected; and if from any cause an election should not be held on the day appointed, said corporation shall not be dissolved, but an election may be held at any meeting of the corporation duly assembled for that purpose.

Sec. 4. All meetings of the corporation, either for the election of officers, or for other purposes, shall be called by the trustees, or a majority of them, who shall cause a notification of the time and place of such meeting, to be put up in at least three public places, within the bounds of the congregation, and at the meeting house door; or by publishing the same to the congregation at some stated meeting, at least ten days before such election shall be held.

Sec. 5. The trustees, or a majority of them, shall have power to manage all the pecuniary concerns, which pertain to the interest and welfare of the corporation; and may fill all vacancies that may occur in their own body; but such appointments shall be valid only till the time fixed for the next annual election; and shall have power to make and cause to be executed, all such by-laws, rules, and regulations, for the government of the corporation, and for conducting its affairs, as shall from time to time be deemed necessary, consistent with the constitution and laws of the United States and of this State.

Sec. 6. The persons named in the first section of this act, or a majority of them, shall be trustees until others shall be elected.

Sec. 7. That any future Legislature shall have power to alter, amend, or repeal, this act: *Provided,* That such alteration, amendment or repeal, shall not affect the title to any estate, real or personal, acquired or conveyed under its provisions.

WM. SAWYER,
Speaker of the House of Representatives.
ELIJAH VANCE,
Speaker of the Senate.

February 4th, 1836.

AN ACT

To amend an act, entitled "An act to regulate the time of holding the Judicial Courts, in the County of Hamilton;" passed February 9, 1835.

Sec. 1. *Be it enacted by the General Assembly of the State of Ohio,* That the county of Hamilton shall compose the Ninth Judicial Circuit; and there shall be two stated civil terms of the Court of Common Pleas, which shall commence and be holden therein, on the first Monday of June, and the first Monday in November, in the year eighteen hundred and thirty-six; and there shall be three stated civil terms in each year thereafter, which shall commence and be holden on the first Monday in February, the first Monday in June, and the first Monday in November, to which stated civil terms, all process of a civil nature shall be returnable, and at which no business of a criminal nature shall be heard or transacted, nor any auction, tavern, or ferry license be granted; and there shall be three stated Criminal terms of the Court of Common Pleas, which shall commence and be holden therein on the third Monday in March, the first Monday in July, and the first Monday in October, in the year eighteen hunded and thirty-six; and there shall be four stated Criminal terms in each year thereafter, which shall commence and be holden therein, on the first Monday in January, the third Monday in March, the first Monday in July, and the first Monday in October; to which stated criminal terms all recognizances and process of a criminal nature shall be returnable; and at which, cognizance shall be taken of all crimes, offences, and misdemeanors; all causes and matters of a probate and testamentary nature, shall be heard and determined; guardians be appointed; executors, administrators, and guardians, be called to account; and auction, tavern, and ferry licences be granted: *Provided,* That nothing herein contained shall be so construed, as to empower the said court of Common Pleas, at the said stated criminal terms to grant orders for the sale of real estate, of deceased persons, of real estate belonging to minors, or to confirm the sales of real estate of deceased persons, or real estate belonging to minors.

Sec. 2. That all process and proceedings of a civil nature, made returnable, or continued to the March term of said court, in the year

1836, by the act to which this is an amendment, be, and the same is hereby made returnable, or continued, as the case may be, to the June term of the said court, in the year 1836, as fixed by this act; and all process, recognizances, and proceedings of a criminal nature, made returnable, or continued to the March term of said court, in the year 1835, by the act to which this is an amendment, be, and the same is hereby made returnable or continued, as the case may be, to the March term of the said court, in the year 1836, as fixed by this act.

Sec. 3.　That the act to regulate the time of holding the Judicial Courts, in the county of Hamilton, passed February 9th, 1835, shall, from and after the first Monday of March, 1836, be, and the same is hereby repealed.

WM. SAWYER,

Speaker of the House of Representatives.

ELIJAH VANCE,

Speaker of the Senate.

February 4th, 1836.

AN ACT

To incorporate the Firemen's Insurance Company, of the town of Springfield.

Sec. 1.　*Be it enacted by the General Assembly of the State of Ohio,* That Ira Paige, William Werden, Pierson Spining, Henry Vinal, Jacob W. Kills, Edward H. Cumming, Reuben Miller, Emery C. Ross, Henry Bretney, and their associates, and those who may hereafter become associated with them, are hereby made a body corporate, to be known by the name of the Springfield Firemen's Insurance Company; and in their corporate capacity, they may make contracts; sue and be sued; and answer and be answered unto, in any court of law or equity in this State, of competent jurisdiction: they shall have a common seal, which they may alter or destroy at pleasure, and may make such by-laws and regulations, for their government, and carry them into execution, as they, or a majority of them, may deem necessary: *Provided,* The same be not incompatible with the constitution or laws of the United States or of this State.

Sec. 2.　That said corporation shall proceed to elect on the first Monday of May, 1836, a president, four directors, and secretary, who shall be stockholders in said company, and who, after being first sworn into office, shall perform the duties enjoined upon them by this act, and by the by-laws established for their government: they shall have power to collect, receive and pay over to such person or persons as may be appointed for that purpose by said company, any funds or moneys subscribed for the insurance of property against fire or casualty; and all funds and moneys so subscribed, shall be receipted for by the proper officers and be considered stock in said company.

Sec. 3.　The president and directors shall hold their offices one year, or until their successors are elected and qualified; and at each yearly meeting of the stockholders, shall lay before them a full and true statement of all accounts and transactions of the company: all obligations, receipts, assignments, transfers and other papers; the acts of said company, shall be signed by the president and countersigned by the secretary.

Sec. 4. It shall be lawful for said company to vest any part of their capital stock, moneys, funds, or other property in any public stocks of this or any other State, and the same to sell or transfer at pleasure, and again invest the same or any part thereof in such stocks or otherwise, whenever said company shall deem it expedient; or they may loan the same or any part thereof to individuals or corporations, on real or personal security, for such a period of time and upon such terms as the president and ditectors shall see most expedient, at a rate of interest not exceeding six per cent. per annum: *Provided,* It shall not be lawful for said company to engage in the business of banking, nor shall said company make, issue or emit any bills of credit as a circulating medium of trade or exchange, under the forfeiture of all the privileges granted by this act.

Sec. 5. The capital stock of said company shall not exceed one hundred thousand dollars, which shall be divided into shares of twenty-five dollars each.

Sec.. 6. Books for subscription shall be opened on the first Monday of April, eighteen hundred and thirty-six, at the Exchange Hotel, in the town of Springfield, in Clark county, and remain open thirty days thereafter, and may be re-opened at such time and place, and remain open for such length of time, as the president and directors shall prescribe, or until all the stock in said company shall be taken: *Provided, however,* That this act shall be void, unless the whole amount of the capital stock shall be subscribed and paid in or secured to be paid in, on or before the first day of February, eighteen hundred and thirty-seven.

Sec. (7.) That any future Legislature may alter or repeal this act: *Provided,* That such amendment or repeal does not affect any property or insurance, effected as aforesaid, under its provisions.

WM. SAWYER,
Speaker of the House of Representatives.
ELIJAH VANCE,
Speaker of the Senate.

February 4th, 1836.

AN ACT

To incorporate the Hillsborough and Aberdeen Turnpike Company.

Sec. 1. *Be it enacted by the General Assembly of the State of Ohio,* That Benjamin Evans, Silas Thomas, William Gilbert, and William Carpenter, of Brown county; Daniel Marlatt, Robert Morrison, Joseph Eylor, and Amos Reece, of Adams county; Thomas Barratt, George W. Barrere, Allen Trimble, and Joshua Woodrow, of Highland county, as commissioners, and their associates, stockholders, as hereinafter provided, their successors and assigns, be, and they are hereby created and declared a body politic and corporate, perpetual, by the name and style of "The Hillsborough and Aberdeen Turnpike Company," to construct and keep in repair a turnpike road, toll gates, and gate keeper's houses, commencing at Hillsborough, in Highland county; thence, by the most eligible route, through Winchester; thence, to William Eckmans, in Adams county; thence, through Decatur to Aberdeen, in Brown county, on the Ohio river; and, by such corporate name and style, said company is hereby made and declared capable, in law and equity, to contract, sue and be sued, make by-laws, not contrary to the constitution or laws of the United States, or of this State; and to have and use a common seal, which they may break, alter, or renew at pleasure; and to acquire, have, hold, sell, transfer and convey property, real and personal, for their corporate use and purpose, but for no other uses or purposes whatsoever.

Sec. 2. That the capital of the company, hereby incorporated, shall consist of one hundred thousand dollars, in shares of fifty dollars each, and may be subscribed and held by individuals, companies or corporations, and shall be appropriated and applied to the uses and purposes, in the first section of this act set forth, and to no other use or purpose; and any person desiring to discharge his subscription to the capital of said company, in labor or materials, on or for said road, shall so specify, at the time of subscribing; in which case, the labor to be performed by such subscriber, shall be assigned, and the value of the same estimated by the principal engineer, superintending the construction of the road; or if materials be subscribed, the value thereof shall be estimated by such principal engineer: *Provided,* That in all cases of subscription to the capital stock of said company, five dollars, in cash, shall be paid to the person or persons, under whose superintendence subscriptions may be received, on each share subscribed; and the residue of such capital stock, whether in cash, labor, or materials, shall be paid, discharged, performed and furnished, on the requisition of the directors, for the time being.

Sec. 3. That books for receiving subscriptions to the capital stock of said company, shall be opened on the tenth day of June next, or such other day as may be agreed upon, at such places, and under the superintendence of such persons, as a majority of said commissioners, or a majority of such of them as consent to act, may designate and appoint; it shall be the duty of said commissioners, or a majority of them, or a majority of such of them as consent to act, to give ten days' notice of the time, places, and persons, at which, and under whose superintendence, will be opened the books for receiving subscriptions to the capital stock of said company; which notice shall be published in some newspaper published, or in general circulation, in each of the counties of Highland, Adams, and Brown; and the books for receiving subscriptions, as aforesaid, shall be kept open as long as said directors shall see fit, unless said sum of one hundred thousand dollars, of said capital stock, shall be sooner subscribed; and that the county commissioners of each county through which said road may pass, be and they are hereby authorized, to subscribe stock in said company, on behalf of their respective counties, to any amount they may deem proper, not exceeding ten thousand dollars, for each county, whenever they shall be authorized by a majority of the people in said county to do so.

Sec. 4. That as soon as it shall be ascertained, that twenty thousand dollars of the capital stock of said company has been subscribed, said commissioners, or a majority of them, or a majority of such of them as consent to act, shall give ten days notice, as provided in the third section of this act, of the time of holding an election, which shall be held at Winchester, in Adams county, for seven directors, to manage and conduct the business and affairs of said company; and on the day thus specified, at Winchester, aforesaid, the stockholders of said company shall proceed to the election, by ballot, of seven directors, stockholders, any five of whom shall constitute a quorum, for the transaction of the business and concerns of said company; the first election for directors, under this act, shall be conducted by two inspectors, who shall be appointed by a majority of such of said commissioners, as may consent to act; and such inspectors shall act under oath; none but stockholders shall vote for, or be elected directors; and the stockholders shall be entitled to one vote, which may be given in person, or by proxy, for each share of stock by him, her, or them owned and held, on the day of election; the seven directors, having the highest number of votes, shall be declared duly elected; but if an election of seven directors shall not be effected, by reason of an equal number of votes being given, in favor of two or more stockholders; in that case, the inspectors of the election shall determine, by lot, amongst the eight or more stockholders, having the highest and an equal number of votes, who shall be directors, to complete the number of seven: *Provided* such determination, by lot, shall not postpone as director, one stockholder having a higher, to another having a lower, number of votes; the directors first elected, under this act, shall hold their office until the first Monday of October next, after their election, and until their successors are elected and qualified; and on said first Monday of October annually, after the first election for directors, there shall be an election for directors of said company; annual elections for directors of said company shall be under the superintendence of the directors, for the time being; who shall designate a place, and shall give the like notice of the time of such annual election, as is required to be given by the commissioners, as aforesaid, of the time and place of holding the first election, under this act; and shall, in like manner, notify the persons elected, and designate a time and place for the persons elected directors, to meet and qualify; and the directors, annually elected, shall proceed, as required of the first directors.

Sec. 5. That within five days, after the first election of directors, under this act, the inspectors of the election shall give notice, in writing, to the seven stockholders, elected directors, of such their election; and shall appoint a day, on which the directors so elected shall meet at Winchester, aforesaid, for organization; and on the day so appointed, which shall not be more than ten days from the day of election, or sooner, if the directors elected can agree, the directors so elected, shall meet at Winchester, and severally take an oath, or affirmation, faithfully and impartially, to discharge the several duties of director of the turnpike company, hereby incorporated; and being thus qualified, such directors shall appoint one of their body president of the board; they shall also appoint a treasurer, who shall not be a director, and they may require and take of the treasurer, bond, in such sum, and with such security, as to them may appear reasonable and necessary, to secure said company; said directors shall also appoint a secretary, who shall keep a full and fair journal of the corporate acts of said company, and shall perform such other duties of secretary, as may be required of him by the directors.

Sec. 6. That the said company shall have a right to lay out, survey, and locate a turnpike road, as specified in the first section of this act, through any improved or unimproved lands, and to take from the lands, occupied by such road, when located as aforesaid, any stone, gravel, timber, or other materials, necessary to construct a good, secure, and substantial turnpike road, as contemplated by this act, and the necessary bridges connected therewith; and if any difference should arise between the owner or owners of any ground, on which said road may be located, or from which such materials are taken, as aforesaid, and the agents of the company, respecting damage, it shall be determined, by three disinterested freeholders, to be appointed by the commissioners of the county, in which the subject of difference lies; who, after being duly sworn, faithfully and impartially to perform the duties, required of them in this act, and taking into consideration, whether the land be, really, rendered more or less valuable, by the road passing through it, shall make out their assessment in writing, of the damage, if any; a copy of which shall be given to the proprietor of the land, and another copy to the agent of the company; and said agent shall pay, or offer to pay, the owner of said land, the amount of such assessed damages, before he shall enter upon and take any such ground or materials, other than to survey the road; and all such assessment of damages, if any should be awarded, shall be paid by the company; but if no damage shall be awarded, then the expense shall be paid by the person who had claimed damages; and in case sufficient materials cannot be procured on the land so as aforesaid required for said road and bridges, said company, or their agents, shall have a right, and they are hereby authorized, to enter upon any unimproved lands, adjoining or in the vicinity of said road, and to dig, cut down, take, and carry away, so much stone, gravel, timber, or other materials, (not previously cut down, taken, approrpriated or prepared, by the owner for any particular use,) as may be necessary to enable said company to construct said road and the necessary bridges, toll gates, and gate keepers' houses; and in case of difference between the owner of any lands, from which materials may be taken, as last aforesaid, such difference shall be determined, and compensation made by said company, in manner provided by the sixth section of this act.

Sec. 7. That in addition to the land, necessary for the construction, use, and repair of said road, said company shall be entitled to, and authorized to acquire, in manner aforesaid, not exceeding one acre of land, at each toll gate, for the erection thereon, and convenient occupation of a gate keeper's house; and said company shall cause such turnpike road to be opened, not exceeding eighty feet wide; at least fifteen feet of which shall be made an artificial road, composed of stone, gravel, wood, or other suitable materials, well compacted together, in such manner as to secure a good, firm, substantial and even road, rising in the middle, with a gradual arch or curve, with sufficient drains on each side, to carry the water therefrom, and shall keep the same in good repair; and in no case shall the ascent in such road be of greater elevation, than four degrees with the horizon.

Sec. 8. That so soon as said company shall have completed such road, or the grading thereof, as aforesaid, or any part of such road, not less than five continuous miles, and so, from time to time, as often as five continuous miles thereof shall be completed, or completely graded, an agent, to be appointed for that purpose, by the commissioners of the proper county, if not otherwise appointed, by or under the Legislature or its authority, shall, on application of said company, examine such road, or part thereof, as aforesaid, and report his opinion to the president of said company; and if such agent shall report said road, or any continuous five miles thereof, to be completed or completely graded, agreeably to the requisitions of this act, said company shall, thereupon, be entitled to erect a toll gate or gates, at suitable distances on said road, and to demand and receive of those traveling or using the same, the tolls allowed by this act.

Sec. 9. That the following shall be the rates of toll demandable and receivable for each and every ten miles of said road when completed, and in the same proportion for any greater or less distance, to wit: For every four wheeled carriage, or wagon, drawn by one horse or ox, eighteen and three fourths cents; for every horse or ox in addition, six and one fourth cents; for every chaise, riding chair, cart, or gig, or other two wheeled carriage, of any kind, drawn by one horse or ox, twelve and a half cents; for every horse or ox in addition, six and one fourth cents; for every sled or sleigh, drawn by one horse or ox, twelve and a half cents; for every coach, chariot, or other four wheeled pleasure carriage, drawn by one horse, (driver included,) twenty-five cents; for every additional horse, six and one fourth cents; for every horse and rider, six and one fourth cents; for every horse, mule or ass, led or driven, six months old and upwards, three cents; for every head of neat cattle, six months old, and upwards, one cent; for every head of sheep or hogs, one fourth of a cent; and for equal distances and like objects, said company shall be entitled to demand and receive one half of the foregoing amounts of tolls on said road, when completely graded, as aforesaid, but not fully completed, as a turnpike road.

Sec. 10. That if any person or persons using said road, shall, with intent to defraud said company, or to evade the payment of tolls, pass through any private gate, or bars, or other ground, except around cross-ways, authorized by law, near to any turnpike gate of said road, every person guilty of, or concerned in such fraudulent practice, shall, for every such offence, be liable to pay said company a sum, not less than two dollars, nor more than ten dollars, to be recovered in action of debt, with costs of suit, before any justice of the peace of the county in which such offence may be committed; and from such judgment of the justice of the peace, an appeal may be taken to the court of common pleas of the proper county.

Sec. 11. That if said company shall fail, for ten days in succession, to keep said road in good repair, and complaint thereof be made to a justice of the peace of the county, in which said road may be out of repair, it shall be his duty, forthwith, to summon three disinterested freeholders of the county to examine the same, and he shall give notice to the toll gatherer, at the nearest gate, of the time when such freeholders will proceed to examine said road; and such freeholders, after taking an oath or affirmation to act impartially, shall proceed to examine said road; and if such

14—L

freeholders shall find said road out of repair, they shall certify their finding to the justice of the peace, who shall immediately transmit a copy of such certificate to the toll gatherer nearest the defective part of said road; and from the time of the toll gatherers receiving such notice, no toll shall be demanded or received for such part of the road, until the same shall be put into complete repair, under the penalty of five dollars for each offence, to be recovered of said company, with costs, on the complaint and for the use of the party aggrieved.

Sec. 12. That if any person shall wilfully or wantonly destroy, or in any manner injure or obstruct any part of said road, or any gate thereon, otherwise than in the just and lawful use thereof, every such person shall be liable to pay said company for every such offence, a sum not less than five dollars, nor more than fifty dollars, to be recovered, with costs, before any justice of the peace of the county in which such offence may have been committed; from which judgment an appeal may be taken to the court of common pleas, but no stay of execution shall be allowed.

Sec. 13. That said company shall put up a post or stone at the end of each mile, with the number of miles from Aberdeen fairly cut or painted thereon; and also in a conspicuous place near each toll gate, shall be placed a board, with the rates of toll fairly painted thereon, with directions to keep to the right.

Sec. 14. That if any person shall wilfuly deface or destroy any guide board, mile post or stone, or painted list or rate of tolls, erected on said road, he shall, on conviction thereof, before a justice of the peace of the proper county, forfeit and pay a sum not less than five dollars, nor more than ten dollars, with costs of suit, in an action of debt, at the suit of said company; and from the judgment of the justice of the peace, in such case, an appeal may be taken to the court of common pleas, but no stay of execution shall be allowed.

Sec. 15. That if any toll gatherer on said road, shall unreasonably detain any person, after payment or tender of the proper amount of toll, or shall demand or receive a greater amount of toll than by this act is authorized, he shall, for any such offence, forfeit and pay a sum, not exceeding twenty dollars, to be recovered with costs of suit, before any justice of the peace of the proper county, in an action of debt, at the suit of the party aggrieved; and from the judgment of the justice, in such case, an appeal may be taken to the court of common pleas: *Provided*, That no action under this section shall be commenced after the expiration of twenty days, from the accruing thereof.

Sec. 16. That there shall be kept a fair account of the whole expense of making and repairing said road, with all incidental expenses; and also a fair account of the tolls received; and the state shall have a right to purchase the same, or any part of the stock thereof, on paying said company a sum of money which, together with tolls received, shall equal the cost and expense of said road, as aforesaid, with ten per cent. interest per annum; and the books of said company shall always be open to the inspection of the agent of the State, appointed for that purpose, by the Legislature; and if the company shall neglect or refuse to exhibit their accounts agreeably to this section, when thereunto required, then all the rights and privileges granted by this act, shall cease.

Sec. 17. That if said company shall not, within five years from the passage of this act, proceed to carry on the work, according to the true intent and meaning of this act, or complete the same within fifteen years, then this act shall be null and void.

WM. SAWYER,
Speaker of the House of Representatives.
ELIJAH VANCE,
Speaker of the Senate.

February 4th, 1836.

AN ACT

To incorporate the town of Jefferson, in the county of Ashtabula.

Sec. 1. *Be it enacted by the General Assembly of the State of Ohio,* That so much of the township of Jefferson, in the county of Ashtabula, as is comprehended in the original recorded town plat of the town of Jefferson, be, and the same is hereby created into and constituted a town corporate, by the name of the town of Jefferson.

Sec. 2. That for the order and good government of said town, and the inhabitants thereof, it shall be lawful for the white male inhabitants, who have resided in said town for the space of six months next preceding said election, having the qualifications of electors of members of the General Assembly, to meet at the usual place of holding elections in said township of Jefferson, on the first Tuesday of April next, and on the first Tuesday of April annually thereafter; and then and there proceed, by a plurality of votes, to elect by ballot, one mayor, one recorder, and five trustees, who shall be householders, and shall hold their respective offices for one year, and until their successors are elected and qualified; such mayor, recorder and trustees, being so elected and qualified, shall constitute a town council, any five of whom shall constitute a quorum for the transaction of any business pertaining to their duties; but any less number shall have no power other than to adjourn from time to time, until a quorum shall have convened, except as hereinafter provided.

Sec. 3. That at the first election to be held under this act, there shall be chosen, *viva voce,* by the electors present, two judges, and a clerk of such election, who shall each take an oath or affirmation, faithfully to discharge the duties required of him by this act; and at all subsequent elections, the trustees, or any two of them, shall be judges: the polls shall be opened between the hours of one and two, and close at four o'clock P. M. of said day; and, at the close of the polls, the vo'es shall be counted, and a true statement thereof proclaimed to the electors present, by one of the judges, and the clerk shall make a true record thereof; and within five days thereafter, said clerk shall give notice to the persons so elected, of their election; and it shall be the duty of such town council, at least ten days before each and every annual election, to give notice of the same by setting up advertisements at three of the most public places in said town.

Sec. 4. That it shall be the duty of the mayor, and in case of his absence or disability to serve, the recorder, to preside at all meetings of the town council; and it shall also be the duty of the recorder to attend all such meetings, and keep a fair and accurate record of their proceedings.

Sec. 5. That the town council shall have power to fill all vacancies which may happen in said board, from the householders, who are qualified electors in said town, whose appointment shall continue until the next annual election, and until their successors are duly elected and qualified; and whenever it may happen that neither the mayor or recorder is present at any such meeting, the trustees shall have power to appoint any one of their number, to perform the duties of mayor and recorder, or both, as the case may be, which appointment shall be *pro tem.*

Sec. 6. That the said mayor, recorder, and trustees of said town, shall be a body corporate and politic, with perpetual succession, to be known and distinguished by the name and title of the Town Council of the town of Jefferson; and shall be capable in law, in their corporate name, to acquire property, real, personal and mixed, for the use of said town, with powers to sell and convey the same; may have a common seal, which they may alter, break, or renew at pleasure; and may sue and be sued, plead and be impleaded, defend and be defended, in any court of competent jurisdiction, whether of law or chancery; and when any suit shall be commenced against said corporation, the first process shall be, by summons, an attested copy of which shall be left with the recorder, or at his usual place of residence.

Sec. 7. That each member of said town council shall, before he enters upon the duties of his office, take an oath, or affirmation, to support the constitution of the United States, and of the State of Ohio, and also an oath of office.

Sec. 8. That the said town council shall have power to ordain and establish by-laws, rules and regulations, for the government of said town, and the same to alter, amend or repeal, at pleasure; to provide in said by-laws for the election of a treasurer, town marshal, and all the subordinate officers which may be thought necessary for the good government and well being of the inhabitants of said town; to prescribe their duties, and determine the period of their appointment, and the fees they shall be entitled to receive for their services, and require them to qualify, previous to their entering upon the duties of their respective offices, and may further require of them a bond with security, conditioned for the faithful performance of their respective duties as an officer of said corporation: the town council shall also have power to affix to the violation of the by-laws and ordinances of the corporation, such reasonable fines and penalties as they may deem proper to enforce obedience of the same, and to provide for the disposition or appropriation of said fines and penalties: *Provided,* Such by-laws and ordinances be not inconsistent with the constitution and laws of the United States, and of this State: *And provided, also,* That no by-law or ordinance of said corporation shall take effect, or be in force, until the same shall have been posted up for two weeks, in one of the most public places within said corporation.

Sec. 9. That the town council shall, at the expiration of each and every year, cause to be made out and posted up as aforesaid, the receipts and expenditures of the preceding year.

Sec. 10. That the said town council shall have power to regulate and improve the streets, lanes and alleys, and to determine the width of side walks: they shall have power to remove all nuisances and obstructions from the streets and commons of said town, or to provide for the removal of the same; and to do all things which a corporation of a similar nature can do, to secure the health, peace, and good order of the inhabitants of said town.

Sec. 11. That for the purpose of more effectually enabling the town council to carry into effect the provisions of this act, they are hereby authorized and empowered to levy a tax on all personal and real property. subject to taxation, within the bounds of said corporation, as the same has been, or shall be appraised and returned on the grand levy of the State: *Provided*, That said tax shall not exceed in any one year, one half of one per centum, on the aggregate amount of all such taxable property within the limits of said corporation; and the said town council shall, between the first Tuesday in April, and the first Tuesday in July, determine the amount of tax to be assessed and collected for the current year.

Sec. 12. That it shall be the duty of the recorder of said corporation, to make out duplicates of taxes, charging each individual, within said corporation, an amount of tax in proportion to the aggregate value of the taxable property belonging to said individual, within the limits of said corporation, as the same appears from the auditor's books of Ashtabula county; and the said auditor shall, at all reasonable office hours, lay open to the inspection of the recorder, any books which may be in his office, affording such information; and the recorder shall be allowed to take abstracts or memorandums. or transcripts therefrom, free of expense, to enable him to make out such duplicates; which duplicates shall be certified by the mayor and recorder; and one of said duplicates shall be delivered to the marshal, or to such other person as shall be appointed collector, whose duty it shall be to collect said tax, in the same manner, and under the same regulations, as the collectors of State and county tax are required by law to collect State and county taxes; and the said marshal or collector, so appointed, shall, immediately after collecting said tax, pay the same over to the treasurer of said corporation, and take his receipt therefor; and the said marshal, or other collector, shall have the same power to sell both real and personal property, as is given, by law, to county treasurers; and, when necessary, the said recorder shall have power to make deeds for real estate, so sold, in the same manner that county auditors are, by law, empowered to do, for lands sold by the county treasurer; and the marshal, or other collector shall receive for his fees such sum as the town council may direct, not exceeding six per centum, on all moneys so by him collected, to be paid by the treasurer, on the order of the recorder.

Sec. 13. That the said town council shall have full power to appropriate any money remaining in the corporation treasury, to the improvement of the streets and alleys, and side walks of said town, when they may deem it necessary so to do; and to make all other improvements of a public nature, which may conduce to the convenience and prosperity of the inhabitants of said town.

Sec. 14. That the mayor of said corporation shall be conservator of the peace throughout said town, and shall, within the same, have all the powers and jurisdiction of a justice of the peace, in all matters either civil or criminal, arising under the laws of this State, to all intents and purposes, whatsoever; and shall give bond for the faithful performance of his duties, in like manner as justices of the peace are required to do, which bond shall be deposited with the corporation treasurer: the said mayor shall perform all the duties required of him by the laws and ordinances of said corporation; and appeals may be taken from the decision of the said mayor, in all cases where appeals are allowed from the decisions of justices of the peace, and in the same manner.

Sec. 15. That the marshal shall be the principal ministerial officer of said town, and shall have the same powers as constables have by law; and his jurisdiction in criminal cases shall be co-extensive with the county of Ashtabula; and he shall execute the process of the mayor, and receive the same fees for his services that constables are allowed in similar cases, for like services.

Sec. 16. That the mayor shall receive the same fees that justices of the peace are entitled to in like cases; and the recorder such fees for his services, as the by-laws and ordinances of such corporation shall prescribe; but the residue of said town council shall receive no pecuniary compensation.

Sec. 17. That if no election should be held by the electors of said town on the first Tuesday of April next, it shall be lawful for any ten householders of said town, to call a meeting of the electors, by giving twelve days notice in three of the most public places therein; which notice shall state the time, place, and object of the meeting, and shall be signed by said householders; and if a majority of the electors of said town shall attend at the time and place mentioned in said notice, it shall be lawful for them to proceed to the election of officers in the same manner, as though the meeting had taken place on the first Tuesday of April; and the officers so elected, shall hold their offices until the first Tuesday of April following, and until their successors be duly elected and qualified.

Sec. 18. That said corporation shall be allowed the use of the jail of said county for the imprisonment of such persons as may be liable to imprisonment under the by-laws and ordinances of said town; and all persons so imprisoned, shall be under the charge of the sheriff or jailor, as in other cases.

Sec. 19. That the Legislature may have power, at any time, to alter, amend, or repeal this act, not thereby affecting, however, in any manner, the rights of individual citizens.

WM. SAWYER,
Speaker of the House of Representatives.
ELIJAH VANCE,
Speaker of the Senate.

February 4th, 1836.

AN ACT

To incorporate "The Western Academy of Natural Sciences."

Sec. 1. *Be it enacted by the General Assembly of the State of Ohio,* That Robert Buchannan, John Locke, Daniel Drake and George Graham, jr. and their associates, who have united in the formation, of an Academy for the cultivation of the Natural Sciences, together with such persons as may hereafter be associated with them for that purpose, be and they are hereby created a body corporate, by the name of the Western Academy of Natural Sciences, at Cincinnati; and by that name are competent to contract and be contracted with, and to sue and to be sued in all courts, with full power to acquire, hold and convey such estate, real, personal and mixed, as said Academy may deem proper and convenient; not exceeding ten thousand dollars; also, to use a common seal, and the same to alter and change at pleasure; also, to make and put in execution such by-laws and rules as they may deem needful and proper for the government of said Academy, and the management of its affairs: *Provided*, That nothing herein contained shall be so construed, as to confer banking powers on this corporation: *And provided also*, Any future Legislature may alter, amend, or repeal this act.

WM. SAWYER,
Speaker of the House of Representatives.
ELIJAH VANCE,
Speaker of the Senate.

February 5th, 1836.

AN ACT

To incorporate the town of Westville.

Sec. 1. *Be it enacted by the General Assembly of the State of Ohio*, That so much of the township of Mad River, in the county of Champaign, as is comprised within the following described limits, which comprises the town plat of Westville, to wit: beginning one hundred and twenty-eight poles south of the north-west corner of section eleven, range eleven; thence west forty poles; thence south eighty poles; thence east one hundred poles; thence north eighty poles; thence west sixty poles to the place of beginning; together with all such additions as may hereafter be recorded thereto, be and the same is hereby created a town corporate, and shall hereafter be known by the name of the town of Westville.

Sec. 2. That it shall be lawful for the white male inhabitants of said town, having the qualifications of electors of the General Assembly, to meet on the first Monday of April next, and on the first Monday of April annually thereafter, and elect by ballot one mayor, one recorder, and five trustees, who shall be householders, and shall hold their offices for one year, and until their successors are elected and qualified, and they shall constitute the Town Council.

Sec. 3. That at the first election, under this act, the electors shall choose, *viva voce*, two judges and a clerk, who shall each take an oath or an affirmation, faithfully to discharge the duties assigned them; and at all elections thereafter, the trustees, or any two of them, shall be judges, and the recorder, clerk; and at all such elections, the polls shall be opened between the hours of ten and eleven, A. M. and close at three o'clock, P. M. of said day; and at the close of the polls, the votes shall be counted and proclaimed, and the clerk shall deliver to each person elected, or leave at his usual place of abode, within three days after, a written notice of his election; and the person so notified, shall within ten days thereafter, take an oath or affirmation to support the constitution of the United States, and of this State, and also an oath of office.

Sec. 4. That the mayor recorder, and trustees, shall be a body corporate and politic, with perpetual succession, by the name of the Town of Westville; shall be capable of acquiring and holding real and personal estate; may sell and convey the same; may have a common seal, and may alter the same; may sue and be sued, plead and be impleaded, answer and be answered unto, in any court of law or equity, in this State or elsewhere; and when any suit is commenced against the corporation, the first process shall be by summons, an attested copy of which shall be left with the recorder, at least ten days before the return day thereof.

Sec. 5. That the mayor, recorder, and a majority of the trustees, shall have the power to make such by-laws and ordinances, and regulations, for the health and convenience of said town, as they may deem advisable; *Provided,* They be consistent with the constitution of the United States, and of this State; and they shall have power to fill all vacancies occasioned by death, removal, or otherwise; to appoint a treasurer, town marshal, and such other subordinate officers, as they may deem necessary; to prescribe their general duties, and to require such security as they may think necessary, to secure the faithful performance of their duties; to remove them at their pleasure; to fix and establish the fees of offices not established by this act, and to impose fines not exceeding two dollars, for refusing to accept any office in said corporation.

Sec. 6. The mayor shall be a conservator of the peace within the limits of said corporation, and shall have the jurisdiction of a justice of the peace, and shall receive the same fees as justices of the peace are entitled to for similar services; he shall give bond and security, as is required of justices of the peace; and an appeal may be had from the decisions of the mayor to the court of common pleas, in the same manner as appeals are taken from the decisions of justices of the peace.

Sec. 7. It shall be the duty of the recorder, to keep a true record of the proceedings of the town council, which record shall, at all times, be open for the inspection of the electors of said town; and the recorder shall preside at all meetings of the corporation in the absence of the mayor, and shall perform such other duties as may be required of him, by the laws and ordinances of said corporation.

Sec. 8. The town council shall have power to lay a tax annually, for corporation purposes, on the property within the limits of said town, returned on the grand levy, made subject to taxation by the laws of this State: *Provided,* That said tax shall not exceed, in any one year, three mills on the dollar; and the recorder shall make out a duplicate thereof, charging thereon each individual, an amount of tax in proportion to his property, as assessed on the grand levy for taxation; which said duplicate shall be certified and signed by the mayor and recorder, and delivered to the marshal, who shall proceed to collect the same, in the same manner, and under the same regulations, as county treasurers are required by law to collect county and State taxes; and said marshal shall, as soon as collected, pay the same over to the treasurer of the corporation.

Sec. 9. That said town council may appropriate any money in the treasury, for the improvement of the streets and side walks, or other improvements, and may have the use of the jail of the county, for the imprisonment of persons liable to imprisonment; and all persons so imprisoned, shall be under the care of the sheriff, as in other cases.

Sec. 10. The town council shall, under no circumstances, have power to license groceries.

Sec. 11. Any future Legislature may alter, amend, or repeal this act: *Provided,* That such alteration, amendment, or repeal, shall not affect private vested rights, or divert the property or funds of the corporation, from the purposes expressed in this act.

WM. SAWYER,
Speaker of the House of Representatives.
ELIJAH VANCE,
Speaker of the Senate.

February 9th, 1836.

AN ACT

To incorporate the Maumee and Kalamazoo Rail Road Company.

Sec. 1. *Be it enacted by the General Assembly of the State of Ohio,* That Horatio Conant, R. A. Forsyth, Oscar White, James Woolcott, Hiram Steel, Robert Gower, Eber Willson, William Wilson, James Kinney, Charles C. P. Hunt, Levi Beebee, and John E. Hunt, together with such other persons as may hereafter become associated with them, in the manner hereinafter prescribed, their successors and assigns, be, and they are hereby created a body corporate, by the name of " The Maumee and Kalamazoo Rail Road Company;" and by that name, shall be, and are hereby made capable in law to purchase, hold, and enjoy, and retain to them, and their successors, all lands, tenements, and hereditaments, necessary for the purposes of this act; and the same to sell, grant, rent, or in any manner dispose of; to contract and be contracted with, to sue and be sued, implead and be impleaded, answer and be answered, defend and be defended; and also to make, have, and use a common seal, and the same to alter, break, or renew at pleasure; and if either of the persons named in this section shall die, refuse or neglect to exercise the powers and discharge the duties hereby created, it shall be the duty of the remaining persons herein before named, or a majority of them, to appoint some suitable person or persons to fill such vacancy or vacancies, so often as the same shall occur.

Sec. 2. That the said corporation are hereby empowered to cause such examinations and surveys to be made between the town of Maumee, and at a point at or near Sylvania, in the county of Lucas, as shall be necessary to ascertain the most advantageous route whereon to construct a rail road, and shall cause an estimate to be made of the probable cost thereof, for

15—L

each mile separately; and the said corporation shall be, and they are hereby invested with the right to construct a rail road, with one or more rail ways, or tracks, from the town of Maumee aforesaid, to a point at or near Sylvania, to intersect the Kalamazoo and Toledo rail road.

Sec. 3. That the capital of said corporation shall be twenty-five thousand dollars, and shall be divided into shares of fifty dollars each; and five dollars on each share shall be paid at the time of subscribing.

Sec. 4. That the above named persons, or a majority of them, or the survivors of them, are authorized to open books for receiving subscription to the capital stock of such company, and shall prescribe the form of such subscription; which books shall be opened within one year from the passing of this act, at such place or places as they may deem expedient, giving twenty days notice in some newspaper printed in the county of Lucas, and in such other place or places as may be thought advisable, of the time and place, or times and places of opening said books: *Provided, however,* That if the publisher of any newspaper, printed in said county, shall neglect or refuse to print such notice, then the required notice shall be published, by affixing the same to the door of the court house in said county, at least twenty days previous to the opening of said books; and said books shall be kept open at least ten days.

Sec. 5. That as soon as said stock, or two thousand dollars thereof, shall have been subscribed, the above named persons, or the same number thereof as shall have given the notice above required, shall give like notice for a meeting of the stockholders to choose directors, at some time at least thirty days thereafter, and at some place within the said county of Lucas; and if, at such time and place, the holders of one half or more of said stock subscribed, shall attend, either in person or by lawful proxy, they shall proceed to choose from the stockholders, by ballot, three directors, each share of capital stock entitling the owner to one vote; and at such election, the persons named in the first section of this act, or those appointed by its provisions to fill vacancies which may have occurred, or any three of them, if no more be present, shall be inspectors of such election, and shall certify in writing, signed by them or a majority of them, what persons are elected directors; and if two or more have an equal number of votes, such inspectors shall determine by lot which of them shall be director or directors, to complete the number required, and shall certify the same in like manner; and said inspectors shall appoint the time and place of holding the first meeting of directors, at which meeting seven shall form a board competent to transact all business of the company, and thereafter a new election of directors shall be made annually, at such time and place as the stockholders at their first meeting shall appoint; and if the stockholders shall, at their first meeting, fail to appoint the day of such election, then it shall be holden in the succeeding year, on the same day of the same month on which said first election was holden, unless the same should be the first day of the week, in which case it shall be holden on the next day succceding; and if no election be made on the day appointed, said company shall not be dissolved, but such election may be made at any time appointed by the by-laws of said company; and directors chosen at any election shall remain directors until others are chosen; and directors chosen at any election shall, as soon thereafter as may be, choose of their own number one person to be president, and another to be treasurer of said company, and another to be secretary of said company; and from time to time may choose such other officers, as by their by-laws they may designate as necessary: *Provided,* That no person shall be a director of such company, who is not a citizen of the State of Ohio.

Sec. 6. That the directors may require payment of the subscription to the capital stock, at such times and in such proportions, and on such conditions as they shall deem fit, under penalty of forfeiture of all previous payments thereon or otherwise, provided they shall never require the payment to be made at any place out of the counties through which said road shall pass; and such directors shall, at least thirty days previous to the appointed time of such required payments, give notice thereof in the manner provided in the fourth section of this act, for giving notice of the opening of the books of subscription for the stock of said company.

Sec. 7. That the directors of said company shall have power to make from time to time all needful rules, regulations and by-laws, touching the business of said company, and to determine the number of tracks or rail-ways upon said road, and the width thereof, and the description of carriages which may be used thereon; to regulate the time and manner in which passengers and goods shall be transported thereon, and the manner of collecting tolls for such transportation, and to fix penalties for the breach of any such rule, or regulation, or by-law, and to direct the mode and condition of transferring the stock of said company; and penalties provided for by said by-laws may be sued for by any person authorized thereto, in the name of said company, and recovered in an action of debt, before any court having jurisdiction of the amount; and said company may erect and maintain toll-houses, and such other buildings and fixtures, for the accommodation of those using said road, and of themselves, as they may deem in any way necessary for their interest or convenience.

Sec. 8. That said company shall have the right to enter upon any land, to survey and lay down said road not exceeding one hundred feet in width, and to take any materials necessary for the construction of said road; and whenever any lands or materials shall be taken for the construction of such road, and the same shall not be given or granted to said company, and the owners thereof do not agree with said company as to the compensation to be paid therefor, the person or persons claiming compensation as aforesaid, or if the owner or owners thereof are minors, insane persons, or married women, then the guardian or guardians of such minor or minors, and insane persons, and the husbands of such married women, may select for themselves an arbitrator, and the said company shall select one arbitrator, and the two thus selected shall take to themselves a third, who shall be sworn and paid as arbitrators in other cases; and the three, or a majority of them, shall award as arbitrators between the parties, and render copies of their award to each of the parties in writing, from which award either party may appeal to the court of common pleas for the county in which such lands or materials may have been situate; and in all cases where compensation shall, in any manner, be claimed for lands, it shall be the duty of the arbitrators and the court to estimate any advantage which the location and constructing of said road may be to the claimant for such compensation; and the value of such advantage, if any, shall be set off against the compensation so claimed of said company; and appeals in such cases shall, when taken, be in all respects proceeded in as appeals in other cases to said court, and be brought into said court by filing the award with the clerk of said court, whose duty it shall be to enter the same on the docket of said court, setting down the claimant or claimants as plaintiff, and said company as defendant; and when the valuation, so ascertained, shall be paid or tendered by said company, said company shall have the same right to retain and own said materials, hold and possess said lands, for the use and purposes of said road, as fully and absolutely as if the same had been granted and conveyed to said company by deed.

Sec. 9. That said company may construct the said rail road across or upon any public road, highway, stream of water or water course, if the same shall be necessary; but the said company shall restore such road, highway, stream of water or water course, to its former state, or in a sufficient manner, not to impair the usefulness of such road, highway, water or water course, to the owner or the public.

Sec. 10. That any rail way company now or yet to be chartered, by law of this State, shall have power to join and unite with the road hereby incorporated, at any point which the directors of such company may think advisable, on such terms as the directors of the said companies may respectively agree; and in case of disagreement, then upon such terms as the supreme court may in chancery determine.

Sec. 11. That said company may demand and receive for tolls upon, and the transportation of persons, goods, produce, merchandize or property of any kind whatsoever, transported by them along said rail way, any sum not exceeding the following rates: on all goods, merchandize or property of any description whatsoever, transported by them, a sum not exceeding three cents per mile per ton for toll; ten cents on a ton per mile for transportation, on all goods, produce, merchandize or property of any description whatsoever, transported by them or their agents; and for the transportation of passengers, not exceeding five cents per mile for each passenger.

Sec. 12. That all persons paying the toll aforesaid, may, with suitable and proper carriages, use and travel upon the said road; always subject, however, to such rules and regulations as said company are authorized to make, by the seventh section of this act.

Sec. 13. That if proceedings be not had, under this act, within three years from the taking effect thereof, and if said road be not completed within ten years thereafter, then the same to be void, and of no effect.

Sec. 14. That so soon as the amount of tolls accruing and received for the use of said road, or any part thereof, according to the provisions of this act, shall exceed five per centum on the amount of capital stock paid in, after deducting therefrom the expenses and liabilities of said company, the directors of said company shall make a dividend of such nett profits among the stockholders, in proportion to their respective shares; and no contingent or accumulating fund exceeding one per centum of the profits of said company, shall remain undivided for more than six months.

Sec. 15. That if any person or persons shall wilfully obstruct, or in any way spoil, injure or destroy said road, or either of its branches, or any thing belonging or incident thereto, or any materials to be used in the construction thereof, or any buildings, fixtures, or carriages, erected or constructed for the use or convenience thereof; such person or persons shall each be liable for every such offence, to treble the damages sustained thereby, to be recovered by an action of debt, in any court having jurisdiction of that amount.

Sec. 16. If the legislature of this State shall, after the expiration of thirty-five years from the passage of this act, make provision by law for the repayment to said company, of the amount expended by them in the construction of said road, together with all moneys expended by them for necessary permanent fixtures at the time of purchase, for the use of said road, with an advance of fifteen per cent. thereon, then said road, with all fixtures and appurtenances, shall vest in and become the property of the State of Ohio.

Sec. 17. Whenever the dividends of said company shall exceed the rate of six per cent. per annum, the Legislature of this State may impose such reasonable taxes on the amount of such dividends, as may be received from other rail road companies.

Sec. 18. That full right and privilege is hereby reserved to the State, or citizens, or any company incorporated by law of this State, to cross the road hereby incorporated: *Provided,* That in so crossing, no injury shall be done to the works of the company incorporated by this act.

WM. SAWYER,
Speaker of the House of Representatives.
ELIJAH VANCE,
Speaker of the Senate.

February 11, 1836.

AN ACT

To incorporate "The Alexander Steam Mill Company," in the county of Athens.

Sec. 1. *Be it enacted by the General Assembly of the State of Ohio* That Ziba Lindly, A. Vanvorhes, William Golden, J. M. Gorsline, Samuel Earhart, W. D. Lindly, James Topping, John Gray and Siba Lindly, jr., and such other persons as may hereafter be associated with them, for the purpose of building a Steam grist and saw Mill, at or near the town of Hibbardsville, in Alexander township, in the county of Athens, be, and are hereby created a body corporate and politic, by and under the name and style of the "Alexander Steam Mill Company:" and by that name and style shall have perpetual succession, and be capable of suing and being sued, contracting and being contracted with, answering and being answered unto, in any court having jurisdiction of the same; and may have a common seal, and the same break, alter or renew, at pleasure, and shall be capable of holding and disposing of, at pleasure, all kinds of property, real, personal or mixed, to the amount of the capital stock of said company, necessary for the objects and purposes of said incorporation.

Sec. 2. That the capital stock of said corporation, shall not exceed ten thousand dollars, to be divided into shares of twenty-five dollars each; and the persons named in the first section of this act, or a majority of them, are hereby authorized and appointed commissioners, to open books of subscription, to the stock of said company, at such place and times, and under such regulations as they shall deem proper.

Sec. 3. That said corporation shall have power to make such by-laws and rules, for its government and regulation, as may be thought necessary and proper: *Provided,* Said by-laws, rules and regulations, are not inconsistent with the constitution and laws of the United States and of this State: *Provided, also,* The fuuds of said company, shall not be used for banking purposes.

Sec. 4. That the private property of each stockholder of said corporation, shall be liable for the debts of the same, to the amount of stock which they severally subscribed: *Provided, always,* That the joint assets and funds of the corporation, shall be first subject to the payments of said debts, before the individual property of said stockholder shall be seized in execution, or other proceedings taken to subject the same to the payment of such debts.

Sec. 5. That any future Legislature shall have power to alter, amend or repeal this act: *Provided,* such alteration, amendment or repeal shall not affect the title to any estate, acquired or conveyed, under the provisions of this act; or divert the same to any other purpose than originally intended.

WM. SAWYER,
Speaker of the House of Representatives.
ELIJAH VANCE,
Speaker of the Senate.

February 16th, 1836.

AN ACT

To extend the time of making payment by the purchasers of the lands of the Salt Reservation, in the county of Jackson.

Sec. 1. *Be it enacted by the General Assembly of the State of Ohio,* That the time for making payment by the purchasers, their assignees and legal representatives, of the lands commonly called the lands of the Salt Reservation, in the county of Jackson, which have been sold in conformity to the provisions of "An act to provide for the sale of the Salt Reservation belonging to the State of Ohio," passed February 7th, 1826, be, and the same is hereby extended to those persons who purchased prior to the first day of June, 1831, and also to such purchasers whose time of payment has expired, and the lands not yet sold, for the term of three years, in addition to the time allowed the purchasers by law at the time of making the respective purchases: *Provided,* That said purchasers, their assignees and legal representatives, shall pay to the agent of the state, on the first day of June next, the full amount of interest which may then be due on any deferred payment; and shall also, annually, thereafter, pay the interest that may accrue on all payments which have or may become due.

Sec. 2. That if any of said purchasers, their assignees or legal representatives, shall fail to pay the interest, as required by the first section of this act, all the benefits and privileges extended by this act to said purchasers, their assignees and legal representatives, shall cease and determine.

WM. SAWYER,
Speaker of the House of Representatives.
ELIJAH VANCE,
Speaker of the Senate.

February, 16th, 1836.

AN ACT

To legalize and confirm certain official acts of the Commissioners of Crawford county.

WHEREAS, by an act of the Legislature, passed March 7th, 1835, the commissioners of the county of Crawford were authorized and required to attach the territory of the Wyandott Reservation in said county of Crawford, to certain townships named in said act, thereby intending to require said Reservation to be attached to the several townships adjoining the same: *And whereas,* The said commissioners, at their June session, 1835, did attach said Reservation to the several townships of said county adjoining thereto, and among others, attached a part of said Reservation to the township of Tymochtee, which was not named in the act aforesaid: *And whereas,* It is necessary for the public convenience that the part of said Reservation set off to said township of Tymochtee by said commissioners as aforesaid, should be and remain attached to said township: Therefore,

Sec. 1. *Be it enacted by the General Assembly of the State of Ohio,* That the official acts of the commissioners of said county of Crawford, in attaching said Reservation to the townships adjoining the same, at their June session, A. D. 1835, be, and the same are hereby legalized, confirmed and made valid.

Sec. 2. That all white persons now, or hereafter resident in that part of said Reservation attached to said township of Tymochtee, shall be, and they are hereby subject to the laws of this State, for the purpose of taxation; and for all civil, criminal and military purposes whatever, in the same manner, and in the same tribunals and places, as other white citizens now are, or hereafter may be, in said township of Tymochtee.

WM. SAWYER,
Speaker of the House of Representatives.
ELIJAH VANCE,
Speaker of the Senate.

February 17th, 1836.

AN ACT

To incorporate the German Reformed Church of Xenia, in Green county.

Sec. 1. *Be it enacted by the General Assembly of the State of Ohio,* That Abraham Hivling, John Ankeny, and Samuel Crumbaugh, and their associates, shall be, and they are hereby declared to be a body politic and corporate, by the name and style of the "German Reformed Church of Xenia, in the county of Green;" to have perpetual succession, and to be capable in their corporate capacity, to contract and be contracted with, to sue and be sued, plead and be impleaded, answer and be answered, defend and be defended, in any court of competent jurisdiction; to have a common seal, and the same to change at pleasure; and to have power to ordain, pass and enforce such by-laws, rules, regulations and ordinances for the good government of said corporation, as they may deem necessary: *Provided,* That such by-laws and ordinances are not repugnant to, or incompatible with the constitution and laws of this State, and of the United States.

Sec. 2. That said association shall be capable in law of purchasing and holding any estate, real or personal, and of receiving any gift, grant, donation, devise or legacy, made or given for the promotion of the objects of said corporation, and in their corporate capacity to sell and convey the same; and the members of the said church (or association) may from time to time, according to their own constitution or rules, elect and appoint such trustees or other officers for the good government and management of its concerns, as may be necessary or expedient, giving always due public notice of such election: *Provided, however,* That the funds of said association, or society, shall never be used for any other purpose than for the erection of a house or houses for religious worship and public instruction: *Provided, also,* That the annual income of all such property does not exceed two thousand dollars.

Sec. 3. That Abraham Hivling, John Ankeny and Samuel Crumbaugh, be, and they are hereby appointed trustees of said association, until others are elected in conformity with the provisions of this act, and their constitution.

Sec. 4. That any future Legislature shall have power to alter, amend, or repeal this act.

WM. SAWYER,
Speaker of the House of Representatives.
ELIJAH VANCE,
Speaker of the Senate.

February 17th, 1836.

AN ACT

To appoint Commissioners to re-establish part of a State Road in the counties of Fairfield and Licking.

Sec. 1. *Be it enacted by the General Assembly of the State of Ohio,* That Ezra Wolf, of Fairfield county, and Benjamin Bean and John Myers, of Licking county, be, and they are hereby appointed commissioners, and Ewell Jeffries, of Fairfield county, surveyor, to re-establish so much of the State road, from Lancaster, in Fairfield county, to Johnstown, in Licking county, as lies between the towns of Havensport and Havana; beginning at Havensport, on the Ohio canal, thence crossing Walnut creek, at Knipper's line, east of his house, in the present road; thence by way of Henry Niswinder's, to pass between his house and barn; thence to the south boundary of Jeremiah Armstrong's land, at a point where the course of Main street, continued southwardly from the town of Havanna, will intersect said south boundary; and thence to the south end of Main street in the town of Havanna.

Sec. 2. That should a vacancy happen in any of the foregoing appointments, by death, removal or otherwise, the commissioners of the county in which the vacancy occurs, shall forthwith fill such vacancy, on being notified of the same.

WM. SAWYER,
Speaker of the House of Representatives.
ELIJAH VANCE,
Speaker of the Senate.

February 17, 1836.

AN ACT

Directing the Sale of School Section Number Sixteen, in the Fifth Township, in the Eighth Range in the Ohio Company's Purchase.

Sec. 1. *Be it enacted by the General Assembly of the State of Ohio,* That each and every eighty acre lot, which is contained within, and composes a part of school section number sixteen, in township number five, in the eighth range of the Ohio Company's Purchase, and county of Washington, and which was granted by Congress for the use of schools, and for the sale of which, the inhabitants have given their assent, in conformity with the provisions of an act entitled "An act to provide for the sale of section sixteen, granted by Congress, for the use of schools," passed January the twenty-ninth, eighteen hundred and twenty-seven; are hereby authorized to be sold, in conformity to the provisions of the above recited act, as soon as practicable or expedient.

WM. SAWYER,
Speaker of the House of Representatives.
ELIJAH VANCE,
Speaker of the Senate.

February 17th, 1836.

AN ACT

To Incorporate the Regular Babtist Church in Newville, in Richland county.

Sec. 1. *Be it enacted by the General Assembly of the State of Ohio,* That Adam Wolfe, William M'Daniel, Abraham Armentrout, Thomas Watts, John Clarke, Joseph Wolfe, William Tucker, Martin Gunter and their associates, and such others as may hereafter become associated with

16—L

them, be, and they are hereby created a body corporate and politic, to be known by the name, style and title of the "Regular Baptist Church in Newville, in Richland county;" with perpetual succession; and by their corporate name may contract and be contracted with, sue and be sued, answer and be answered unto, plead and be impleaded, defend and be defended, in all courts of law and equity in the State of Ohio, or elsewhere; they may have a common seal, which they may break, alter and renew at pleasure; and shall be capable of holding property, real, personal or mixed, either by purchase, gift, grant, devise or legacy, and may sell, alien, dispose of and convey the same: *Provided*, That, the annual income of said property shall not exceed the sum of eight hundred dollars.

Sec. 2. There shall be elected on the Saturday preceding the first Lord's day in April, A. D. 1836, and on Saturday preceding the first Lord's day in April, annually, by the members of said church, three trustees, a treasurer and clerk, who shall hold their offices respectively, for the term of one year, and until their successors shall be duly elected; but if by negligence or casualty the elections should not be held on the day appointed in this act for the annual election, said corporation shall not be then dissolved, but an election may be holden at any meeting of the members of the said church duly notified and assembled for that purpose.

Sec. 3. All such property as may be holden by said church, shall be under the control and management of the trustees, a majority of whom shall have power to make any contract in behalf of said church, which may become necessary to carry into effect the objects of said corporation, and to manage all pecuinary and prudential concerns which appertain to the interest and welfare of said church: *Provided*, They shall not have power to sell or alienate any real estate belonging to the said corporation, unless directed so to do by a resolution of the church, passed at a regular meeting for business.

Sec. 4. The property and funds which now belong or may hereafer belong to said church, shall be appropriated exclusively to the support of public worship, in such manner and form as said church, from time to time, may deem proper and advisable: *Provided*, Said church as a body, shall not appropriate any part of said property or funds in any other way than for the benefit of the Regular Baptist Church as above described, and for no other purpose.

Sec. 5. The corporation shall have power to make such by-laws, rules and regulations as may be deemed proper for the regulation and good government of said church: *Provided*, The same be not inconsistent with the constitutions and laws of the United States, and of the State of Ohio: *And Provided, also*, That said by-laws, rules and regulations shall be agreed to by a meeting of said corporation specially held for that purpose, of which meeting the members shall be duly notified by giving at least ten day's previous notice; and that original process against said corporation shall be by a summons, an attested copy of which, shall be left at the residence of one of the trustees at least five days before the return day thereof, and such service shall be deemed sufficient to bind said corporation.

Sec. 6. That Adam Wolfe, William M'Daniel, and Abraham Armentrout, be, and they are hereby appointed trustees until the first annual election is held, and until others are elected.

Sec. 7. Any future Legislature shall have power to alter, amend or repeal this act: *Provided,* Such alteration, amendment or repeal shall not affect the title to any property acquired or conveyed under its provisions.

WM. SAWYER,
Speaker of the House of Representatives.

ELIJAH VANCE,
Speaker of the Senate.

February 17, 1836.

AN ACT

To authorize Joseph Ridgway, (Senr.) and P. B. Wilcox, administrators of Ralph Osborn, deceased, to complete the real contracts and sell the real estate of said decedent.

Sec. 1. *Be it enacted by the General Assembly of the State of Ohio,* That Joseph Ridgway, Senr. and P. B. Wilcox, administrators of Ralph Osborn, late of Franklin county, deceased, be, and they are hereby authorized and empowered to convey, by a deed or deeds in fee simple, all lands and tenements contracted to be sold by said Osborn, but not conveyed in his life time; and also to sell and convey, by a deed or deeds in fee simple, the lands and tenements of which the said Osborn died, seized, or, which he owned at the time of his death; which deeds being executed according to law, shall vest in the grantee or grantees all the right, title and estate which the said Osborn had at the time of his death.

Sec. 2. That before any such sales shall be made or deeds executed, the said administrators shall give bond and security to the satisfaction of the Court of Common Pleas of said Franklin county, that they will faithfully account for all moneys received on such sales and execution of said deeds; which bond shall be made payable to the State of Ohio, and may be prosecuted as other official bonds.

WM. SAWYER,
Speaker of the House of Representatives,

ELIJAH VANCE,
Speaker of the Senate.

February 18, 1836.

AN ACT

To incorporate the Preacher's Aid Society of the Methodist Protestant Church.

Sec. 1. *Be it enacted by the General Assembly of the State of Ohio,* That Joseph Sharp, William Marshall, William Camp, William Hamilton, John Vanderbarack, Henry Nash, Olcut White, Cornelius Springer, and Samuel Fairbank, of the county of Muskingum, and their successors qualified and appointed as hereinafter mentioned, be and they are hereby created a body corporate and politic, by the name and style of the Preacher's Aid Society, of the Methodist Protestant Church; and are hereby fully empowered to carry into effect the benevolent and charitable purposes in this act set forth; and by the name aforesaid, shall be capable in law to sue and be sued, plead and be impleaded, defend and be defended, in all courts of law and equity, in all manner of suits, complaints or causes whatever.

Sec. 2. That the said trustees, and their successors in office, by the name and style aforesaid, shall be capable in law to take, receive, possess and enjoy, all manner of lands, tenements, rents, hereditaments, and any sum or sums of money, and any kind or portion of goods, given, granted or devised, unto them or their successors, by any person or persons, body politic or corporate, agreeably to the intention of the donors, [respectively,] and according to the objects and condition in this act set forth: *Provided,* That the annual income of all such property, shall not exceed the sum of two thousand dollars.

Sec. 3. That in case of the death, resignation or expulsion of any one or more members of said corporation, or of their successors, then it shall be the duty of the remaining trustees to nominate double the number of those whose seats may have been vacated, as aforesaid, and to make a representation thereof in writing. to the ensuing Pittsburg Annual Conference of the Methodist Protestant Church, (a principal part of which lies within the State of Ohio,) at their next annual assembly, whose duty it shall be immediately to elect, by a majority of votes, a person or persons, as the case may be, out of the whole number nominated by the trustees as aforesaid, to fill up such vacancy or vacancies, in order to keep up the number of nine trustees forever; and upon every such choice, a certificate shall be issued from the said annual conference, signed by the president and secretary, and directed to the trustees of said corporation, containing the name or names of the person or persons so chosen, which certificate shall he registered in the books of said corporation, and the person or persons so chosen, shall be vested with all the powers and immunities of a member of said corporation: *Provided, however,* That no person shall be eligible as a trustee of said corporation who has not been a member of said church for at least five years next preceding his election, and shall not be at least twenty-five years of age, and a citizen of the State.

Sec. 4. That the said corporation shall meet at least once in every year, for the transaction of their necessary business, at such time and place in this State, as a majority of them may think proper; and when so met, they shall have the power to make such by-laws and regulations for their government, in the management of their affairs, as a majority of them may judge necessary; and also, at every such annual meeting, they shall choose by a majority of votes, a president and secretary out of their own body, whom, if it be thought proper, may be continued in office from year to year: *Provided,* That such by-laws be not inconsistent with the laws of the United States and of this State.

Sec. 5. That if at any time, a majority of the trustees should deem it expedient, by deed or otherwise, to sell, convey or otherwise dispose of any part or parcel of the estate, real or personal, belonging to such corporation, in such case it shall be their duty to make a representation thereof in writing to the ministers and laymen in the Pittsburgh annual conference assembled, who shall judge of the expediency of such proposed sale; and if two thirds of the ministers and laymen assembled as aforesaid, shall consent thereto, a certificate shall be issued from the said annual conference, signed by the president and secretary, declaring such approbation and specifying the kind and amount of property to be sold or otherwise disposed of, which certificate shall be transmitted to the said trustees, who shall cause the same to be recorded in the books of the corporation: *Provided always*, That the money arising from said sale shall be vested, as soon as practicable, in such other securities and property, as in the judgment of a majority of them, will be most productive and safe: *And provided further*, That the annual interest or income arising from the money so vested, shall be exclusively applied in the manner and for the purposes in this act set forth.

Sec. 6.   That the annual rents, interest and income of the estate, real and personal, which may at any time belong to the said corporation and their successors, shall by them be held subject to the exclusive order and control of the ministers and laymen in the Pittsburgh annual conference assembled; and they are hereby vested with full powers to appropriate and point out the mode of applying the same to the objects, under the limitations, and for the uses and purposes herein mentioned and expressly declared.

Sec. 7.   That the fund hereby intended to be established, is expressly for the purpose of relieving the distressed, and supplying the deficiencies of the itinerant superannuated, and worn out ministers of the Methodist Protestant Church, within the bounds of the Pittsburgh district, who remain in connection with and continue subject to the order and discipline of said church; and also for the relief of the widows and orphans of such ministers as aforesaid, and for no other use, intent or purpose whatever; *Provided*, That no sum exceeding one hundred dollars shall be appropriated to an unmarried minister, in any one year; also that no sum exceeding two hundred dollars shall be applied to a married minister in any one year; and that no sum exceeding one hundred dollars in any one year shall be applied to the use of each widow, as hereinbefore mentioned and described; and also, that no sum exceeding sixteen dollars shall be applied in any one year, to the use of each child or orphan of such ministers, as are herein before particularly mentioned and described.

Sec. 8.   That no sum or sums of money, under any pretence whatever, shall be drawn from the fund hereby intended to be established, other than for the purposes and under the limitations and restrictions, herein before expressly mentioned and declared: *Provided nevertheless*, That the trustees of said corporation and their successors, shall have power to draw and apply from time to time, so much money belonging to said fund, as in the judgment of a majority of them, may be wanting to defray all the necessary expenses of conducting the business of said corporation.

Sec. 9.   That it shall be the duty of the trustees to cause regular and fair accounts to be kept, (in a book provided for that purpose) of the funds of said corporation, as well as it respects the kind and amount of the capital stock and of the annual interest and income thereof, as of all the moneys which shall from time to time be drawn therefrom, for the object herein before mentioned; and further, it shall be the duty of the trustees and their successors, to prepare and lay before the ministers and laymen of the Pittsburgh annual conference, at their annual meeting, a statement of the affairs and funds of said corporation, for their examination, which shall be signed by the president and secretary.

Sec. 10. That if ever the Methodist Protestant Church should abandon the principle of representation, by refusing to admit laymen into the councils of the church, by any conventional act or otherwise, as now provided for in the discipline thereof, then, and in that case, this corporation shall transfer all the moneys, lands, tenements, goods and chattles, belonging to the said corporation, to the benefit of the Methodist Church of the United States of America, which admits and practices in its government, upon the principle of lay representation; and if there be no such Methodist Church in the United States of America, then it shall transfer the property above named to the State of Ohio, for the benefit of the general school fund, and cease any longer to be a body corporate: *Provided,* That any future Legislature shall have power to alter, amend or repeal this act: *Provided also,* Such alteration or repeal shall not affect the title to any estate real or personal, acquired or conveyed under its provisions, or divert the same to any other purpose than originally intended.

WM. SAWYER,
Speaker of the House of Representatives.
ELIJAH VANCE,
Speaker of the Senate.

February 18, 1836.

AN ACT

To enable the County Commissioners of the county of Putnam, to purchase, for the use of the county of Putnam, lands therein named.

Whereas, by an act, entitled "An act to organize the county of Putnam, and establish its seat of justice," passed January 3d, 1834, there was granted to said county, one hundred and sixty acres of land, to be taken out of fractional section five, township one, and range six, east, lying and being in said county, including therein, the place selected for the seat of justice of said county, by commissioners appointed by a resolution of the General Assembly of Ohio, passed February 12th, 1829, the whole of said section, belonging to the State, having been selected for canal purposes: *And whereas,* The whole of the remainder of said section is yet not sold by the State, and the county commissioners of said Putnam county are desirous of purchasing the same, for the use and benefit of the seat of justice of said county: Therefore,

Sec. 1. *Be it enacted by the General Assembly of the State of Ohio,* That the county commissioners of the county of Putnam, be, and they are hereby authorized to purchase, for the use and benefit of the town of Kalida, the seat of justice of Putnam county, the residue of section number five, in township number one, and range number six, east; lying and being in the

county of Putnam aforesaid, and which now remains unsold, after taking
out of said section, the one hundred and sixty acres already granted to said
county.

Sec. 2. That the director of the town of Kalida, be, and he is hereby
constituted and appointed director, to superintend, under the direction of
the commissioners of the county, all things in relation to the purchase and
sale of said land, in the same manner, and with the same powers, as is by
law conferred on township directors.

Sec. 3. That said director shall, some time in the month of May next,
under the direcction of the commissioners of said county, (cause) to be surveyed and laid out by metes and bounds, the balance of said fractional section number five, town one and range six, east, which now remain unsold,
after taking out the one hundred and sixty acres, as named in the first section of this act; and shall immediately thereafter make out three copies of
the plat and field notes of the survey of said land, one of which he shall
carefully preserve, one he shall forward to the register of the canal land
office for the district in which the lands lie, and the other he shall forward
to the Governor.

Se. 4. That it shall be the duty of the Governor, upon receiving the
plat and field notes of said land, to execute a deed of conveyance in behalf
of the State for said land, to the county commissioners of the county of
Putnam, for the use and benefit of the town of Kalida, the seat of justice
of said county, and transmit the same to the said county commissioners.

Sec. 5. That upon receiving the deed of conveyance, as required by
the foregoing section of this act, it shall be the duty of the county com-
missieners aforesaid, to have the said deed recorded; and they shall forthwith cause the whole of said land, in said deed conveyed, to be laid out in
lots or parcels of ground, not containing less than four, nor more than ten
acres each, with necessary and proper avenues to go to and from said lots;
and the said commissioners shall cause the plat of said premises so laid as
aforesaid, to be recorded in the recorder's office of said county.

Sec. 6. That the county commissioners of the county of Putnam, and
their successors in office, shall have the care, management and superintendence of the whole of the premises and lots of ground, and the sale thereof; and they are hereby authorized to cause said lots to be sold at public
or private sale, and with or without a credit for the purchase money, and if
sold on a credit, to direct in what manner the purchase money shall be secured; and the said county commissioners and their successors in office,
shall execute deeds of conveyance for all lots or parcels of ground that
may be sold, whenever the same shall be fully paid for.

Sec. 7. That it shall be the duty of the aforesaid director to sell said
lots of ground under the direction of the county commissioners, and to collect and receive all moneys arising from the sale of said lots, and pay the
same over, from time to time, as collected, to the treasurer of Putnam county; and the said director shall keep an accurate account of all sales by him
made, and shall settle his accounts in relation to his office of director once
in every year, with the county commissioners; and the said director shall
receive such compensation for his services as the said county commissioners
shall deem just and reasonable.

Sec. 8. That the proceeds of the sale of said lots, as provided for by this act, shall be applied as follows: first, to the payment of the purchase money for said land at the rate of three dollars per acre, with interest on the purchase from the time of sale till the same be paid; to be paid into the State treasury, for the benefit of the canal fund; secondly, to the payment of the expenses necessarily incurred in laying off said tract of land, as by this act is required, and in making such sales; thirdly, all the residue, if any, shall remain in the county treasury, for the use and benefit of said Putnam county, in the erection of a court house and other public buildings in the town of Kalida, the seat of justice of said county.

Sec. 9.   That to secure the payment of the purchase money, as named in the eighth section of this act, the directors of the town of Kalida shall make, execute, and deliver to the Treasurer of State a bond with sufficient security for the sum of four thousand dollars, conditioned for the faithful paying over the purchase money aforesaid, in five annual instalments; which bond shall be executed and delivered previous to the execution and delivery of the deed, provided for in the fourth section of this act.

WM. SAWYER,
Speaker of the House of Representatives.
ELIJAH VANCE,
Speaker of the Senate.

February 18, 1836.

AN ACT

To extend the time of making payment by the purchasers of certain School sections in the county of Butler.

Sec. 1.   *Be it enacted by the General Assembly of the State of Ohio,* That the time for making payment by the purchasers, their assigns or legal representatives, of fractional section sixteen, township one, range two, between the Miami rivers, in the county of Butler, which has been sold in conformity with the provisions of [an] act entitled, " An act to provide for the sale of section sixteen, granted by Congress for the use of schools," passed January the twenty-ninth, one thousand eight hundred and twenty-seven, be, and the same is hereby extended to the first day of January, in the year one thousand eight hundred and thirty-nine: *Provided,* That said purchasers, their assigns, or legal representatives, shall pay to the treasurer of said county, on or before the eleventh day of August next, the full amount of interest which then may be due on any deferred payment, and shall also, annually thereafter, pay the interest that may accrue on said deferred payments.

Sec. 2.   That the time of making payment by the purchasers of section twenty-two, town three, range three, given to fractional townships one and two, range three, in lieu of section sixteen, be extended agreeably to the provisions of the first section of this act.

Sec. 3.   That the time of making payment by the purchasers of school section sixteen, township five, range two, and section sixteen, township three, range one, west of the Great Miami river, in the county of Butler, be, and the same is hereby extended to the first day of January, one thousand eight hundred and forty-one: *Provided,* Said purchasers, their assigns or legal representatives, shall pay to the treasurer of said county, on or before the twenty-fifth day of March, one thousand eight hundred and thirty-seven, the full amount of interest which then may be due on any deferred payment; and shall also annually thereafter pay the interest that may accrue on said deferred payment.

Sec. 4. That the time of making payment of such sum or sums as may be now due, or which may hereafter become due from the purchaser or purchasers of school section numbered sixteen, township three and range two, west of the Great Miami river, in the county of Butler, be, and the same is hereby extended to the first day of January. one thousand eight hundred and forty-one: *Provided,* Said purchaser or purchasers, his, her, or their assigns or legal representatives, shall pay to the treasurer of Butler county, on or before the twenty-fifth day of March, one thousand eight hundred and thirty-seven, the full amount of interest which may be then due on such deferred payments; and shall also, annually thereafter, pay as aforesaid, the interest that may accrue on such defferred payments: *Provided, further,* That nothing in this section contained, shall be so construed, as to prevent the purchasers aforesaid, from paying the whole amount which he, she, or they may owe, by reason of the foregoing purchase, with interest thereon, at any time after the said twenty-fifth day of March, eighteen hundred and thirty-seven: *Provided,* Said purchaser, or purchasers, or any of them, shall elect so to do.

Sec. 5. That if any of said purchasers, their assigns or legal representatives, shall fail to pay the interest as required in the first, third and fourth sections of this act, all the benefits and privileges extended by this act to said purchasers, their assigns and legal representatives, shall cease and determine.

WM. SAWYER,
Speaker of the House of Representatives.
ELIJAH VANCE,
Speaker of the Senate.

February 18, 1836.

AN ACT

To lay out and establish a graded State Road in the counties of Fairfield and Perry.

Sec. 1. *Be it enacted by the General Assembly of the State of Ohio,* That Gideon Martin and Isaac Hite, of the county of Fairfield, and John Vannatta, of the county [of] Perry, be, and they are hereby appointed commissioners, and Ewel Jeffries, of the county of Fairfield, surveyor, to lay out and establish a graded State road, beginning at the town of Lancaster, in the county of Fairfied, passing through Bremen, in said county, thence to Cropingville, in Perry county; thence to Mount Hope, in said county; thence to Bristol, in said county of Perry, so as to intersect the graded state road from M'Connellsville, in Morgan county, at the point last named.

17—L

Sec. 2. That the said road shall, in no case, exceed an angle of five degrees with the horizon; and the commissioners aforesaid, shall, in all cases, be governed by the act defining the mode of laying out and establishing State roads, passed March 14, 1831.

Sec. 3. That should either of the commissioners or surveyor die, or remove out of the county, or refuse to serve, the commissioners of the county in which such vacancy shall happen, shall forthwith, on being notified of such vacancy, appoint some suitable person to fill the same.

WM. SAWYER,
Speaker of the House of Representatives.
ELIJAH VANCE,
Speaker of the Senate.

February 18, 1836.

AN ACT

To authorize the County Auditor of Wayne county, to sell certain School Lands therein named.

Sec. 1. *Be it enacted by the General Assembly of the State of Ohio,* That the County Auditor of Wayne county be, and he is hereby authorized to sell all, or any part of the south east quarter of section sixteen, in the township of Canaan, in Wayne county, in lots of not less than ten acres each; and that he shall in all other respects be governed by the laws now in force, for the sale of lands granted by Congress for the use of schools.

Sec. 2. That the said Auditor shall direct the surveyor' to lay out the said quarter section into such lots, as may, by the trustees of the township of Canaan, be directed, and make a out plat of the same, which shall be deposited in the Auditors office of said Wayne county.

WM. SAWYER,
Speaker of the House of Representatives.
ELIJAH VANCE,
Speaker of the Senate.

February 18th, 1836.

AN ACT

Further to amend the act, entitled "An act to incorporate the Sandy and Nimishillen Navigation Company," passed February 13th, 1832.

Sec. 1. *Be it enacted by the General Assembly of the State of Ohio,* That the president and directors of the Sandy and Nimishillen Navigation Company, be, and they are hereby authorized, to borrow such sum, or sums of money, as may be necessary for the completion of Canal and slack-water Navigation, as is contemplated and declared by the act, to which this is an amendment; and they are hereby authorized to pledge the capital stock of said company, now subscribed, or that may hereafter be subscribed, together with the revenues thereof, as security for the payment of the principal and interest, of such sum or sums, by them borrowed for the use of said company, under the provisions of this act.

Se 2. That it shall be the duty of the proper officers of said company to give sixty days notice of any call, for the payment of any instalment or instalments, due on the capital stock of said company, in two of the newspapers printed in each county in which any stockholder may at the time reside, and not otherwise.

WM. SAWYER,
Speaker of the House of Representatives.
ELIJAH VANCE,
Speaker of the Senate.

February 18, 1836.

AN ACT

To incorporate the Methodist Episcopal Church of the town of Lancaster.

Sec. 1. *Be it enacted by the General Assembly of the State of Ohio,* That George Kauffman, Hugh H. Waite, Ezra Schleich, William Hunter, Robert R. Claspill, John S. Walters, Robert Fielding, George H. Smith, Walter MD'onald, Amos Hunter, James Cranmer, and their associates, who are, or shall hereafter be connected with them, be, and they are hereby created a body politic and corporate, by the name and style of "The Methodist Episcopal Church of Lancaster;" and as such shall have perpetual succession; and by their corporate name, may contract and be contracted with, sue and be sued, plead and be impleaded, answer and be answered, defend and be defended, in any court of law and equity; may have a common seal, and alter the same at pleasure.

Sec. 2. That said corporation shall have power to purehase, receive, hold and enjoy, any estate, real personal and mixed, the annual income of which shall not exceed two thousand dollars, for church purposes, and such other expenses as may be incident to the support of public worship.

Sec. 3. That for the better management of the affairs of said congregation, there shall be elected, by ballot on the first Monday of December, one thousand eight hundred and thirty-six, by the male members of said church who are in full connection, above the age of twenty-one years, nine trustees who shall be members of said church, three of whom shall be elected for one year, three for two years, and three for three years; and as their several terms of office shall expire, their successors shall, on the first Monday of December in each year, be elected as aforesaid, to serve three years, so as to create a vacancy of three trustees, to be filled as aforesaid, in each year.

Sec. 4. That said trustees, any five of whom shall be a quorum to transact business, shall have the entire management and control of all the property of the corporation; erect suitable buildings for public worship, and hold all the property of the corporation in trust for the benefit of the members thereof foreever; and shall have power to do any act, or acts in relation to the same as, in their opinion, may be necessary to advance the interests of the corporation.

Sec. 5. That the trustees shall have power to adopt and establish such by-laws and ordinances as may be deemed necessary for the good government of the corporation: *Provided*, That the same be not contrary to the Constitution and laws of the United States, and the State of Ohio; and they shall have further power to fill any vacancy that may happen in their own body, until their next annual election thereafter: *Provided*, that a failure to meet, and hold any election required by this act, shall not be considered a forfeiture of this charter; but the officers previously chosen shall serve until their successors are elected, which election may be held at any meeting duly notified by them for that purpose.

Sec. 6. That it shall be the duty of the trustees to permit the preachers and ministers of the Episcopal Church, who shall be duly authorized by the General, or Annual Conferrence of said Church, to expound God's Holy Word, in any house held by them in trust for that purpose.

Sec. 7. That until the first annual election, required to be held under the provisions of this act, Ezra Schleich, Hugh H. Waite, Geo. Kauffman, William Hunter, Robert R. Claspill, John S. Walters Walter M'Donald, Rober Fielding and George H. Smith, be and the same are hereby appointed trustees, to take charge of and manage the property and affairs of said corporation.

Sec. 8. That original process against said corporation shall be served by leaving an attested copy with one or more of the trustees, at least ten days before the return day, and such service shall be deemed sufficient to bind said corporation.

Sec. 9. That any future legislature shall have the power to modify or repeal this act: *Provided*, That such modification or repeal shall not affect the title to any real estate, or personal, acquired or conveyed under its provisions.

WM. SAWYER,
Speaker of the House of Representatives.
ELIJAH VANCE,
Speaker of the Senate.

February 18th, 1836.

AN ACT

To lay out and establish a graded State Road from Concord, in the county of Muskingum, to Newcastle, in Coshocton county.

Sec. 1. *Be it enacted by the General Assembly of the State of Ohio,* That John G. Pigman, and Alexander Slaughter, of Coshocton county, and Daniel Stillwell, of Muskingum county, be, and they are hereby appointed commissioners, and George Smith, of Muskingum county, surveyor, to lay out and establish a graded state road, commencing at the town of Concord, in the county of Muskingum; thence to Adams' mill, on the Ohio canal; thence to Moscow, in Coshocton county; thence to Newcastle, in said county.

Sec. 2. That said road shall, in no case, exceed an angle of five degrees with the horizon.

Sec. 3. That the commissioners aforesaid shall, in all respects, be governed by the law in force defining the mode of laying out and establishing State roads, except in the appointment of a surveyor, which is provided for in the first section of this act.

Sec. 4. That should a vacancy happen in any of the foregoing appointments by death, removal, or otherwise, the commissioners of the county in which the vacancy occurs, shall forthwith fill such vacancy, as often as it may occur, on being notified of the same.

WM. SAWYER,
Speaker of the House of Representatives.
ELIJAH VANCE,
Speaker of the Senate.

February 18, 1836.

AN ACT

To incorporate the Highland Library Association.

Sec. 1. *Be it enacted by the General Assembly of the State of Ohio,* That Francis Carter, William O. Collins, William Scott and their associates, be, and they are hereby created and declared a body corporate and politic, by the name and style of the "Highland Library Association;" and by that name shall have perpetual succession; be capable of suing and being sued, pleading and being impleaded; may have a common seal, and may alter the same at pleasure.

Sec. 2. That the said corporation may purchase, receive, hold and convey any estate, personal or mixed, *Provided,* The annual income of said estate shall not exceed the sum of one thousand dollars.

Sec. 3. That the members of said corporation may from time to time elect such officers as may be deemed necessary for the institution, and make all necessary by-laws, and may annex to the same reasonable pecuinary fines for the breach thereof: *Provided,* That any future Legislature shall have power to alter, or repeal this act.

WILLIAM MEDILL,
Speaker pro tem. of the House of Representatives.
ELIJAH VANCE,
Speaker of the Senate.

February 29th, 1836.

AN ACT

To amend the act entitled, "An act to extend the time of making payment by the purchasers of School section sixteen, township two, range four, between the Miami rivers, in the county of Butler," passed February 23d, 1835.

Sec. 1. *Be it enacted by the General Assembly of the State of Ohio,* That the time for making payment by the purchasers of school section sixteen, town two, range four, between the Miami rivers, as set forth in the act to extend the time of making payment by the purchasers of school section sixteen, township two, range four, between the Miami rivers, in the county of Butler, passed February 23d, 1835, be, and the same is hereby extended to the first day of January, one thousand eight hundred, thirty-nine: *Provided,* That said purchasers, their assigns, or legal representatives, shall pay the treasurer of said county, on or before the eleventh day of August, annually, all interest that may accrue on said deferred payments; any thing in the act to which this is an amendment, to the contrary, notwithstanding.

WILLIAM MEDILL,
Speaker pro tem. of the House of Representatives.
ELIJAH VANCE,
Speaker of the Senate.

February 29, 1836.

AN ACT

Authorizing the Commissioners of Hamilton county, to alter a part of the State road leading from Cincinnati, westwardly, to the State line.

Sec. 1. *Be it enacted by the General Assembly of the State of Ohio,* That the commissioners of Hamilton county, by and with the consent of the owner or owners of the land through which they may pass, are hereby authorized to alter the site of that part of the state road leading from Cincinnati, westwardly, to the State line; beginning at a point in said state road at the east side of the village of Cleves; thence eastwardly on the best ground to the top of the hill to intersect the old road.

WILLIAM MEDILL,
Speaker pro tem. of the House of Representatives.
ELIJAH VANCE,
Speaker of the Senate.

February 29, 1836.

AN ACT

Providing for the sale of Section Sixteen, in the township of Read, in the county of Seneca.

Sec. 1. *Be it enacted by the General Assembly of the State of Ohio,* That

it shall be the duty of the assessor of Seneca county, on or before the first day of April next to provide himself with a suitable book for that purpose, and proceed to take the votes of all the white male inhabitants over the age of twenty-one years, residing in the bounds of original surveyed town. ship number three, north, of range seventeen, in the county of Seneca, afore. said, who have resided therein for twelve months next preceding the first day of April aforesaid, whether such white male inhabitants be, or be not citizens of the United States; and it shall further be the duty of said assess. or, between the first day of April and the twenty-fifth day of May next, to call upon all the white male inhabitants residing in the township afore. said, and request any such inhabitant to give his vote for or against a sale of the school land, aforesaid, by signing his name under the head of the proper columns; and if such inhabitant be unable to write, the assessor aforesaid, shall write the name of such inhabitant, to which he shall affix his mark of approbation; which said vote taken as aforesaid, shall be en. tered in said book by said assessor, in form following, to wit: The votes of the white male inhabitants over the age of twenty-one years, residing within the bounds of said original surveyed township, (there being twenty of said inhabitants within the same,) for and against the sale of the said section sixteen; it being the tract granted by Congress for the use of schools in . said original surveyed township.

Names of those who voted in favor of a sale.	Names of those who voted against the sale.

Which said list of votes so taken as aforesaid, the assessor shall deliver to the county auditor of said Seneca county, forthwith, after having taken the same as aforesaid; and if it shall appear from said list, that a majority of the white male inhabitants aforesaid, have voted in favor of a sale, then a sale of said school section may be made in the manner hereinafter prescribed.

Sec. 2. That Isaac H. Bennet, James Harrison, and John B. Case, of the county of Seneca, be, and they are hereby appointed commissioners, whose duty it shall be to view and appraise said school section sixteen, so soon as the assessor shall have performed the duties required of him by the first section of this act, they having first taken an oath or affirmation, before some person competent to administer the same, faithfully and im. partially to appraise said land.

Sec. 3. That should either of the commissioners die, or refuse to per. form the duties required by this act, or remove out of said county of Sen. eca, then the county commissioners of said county shall fill such vacancy so often as it may occur.

Sec. 4. That the commissioners appointed by virtue of this act are hereby authorized, if they deem it expedient, to take to their assistance the surveyor of Seneca county, who, under their direction, shall make such surveys, divisions and maps thereof as may be necessary, for the perform. ance of the duties required of them by this act; and said commissioners and surveyor shall each receive for his services one dollar and fifty cents for each day he may be employed in said service, to be paid out of the county treasury of said county of Seneca, which shall be refunded to said treas. ury in manner hereinafter provided.

Sec. 5. That so soon as said school section sixteen has been surveyed under the direction of said commissioners, and maps thereof made as pro-

vided in the fourth section of this act, the said commissioners shall cause
to be delivered to the auditor of Seneca county, such surveys and divisions and map thereof, and the separate appraisement of such lot laid off
in said school section, if the same shall have been divided into lots, and
otherwise the appraisement of the entire section so made under the requirements of this act; and it shall be the duty of such auditor, after having
given thirty days previous notice thereof by advertisement in some newspaper printed in Seneca county, and if no newspaper be published in said
county, or if the publisher of any newspaper in said county shall refuse to
publish the same, then the notice shall be given by affixing such notice on
the door of the court house in said county, and in five other public places
in said county, three of which shall be in said township of Read, thirty
days previous to such sale; and the affidavit of one or more [of] such commissioners, certifying the manner, time, and places of publishing such notices, shall be conclusive evidence of such fact, to offer such section, or such
lots laid off in such section separately for sale, between the hours of ten
o'clock A. M. and of five o'clock P. M. on the day designated in such notice, and shall sell the same, and each of the same to the highest bidder:
Provided, That neither said section, nor any part of said section, shall be
sold for less than its appraised value, and that one-fourth of the money bid
for the same shall be paid at the time of sale; and the remaining three-
fourths of the money so bid, shall be payable in three equal annual instalments, payable annually, and successively after the day of said sale, with
interest at the rate of six per cent. per annum, on all moneys unpaid, to be
computed from said day of sale; and said commissioners may continue said
sale, by adjournment, from day to day, [for] three successive days, if any
portion of such section shall remain unsold; and if at the expiration of said
three days, any portion of such land shall remain unsold, the sale thereof
may be adjourned for a time not exceeding three months; and said commissioners shall in like manner proceed, giving like notice of each succeeding sale, until the whole be sold.

Sec. 6. That on the sale of said lands so made as aforesaid, the auditor of said county shall take a bond from each purchaser, with at least
one sufficient surety, conditioned for the payment to the treasurer of Seneca county, of all the moneys due for said land, or for any part thereof,
with the interest thereon to become due or accruing, to be applied to the
use of schools in said township of Read; and said auditor, on the final
payment of said bond according to the conditions thereof, shall make and
execute a deed of said land to the purchaser or purchasers thereof, his or their
heirs and assigns, in fee simple; and said purchase money, when received,
shall be deposited in the common school fund, for the benefit of said township:
Provided, That if any person or persons who shall purchase any part of
said school section, under the provisions of this act, shall be desirous of
completing the payment for the same, within a less time than that required by the obligation of the bond, he shall be allowed to complete payment for the same at any time, and shall be entitled to receive a deed in
fee simple for said land, in the manner herein provided.

Sec. 7. That the auditor of said county shall be entitled to receive for
all conveyances as he may be required to make by virtue of this act, twelve
and a half cents for each hundred words contained therein, and in like pro-

portion for any smaller number; and that the asesssor be entitled to receive for his services performed under the provisions of this act, the sum of one dollar and fifty cents per day, for each day he may be necessarily employed in said service.

Sec. 8. That the treasurer of said county shall, out of the first moneys that may come to his hands of the interest of said purchase moneys, pay the said assessor, commissioners, surveyor, and auditor, the fees and compensation herein before specified, to be paid to said commissioners, surveyor, and auditor, as well as all necessary fees and expenses for acknowledging said deeds, and for publishing the advertisements, made necessary by the requirements of this act.

Sec. 9. That the act entitled "An act directing the sale of a certain school section numbered sixteen, in Read township, in the county of Seneca," passed March 4, 1835, be, and the same is hereby repealed.

WILLIAM MEDILL,
Speaker pro tem, of the House of Representatives.
ELIJAH VANCE,
Speaker of the Senate.

February 29, 1836.

AN ACT

To lay out and establish a State road from the town of Piketon, in the county of Pike, to the town of Adelphi, in the county of Ross,

Sec. 1. *Be it enacted by the General Assembly of the State of Ohio,* That Samuel Reed, of the county of Pike, James Tomlinson and David Rowell, of the county of Ross, be, and they are hereby appointed commissioners, and Richard Bayes, of Pike county, surveyor, to lay out and establish a state road; commencing at the town of Piketon, in the county of Pike; thence the nearest and best way to the town of Richmond, in the county of Ross; from thence the nearest and best way to the town of Londonderry, in said county of Ross; and from thence the nearest and best way to intersect the state road leading to Tarlton, at the town of Adelphi, in said county of Ross.

Sec. 2. That the expenses of viewing, laying out and establishing said road shall be paid as pointed out in the act entitled "An act defining the mode of laying out and establishing State roads;" and the commissioners shall be governed in all respects by the provisions of said act; and if any one of the commissioners aforesaid, should die, refuse to serve, or remove out of the county in which he now resides, the county commissioners thereof, shall, as soon as convenient, proceed to appoint some suitable person to fill such vacancy as often as the same may occur.

WILLIAM MEDILL,
Speaker pro tem. of the House of Representatives.
ELIJAH VANCE,
Speaker of the Senate.

February 29th, 1836.
18—L

AN ACT

For the relief of I. H. Butler & Son.

Whereas, I. H. Butler & son contracted to construct section No. 207, on the Ohio canal, south of the Licking summit, including a culvert across Sunfish creek, of two arches, each forty feet space; which culvert was destroyed by an unusual freshet, in the month of July, 1831, by which casualty the said contractors have sustained heavy losses in the completion of the said work, and have not, as they alledge, received adequate remuneration therefor: Therefore,

Sec. 1. Be it enacted by the General Assembly of the State of Ohio, That the board of canal commissioners, and their successors in office, be, and they are hereby authorized to inquire into the circumstances of the case, and to decide, according to the principles of justice and equity, on the claim for the losses sustained in consequence of the casualty aforesaid, and if it shall appear that the said contractors are entitled to any remuneration, they shall determine the amount so to be allowed, and shall cause the same to be paid to the said contractors, out of the canal fund.

WILLIAM MEDILL,
Speaker pro tem. of the House of Repeesentatives.

ELIJAH VANCE,
Speaker of the Senate.

February 29, 1836.

AN ACT

To incorporate the Sandusky Canal and Slackwater Navigation Company.

Sec. 1. Be it enacted by the General Assembly of the State of Ohio, That Rodolphus Dickison, John Bell, Sardis Birchard, Jaques Hulbard, James Justice, James Moore, and Platt Brush, of the county of Sandusky; and Henry Ebert, Jacob Stem, Andrew Lugenbeel, Lorenzo Abbott, John Walker, Agreen Ingraham, John Park, Vincent Bell, and Josiah Hedges, of the county of Seneca; and Joseph M'Cutchen, Joseph H. Larwell, and Joseph Chaffee, of the county of Crawford; and their associates, as well in their own person, as those who shall succeeed them, be, and are hereby created a body politic and corporate, by the name and style of "The Sandusky Canal and Slackwater Navigation Company," for the purpose of constructing a canal, or slackwater navigation, commencing at Lower Sandusky, in Sandusky county; thence to a point on the west side of the Sandusky river, between the toll bridge of Josiah Hedges and opposite to the mouth of Rocky creek, in Seneca county; and thence to the mouth of Tymochtee creek, in the county of Crawford; said canal, or slackwater navigation, to be determined on actual survey and examination, to be made under the superintendence of the directors for the time being, of the company hereby created; and said company shall have perpetual succession, and shall be capable of holding capital stock to the amount of three hundred thousand dollars, together with the increase and profits thereof, with the power of taking, purchasing, and holding, to them, their successors and assigns, in fee simple, and for any less estate, any such land, tenements, hereditaments, and estates, real, personal, or mixed, as shall be necessary for them in the prosecution of their work, or as shall be necessary for carrying the same into complete effect; and shall be capable of suing and being sued, pleading and being impleaded; and may have a common seal, and break, alter, or renew the same at pleasure: *Provided*, That nothing in this act contained shall be so construced as to give to the corporation, hereby created, exclusive privileges, rights and immunities, to the detriment of any of the public works of the State that have been, or hereafter may be, constructed.

Sec. 2. That if the corporation, hereby created, shall not, within five years from the first day of September next, after the passage of this act, commence, and within five years thereafter, construct, finish, and put into operation, the said canal, or slackwater navigation, then said corporation shall thenceforth cease, and this act shall be null and void.

Sec. 3. That the persons named in the first section of this act, or any two of them, who may consent to act as such, shall be commissioners for receiving subscriptions to the capital stock of said company; whose duty it shall be, at such time as may be agreed on by the persons hereinbefore named, being within the limits for commencing said work, to cause books to be opened at Lower Sandusky, in the county of Sandusky, and in Tiffin, in the county of Seneca, and such other places as the persons named in the first section of this act shall see fit, on the same or different days, under their own supervision, or under the management of such person as they may appoint, for receiving subscriptions to the capital stock of said company; each subscriber to be a member of said corporation, for all purposes; and public notice shall be given in such manner as shall be deemed advisable by said commissioners, of the times and places of opening said books; and the said commissioners, or a majority of them, may prescribe the form of said subscription.

Sec. 4. That whenever fifty thousand dollars to the capital stock of said company shall have been subscribed, it shall be the duty of the said commissioners, or a majority of them, to call a meeting of the subscribers, by causing notice to be published in one or more newspapers, in general circulation in the respective places where said subscription books may have been opened, and stock subscribed, at least twenty days previous thereto, specifying the time and place of such meeting, which shall be at some convenient town, or place, near the route of the contemplated canal, or slackwater navigation; at which meeting, the stockholders who may attend, in person, or by lawful proxy, shall elect, by ballot, seven directors, who shall hold their offices until the expiration of one year, and until their successors shall have been chosen and duly qualified; and the said commissioners shall be inspectors of the first election of directors of said corporation; and shall certify, under their hands, those duly elected, and shall deliver over to them the said certificates and subscription books.

Sec. 5. That the capital stock of said company shall be divided into shares of one hundred dollars each, which shall be deemed personal property, and transferable in such manner as the by-laws of said company shall prescribe.

Sec. 6. That the management of the concerns of said corporation shall be entrusted to seven directors, to be elected annually by the stockholders by ballot; and the directors first chosen, and such directors as shall thereafter be chosen, at any subsequent election, shall, immediately thereafter, meet and elect one of their number, who shall be president thereof, until another election; and also appoint a treasurer and secretary, who may be removed at the pleasure of said president and directors, and others appointed in their places; and a majority of said directors shall constitute a board for every purpose within the provisions of this act.

Sec. 7. That in case it should at any time happen, that the election of directors should not be made on any day when, pursuant to this act, it ought to be made, the said corporation, for that cause, shall not be deemed to be dissolved, but such election may be held at any other time directed by the by-laws of said corporation.

Sec. 8. That each subscriber shall pay to the commissioners, or to the person appointed by them to receive subscriptions to the capital stock of said company, at the time of subscribing, the sum of five dollars on each share for which he shall subscribe, and the same shall be deemed and taken as an instalment paid on account of the stock to which he shall become entitled by such subscription; and the commissioners shall pay over all moneys so paid, to the directors elected, pursuant to the sixth section of this act.

Sec. 9. That the books of subscription shall remain open as long as the president and directors shall see fit, and each subscriber shall be bound to pay, from time to time, such instalment on his, her, or their stock, as the said president and directors may lawfully require, they giving at least thirty days notice of the time and place of making the payment required, in such public newspapers in the State of Ohio and elsewhere, as will be best calculated to give information thereof to the stockholders; but no assessment shall ever be made, so as to render any subscriber liable to pay more than one hundred dollars for a share.

Sec. 10. That if any subscriber shall fail or neglect to pay any instalment, or part of any subscription, by him previously subscribed, for the space of sixty days after the same shall be due and payable, the stock shall be forfeited to the company, and may be sold by the president and directors for the benefit of said company, after thirty days notice, given in some newspaper in general circulation; and if said shares, so sold, shall not amount to a sum sufficient to discharge the balance due on said shares, the said subscribers shall be personally liable for the balance still remaining due; and if said shares shall sell for a sum more than sufficient to pay said balance, the same shall be paid over to said subscriber, or subscribers, on demand.

Sec. 11. That at all elections of directors for said company, and at all general meetings of the stockholders, each stockholder shall be entitled to one vote, for each share of the capital stock of said company; and every executor, administrator, trustee, or guardian, shall be entitled to like privilege of voting, on behalf of the estate, copartnership, corporation, or society, of which he may be such executor, administrator, trustee, or guardian: *Provided,* That no share subscribed for, shall confer the privilege of voting on such subscriber, unless the sum of five dollars, as the first instalment, and all other instalments called for, by the president and directors, according to the ninth section of this act, shall have been fully paid.

Sec. 12. That if any vacancy should occur by 'death resignation, or a refusal to act, of any president, or director, before the expiration of the year for which he was elected, a person to fill such vacancy shall be appointed by the president and directors of said company, or a majority of them.

Sec. 13. That at the regular annual meeting of the stockholders of said company, it shall be the duty of the president and directors in office for the preceding year, to exhibit a clear and accurate statement of the affairs of said company; and that at any general meeting of the stockholders, a majority in value of all the stockholders in said company, may remove from office, any president, or any of the directors, and may appoint others in their stead.

Sec. 14. That every president and director of said company, before he acts as such, shall take an oath, or affirmation, that he will well and truly discharge the duties of his office, to the best of his skill and judgment.

Sec. 15. That the president and directors shall annually, or semi-annually, declare and make such dividends as they may deem proper; of the nett profits arising from the resources of said company, after deducting the necessary current, and probable contingent, expenses; and they shall divide the same amongst the proprietors of the stock of said company, in proportion to their respective shares.

Sec. 16. That the president and directors of said company, or a majority of them, or any person or persons authorized by a majority of them, may agree with the owner of any land, earth, timber, gravel, stone, or other materials, for the purchase, use or occupation of the same; and if they cannot agree, or if the owner or owners, or any of them, be a feme covert, minor, non compos mentis, or out of the county in which the property wanted, may lie, application may be made to any justice of the peace of said county, who shall thereupon issue his warrant, under his hand and seal, to the the sheriff of said county, or to some disinterested (person,) if the sheriff shall be interested, requiring him to summon a jury of twelve disinterested inhabitants of said county, to meet on the land, or near to other property, or materials, to be valued on a day named in said warrant, not less than ten, nor more than twenty days, after the issuing the same; and if, at the same time and place, any of said persons do not attend, the sheriff, or summoner, shall immediately summon as many persons as may be necessary, with the persons in attendance, to furnish a pannel of twele jurors, and from them, each party, or its, his, her, or their agent, or if either be not present, in person, or by agent, the sheriff, or summoner, for it, him, her, or them, may strike off three jurors, and the remaining nine shall act as a jury of inquest of damages; and before they act as such, the said sheriff, or summoner, shall administer to each of them, an oath or affirmation, that they will justly and impartially value the damages, which the owner or owners may sustain, by the use or occupation of such land or materials, or both, as may be required by said company; and the jury, in estimating the damages, in case it be for the land used for said canal, shall take into the estimate the benefits resulting to said owner or owners, from constructing said canal or slackwater navigation, through, along, or near the property of said owner, or owners, in extinguishment of the claim for damages; and the said jury shall reduce their inquisition to writing, and sign the same; and it shall then be returned to the clerk of the court of common pleas for the county, and by such clerk filed in his office, and shall be confirmed by said court at its next session, if no sufficient cause to the contrary be shown; and when confirmed, shall be recorded by said clerk, at the expense of said company; but if set aside, said court may direct another inquisition to be taken, in the same manner above prescribed; and such inquisition shall describe the property taken, or the bound of the land to be occupied; and the amount of such valuation, when paid or tendered to the owner or owners of such property, or his, her, or their legal representatives, shall entitle said company to the said property, or the use and occupation of said land, so long as the same shall be used for said canal, or slackwater navigation—and the valuation, if not received when tendered, may, at any time thereafter, be received from the said company, without costs, by the said owner or owners, or their legal representatives; and that such sheriff, or summoner, shall be entitled to receive, from said company, the same fees as are allowed for like services, in case of appraisement of real estate previous to sale under execution.

Sec. 17.   That said company, in designating and running out the line of the said canal, or slackwater navigation, may enter upon, and use the channel of the Sandusky river, and the water thereof, or so much of the same as may be necessary, for the construction, and use of the said canal, or slack water navigation, together with a sufficient quantity of land upon each side of said river, for a towing and heel path, compensation to be made for the same in the manner prescribed in the sixteenth section of this act.

Sec. 18. That in all cases, it shall be competent for said company and any corporation or corporations, person or persons, injured by the location or construction thereof, to refer the question of damages to such arbitrators as they may agree upon, whose award, when made, and returned to the court of common pleas, within and for the county wherein the damages have been sustained and affirmed, by said court, shall be final; and said court may enter judgment accordingly.

Sec. 19.   That if, after the location of said canal, or slack water navigation, as aforesaid, any alterations shall be made in the course thereof, the damages may be estimated in the same way, and the same proceeding had in manner provided in this act.

Sec. 20.   That upon payment by the said company, of such damages, to the person or persons, corporation or corporations, to whom the same may have been assessed or awarded, as in this act before provided, then the said company shall be deemed to be seized and possessed of the use of all such lands or real estate, not exceeding one hundred feet in width, as shall have been assessed or appraised, by commissioners and arbitrators so chosen, as before provided, so long as the same shall be used for such canal, or slack water navigation; and it shall be the duty of the commissioner and arbitrators, so chosen, to embrace in their reports or awards, a description of the lands, or real estate, for which they shall assess damages as aforesaid.

Sec. 21. That in any suit instituted against the corporation, the service of legal process on the president, or any one of the directors, or on the treasurer, or secretary of said corporation, at least ten days before the return day thereof, shall be deemed and held in all courts and places, a sufficient and valid service on said corporation.

Sec. 22. That whenever, in the construction of said canal, or slack water navigation, it shall be necessary to unite with, or intersect, any established road or ways, it shall be the duty of the president and directors of said company, so to construct the canal, or slackwater navigation, across such established road or way, as not to impede the passage or transportation of persons, or property, along the same; and when it shall be necessary to pass through the land of any individual, it shall also be their duty, to provide such individual proper wagon ways across the said canal, or slack water navigation, from one part of his land to another.

Sec. 23. That it shall be lawful for said company, annually to fix, regulate and receive the tolls and charges by them to be received, for the transportation of property or persons on the canal and slack water navigation authorized by this act, for the sole benefit of said company: *Provided,* That the nett proceeds of such tolls and charges thus fixed, regulated and received by said company, shall at no time exceed ten per centum per annum, on the capital invested in the construction and necessary expenditures of said canal or slack water navigation: *Provided, however,* That this restriction in the amount of tolls and charges, shall not be construed, so as to prevent said company from fixing and receiving the highest rate of tolls and duties, together with the charges of freight to which property of a similar kind is subject, as the costs of transportation on the Ohio canal, during the same period of time.

Sec. 24. That if any person or persons, shall wilfully, by any means whatever, injure, impair or destroy, any part of the canal, or slack water navigation, constructed by said company under this act, or any of the necessary works, boats or machines, of said company, such person, so offending, shall, for every such offence, forfeit and pay to the said company, treble damages, which may be recovered, in the name of the company, by an action of debt, in any court having jurisdiction of the same; and shall also be subjected to indictment, and, upon conviction of such offence, shall be punished by fine, not exceeding one hundred dollars, and imprisoned not exceeding three months, at the discretion of the court.

Sec. 25. That this act shall be considered a public act, and shall be favorably construed, for the purposes therein expressed and declared, in all courts and places whatsoever.

Sec. 26. That if, at any time after said canal or slack water navigation may be located, any unforseen obstacles, impediments, or inconveniences occur on the route located, between the points herein named, the said corporation shall have power to deviate from the course marked out, so far, and in such manner, as may be calculated to surmount, overcome, or avoid such obstacles, impediments and inconveniences, said corporation, satisfying the damages that may be occasioned thereby, to be assessed in the manner provided for by this act; and the said corporation shall, from time to time, make such alteration in the route of said canal, or slack water navigation, as may be necessary or expedient, satisfying all damages in manner as aforesaid: *Provided,* That the State shall at any time after the expiration of fifty years, from the passage of this act, have the right to purchase the said canal, by paying to said company, the amount expended by them, in the location, construction and repairs of the same, together with fifteen per cent. thereon: *Provided, also,* That the sum so to be paid by the State, shall not, together with the tolls received by the company, be less than the amount expended by them, with eight per centum per annum, thereon.

WILLIAM MEDILL,
Speaker pro tem. of the House of Representatives.
ELIJAH VANCE,
Speaker of the Senate.

February 26, 1836.

AN ACT

For the relief of Charles Steward.

Sec. 1. *Be it enacted by the General Assembly of the State of Ohio,* That if Charles Steward, or his legal representatives, shall pay to the treasurer of the county of Richland, one third of the money from him due for part of section sixteen, in township number twenty-one, of range sixteen, in said county, together with all interest due thereon, in one year from the passage of this act, and the remaining two thirds in two equal instalments annually thereafter, with interest thereon, year by year, as the same becomes due, then the said Charles Steward, and his heirs, shall be entitled to receive a deed of said lands, in the same manner as if the original terms of sale had been strictly complied with.

WILLIAM MEDILL,
Speaker pro tem. of the House of Representatives,
ELIJAH VANCE,
Speaker of the Senate,

February 29, 1836,

AN ACT

Making a special appropriation of the three per cent. fund, within the county of Jackson.

Sec. 1. *Be it enacted by the General Assembly of the State of Ohio,* That two hundred dollars of the three per cent. fund, which has, or may hereafter become due to the county of Jackson, be, and the same is hereby directed to be expended under the direction of the county commissioners of said county, in the erection of a bridge across the south fork of Salt creek, on the state road leading from the town of Jackson, in said county, to Chillicothe, in Ross county, at or near the residence of the widow How.

Sec. 2. That the amount hereby appropriated shall be charged to the said county of Jackson, and deducted out of any moneys which may hereafter be appropriated to said county in the distribution of the three per cent. fund.

WILLIAM MEDILL,
Speaker pro tem. of the House of Representatives.

ELIJAH VANCE,
Speaker of the Senate.

February 29, 1836.

AN ACT

Providing for the adjustment of the claims of the Warren County Canal Company, and the completion of said Canal.

Sec. 1. *Be it enacted by the General Assembly of the State of Ohio,* That the canal commissioners are hereby authorized and required, in the name, and for the use of the State of Ohio, to enter upon and take possession of the line of the Warren county canal, and to cause the same to be completed, from and to the points designated in the act entitled "An act incorporating the Warren County Canal Company," passed 22d February, 1830; and the same shall become an appendage to, and part and parcel of the Miami canal.

Sec. 2. That the laws now in force, in relation to the location, construction, regulation, and protection of the canals of this State, are hereby extended to the Warren county canal.

Sec. 3. That it shall be the duty of the directors of the Warren County Canal Company, to make out, under oath or affirmation, an accurate account of all money by them expended, or for which they may be liable on account of said Warren county canal, in a plain and intelligible manner, enter the same on the books of the company, and furnish a certified copy thereof to the acting canal commissioners, for the use of the State; which sum, or so much thereof as the company shall have paid, shall be refunded to the company, without interest, on the completion of said canal, after deducting therefrom fifty per cent.

Sec. 4. That the faith of the State is hereby pledged for the completion of said Warren county canal, within two years from this date, and the final repayment to the company, agreeably to the condition of the preceding section.

Sec. 5. That the Warren County Canal Company shall continue to

19—L

exercise their corporate powers, until the business of said company shall be finally closed.

WILLIAM MEDILL,
Speaker pro tem. of the House of Representatives.
ELIJAH VANCE,
Speaker of the Senate.

February 29, 1836.

AN ACT

To repeal part of an act to lay out and establish certain State roads in the counties of Carroll, Columbiana, Trumbull, and Harrison.

Sec. 1. *Be it enacted by the General Assembly of the State of Ohio,* That so much of an act, passed February 5th, 1834, entitled "An act to lay out and establish certain state roads in the counties of Carroll, Columbiana, Trumbull, and Harrison," as authorizes the laying out and establishing a graded state road north of, and including the village of Georgetown, in Columbiana county, to Warren, in Trumbull county, be, and the same is hereby repealed.

WILLIAM MEDILL,
Speaker pro tem. of the House of Representatives.
ELIJAH VANCE,
Speaker of the Senate.

February 29, 1836.

AN ACT

To authorize the commissioners of Carroll county to borrow money.

Sec. 1. *Be it enacted by the General Assembly of the State of Ohio,* That the county commissioners of the county of Carroll, or their successors in office, be, and they are hereby authorized to borrow for, and on the credit of said county, a sum of money not exceeding five thousand dollars, at a rate of interest not exceeding seven per centum per annum; which money, when so borrowed, shall be applied to the payment of any debt or debts, which is, are, or may hereafter be due from said county, for the execution and completion of the public buildings in said county, or otherwise.

Sec. 2. That the said commissioners are hereby authorized to pledge and apply the revenues of said county, for and in the payment of any loan or loans which may be effected by them, under the provisions of this act.

WILLIAM MEDILL,
Speaker pro tem. of the House of Representatives.
ELIJAH VANCE,
Speaker of the Senate.

February 29, 1836,

AN ACT

To incorporate the Etna Iron Company

Sec. 1. *Be it enacted by the General Assembly of the State of Ohio,* That Gregory Powers, Robt. R. Dubois, Fred. Measworth, Erastus Torroy, and Daniel J Garrat, together with those who may hereafter become stockholders, their successors and assigns, be, and they are hereby created a body corporate and politic, with perpetual succession, to be known and distinguished by the name and style of the "Ætna Iron Company," for the purpose of forging and manufacturing iron, and by that name shall be, and are hereby made a body in law, to have, purchase, receive, possess, enjoy and retain, to them and their successors, all such lands, tenements, and hereditaments, as shall be requisite for their accommodation and convenience in the transaction of their business, and such as may be in good faith conveyed to them by way of security, or in satisfaction of debts, or purchases at sale, upon judgments obtained for such debts, the same to grant, sell, or dispose of; to sue and be sued, to plead and be impleaded, answer and be answered unto, defend and be defended, in all courts having competent jurisdiction; and also to make, have, and use a common seal, and the same to break, alter or renew at pleasure.

Sec. 2. That the stockholders, or a majority of them, shall have power to make such by-laws and rules, for regulating the concerns of said corporation, as they shall think necessary and expedient, and also respecting the management and disposition of the stock, property and estate of said corporation, the duties of the officers, artificers and agents, by them to be employed, the election of directors, and all such as appertain to the interest of said corporation: *Provided,* That such by-laws and rules be not inconsistent with the constitution and laws of the United States, and of this State

Sec. 3. That the capital stock of said corporation shall not exceed one hundred thousand dolars, and shall be divided into shares of one hundred dollars each, to be subscribed for, and paid, at such time, and in such proportion, and under such penalties, as the by-laws and rules of said corporation may prescribe; and that each share shall be entitled to one vote: *Provided,* That the funds of said corporation shall not be used for any other pupose than that of manufacturing and forging iron.

Sec. 4. That each and every stockholder, or his assigns, shall be held liable in his individual capacity for the amount of his or their stock subscribed or owned; and that the debts of said company shall at no time exceed the amount of stock subscribed; and if such debts should at any time exceed the amount of stock subscribed, then the directors acting for the company, at the time such excess of debt was created, and authorizing the creating of the same, shall be individually liable for such excess of debt; and should the property of such directors so made liable be insufficient to satisfy such excess of debt, then the stockholders shall be individually liable for such excess of debt.

Sec. 5. That if any stockholder or stockholders of said company shall, at the time of his, her, or their subscribing to the stock of said company, or purchasing the same, be desirous to become responsible for the debts of the company only to the amount of his or their stock subscribed or purchased, it shall be lawful for him or them so to be exempt from liability for all the debts of the company, arising after the time of his or their acquiring an interest in such company: *Provided,* He or they shall from that time, in no manner or form, either by voting for officers of the company, or in any other way interfere with, or attempt to govern or direct the business and affairs of said company: *And provided, further,* That he or they shall, within ten days from the time his or their interest shall accrue, give notice of the exact amount of his or their stock, and that the same is holden, subject to the privileges and restrictions in this section of this act contained, in some newspaper in general circulation in the county in which this company is established; which notice shall also be entered, by the proper officer, upon the books of the company: *Provided, however,* That no more than two-fifths of the capital stock of this company shall be exempt from liability, under the provisions of this scetion.

Sec. 6. That no transfer of stock shall be valid or effectual, until such transfer shall be entered or registered in the book or books, to be kept by the company for that purpose; and further, that such transfer of stock shall be made subject to the debts or demands due from the person transferring to said company, at the time of making such transfer.

Sec. 7. That the members of said company shall meet at some convenient place, at the Cuyahoga Falls, on or before the first Monday of May next, for the purpose of organizing themselves under this act.

Sec. 8. That the capital stock and funds of said company shall be applied exclusively to the manufacturing of iron from the raw material, or otherwise, and no portion of said funds shall ever be employed in banking purposes: *Provided,* That any future Legislature may alter or repeal this act; but any modification or repeal shall not affect the title to any estate, real or personal, acquired or conveyed under its provisions, or divert the same to any other use than originally intended.

WILLIAM MEDILL,
Speaker pro tem. of the House of Representatives.
ELIJAH VANCE,
Speaker of the Senate.

February 29th, 1836.

AN ACT

To extend the corporate limits of the town of Wilmington, in the county of Clinton.

Sec. 1. *Be it enacted by the General Assembly of the State of Ohio,* That the limits of the corporation of the town of Wilmington, in the county of Clinton, in this State, be, and the same are hereby extended so as to include all that part of said town of Wilmington, known and designated on the plat of said town as Thatcher's addition.

WILLIAM MEDILL,
Speaker pro tem. of the House of Representatives.
ELIJAH VANCE,
Speaker of the Senate.

February 29, 1836.

AN ACT

To incorporate the Dayton Cotton Manufactory.

Sec. 1. *Be it enacted by the General Assembly of the State of Ohio,* That David Z. Cooper, Isaac N. Partrage, Amos A. Richards, Augustus George, Alexander Grimes, Joseph Barnett, Peter Aughinbaugh, J. D. Loomis, Edwin Smith, David Stone, Ralph P. Lowe, John Rench, Hebert Jewett, and Peter P. Lowe, together with those who may hereafter become stockholders, their successors and assigns, be, and they are hereby created a body corporate and politic, with perpetual succession, to be known and distinguished by the name and title of the Dayton Cotton Manufactory, for the purpose of manufacturing cotton and woollen fabrics and machinery; and by that name shall be, and are hereby made a body in law, to have, purchase, receive, possess, enjoy and retain, to them and their successors, all such lands, tenements and hereditaments, as shall be requisite for their accommodation and convenience in the transaction of their business, and such as may be in good faith conveyed to them by way of security, or in satisfaction of debts, or purchases at sales, upon judgments obtained for such debts: the same to grant, rent, sell or dispose of; to sue and be sued, to plead and be impleaded, answer and be answered unto, defend and be defended, in all courts having competent jurisdiction; and also to make, have, and use a common seal, and the same to break, alter, or renew, at pleasure.

Sec. 2. That the stockholders, or a majority of them, shall have power to make such by-laws and rules for regulating the concerns of said corporation, as they shall think necesssary and expedient, and also respecting the management and disposition of the stock, property and estate of said corporation, the duties of the officers, artificers, and agents, by them to be employed, the election of directors, and all such as appertain to the interest of said corporation: *Provided,* That such by-laws and rules be not inconsistent with the constitution and laws of the United States, and of this State.

Sec. 3. That the capital stock of said corporation shall be fifty thousand dollars, with power for the stockholders, or a majority of them, to increase the stock to one hundred and fifty thousand dollars, in shares not exceeding five hundred dollars each, to be subscribed for and paid at such times, and in such proportion, and under such penalties, as the by-laws and rules of said corporation may prescribe; and that each share shall be entitled to one vote: *Provided,* That no subscription or transfer of stock shall be valid, until such subscription or transfer shall have been registered in a a book to be kept by said company for that purpose, and also recorded in the books of the recorder of the county of Montgomery: *Provided, also,* That the funds of said corporation shall not be used for any other purpose than that of manufacturing cotton and woollen fabrics and machinery; and the stock of said corporation shall be considered personal estate.

Sec. 4. That each and every stockholder, or his assigns, shall be held liable in his individual capacity for the amount of his or her stock subscribed; if such debts should at any time exceed the amount of stock sub-

pany, then the individual stockholders of said company, shall be held individually liable for all unsatisfied claims against said company, in proportion to the amount of stock held or owned by them respectively.

Sec. 5. This act shall be taken in all courts of justice and elsewhere, as a public act, and any future Legislature shall have power to alter or modify this act.

WILLIAM MEDILL,
Speaker pro tem. of the House of Representatives.
ELIJAH VANCE,
Speaker of the Senate.

February 29th, 1836.

AN ACT

Authorizing the commissioners of Hamilton county to erect a free bridge over the river Whitewater.

Sec. 1. *Be it enacted by the General Assembly of the State of Ohio,* That the commissioners of Hamilton county shall, on the payment by the citizens of a sum not less than three thousand dollars, or on the payment of the same being secured to them, appropriate a certain portion of the road tax annually assessed in said county, for the purpose of erecting a good, safe and substantial bridge across the Whitewater river, at or near the point where the state road leading from Cincinnati, through Cleves and Elizabethtown, to the State line, crosses said river: *Provided,* That the appropriations so made shall be such as to complete said bridge within four years from the time of commencement.

Sec. 2. That the commissioners of Hamilton county for the time being, and their successors, shall be capable of receiving any gift or donation for the purpose aforementioned; and as a board of commissioners may contract and be contracted with, sue and be sued, plead and be impleaded, answer and be answered, defend and be defended, in any court of competent jurisdiction; and may appoint all such agents as may be necessary for managing the erection of said bridge, and allow them such compensation as they shall think just and right.

Sec. 3. That as soon as said bridge is completed, or so far completed as to admit of the safe passage of wagons, horses, cattle, &c., the same shall be free, and forever remain so.

WILLIAM MEDILL,
Speaker pro tem. of the House of Representatives.
ELIJAH VANCE,
Speaker of the Senate.

February 29, 1836.

AN ACT

To legalize the sale of section sixteen, in township one, in the Twelve Mile Reserve, at the foot of the Rapids.

WHEREAS, an act providing for the sale of school section sixteen, in the

153

Twelve Mile Reserve, in the county of Wood, passed by the General Assembly, on the fifth day of March, 1835, describes the same as being in township number three, whereas it should have been township number one: *And whereas*, the auditor of Wood county, in pursuance of the provisions of said act, sold section sixteen, in township number one, without discovering the error in the description: Therefore,

Sec. 1. *Be it enacted by the General Assembly of the State of Ohio,* That the proceedings and sale aforesaid of section sixteen, in township number one, shall be as valid in all respects as if the said section had been described in said act as being in township number one.

WILLAM MEDILL,
Speaker pro tem. of the House of Representatives.
ELIJAH VANCE,
Speaker of the Senate.

February 29, 1836.

AN ACT

To incorporate the town of Batavia, in the county of Clermont.

Sec. 1. *Be it enacted by the General Assembly of the State of Ohio,* That so much of the township of Batavia, in the county of Clermont, as is included in the following bounds, towit: Beginning on the bank of the east fork of the Little Miami, so that a line running south 50 degrees east, will include Sarah Cotes' stone house; thence south 50 degrees east, so far that a line running north 40 degrees east, will include the whole town plat, with the additions thereto; thence north 40 degrees east, so far, that a line running 50 degrees west, will include William M. Ely's dwelling house, and yard immediately around said house; thence north 50 degrees west, to the east fork of the Little Miama, aforesaid; thence up the same, with its meanders, to the beginning: be, and the same is hereby created into, and constituted a town corporate, by the name of the Town of Batavia.

Sec. 2. That for the order and good government of said town, and inhabitants thereof, it shall be lawful for the white male householders thereof, who have resided therein for the space of three months next preceeding the day of election, having the qualifications of elector of members of the General Assembly, to meet at some convenient place in the said town of Batavia, on the second Saturday of March next and on the second Saturday of March, annually, thereafter, and there proceed, by a plurality of votes, to elect by ballot, one mayor, one recorder, and five trustees, who shall be householders of said town; who shall hold their offices until the next annual election, and until their successors are elected and qualified; and such mayor, recorder and trustees, so being elected and qualified, shall constitute the Town Council of said town, any five of whom shall constitute a quorum, for the transaction of business, pertaining to their duties.

Sec. 3. That at the first election, to be holden under this act, there shall be chosen *viva voce*, by the electors present, two judges and a clerk of said

20—L

election, who shall each take an oath or affirmation faithfully to discharge the duties required of them by this act; and at all subsequent elections, the trustees, or any two of them, shall be judges, and the recorder, or in his absence, some other person, to be appointed by the judges, shall be clerk: the polls. shall be opened between the hours of ten and eleven o'clock in the forenoon, and, closed at three o'clock, in the afternoon of said day; and at the close of the polls, the votes shall be counted, and a true statement thereof proclaimed to the voters' present, by one of the judges, and the clerk shall make a true copy thereof, and within five days thereafter, he shall give notice to the persons so elected, of their election; and it shall be the duty of the town council, at least ten days before each and every annual election, to give notice of the same by setting up advertisements at three of the most public places in said town.

Sec. 4. That the mayor, and in case of his absence, the recorder, shall preside at all meetings of the town council; and the recorder shall attend all meetings of the town council, and make a fair and accurate record of all their proceedings.

Sec. 5. That the town council shall have power to fill all vacancies which may happen in said board, from the householders, who are qualified electors in said town, who shall hold their appointment until the next annual election, and until their successors are elected and qualified; and in the absence of the mayor and recorder from any meeting of the town council, the trustees shall have power to appoint any two of their number, to perform the duties of mayor and recorder, for the time being.

Sec. 6. That the mayor, recorder, and trustees of said town, shall be a body corporate and politic, with perpetual succession, to be known and distinguished by the name and style of the "Town Council of the town of Batavia;" and shall be capable in law, by their corporate name, to acquire property, real, personal and mixed, for the use of said town, and may sell, and convey the same at pleasure; they may have a common seal, which they may break, alter, or renew at pleasure; they may sue and be sued, plead and be impleaded, defend and be defended, in all manner of actions, and in all courts of law and equity; and whenever any suit shall be commenced against said corporation, the process shall be served by copy, which shall be left with the recorder, or at his usual place of residence, at least five days before the return day thereof.

Sec. 7. That each member of said town council, before entering upon the duties of his office, shall take an oath, or affirmation, to support the constitution of the United States, and the constitution of this State, and also an oath of office.

Sec. 8. That the town council shall have power to make, ordain and establish by-laws, rules and regulations, for the government of said town, and to alter, amend or repeal, the same at pleasure; to provide for the appointment of a treasurer, town marshal, and such other subordinate officers, as they may think necessary; to prescribe their duties, and determine the periods of their appointments, to fix the fees they shall be entitled to for their services; and the treasurer, marshal, and other officers shall, before entering upon the duties, take an oath of office, and shall respectively give bonds with security, in such sums as shall be determined by the town council, payable to the State of Ohio, conditioned for the faithful performance of their respective duties: the town council shall also have power to fix reasonable fines and penalties for any violation of the laws and ordinances of the corporation, and to provide for the collection and disposition of the same: *Provided,* Such by-laws, ordinances, rules and regulations be not inconsistent with the constitution and laws of the United States, and of this State: *And Provided, also,* That no by-law, ordinance, rule or regulation shall take effect or be in force, until the same shall have been posted up for two weeks, in one or more of the most public places in said corporation.

Sec. 9. That the town council shall, at the expiration of each and every year, cause to be made out and posted up as aforesaid, the receipts and expenditures of the preceding year.

Sec. 10. That the town council shall have power to regulate and improve the streets, lanes and alleys, and to determine the width of the side walks in said town: they shall have power to remove all nuisances and obstructions from the streets and commons of said town, and to do all things which similar corporations have power to do.

Sec. 11. That for the purpose of more effectually enabling said town council to carry into effect the provisions of said act, they are hereby authorized and empowered to levy a tax on all the real and personal property, subject on the grand levy to taxation, within the limits of said town, upon the appraisement made and returned upon said grand levy: *Provided,* That said tax, so levied by said town council, shall not in any one year exceed one half of one per centum, on the aggregate amount of all such taxable property within the limits of said town; and the said town council shall, annually, between the first day of April, and the first day of July, determine the amount of tax to be assessed and collected for the current year.

Sec. 12. That it shall be the duty of the recorder of said corporation, to make out duplicates of taxes, charging each individual, within said corporation, an amount of tax in proportion to the aggregate value of the taxable property belonging to such individual, within the limits of said corporation, as the same appears upon the books of the auditor of said county of Clermont; and the said recorder shall have power of inspecting the books of said auditor, and to take any minutes or transcripts therefrom as may be necessary to aid him in the discharge of the duties hereby enjoined upon him, free of. expense: when said recorder shall have made out said duplicates, as aforesaid, he shall deliver one of such duplicates to the marshal of said town, or to such other person as may be appointed collector, whose duty it shall be to collect taxes charged thereon in the same manner, and under the same regulations, as are provided by law for the collection of State and county taxes: and the said marshal or collector, shall, immediately after collecting said tax, pay the same over to the treasurer of said corporation, and take his receipt therefor; and the said marshal, or collector, shall have the same power to sell both real and personal property, as is given, by law, to county treasurers; and when necessary, the recorder shall have power to make deeds for real estate, so sold, in the same manner that county auditors are, by law, empowered to do, for lands sold by the county treasurer; and the marshal, or collector shall receive such fees for his services, as the town council may direct, not exceeding six per cent. on all moneys so by him collected, to be paid by the treasurer, on the order of the recorder.

Sec. 13. That the said town council shall have power to appropriate any money remaining in the corporation treasury, to the improvement of the streets alleys, and side walks of said town, whenever they may deem it necessary, and to make any other improvement which may conduce to the health and comfort of said town.

Sec. 14. That the mayor of said town shall be a conservator of the peace within the limits of said corporation, and shall have therein all the powers and jurisdiction of a justice of the peace, in all matters, civil or criminal, arising under the laws of this State: he shall perform all the duties enjoined upon him by the laws and ordinances of the corporation; and shall give bond in the same manner that justices of the peace are by law required; and appeals may be taken from the decision of the said mayor, in all cases, where by law appeals are allowed from the decisions of justices of the peace, and in the same manner.

Sec. 15. That the marshal shall be the principal ministerial officer of said corporation, and shall have the same power as constables have by law; and his authority, in the execution of criminal process, shall be coextensive with the limits of said county of Clermont, and he shall receive for his services such fees as are allowed by law to constables in similar cases, for like services.

Sec. 16. That the mayor shall receive for his services such fees as are allowed by law to justices of the peace, for similar services, in like cases: the recorder shall receive such fees for his services, as shall be fixed by the by-laws and ordinances of the corporation.

Sec. 17. That if no election shall be held by the electors of said town, on the second Saturday of March next, it shall be lawful for any ten householders of said town, to call a meeting of the electors, by giving ten days notice thereof, in writing, to be posted up in one or more public places in said town; which notice shall state the time, and place, and object of meeting, and shall be signed by the said householders; and if a majority of the qualified electors of said town shall attend at the time and place speified in said notice, it shall be lawful for them to proceed to the election of officers in the same manner as hereinbefore provided for; and the officers so elected shall hold their offices until the second Saturday of March following, and until their successors are elected and qualified.

Sec. 18. That the said corporation shall be allowed the use of the county jail, for the imprisonment of such persons as may be liable to imprisonment under the laws and ordinances of said town; and all persons so imprisoned, shall be under the charge of the sheriff or jailor, as in other cases.

Sec. 19. That any future Legislature shall have power to alter, amend, or repeal the act.

WILLIAM MEDILL,
Speaker pro tem. of the House of Representatives.
ELIJAH VANCE,
Speaker of the Senate.

February 29, 1836.

AN ACT

To incorporate the Ashtabula, Warren and East Liverpool Rail Road Company.

Sec. 1. *Be it enacted by the General Assembly of the State of Ohio,* That Matthew Hubbard, Horace Wilder, Roger W. Griswold, Joab Austin, Gaius W. St. John, of the county of Ashtabula; Ephraim Brown, John Crowell, Zalmon Fitch, George Parsons, Charles Smith, Cornelius Tomson, Asahel Medbury, of the county of Trumbull; and Elderkin Potter, John Smith, David Hanna, John Dixon, John Patrick, and William G. Smith, of Columbiana county; be, and they are hereby appointed commissioners, under the direction of a majority of whom, subscriptions may be received to the capital stock of the Ashtabula, Warren and Liverpool Rail road Company, hereby incorporated; and they, or a majority of them, may cause books to be opened at such times and places as they may direct, and for the purpose of receiving subscriptions to the capital stock of said company, after giving such notice of the time and place of opening the same, in the counties of Ashtabula, Trumbull and Columbiana, or such other places as they may deem expedient, by publication in a newspaper printed nearest the place of opening the books for at least thirty days; and that, upon the first opening of said books, they shall be kept open for at least ten days in succession, from ten o'clock, A. M. until two o'clock, P. M.; and if, at the expiration of that period, such subscription to the capital stock of said company, as is necessary to its incorporation, shall not have been obtained, then said commissioners, or a majority of them, may cause said books, by giving notice as aforesaid, to be opened from time to time, after the expiration of said ten days, for the space of three years thereafter; and if any of said commissioners shall die, resign or refuse to act, during the continuance of the duties devolved upon them by this act, another or others may be appointed in his or their stead, by the remaining commissioners, or a majority of them.

Sec. 2. That the capital stock of The Ashtabula, Warren and Liverpool rail road company, shall be one million five hundred thousand dollars, and shall be divided into shares of fifty dollars each, which shares may be subscribed by individuals only; and it shall and may be lawful for said corporation to commence the construction of the said rail road or way, and enjoy all the powers and privileges conferred by this act, as soon as the sum of fifty thousand dollars shall be subscribed to said stock.

Sec. 3. That all persons who shall become stockholders pursuant to this act, shall be, and are hereby created a body corporate, and shall be and remain a corporation forever, under the name of The Ashtabula, Warren and Liverpool Rail Road Company; and by that name, shall be capable in law of purchasing, holding, selling, leasing and conveying estates, real, personal, and mixed, so far as the same shall be necessary for the purposes hereinafter mentioned, and no further; and shall have perpetual succession; and by said corporate name, may contract and be contracted with, sue and be sued; and may have and use a common seal, which they shall have power to alter or renew at their pleasure; and shall have, enjoy, and may exercise, all the powers, rights and privileges, which corporate bodies may lawfully do, for the purposes mentioned in this act.

Sec. 4. That upon all subscriptions there shall be paid at the time of subscribing, to the said commissioners or their agents, appointed to receive such subscriptions, five per cent. on every share subscribed; and the residue thereof shall be paid in such instalments, and at such times, as may be required by the president and directors of said company: *Provided*, No payment other than the first shall be demanded, until at least thirty days public notice of such demand shall have been given by said president and directors in some newspaper of general circulation in the State of Ohio, and in at least one newspaper in each county through which said road passes; and if any stockholder shall fail or neglect to pay such instalment or part of said subscription thus demanded, for the space of sixty days next after the time the same shall be due and payable, the said president and directors, upon giving at least thirty days previous notice thereof, in manner aforesaid, may, and they are hereby authorized, to sell at public vendue so many of the shares of the said delinquent stockholder or stockholders, as shall be necessary to pay such instalment, and the expenses of advertising and sale, and transfer the shares so sold to the purchasers; and the residue of the money arising from such sale, after paying such instalments and expense, shall be paid to said stockholder on demand.

Sec. 5. That at the expiration of ten days, for which the books are first opened, if one thousand shares of said capital stock shall have been subscribed; or, if not, as soon thereafter as the same shall be subscribed, if within three years after the first opening of the books, the said commissioners, or a majority of them, shall call a general meeting of the stockholders, at such time and place as they may appoint, and shall give at least sixty days previous notice thereof; and at such meeting the said commissioners shall lay the subscription books before the stockholders then and there present; and thereupon the said stockholders, or a majority of them, shall elect thirteen directors by ballot, a majority of whom shall be competent to manage the affairs of said company; they shall have the power of electing a president of said company, from among the directors, and of allowing him such compensation as they may deem proper; and in said election, and on all other occasions wherein a vote of the stockholders of said company is to be taken, each stockholder shall be allowed one vote for every share owned by him or her; and every stockholder may depute any other stockholder to vote and act for him or her, as his or her, or their proxy; and the commissioners aforesaid, or any three of them, shall be judges of the first election of said directors.

Sec. 6. That to continue the succession of the president and directors of said company, seven directors shall be chosen annually on the third Monday of October in every year, in the town of Warren, Trumbull county, or at such other place on the line of said road, as a majority of the directors shall appoint; and if any vacancy shall occur by death, resignation, or otherwise, of any president or director, before the year for which he was elected shall expire, a person to fill such vacant place for the residue of the year may be appointed by the president and directors of said company or a majority of them; and that the president and directors of said company shall hold and exercise their offices until a new election of president and directors; and that all elections which are by this act, or the by-laws of the company, to be made, on a particular day or at a particular time, if not made on such day or time, may be made at any time within thirty days thereafter.

Sec. 7. That a general meeting of the stockholders shall be held annually at the time and place appointed for the election of directors of said company; that meetings may be called at any time during the interval between the said annual meetings, by the president and directors, or a majority of them, or by the stockholders owning at least one fourth of the stock subscribed, upon giving at least thirty days notice of the time and place of holding the same, as provided in the fifth section of this act; and when any such meetings are called by the stockholders, such notice shall specify the particular object of the call; and if, at any such meeting, a majority in value of the stockholders are not present, in person or by proxy, such meeting shall be adjourned from day to day without transacting any business, for any time not exceeding three days; and if, within said three days, stockholders holding a majority in value of the stock subscribed, do not thus attend, such meeting shall then proceed to business.

Sec. 8. That (at) any regular annual meeting of the stockholders of said company, it shall be the duty of the president and directors in office for the previous year, to exhibit a full, clear and distinct statement of the affairs of the company; that (at) any called meeting of the stockholders, a majority of those present, in person or by proxy, may require similar statements from the president and directors, whose duty it shall be to furnish them when thus required; and that at all general meetings of the stockholders, a majority in value of all the stockholders in said company may remove from office any president or any of the directors of said company, and may appoint others in their stead.

Sec. 9. That any president and director of said company, before he acts as such, shall take an oath or affirmation, as the case may be, that he will well and truly discharge the duties of his said office to the best of his skill and abilities.

Sec. 10. That the said president and directors, or a majority of them, may appoint all such officers, engineers, agents or servants whatsoever, as they may deem necessary for the transaction of the business of the company, and may remove any of them at their pleasure; that they, or a majority of them, shall have power to determine by contract the compensation of all officers, engineers, agents or servants, in the employ of said company, and to determine by their by-laws the manner of adjusting and settling all accounts against the said company; and also the manner and evidence of transfers of stock in said company, and they, or a majority of them, shall have power to pass all by-laws which they may deem necessary or proper for exercising all the powers vested in the company hereby incorporated, and for carrying the objects of this act into effect.

Sec. 11. That the said corporation shall be, and they are hereby vested with the right to construct a double or single rail road, or way, from Ashtabula harbor, in the county of Ashtabula, through Warren, in the county of Trumbull, to Liverpool, in the county of Columbiana, and to connect the same by branches with any other rail road constructed in the vicinity of said road, with the consent of the company with which it is proposed to unite said road: *Provided*, That no branch shall be constructed until the main route from Ashtabula harbor to Liverpool, on the Ohio river, has been completed; to transport, take, and carry property and persons upon the same, by the power and force of steam, of animals, or of any mechanical or other powers, or of any combination of them, which the said corporation may choose to employ.

Sec. 12. That the president and directors of said company shall be, and they are hereby invested with all rights and powers necessary for the location, construction, and repair of said road, not exceeding one hundred feet wide, with as many sets of tracks as the said president and directors may deem necessary; and that they may cause to be made, contract with others for making said rail road, or any part of it; and they, or their agents, or those with whom they may contract for making any part of the same, may enter upon, and use and excavate, any land which may be wanted for the site of said road, or for any other purpose necessary and useful in the construction, or in the repair of said road or its works; and that they may build bridges, may fix scales and weights, may lay rails, may take and use any earth, timber, gravel, stone, or other materials, which may be wanted for the construction or repair of any part of said road, or any of its works; and may make and construct all works whatsoever, which may be deemed necessary in the construction or repair of said road.

Sec. 13. That the president and directors of said company, or a majority of them, or any persons authorized by them, or a majority of them, may agree with the owner or owners of any lands, earth, timber, gravel, stones, or other materials, or any improvements which may be wanted for the construction or repair of said road, or any of their works, for the purchase, use, or occupation of the same; and if they cannot agree, and if the owner or owners, or any of them, be a *feme covert*, under age, *non compos mentis*, or out of the county in which the property wanted may lie, when such lands and materials may be wanted, application may be made to any justice of the peace of said county, setting forth the facts in writing and under oath; who shall thereupon issue his warrant. under his hand and seal, directed to the sheriff of said county, or to some disinterested person, if the sheriff shall be interested, requiring him to summon a jury of twelve men, inhabitants of said county, not related, or in any wise interested, to meet on the land or near to the other property or materials to be valued, on a day named in said warrant, not less than ten nor more than twenty days after the issuing of the same; and if, at the said time and place, any of said persons summoned do not attend, the said sheriff, or summoner, shall immediately summon as many persons as may be necessary, with the persons in attendance, to furnish a pannel of twelve jurors in attendance, and from them, each party, or his, her, or their agent, if either be not present in person or by agent, the sheriff or summoner, for him, her, or them, may strike off three jurors, and the remaining six shall act as a jury of inquest of damages; and before they act, the said sheriff or summoner, shall administer to each of them an oath or affirmation, as the case may be, that they will faithfully and impartially value the damages which the owner or owners will sustain by use or occupation of the same, required by said company; and the jury estimating the damages, if for the ground occupied by said road, shall take into the estimate the benefits resulting to said owner or owners, by reason of said road passing through or upon the land of such owner or owners, towards the extinguishment of such claim for damages; and the said jury shall reduce their inquisition to writing, and shall sign and seal the same; and it shall then be returned to the clerk of the court of common pleas of said county, and by such clerk filed in his office; and shall be confirmed by the said court at its next session, if no sufficient cause to the contrary be shown; and when confirmed, shall be recorded by said clerk, at the expense of said company; but if set aside, the court may direct another inquisition to be taken in manner above prescribed; and such inquisition shall describe the property taken, or the bounds of the land condemned; and such valuation when paid, or tendered to the owner or owners of said property, or his, her, or their legal representatives, shall entitle said company to the full right of such personal property, and to the use and occupation of such landed property, in the same thus valued, as fully as if it had been conveyed by the owner or owners of the same; and the valuation, if not received when tendered, may at any time thereafter be received from the company without cost, by the owner or owners, his, her, or their legal representative or representatives; and that such sheriff or summoner, and jurors, shall be entitled to demand and receive from the said company the same fees as are allowed for like services in cases of fixing the valuation of real estate previous to sale under execution.

Sec. 14. That whenever, in the construction of such road, it shall be necessary to cross or intersect any established road or way, it shall be the duty of the president and directors of said company so to construct the said rail road or way as not to impede the passage or transportation of persons or property along the same; or when it shall be necessary to pass through the land of any individual, it shall also be their duty to provide for such individual proper wagon ways across said road, from one part of his land to another, without delay.

Sec. 15. That if said company shall neglect to provide proper wagon ways across said road, as required by the fourteenth section of this act, it shall be lawful for any individual to sue said company, and to be entitled to such damages as a jury may think him or her entitled to, for such neglect on the part of said company.

Sec. 16. That if it shall be necessary for such company in the selection of the route or construction of the road to be by them laid out and constructed, or any part of it, to connect the same with, or to use any turnpike road or bridge, made or erected by any company or persons incorporated, or authorized by any law of this State it shall be lawful for the said president and directors, and they are hereby authorized, to contract or agree with any such other corporation or persons, for the right to use such road or bridge, for the transfer of any of the corporate or other rights and privileges of such corporation or persons, to the said company hereby incorporated: and every such other incorporation or persons incorporated by, or acting under the laws of this State, is, and are hereby authorized to make such arrangement, contract or transfer, by and through the agency of the person authorized by their respective acts of incorporation, to exercise their corporate powers, or by such persons as by any law of this State, are entrusted with the management and direction of said turnpike, road or bridge, or any other rights and privileges aforesaid; and any contract or agreement or transfer, made in pursuance of the power and authority hereby granted, when executed by the several parties, under their respective corporate seals, or otherwise legally authen-

21—L

ticated, shall vest in the company hereby incorporated, all such road, part of road, rights and privileges, and the right to use and enjoy the same, as fully to all intents and purposes as they now are or might be used and exercised by the said corporation or persons in whom they are now vested.

Sec. 17. That the said president and directors shall have power to purchase, with the funds of the company, and place on any rail road constructed by them under this act, all machines, wagons, vehicles or carriages of any description whatsoever, which they may deem necessary or proper for the purpose of transportation on said road, and that they may demand and receive for tolls upon, and the transportation of persons, goods, produce, merchandize, or other property of any kind whatsoever, transported by them along said rail road, any sum not exceeding the following rates: on all goods, merchandize, or other property of any description whatsoever, transported by them, a sum not exceeding one and one half cents per mile for tolls; and five cents on a ton per mile for transportation on all goods, produce, merchandize, or property of any description whatsoever, transported by them or their agents; and for the transportation of passengers, not exceeding three cents per mile for each passenger, and it shall be lawful for any other company, or any person or persons whatsoever, to transport in proper cars or carriages, any persons, merchandize, produce or property of any description whatsoever, along said road or any part thereof, subject to such rules and regulations as the said president and directors may prescribe under the provisions of this act; and the said road, with all their works, improvements and profits, and all machinery used by them on said road for transportation, are hereby vested in said company, incorporated by this act, and their successors forever; and the shares of the capital stock of said company shall be deemed and considered personal property, transferable by assignment, agreeable to the by-laws of said company.

Sec. 18. That it shall be lawful for the president and directors of said company, when they may deem it necessary, to borrow any sum of money from any person, or persons, corporation or company, not exceeding the amount which shall have been paid in by the stockholders of the said company, for the purpose of completing the aforesaid rail road, or for otherwise carrying into effect the provisions of this act, and by their corporate seal to mortgage or pledge the capital stock of the said company for the payment of the same: *Provided*, That such loan shall have been agreed to by a majority in value of all the stockholders of said company.

Sec. 19. That the said president and directors, shall, semi-annually, declare and make a dividend of all the nett profits arising from the resources of said company, and shall divide the same amongst the stockholders of said company in proportion to their respective shares; reserving from the same, a sum sufficient to meet the current contingent expenses and debts of the company.

Sec. 20. That if any person or persons shall wilfully, by any means whatsoever, injure, impair or destroy any part of the said rail road, constructed by said company, under this act, or any of the works, buildings or machinery of said company, such person or persons, so offending, shall each of them, for every such offence, forfeit and pay to the said company, any sum not exceeding three fold the damages, which may be recovered in the name of the company, by an action of debt in the court of common pleas for the county wherein the offence shall have been committed; and shall also be subject to an indictment in said court, and upon conviction of such offence, shall be punished by fine and imprisonment, at the discretion of the court.

Sec. 21. That if said rail road shall not be finished within twenty years from the passage of this act, then this act shall be null and void.

Sec. 22. That the State shall have the right, after the expiration of thirty-five years from the passage of this act, to purchase and hold the same, for the use of the State, by paying to said company the amount expended by them in the location, construction and permanent fixtures of said road, with fifteen per centum thereon: *Provided, however*, That the sum so to be paid by the State together with tolls received by the company, shall not be less than the amount by them expended upon said road and fixtures, with six per centum per annum thereon: of which cost and tolls an accurate account shall be kept and submitted to the General Assembly, duly attested by the oath of the officers of said company, if the General Assembly shall require it; any future Legislature may alter or amend this act, so far as to regulate the rate of tolls to be charged by said company for the transportation of the mail.

Sec. 23. That this act is hereby declared to be a public act, and shall be so construed in all courts of justice and elsewhere.

WILLIAM MEDILL,
Speaker pro tem. of the House of Representatives.
ELIJAH VANCE,
Speaker of the Senate.

February 29th, 1836.

AN ACT

To incorporate the Cuyahoga and Erie Rail Road Company.

Sec. 1. *Be it enacted by the General Assembly of the State of Ohio,* That James Butler, Van R. Humphrey, Augustus Baldwin, Israel Town, George B. Depeyster, Nathan Button, William Pomeroy, Charles L. Rhodes, Thomas Earl, and Joshua Woodward, of Portage county; Charles M. Giddings, Harman C. Baldwin, S. J. Andrews, and Frederick Whitlesey, of Cuyhoga county, be, and they are hereby appointed commissioners, under the direction of a majority of whom, subscriptions may be received to the capital stock of the Cuyahoga and Erie Rail Road Company, hereby incorporated; and they, or a majority of them, may cause books to be opened in the counties of Cuyahoga, and Portage, at such times and places as they may direct, and for the purpose of receiving subscriptions to the capital stock of said company, after having given thirty days notice of the time and place of opening the same; and that, upon the first opening of said books, they shall be kept open for at least ten days in succession, from ten o'clock A. M. until two o'clock P. M.; and if, at the expiration of that period, such a subscription to the capital stock of said company, as is necessary to its incorporation, shall not have been obtained, then said commissioners, or a majority of them, may cause said books to be opened from time to time, after the expiration of said ten days, and for the space of three years thereafter; and if any of said commissioners shall die, resign, or refuse to act, during the continuance of the duties devolved upon them by this act, another or others may be appointed in his or their stead, by the remaining commissioners, or a majority of them.

Sec. 2. That the capital stock of the Cuyahoga and Erie rail-road Company, shall be one hundred and fifty thousand dollars, and shall be divided in shares of fifty dollars each; and it shall and may be lawful for said corporation, to commence the construction of the said rail road or way, and enjoy all the powers and privileges conferred by this act, so soon as the sum of ten thousand dollars shall be subscribed to said stock.

Sec. 3. That all persons who shall become stockholders pursuant to this act, shall be, and they are hereby created a body corporate, and shall be and remain a corporation forever, under the name of the Cuyahoga and Erie Rail Road Company; and by that name shall be capable in law of purchasing, holding, selling, leasing, and conveying estates, real, personal, and mixed, so far as the same shall be necessary for the purposes hereinafter mentioned, and no further; and shall have perpetual succession; and by said corporate name may contract and be contracted with; sue and be sued; and may have and use a common seal, which they shall have power to alter or renew at pleasure; and shall have, enjoy, and may exercise, all the powers, rights, and privileges, which corporate bodies may lawfully do, for the purposes mentioned in this act.

Sec. 4. That upon all subscriptions, there shall be paid at the time of subscribing, to the said commissioners or their agents, appointed to receive such subscription, the sum of five dollars on every share subscribed; and the residue thereof shall be paid in such instalments, and at such times, as may be required by the president and directors of said company: *Provided,* No payment other than the first shall be demanded, until at least thirty days public notice of such demand shall be given by said president and directors in some newspaper of general circulation in the State of Ohio; and in the said counties of Portage and Cuyahoga: and if any stockholder shall fail or neglect to pay any instalment or part of said subscription thus demanded, for the space of sixty days next after the time the same shall be due and payable, the said president and directors, upon giving at least thirty days previous notice thereof, in manner aforesaid, may, and they are hereby authorized to sell at public vendue so many of the shares of the said delinquent stockholder or stockholders, as shall be necessary to pay such instalment, and the expenses of advertising and sale, and transfer the shares so sold to the purchasers; and the residue of the money arising from such sale, after paying such instalment and expense, shall be paid to said stockholder on demand.

Sec. 5. That at the expiration of ten days, for which the books are first opened, if seventy-five shares of said capital stock shall have been subscribed; or if not, as soon thereafter as the same shall be subscribed, if

within three years after the first opening of the books, the said commissioners, or a majority of them, shall call a general meeting of the stockholders,
at such time and place as they may appoint, and shall give at least sixty
days previous notice thereof; and at such meeting the said commissioners
shall lay the subscription books before the stockholders then and there present; and thereupon the said stockholders, or a majority of them, shall
elect twelve directors by ballot, a majority of whom shall be competent
to manage the affairs of said company: they shall have the power of electing a president of said company, either from among said directors or others,
and of allowing him such compensation as they may deem proper; and in
said election, and on all other occasions wherein a vote of the stockholders
of said company is taken, each stockholder shall be allowed one vote for
every share owned by it, him or her; and every stockholder may depute
any other person to vote, and act for him or her, as his or their proxy:
and the commissioners aforesaid, or any of them, shall be judges of the first
election of said directors.

Sec. 6.   That to continue the succession of the president and directors
of said company, twelve directors shall be chosen annually on the third
Monday of October in every year, in the town of Franklin, in the county
of Portage, or at such other place as a majority of the directors shall appoint: and if any vacancy shall occur by death, resignation, or otherwise,
of any president or director, before the year for which he was elected had
expired, a person to fill such vacant place for the residue of the year may
be appointed by the president and directors of said company, or a majority of them; and that the president and directors of said company shall
hold and exercise their offices until a new election of president and directors; and that elections which are by this act, or by the by-laws of the
company, to be made, on a particular day or at a particular time, if not
made on such a day or time, may be made at any time within thirty days
thereafter.

Sec. 7.   That a general meeting of the stockholders shall be held annually at the time and place appointed for the election of president and directors of said company; that meetings may be called at any time during
the interval between the said annual meetings, by the president and directors, or a majority of them, or by the stockholders owning at least one
fourth of the stock subscribed, upon giving at least thirty days public notice of the time and place of holding the same; and when any such meetings are called by the stockholders, such notice shall specify the particular
object of the call; and if at any such called meeting, a majority in value
of the stockholders of said company are not present, in person or by
proxy, such meeting shall be adjourned from day to day without transacting any business, for any time not exceeding three days, and if, within said
three days, stockholders holding a majority in value of the stock subscribed, do not thus attend, such meeting shall be dissolved.

Sec. 8.   That at the regular meetings of the stockholders of said company, it shall be the duty of the president and directors in office for the
previous year, to exhibit a clear and distinct statement of the affairs of the
company; that (at) any called meeting of the stockholders, a majority of
those present, in person or by proxy, may require similar statements from
the president and directors, whose duty it shall be to furnish them when

thus required, and that at all general meetings of the stockholders, a majority in value of all the stockholders of said company, may remove from office any president or any of the directors of said company, and may appoint officers in their stead.

Sec. 9. That any president and director of said company, before he acts as such, shall take an oath or affirmation, that he will well and truly discharge the duties of his said office to the best of his skill and judgment.

Sec. 10. That the said president and directors, or a majority of them, may appoint all such officers, engineers, agents or servants, whatsoever, as they may deem necessary for the transaction of the business of the company, and may remove any of them at their pleasure; that they, or a majority of them, shall have power to determine by contract the compensation of all engineers, officers, agents or servants, in the employ of said company, and to determine by their by-laws the manner and evidence of transfers of stock in said company: and they, or a majority of them, shall have power to pass all by-laws which they may deem necessary or proper for exercising all the powers vested in the company hereby incorporated, and for carrying the objects of this act into effect: *Provided, only,* That such by-laws shall not be contrary to the laws of this State, or of the United States.

Sec. 11. That said corporation shall be, and they are hereby vested with the right to construct a double or single Rail-road, or way, from Cleveland, in the county of Cuyahoga, to Franklin, in the county of Portage; to transport, take and carry property and persons upon the same, by the power and force of steam, of animals, or of any mechanical or other power, or of any combination of them, which the said corporation may choose to employ.

Sec. 12. That the president and directors of said company shall be, and are hereby invested with all rights and powers necessary for the location, construction and repair of said road, not exceeding one hundred feet wide, with as many sets of tracks as the said president and directors may deem necessary; and they may cause to be made, contract with others for making said Rail-road, or any part of it; and they, or their agents, or those with whom they may contract for making any part of the same, may enter upon, and use and excavate any land which may be wanted for the site of said road, or for any other purpose necessary and useful in the construction or in the repair of said road or its works; and that they may build bridges, and fix scales and weights, may lay rails, may take and use any earth, timber, gravel, stone, or other materials which may be wanted, for the construction or repair of any part of said road, or any of its works; and may make and construct all works whatsoever, which may be necessary in the construction or repair of said road.

Sec. 13. That the president and directors of said company, or a majority, of them, or any persons authorized by them, or a majority of them, may agree with the owner or owners of any lands, earth, timber, gravel, or stone, or other materials, or any improvements which may be wanted for the construction or repair of said road, or any of their works, for the purchase, or use or occupation of the same: and if they cannot agree, and if the owner or owners, or any of them, be a married woman, insane person, or idiot, or out of the county in which the property wanted may lie, when such lands and materials may be wanted, application may be made to any justice of the peace of such county, who shall thereupon issue his warrant under his hand and seal, directed to the sheriff of said county, or to some disinterested person if the sheriff shall be interested, requiring him to summon a jury of twelve men, inhabitants of said county, not related or in any wise interested, to meet on the land or near to the other property or materials to be valued, on a day named in said warrant, not less than ten nor more than twenty days after the issuing of the same: and if, at the same time and place, any of said pesons do not attend, the said sheriff, or summoner, shall immediately summon as many persons as may be necessary, with the persons in attendance, to furnish a pannel of twelve jurors in attendance, and from them, each party, or its, his, or her or their agent, the sheriff, or summoner, for him, her, it or them, may strike off three jurors, and the remaining six shall act as a jury of inquest of damages; and before they act as such, the said summoner or sheriff, shall administer to each of them an oath or affimation, as the case may be, that they will faithfully and impartially value the damages which the owner or owners will sustain by use or occupation of the same, required by said company; and the jury estimating the damages, if for the ground occupied by said road, shall take into the estimate the benefits resulting to said owner or owners, by reason of said road passing through or upon the land of such owner or owners, towards the extinguishment of such claim for damages; and the said jury shall reduce their inquisition to writing, and shall sign and seal the same; and it shall then be returned to the clerk of the court of common pleas for said county, and by such clerk filed in his office; and shall be confirmed by the said court at its next session, if no sufficient cause to the contrary be shown; aud when confirmed, shall be recorded by said clerk, at the expense of said company: but if set aside, the court may direct another inquisition to be taken in the manner above described; and such inquisition shall describe the property taken, or the bounds of the land condemned; and such vuluation when paid, or tendered to the owner or owners of said property, or his, her or their legal representatives, shall entitle said company to the full right to said personal property, and the use and occupation of such landed property, for the purpose of said road, thus valued, as fully as if it had been conveyed by the owner or owners of the same; and the valuation, if not received when tendered, may at any time thereafter be received, from the company without cost, by the owner or owners, his, her or their legal representative or representatives: and that such sheriff or summoner, and jurors, shall be entitled to demand and receive from the said company the same fees as are allowed for like services in cases of fixing the valuaton of real estate previous to sale under execution.

Sec. 14. That whenever, in the construction of said road, it shall be necessary to cross or intersect any established road or way, it shall be the duty of the said president and directors of said company, so to construct the said rail-road across such established road or way, as not to impede the passage or transportation of persons or property along the same; or when it shall be necesary to pass through the land of any individual, it shall also be their duty to provide for such individual, proper wagon ways across said road, from one part of his land to another, without delay.

Sec. 15. That if said company should neglect to provide proper wagon ways across said road, as required by the fourteenth section of this act, it shall be lawful for any individual to sue said company, and be entitled to such damages as a jury may think him or her entitled to, for such neglect on the part of said company.

Sec. 16. That if it shall be necesary for such company, in the selection of the route or construction of the road to be by them laid out and constructed, or any part of it, to connect the same with or to use any turnpike road or bridge, made or erected by any company or persons incorporated, or authorized by any law of this State, it shall be lawful for the said president and directors, and they are hereby authorized to contract or agree with any such other corporation or persons, for the right to use such road or bridge, or for the transfer of any of the corporate or other rights or privileges of such corporation or persons, to the said company hereby incorporated; and every such other incorporation, or persons incorporated by, or acting under the laws of this State, is, and are hereby authorized to make such an agreement, contract or transfer, by and through the agency of the person authorized by their respective acts of incorporation, to exercise their corporate powers, or by such persons as by any law of this State, are intrusted with the management and direction of said turnpike, road or bridge, or of any of the rights and privileges aforesaid; and any contract, agreement or transfer, made in pursuance of the power and authority hereby granted, when executed by the several parties under their respective corporate seals, or otherwise, legally authenticated, shall vest in the company hereby incorporated, all such road, part of road, rights and privileges, and the right to use and enjoy the same, as fully to all intents and purposes as they now are or might be used and exercised by the said corporation or persons in whom they are now vested.

Sec. 17. That the said president and directors shall have power to purchase, with the funds of the company, and place on any rail-road constructed by them under this act, all machines, wagons, vehicles or carriages of any description whatsoever, which they may deem necessary or proper for the purposes of transportation on said road; and that they shall have power to charge for tolls and the transportation of persons, goods, produce, merchandize or property of any kind whatsoever, transported by them along said rail-way, any sum not exceeding the followin rates, on all goods, merchandize, or property of any description whatsoever, transported by them, a sum not exceeding one and a half cents per mile for tolls, and five cents per mile per ton, for transportation on all goods, produce, merchandize, or property of any description whatsoever, transported by them, or their agents; and for the transportation of passengers not exceeding three cents per mile for each passesenger; and it shall be lawful for any other company, or any other person or persons whatsoever, paying the tolls aforesaid, to transport any persons, merchandize, produce, or property of any description whatsoever, along said road, or any part thereof, without license, or permission of the president and directors of said company: and the said road, with all their works, improvements and profits, and all machinery on said road for transportation, are hereby vested in said company, incorporated by this act, and their successors forever; and the shares of the capital stock of said company shall be deemed and considered personal property, transferable by assignment, agreeable to the by-laws of said company.

Sec. 18. That any other rail road company, now or hereafter to be chartered by the law of this State, may join and connect said road with the road hereby contemplated, and run cars upon the same, under the rules and regulations of the Cuyahoga and Erie Rail road Company, as to the construction and speed of said cars; and full right and privilege is hereby reserved to the State, or the citizens, or any incorporated company, by authority of this State, to cross the Rail road hereby incorporated: *Provided,* That in so crossing, no injury shall be done to the works of the company hereby incorporated.

Sec. 19. That the president and directors shall, semi-annually, declare and make such dividend as they may deem proper, of the nett profits arising from the resources of said company, deducting the probable amount of the outstanding debts due by said company, and the necessary current and contingent expenses, and that they shall divide the same amongst the stockholders of said company, in proportion to their respective shares.

Sec. 20. That if any person or persons shall wilfully, by any means whatsoever, injure, impair or destroy any part of said Rail road, constructed by said company, under this act, or any of the works, buildings, (or) machinery of said company, such person or persons, so offending, shall, each of them, for every such offence, forfeit and pay to the said company any sum not exceeding three fold the damages, which may be recovered in the name of the company, by an action of debt, in the court of common pleas for the county wherein the offence shall be committed, and shall also be subject to an indictment in said court, and upon conviction of such offence, shall be punished by fine and imprisonment, at the discretion of the court.

Sec. 21. That if said rail road shall not be commenced in three years from the passage of this act, and shall not be finished within fifteen years from the time of the commencement thereof, then this act to be null and void.

Sec. 22. If the Legislature of this State shall, after the expiration of thirty-five years from the passage of this act, make provisions by law for the repayment to said company of the amount expended by them in the construction of the said rail road, and if the value of the necessary permanent fixtures thereto at the time, with an advance of fifteen per cent. thereon, then said road and fixtures shall vest in, and become the property of the State of Ohio; of which expenditures an accurate statement in writing, attested by the oaths or affirmations of the officers of said company, shall be submitted to the General Assembly, if required.

Sec. 23. Whenever the dividend of said company shall exceed the rate of six per cent. per annum, the Legislature of this State may impose such reasonable taxes on the amount of such dividends as may be received from other rail road companies.

Sec. 24. That this act is hereby declared to be a public act, and shall be so construed in all courts of justice, and elsewhere.

WILLIAM MEDILL,
Speaker pro tem. of the House of Representatives.
ELIJAH VANCE,
Speaker of the Senate.

February 29, 1836.
22—L

An act

To incorporate the Cleveland and Warren Rail Road Ccompany.

Sec. 1. *Be it enacted by the General Assembly of the State of Ohio,* That Charles Dennison, Edmund Clark, Leonard Case, John W. Willey, Gurdon Fitch, Eben Hosmer, Hezekiah Dunham, of the county of Cuyahoga; Chauncey Eggleston, Alanson Baldwin, William R. Henry, Elisha Garrett and William Quinby, of the county of Portage; Daniel Gilbert, James L. Vangorder, David Tod, Zalmon Fitch, Rufus P. Spalding, Charles White, Mathew Birchard and Eli Baldwin, of the county of Trumbull; together with such other persons as may hereafter become associated with them, in the manner hereinafter prescribed, their successors and assigns, be, and they are hereby created a body corporate and politic, by the name of " The Cleveland and Warren Rail road Company;" and by that name shall be, and are hereby made capable in law, to have, hold, purchase, receive and possess, enjoy and retain to them, and their successors, all such lands, tenements and hereditaments, with their appurtenances, as shall be necessary or in any wise convenient for the transaction of their business, and such as may in good faith be conveyed to them, by way of security, or in payment of debts; and the same to sell, grant, rent, or in any wise dispose of; to sue and be sued, plead and be impleaded, answer and be answered, defend and be defended; and also, to have and use a common seal, and the same to alter, break or renew at pleasure; and they shall be, and hereby are invested with all the powers and privileges, which are by law incident to corporations of a similar nature, and which are necessary to carry into effect the objects of this association; and if either of the persons named in this section shall die, or refuse or neglect to exercise the powers, and discharge the duties hereby created, it shall be the duty of the remaining persons herein before named, or a majority of them, to appoint some suitable person, or persons, to fill such vacancy or vacancies, so often as the same shall occur.

Sec. 2. That the said corporation shall be, and is hereby, vested with the right to construct a rail road with one or more tracts, or ways, from some point in Cleveland, in the county of Cuyahoga, to the village of Warren, in the county of Trumbull, through the township of Aurora, and the centre of said Auroa, if the same can he done without an additional expense of two thousand dollars to the company, and also passing through Garrettsville, Bedford Centre and Newburgh, if practicable and expedient; and to transport, take and carry persons and property, upon the same, by the power and force of steam, of animals, or any other mechanical or other power, or any combination of them, which said corporation may choose to employ.

Sec. 3 That the capital stock of said company, shall be divided into shares of one hundred dollars each.

Sec. 4. That the said corporation, shall be, and is hereby authorized, to raise, by subscription within the period of three years from the passage of this act, as capital stock, sufficient funds for the accomplishment of the objects aforesaid; and for that purpose, the persons named in the first section of this act, or a majority of them, so soon after the taking effect of this act, as they shall judge proper, shall cause books to be opened, at such times, and places as they shall think fit, in the States of Ohio, Pennsylvania, Maryland, and €lsewhere, under the management of such persons as they shall appoint, for receiving subscription, to the capital stock of said company, and keep the same open at least ten days; and each subscriber shall be a member of said corporation, for all purposes; and public notice shall be given, in such manner as may be deemed advisable by said corporation, of the times and places of opening books, and the above named persons, or a majority of them, may prescribe the form of said subscription; and whenever the sum of one hundred thousand dollars, or a greater part of said stock, shall have been subscribed, it shall be the duty of said persons, or a majority of them, to call a meeting of the stockholders, by causing notice to be published in one or more newspapers, in general circulation in the respective places in which stock shall have been subscribed, at least thirty days previous thereto, of the time and place of holding said meeting, which place shall be at some convenient point, on or near the route of said rail road; at which meeting, the stockholders who shall attend for that purpose, eitheir in person or by lawful proxy, shall elect, by ballot, seven directors, who shall hold their offices during one year, and until others shall be chosen and qualified in their places; and the persons named in the first section, or a majority of them, shall be inspectors of the first election of directors of the said corporation, and shall certify, under their hands, the names of those duly elected; and shall deliver over to them, the said certificates and subscription books, and at said election, and at all other elections, or voting of any description, every member shall have a right of voting by himself, or proxy duly authorized in writing; and each share shall entitle the holder to one vote; and the management of the concerns of said corporation shall be entrusted to seven directors, to be elected annually, bv the stockholders, by ballot; and the directors first chosen, and such directors as shall hereafter be chosen, at any subsequent election, shall immediately thereafter, meet and elect one of their number, who shall be president thereof, until another election; and also elect a treasurer and secretary; who may be removed at the pleasure of the said president and directors, and others elected in their places; and a majority of said directors shall constitute a board, for every purpose within the provisions of this act.

Sec. 5. That in case it should at any time happen, that the election of directors shall not be made, on any day, when pursuant to this act it ought to be made, the said corporation shall not, for that cause, be deemed to be disolved, but such election may be held at any other time, directed by the by-laws of said corporation.

Sec. 6. That the books of subscription shall remain open as long as the president and directors of said company shall see fit; and each subscriber shall be bound to pay, from time to time, such instalments on his stock, as the said president and directors may lawfully require, they giving at least thirty days previeus notice, of the time and place of making the payments required, in at leass one newspaper, in general circulation in each of the counties through which the road may pass; but no assessment shall ever be made so as to render any subscriber liable to pay more than one hundred dollars for a share; if, however, after the closing of said books, or at any time, it shall appear that sufficient funds have not been raised, the president and directors of said company, or its officers duly authorized for that purpose, may, at any time, and from time to time, raise the necessary funds, by creating and selling additional shares, in such manner and upon such terms, as the president and directors shall prescribe; and the holders of such additional shares, shall thenceforward be members of said corporation for all purposes.

Sec. 7. That if any subscriber shall neglect to pay his subscription, or any portion thereof, for the space of thirty days after he is required so to do, by the said president and directors, notice having been given, as required in this act, the treasurer of said corporation, or other officer duly author. ized for that purpose, may make sale of such share or shares, at public auction, to the highest bidder, giving at least thirty days notice thereof, in some newspaper in general circulation at the place of sale; and the same shall be transferred by the treasurer, to the purchaser; and such delinquent subscriber shall be ehld personally accountable to to the corporation for the balance, if his share or shares shall be sold for less than the amount remaining due thereon, and shall be entitled to the overplus, if the same be sold for more than the amount so remaining due, after deducting the costs of sale.

Sec. 8. That it shall and may be lawful for any State, or for the government of the United States, to subscribe for any number of shares of stock in said company. upon the same terms as other subscribers are authorized to take and subscribe for the same.

Sec. 9. That said corporation be, and they are hereby authorized, to cause such examination and surveys to be made by their agents, surveyors and engineers, of the ground lying in the vicinity of said routes as shall be necessary to determine the most eligible and expedient route, whereon to construct said rail road; and the examination being made, and the route determined, it shall be lawful for said corporation, by themselves or lawful agents, to enter upon, and take possession of, all such lands, materials and real estate, as may he indispensable for the construction and maintenance of said rail road, and the examination requisite and appertaining therto; but all lands, materials or real estate [thus] entered upon, used or occupied, which are not donations, shall be purchased by the corporation, of the owner or owners thereof, at a price to be mutually agreed between them; and in case of disagreemeet, as to the price, it shall be the duty of the commissioners of the proper county, upon a notice given them by either party, in writing, and making satisfactory proof that the opposite party has had at least three days notice of the intended application, to appoint three disinterested freeholders, of the proper county, to determime the damages which the owner or owners of the lands, materials or real estate, so entered upon, or used by the said corporation, has or have. sustained by the occupation or use of the same; and upon payment by said corporation, of such damages, to the person or persons to whom the same may be awarded, as aforesaid, then the said corporation shall be deemed to be, and stand seized and possessed of the use, for the purpose of said road, of all such lands, materials or real estate, as shall have been appraised; and it shall be the duty of said appraisers, to deliver to the said corporation, a written statement, signed by them, or a majority of them, of the award they shall make, containing a description of the lands, materials or real estate appraised; to be recorded by the said corporation, in the commissioners' office in said county: *Provided,* That either party shall have power, except in cases only where materials are used, to appeal from the decision of the said appraisers, to the court of common pleas, of the proper county, at any time within twenty days after the appraisers shall have made their return, as aforesaid, and said court shall proceed thereon, as in cases of appeals, on application for damages in laying out and establishing county roads.

Sec. 10. That the appraisers authorized by the foregoing section of this act, before they proceed to estimate damages, shall severally take an oath or affirmation, faithfully, impartially and honestly to discharge their said duty, by returning the true amount of damages, over and above the benefits arising from said road, estimated in cash; and the said apprisers shall, severally, be entitled to receive from said corporation, one dollar per day, for every day they may [be] necessarily employed: *Provided, however,* That if said applicant or applicants, shall not obtain an award of damages, then, and in such case, said applicant or applicants shall pay all costs.

Sec. 11. That the said corporation shall have power to determine the width, not exceeding one hundred feet, and dimensions of said rail roads, whether it shall be a double or single track; to regulate the time and manner in which passengers and property shall be transported thereon; and the manner of collecting tolls for such transportation; and to erect and maintain buildings for the accommodation of the business of the corporation, as they may deem advisable, for their interest.

Sec. 12. That said corporation may construct the rail road across, or upon, any road, canal, highway, stream of water or water course, if the same shall be necessary; but the said corporation shall restore such road, canal or highway, stream of water or water course, thus intersected or crossed, to its former state of usefulness, or in such a manner as not to impair its convenience, usefulness or value, to the owner or public, without delay.

Sec. 13. That said company may demand and receive, per tons upon and transportation of goods, produce, merchandize, or property of any kind whatsoever, transported by them along said rail way, any sum not exceeding the following rates: on all goods or property of any description transported by them, a sum not exceeding one and a half cents per mile for toll, five cents per mile, per ton, for transportation; and for transportation of passengers not exceeding three cents per mile for each passenger; and all persons paying the tolls aforesaid, may with suitable and proper cars, transport persons or property on said rail road, subject to the by-laws of said company; as to the construction and speed of said cars.

Sec. 14. That at the regular annual meeting of the stockholders of said company, it shall be the duty of the president and directors in office for the previous year, to exhibit a clear and distinct statement of the affairs of the company, and the president and directors shall annually or semi-annually, declare and make such dividend as they may deem proper, of the nett profits arising from the resources of said company, deducting the necessary current and probable contingent expenses; and they shall divide the same among the stockholders of said company in proportion to their respective shares in the stock paid into the company.

Sec. 15. That the said president and directors, or a majority of them, may appoint all such officers, engineers, agents or servants whatsoever, as they may deem necessary for the transaction of the business of the company, and may remove any of them at their pleasure: and they, or a majority of them, shall have power to determine the compensation of all such engineers, officers, agents or servants, and to contract with them for their respective services; and to determine by their by-laws the manner of adjusting and settling all accounts against the said company; and also, the manner and evidence of the transfer of stock in said company: and they, or a majority of them, shall have power to pass all by-laws which they may deem necessary or proper for exercising all the powers vested in the company hereby incorporated, and for carrying into effect the object of this act.

Sec. 16. That the State shall have power, at any time after the expiration of thirty-five years from the passage of this act, to purchase and hold said road, for the use of this State, at a price not exceeding the original cost for the construction of said road, and the necessary permanent fixtures, at the time of purchase, and fifteen per cent. advance theron, of which cost an accurate statement in writing, shall be submitted to the General Assembly, duly attested by the oaths of the officers of said company, if the General Asrembly shall require it: *Provided*, That the sum thus to be paid by the State, shall not, together with the tolls received by the company, be less than the amount of expenditures by them made, and six per centum thereon.

Sec. 17. That in any suit instituted against said corporation, service of process made upon any one of the directors, at least ten days before the return day thereof, shall in all courts and places, be deemed and held a sufficient and valid service on the said corporation.

Sec. 18. That when the rail-road shall be completed, the president and directors of said company, shall make out a minute, full and detailed statement, in writing, of the expenses incurred by the said corporation, in locating, exploring of routes, and constructing said rail-road; which report shall be verified by the oaths of said president and directors, and filed by them in the office of the Secretary of this State; and if after the first location of the route of said rail-road, or the completion of the same, as aforesaid, any alteration shall be made in the course thereof, or in any of its branches or connections, the said president and directors shall, in like manner, from time to time, make out and file statements of the expenses incurred by such alterations, branches or connections, as aforesaid.

Sec. 19. That any rail-road company, now, or hereafter to be chartered or created by law of this State, shall have power to join and unite with the road hereby incorporated, at any point which the directors of said company may think advisable; or any cars, carriages, or other vehicle, used on either road, joined or intersected, may run, pass and occupy the intesected or united road, without reloading, or change of cargo or passengers, subject, however, to the rules and regulations, to the tolls and charges, common on the road so used and occupied.

Sec. 20. That if any person shall wilfully obstruct, or in any way spoil, injure and destroy said road, or any part thereof, or either of its branches, or any part thereof, or any thing belonging or incident thereto, or any materials to be used in the construction thereof, or any building, fixture or carriage, erected or constructed for the use or convenience thereof, or used thereon, such person or persons shall each be liable, for every such offence, in treble the damages sustained thereby, to be recovered by action of debt, in any court having jurisdiction thereof; and shall also be subject to an indictment in the court of common pleas of the county where such offence was committed; and upon conviction thereof, shall be punished by fine, not exceeding one hundred dollars, and imprisonment in the county jail, not exceeding twenty days.

Sec. 21. That whenever the Legislature of the State of Pennsylvania shall pass a law authorizing the construction of a rail-road from Pittsburg, in said State, or from any other point below, on the Ohio river, running in a direction towards Cleveland, aforesaid, to the line of this State, then the corporation hereby erected, shall have power to extend and prolong the road, hereby provied for, easterly, from Warren to a point on the line of this State, where the same may be united with such road, authorized by said State of Pennsylvania.

Sec. 22. That when it shall be necessary to pass through the land of any individual, it shall be the duty of said company to provide for such individual proper wagon ways across said road, from one part of his land to another, without unnecessary delay.

Sec. 23. That if said road shall not be commenced within three years from the passage of this act, and completed within ten years thereafter, then this act to be void and of no effect.

Sec. 24. Whenever the dividends of said company shall exceed the rate of six per cent. per annum, the Legislature of this State may impose such reasonable taxes on the amount of such dividends as may be received from other rail-road companies.

WILLIAM MEDILL,
Speaker pro tem. of the House of Representatives.
ELIJAH VANCE,
Speaker of the Senate.

February 29, 1836.

AN ACT

To incorporate the Columbus, Delaware, Marion and Upper Sandusky Rail Road Company

Sec. 1. *Be it enacted by the General Assembly of the State of Ohio,* That Joseph Ridgway, William Neil, John N. Champion, Lyne Stirling, junr., Wray Thomas, Robert Brotherton, and Moses H. Kirby, of the county of Franklin; William Little, Ezra Griswold, Hosea Williams, Caleb Howard, and David T. Fuller, of the county of Delaware; John E. Davidson, Sanford S. Bennet, Elisha Hardy, Carey, A. Darlinton, Eber Baker, George H. Bushby, and Nathan Peters, of the county of Marion; John Carey, Joseph Chaffer, G. C. Worth, and William Walker of the county of Crawford; be and they are hereby appointed commissioners, under the direction of a majority of whom, subscrptions may be received to the capital stock of the Columbus, Delaware, Marion and Upper Sandusky Rail road company, hereby incorporated; and they or a majority of them, may cause books to be opened in the counties aforesaid, at such other times and places as they may direct, for the purpose of receiving subscriptions tothe capital stock of said company, after having given at least twenty days previous notice, of the time and place or places ofopening the same, by advertisement in some newspaper in general circulation in the place or places where said books are to be opened and that upon the first opening of said books, they shall be kept open for at least ten successive days, from ten o'clock, A. M. until 3 o'clock, P.M.; and if, at the expiration of that period the whole amount of the capital stock of said company, as herein after declared, shall not have been subscribed, then said commissioners, or a majority of them, may cause said books to be opened, from time to time, after the expiration of ten days, for the space of three years thereafter, and if any of the said commissioners shall die, resign, or refuse to act, during the continuance of the duties devolved upon them by this act, another, or others may be appointed in his or their stead, by the remaining commissioners, or a majority of them.

Se 2.   That the capital stock of the Columbus, Delaware, Marion and Upper Sandusky Rail-road Company, shall be five hundred thousand dollars; and shall be divided into shares of fifty dollars each; which shares may be subscribed for by individuals only, and it shall and may be lawful for said corporation to commence the construction of the said Rail-road or way, and enjoy all the powers and privileges conferred by this act, as soon as the sum of thirty thousand dollars shall be subscribed to said stock.

Sec. 3.   That all persons who shall become stockholders, pursuant to this act, shall be, and they are hereby created a body corporate, with perpetual succession, under the name of the Columbus, Delaware, Marion and Upper Sandusky Rail-road Company; and by that name shall be capable of purchasing, holding, selling, leasing and conveying estates, real personal or mixed, so far as the same may be necessary, for the purpose hereinafter mentioned, and no further; and by said corporate name, may contract and be contracted with, sue and be sued, and may have and use a common seal, which they may alter or renew at pleasure; and shall have, enjoy, and may exercise all powers, rights and privileges, which corporate bodies may lawfully do, for the purposes mentioned in this act.

Sec. 4.   That there shall be paid to said commissioners, or their agent or agents appointed to receive subscriptions to the capital stock of said company, at the time of subscribing for the same, five dollars, on each share subscribed; and the residue thereof shall be paid in such instalments, and at such times, as may be required by the president and directors of said company: *Provided*, That no payment, other than the first, shall be demanded, until at least twenty days notice of such demand, shall have been given by said president and directors, in some newspapers in general circulation in this State; and if any stockholder or stockholders shall fail to pay any instalment, or part of said subscription thus demanded, for the space of sixty days, next after the same shall have been due and payable, the said president and directors, upon giving at least twenty days previous notice thereof, in manner last aforesaid, may, and they are hereby authorized to sell at public auction, so many of the shares of such delinquent stockholder or stockholders, as shall be necessary to pay such instalment; and the expense of advertising, selling and transferring the same; and to transfer the share or shares, so sold, to the purchaser; and the residue of the money arising from such sale, after paying the instalment and expense aforesaid, shall be paid to such stockholder or stockholders on demand.

Sec. 5. That at the expiration of the ten days, for which the books are first opened, if thirty thousand dollars of said capital stock, shall have been subscribed; or if not, as soon thereafter as the same shall be subscribed, if within three years after the opening of the books, the said commissioners, or a majority of them, shall call a general meeting of the stockholders, at such time and place as they may appoint, giving, however, at least sixty days notice previous to the time of such meeting, by advertisement in some newspaper printed in the counties through which said road passes and at such meeting, the commissioners shall lay the subscription books before the stockholders then and there present, and thereupon the stockholders, or a majority of them, shall elect, by ballot, twelve directors, a majority of whom shall be competent to manage the affairs of said company; they shall have the power to elect a president of said company, either from among the directors, or others; and of allowing him such compensation for his services, as they may deem proper; and in said election, and on all other occasions, wherein a vote of the stockholders of said company is to be taken, each stockholder shall be allowed one vote for each share he, she, or they may own of the capital stock of said company; and every stockholder may depute any other person to vote and act for him, her, or them, as his, her, or their proxy; and the commissioners aforesaid, or any three of them, shall be judges of the first election of said directors.

Sec. 6. That to continue the succession of the president and directors of said company, twelve directors and a president shall be chosen annually, on the third Monday of October, in each year, in the town of Marion, or at such other place as a majority of the directors shall appoint: and if any vacancy shall occur, by death, resignation, or otherwise, of any president or director, before the year for which he was elected shall have expired, a person to fill such vacant place for the residue of the year, may be appointed by the president and directors of said company, or a majority of them and that the president and directors of the company, shall hold and exercise their offices, until their successors are elected and qualified to serve; and all elections which are, by this act, or the laws of the company, to be made on any particular day, or at any particular time, if not made on such day or time, may be made at any subsequent time and place appointed by the stockholders for the purpose; and said corporation shall not, by any such failure to hold an election at the time and place appointed by this act, be dissolved.

Sec. 7. That a general meeting of the stockholders of said company, shall be held annually at the time and place appointed for the election of the president and directors of said company, that they may be called at any time during the interval between the said annual meetings, by the president and directors, or a majority of them, or by the stockholders owning at least one fourth of the stock subscribed, by giving at least thirty days public notice of the time and place of holding the same; and when any such meetings are called by the stockholders, such notice shall specify the particular object of the call; and if at any such called meeting, a majority, in value, of the stockholders of said company, shall not be present, in person or by proxy, such meeting shall be adjourned, from day to day without transacting any business, for any time not exceeding three days; and if within said three days, stockholders, holding a majority in value of the stock subscribed, do not thus attend, such meeting shall be dissolved.

Sec. 8. That at the regular annual meeting of the stockholders of said company, it shall be the duty of the president and directors, in office for the previous year, to exhibit a clear and distinct statement of the affairs of the company; and that at any called meeting of the stockholders, a majority of those present, in person or by proxy, may require similar statements of the said president and directors, whose duty it shall be to furnish them, when thus required; and that at all general meetings of the stockholders, those holding a majority, in value, of all the stock subscribed, may remove from office any president, or any of the directors of said company, and appoint others in their stead.

Sec. 9. That every president and director of said company, before he acts as such, shall take an oath or affirmation that he will well and truly discharge the duties of his said office, to the best of his skill and judgment.

Sec. 10. That the said president and directors, or a majority of them, may appoint all such officers, engineers, agents, or servants whatsoever, as they may deem necessary, for the transaction of the business of the company, and may remove any of them at pleasure; that they, or a majority of them, shall have power to determine, by contract, the compensation of all the engineers, officers, agents or servants, in the employ of said company; and to determine by their laws. the manner of adjusting and settling all accounts against the said company, and also the manner and evidence of transfers of stock, in said company; and they, or a majority of them, shall have power to pass all by-laws which they may deem necessary or proper, for exercising all the powers vested in the company hereby incorporated, and for carrying the objects of this act into effect: *Provided, however,* That such by-laws shall not be contrary to the laws of the United States, or of this State.

Sec. 11. That if the capital stock of said company shall be deemed insufficient for the purposes contemplated by this act, it shall and may be lawful for the president and directors, or a majority of them from time to time, to increase the capital stock, by the addition of so many shares as they may deem necessary, not exceeding in amount, five hundred thousand dollars, for which they may, at their option, cause subscriptions to be received, giving notice, in the manner herein before prescribed; or may sell the same for the benefit of the company.

Sec. 12. That said corporation be, and they are hereby vested with the right to construct a double or single rail road or way, from some point in the city of Columbus, in the county of Franklin; thence to Delaware, in the county of Delaware; thence to Marion, in the county of Marion; thence (as near by Little Sandusky, in the county of Crawford, as may be found advantageous) to intersect the Mad river and Lake Erie rail road, at or near Upper Sandusky, in the county of Crawford; making such other intermediate points, as may hereafter be found necessary; and to transport, take and carry persons and property upon the same, by the power and force of steam, of animals, or of any mechanical or other power, or of any combination of them, which the said corporation may choose to employ.

Sec. 13. That the president and directors of said company shall be, and they are hereby invested with all the rights and powers necessary for the location, construction, and repairs of said road, not exceeding one hundred feet wide, with as many sets of tracks as the said president and directors may deem necessary; and they may cause to be made, or contract with others for making said rail road, or any part of it; and they or their agents, or those with whom they may contract for making any part of the same, may enter upon, use and excavate any land which may be wanted for the site of said road, or for any other purpose necessary or useful in the construction or repair of said road, or its works; and that they may build bridges, fix scales and weights, lay rails, take and use any earth, timber, gravel, stone, or other materials, which may be wanted for the construction of said road, or any part thereof, or of any of its works; and may make and construct all works whatsoever, which may be necessary in the construction of said road.

Sec. 14. That the president and directors of said company, or a majority of them, or any person or persons authorized by a majority of them, may agree with the owner or owners of any land, timber, gravel, stone, earth, or other materials, or any improvement which may be wanted for the construction or repair of said road, or any of its works, for the purchase, use or occupation of the same; and if they cannot agree, or if the owner or owners, or any of them, be a married woman, under age, or of unsound mind, or out of the county within which the property wanted may lie when such land or materials may be wanted, application may be made to any justice of the peace of such county, who shall thereupon issue his warrant, under his hand and seal, to the sheriff of the county, or to some disinterested person, if the sheriff shall be interested, requiring him to summon a jury of twelve men, of said county, (not related, or in any wise interested) to meet, on the land, or near to the other property, or materials, to be valued on a day named in said warrant, not less than ten, nor more than twenty days, from the date thereof; and if, at the said time and place, any of said persons summoned do not attend, the said sheriff, or summoner, shall immediately summons as many persons as may be necessary, with the persons in attendance, to furnish a pannel of twelve jurors, in attendance; and from them, each party, his, her, or their agent, or if either be not present, in person, or by agent, the sheriff, or summoner, for him, it, her, or them, may strike off three jurors, and the remaining six shall act as a jury of inquest of damages; and before they act as such, the said sheriff, or summoner, shall administer to each of them, an oath, or affirmation, that they will justly and impartially value the damages, which the owner or owners will sustain (if any) by the use and occupation of such land, property, earth, stone, or other materials, by said company; and the jury estimating the damages, if for land occupied by said road, shall take into the estimate the benefits resulting to said owner or owners, by reason of said road passing through, or upon said land, towards the extinguishment of said claim for damages; and the said jury shall reduce their inquisition to writing, and shall sign and seal the same; and it shall then be returned to the clerk of the court of common pleas of said county, and by said clerk filed in his office, and shall be confirmed by said court at its next or some subsequent term, if no sufficient cause to the contrary be shown; and when confirmed, shall be recorded by said clerk, at the expense of said company; but if set aside, the said court may direct another inquisition to be taken, in the manner above prescribed; and such inquisition shall describe the property taken, or the bounds of the lands condemned; and such valuation, when paid or tendered to the owner or owners of said property, or land, or his, her, or their legal representatives, shall entitle said company to the right and interest in said personal property, and to the use and occupation of said landed property for the purposes of said road, thus valued, as fully as if it had been conveyed by the owner or owners; and the valuation, if not received when tendered, may, at any time thereafter, be recovered from said company, without costs, or interest; and that said sheriff, or summoner, and jurors shall be entitled to demand and receive from said company, the same fees as are allowed for like services, in cases of fixing the value of real estate previous to sale, under execution at law.

Sec. 15. That whenever in the construction of said road, it shall be necessary to cross or intersect any established road, or way, it shall be the duty of the president and directors of said company, so to construct said rail-road as not to impede or obstruct the transportation of persons or property along such established road or way; or when it shall be necessary to pass through the land of any individual, it shall be also their duty to provide for such individual, proper wagon ways across said road, from any part of his land to another.

Sec. 16. That if said company shall neglect to provide proper wagon ways across said road, as required by the fifteenth section of this act, it shall be lawful for any individual or individuals to sue said company, and recover such damages as a jury may think him, her or them, entitled to, for such neglect, with costs of suit.

Sec. 17. That whenever it shall be necessary for said company to have, use or occupy any land or materials in the construction or repair of said road, or any part thereof, or their works or necessary buildings, the president and directors of said company, or their agent or agents, or those employed by them in making or repairing the same, may immediately take and use the same, they having first caused the property wanted to be viewed and appraised by a jury, (formed in the manner hereinbefore prescribed,) in those cases where the property is to be changed or altered, by admixture with other substances, before such alteration is made; and the inquest of said jury, after tender of the valuation, shall be a bar to all actions for the taking or using such property.

Sec. 18. That if it shall be necessary for the said rail road company, in the selection of the route or construction of the road, by them to be laid out and constructed, or any part of it, to connect the same with, or to use any turnpike road or bridge, made or erected by any company, or person or persons incorporated or authorized by any law of this State, it shall be lawful for said president and directors to contract and agree with any such other corporation, person or persons, for the right to use said road or bridge, or for the transfer of any of the corporate or other rights and privileges of such corporation, person or persons, to the said company hereby incorporated; and every such other corporation, person or persons incorporated, or acting under the laws of this State, is, and are hereby authorized to make such agreement, contract or transfer, by and through the agency of the person or persons authorized by their respective acts of incorporation, to exrecise their corporate powers, or by such person or persons as, by any law of this State is, are, or shall be entrusted with the management and direction of such turnpike road or bridge, or any of the rights or privileges aforesaid; and every contract, agreement, or transfer, made in pursuance of the authority hereby granted, when executed by the parties, under their respective corporate seals, or otherwise legally authenticated, shall vest in the company hereby incorporated, all such road, part of road, rights, privileges, and the right to use and enjoy the same, as fully as they might be used, exercised and enjoyed by said corporation, person or persons, of whom they were obtained.

Sec. 19. That the said president and directors shall have power, and they are hereby authorized, to purchase with the funds of said company, and place on the rail road constructed by them under this act, all machines, vehicles, wagons or carriages, of any description whatsoever, which they may deem necessary and proper for the purposes of transportation on said road; and they shall have power to charge for tolls, and the transportation of persons, goods, produce, merchandize or other property of any kind whatsoever, transported by them along said rail way, any sum not exceeding the following rates: on all goods, merchandize, or property of any description whatsoever, a sum not exceeding one and a half cents per mile for tolls, and five cents per mile per ton for transportation, on all goods, produce, merchandize or other property of any description whatsoever, transported by them or their agent, and for the transportation of passengers not exceed three cents per mile for each passenger; and any other company, person or persons, paying the tolls aforesaid, may, with suitable and proper cars, transport persons or property on said road, subject to the by-laws of said company as to the construction and speed of said cars; and the said road, with all its works, improvements and profits, and all machinery used on said road for transportation, are hereby invested in the company hereby incorporated, and their successors forever; and the shares of the capital stock of said company shall be deemed and considered personal property, transferable by assignment, agreeably to the by-laws of said company.

Sec. 20. That the president and directors of said company shall semi-annually declare and make such dividend as they may deem proper, of the nett profits arising from the resources of said company, after deducting outstand standing debts, the necessary current and contingent expenses; and that they shall divide the same among the stockholders in proportion to the amount of stock by them subscribed and paid in.

Sec. 21. That any other rail road company now, or hereafter to be chartered, may join and connect any rail road with the road hereby contemplated, and run cars upon the same under the rules and regulations of the president and directors of this rail road company as to the speed and construction of said cars; and full right and privilege is hereby reserved to the

State, or the citizens, or any company incorporated by law of this State, to cross the road hereby incorporated: *Provided*, That in so crossing, no injury shall be done to the works of the company hereby incorporated.

Sec. 22.   That if any person or persons shall wilfully, by any means whatever, injure, impair or destroy any part of said rail road, constructed by said company under this act, or any of the necessary works, buildings or machinery of said company, such person or persons so offending shall each of them, for every such offence, forfeit and pay to the said company a sum not exceeding three fold the damages, which may be recovered in the name of the president and directors of said company, by an action of debt in the court of common pleas of the county wherein the offence shall be committed, and shall also be subject to an indictment in said court; and on conviction of such offence, shall be punished by fine and imprisonment, at the discretion of the court.

Sec. 23.   That if this road shall not be commenced in five years from the passage of this act, and completed within fifteen years from the time of commencement thereof, then this act shall be null and void.

Sec. 24.   If the Legislature of this State shall, after the expiration of thirty-five years from the passage of this act, make provisions by law for the repayment to the said company of the amount expended by them in the construction of said road, together with all moneys expended by them for necessary permanent fixtures, at the time of purchase for the [use] of said road, with an advance of fifteen per cent. thereon, then said road, with all fixtures and appurtenances, shall vest in and become the property of the State of Ohio, of which cost an accurate account shall be kept and submitted to the General Assembly, duly attested by the oaths of the officers of said company, whenever the General Assembly shall demand the same.

Sec. 25.   Whenever the dividends of said company shall exceed the rate of six per cent. per annum, the Legislature of this State may impose such reasonable taxes on the amount of such dividends as may be received from other rail road companies.

Sec. 26.   This act is hereby declared to be a public act, and shall be so received and construed in all courts of justice and elsewhere.

WILLIAM MEDILL,
Speaker pro tem. of the House of Representatives.
ELIJAH VANCE,
Speaker of the Senate.

February 29, 1836.

To incorporate the Presbyterian Congregation, in Carrollton.

Sec. 1.   *Be it enacted by the General Assembly of the State of Ohio,* That James Sinclair, James Cameron, James Davis, John Thompson, John Dunlap, John S. Hunter, John Ebersole, John M'Cormick, Josiah B. Emery, Jonathan M'Elderry, William Harkless, Daniel Van Horne, Daniel M'Cook, James Hanna, William Holmes, and William Ogle, and their as sociates for the time being, be, and they are hereby created a body corporate and politic, by the name of "The Presbyterian Congregation, in Carrollton," and as such shall remain and have perpetual succession; subject however to such future regulations as the Legislature may think proper to make, touching matters of mere temporal concernment.

Sec. 2. That the said corporation shall be capable in law, by the name aforesaid, of suing and being sued, pleading and being impleaded, in any action or suit, in any court having competent jurisdiction.

Sec. 3. That the said corporation, by the name aforesaid, shall be capable in law of having, receiving, acquiring, and holding, either by trust, grant, devise or purchase, any estate, real, personal or mixed, which may become the property of said corporation: *Provided*, The annual income of all such property shall not exceed the sum of two thousand dollars: *And provided, also*, That all such property shall be considered as held in trust, under the management and at the disposal of said corporation, for the purpose of promoting the interest of said congregation, defraying the expenses incident to their mode of worship, and maintaining any institutions of charity or education that may therewith be connected: *Provided, moreover*, That when money or other property shall be given, granted, bequeathed or devised to said congregation for any particular use or purpose, it shall be faithfully applied to such end or purpose.

Sec. 4. That on the third Monday of October, one thousand eight hundred and thirty-six, and on the third Monday of October, in each and every year, after the year eighteen hundred and thirty six, there shall be elected five trustees, and such other officers as the said congregation may deem necessary; who shall hold their offices for one year, and until their successors shall be elected: *Provided*, That a failure to make an election on the day appointed, shall not work a forfeiture of the privileges of the corporation; but in every such failure, from any cause, the trustees, or any two of them, shall have power to appoint such other day for an election as they may judge fit.

Sec. 5. That all elections shall be by ballot, and shall be determined by a plurality of votes; each male supporter, by subscription of said congregation, being entitled to one vote, in this, as in all other matters, touching the interest of the corporation.

Sec. 6. That extra meetings of the congregation shall and may be called by the trustees, or any two of them, at any time, on their giving ten days previous notice, by advertisement in three public places in Carrollton, one of which shall be on the door of the house used by said congregation as a place of public worship.

Sec. 7. That the trustees, or a majority of them, may establish a common seal, which they may alter, change or renew, at pleasure; and shall have power and authority to make all contracts in behalf of the corporation, and to manage all pecuniary and prudential matters, and other concerns pertaining to the good order, interest, and welfare of the congregation; and to make such rules, regulations or by-laws, consistent with the constitution and laws of the United States, and of the State of Ohio, as they may deem advisable, from time to time, for their own government and for that of the corporation: *Provided*, That they shall make no by-laws, or pass any order for the imposing or assessing of any taxes, or for the sales of any property, on account of the corporation, unless by the consent of said corporation, expressed by a majority of the male supporters of said congregation present, upon a day legally advertised for that purpose.

Sec. 8. That all process against the said corporation shall be by summons, and the leaving a copy of such summons with any one of the trustees, shall be deemed in law a sufficient service to bind said corporation.

Sec. 9. That John S. Hunter, John Thompson, William Holmes, James Hanna, and John M'Cormick, be, and they are hereby constituted trustees of said congregation, with full power to act until the first annual meeting, and until their successors are chosen.

WILLIAM MEDILL,
Speaker pro tem. of the House of Repeesentatives.

ELIJAH VANCE,
Speaker of the Senate.

February 29, 1836.

AN ACT

To amend the act entitled "An act to incorporate the Union Bridge Company," passed February 11th, 1832.

Sec. 1. *Be it enacted by the General Assembly of the State of Ohio,* That for the purpose of further enabling the Union Bridge Company to construct a substantial and permanent bridge across the Little Miami river, at or near Turpin's Ferry, in Hamilton county, and to construct and secure a good substantial turnpike road from said bridge to some eligible point on the Cincinnati, Columbus and Wooster turnpike road, and of keeping the same in good repair, and said company shall have the right to enter on any lands in the vicinity of the site of said bridge, and take from thence stone, gravel, sand, earth, or other materials, necessary for the construction of said road, and the embankments of said bridge: *Provided,* That nothing herein contained shall be [so] construed as to prohibit persons on whose lands they may enter, and therefrom remove materials aforesaid, from claiming and receiving damages as hereinafter provided.

Sec. 2. That if any person or persons, on whose lands said company may enter, for the purpose of removing any of the aforenamed materials, should claim or demand damages therefor, and the person or persons so claiming and the said company not be able to agree upon the amount of damages, it shall be the duty of the sheriff of Hamilton county, on application of either of the said parties, to appoint three disinterested freeholders, who, upon a day to be named by said sheriff, shall meet, and after taking an oath or affirmation to faithfully and impartially discharge the duties by this act required of them, shall proceed to examine any claim or claims that may be submitted to them; make out their assessment, or assessments, in writing, of the damages, if any; a copy of which shall be given to the proprietor or proprietors of the land, and another copy to the company, or their agent; and the said company, or their agent shall pay, or offer to pay the owner or owners of such land, the amount of such assessed damages, before they or he shall enter upon, or take any materials for the purpose aforesaid; and in all cases where damages are assessed the company shall pay all expenses of such assessment, and where no damages are assessed, the person or persons claiming the same shall pay the expenses.

WILLIAM MEDILL,
Speaker pro tem. of the House of Representatives.
ELIJAH VANCE,
Speaker of the Senate.

February 29, 1836.

AN ACT

To incorporate the town of Higginsport, in the county of Brown.

Sec. 1. *Be it enacted by the General Assembly of the State of Ohio,* That so much of the township of Lewis, in the county of Brown, as included within the bounds, of the town plat of the town of Higginsport, in said county of Brown, as the said town plat now stands on record, in the office of the recorder of said county, be and the same is hereby created into, and, constituted a town corporate, by the name of the Town of Higginsport.

Sec. 2. That for the order and good government of said town, and inhabitants thereof, it shall be lawful for the white male householders thereof, who have resided therein for the space of three months next preceding the day of election, having the qualifications of electors of members of the General Assembly, to meet at some convenient place in the said town of Higginsport, on the fourth Saturday of May next, and on the fourth Saturday of May annually, thereafter, and then and there proceed, by a plurality of votes, to elect by ballot, one mayor, one recorder, and five trustees, who shall be householders in said town; who shall hold their office until the next annual election, and until their successors are elected and qualified; and such mayor, recorder and trustees, so being elected and qualified, shall constitute the Town Council of said town, and any five of whom shall constitute a quorum, for the transaction of business, pertaining to their duties

Sec. 3. That at the first election, to be holden under this act, there shall be chosen *viva voce*, by the electors present, two judges and a clerk of said election, who shall take an oath or affirmation faithfully to discharge the duties required of them by this act; and at all subsequent elections, the trustees, or any two of them, shall be judges, and the recorder, or in

24—L

his absence, some other person, to be appointed by the judges, shall be clerk: the polls shall be opened between the hours of ten and eleven o'clock in the forenoon, and, closed at three o'clock, in the afternoon of said day; and at the close of the polls, the votes shall be counted, and a true statement thereof proclaimed to the voters present, by one of the judges; and the person having the highest number of votes, shall be declared duly elected; and the clerk shall make a true copy thereof, and within five days thereafter, he shall give notice to the persons so elected of their election; and it shall be the duty of the town council, at least ten days before each and every annual election, to give notice of the same, by setting up advertisements at three of the most public places in said town.

Sec. 4. That the mayor, and in case of his absence, the recorder, shall preside at all meetings of the town council; and the recorder shall attend all meetings of the town council, and make a fair and accurate record of all their proceedings.

Sec. 5. That the town council shall have power to fill all vacancies which may happen in said board, from the householders, who are qualified electors in said town, who shall hold their appointments until the next an nual election, and until their successors are elected and qualified; and in the absence of the mayor and recorder from any meeting of the town council, the trustees shall have power to appoint any two of their number, to perform the duties of mayor and recorder, for the time being.

Sec. 6. That the mayor, recorder, and trustees of said town, shall be a body corporate and politic, with perpetual succession, to be known and distinguished by the name and style of the "Town Council of the town of Higginsport" and shall be capable in law, by their corporate name, to acquire property, real, personal and mixed, for the use of said town, and may sell, and convey the same at pleasure; they may have a common seal, which they may break, alter, or renew at pleasure; they may sue and be sued, plead and be impleaded, defend and be defended, in all manner of actions, and in all courts of law and equity; and whenever any suit shall be commenced against said corporation, the process shall be served by copy, which shall be left with the recorder, or at his usual place of residence, at least five days before the return day thereof.

Sec. 7. That each member of said town council, before entering upon the duties of his office, shall take an oath, or affirmation, to support the constitution of the United States, and the constitution of this State, and also an oath of office.

Sec. 8. That the town council shall have power to make, ordain and establish by-laws, rules and regulations, for the government of said town, and to alter, or repeal, the same at pleasure; to provide for the appointment of a treasurer, town marshal, and such other subordinate officers, as they may think necessary; to prescribe their duties, and determine the period of their appointments, and to fix the fees they shall be entitled to for their services; and the treasurer, marshal, and other officers shall before entering upon their duties, take an oath of office, and shall respectively give bond with security, in such sum as shall be determined by the town council, payable to the State of Ohio, conditioned for the faithful performance of their respective duties: the town council shall also have power to fix reasonable fines and penalties for any violation of the laws and ordinances of the corporation, and to provide for the collection and disposition of the same: *Provided,* Such by-laws, or ordinances, rules and regulations be not inconsistent with the constitution and laws of the United States, and of this State: *And Provided, also,* That no by-law, ordinance, or regulation shall take effect or be in force, until the same shall have been posted up for two weeks, in two of the most public places in said corporation.

Sec. 9. That the town council shall, at the expiration of each and every year, cause to be made out and posted up as aforesaid, the receipts and expenditures of the preceding year.

Sec. 10. That the town council shall have power to regulate and improve the streets, lanes and alleys, and determine the width of the side walks in said town: they shall have power to remove all nuisances and obstructions from the streets and commons of said town, and to do all things which similar corporations have power to do: *Provided,* They shall never have power to grant license to retail spirituous liquors.

Sec. 11. That for the purpose of more effectually enabling said town council to carry into effect the provisions of said act, they are hereby authorized and empowered to levy a tax on all the real and personal property, subject on the grand levy to taxation, within the limits of said town, upon the appraisement made and returned upon said grand levy: *Provided,* That said tax, so levied by said town council, shall not in any one year exceed one half of one per centum, on the aggregate amount of all such taxable property within the limits of said town; and the said town council shall, annually, between the first day of April, and the first day of July, determine the amount of tax to be assessed and collected for the current year.

Sec. 12. That it shall be the duty of the recorder of said corporation, to make out duplicates of taxes, charging each individual, within said corporation, an amount of tax in proportion to the aggregate value of the taxable property belonging to such individual, within the limits of said corporation, as the same appears upon the books of the auditor of said county of Brown; and the said recorder shall have power of inspecting the books of said auditor, and to take any minutes or transcripts therefrom, as may be necessary to aid him in the discharge of the duties hereby enjoined upon him, free of expense: when said recorder shall have made out said duplicates, as aforesaid, he shall deliver one of such duplicates to the marshal of said town, or to such other person as may be appointed collector, whose duty it shall be to collect the taxes charged thereon, in the same manner and under the same regulations, as are provided by law for the collection of State and county taxes: and the said marshal or collector, shall, immediately after collecting said taxes, pay the same over to the treasurer of said corporation, and take his receipt therefor; and the said marshal, or collector, shall have the same power to sell both real and personal property, as is given, by law, to the county treasurer; and when necessary, the recorder shall have power to make deeds for real estate, so sold, in the same manner that county auditors are, by law, empowered to do, for lands sold by the county treasurer; and the marshal, or collector shall receive such fees for his services, as the town council may direct, not exceeding six per centum on all moneys so by him collected, to be paid by the treasurer, on the order of the recorder.

Sec. 13. That the said town council shall have power to appropriate any money remaining in the corporation treasury, to the improvement of the streets, alleys and side walks of said town, whenever they may deem it necessary, and to make any other improvements which may conduce to the health and comfort of said town.

Sec. 14. That the mayor of said town shall be a conservator of the peace within the limits of said corporation, and shall have therein all the powers and jurisdiction of a justice of the peace, in all matters, civil or criminal, arising under the laws of this State: and shall give bond and security, as justices of the peace are required to do; he shall perform all the duties enjoined upon him by the laws and ordinances of the corporation; and appeals may be taken from the decision of the said mayor, in all cases, where by law appeals are allowed from the decisions of justices of the peace, and in the same manner.

Sec. 15. That the marshal shall be the principal ministerial officer in said corporation, and shall have the same power as constables have by law; and his authority, in the execution of criminal processs, shall be coextensive with the limits of said county of Brown, and he shall receive for his services such fees as are allowed by law to constables, in similar cases, for like services.

Sec. 16. That the mayor shall receive for his services such fees as are allowed by law to justices of the peace, for similar services, in like cases; the recorder shall receive such fees for his services, as shall be fixed by the by-laws and ordinances of the corporation.

Sec. 17. That if no election shall be held by the electors of said town, on the fourth Saturday of May next, it shall be lawful for any ten householders of said town, to call a meeting of the electors, by giving ten days notice thereof, in writing, to be posted in one or more of the most public places in said town; which notice shall state the time, and place, and object of said meeting, and shall be signed by the said householders; and if a majority of the qualified electors of said town shall attend at the time and place specified in said notice, it shall be lawful for them to proceed to the election of officers, in the same manner as hereinbefore provided for; and the officers so elected shall hold their offices until the fourth Saturday of May following, and until their successors are elected and qualified.

Sec. 18. That the said corporation shall be allowed the use of the county jail, for the imprisonment of such persons as may be liable to imprisonment under the laws and ordinances of said town; and all persons so imprisoned, shall be under the charge of the sheriff or jailor, as in other cases.

Sec. 19. That any future Legislature shall have power to alter, amend, or repeal this act.

WILLIAM MEDILL,
Speaker pro tem. of the House of Representatives.
ELIJAH VANCE,
Speaker of the Senate.

February 29, 1836.

AN ACT

To lay out and establish a graded State road in the counties of Morgan, Perry and Hocking.

Sec. 1. *Be it enacted by the General Assembly of the State of Ohio,* That William Pugh, of Morgan county; John Colborn, of Perry county; and Adam Smith, of Hocking county, be, and they are hereby appointed commissioners, and James Brown, of Perry county, surveyor, to lay out and establish a graded state road, beginning at or near the town of M'Connelsville, in the county of Morgan; thence the nearest and best route to Logan, in the county of Hocking.

Sec. 2. That said road shall in no case exceed an angle of five and an half degrees with the horizon; and the commissioners aforesaid shall in all cases be governed by the act defining the mode of laying out and establishing state roads, passed March 14th, 1831.

Sec. 3. That should either of the commissioners or surveyor die, or remove out of the county, or refuse to serve, the commissioners of the county in which such vacancy shall happen, shall forthwith, on being notified of such vacancy, appoint some suitable person to fill the same.

WILLIAM MEDILL,
Speaker pro tem. of the House of Representatives.
ELIJAH VANCE,
Speaker of the Senate.

February 29, 1836.

AN ACT

To lay out and establish a graded State road in the counties of Holmes and Tuscarawas.

Sec. 1. *Be it enacted by the General Assembly of the State of Ohio,* That Robert Martin, of Holmes county, and John Patton and Christopher Ritter, of Tuscarawas county, be, and they are hereby appointed commissioners, and Anson Wheaton, of Holmes county, surveyor, to lay out and establish a graded state road, commencing in the town of Millersburg; thence the nearest and best route to the town of Berlin; thence the nearest and best route to Waynesburg, in Holmes county; thence the nearest and best route to Bolivar, in Tuscarawas county.

Sec. 2. That said road shall in no case exceed an angle of four degrees with the horizon.

Sec. 3. That the said commissioners are hereby authorized to receive and appropriate on said road, all such subscriptions and donations as may be made for opening and improving the same.

Sec. 4. That the commissioners aforesaid shall in all respects be governed by the laws in force, defining the mode of laying out and establishing state roads; and should either of said commissioners die, remove

out of the county, or refuse to serve, the commissioners of the county in
which such vacancy may occur, are hereby authorized to fill the same.

WILLIAM MEDILL,
Speaker pro tem. of the House of Representatives.
ELIJAH VANCE,
Speaker of the Senate.

February 29th, 1836.

AN ACT

To incorporate "The Wellsville Literary Institute."

Sec. 1. *Be it enacted by the General Assembly of the State of Ohio,*
That Joshua A. Riddle, Henry Cope, William D. Peters, Albert G. Catlett,
James Aten, Joseph Boyce, William G. Murdock, James Stewart, Benjamin Wilson, John F. Patterson, Alexander Wells, Albert G. Richardson,
and their associates, be, and they are hereby created a body corporate and
politic, by the name of "The Wellsville Literary Institute;" and by that
name, shall have perpetual succession; be capable of suing and being
sued, pleading and being impleaded; may have a common seal, and the
same break or alter at pleasure.

Sec. 2. That the said corporation may purchase, receive, hold and convey any estate, real, personal, or mixed: *Provided,* The annual income of
said estate shall not exceed two thousand dollars: *And provided also,* That
no part of the stock of said corporation, or property owned by it, shall at
any time be used or employed for any other than literary and scientific
purposes; the purchase of books, maps, charts, pamphlets, newspapers,
or other useful publications; lands and buildings necessary for the business of the association, and its other necessary expenses.

Sec. 3. That the members of said corporation may, from time to time,
elect such officers as may be deemed necessary, in the manner pointed out
in the constitution of said association; make all such by-laws as may be
deemed necessary to the good government of the same; and affix such
pecuniary penalties and fines, for breaches thereof, as they may deem reasonable and necessary.

Sec. 4. That any future Legislature may alter, amend, or repeal this
act.

WILLIAM MEDILL,
Speaker pro tem. of the House of Representatives.
ELIJAH VANCE,
Speaker of the Senate.

February 29, 1836.

AN ACT

To incorporate the Trustees of the Putnam Classical Institute.

WHEREAS, certain individuals in the town of Putnam, in the county of

Muskingum, for the purpose of advancing the cause of education, have associated themselves together, and organized a board of Trustees; *And whereas,* an act of incorporation would greatly facilitate the object they have in view: Therefore,

Sec. 1. *Be it enacted by the General Assembly of the State of Ohio,* That William H. Beecher, Levi Whipple, Alva Buckingham, Julius C. Guthrie, Solomon Sturges and Albert A. Guthrie, and their successors, be, and they are hereby declared to be a body corporate and politic, with perpetual succession, to be known and distinguished by the name and style of the "Trustees of the Putnam Classical Institute."

Sec. 2. That the said trustees, by their corporate name aforesaid, shall be competent to sue and be sued, plead and be impleaded, defend and be defended, in all courts of law or equity; may have a common seal, and alter the same at any time; and may fill all vacancies in their own body, which may occur by death or otherwise; and may add to their number at discretion.

Sec. 3. That the said rtustees, (a majority of whom shall constitute a board,) shall have power to appoint a president, secretary, and treasurer, and such other officers and agents as they may deem necessary; and the said other officers may or may not be of their own number; and the said trustees may ordain and establish such laws, rules and regulations for the government of said corporation, as they may deem proper: *Provided,* That the same be not inconsistent with the constitution and laws of the United States and of this State.

Sec. 4. That the trustees, in their corporate capacity, and their successors in office, shall be capable in law, of receiving and acquiring, either by purchase, devise, gift, bequest, or otherwise, property, real, personal, or mixed; to be used, improved, expended or conveyed, for the benefit of said Institute: *Provided,* That such property shall be held and used only for literary purposes: *Provided further,* That any future Legislature shall have power to alter, amend, or repeal this act: *Provided,* Such alteration, repeal, or amendment shall not affect the title to any estate, real or personal, acquired or conveyed, under its provisions, or divert the same to any other use than originally intended.

WILLIAM MEDILL,
Speaker pro tem. of the House of Representatives.
ELIJAH VANCE,
Speaker of the Senate.

February 29th, 1836.

AN ACT

To incorporate the Bedford Lyceum, in the county of Cuyahoga.

Sec. 1. *Be it enacted by the General Assembly of the State of Ohio,* That George Thompson, Sidney Smith, Julius S. Benedict, C. G. Dyer, D. B. Dunham, John Tinker, and James Efselstyn, and their associates, together with such other persons as may become associated with them, are hereby constituted a body politic and corporate, with perpetual succession, by the name of the "Bedford Lyceum," to be located in the township of Bedford, in said county; by which name they may contract and prosecute and defend suits, and may acquire, hold control, and dispose of real and personal property, not exceeding the annual value of one thousand dollars; which shall be applied to no other than literary purposes, the purchase of books, maps, charts, pamphlets, and newspapers, and the expenses of the institution.

Sec. 2. They shall have power to form a constitution and by-laws, for the good government of the association, the regulation of its fiscal concerns, the admission of members, and the appointment of its officers, together with such other powers as may be necessary to the corporate existence and proper and efficient management of its affairs.

See. 3. Any future Legislature may alter or repeal this act.

WILLIAM MEDILL,
Speaker pro tem. of the House of Representatives.

ELIJAH VANCE,
Speaker of the Senate.

Mar. 1, 1836.

AN ACT

To lay out and establish a State road in the counties of Putnam and Williams.

Sec. 1. *Be it enacted by the General Assembly of the State of Ohio,* That Ephraim Doty, Jacob Hall, and David Hull, of Williams county, be, and they are hereby appointed commissioners, to lay out and establish a state road, commencing at Greer's Mill, in Putnam county, to Defiance, in Williams county; thence running northwestardly, up Bean creek, at or near Ephraim Doty's; thence crossing Bean creek on the school section, at or near where the county road now crosses; thence up Bean creek, to Evans Port; thence up Bean creek to the state line.

Sec. 2. That in case either of the commissioners refuse to serve, or remove out of the county, his place shall be supplied by the commissioners of the county where the vacancy shall happen, as often as it may occur.

Sec. 3. That the commissioners shall be governed in all respects by the law now in force defining the mode of laying out and establishing state roads, passed March 14th, 1831, and the expenses of laying out and establishing said road shall be paid as pointed out in said act.

WILLIAM MEDILL,
Speaker pro tem. of the House of Representatives.

ELIJAH VANCE,
Speaker of the Senate.

March 1, 1836.

AN ACT

To lay out and establish a State road in the counties of Wood, Henry, Putnam, and Van Wert.

Sec. 1. *Be it enacted by the General Assembly of the State of Ohio,* That Edward Howard, of Wood county; Jacob Dewese, of Putnam county; and Ansel Blossom, of Van Wert county, be, and they are hereby appointed commissioners to lay out and establish a State road, commencing at Gilead, in Wood county; running thence to Franconia, in Putnam county; thence to the county seat of Van Wert county; thence to Wiltshire, in said county; thence to the state line, in a direction to Indianapolis.

Sec. 2. That in case either of the commissioners die, refuse to serve, or remove out of the county, his place shall be supplied by the commissioners of the county where the vacancy happens, as often as it may occur.

Sec. 3. That the commissioners aforesaid shall be governed in all respects by the law now in force defining the mode of laying out and establishing state roads, passed March 14th, 1831; and the expenses of laying out and establishing said road, shall be paid as pointed out in said act.

WILLIAM MEDILL,
Speaker pro tem. of the House of Representatives.
ELIJAH VANCE,
Speaker of the Senate.

Mar. 1, 1836.

AN ACT

To incorporate the Methodist Protestant Church of Wellsville, Columbiana county.

Sec. 1. *Be it enacted by the General Assembly of the State of Ohio,* That Joseph Wells, George Gibbuns, Samuel Gellingham, John Gray, Stephen Fawcett, Robert Pile and Abraham Dayhoff, and their associates, together with such other persons as may hereafter be associated with them, be, and they are hereby created, a body corporate and politic, by the name of "The Methodist Protestant Church of Wellsville;" and as such shall remain and have perpetual succession; and by their corporate name, may contract and be contracted with, sue and be sued, answer and be answered unto, plead and be impleaded, defend and be defended, in any court of competent jurisdiction, in all manner of actions, causes and complaints whatever; and may have a common seal, which they may change, alter, or renew at pleasure.

Sec. 2. That the said corporation, by the name and style aforesaid, shall be capable, in law, of holding property, real ,personal or mixed, either by purchase, gift, grant devise or legacy, which may become the property of said corporation, to any amount not exceeding four thousand dollars: *Provided,* That all such property shall be considered as held in trust, under the management and at the disposal of said corporation, for the pur-

25—L

pose of promoting the interest of said society or congregation, defraying the expenses incident to their mode of worship, and maintaining or supporting any institution of charity or education connected therewith: *Provided, further*, That when any money or other property, shall be given, granted, bequeathed or devised to said congregation, for any particular use or purpose, it shall be faithfully applied to such use or purpose; and that the property and other concerns of the corporation, shall be under the management and control of trustees, to be appointed agreeable to the direction of the congregation.

Sec. 3. That on the first Monday of May next, in the year one thousand eight hundred and thirty-six, and on the first Monday in May, each and every year thereafter, the members of said society shall elect seven trustees, and such other officers as they may deem necessary, who shall hold their offices for one year, and until their successors shall be elected: *Provided* That in case of any failure to elect officers as aforesaid, the trustees may call a meeting at such time and place as they may think proper, for the purpose of electing such officers.

Sec. 4. That the four first named persons in the first section of this act, be, and they are hereby appointed trustees, until the first election, and until others are elected in their places.

Sec. 5. That the trustees, or any four of them, shall have power to call a meeting of the corporation, either for the election of officers, or for the transaction of other business of the society, by giving or causing to be given to the society, immediately after public worship, ten days previous notice; or by causing notification thereof to be put up, in three or more public places, within the limits of said congregation, at least fifteen days before said meeting.

Sec. 6. That any meeting of the congregation, duly assembled, may adopt and establish such by-laws and ordinances, as may be deemed proper and necessary for the good government of said corporation.

Sec. 7. That original process against said corporation, shall be by summons; which shall be served by leaving an attested copy with one or more of the trustees, at least ten days before the return day thereof, and such service shall be deemed sufficient in law to bind said corporation.

Sec. 8. That any future Legislature shall have power to modify or repeal this act: *Provided*. That such modification or repeal, shall not affect the title to any real or personal estate, acquired or conveyed under its provisions.

WILLIAM MEDILL,
Speaker pro tem. of the House of Representatives.
ELIJAH VANCE,
Speaker of the Senate.

March 1st, 1836.

AN ACT

To incorporate the Savings' Institute in the town of Newark, in the county of Licking.

Sec. 1. *Be it enacted by the General Assembly of the State of Ohio,*

That Asa Beckwith, Hezekiah S. Sprague, John Woolf, Richard Harrison, William Spencer and Israel Dille, and their associates and successors, be, and they are hereby constituted a body corporate and politic, by the style of "TheSavings' Institute of the town of Newark," for the purpose of receiving money on deposite, and loaning the same on interest, for the benefit of the persons so making such deposite, and for no other purpose whatever; and said corporation shall be capable in law of suing and being sued, of defending and being defended, and of answering and being answered, in any court of law or equity in this State.

Sec. 2. That said corporators, or a majority of them, after ten days notice thereof being previously given, shall meet at the court house in said town of Newark, and may then and there create a capital stock of any sum not exceeding five hundred dollars, to be divided into shares of two dollars, and may open books for the subscription of said stock; which may be loaned on interest in the same manner as moneys deposited, and the principal shall remain as a perpetual fund, for the security of such persons as may make deposites in said corporation; and that after one hundred dollars of said stock has been subscribed, the stockholders may proceed to the election of a president, five trustees and a treasurer, who shall form a board of directors, and who shall hold their offices for the space of one year; and in case of a vacancy, shall have power to fill the same from among the stockholders aforesaid: *Provided*, That no person shall be allowed to take more than ten shares of said stock, unless the whole amount of stock created as above mentioned, be not taken within one year from the time of opening said books; and every stockholder shall be entitled to one vote for each share of stock he may own, not exceeding ten shares, and one vote for every five shares he may own in addition; but no person shall be entitled in any case to more than fifteen votes in said corporation.

Sec. 3. The treasurer shall, within five days after his election, give bond, with good and sufficient security, to the approval of the president and directors, in any sum not less than three times the amount of the stock created as aforesaid, conditioned that he will faithfully account for and pay over all moneys paid into, or deposited with him, as such treasurer; and that he will faithfully discharge all the duties imposed upon him by the by-laws and constitution of said corporation; and said treasurer may be allowed any sum not exceeding two per cent. as a compensation for his services.

Sec. 4. That said bond of the treasurer's shall be made payable to the Savings' Institute, and shall be filed in the office of the treasurer of Licking county, for the benefit of all persons interested.

Sec. 5. That the treasurer shall keep a true and fair record of the business of said institution; and shall settle with the said president and directors as often at least as once a year; and shall pay over to all persons making deposites with him, the amount of his or their principal deposited, according to the terms of the deposite, together with interest as has actually been received therefor, deducting not more than two and a half per cent. from interest, for contingent expenses and compensation of said treasurer.

Sec. 6. That said stockholders, or a majority of them, shall have power to form a constitution and code of by-laws for the government and regulation of said institute; they may adopt a common seal, which they may alter at pleasure; and regulate the times of holding their elections and other meetings, and make such rules and regulations respecting deposites and loans as they may think necessary and proper, not inconsistent with the provisions of this act: *Provided*, That said president and directors may, if they think necessary, for the safety of the moneys of the corporation, require of the said treasurer other and further security; and in case he fails to comply within three days from the time of such request, they may declare his office vacant, and proceed to the appointment of a new treasurer, who shall hold his office until his successor is duly elected and qualified: *Provided*, That any future Legislature may alter or repeal this act.

WILLIAM MEDILL,
Speaker pro tem. of the House of Representatives.
ELIJAH VANCE,
Speaker of the Senate.

March 1, 1836.

AN ACT

To vacate part of the town of Washington, in the county of Guernsey.

Sec. 1. *Be it enacted by the General Assembly of the State of Ohio,* That the owner or owners of lots, number sixteen and eighteen, Robb's addition of the town plat of Washington, in the county of Guernsey, are authorized and empowered to vacate said town plat so far as relates to said lots, together with so much of the streets and alleys as pass through said lots: *Provided*, That the proceedings thereon shall be acknowledged by proper instrument in writing before a justice of the peace, and recorded in the recorder's office in the county of Guernsey, within six months from the passage of this act.

WILLIAM MEDILL,
Speaker pro tem. of the House of Representatives.
ELIJAH VANCE,
Speaker of the Senate.

March 1, 1836.

AN ACT

Making a special appropriation of the Three per cent. Fund in the county of Seneca.

Sec. 1. *Be it enacted by the General Assembly of the State of Ohio,* That one hundred dollars of the three per cent. fund belonging to the county of Seneca, be expended under the direction of Ebenezer Smith, a resident of said county, in the making of a bridge over Beaver creek, where the state road from Tiffin to Sandusky City intersects the same, and to the grading of the hills on each side of said creek.

Sec. 2. That when the commissioners of Seneca county are satisfied that the said sum of one hundred dollars has been faithfully expended, according to the true intent and meaning of this act, they shall direct the auditor of said county to issue his order on the county treasurer for that amount of the three per cent. fund in his hands, if he should have that amount, if not, then out of the first he may receive from the Treasurer of State.

Sec. 3. That should the said Ebenezer Smith, on any account, fail to perform the duties of the above appointment, or a vacancy should otherwise happen in said office, the commissioners of Seneca county shall appoint a superintendent, to direct the expenditure and application of said money agreeably to the provisions of this act.

WILLIAM MEDILL,
Speaker pro tem. of the House of Representatives.
ELIJAH VANCE,
Speaker of the Senate.

March 1, 1836.

AN ACT

To incorporate the Bedford Library Company in Cuyahoga county.

Sec. 1. *Be it enacted by the General Assembly of the State of Ohio,* That J. P. Robinson, E. G. Dyer and D. G. Moss of Bedford, in the county [of] Cuyahoga, and their associates, together with such other persons as may be hereafter associated with them are hereby created a body corporate, by the name of the "Bedford Library Company," with perpetual succession; and by their corporate name may contract and prosecute and defend suits, and may hold, enjoy and dispose of real and personal property, not exceeding the annual value of two thousand dollars, which shall be used solely for the purposes of a Library company in Bedford aforesaid; and the corporation may appoint such officers and make such regulations and by-laws for the government of its members, and the management of its affairs, as may be necessary and expedient.

Sec. 2. Any future Legislature may alter or repeal this act.

WILLIAM MEDILL,
Speaker pro tem. of the House of Representatives.
ELIJAH VANCE,
Speaker of the Senate.

March, 1st, 1836.

AN ACT

To lay out and establish a State road in the counties of Montgomery and Butler.

Sec. 1. *Be it enacted by the General Assembly of the State of Ohio,* That John Shelby and Michael Gunckel, of the county of Montgomery, and

Jacob Ogle and John K. Wilson, of the county of Butler, be, and they are hereby appointed commissioners, and William H. Long, of the county of Montgomery, surveyor to lay out and establish a state road, commencing at Dayton, in the county of Montgomery; running thence through Germantown, in said county, to Oxford, in Butler county.

Sec. 2. That the said road commissioners shall in all respects, be governed by, and the expenses of laying out and establishing said road, be paid in accordance with the provisions of the act, entitled, "An act defining the mode of laying out and establishing state roads," passed March 14th, 1831, except the appointment of a surveyor, which is provided for in the first section of this act.

Sec. 3. That should any vacancy at any time occur in the said board or road commissioners, or either of them refuse to serve, it shall be the duty of the county commissioners of the county in which such vacancies, or refusal may happen, to fill the same from time to time, as often as the same may occur, by the appointment of a suitable person without delay.

WILLIAM MEDILL,
Speaker pro tem. of the House of Representatives.
ELIJAH VANCE,
Speaker of the Senate.

March 2, 1836.

AN ACT

To lay out and establish a State road in the counties of Henry, Putnam, Hardin and Logan.

Sec. 1. *Be it enacted by the General Assembly of the State of Ohio,* That John Patrick, of the county of Henry, Jonathan Carter, of the county of Hardin, and John Watt, of the county of Logan, be, and they are hereby appointed commissioners, and William Scott, of the county of Hardin, surveyor, to lay out and establish a state road, commencing at Napoleon, the county seat of Henry county; thence through the village of Ottawa, in Putnam county; thence to the village of Roundhead, in Hardin county, thence to Bellefontaine, in Logan county.

Sec. 2. That the commissioners and surveyor aforesaid, shall be governed in all respects, by the law now in force, establishing the mode of laying out and establishing state roads, passed March 14th, 1831.

Sec. 3. That should a vacancy happen in any of the foregoing appointments, by death, removal or otherwise, the county commissioners of the proper county, shall fill such vacancy as often as it may occur.

WILLIAM MEDILL,
Speaker pro tem. of the House of Representatives.
ELIJAH VANCE,
Speaker of the Senate.

March 2d, 1836.

AN ACT ·

To lay out aud establish a graded State road in the counties of Coshocton and Muskingum.

Sec. 1. *Be it enacted by the General Assembly of the State of Ohio,* That James Shores, and William Galloway, of Coshocton county, and Hugh F. Hogan, of Muskingum county, be, and they are hereby appointed commissioners, and Lewis Wright, of Coshocton county, surveyor, to lay out and establish a graded state road, commencing at the river road, (so called,) leading from Coshocton to Mount Vernon, at or near Cosner's ford, over the Walhonding river, in Coshocton county, and running thence to the town of Zeno; thence to William Galloway's saw mill; thence to the town of Pleasantville; thence to the town of Moscow; thence to Norris' bridge, on the Ohio canal; thence to the town of Dresden, in Muskingum county.

Sec. 2. That said road, in no case shall exceed an angle of five degrees with the horizon.

Sec. 3. That the commissioners aforesaid, shall in all respects, be governed by the law in force, defining the mode of laying out and establishing state roads, passed March 14th, 1831.

Sec. 4. That should any vacancy or vacancies happen in any of the foregoing appointments, by death, removal or otherwise, the commissioners of the county in which such vacancy or vacancies may happen, shall forthwith fill the same as often as it may occur, on being notified of the same.

WILLIAM MEDILL,
Speaker pro tem. of the House of Representatives.
ELIJAH VANCE,
Speaker of the Senate.

March 2d, 1836.

AN ACT

To incorporate the Freewill Baptist Huron Quarterly Meeting, in the county of Huron.

Sec. 1. *Be it enacted by the General Assembly of the State of Ohio,* That John Wheeler, T. J. Carlton, Daniel Ruggles, Luther Palmer, Seth C. Parker, Jeremiah Chapman, Marcus Mugg, S. B. Russell, S. W. Husted, Luther Hodge, E. Curtis, and their associates, and such other persons as may be hereafter associated with them, be, and they are hereby created a body corporate and politic, by the name and style of "The Freewill Baptist Huron Quarterly Meeting;" and as such shall remain and have perpetual succession; and by their corporate name may contract and be contracted with, sue and be sued, answer and be answered, plead and be impleaded, defend and be defended, in any courts of competent jurisdiction: and may have a common seal, and alter the same at pleasure.

Sec. 2. That said corporation shall have power to purchase, hold and enjoy, any estate, real, personal, or mixed, and the same to convey at pleasure: *Provided,* That the annual income of all such property shall not exceed the sum of two thousand dollars: *And provided also,* That all such property shall be considered as held in trust, under the management, and at the disposal of the trustees of said corporation, for the purpose of promoting the interests of said corporation, and defraying the expenses incident to their mode of worship: *And provided, further,* That when money, or other property, shall be given, granted, bequeathed, or devised, to said corporation, for any particular use or purpose, the same shall be faithfully applied to such use or purpose, and to no other.

Sec. 3. At the quarterly meeting of said society, on the last Saturday of December, annually, there shall be chosen, by ballot, by the members present, nine trustees, any five of whom shall be a quorum for the transaction of business; and shall have power to enact all such rules, regulations and by-laws as may be deemed necessary for the good order and government of said corporation: *Provided,* Such rules, regulations, and by-laws be not contrary to the constitution and laws of this State, or of the United States.

Sec. 4. That all members present at said quarterly meeting shall be entitled to vote in the transaction of any business in which the corporation may be interested.

Sec. 5. That original process against said corporation shall be served by leaving an attested copy with any three of said trustees, at least ten days before the return day thereof; and all suits instituted against said corporation shall be in their corporate name.

Sec. 6. That the first nine persons mentioned in the first section of this act, be, and they are hereby constituted trustees of said corporation; with full power to act as such, until the last Saturday in December next, and until their successors are chosen.

Sec. 7. That any future Legislature may alter, amend or repeal this act.

WILLIAM MEDILL,
Speaker pro tem. of the House of Representatives.
ELIJAH VANCE,
Speaker of the Senate.

March 2d, 1836.

AN ACT

To incorporate the Wooster, Massillon and Canton McAdamized Road Company.

Sec. 1. *Be it enacted by the General Assembly of the State of Ohio,* That David Robinson, Joseph Stibbs, Joseph S. Lake, John Goudy, and Nathan Eldirge, of Wayne county; William Henry, Charles B. Cummings, James Duncan, Charles R. Skinner, Jacob Miller, John Harris, George Dewalt, William Christmas, James Hazlett and John Shorb, of the county of Stark; and their associates, be, and they are hereby created a body politic and corporate, for the purpose of constructing a turnpike road; commencing at the east end of Liberty street, in the town of Wooster; thence eastwardly through Dover, in said county of Wayne; thence through East Greenville, and Brookfield, in Main street, in the town of Massillon, to Canton, in the county of Stark; by the name and style of " The Wooster, Massillon and Canton McAdamized Road Company;" and by that name, they and their successors shall have perpetual succession, and all the privileges and immunities incident to a corporation; and shall be capable of holding capital stock to the amount of two hundred thousand dollars, and the increase and profits thereof; and of taking, purchasing, and holding to them, their successors and assigns, in fee simple, any such lands, tenements, hereditaments and property, real and personal, or mixed, as shall be necessary for them in the prosecution of their works; and shall be capable of suing and being sued, pleading and being impleaded, answering and being answered, and of doing all matters and things, that a corporation or body politic, created and established for like purposes, may lawfully do; and may have a common seal, which they may alter or renew at pleasure.

Sec. 2. The above named persons, or any five of them, are authorized to open books for receiving subscriptions to the capital stock of said company, within one year, at such time and place as they may see proper, after giving at least thirty days notice, in one or more newspapers printed in the counties of Wayne and Stark; and the said books shall be kept open under such regulations as shall be directed by the commissioners hereinbefore named, or a majority of them.

Sec. 3. The capital stock of said company shall be divided into shares of fifty dollars each; and when five hundred shares of said stock are subscribed, the commissioners herein named shall call a meeting of the stockholders, by giving thirty days notice as aforesaid, for the purpose of electing nine directors; at which election at least three of said commissioners shall be present, one of whom shall preside; all votes for directors shall be by ballot, each stockholder having one vote for each and every share he may own; stockholders may also vote by proxy, under such regulations as may be prescribed by said commissioners; and the directors thus elected, shall qualify themselves by an oath or affirmation of office; and as soon as organized, proceed to elect from their number a president, whose duty it shall be to sign all contracts and obligations on behalf of the company; all elections for directors thereafter, shall be on the first Monday of January, annually.

Sec. 4. The president and directors shall hold their offices for one year, and until their successors are elected and qualified; they shall, in all cases, manage the concerns of the company, appoint such other officers and agents as may be necessary, fill all vacancies that may happen, until the next annual election; and may require an oath of any of the agents so by them appointed; may call special meetings of the stockholders, by giving notice as before directed; keep a record of their proceedings relative to the company, and do all other matters and things touching the concerns of the company contemplated by this act, and make all by-laws for the government of said corporation: *Provided*, Such by-laws are not inconsistent with the constitution and laws of the United States, and this State.

Sec. 5. That if any stockholder shall neglect or refuse to pay any instalments due, after sixty days notice having been previously given thereof, and the time and place of payment mentioned therein, it shall be the duty of the board of directors to collect the deficient instalment by suit, with interest and costs thereon, from the time such instalment became due; and no delinquent stockholder shall have a right to vote at any meeting of the stockholders, on any share or shares for which he may be delinquent.

Sec. 6. Said corporation shall have the right to survey, lay out and make said road through any improved or unimproved lands, on the best ground and most advantageous route between the various points mentioned in the first section of this act; and use any stone, gravel, timber, or other materials necessary to construct a good, secure and substantial road, found upon the line of said road, when surveyed and laid off; and in case such materials aforesaid be not found on said line, then, and in that case, said company, or their agents, shall have a right to enter upon any unimproved lands adjoining, or in the vicinity of said road, and to dig, cut down, take, and carry away so much stone, gravel, timber or materials, not previously appropriated by the owner or owners to any particular use, as may be necessary to enable said company to construct said road, and the necessary bridges; and if any difference should arise between the owner or owners of any ground on which said road may be located, or from which such materials are taken as aforesaid, and the agents of the company, respecting damages, it shall be determined by three disinterested freeholders, to be appointed by the commissioners of the county in which the subject of difference lies; who, after being duly sworn faithfully and impartially to perform the duties required of them by this act, shall take into the estimate the benefits resulting to said owner or owners, from constructing said road through, along or near such land, which estimate shall be in extinguishment of damages; and which estimate, together with the damages, shall be by them made out in writing, and one copy be delivered by them to the owner or owners of such land, and one copy to the agent of said company; and said agent shall pay, or offer to pay, the owner or owners of said land the amount of damages assessed, before he shall enter upon such grounds, or take any materials, except to survey said road; and all expenses of such assessment of damages shall be paid by said company; and such appraisers shall receive for their services, one dollar and fifty cents per day, for each and every day they may be so employed, to be paid as aforesaid: *Provided,* That nothing in this act shall be so construed as shall prevent an appeal from such decision to the court of common pleas for said county.

Sec. 7. That the president and directors of said company shall cause the said road to be opened, not exceeding eighty feet wide, at least twenty feet of which shall be made an artificial road, and composed of stone or gravel, (except the bridges, which may be made of wood or stone, as said company may determine,) of the best materials that can be obtained, well compacted together in such a manner as to secure a firm, substantial, and even road, rising in the middle, with a gradual arch or curve, with sufficient drains on each side of the road to convey the water therefrom, and shall maintain and keep the same in good repair; and in no case shall the ascent in said road exceed, or be of greater elevation, than five degrees with the horizon.

Sec. 8. So soon as said company shall have completed said road as aforesaid, or any part thereof, not less than ten continuous miles, and so from time to time, as ten continuous miles of said road shall be completed, an agent, to be appointed by the commissioners of the proper county, if not otherwise appointed by direction of the Legislature, shall, on application of the company, examine the same, and report his opinion in writing to the president of the company; and if such report shall state the road, or any ten continuous miles to be completed, agreeably to the provisions of this act, the company may then erect a gate or gates, at suitable distances, and demand and receive of persons travelling said road, the tolls allowed by this act.

Sec. 9. The following shall be the rates of toll, for each and every ten miles of said road, and in that proportion for a greater or less distance, to wit: for every four wheeled carriage, not exceeding two and one half inches on the tread, drawn by two horses, or oxen, twenty-five cents; for every horse or ox in addition, six and one-fourth cents; for every two wheeled carriage, not exceeding two and one-half inches in the tread, drawn by two horses or oxen, eighteen and three-fourth cents; for every horse or ox in addition, six and one-fourth cents; for every four wheeled carriage, of four inches or upwards on the tread, drawn by two horses or oxen, twelve and one half-cents; and for every horse or ox in addition, five cents; for every two wheeled carriage, of four inches or upwards on the tread, ten cents; and for every horse or ox in addition, five cents; for every sled or sleigh drawn by two horses or oxen, twelve and a half cents; for every horse or ox in addition, six and one-fourth cents; for every sled or sleigh drawn by one horse, ten cents; for every horse and rider, six and one fourth-cents; for every horse, mule or ass, six months old, led or driven, three cents; for neat cattle, six months old, twenty-five cents for every score, and a less number in proportion; for every score of sheep or hogs twelve and one half cents; for every four wheeled pleasure carriage, drawn by two horses, thirty one and one fourth cents; for every horse in addition, ten cents; for every two or four wheeled carriage, drawn by one horse, twenty-five cents; for every horse in addition, ten cents: *Provided,* That said company may erect one gate every five miles, upon said road, at which half toll shall be demanded and collected: *Provided, also,* That all persons going to, or returning from public worship; all militia men going to, or returning from their respective muster grounds; all funeral processions; and all persons going to or returning from elections, shall pass toll free.

Sec. 10. That if any person or persons using said road, shall, with intent to defraud said company, or evade the payment of toll, pass through any private gates, or bars, or along any other ground near to any turnpike, which shall be erected pursuant to this act, or shall practice any fraudulent means to evade the payment of such tolls, each and every person concerned in such fraudulent practices, shall, for every such offence, forfeit and pay the company the sum of five dollars, to be recovered with costs of suit, before any justice of the peace, in any county through which the said road may pass, and such offence may be committed.

Sec. 11. If said company shall fail for ten days in succession, to keep said road in good repair, and complaint be made thereof, to a justice of the peace, in the county in which said road is out of repair, it shall be his duty forthwith, to summons three disinterested freeholders to examine the same, and he shall give notice to the toll gatherer at the nearest gate, of the time when said freeholders will proceed to examine the same; and the said freeholders, after having taken an oath or affirmation to act impartially, shall proceed to examine said road; and if the same is out of repair, they shall certify it to the justice of the peace, who shall immediately transmit a copy of such certificate to the nearest toll gatherer where such defective part of said road lies; and from the time of receiving such notice, no toll shall be demanded or received, for such part of the road, until the same shall be put in complete repair, under the pealty of five dollars for every such offence; to be recovered, with costs of suit, of said company, on the complaint, and for the use of the party aggrieved.

Sec. 12. That the said company shall put a post or stone at the end of each mile, with the number of miles from Wooster, fairly cut or painted thereon, and also in a conspicuous place, near each toll gate shall be placed a board with the rates of tolls fairly painted thereon, and directions to keep to the right.

Sec. 13. If any person or persons shall, wantonly or wilfully destroy, or in any manner injure or obstruct any part of said road, or any gate thereon, otherwise than in the just and lawful use thereof, he or they shall be liable to not more than fifty, nor less than five dollars for every such offence, the one half thereof to go to the county in which the offence is committed, and the other half to the informer; and shall, moreover, be liable for all damages to the company, and for all injuries occuring to travelers in consequence of any such damage to, or obstruction of such road; all damages or costs awarded to the company or to travellers, under this section, by a court, or justice of the peace having competent jurisdiction, shall be collected forthwith, by execution and sale of property, without any delay or stay of execution.

Sec. 14. That any person wilfully defacing or destroying any guide board, mile stone, post, or printed list of rates of tolls erected on said road, shall, on conviction thereof, before any justice of the peace, be fined in any sum not exceeding twenty dollars, at the suit of any person, for the use of said company.

Sec. 15. That if any toll gatherer on said road, shall unnecessarily delay any passenger after the toll has been paid, or offered to be paid, or shall demand or receive greater toll than is by this act allowed, he shall for every such offence, forfeit and pay a sum not exceeding twenty dollars, to be recovered as other fines provided for by this act, for the use of the party agrieved.

Sec. 16. That said company shall be and they are hereby authorized and entitled to demand and receive, the like tolls from persons conveying the United States Mail, as from other persons, and in case of neglect or refusal on the part of any person or persons, engaged in the transportation of the mails to pay the tolls by this act authorized to be demanded and received, said company may proceed to collect the same by an action of debt, but shall not obstruct or delay the passage of the mail.

Sec. 17. That if said company shall not, within two years from and after the passage of this act, commence the construction of said road, and within ten years thereafter complete the same, it shall be lawful for the State to resume all the rights and privileges granted by this act: *Provided*, Nothing contained in this section shall be so construed as to affect any real estate, or property acquired under the provisions of this act: *Provided, also*, That this act may be altered or amended by any future Legislature, not inconsistent with the foregoing provision.

Sec. 18. That all fines, penalties, and forfeitures incurred against the provisions of this act, shall be sued for and collected by action of debt, in the name of any person who may prosecute; and when collected, shall be appropriated as directed by this act.

WILLIAM MEDILL,
Speaker pro tem. of the House of Representatives.
ELIJAH VANCE,
Speaker of the Senate.

March 2, 1836.

AN ACT

To incorporate the Hamilton, Rossville, Darrtown, Oxford and Fair Haven Turnpike Company.

Sec. 1. *Be it enacted by the General Assembly of the State of Ohio,* That William Bebb, Issac Matthias, Robert Becket, James Bradbury, Willis Davis, E. D. Crookshank, Hugh Herron, John Clark, Ebenezer Elliot Nathan Brown, F. J. Porter, A. Porter, James Elliot, and Thomas Pinkerton of the counties of Butler and Preble, in the State of Ohio, be and they are hereby appointed commissioners, under the direction of a majority of whom subscriptions may be received to the capital stock of "The Hamilton, Rossville, Darrtown, Oxford, and Fairhaven Turnpike Company," which is hereby incorporated.

Sec. 2. That so soon as said commissioners, or a majority of them, shall have organized themselves, by written articles of association, for the government of said company, in which this act shall be recognized, they may cause books to be opened at Hamilton, Rossville, Darrtown, Oxford, Fairhaven, and at such other places as a majority of them may direct, for the purpose of receiving subscriptions to the capital stock of said company, having given at least thirty days previous notice of the times and places of opening said books of subscription; and if any of said commissioners shall die, resign, or refuse to act, a majority of said commissioners shall have power to fill such vacancy or vacancies: *Provided,* That it shall be the duty of the commissioners to open said books for subscriptions, between the first day of April and the first day of September, 1836.

Sec. 3. That said company shall be capable of holding capital stock to the amount of two hundred thousand dollars, divided into shares of fifty dollars each; that when one fifth or a greater portion of said stock shall have been subscribed, in the manner hereinbefore pointed out, then the said subscribers, and such subscribers as may thereafter become associated with them, their legal representatives, successors, and assigns, shall be, and are hereby constituted a body politic and corporate, under the name of the Hamilton, Rossville, Darrtown, Oxford, and Fairhaven Turnpike Company; and by that name they and their successors shall have perpetual succession, and all the rights, privileges and immunities incident to a corporation; and shall, in their corporate name, be capable of taking and holding capital stock to the amount of two hundred thousand dollars, together with the increase and profits thereon, and of purchasing, securing, holding, selling, leasing, and conveying estate, real, personal, and mixed, so far as shall be necessary for the purposes hereinafter mentioned, and no farther; and shall, in their corporate name and capacity, be capable of suing and being sued, pleading and being impleaded, answering and being answered, in any cause or action, bill or plaint, in any court of competent jurisdiction, in this State, or elsewhere; and may have and use a common seal, and the same may alter at pleasure; and it shall be lawful for any individual, body politic or corporate, or other company or association, or for the county commissioners of any county through which such road may pass, for and on behalf of said county, to subscribe for and own any part of the capital stock of said turnpike company, and upon payment thereof, to be entitled to all the privileges and profits which individual stockholders enjoy.

Sec. 4. That the commissioners hereby appointed, and the president and directors of said company, after they shall have been elected, shall have full power to collect all moneys subscribed to the capital stock of said company: *Provided*, That not more than one tenth part of each share shall be demanded at the time of subscribing, nor more than that sum at any subsequent instalment; and that at least thirty days notice shall be given of the time and place of paying said instalments; and no instalment shall be required in less than thirty days from the day of payment of any preceding instalment.

Sec. 5. That whenever one fifth part, or a greater amount of the capital stock of said company shall have been subscribed, it shall be the duty of the commissioners hereinbefore named, or a majority of them, to call a meeting of the subscribers, at such time and place as they may appoint, by giving at least twenty days previous notice thereof, in some newspaper in Hamilton or Rossville, and lay before the subscribers who then and there may be present, the subscription of said company; and thereupon the subscribers present shall proceed to elect, by ballot, nine directors, to manage the affairs of said company; and at such election at least three of the commissioners named in the first section of this act shall preside; and the directors thus elected shall hold their office until the first Monday of April thence next ensuing, and until their successors shall have been chosen and qualified; said directors shall have power to elect a president and secretary from their own number, and a treasurer from among the stockholders, and to perform all duties required of them by this act.

Sec. 6. That the stockholders shall annually, on the first Monday of April, meet at some convenient point on said road, and elect nine directors; but a failure to elect on said day shall not work a dissolution of said corporation, but said election may be held on any other day, after twenty days previous notice thereof; in all elections and in all meetings of said company, each stockholder shall be entitled to one vote for each share he may hold, and shall moreover vote by proxy, in such manner as may be prescribed by the by-laws of said company.

Sec. 7. That the directors, when elected, shall take an oath faithfully to discharge their duties; and they shall have power to fill all vacancies which may happen in their own body, or in the offices of their president, secretary, or treasurer.

Sec. 8. That the president and directors of said company shall have power to manage the concerns of said company; to employ and dismiss at pleasure, such engineer or other agents, as they'may deem expedient, and to fix their compensation; to borrow, on behalf of said company, any sum or sums of money not exceeding two hundred thousand dollars, for any term not exceeding thirty years; said money so borrowed to be appropriated for the construction of said turnpike road, and for no other purpose whatsoever; and the individual property of all the stockholders, real and personal, to be liable to the payment of said money so borrowed, in proportion to their respective interests in said company: and said directors, or a majority of them, shall have power to contract with any person or persons on behalf of said company, for laying out and constructing a turnpike road, from Hamilton or Rossville, in the county of Butler, through Darrtown in said county, and Fairhaven in Preble county, to meet the turnpike road to be constructed from Richmond, Indiana, towards Hamilton, at the most convenient and eligible point on the line between Ohio and Indiana; they shall have further power to construct a lateral or branch from the most eligible point on said road, to the town of Oxford, in the county of Butler; and said president and directors shall moreover have power on behalf of said company, to do and perform any act necessary to carry into effect the object of said company; and to ordain such regulations and by-laws as they may deem necessary for its control and government: *Provided*, Such by-laws and regulations be not inconsistent with the constitution and laws of the United States, or of this State.

Sec. 9. That any three or more of the stockholders of said company, owning at least one hundred shares of the capital stock, shall have power to call a special meeting of the stockholders, at some convenient point on said road, by giving at least thirty days previous notice of such meeting, by advertisement, published in some newspaper published in Hamilton or Rossville: that at such special meeting the stockholders, or a majority of those present, may require a full and fair exhibit of the affairs of said company, from the president and directors, whose duty it shall be to furnish the same; and that at any meeting of the stockholders of said company convened as aforesaid, a majority in value of all the stockholders concurring, may remove from office any president or director of said company, and elect others in their stead.

Sec. 10. That whenever any subscriber shall fail or neglect to pay any instalment on his stock, called for by the company, after sixty days notice of the time and place of payment, in manner required by this act, he or she shall for every month the same remains unpaid, forfeit and pay to said company five per cent. on the amount of said instalment; and it shall be the duty of said president and directors, after three months shall have elapsed from the time the same becomes due and payable, to sue for and collect the balance of such instalment, with interest, penalty and cost thereon, from the time such instalment had become due; and should any instalment remain due and unpaid for the space of one year after the same becomes due and payable, the said president and directors may, after giving sixty days notice of the time and place, sell the stock of such delinquent subscriber, for the best price that can be obtained for the same; and if the proceeds of any such sale shall exceed the amount due the company thereon, the surplus, after paying the expenses of sale shall bepaid to the subscriber so failing, or his legal representatives; and the purchaser of such stock shall become a stockholder in said company, subject to all the rules and entitled to all the privileges thereof, to the amount of stock by him or her owned: *Provided,* That each and every original stockholder, or his or her assigns, shall be liable in his or her individual capacity for all debts of the corporation, to the full amount of his or their stock subscribed and not paid unto said corporation: *Provided, also,* That the joint funds of the company shall be first liable.

Sec. 11. That said president and directors shall have a right to lay out, open and construct said road through any improved or unimproved lands on the route through which it may be located between the points aforesaid, and to take from the lands occupied by said road, any stone, gravel, timber, or other materials necessary for its construction; and in case sufficient materials cannot be found on the lands so occupied, said company, or their agents, shall have a right to enter upon any improved lands in the vicinity of said road, and dig, cut down, take, and carry away, so much stone, gravel, or other materials, as may be necessary for the construction of said road.

Sec. 12. That if difference shall arise between the owners of said lands and the company, or its agents, respecting the amount of damages sustained, by the location of said road, or the value of said materials, said value or damages shall be ascertained by three disinterested freeholders of the county, to be appointed by the commissioners of said county, who taking into consideration whether the premises through which said road may pass, or from which such materials may be taken, will be rendered more or less valuable in consequence of said road, they shall assess the damages, if any, and make out their award in writing, a copy of which shall be delivered to the proprietor of such lands, and another copy to the agent of said company; and said company or their agent shall pay or offer to pay, in money, to such proprietor the amount of such awarded damages, together with the costs of assessment, before said company shall enter upon and take possession of any such ground or materials, other than survey and locate [of] said road; but if no damages be awarded to such claimant he shall pay the costs: *Provided,* That before said freeholders proceed to the discharge of their duties they shall take an oath or affirmation faithfully to discharge their duties under this section.

Sec. 13. That said company shall cause said road to be opened not exceeding one hundred feet in width, at least twenty-four feet of which shall be made an artificial road composed of stone, gravel, wood, or other substantial materials, well compacted together, in such manner and after such plan as said company may deem most eligible to make a firm and substantial road, rising in the middle with a gradual arch; and said company shall maintain and keep the same in good repair; and in no case shall the ascents and decents in said road, when completed, exceed one angle of five degrees with the horizon.

Sec. 14. That whenever in the construction of said road, it shall be necessary to cross or intersect any established road or way, it shall be the duty of said company so to construct said turnpike across said road or way, as not to impede the passage of persons or the transportation of property thereon.

Sec. 15. That so soon as said company shall have completed said road or way, or any part thereof, not less than five miles together, and so from time to time, as often as five miles in addition shall have been completed, an agent to be appointed by the Governor, shall on application of the company, examine said road so completed, and report his opinion thereof in writing to the president of said board, and to the Governor; and if said report shall state said road, or any continuous five miles thereof, to be completed according to the provisions of this act, the company may then erect a gate across said road, at suitable distances, and demand and receive from persons travelling on said road the tolls allowed by this act: *Provided,* That no gate shall be erected within any town or village, or within twenty rods of the inlots of any town.

Sec. 16. That said company be, and they are hereby authorized to demand and receive from persons travelling said road, the following tolls for every ten miles travel on said road, and in suitable proportion for a less distance, to wit: for every four wheeled carriage drawn by two horses, or oxen, twenty-five cents; for every horse or ox in addition, six and one fourth cents; for every two wheeled carriage drawn by two horses or oxen, eighteen and three fourths cents; for every horse or ox in addition, six and one fourth cents; for every sled or sleigh drawn by two horses or oxen, twelve and a half cents; for every horse or ox in addition, six and one fourth cents; for every horse and rider, six and a fourth cents; for every horse, mule or ass, six months old and upwards, three cents; for every head of neat cattle, six months old or upwards, one cent; for every head of sheep or hogs, one half cent; for every four wheeled pleasure carriage drawn by two horses, thirty-seven and a half cents; for every horse in addition, six and one fourth cents; for every two wheeled pleasure carriage drawn by one horse, twenty-five cents; for every chaise, riding chair, gig or cart, or other two wheeled carriage of any kind drawn by one horse, twelve and a half cents; *Provided,* That all persons going to or returning from public worship, all funeral processions, all militia men, going to or returning from public muster, all jury men, going to or returning from courts, the armies, troops and baggage of the United States, shall pass the same free from the payment of any tolls whatever.

Sec. 17. That said company shall, when said road is completed, or any continuous five miles thereof, before they proceed to collect toll, set up a post or stone at the end of each mile, with the number of miles from Hamilton or Rossville fairly designated thereon, and also shall place in some conspicuous place near each toll gate, a board or canvass, on which shall be printed in legible characters the rate of tolls allowed by this act.

Sec. 18. That if any person using said road shall, with the intent to defraud said company, pass through any private gate or bars, or on any other ground, (except around cross ways allowed by law,) near to any turnpike gate which shall be erected in pursuance of this act, with intent to evade or lessen the payment of said toll, every person so offending shall for every such offence forfeit and pay to said company five dollars, to be recovered in an action of debt, before any justice of the county where the offence shall have been committed, with cost, and without stay of execution.

27—L

Sec. 19. That if any person shall wantonly or wilfully destroy, or in any manner injure or obstruct any part of said road, or any gate thereon, otherwise than in the lawful use thereof, every such person shall, on conviction thereof before any justice of the peace having competent jurisdiction thereof, be fined in any sum not exceeding fifty nor less than five dollars for every such offence, to be recovered in an action of debt in the name of the State of Ohio, one half to go to the person prosecuting, and the other half to the use of the Deaf and Dumb Asylum; and such person shall also be liable to said company for all such damage, and for all damage resulting to travellers from such offence, to be collected in any court of competent jurisdiction, without delay or stay of execution.

Sec. 20. That any person wilfully defacing or destroying any guide post, or mile post, or stone, or printed list of rates of toll, erected on said road, shall on conviction thereof before any justice of the peace of the county where the offence shall be committed, forfeit and pay a sum not exceeding fifty dollars, to be recovered with costs of suit, in any proper action at the suit and for the use of said company.

Sec. 21. That all persons driving carriages, wagons, or any other vehicle, or riding on horse back on said road, shall on meeting any carriage, wagon, or other vehicle, keep to the right, so as to leave at least one half part of the road free; that said company shall have power by their by-laws to impose such pecuniary penalties for the violation of the provisions of this section, as they may deem expedient; and any person violating the provisions of this section to the damage of any person, shall be liable to an action of damages, at the suit of the party so injured, before any court of competent jurisdiction.

Sec. 22. That if the toll gatherers on said road shall unreasonably detain any passenger after the toll has been paid or tendered, or shall demand or receive greater toll than is by this act allowed, he shall for every such offence forfeit and pay a sum not exceeding twenty dollars, to be recovered with costs before any justice of the peace having competent jurisdiction, at the suit and for the use of the person aggrieved: *Provided*, That no suit shall be brought under this section after twenty days from the time of incurring the penalty.

Sec. 23. That the directors shall annually or semi-annually as, they may determine, declare such dividends of the nett profits of said company, as they may deem proper; and they shall at all annual meetings of said company, exhibit a fair statement of its affairs.

Sec. 24. That should it be deemed avisable by the commissioners under this act, or a majority of them, to construct a lateral branch of said road extending from a point at or near the town of Oxford, in the county of Butler, to the State line, at or near the college corner, so as to intersect a turnpike road proposed to be made from Centreville, by way of Liberty, in Indiana, and terminating at or near said college corner, aforesaid: then and in that case, said commissioners shall be, and they are hereby authorized to open books at such points as a majority of them may direct, for the purpose of receiving additional subscriptions to the capital stock, equal to the sum necessary to the construction of said lateral branch of said road herein contemplated; and in opening said books, receiving subscriptions, and constructing said lateral branch, the corporation shall be governed in all respects by the foregoing provisions of this act: and when said lateral branch, or any part thereof, shall have been made in pursuance of the provisions of this act, said corporation shall have power to ask and demand the same rates of toll per mile, upon the same, as may be charged by virtue of this act upon the main line of road.

Sec. 25. That said commissioners, or a majority of them, shall determine, at the first meeting, at what point, either of Hamilton or Rossville, said road shall commence, and the stock thereof subscribed shall be with reference to such point.

Sec. 26. Said company shall commence said road within three years, and complete the same within fifteen years, otherwise their powers and privileges to cease.

WILLIAM MEDILL,
Speaker pro tem. of the House of Representatives.
ELIJAH VANCE,
Speaker of the Senate.

March 2, 1836.

AN ACT

To incorporate the Vermillion and Birmingham Rail-road Company.

Sec. 1. *Be it enacted by the General Assembly of the State of Ohio,* That James R. Ford, Charles P. Judson, Daniel B. Standerd, Orange A. Leonard, Jonathan Bryant, Cyrus Butler, Perus Starr, Philip E. Bronson, Ebenezer Warner, James R. Tolles, George A. Boalt, and William Adams, of the county of Huron, together with such other persons as may thereafter become asociated with them, in the manner hereinafter prescribed, their successors and assigns, be, and they are hereby created a body corporate and politic, by the name and style of "The Vemillion and Birmingham Rail-road Company;" and by that name shall be, and are hereby made capable in law, to have, hold, purchase, receive and possess, enjoy and retain to them, and their successors, all such lands, tenements and hereditaments, with their appurtenances, as shall be necessary or in any wise convenient for the transaction of their business, and such as may in good faith be conveyed to them, by way of security, or in payment of debts; and the same to sell, grant, rent, or in any manner dispose of; to contract and be contracted with, sue and be sued, implead and be impleaded, answer and be answered, defend and be defended, in courts of record, or elsewhere; and also, to make, have, and use a common seal, and the same to alter at pleasure; and they shall be, and are hereby invested with all the powers and privileges, which are by law incident to corporations of a similar nature, and which are necessary to carry into effect the objects of this association; and if either of the persons named in this section shall die, refuse or neglect to exercise the powers and duties hereby required, it shall be the duty of the remaining persons herein before named, or a majority of them, to appoint some suitable person, or persons, to fill such vacancy or vacancies.

Sec. 2. That the said corporation are hereby empowered to cause such examinations and surveys to be made, between the village of Birmingham, and the mouth of the Vermilion river, in the county of Huron, as · may be necessary to ascertain the most advantageous route whereon to construct a rail-road, and shall cause an estimate to be made of the probable cost thereof, for each mile separately; and the said corporation shall be, and they are hereby invested with the right to construct a rail-road, with one or more tracks, from some point on the west side, and near the mouth of the Vermilion aforesaid, to some point within the village plat of Birmingham, where it shall be deemed expedient; and the said corporation shall have the right to take, transport, or carry persons and property, upon said road, when constructed, by the force of steam, animal, mechanical, or other power, or any combination of them, which the said corporation may choose to employ.

Sec. 3. That the capital stock of said company shall be thirty thousand dollars, and shall be divided into shares of fifty dollars each; and the persons named in the first section of this act, or a majority of them, after having given three weeks notice in one or more of the newspapers published in said county of Huron, or causing written notices to be posted up in three or more of the most public places on said route, may cause books to be opened, at such times and places as they may direct, for the purpose of reciving subscriptions to the capital stock of said company; and at the first opening of said books, they shall be kept open at least three days in succession, from nine o'clock A. M. to five o'clock P. M.; and if, at the expiration of that time, such subscription to the capital stock of said company as is necessary to its corporation, shall not have been obtained, the aforesaid persons may cause said books to be opened, from time to time, giving the notice required as aforesaid, for the term of three years thereafter.

Sec. 4. That as soon as said stock, or ten thousand dollars thereof, shall have been subscribed, the above named persons, or the same number thereof as shall have given the notice above required, shall give like notice for a meeting of the stockholders of said company, to choose directors, at some time at least three weeks thereafter, and at such place as shall be designated in said notice: the holders of one half, or more, of said capital stock, shall attend, either in person, or by lawful proxy; they shall proceed to choose from the stockholders, by ballot, nine directors, each share of the capital stock entitling the owner thereof to one vote; and, at such election, the persons named in the first section of this act, or those appointed to fill vacancies, or any three of them, if no more be present, shall be inspectors of such election, and shall certify, in witness signed by them, or a majority of them, what persons are elected directors; and said inspectors shall appoint the time and place of holding the first meeting of directors, at which meeting five shall form a board competent to transact all business of the company; and thereafter, a new election of directors shall be made annually, at such time and place as a majority of the stockholders, at their previous meeting, shall appoint; and if no election be made on the day appointed, said company shall not thereby be dissolved, but such election may be made at any time appointed by the by-laws of said company; and the directors chosen at any election, shall hold their offices until their successors

213

are chosen; and the said board of directors shall be competent to manage the affairs of said company; they shall have power to elect a president, treasurer, and secretary of said company, either from amongst the directors or stockholders of said company, and of allowing him or them such compensation for his or their services, as they may deem proper; and from time to time, may choose such other other officers as, by their by-laws, they may designate as necessary.

Sec. 5. That upon every subscription, there shall be paid, at the time of subscribing, to the persons named in the first section of this act, or their agents, the sum of five dollars on every share subscribed for, and the residue shall be paid in such instalments, and at such time after the commencement of the work, as may be required by the president and directors of said company: *Provided*, That notice of such demand shall have been given, as is required in the third section of this act; and if any stockholder shall fail, or neglect to pay, any instalment, or part of said subscription thus demanded, for the space of sixty days after the same shall be due and payable, the president and directors of said company may sell, at public vendue, so many shares of such delinquent stockholder, as may be necessary to pay said instalment, and all necessary expenses incurred in making said sale; and may transfer the shares so sold, to the purchaser, and shall pay the overplus, if any, to such delinquent stockholder.

Sec. 6. That the directors of said company shall have power to make, from time time, all needful rules, regulations, and by-laws, touching the business of said company, not imcompatible with the laws and constitution of this State, and of the United States, and to determine the number of tracks or rail-ways, upon said road, and the width thereof, and the description of carriages which may be used thereon; to regulate the time and manner in which passengers and property shall be transported thereon, and the manner of collecting tolls for such transportation; and to fix penalties for the breach of any such rule, regulation, or by-law, and direct the mode and condition of transferring the stock of said company; and penalties provided for by said by-laws, may be sued for by persons authorized thereto, in the name of said company, and recovered in action of debt, before any court having competent jurisdiction; and said company may fix scales and weights, erect and maintain toll-houses, and such other buildings and fixtures for the accommodation of those using said road, and of themselves, as they may deem expedient and necessary.

Sec. 7. That said company shall have a right to enter upon any lands, to survey, and lay down said road, not exceeding one hundred feet in width, and to take any materials necessary for the construction, or repair of said road; and whenever any land, or materials shall be taken for the construction or repairs of said road, and the same shall not be given or granted to said company, and the owners thereof do not agree with said company as to the value to be paid therefor, the person or persons, his, her, or their agents, claiming damages as aforesaid, or if the owner, or owners thereof, are minors, insane persons, or married women, then the guardian, or guardians, of said minor or minors, or insane persons, or the husband of such married women, may select, for themselves, one arbitrator, and the company shall select one arbitrator, and the two, thus selected, shall take to themselves a third, who shall be sworn and paid as arbitrators in other cases; and the three, or a majority of them shall award as arbitrators between the parties, taking into consideration the benefits resulting to said owner, or owners, by reason of said road passing through, or upon, said owner or owners premises, towards the mitigation of such claim for damages, and to render copies of their award to each of the parties in writing; from which award, either party may appeal to the court of common pleas, for the county. in which such lands or materials may be 'situate; and appeals in such cases shall, when taken, be in all respects proceded in as appeals in other cases to said court, and be brought into said court, by filing the award with the clerk of said court, whose duty it shall be to enter the same on the docket of said court, setting down the claimant, or claimants, as plaintiffs, and said company as defendants; when the valuation, so ascertained, shall be paid, or tendered by said company, said company shall have the right to retain the use and occupancy of said lands and materials, as fully and absolutely, as if the same had been granted and conveyed to said company by deed.

Sec. 8. That the said company may construct the said rail-road through any land, across or upon any public road, highway, stream of water, or water course, if the same shall be necessary; but the said company shall restore such lands, road, highway, stream of water, or water course, to its former state, or in such manner as not to impair the usefulness of such lands, highway, water, or water course, to the owner or the public, without unnecessary delay.

Sec. 9. That if said company should neglect or refuse to restore the lands, road, highway, stream of water or water course, as is required in the eighth section of this act, it shall be lawful for any individual, his or her agent, to sue said company, and to be entitled to such damages as a jury may think him or her entitled to for such neglect or refusal.

Sec. 10. That said company may demand and receive for tolls upon, and the transportation of persons, goods, merchandize, produce, or property of any kind whatsoever, transported by them along said rail-way, any sum not exceeding the following rates: on all goods, merchandize, or property of any description whatsoever, transported by them, any sum not exceeding two and a half cents per mile for toll, and eight cents on a ton per mile for transportation; and for the transportation of passengers, not exceeding four cents per mile for each passenger.

Sec. 11. That all persons, paying the toll aforesaid, may, with suitable and proper carriages, use, and travel upon said rail-road; always subject, however, to such rules and regulations as said company are authorized to impose, by the sixth section of this act.

Sec. 12. That so soon as the amount of tolls accruing and received for the use of said road, or according to the provisions of this act, shall exceed five per cent. on the amount of capital stock paid in, after deducting therefrom the expenses and liabilities of said company, the directors of said company shall make a dividend of such nett profits among the stockholders in proportion to their respective shares; and no contingent or accumulating fund, exceeding one per centum of the freight of said company, shall remain undivided more than six months; and that whenever the dividends of said company shall exceed the sum of six per cent. per annum, the Legislature of this State may impose such reasonable tax on such dividends as may be levied on other rail-road companies.

Sec. 13. That if any person or persons shall wilfully obstruct, or in any way spoil, injure or destroy said road, or any thing belonging or incident thereto, such person or persons shall each be liable for every such offence to treble the damages sustained thereby, to be recovered by an action of debt, in any court having competent jurisdiction.

Sec. 14. [That] the State shall have power at any time after the expiration of thirty-five years from and after the passage of this act, to purchase and hold the same for the use of the State, at a price not exceeding the original cost for the construction of said road and the necessary permanent fixtures at the time of purchase, and fifteen per cent. thereon; of which cost an accurate account shall be kept, and be submitted to the General Assembly, duly attested by the oath of the officers of said company, whenever the General Assembly shall require the same; and the right to alter or amend this act whenever the Legislature shall deem the same expedient and proper, is hereby reserved.

Sec. 15. That any other rail-road now, or hereafter to be chartered, may join and connect any rail-road with the road hereby contemplated, and run cars upon the same under the rules and regulations of the president and directors of this rail-road company, as to the construction and speed of said cars; and full right and privileges is hereby reserved to the State or citizens, or any company incorporated by law of this State, to cross this road: *Provided*, That in so crossing, no injury shall be done to the works of the company hereby incorporated.

Sec. 16. That if said rail-road shall not be commenced within three years from the passage of this act, and shall not be completed within ten years thereafter, then this act to be void and of no effect.

Sec. 17. That the president and directors of said company shall have power at any time during the ten years mentioned in the preceding section, to cause an examination and survey to be made between Birmingham and the town of Ashland, in the county of Richland; and if found practicable, said company may extend the road hereby incorporated to Ashland, or to any intermediate point between the places aforesaid, and shall be governed therein in all respects under the provisions of this act; and the said company are hereby authorized to increase their capital stock to an amount proportionate to the increased distance, sufficient to construct said rail-road; and shall cause books to be opened for subscription for such increase of capital stock, in the same manner and under the same restrictions as are provided for in the third section of this act.

Sec. 18. This act is hereby declared to be a public act, and shall be so considered in all courts of justice and elsewhere.

WILLIAM MEDILL,
Speaker pro tem. of the House of Representatives.
ELIJAH VANCE,
Speaker of the Senate.

March 2, 1836.

AN ACT

To lay out and establish a State road in the counties of Franklin and Licking.

Sec. 1. *Be it enacted by the General Assembly of the State of Ohio,* That Michael Niswanger and Noble Landen, of Franklin county, and Jacob Baker of Licking county, be and they are hereby appointed commissioners, and Abraham Boring, of Licking county, surveyor, to lay out and establish a state road, commencing at Columbus, in Franklin county; thence along the old state road to Allum creek; thence up Allum creek to Adam Read's; thence to Noble Landon's in Plain township; thence to Johnstown, in Licking county.

Sec. 2. That the commissioners aforesaid shall be governed, in all respects; by the law now in force defining the mode of laying out and establishing state roads, passed March the fourteenth, eighteen hundred and thirty-one; and the expenses of laying out and establishing said road, shall be paid as pointed out in said act.

Sec. 3. That in case either of the commissioners die, refuse to serve, or remove out of the county, his place shall be supplied by the commissioners of the county, where the vacancy shall happen, as often as it may occur.

WILLIAM MEDILL,
Speaker pro tem. of the House of Representatives.
ELIJAH VANCE,
Speaker of the Senate.

March 2, 1836.

AN ACT

To incorporate the town of M'Connellsville.

Sec. 1. *Be it enacted by the General Assembly of the State of Ohio,* That so much of the township of Morgan, in the county of Morgan, as is included in the recorded town plat, and the additions thereto, of the town of M'Connellsville, be, and the same is hereby created a town corporate.

Sec. 2. That it shall be lawful for the white male inhabitants of said town, having the qualifications of electors of the General Assembly, to meet on the first Monday of May next, and on the first Monday of May annually thereafter, and elect, by ballot, one mayor one recorder, and five trustees, who shall be householders, and shall hold their offices for one year, and until their successors are elected and qualified, and they shall constitute the town council,

Sec. 3. That at the first election under this act, the electors shall choose *viva voce,* two judges and a clerk, who shall each take an oath or affirmation faithfully to discharge the duties assigned them; and at all elections thereafter, the trustees, or any two of them, shall be judges, and the recorder clerk; and at all such elections the polls shall be opened between the hours of nine and ten, A. M. and close at three o'clock, P. M.

of said day; and at the close of the polls the votes shall be counted and proclaimed; and the clerk shall deliver to each person elected, or leave at his usual place of abode, within five days after, a written notice of his election; and the person so notified shall, within ten days thereafter, take an oath or affirmation to support the constitution of the United States, and of this State, and also an oath of office.

Sec. 4. That the mayor, recorder and trustees shall be a body corporate and politic, with perpetual succession, by the name of the town of M'Connellsville; shall be capable of acquiring and holding real and personal estate, and may sell and convey the same; and may have a common seal, and may alter the same; may sue and be sued, plead and be impleaded, answer and be answered unto, in any court of law or equity in this State, or elsewhere: and when any suit is commenced against the corporation, the first process shall be by summons, an attested copy of which shall be left with the recorder, at least ten days before the return day thereof.

Sec. 5. That the mayor, recorder, and a majority of the trustees shall have the power to make such by-laws, and ordinances, and regulations, for the health and convenience of said town, as the may deem advisable: *Provided,* They be consistent with the constitution and laws of the United States, and of this State; and they shall have power to fill all vacancies occasioned by death, removal, or otherwise; to appoint a treasurer, town marshal, and such other subordinate officers as they may deem necessary, to secure the faithful performance of their duties; and to remove them at pleasure; to fix and establish the fees of officers, not established by this act; and to impose fines, not exceding two dollars, for refusing to accept any office in said corporation.

Sec. 6. The mayor shall be conservator of the peace within the limits of said corporation, and shall have the jurisdiction of a justice of the peace, and shall receive the same fees as justices of the peace are entitled to for similar services; he shall give bond and security, as is required of justices of the peace; and an appeal may be had from the decisions of the mayor to the court of common pleas, in the same manner as appeals are taken from the decisions of justices of the peace.

Sec. 7. It shall be the duty of the recorder to keep a true record of the proceedings of the town council, which record shall at all times be open for the inspection of the electors of said town; and the recorder shall preside at all meetings of the corporation, in the absence of the mayor, and shall perform such other duties as may be required of him by the laws and ordinances of said corporation.

Sec. 8. The town council shall have power to levy a tax annually, for corporation purposes, on the property within the limits of said town, returned on the grand levy, made subject to taxation by the laws of this State: *Provided,* That said tax shall not exceed in any one year two and a half mills on the dollar; and the recorder shall make a duplicate thereof, charging thereon each individual an amount of tax in proportion to his property, as assessed on the grand levy for taxation; which said duplicate shall be certified and signed by the mayor and recorder, and delivered to the marshal, who shall proceed to collect the same, in the same manner, and under the same regulations as county treasurers are required by law to collect county and State taxes; and said marshal shall, as soon as collected, pay the same over to the treasurer of the corporation.

Sec. 9. That said town council may appropriate any money in the treasury for the improvement of the streets and side walks, or other improvements; and may have the use of the jail of the county, for imprisonment; and all persons so imprisoned shall be under the care of the sheriff, as in other cases.

Sec. 10. That the town council shall under no circumstances have power to license groceries.

Sec. 11. That any future Legislature may alter, amend or repeal this act: *Provided*, That such alteration, amendment or repeal shall not affect private vested rights, or divert the property or funds of the corporation from the purposes expressed in this act.

WILLIAM MEDILL,

Speaker pro tem. of the House of Repeesentatives.

ELIJAH VANCE,

Speaker of the Senate.

March 2, 1836.

AN ACT

Providing for the sale or leasing of Section sixteen, or lands in lieu thereof, in the townships of Sandusky and Jackson, in the county of Crawford.

Sec. 1. *Re it enacted by the General Assembly of the State of Ohio*, That it shall be the duty of the assessor of Crawford county, on or before the first day of April next, to provide himself with a suitable book for that purpose, and proceed to take the votes of all the white male inhabitants over the age of twenty-one years, residing in Sandusky and Jackson townships, it being composed of originally surveyed townships sixteen and seventeen, in range twenty-one, in said county, who have resided therein for twelve months next preceding the said first day of April, whether such white male inhabitants be, or be not citizens of the United States; and it shall further be the duty of said assessor, between said first day of April, and the first day of May next, to call upon all the white male inhabitants residing in the townships aforesaid, and request any such inhabitant to give his vote for or against a sale of the school land aforesaid, by signing his name under the head of the proper columns; and if such inhabitant be unable to write, said assessor shall write the name of such inhabitant, to which he shall fix his mark or assent; which said vote shall be taken in said book by said assessor, in form following, to wit: The vote of the white male inhabitant over the age of twenty-one years, residing within the bounds of originally surveyed townships, sixteen and seventeen, in range twenty-one, in the county of Crawford, there being twenty of said inhabitants within the same, for and against the sale of section sixteen, or lands in lieu thereof in said townships, granted by Congress for the use of schools in said original townships.

Names of those who voted in favor of a sale.	Names of those who voted against a sale.

Which said list of votes, taken as aforesaid, the assessor shall deliver to the county auditor of said county forthwith.

Sec. 2. That James Clement, Jacob Andrews and Abraham Hahn, are hereby appointed commissioners, whose duty it shall be to view and appraise said school section sixteen, or lands in lieu thereof, so soon as the assessor shall have performed the duties required of him by the first section of this act, they having first taken an oath or affirmation, before some person competent to administer the same, faithfully and impartially to appraise said land; and should either of said commissioners die, or refuse to perform the duties aforesaid, or remove out of said county, then the commissioners of said county shall fill such vacancy so often as the same shall occur.

Sec. 3. That the commissioners appointed by virtue of this act, are hereby authorized, if they deem it expedient, to take to their assistance the surveyor of said county, who under their direction shall make such surveys, divisions and maps thereof, as may be necessary for the performance of the duties required of them by this act; and said commissioners and surveyor shall each receive for his services, one dollar and fifty cents for each day he may be employed in said service, be paid from the treasury of said county, which shall be refunded to said treasury, in manner hereinafter provided.

Sec. 4. That so soon as said school section sixteen or lands in lieu thereof, has been surveyed under the direction of said commissioners, and maps thereof made as provided in the third section of this act, the said commissioners shall cause to be delivered to the auditor of said county, such surveys and divisions and map thereof, and the separate appraisement of each lot laid off in said lands, if the same shall have been divided into lots, and otherwise, the appraisement of the entire section so made under the requirements of this act; and it shall be the duty of such auditor, after giving thirty days previous notice thereof, by advertisment in some newspaper published in said county, and if no newspaper be published in said county, or if the publisher of any newspaper shall refuse to publish the same, then the notice shall be given by affixing such notice on the door of the court house in said county, and in five other public places in said county, three of which shall be in said townships of Sandusky and Jackson, thirty days previous to such sale; and the affidavit of one or more of such commissioners, certifying the manner, time, and places of publishing such notices, shall be conclusive evidence of such fact, to offer such section, or such lots laid off in such section separately, for sale, between the hours of ten o'clock A. M. and five o'clock P. M. on the day designated in such notice, and shall sell the same, and each of the same, to the highest bidder; *Provided,* That neither said lands, nor any part of said lands, shall be sold for less than its appraised value, and that one fourth of the money, bid for the same, shall be paid at the time of sale; and the remaining three-fourths of the money so bid, shall be payable in three equal instalments, payable annually, and successively after the day of said sale, with interest at the rate of six per cent. per annum, on all moneys unpaid, to be computed from said day of sale: and said commissioners may continue said sale, by adjournment, from day to day, for three successive days, if any portion of such land shall remain unsold; and if at the expiration of said three days, any portion of such land shall remain unsold, the sale thereof may be adjourned for a time not exceeding three months, and said commissioners shall in like manner proceed giving like notice of each succeeding sale, until the whole be sold.

Sec. 5. That on the sale of said lands so made as aforesaid, the auditor of said county shall take a bond from each purchaser, with at least one sufficient surety, conditional for the payment to the treasurer of said county, of all the moneys due for said land, or for any part thereof, with the interest thereon becoming due or accruing, to be applied to the use of schools in said townships of Sandusky and Jackson; and said auditor, on the final payment of said bond according to the conditions thereof, shall make and execute a deed or deeds of said land to the purchaser or purchasers thereof, in fee simple; and the said purchase money, when received, shall be deposited in the school fund, for the benefit of said townships.

Sec. 6. That the auditor of said county shall be entitled to receive for all conveyances he may be required to make by virtue of this act, twelve and a half cents for each hundred words contained therein, and in like proportion for any smaller number; and that the assessor be entitled to receive for his services, performed under the provisions of this act, the sum of one dollar and fifty cents per day, for each day he may be necessarily employed in said service.

Sec. 7. That the treasurer of said county shall, out of the first moneys that shall come to his hands of the interest of said purchase money, pay the said assessor, commissioners, surveyor, and auditor, the fees and compensation herein before specified, to be paid to said assessor, commissioners, surveyor, and auditor, as well as all necessary fees and expenses for acknowledging said deeds, and for publishing the advertisements, made necessary by the requirements of this act.

WILLIAM MEDILL,
Speaker pro tem. of the House of Representatives.
ELIJAH VANCE,
Speaker of the Senate.

March 2, 1836.

AN ACT

To define, more particularly, the duties of the Sheriff of Hamilton county, in certain cases.

Sec. 1. *Be it enacted by the General Assembly of the State of Ohio,* That it shall be the duty of the sheriff of Hamilton county, in addition to the duties already imposed by law on sheriffs of counties in general, to visit daily, by himself or deputy, every cell and apartment of the jail of said county, and cause the same to be daily swept, and all dirt and filth to be removed therefrom.

Sec. 2. That the said sheriff shall, at the expense of tth said county, procure a suitable book, to be called the jail calendar, in which the said sheriff shall enter or cause to be entered the names of all persons committed to said jail on criminal process, carefully noting their ages, color, times when committed, the causes of commitment, the magistrate by whom committed, also the times when discharged, and in what manner, whether by acquittal, by order of the magistrate who committed, by habeas corpus, committed to the penitentiary, transmitted to other states, or other counties in this State, consigned to capital punishment, and all escapes and deaths; which calendar shall be the property of the said county, and shall at all reasonable hours of the day be open to the inspection of any citizen of said county, who may wish to examine the same; and the said sheriff, on going out of office, shall deliver up said calendar te his successor in office; and [in] case of the death of said sheriff, his personal representatives shall in like manner deliver up said calendar.

Sec. 3. That it shall further be the duty of the said sheriff to keep in a book for that especial purpose, a regular and accurate account of all expenses by him made for the support of all such persons committed to said jail, and whom the said county is, by law, obliged to support, and shall make distinct charges for every distinct item of such expense, and the time when the same occurred, and shall make a distinct and separate statement of all such extra allowances as may be ordered for the prisoners by the attending physician; and when, in the opinion of the attending physician, an extra allowance is needed, he shall make the order therefor, in said book, with his own hand, the date of its commencement, and the name of the prisoner for whom ordered.

Sec. 4. That the county commissioners of said county, in settling with said sheriff for the support of prisoners, shall require said book of accounts and said calendar to be brought before them; and the said commissioners shall not allow any item or items of said sheriff's account for extra allowances, which have not been ordered by the attending physician of said jail, as pointed out in the third section of this act.

Sec. 5. That said sheriff shall receive, for keeping and providing for a person in jail, per day, eighteen and three-fourth cents, and no more, except in the cases provided for in the third section of this act, any law to the contrary notwithstanding; and no fees shall be allowed said sheriff for letting out of, or receiving into the said jail, under the direction of the county commissioners of said county, such prisoners as have been, or may be hereafter sentenced to be imprisoned in said jail at hard labor, by the court of common pleas of said county.

Sec. 6. That if the said sheriff shall refuse or neglect to perform the duties which, by this act, he is required to perform, he shall, upon conviction therof, be fined in any sum not exceeding one thousand dollars, at the discretion of the court; to be recovered by indictment, to and for the use of said county.

WILLIAM MEDILL,
Speaker pro tem. of the House of Representatives.
ELIJAH VANCE,
Speaker of the Senate.

March 2. 1836.

AN ACT

To revive and amend An act to incorporate the Nelson Academy, passed January 24, 1828.

Sec. 1. *Be it enacted by the General Assembly of the State of Ohio,* That the act to incorporate the Nelson Academy, passed January 24, 1828, be, and the same is hereby revived.

Sec. 2. That Marcus A. Bierce, Wells Clark, Stephen Baldwin, Orrin Smith, Stephen Skiff, Uriel Mills, John G. Stevens and Daniel Everett, with their associates, be, and they are hereby declared a body politic and corporate, by the name of "The Nelson Academy;" and as such, are entitled to all the privileges, and subject to all the duties required of the original corporators, named in the act to which this is an amendment.

Sec. 3. That in case the stockholders of this academy shall fail to elect, on the second Monday of April, annually, as required by the 2d section of the act to which this is an amendment, further time shall be allowed to said stockholders, from said second Monday of April, annually, not exceeding six months therefrom, to hold such meeting.

Sec. 4. That so much of the act to which this is an amendment, as is inconsistent with the provisions of this act, be, and the same is hereby repealed.

Sec. 5. That any future Legislature shall the power to alter, amend, or repeal this act.

WILLIAM MEDILL,
Speaker pro tem. of the House of Representatives.
ELIJAH VANCE,
Speaker of the Senate.

March 2, 1836.

AN ACT

To amend an act entitled "An act to incorporate the Oxford and Miami Rail road Company," passed March 9th, 1835.

Sec. 1. *Be it enacted by the General Assembly of the State of Ohio,* That said corporation may demand and receive from all persons using or travelling upon said rail-road, the following rates of toll, to wit: for every ton weight of goods, of freights of any description, eight cents, for every mile the same shall pass upon said rail-road, and a rateable proportion for any greater or less quantity; for every pleasure carriage or carriages, used for the conveyance of passengers, four cents per mile, in addition to the toll by weight, upon the load: all persons paying the toll aforesaid, may, with suitable and proper carriages, use and travel upon the said rail-road, subject to such regulations and rules as said corporation are authorized to make by the seventh section of the act to which this is an amendment.

Sec. 2. That the time named in the fourth section of the act to which this is an amendment, to open books for receiving subscriptions to the capital stock of said corporation, shall be extended one year from the passage of this act.

Sec. 3. That if the corporation created by the act to which this is an amendment, shall not within two years from the passage of this act, commence, and within seven years put in operation said rail-road, from Oxford to the town of Hamilton or Rossville, then this act shall be null and void.

Sec. 4. That so much of the fourth, ninth and fifteenth sections of the act to which this is an amendment, as is inconsistent with the provisions of this act, be, and the same· is hereby repealed.

WILLIAM MEDILL,
Speaker pro tem. of the House of Representatives.
ELIJAH VANCE,
Speaker of the Senate.

March 2, 1836.

AN ACT

To amend an act to incorporate the Pennsylvania and Ohio Canal Company, passed Jan. 10th, 1827, and the act amendatory thereof, passed Feb. 20th, 1835.

Sec. 1. *Be it enacted by the General Assembly of the State of Ohio,* That the capital stock of said company shall henceforth be deemed and held as personal property, and any share or shares of any stockholder may be assigned and transferred on the books of said company, in person, or by power of attorney, executors, administrators, guardians, and trustees, in such manner as shall be prescribed by the by-laws of the board of directors; but no stockholder indebted to the corporation shall be permitted to transfer his stock while such indebtedness exists, or receive a dividend thereon until all instalments which shall have been required to be paid by the board of directors shall be fully paid, any thing contained in said acts to the contrary notwithstanding.

Sec. 2. That the period at which the states of Pennsylvania and Ohio shall have the right to purchase that part of said canal which lies within their respective territorial limits, shall be, and hereby is extended to the term of fifty years from and after the completion of the same, after which period the said States shall each have the right to purchase for the sole use and benefit of such State, such portion thereof as lies within its limits, by paying to said corporation the amount expended by said company, in locating, constructing and repairing said canal within such State, together with fifteen per centum thereon: *Provided, however,* That the sum so to be paid by said States respectively for so much of said canal as lies within their territorial limits, shall not, together with the tolls received by said company on such portion thereof, be less than the amount of expenditures thereon, and six per centum per annum thereon.

Sec. 3. That the canal commissioner or board of public works shall determine the point of intersection with the Ohio canal, and that so much of the aforesaid acts as are contrary or inconsistent with the provisions herein contained, be, and the same is hereby repealed.

WILLIAM MEDILL,
Speaker pro tem. of the House of Representatives.

ELIJAH VANCE,
Speaker of the Senate.

March 2d, 1836.

AN ACT

To amend an act entitled "An act to incorporate the town of Richmond," in Jefferson county.

WHEREAS, the town of Richmond has it in contemplation to grade and McAdamize Main street, in said town: *And whereas,* Doubts are entertained as to the power of the corporation to borrow money for town purposes: Therefore,

Sec. 1. *Be it enacted by the General Assembly of the State of Ohio,* That the town council of the town of Richmond is hereby expressly authorized to borrow money for town purposes; and to make and publish all necessary ordinances for such purpose.

Sec. 2. That it shall be the duty of the town council, at their annual meeting for fixing the rate of taxation, to levy, assess and make all necessary provision for the collection of so much tax, as will be sufficient to cover any amount of principal or interest due, or to become due within the current year, on any sum borrowed by said council: *Provided,* The said tax or sum to be collected shall not exceed five hundred dollars in any one year.

Sec. 3. That the town council shall have power to alter or change the location of any cross street, lane or alley in said town, or to vacate the same, whenever it may be deemed advantageous to the citizens generally: *Provided,* That any individual or individuals who may sustain damages thereby, be compensated for the same.

Sec. 4. That all acts, or parts of acts, which may conflict, in any manner, with this act, are hereby repealed.

WILLIAM MEDILL,
Speaker pro tem. of the House of Representatives.

ELIJAH VANCE,
Speaker of the Senate.

March 2d, 1836.

AN ACT

To lay out and establish a graded State road in the counties of Perry and Hocking.

Sec. 1. *Be it enacted by the General Assembly of the State of Ohio,* That Adam Binckley, and Jos Rush, of the county of Perry, and John

Westenhaver, of the county of Hocking, be, and they are hereby appointed commissioners, and James Brown, of the county of Perry, surveyor, to lay out and establish a graded state road, beginning at the town of Somerset, in the county of Perry; passing through the town of Mount Hope, in said county; thence to the town of Logan, in the county of Hocking.

Sec. 2. That the said road shall in no case exceed an angle of five degrees with the horizon; and the commissioners aforesaid, shall in all cases be governed by the act defining the mode of laying out and establishing state roads, passed March 14th, 1831.

Sec. 3. That should either of the commissioners or surveyor die, or remove out of the county, or refuse to serve, the commissioners of the county in which such vacancy shall happen, shall forthwith, on being notified of such vacancy, appoint some suitable person to fill the same, as often as it may occur.

WILLIAM MEDILL,
Speaker pro tem. of the House of Representatives.

ELIJAH VANCE,
Speaker of the Senate.

March 3d, 1836.

AN ACT

To lay out and establish a graded State road in the counties of, Morgan and Perry.

Sec. 1. *Be it enacted by the General Assembly of the State of Ohio,* That Samuel Aikens, of the county of Morgan, and Robert Criswell, and Henry Hasleton, of the county of Perry, be, and they are hereby appointed commissioners, and John Talley, of the county of Morgan, surveyor, to lay out and establish a graded state road, beginning at the Muskingum river, in the town of Malta, in the county of Morgan, passing through Morgansville, in said county; thence to Bristol, in Perry county, or to intersect said road leading from M'Connelsville, in Morgan county, to Bristol, in Perry county, as the situation of the ground will permit.

Sec. 2. That the said road shall [in] no case exceed an angle of five and a half degrees with the horizon; and the commissioners aforesaid shall in all cases be governed by the act defining the mode of laying out and establishing state roads, passed March 14th, 1831.

Sec. 3. That should either of the commissioners or surveyor die, or remove out of the county, or refuse to serve, the commissioners of the county in which such vacancy shall happen, shall forthwith, on being notified of such vacancy, appoint some suitable person to fill the same.

WILLIAM MEDILL,
Speaker pro tem. of the House of Representatives.

ELIJAH VANCE,
Speaker of the Senate.

March 3, 1836.
29—L

AN ACT

To incorporate the City of Ohio.

Sec. 1. *Be it enacted by the General Assembly of the State of Ohio,* That so much of the township of Brooklyn, in the county of Cuyahoga, as is contained in the following bounds, viz: Beginning at the point of intersection of the west line of original surveyed lot, No. 50, in said township, with the southern shore of Lake Erie; thence south on said west line of lot, No. 50, its whole length, to the northwest corner of lot, No. 49; thence south the whole length of the west line of said lot, No. 49, to the northwest corner of lot, No. 48; thence south on the west line of said lot No. 48, to the centre of Walworth or Spring run, so called; thence following down the centre of said run to its intersection with the east line of original lot, No. 69, in said township; thence north along the east line of said lot, No. 69, to the northeast corner thereof; thence northwestardly and northwardly along the westwardly line of the farm conveyed to Joel Scranton by Alfred Kelley, to the Cuyahoga river, to the centre of said river; thence down the centre of said river, to the extreme northerly end of the west pier of the present harbor; thence northerly in Lake Erie, on the line of the townships of Brooklyn and Cleveland, to the north line of the township of Brooklyn; thence westerly, on the north line of the township of Brooklyn, to a point due north from the place of beginning; thence south to said place of beginning; shall be, and hereby is declared to be a City; and the inhabitants thereof, are created a body corporate and politic, by the name and style of the "City of Ohio;" and by that name, shall be capable of contracting and being contracted with, of suing and being sued, pleading and being impleaded, answering and being answered unto, in all courts and places, and in all matters whatsoever; with power of purchasing, receiving, holding, occupying and conveying real and personal estate; and may use a corporate seal, and change the same at pleasure; and shall be competent to have and exercise all the rights and privileges, and be subject to all the duties and obligations appertaining to a municipal corporation.

Sec. 2. That the government of said city, in the exercise of its corporate powers, and management of its fiscal, prudential and municipal concerns, shall be vested in the mayor and council; which council shall consist of four members from each ward, and shall be denominated the City Council; and also such other officers as are hereafter mentioned and provided for.

Sec. 3. That the city shall, until the city council see fit to increase, alter or change the same, be divided into three wards, in the following manner, to wit: The first ward shall comprise all the territory lying northerly of the centre of Detroit street, to its intersection with River street; thence northerly through the centre of River street, to its intersection with Centre street; thence through the centre of said street, to the float bridge, and to the centre of the Cuyahoga river: the second ward shall comprise all the territory lying southerly of the said described boundary of the first ward, and northerly of the centre of Prospect and Franklin streets, to the intersection of Franklin with Columbus street; thence with the centre or Columbus street, to the centre of the Cuyahoga river: the third ward shall include all the territory not embraced in the first and second wards, and lying southerly of the above described southerly boundary of the second ward, until the wards shall be altered, or increased in number, by the city council.

Sec. 4. That the mayor of said city shall be elected by the qualified voters thereof, on the last Monday of March, annually, and shall hold his office for the term of one year, and until his successor shall be chosen and qualified; it shall be his duty to preside at the meetings of the city council, when other duties will permit; to recommend to said council such measures as he may deem expedient; and when presiding at the meetings of the city council, he shall have a casting vote, when the votes of the members are tied; to be vigilant and active at all times in causing the laws and ordinances of said city to be put in force and duly executed; to inspect the conduct of all subordinate officers in the government thereof; and as far as in his power, to cause all negligence, carelessness and positive violation of duty, to be prosecuted and promptly punished; he shall keep the seal of said city; sign all commissions, licenses, and permits, which may be granted by or under the authority of the city council; and shall keep an office in some convenient place in said city, to be provided by the city council; he shall perform such duties and exercise such powers as, from time to time, devolve upon him by the ordinances of said city, not inconsistent with the provisions of this act, and the character and dignity of his office; and generally do and perform all such other duties and exercise such other powers as pertain to the office of mayor; he shall, in his judicial capacity, have exclusive original jurisdiction of all cases for the violation of the ordinances of said city; and he is hereby vested with powers coequal with justices of the peace, within the county of Cuyahoga; shall have power to exercise the same jurisdiction and authority, in civil and criminal cases, within the limits of said county, and shall be entitled to the same fees as justices of the peace in like cases; all process shall be directed to the city marshal, who is hereby authorized and empowered to exercise the same powers, in serving such process, levying execution, and making distress on delinquents, in civil and criminal cases; and shall be entitled to the same fees as constables are for the like services: and in case of misconduct in office, of the mayor, recorder, treasurer, marshal, councilmen, or any subordinate officer, the city council have hereby power to remove him, or any of them, by an agreement of a majority of two-thirds concurring; and the mayor shall have power, and it shall be lawful for him, to award all such process, and issue all such writs as shall be necessary to enforce the due administration of right and justice throughout said city, and for the lawful exercise of his jurisdiction, agreeable to the usages and principles of law: *Provided,* That in all cases brought before the said mayor, for the violations of the ordinances of said city, and when the said mayor shall adjudge the defendant or defendants to pay a fine of fifteen dollars or upwards, exclusive of costs, the defendant or defendants, shall have a right of appealing from said judgment to the court of common pleas of Cuyahoga county, upon giving bonds in double the amount of said judgment and costs, and with such security as shall be approved of by said mayor, within ten days from the rendition of said judgment; which bond shall be conditioned to pay the judgment and costs, which may be recovered against him, her, or them, in the said court of common pleas; which appeal, when [perfected] by giving bond as aforesaid, shall entitle the party appealing, to the same rights and privileges, subject to the same conditions, restrictions and limitations, as by the laws of the State, are prosecuted; and it shall be sufficient to set forth in the indictment, the offence, in the words of the ordinance said to be violated; and to refer to said ordinance, by title only, without reciting such ordinance, and by concluding said indictment, against the peace, and dignity of the State of Ohio; and the said court of common pleas of Cuyahoga county, is hereby authorized, empowered and directed, to take cognizance and hear and determine all such causes as shall be brought before them by appeal as aforesaid, and assess such fine, and pass such judgment against such defendant or defendants as shall be prescribed by the ordinances of the city; the mayor shall moreover have authority to take and certify the acknowledgments of all deeds for the conveyance or incumbrance of real estate, in the State of Ohio; and it shall be lawful for him to order any persons brought before him, charged with the commission of any criminal offence, in any State or Territory of the United States, upon proof, by him adjudged, to direct such accused person to be delivered to some suitable person or persons, to be conveyed to the proper jurisdiction for trial.

Sec. 5. That the qualified electors of each ward in said city shall, on the last Monday of March next, elect by ballot, four members of the city council, in each ward, who shall have resided in said city one year, and possess the qualifications of electors, and shall be residents and inhabitants in the ward in which they shall be elected, and the members so elected, shall meet in each ward within five days, and determine by lot the time they shall severally serve, two shall serve one year, and two shall serve two years, so that one half of them shall be out every year; and at every annual election, which shall be on the last Monday of March in every year, there shall be elected two new members of said council, in each ward, who shall continue in office two years, and until their successors shall be elected and qualified; and the members so elected shall, when assembled together and duly organized, constitute the city council, a majority of the whole number of whom shall be necessary to constitute a quorum for the transaction of business; they shall be judges of elections and qualifications of their own members, and shall determine the rules of their proceedings, and shall keep a journal thereof, which shall be open to the inspection and examination of every citizen; and may compel the attendance of absent members, in such manner and under such penalties as they think fit to [prescribe]; they shall meet in the council chamber, or some other convenient place in said city, within five days after the election, and after having taken the oath of office before the mayor, or some other officer qualified to administer oaths, they shall elect from their own body, a president, who shall, in case of the absence of the mayor, preside in their meetings for one year; and a recorder and treasurer, who shall hold their offices for one year and until their successors are elected and qualified.

Sec. 6. That the city council shall provide the places and fix the times of holding their meetings, not herein otherwise provided for, which at all times shall be open for the public; they shall appoint all city surveyors, clerk of the market, street commissioners, health officers, weighers of hay, measurers of wood and coal, wharf masters, and such other city officers, whose appointment or election is not herein otherwise provided for, as shall be necessary for the good government of said city, and the due exercise of its corporate powers, and which shall have been provided for by ordinance; and all city officers, whose time of service is not prescribed, and whose powers and duties are not defined in and by this act, shall perform such duties, exercise such powers, and continue in office for such term of time, not exceeding one year, as shall be prescribed by ordinance.

Sec. 7. That the city council shall have the custody, care, superintendence, management and control of all the real and personal estate, moneys, funds and revenues, which from time to time may be owned by, or of right belong to said city; with full power to purchase, hold, possess, use, occupy, sell and convey the same, for the use and benefit of said city, and the inhabitants thereof: *Provided*, That the city council shall not have power to sell any public landing, wharf or wharves, dock or docks, basin or basins, or any interest therein, or part thereof, which now is, or hereafter may be used and kept for the accommodation and convenience of the merchants, and others engaged in the trade, commerce and navigation of said city.

Sec. 8. That the said city council shall have power, and it is hereby made their duty, to make and publish, from time to time, all such ordinances as shall be necessary to secure to said city, and the inhabitants thereof, against injury from fire, thieves, robbers, burglars, and all other persons violating the public peace; for the suppression of riots, and gambling, and indecent and disorderly conduct; for the punishment of all lewd and lascivious behaviour in the streets or other public places of said city; and for the apprehension and punishment of all vagrants and idle persons; they shall have power, from time to time, to make and publish all such by-laws and ordinances, as they shall deem necessary, to provide for the safety, preserve the health, promote the prosperity and improve the morals, order, comfort and convenience of said city, and the inhabitants thereof: to impose fines, forfeitures, and penalties, on all persons offending against the laws and ordinances of said city, and provide for the prosecution, recovery and collection thereof; and shall have power to regulate, by ordinance, the keeping and sale of gunpowder within the city.

Sec. 9. That the said city council shall have power to establish a board of health for said city: invest it with such powers, and impose upon it such duties, as shall be necessary to secure said city, and the inhabitants thereof, from the evils, distress and calamities of contagious, infectious and malignant diseases: provide for its proper organization, and the election or appointment of the necessary officers thereof; and make such by-laws, rules and regulations for its government and support, as shall be required for enforcing the most prompt and efficient performance of its duties, and the lawful exercise of its powers: they shall have power, whenever the public peace of said city shall require it, to establish a city watch, and organize the same under the general superintendence of the city marshal, or other proper officer; prescribe its duties and define its powers, in such a manner as will most effectually preserve the peace of said city, secure the inhabitants thereof from personal violence, and their property from fire and unlawful depredations: they shall establish and organize all such fire companies, and provide them with the proper engines and other instruments, as shall be necessary to extinguish fires and preserve the property of the inhabitants of said city, from conflagration; and provide such by-laws and regulations for the government of the same, as they shall think fit and expedient; and each and every person who may belong to such fire company, shall, in time of peace, be exempted from the performance of military duty, under the laws of this State: they shall erect, establish and regulate the markets and market places of said city, for the sale of provisions, vegetables and other articles, necessary for the sustenance, comfort and convenience of said city, and the inhabitants thereof; to assize and regulate the sale of bread; and they shall have power to establish and construct landing places, wharves, docks and basins in said city, at or on any of the city property.

Sec. 10. That for the purpose of more effectually securing said city from the destructive ravages of fire, the said city council shall have power and authority, and for such purpose they are hereby empowered and authorized, on the application of three-fourths of the whole number of owners or proprietors of any square, or fractional square, in said city, to prohibit, in the most effectual manner, the erection of any building, or the addition to any building before erected, more than ten feet high, in any square or fractional square, except the outer walls thereof shall be composed entirely of brick or stone and mortar, and to provide for the most prompt removal of any building, or any addition to any building, which may be erected, contrary to the true intent and meaning of this section; and the said city council shall have the power, and it is hereby made their duty, whenever in their opinion the public good shall require it, to cause the streets of said [city] to be suitably lighted, in such manner as they may, from time to time prescribe and ordain.

Sec. 11. That the said city council shall have power, and it is hereby made their duty, to regulate, by good and wholesome laws and and ordinances for that purpose. all taverns, ale and porter shops and houses, and places where spirituous liquors are sold by a less quantity than a quart, and all houses of public entertainment, within said city; all theatrical exhibitions and public shows; and all exhibitions of whatever name or nature, to which admission is obtained on the payment of money, or any other reward; the sale of all horses and other domestic animals, at public auction, in said city; and impose reasonable fines and penalties for the violation of any such laws and ordinances: and the said city council shall have full and exclusive powers to grant or refuse license to showmen, and keepers and managers of theatrical exhibitions, and all other exhibitions for money or reward, auctioneers for the sale of horses and other domestic animals, at public auction, in said city: and in granting any such license, it shall be lawful for said city council to exact, demand and receive such sum or sums of money, as they shall think fit and expedient; to annex thereunto, such reasonable terms and conditions, in regard to time, place and other circumstances under which such licenses shall be acted upon, as in their opinion the peace, quiet and good order of society, in said city may require; and for the violations of such reasonable terms and conditions as aforesaid, the mayor shall have power to revoke or suspend such license, whenever the good order and welfare of said city may require it, in such manner as may be provided for by ordinance.

Sec. 12. That the city council shall have power, and they are hereby authorized to require and compel the abatement of all nuisances within the limits of said city, under such regulations as shall be prescribed by ordinance; to cause all grounds therein, where water shall at any time become stagnant, to be raised, filled up or drained; and to cause all putrid substances, whether animal or vegetable, to be removed; and to effect these objects, the said city council may, from time to time, give order to the proprietor or proprietors, or to his or her agent, and to the non-resident proprietors, who have no agents therein, by a publication in one or more of the newspapers printed in said city, or vicinity, for the period of six weeks, of all or any grounds, subject at any time to be covered with stagnant water, to fill up, raise or drain such grounds at their own expense: and the said city council shall designate how high such grounds shall be filled up and raised, or in what manner they shall be drained; and fix some reasonable time for filling up, raising and draining the same; and if such proprietor or proprietors, or agent, shall refuse or neglect to fill up, raise, or drain such grounds, in such manner, and within such time, as the said city council shall have designated and fixed, they shall cause the same to be done at the expense of the city, and assess the amount of the expense thereof, on the lot or lots of ground so filled up, raised or drained, as aforesaid, and place the assessment so made as aforesaid, in the hands of the city marshal, who shall proceed to collect the same, by a sale of such lot or lots, if not otherwise paid, in the same manner, with the same powers, and under the same regulations, and shall make good and sufficient deed thereof to the purchaser, subject to the same right of redemption by the proprietor or proprietors, their heirs or assigns, as the law prescribes for the time, for the sale of lands for the non-payment of State and county taxes; but no penalty for the non-payment of any such taxes or assessments, shall exceed twenty-five per cent.

Sec. 13. That said city council shall cause the streets, lanes, alleys and commons of said city, to be kept open and in repair, and free from all kinds of nuisances; but it shall be lawful for them to continue any building, or erection now standing thereon, if in their opinion the interest and general health of said city, will not be injured thereby; they shall have the exclusive power of appointing supervisors and other officers of streets, within the said city: they shall have the power, whenever the public convenience or safety shall require it, to prohibit hogs, cattle, horses, and other descriptions of animals, from running at large in the streets, lanes, and alleys, commons and other public places in said city: they shall have power to license and regulate all carts, wagons, drays, and every description of two and four wheeled carriages, which may be kept in said city for hire; all livery stables, brokers and loan offices; and to provide for the inspection, and appointment of inspectors of all articles of domestic growth, produce or manufacture, which may be brought to said city, sold or purchased therein, for exportation, and not included in the inspection laws of the State.

Sec. 14. That to defray the current expenses of said city, the said city council shall have power to levy and collect taxes on the real and personal property therein, on the basis of city taxation hereinafter provided; and it shall be the duty of the city recorder, to calculate and make a duplicate record of city taxes, on said basis of city taxation, in the same manner as required of the county auditor, in making duplicates of State, county, and other taxes, based upon the grand list of taxable property in this State, and deliver the duplicate of such city taxes, to the city marshal, at such time as he may be directed so to do, by the ordinances of the city council; and it shall be the duty of the city marshal to proceed in enforcing the collection of said taxes, in the same manner, by distress and sale of personal property, and advertisement and sale of real estate, as is prescribed by the several acts regulating the mode of taxation in this State; and on sale of real estate for taxes, the city recorder shall have power to execute a deed of such real estate, as may be so forfeited and sold for city taxes, which deed shall be good and valid in law, as the county auditor's deed for lands sold for taxes under the said laws, regulating the mode of taxation in this State: the same time and privilege of redemption shall be incident to said sales of real estate for city taxes, as are provided in said State laws, regulating the mode of taxation; and the said city marshal shall pay over to the city treasurer, all moneys so collected by him, as aforesaid, within such time, and under such penalties for neglecting or refusing to pay over, as said city council shall prescribe; and the city recorder and marshal shall receive such suitable compensation for the services aforesaid, as the city council shall, from time to time, fix by ordinance; and the said city council shall have power whenever, in their opinion, the interest of said city shall require it, to levy and collect taxes on dogs and other domestic animals, not included in the list of taxable property for State and county purposes, to be collected in the same manner as is provided in this section for the collection of city taxes: *Provided*, The amount of taxes levied as aforesaid, shall not, in any one year exceed one per centum on the aggregate value of taxable property in said city.

Sec. 15. That the said city council shall have power to levy and collect a special tax, from the real estate of any section, square, or part of square, or market place of said city, on the petition of the owner or owners of not less than two thirds in value thereof, for opening, paving, repairing or improving any street, lane or alley, bounding on, or within the same, or for the purpose of lighting any section, lane or alley, bounding on, or within the same: *Provided*, That for the purpose of lighting such street, lane or alley, the owner or owners of not less than two thirds of the real estate, bounded on or within the same, and both sides thereof shall petition therefor; the city council shall moreover have power, when two thirds of the members shall deem it necessary, to assess a special tax, for supplying said city, or any portion thereof, with a night watch.

Sec. 16. There shall be annually elected at the same time and in the same manner as the members of the city council, one assessor for each ward in said city, whose duty it shall be, after having been duly sworn or affirmed, to proceed, between the last Monday in March and the second Tuesday in May thereafter, to assess all the real and personal property, or capital of any kind, within the said city, subject to taxation for State, county or township purposes, and also all buildings of a less value than two hundred dollars, within said city; and shall make returns of their assessment roll to the office of the city recorder, on or before the second Tuesday in May; and after said assessment shall be equalized and established by the authority of the city council, to whom, as a board of equalization, any person dissatisfied with the assessment of any or all of his taxable property as so taken by said assessors, may appeal to said city council, who shall annually, on the fourth Tuesday in May, hold a special meeting for the purpose of hearing and determining on said appeals, with power to adjourn from day to day, until such appeals are disposed of, and whose determination thereon shall be final and conclusive; and said assessment, when so established, shall form the basis of all city taxation, for general purposes.

Sec. 17. That the said city council shall have power, whenever in their opinion the public good shall require it, to erect a city prison, and to regulate the police or internal government of the same; that the said city prison may contain cells for solitary confinement, and such apartments as may be necessary for the safe keeping, accommodation, and employment of all such persons as may be confined therein; that the city council shall have power to pass all such ordinances as may be necessary for the apprehension and punishment of all common street beggars, common prostitutes, and persons disturbing the peace of said city, who, upon conviction thereof, before the mayor, in such manner as the said city council shall prescribe, may be fined in any sumnot exceeding one hundred dollars, or be confined in the cells, or kept at hard labor, in said city prison, for any length of time not exceeding fifteen days: that any person convicted before the mayor, under the provisions of this act, of any offence which by the laws of the State of Ohio, is punishable in whole, or in part, by confinement in the county jail, may be confined in the cells of the city prison for any time not exceeding that specified by the laws of this State, for the punishment of such offence, for the said term of confinement: *And provided, also,* That until such city prison shall be prepared for the reception of prisoners, the said city shall be allowed the use of the county jail of Cuyahoga county, for the confinement of all such persons as may be convicted before the mayor, and who shall be liable to imprisonment under the laws of this State, or the ordinances of said city; and all persons so imprisoned shall be under the charge of the sheriff of said county, who shall receive and discharge such persons in and from said jail, in such manner as shall be provided by the ordinances of said city, or otherwise, by due course of law; and after the said city prison shall be erected and prepared for the reception of prisoners, the marshal of said city, in the control, government and management thereof, shall have the same power and authority, and be subject to the same liabilities as by the laws of this State now are, or hereafter may be conferred and imposed upon the sheriffs of the several counties, in the control, government, and management of the county jails, and all such other powers and duties as the city council may prescribe, to enforce any sentence of hard labor pronounced against any person by the said mayor.

Sec. 18. That all moneys raised, received, or collected, by means of any tax, license, penalty, fine, forfeiture, or otherwise, under the authority of this act, or which may belong to said city, shall be paid into the city treasury, and shall not be drawn therefrom, except by order, or under the authority of the city council; and it shall be the duty of said city council to liquidate and settle all claims and demands against said city, and

30—L

to require all officers, agents or persons entrusted with the disbursement or expenditure of the public money, to account to them therefor, at such time and in such manner as they may direct; and they shall annually publish, for the information of the citizens, a particular statement of the receipts and expenditures of all public money belonging to said city, and also of all debts due and owing to and from the same; and the city council shall have power to pass all such laws and ordinances as may be necessary and proper to carry into effect the powers herein and by this act granted.

Sec. 19. That every law or ordinance of said city, before it shall be of any force or validity, or in any manner binding on the inhabitants thereof, or others, shall be agreed to, and ordered to be engrossed for its final passage, by a majority of all the members of the city council; it shall then be reconsidered by the city council, and if in its final passage it shall be adopted by a majority of all the members, it shall become a law for said city; and all questions on the final passage of any law or ordinance, or the adoption of any resolutions, shall be taken by yeas and nays, and the names of the persons voting for or against the same shall be entered in the journals of said council; and all the laws and ordinances passed and adopted as aforesaid, shall be signed by the president of the council, and the city recorder, and immediately published in one or more of the newspapers published in said city, or vicinity.

Sec. 20. That it shall be the duty of the city recorder to make and keep a just and true record of all and every law and ordinance made and established by the city council, and all their proceedings in their corporate capacity; and the record so made shall at all times be open to the inspection of any elector of said city: and he shall perform such duties, and exercise such powers as may be lawfully required of him by the ordinances of said city; and he shall preside over the meetings of the city council, in the absence of the mayor and president, until otherwise directed by the city council.

Sec. 21. That the city treasurer shall give bond with security to the recorder, to be approved by the city council, before he enters on the duties of his office, conditional for the faithful discharge thereof; he shall pay over all moneys by him received, to the order of the mayor or president of the city council, countersigned by the city recorder; but no money shall be drawn from the treasury but by appropriations made by the city council; and the treasurer shall, when required, submit his books and vouchers to their inspection; and he shall perform such duties and exercise such powers as may be lawfully required of him by the ordinances of said city.

Sec. 22. That there shall be elected annually by the city council, a city marshal, who shall hold his office one year, and until his successor shall be elected and qualified; who shall perform such duties and exercise such powers, not herein specified, as may be lawfully required of him by the ordinances of said city, and shall receive such fees and compensations as the said city council shall direct: the said marshal shall execute and return all writs and other processes directed to him by the mayor, or when necessary in criminal cases, or for violations of the city ordinances, may serve the same in any part of Cuyahoga county; it shall be his duty to suppress all riots, disturbances, and breaches of the peace; to apprehend all rioters, and disorderly persons, and disturbers of the public peace in said city, and all persons in the act of committing any indictable offence against the laws of this State, or ordinances of said city, or fleeing from justice after having committed any such offence, and him, her, or them forthwith to take into custody and bring before the mayor for examination; and in case of resistance may call to his aid and command the assistance of all by-standers, and others in the vicinity; he shall have power to appoint one or more deputies, and at pleasure to dismiss or discharge them from office; and shall in all things be responsible for the correct and faithful discharge of their duties, and liable for all negligence, carelessness and misconduct in office, and positive violations of duty, which they, or either of them may be guilty of in the performance of the duties of their official stations.

Sec. 23. That the mayor, councilmen, marshal, treasurer, city recorder, and all other officers under the government of the said city, shall, before entering on the duties of their respective offices, take an oath or affirmation to support the constitution of the United States. and of this State, and faithfully and impartially to perform the several duties of the office to which they may be respectively elected, or appointed, and when required shall give such bonds to said city, with good and sufficient security, in such sum or sums, and with such conditions thereto as the city council may from time to time direct, and in all cases not hereinbefore provided for, shall respectively be allowed, and receive such fees and compensation for their services, and be liable to such fines, penalties and forfeitures for negligence, carelessness, and misconduct in office, and positive violation of duty, as the said city council shall by ordinance order and determine.

Sec. 24. That in all elections for city officers, not otherwise provided for, it shall be the duty of the mayor to issue a proclamation to the qualified voters of said city, or to those of the respective wards, as the case may require, setting forth the time of said election, the place or places where the same shall be held, the officer or officers to be chosen, and cause such proclamation to be published in one or more newspapers printed in said city, or vicinity, at least ten days previous to said election; and every such election shall be opened between the hours of eight and ten o'clock, in the forenoon, and continue open until four o'clock in the afternoon, and shall in all things be conducted agreeably to the laws regulating township elections, for the time being; and it shall be the duty of the judges of such elections, in the several wards, within two days thereafter, to make and direct the return thereof to the mayor of the said city, at his office, in the same manner that election returns are required to be made to the clerk of the court of common pleas, by the act entitled "An act to regulate elections:" *Provided*, That in all elections of mayor, the returns thereof shall be made and directed to the president of the city council; and the said mayor, or president of the city council, as the case may be, shall, within five days after any such election, open the returns which have been made to him, as aforesaid, and shall make an abstract of all the votes and file the same with the city recorder, and who shall make a record thereof in a book to be kept by him for that purpose, and the person or persons having the highest number of votes shall be declared duly elected; but if from any cause, the qualified voters of said city, or of the respective wards, as the case may be, shall fail to effect any election at the time, and in the manner herein provided, the mayor shall forthwith issue his proclamation, for the second, or other election, which in all things shall be notified, conducted, regulated, and the returns thereof made, as in and by this act is prescribed; and the person or persons who shall be chosen at any such second, or other election, shall hold his or their office, until the next stated period for the choice of a successor, or successors; and it shall be the duty of the mayor, or president of the city council, immediately to notify such person or persons as may be elected, as aforesaid, of his or their election, by causing a written notice thereof to be served upon him or them, by the city marshal, or his deputy; and every person so chosen, or elected, as aforesaid, shall within ten days after being so notified of his election, cause himself to be qualified to enter upon the duties of his office, and in default thereof, the office to which he shall have been elected, shall be deemed and considered in law to be vacant: and it shall be the duty of the city council to prescribe the time and manner, and provide the place or places of holding all elections in said city, for city officers, and of making the returns thereof, not herein otherwise directed and prescribed.

Sec. 25. That each and every white male inhabitant, above the age of twenty-one years, having the qualifications of an elector, for members of the General Assembly of the State of Ohio, and having residence in said city one year next preceeding an election for city officers, shall be deemed a qualified voter of said city, and shall be entitled to vote in the ward in which he resides, for mayor, and members of the city council: *Provided*, That no person shall be capable of holding any office under the government of said city, who has not resided therein, or been an inhabitant thereof, at least one year next preceding his election or appointment.

Sec. 26. That the city council, two-thirds of all the members concurring therein, shall have power to borrow money for the discharge and liquidation of any debt of the city, and to pledge for the payment of the interest and the re-payment of the principal, the property and resources of the city, in such manner, and upon such terms and conditions, as by an ordinance voted for by two-thirds of the members elected, as aforesaid, may be prescribed.

Sec. 27. That said city council shall have power, on the petition of the owners of two thirds of the value of any square or section of said city, to lay out and establish a new street, or streets, alley or alleys, through or across such square or section: *Provided*, Notice of the presenting of such petition be given by publication thereof in one more newspapers published in said city, or vicinity, for three weeks in succession, the last of which shall be at least sixty days before presenting said petition: *And Provided, also*, That if any person shall claim damages in consequence of the laying out of any such new street or alley, and shall file notice thereof, in writing, in the office of the city recorder, within ten days after the order for laying out of said street or alley shall have been made, the said city council shall cause the damages, if any, over and above the benefit to the property claimed to have been injured, to be assessed under oath, by three disinterested, judicious freeholders, of said city, to be appointed by said council, for the purpose; which shall be paid within three months after the making of the said order by the persons petitioning for the laying out of such new street or alley, or in default thereof, the order laying out the said street or alley shall be null and void.

Sec. 29. That the city council shall have power to levy a special tax to defray the expense of grading, paving, or otherwise improving, any road, street, lane, alley, square, market place, or common, within said city, by a discriminating assessment upon the land and ground bound and abutting on such road, street, alley, lane, market place, square, or common, or near thereto, in proportion to the benefit accruing to such land or ground; and the city council shall appoint a committee of three disinterested, judicious freeholders, of said city, to estimate the cost of any such projected improvements, and to assess the expense on the land and ground as aforesaid; and the city council shall give notice in one or more of the newspapers published in said city, or vicinity, for six consecutive weeks of the improvement to be made, in order that any one damaged, by reason of such improvements, may file his claim, in writing, in the office of the city recorder, within ten days after the expiration of the said six weeks notice, and the said committee shall assess the damages, if any, of such claimants, and shall add the same to the cost of the improvement, as a part of the expese thereof, to be assessed, as aforesaid; and said committee, within twenty days after the time shall have expired for filing claims for damages (unless for good cause, the council shall grant them further time,) shall make return to the office of the city auditor, setting forth the estimated cost of such projected improvement, including the damages awarded by them to the claimants, together with the names of such claimants, and grounds of claim, with the amount awarded them, severally, set opposite their respective names; and also, a brief disction of the lands and grounds upon which they shall have assessed the expense of the improvement, with the names of the owners, or persons liable to pay the assessment, respectively annexed, and the amount thereon assessed, set opposite their respective names, and and if the name of the person owing, or liable for the tax, is unknown, the fact shall be stated by writing "unknown owners," in place of the name; and the city council, if they order and direct the improvement to be made, shall direct the city auditor, whose duty it shall be, to annex the duplicate of taxes, so assessed, to the annual assessment roll, hereafter specified, and to deliver it, therewith, on or before the first Monday in July following, to the city marshal, to be by him collected, at the same time, and in the same manner, as the annual taxes; and the proceedings of said collector shall, in all respects, be the same as in the collection of the annual taxes of said city, and he shall, in like manner, pay the same into the city treasury; and in case of any tax being returned unpaid and delinquent, the proceedings shall in all respects be the same as in cases of delinquency in the payment of the annual taxes, with the addition of the like interest and penalty; and when the improvements so ordered, shall be completed, each claimant shall be entitled to receive, from the city treasury, the amount of damages, so by the return of said committee, awarded him; and the city council shall cause the public streets, roads, lanes, alleys, and highways, and the public square, and other public grounds that now exist within the limits of said city, to be, by the surveyor of the county of Cuyahoga, or some other competent surveyor, to be surveyed, described, and permanently marked, and the plat thereof recorded by the city recorder, in a book to be provided for that purpose; in which book shall also be recorded, a plat of any new street which may hereafter be established by said council under the provisions of this act, and also, of any change or alteration in any of the streets or highways of the city; and such survey and record, shall be, thereafter, conclusive evidence of the position and limits of such street, lane, alley, highway, square, or public ground; subject, however, to such alterations as may be made therin, agreeable to the provisions of this act.

Sec. 29. That said city council shall have the general superintendence of all the common schools in said city, and from time to time, shall make such regulations for the division of said city [into] school districts, and for the erection of school houses theerin, and such provisions for the government and instruction of children therein, as to them shall appear proper and expedient.

Sec. 30. That the trustees of the township of Brooklyn, shall appoint two suitable persons in each ward, to be judges of the first election, also, suitable persons to be clerks, in each ward, and procure a suitable place in each ward, for holding the election; and at every annual election thereafter, the city council shall appoint two of their members in each ward, who are not candidates for election, to be judges, and make such other arrangements, by ordinances, respecting said election, as shall be lawful and convenient for the citizens of the several wards.

Sec. 31. That this act shall be taken and received in all councils, and by all judges, magistrates, and other public officers, as a public act, and all printed copies of the same, which shall be printed by, or under the authority of the General Assembly, shall be admitted as good evidence thereof, without any other proof whatever.

Sec. 32. That any future Legislature may alter, amend or repeal this act.

WILLIAM MEDILL,
Speaker pro tem. of the House of Representatives.
ELIJAH VANCE,
Speaker of the Senate.

March 3, 1836.

AN ACT

To incorporate the Duck creek Bridge Company.

Sec. 1. *Be it enacted by the General Assembly of the State of Ohio,* That G. S. B. Hempstead, Jonas Moore, and their associates, be, and they are hereby created a body corporate and politic, by the name and style of "The Duck creek Bridge Company;" and as such, shall remain and have perpetual succession; and by their corporate name, may contract and be contracted with, sue and be sued, answer and be answered, plead and be impleaded, defend and be defended, in any court of competent jurisdiction.

Sec. 2. That the said corporation be, and they are hereby authorized to erect a toll bridge across Duck creek, in the county of Washington, at its mouth, where the road from Marietta to Wheeling crosses the same.

Sec. 3. That if the said company shall erect and complete said bridge, in a substantial manner, of proper width, and being in other respects of sufficient strength and dimensions, so as to admit of the safe passage of passengers, teams, and carriages, of the usual dimensions, within three years from the passage of this act, they shall, from the time of completing said bridge, enjoy all the privileges secured to them by this act.

Sec. 4. That after the completion of said bridge, as aforesaid, the proprietors thereof are hereby authorized to demand and receive from passengers who may cross said bridge, the following rates of toll, to wit: For each foot passenger, two cents; for each horse and rider, six and one-fourth cents; for each horse, mule or ass, one year old, two cents; for each wagon or cart, drawn by two horses or oxen, twelve and one half cents; for each horse or ox in addition, three cents; for each carriage, wagon or cart, drawn by one horse, ten cents; for each horse in addition, two cents; for each sleigh or sled, drawn by one horse or ox, six and one-fourth cents; for each horse in addition, four cents; for each sled, drawn by one yoke of oxen, twelve and one half cents; for each yoke of oxen in addition, four cents; for each stage coach or other pleasurable carriage, drawn by four horses, and driver, twenty-five cents; the same drawn by two horses, eighteen and three-fourth cents; for each wagon, drawn by four horses, twenty-five cents; for each horse in addition, six and one-fourth cents; for each head of neat cattle, one year old and upwards, one cent; the same under one year old, one half cent; and for each head of sheep and hogs, one half cent.

Sec. 5. That the proprietors of said bridge shall, previous to receiving any tolls, set up and keep, in some conspicuous place over or near the gate to be erected on said bridge, a board, on which shall be painted or printed, in a plain and legible manner, the rates of toll allowed by this act.

Sec. 6. That if the proprietors of said bridge shall demand and receive any higher or greater toll than is by this act allowed, they shall be subject to the like fines and penalties which are, or may be provided, in case of ferries; and, in ten years after the completion of said bridge, it shall be in the power of every Legislature to make such alteration in the rates of toll herein established, as to them shall appear, from time to time, equitable and right.

Sec. 7. That the said company shall have power to adopt such by-laws, rules and regulations, for the government of the same, as they may deem expedient, not inconsistent with the constitution and laws of the United States or of this State.

Sec. 8. That the said company shall pay unto Nahum Ward, or his legal representative, such sum or sums of money for all such materials and labor as has heretofore been prepared and brought upon the ground by said Ward, for the purpose of building said bridge, as the county commissioners of Washington county shall value said materials and labor at; and said county commissioners are hereby authorized and required, on or before the first Monday in June next, to proceed and value the same; which valuation they shall deliver in writing to the said Nahum Ward on demand:

Provided, That said commissioners shall value no materials or labor except such as, in their opinion, will be useful in building said bridge, and such as were prepared and on the ground previous to the first day of January, eighteen hundred and thirty-six.

WILLIAM MEDILL,
Speaker pro tem. of the House of Representatives.
ELIJAH VANCE,
Speaker of the Senate.

March 3, 1836.

AN ACT

To amend an act, entitled "An act to incorporate the town of Lancaster, in Fairfield county," passed February 4th, 1831.

Sec. 1. *Be it enacted by the General Assembly of the State of Ohio,* That so much of the townships of Hocking and Bern, as is included in the plat of in lots of the town of Lancaster, Carpenter's addition thereto, the Bank addition thereto, out lot number four, east of said town of Lancaster as laid out into in lots, a tier of in lots laid out on the north end of out lot number six, east of said town, and all other in lots, out lots and additions that now are, or shall hereafter be laid out, be, and the same are hereby erected into and constituted a town corporate, by the name of the Town of Lancaster.

Sec. 2. That for the good order and government of said town and of the inhabitants thereof, there shall henceforth be elected by the free white male inhabitants of said town, having the qualifications of electors of members of the General Assembly, on the third Monday of April annually, nine trustees and a town marshal, who shall continue in office until their successors are elected and qualified; and it shall be the duty of said trustees, within five days after being notified of their election, as is prescribed for by the act of which this is an amendment, to assemble at the town hall, in said town, and after having taken an oath or affirmation to support the constitution of the State of Ohio, and an oath of office, to be administered by any person legally qualified, they shall proceed to elect by ballot, from among themselves, a president and recorder; and shall in like manner appoint a treasurer, who shall be a qualified voter of said corporation, but not one of their own body; and when said trustees are so elected and qualified, they shall be a body politic and corporate, with perpetual succession, to be known by the name and title of the "Town Council of the town of Lancaster."

Sec. 3. That said town council be, and they are hereby authorized to borrow money for town purposes; and to make and publish all necessary ordinances for that purpose: *Provided,* That the debt so created shall at no one time exceed the sum of ten thousand dollars.

Sec. 4. That it shall be the duty of said town council, at their annual meeting for fixing the rate of taxation, to levy and assess, and make all necessary provisions for the collection of so much tax, or other means within the control of said corporation, as will be sufficient to cover any amount of principal or interest due, or to become due, within the then current year, on any sum borrowed by said council: *Provided*, That said town council shall not in any one year levy a tax for the above purposes, exceeding the sum of one per cent. on the valuation of the taxable property within the limits of said corporation: *And provided further*, That the levying of said taxes for the purposes aforesaid, shall not affect the right of said town council to levy taxes under the act to which this is an amendment, for the purposes in said act specified.

Sec. 5. That it shall be the duty of said town council to cause all by-laws and ordinances, by them enacted for the government of said town, to be published at least one week in some public newspaper printed in said town, of general circulation therein; upon which publication, and not before, said by-laws and ordinances shall be in full force.

Sec. 6. That so much of the act to which this is an amendment, as is inconsistent with the provisions of this amendment, be, and the same is hereby repealed.

Sec. 7. That said town council, and their successors in office, shall have full power and authority to enact and enforce ordinances and by-laws in relation to such grounds as now are, or hereafter may be purchased by them for the use of said town, for the burial of the dead, notwithstanding said grounds may not lie within the incorporated limits of said town: *Provided*, That such by-laws and ordinances shall be consistent with the chartered privileges of said town.

Sec. 8. That said town council shall further have full power and authority to subdivide or lay out said burying grounds into lots, and to dispose of said lots to the religious societies of said town, conferring to said religious societies the exclusive right to bury their dead in their respective lots: *Provided*, That all such dispositions of lots shall be by public sale; pursuant to which sales, the said town council shall, on payment of the purchase money, execute a suitable grant to the society purchasing; securing to said society the exclusive right to enter within said lots upon condition that said religious societies shall continue to keep their respective lots in order, agreeably to such regulations as shall from time to time be prescribed by said town council: *Provided, also,* That said town council shall reserve suitable portions of said grounds for the general use of said town as a burying ground.

Sec. 9. That obedience to all by-laws and ordinances passed in relation to said burial ground, shall be enforced; and punishments for infractions of said by-laws and ordinances shall be inflicted by prosecution or suit before the president of said town council, reserving nevertheless the right of appeal to the court of common pleas.

Sec. 10. That it shall and may be lawful for the friends or relatives of deceased persons who have been buried in any grave yard within the incorporated limits of said town, to remove the remains of such deceased persons and inter the same in the new burying grounds; and in like manner it shall and may be lawful for the town council aforesaid, by and with the consent of the relatives of deceased persons buried within the limits of said

31—L

incorporation to remove the remains of said deceased persons, and re-inter the same as aforesaid.

WILLIAM MEDILL,
Speaker pro tem. of the House of Representatives.
ELIJAH VANCE,
Speaker of the Senate.

March 3, 1836.

AN ACT

To incorporate the Seneca county Academy.

Sec. 1. *Be it enacted by the General Assembly of the State of Ohio,* That Samuel Waggoner, Sidney Smith, Joshua Maynard, Chauncey Rundell, Timothy P. Roberts, Sela Chapin, junior, and Calvin Bradley, of the county of Seneca, together with such other persons as may hereafter be associated with them, for the purpose of establishing an Academy in the town of Republic, in the township of Scipio, in the county of Seneca, be, and they are hereby created a body politic and corporate, with perpetual succession, by the name of the "Seneca county Academy;" and by that name, shall be competent to contract and be contracted with, to sue and be sued, answer and be answered unto, in all courts of law and equity; and to acquire, possess and enjoy, and to sell, convey, and dispose of, property both real and personal; and shall possess all the powers usually incident to such corporations: *Provided,* That the annual income of such property shall not exceed two thousand dollars.

Sec. 2. That any three of the above named persons shall have power to call a meeting, by giving ten days previous notice thereof, by advertisements set up at three of the most public places in the township of Scipio aforesaid.

Sec. 3. That said corporation shall have power to form a constitution and adopt by-laws for its government, to prescribe the number and title of its officers, and define their powers and duties, to prescribe the manner in which members may be admitted and dismissed, and other powers necessary for the efficient management of its corporate concerns.

Sec. 4. That any future Legislature may modify or repeal this act.

WILLIAM MEDILL,
Speaker pro tem. of the House of Representatives.
ELIJAH VANCE,
Speaker of the Senate.

March 4, 1836.

AN ACT

To incorporate the Madison Liberal Institute, in the county of Hamilton.

Sec. 1. *Be it enacted by the General Assembly of the State of Ohio,* That

Ebenezer Ward, Enion Singer, John Armstrong, Hiram Badine, Timothy Day, together with such other persons as may be hereafter associated with them, for the purpose of establishing an academic institution, and for no other purpose, in the town of Madison, in the county of Hamilton, be, and they are hereby created a body politic and corporate, with perpetual succession, by the name of "The Madison Liberal Institute;" and by that name shall be competent to contract and be contracted with, to sue and be sued, to answer and be answered unto, in all courts of law and equity; and to acquire, possess, and enjoy, and to sell convey, and dispose of property, both real and personal: *Provided.* That the annual income of such property shall not exceed two thousand dollars.

Sec. 2. That any three of the above named persons shall have power to call a meeting by giving ten days previous notice thereof, by advertisement set up in three of the most public places in the town of Madison.

Sec. 3. That said corporation shall have power to form a constitution and adopt by-laws, for its government; to prescribe the number and title of its officers, the time and manner of electing them, and define their powers and duties; to prescribe the manner in which members may be admitted and dismissed; and all other powers necessary to the efficient management of its corporate concerns: *Provided,* That the constitution, by-laws, and regulations of the corporation be consistent with the constitution and laws of the United States, and of this State.

Sec. 4. That any future Legislature may modify or repeal this act: *Provided,* That the title to any property, real or personal, acquired or conveyed under its provisions, shall not be thereby affected.

WILLIAM MEDILL,
Speaker pro tem. of the House of Representatives.

ELIJAH VANCE,
Speaker of the Senate.

March 4, 1836.

AN ACT

To lay out and establish a graded State road in the counties of Muskingum, Perry, and Hocking.

Sec. 1. *Be it enacted by the General Assembly of the State of Ohio,* That Nicholas Pierce, of Muskingum county; Thomas Wright, of Perry county; and Elie Barker, of Hocking county, be, and they are hereby appointed commissioners, and James Brown, of Perry county, surveyor, to lay out and establish a graded state road, beginning at Newton Mills, in Muskingum county; thence to Rehobeth, and New Lexington, in Perry county; thence to Logan, in Hocking county.

Sec. 2. That said road shall in no case exceed an angle of five degrees with the horizon; and the commissioners aforesaid shall, in all cases not provided for in this act, be governed by the act defining the mode of laying out and establishing state roads, passed March 14th, 1831.

Sec. 3. That should either of the commissioners, or surveyor die, or remove out of the county, or refuse to serve, the commissioners of the county in which such vacancy shall happen, shall forthwith, on being notified of such vacancy, appoint some suitable person to fill the same.

WILLIAM MEDILL,

Speaker pro tem. of the House of Representatives.

ELIJAH VANCE,

Speaker of the Senate.

March 4, 1836.

AN ACT

To incorporate the Methodist Episcopal Church and Society, in the town of Burlington, county of Lawrence.

Sec. 1. *Be it enacted by the General Assembly of the State of Ohio,* That William Gillen, Andrew P. Kauns, Curtis Scovel, Charles M'Coy, John M'Coy, John Bryan, Thomas Kerr, and their associates, together with such persons which may hereafter be associated with them, be, and they are hereby created a body politic and corporate, by the name of the Methodist Episcopal Church and Society of Burlington; and as such shall remain and have perpetual succession, and by their corporate name may contract and be contracted with, sue and be sued, answer and be answered, defend and be defended, plead and be impleaded, in any court of competent jurisdiction, in all manner of actions, causes and complaints whatsoever; and may have a common seal which they may alter at pleasure.

Sec. 2. That said corporation shall be capable in law and in equity, in their corporate name aforesaid, of having, receiving, acquiring and holding, by purchase, gift, grant, devise or legacy, any estate, real, personal or mixed, for the use of said corporation: *Provided,* That the annual income of all such property shall not exceed the sum of two thousand dollars; and that all the property of whatever kind, shall be considered as held in trust, under the management and at the disposal of said corporation, for the purpose of promoting the interest of said society, and maintaining any institution of charity: *And provided, also,* That where money or other property shall be given, granted, devised, or bequeathed, for the purposes of education, shall be faithfully applied to such purpose, and no other.

Sec. 3. That for the better managing of the affairs of said society, and promoting the interests thereof, there shall be elected on the first Saturday in June next, and annually thereafter, seven trustees, and such other officers as the corporation may deem necessary, who shall hold their offices for one year and until their successors shall be elected: *Provided,* That if from any cause an election of officers should not be made on the day appointed for the annual election, the society may elect their officers at any meeting of the corporation duly assembled.

Sec. 4. That William Gillen, Andrew P. Kauns, Curtis Scovil, Charles M'Coy, John M'Coy, John Bryan, and Thomas Kerr, named in the first section of this act, be, and they are hereby appointed trustees until the first annual election, and until others are elected in their place.

Sec. 5. That all elections of the corporation shall be by ballot; and the person or persons having a majority of the votes for any office, shall be considered duly elected; and all matters of the corporation shall be determined by a majority of the members present, at any meeting of the society duly assembled.

Sec. 6. That the trustees, a majority of whom shall be a quorum for the transaction of business, shall have the management and control of all the property and concerns of the corporation, and they, or a majority of them, shall have power to call a meeting of the society, either for the election of officers, or for the transaction of any other business of the society, by giving to said society, immediately after public worship, at least five days previous notice of said meeting, or by causing notifications thereof to be set up in three or more public places within the limits of said society, at least ten days previous to such meeting.

Sec. 7. That any meeting of the society, duly assembled, may adopt and establish such by-laws and ordinances, as may be deemed proper and necessary for the good government of said corporation: *Provided*, That such by-laws and ordinances shall be compatible with the constitution and laws of the United States, and of this State.

Sec. 8. That original process against the corporation shall be served by leaving an attested copy with one or more of the trustees, at least five days before the return day thereof; and such service shall be deemed sufficient to bind the corporation.

Sec. 9. That any future Legislature shall have power to modify or repeal this act: *Provided*, That such modification or repeal shall not affect the title to any estate, real or personal, acquired or conveyed under its provisions.

WILLIAM MEDILL,
Speaker pro tem. of the House of Representatives.

ELIJAH VANCE,
Speaker of the Senate.

March 4, 1836.

AN ACT

To incorporate the Congregational Church and Society of Ravenna.

Sec. 1. *Be it enacted by the General Assembly of the State of Ohio,* That John N. Skinner, Isaac Swift, Timothy Carnahan, Adam Poe, R. I. Thompson, Charles Clapp, and their associates, together with such other persons as may hereafter be associated with them, be, and they are hereby declared a body corporate and politic, by and with the name and style of the "Congregational Church and Society of Ravenna;" with perpetual succession, and capacity of contracting and being contracted with, suing and being sued, answering and being answered, pleading and being impleaded, defend and being defended, in all courts of law and equity, and may also have a common seal, which they may break, alter or renew at pleasure.

Sec. 2. That they shall have power to make, pass, and enforce, from time to time, such rules, by-laws, and regulations as they may deem proper for the good regulation of said association: *Provided,* That such rules, by-laws, and regulations shall not be repugnant to the constitution or laws of this State and of the United States.

Sec. 3. That said association shall be capable in law of purchasing and holding any estate, real or personal, and of receiving any gift, grant, donation or legacy, made or to be made, to said association; with full power to sell, dispose of, and convey the same: *Provided,* That the annual income of such property shall not exceed two thousand dollars.

Sec. 4. That John N. Skinner, Isaac Swift, Timothy Carnahan, Adam Poe, R. I. Thompson, Charles Clapp, be, and they are hereby appointed trustees of said association, until others are appointed in conformity with the rules, by-laws and regulations made by said association.

Sec. 5. That any future Legislature shall have power to modify or repeal this act: *Provided,* That such modification or repeal shall not affect the title to any estate, real or personal, acquired or conveyed under its provisons.

WILLIAM MEDILL,
Speaker pro tem. of the House of Representatives.
ELIJAH VANCE,
Speaker of the Senate.

March 4, 1836.

AN ACT

To incorporate the First Presbyterian Church of Lower Sandusky, in the county of Sandusky.

Sec. 1. *Be it enacted by the General Assembly of the State of Ohio,* That Jaques Hulburd, William C. Otis, and Samnel Crowell, and their associates, and such other persons as may hereafter be associated with them, be, and they are hereby created and declared a body corporate and politic, by the name of "The First Presbyterian Church of Lower Sandusky, in the county of Sandusky," and as such shall remain and have perpetual succession; and by their corporate name may contract and be contracted with, sue and be sued, plead and be impleaded, defend and be defended, in any court of competent jurisdiction, and in all manner of actions, causes and complaints whatsoever; and may have a common seal, which they may change or alter at pleasure.

Sec. 2. That said corporation, by the name and style aforesaid, shall be capable in law of holding property, real and personal, or mixed, either by purchase, gift, grant, devise or legacy, which may become the property of the corporation: *Provided,* That the annual income shall not exceed two thousand dollars: *Provided, also,* That all such property shall be considered as held in trust, under the management and at the disposal of said corporation, for the purpose of promoting the interest of said church, defraying the expenses incident to their mode of worship, and maintenance of any institutions of charity or education that may be therewith connected: *Provided, moreover*, That when money or other property shall be given, granted, devised or bequeathed to said church for any particular use or purpose, it shall be faithfully applied to such use or purpose: the property and other concerns of the corporation shall be under the management and control of trustees, to be appointed agreeably to the directions of the church; a majority of the trustees shall be a quorum for the transaction of business.

Sec. 3. That on the first Monday in January, one thousand eight hundred and thirty-seven, there shall be elected by said church, three trustees, and on the first Monday in January thereafter, one trustee, and such other officers as the church may deem necessary, who shall hold their offices as hereinafter pointed out, and until their successors shall be elected.

Sec. 4. That Jaques Hulburd, William C. Otis and Samuel Crowell, [named] in the first section of this act, be, and they are hereby appointed trustees until the first annual election, and until others are elected in their places; the offices of one of said trustees shall become vacant yearly, as follows: the first mentioned, on the first Monday of January, one thousand eight hundred and thirty-seven; the second on the first Monday of January, one thousand eight hundred and thirty-eight; and the third on the first Monday of January, one thousand eight hundred and thirty-nine.

Sec. 5. That all elections of the corporation shall be by ballot, and the person or persons having a majority of the votes, shall be considered duly elected: and all matters of the corporation shall be determined by a majority of the members present, at any meeting of the church duly assembled.

Sec. 6. That the trustees, or a majority of them, shall have power to call a meeting of the church, either for the election of officers, or for the transaction of any other business of the church, by causing or giving to the church immediately after public worship, ten days' previous notice of said meeting, or causing notifications thereof to be put up in three or more public places within the limits of the church, one of which to be at the usual place of holding public worship, at least fifteen days previous to such meeting.

Sec. 7. That any meeting of the corporation duly assembled, may adopt such by-laws and ordinances as may be deemed proper and necessary for the good government of said corporation.

Sec. 8. That original process against the corporation shall be served by summons, which shall be served by leaving an attested copy with one or more of the trustees, at least ten days before the return day thereof; and such service shall be deemed sufficient in law to bind the corporation.

Sec. 9. That any future Legislature shall have power to modify or repeal this act.

WILLIAM MEDILL,
Speaker pro tem. of the House of Representatives.
ELIJAH VANCE,
Speaker of the Senate.

March 4, 1836.

AN ACT

To incorporate the First Presbyterian Church, in the town of Knoxville, in Jefferson county.

Sec. 1. *Be it enacted by the General Assembly of the State of Ohio,* That Samuel Hunter, James Alexander, John Maxwell, Andrew Robinson, and David Sloane, and their associates, be, and they are hereby declared to be a body politic and corporate, by the name and style of "The First Presbyterian Church," in the town of Knoxville, in Jefferson county; to have perpetual succession, and to be capable in their corporate capacity, to contract and be contracted with, sue and be sued, plead and be impleaded, answer and be answered, defend and be defended, in any court of competent jurisdiction; to have a common seal; and to have power to ordain, pass, and enforce such by-laws and ordinances for the regulation and good government of said association, as they may deem necessary: *Provided,* That such by-laws and ordinances are not incompatible with the constitution and laws of this State, or of the United States.

Sec. 2. That said association shall be capable in law of purchasing and holding any estate, real or personal, and of receiving any gift, grant, donation or legacy, made or given for the promotion of the objects of said association, and in their corporate capacity to sell and convey the same; and said association may from time to time, elect and appoint such trustees, or other officers, for the good government and management of its concerns, as may be deemed necessary and expedient: *Provided, however,* That the funds of said association shall not at any time exceed five thousand dollars; and also, that said funds shall never be used for any other purpose than for the purchase of suitable sites, and for the erection of suitable buildings for religious worship and public instruction.

Sec. 3. That Samuel Hunter, James Alexander, John Maxwell, Andrew Robinson, and David Sloane, be, and they are hereby appointed trustees of said association, until others are elected in conformity with the by-laws and ordinances made by said association.

Sec. 4. That any future Legislature may amend or repeal this act.

WILLIAM MEDILL,
Speaker pro tem. of the House of Representatives.

ELIJAH VANCE,
Speaker of the Senate.

March 4, 1836.

AN ACT

To incorporate the Toledo and Sandusky City Rail-Road Company.

Sec. 1. *Be it enacted by the General Assembly of the State of Ohio,* That George M'Kay, Stephen B. Comstock, William P. Daniels, and Andrew Palmer of Toledo, in the county of Lucas; Samuel M. Lockwood, of the county of Sandusky; John G. Camp, Oran Follett, and Isaac A. Mills, of Sandusky City, in the county of Huron; together with those who may hereafter become stockholders, in the manner hereinafter prescribed, their successors and assigns, be, and they are hereby created a body corporate, by the name and style of the "Toledo and Sandusky Rail-Road Company;" and by that name and style shall be, and hereby are made capable in law, to have, purchase, receive, possess and enjoy, real and personal estate, and retain to them, their successors and assigns, all such lands, tenements and hereditaments, as shall be requisite for their accommodation and convenience in the transaction of their business, and such as may be in good faith conveyed to them by way of security, or in satisfaction of debts, or by donation and purchase, and the same to sell, grant, rent or otherwise dispose of; to sue and be sued, plead and be impleaded, answer and be answered unto, defend and be defended, in courts of record and elsewhere; and also to make, have and use a common seal, and the same to alter, break, renew, or change at pleasure.

Sec. 2. That the said corporation shall be, and are hereby vested with the right and authority to construct a single or double rail-road from Sandusky City to Toledo, by such route as after due examination and survey shall be found most eligible, with the privilege of extending said route to some point on the west line of the State of Ohio, and shall pass within five miles of the town of Maumee if practicable and also of constructing branches on such routes or lines as may hereafter be deemed most eligible and proper, to the towns of Lower Sandusky and Port Clinton, in the county of Sandusky, and to the town of Maumee in the county of Lucas; to transport, take and carry persons and property upon the same, by the power and force of steam, of animals, or any other mechanical or other power, or combination of them, which said corporation may choose to employ.

Sec. 3. That that the capital stock of said company shall be five hundred thousand dollars, and shall be divided into shares of fifty dollars each; and the shares of the capital stock of said company shall be deemed personal property, transferable by assignment, agreeably to the by-laws of said company.

Sec. 4. That the above named persons, or a majority of them, who may consent to act as such, shall be commissioners, who may authorize any three of their number to open books for receiving subscriptions to the capital stock of said corporation within twelve months after the passing of this act, in the counties through which said road passes, and at such other place or places as they may deem expedient; not less than ten days notice shall be previously given by them, in one or more newspapers printed in the place where the books are to be opened, of the time and place of opening said books; and as soon as the stock shall be subscribed, or fifty thousand dollars thereof, they may give a like notice for a meeting of the stockholders to choose directors, at the time and place appointed; and five directors shall be chosen by ballot, who shall be citizens of the State of Ohio, by such of the stockholders as shall attend for that purpose, either in person or by lawful proxies: each share of the capital stock shall entitle the owner to a vote; the persons named in the first section of this act, or any three appointed by a majority of them, shall be inspectors of such election, and shall certify, under their hands, what persons are elected directors, and appoint the time and place of the first meeting of the directors: five directors, or a majority of them, shall form a board, and be competent to transact all the business of the corporation; a new election of the directors shall be held annually, at such time and place as the stockholders at their first meeting, shall appoint; but if no election shall be made on the day ppointed, such election shall be held at any other time appointed by the by-laws of the corporation; and the directors chosen at any election shall, as soon thereafter as may be convenient, choose out of their number or otherwise, as they may elect one person to be president, and another to be treasurer of said corporation; and if any vacancy shall occur in said board by death, resignation, or otherwise, such vacancy shall be filled by the remaining directors, or a majority of them.

Sec. 5. That upon every subscription there shall be paid, at the time of subscribing, to the person authorized to open said books, the sum of five dollars on each share subscribed; and the residue thereof shall be paid in such instalments, and at such times, as may be required by the president and directors of said company, to the treasurer thereof: *Provided*, No payment other than the first shall be demanded until at least thirty days public notice of such demand shall have been given, by said president and directors, in a newspaper printed in the towns of Toledo and Sandusky: and if any stockholder shall fail or neglect to pay any instalment or part of said subscription thus demanded, for the space of thirty days next after the time the same shall be due and payable, the said president and directors, upon giving twenty days notice thereof, in manner aforesaid, may, and they are hereby authorized to sell at public auction so many of the shares of such delinquent stockholder or stockholders as shall be necessary to pay such instalment and the expenses of advertising and sale, and transfer the shares so sold to the purchaser; and the residue of the money arising from such sale, after paying such instalment and expense, shall be paid to such delinquent stockholder, on demand.

Sec. 6. That the said corporation be, and they are hereby authorized, to cause such examinations and surveys to be made on the ground lying between the aforementioned points as shall be necessary to determine the most eligible route whereon to construct said rail road; and it shall also be lawful for said corporation, by its members or lawful agents, to enter upon and take possession of all such lands and real estate as may be necessary for the construction and repairs of the said rail-road and the requisite erections; and the president and directors of said company may agree with said owner or owners of any land, earth, timber, gravel, stone or other materials, or any articles whatever, which may be wanted in the construction or repair of said road, or any of its works, for the purchase or occupation of the same; and in case of disagreement with the owner as to the price of any land required for said rail road, or as to the price of such materials, not previously appropriated by the owner to any particular use, found on any unimproved land adjoining or near said road, or if the owners are under any disability in law to contract, or out of the county, application may be made to any justice of the peace of the proper county, who shall thereupon issue his warrant under his hand seal, to the sheriff of the proper county, requiring him to summon a jury of six disinterested freeholders of such county, to appear at or near the land, or materials, or property to be valued, on a day named in said warrant, not less than five nor more than ten days after the issuing of the same; and if any of the persons summoned do not attend, the said sheriff shall immediately summon as many as may be necessary to furnish a pannel of six jurors, who shall act as a jury of inquest of damages, having an oath or affirmation first administered to each by said sheriff, justly and impartially to value the damages which the owner or owners will sustain by the use or occupation of the land, materials or property required by said company, and the jury estimating the damages, if for the ground occupied by said road, shall take into the estimate the benefit resulting to said owner or owners, by reason of said road passing through or upon the lands of such owner or owners towards the extinguishment of such claim for damages; and the said jury shall reduce their inquisition to writing, and shall sign and seal the same; and such valuation, when paid or tendered to the owner or owners of said property, his, her or their legal representatives, shall entitle said company to the land, estate and interest, in the same thus valued, as fully as if it had been conveyed by the owner or owners of the same, for such term of time as said company shall occupy the same as a rail road, and the inquest of the jury, after confirmation and after payment or tender of the valuation, shall be a bar to all actions, for taking or using such property; and that such sheriff and jurors shall be entitled to receive from the said company the same fees as are allowed for like services in cases of fixing the valuation on real estate, previous to sale, under execution: *Provided*, That either party may, within ten days, appeal from the decision of said jury of inquest, to the court of common pleas of the proper county, in which such lands are situated; and the said court shall proceed thereon as in cases of appeals for damages in laying out State roads.

Sec. 7. That the said corporation shall have power to determine the width and dimensions of the said rail road, or any part thereof, not exceeding one hundred feet in width, and whether it shall be a double or single track; to regulate the form and manner of its construction, and the time and manner in which passengers and property shall be transported thereon, and the manner of collecting tolls for such transportation, and to erect and maintain buildings for the accommodation of the business of the corporation, as they may deem advisable for their interests.

Sec. 8. That the said corporation may construct their rail road across or upon any road or highway, or across any river, stream or water course, if the same shall be necessary; but in such case it shall be the duty of said corporation so to construct said rail road, as conveniently to admit of the passage or transportation of persons or property upon any such road, highway, river, stream or water course; and when it shall be necessary to pass through the lands of any individual, it shall be their duty to provide such individual proper wagon ways across said rail road, from one part of his land to another: *Provided*, Said rail road shall not be so constructed as in any manner to obstruct, impede or delay the navigation of the Sandusky, Maumee or Portage rivers.

Sec. 9. That the said corporation shall have power to purchase, with the funds of the company, and place on the rail road constructed by them under this act, all machines, wagons, vehicles or carriages of any description, whatsover, which they may deem necessary or proper for the purposes of transportation on said road; and may demand and receive from all persons using or travelling upon said rail road, the following rate of toll, per mile, to wit: for every ton weight of goods, or freight of any description, eight cents for every mile the same shall pass upon said rail road, and a rateable proportion for any greater or less quantity; for every pleasure car. riage, used for the conveyance of passengers, four cents per mile, in addi. tion to the toll by weight upon the load: and it shall be lawful for any other company, person or persons, paying the tolls aforesaid, with suitable and proper cars, to transport upon said [road,] persons or property of any description whatsoever, subject to the by-laws of the company as to the construction and speed of said cars; and the said road, with all the works, improvements, profits and machinery for transportation, are hereby vest. ed in said company, incorpoeated by this act, and their successors, for. ever.

Sec. 10. That at the regular annual meeting of the stockholders of said company, it shall be the duty of the president and directors in office for the previous year, to exhibit a clear and distinct statement of the affairs of the company; and the president and directors shall, annually or semi-annually, declare and make such dividend as they may deem proper, of the nett pro. fits arising from the resources of said company, deducting the necssary cur. rent and probable coutingent expenses, and they shall divide the sum among the stockholders of said company, in proportion to their respective shares.

Sec. 11. That the president and directors, or a majority of them, may appoint all such officers, engineers, agents or servants whatsoever, as they may deem necessary for the transaction of the business of the company, and may remove any of them at pleasure; that they, or a majority of them, shall have power to determine by contract the compensation of all the en. gineers, officers, agents, or servants in the employ of said company; and they, or a majority of them, shall have power to pass all by-laws which they may deem necessary or proper for exercising all the powers vested in the company hereby incorporated, and for carrying the objects of this act into effect.

Sec. 12. That [if] it shall be necessary for the said rail-road company, in the selection of the route, or construction of the road, by them to be laid out and constructed, or any part of it, to connect the same with, or to use any road, street, or bridge, made or erected by any company or persons incorporated or authorized by any law of this State, it shall be lawful for the said president and directors, and they are hereby authorized to contract and agree with any such other corporation or persons, for the right to use such road, street or bridge, or for the transfer of any of the corporate or other rights or privileges of such corporation or persons, to the said com- pany hereby incorporated; and every such other corporation and persons incorporated by, or acting under the laws of this State, are hereby authori- zed to make such an agreement, contract, or transfer, by and through the agency of the persons authorized by their acts of incorporation to exercise the corporate powers, or by such persons as by any law of this State are entrusted with the direction and management of such road, street or bridge, or any of the rights or privileges aforesaid; and every contract, agreement or transfer, made in pursuance of the power and authority hereby granted, when executed by the several parties, under their respective and corporate seals, or otherwise legally authenticated, shall vest in the company hereby incorporated all such roads, parts of roads, streets, rights and privileges, and the right to use and enjoy the same as fully, to all intent and purposes, as they now are, or might be used and exercised by the said corporations or persons in whom they are now vested.

Sec. 13.   That if at any time after said rail-road and improvements may be located, any unforeseen obstacles, impediments or inconveniences occur on the route located, or its branches, the said corporation shall have power to deviate from the course marked out, so far, and in such manner, as the said directors may deem best calculated to surmount, overcome or avoid said obstacles, impediments, or inconveniences; said corporation satisfying the damages that may be occasioned thereby, to be assessed in the manner provided by the sixth section of this act; and the said corporation shall from time to time make such alterations in the course of said rail-road and improvements as they may deem necessary or convenient, satisfying all damages in manner aforesaid.

Sec. 14.   That if any person or persons shall wilfully, by any means whatever, injure, impair or destroy any part of the rail-road constructed by said company, under this act, or any of the works, buildings or machinery of said company, such person or persons, so offending, shall each of them, for every such offence, forfeit and pay to the said company a sum not exceeding three fold the damages, which may be recovered in the name of said company, by an action of debt in the court of common pleas of the county wherein the offence shall be committed, and shall also be subject to an indictment in the said court; and upon conviction of such offence, shall be punished by fine, not exceeding one hundred dollars, and imprisonment in the jail of such county, not more than thirty days.

Sec. 15.   That this act shall be favorably construed to effect the purposes thereby intended, and copies thereof, printed by the authority of the State, shall be received as evidence thereof.

Sec. 16.   That if the corporation hereby created shall not, within two years from the passage of this act, commence, and within five years put in operation the main branch of said road from Toledo to Sandusky City. then this act shall be null and void; and if they shall not, within ten years, construct and put in operation that part lying west of Toledo, to the west line of the State, then this act shall be null and void, so far as relates to the extension from the said Toledo to the west line of the State.

Sec. 17.   That full right and privilege is hereby reserved to the State, or the citizens thereof, or any company hereafter to be incorporated under the authority of this State, to connect with or cross the road hereby provided for, any other rail-road leading from the main route to any part or parts of this State: *Provided*, That in forming such connection or crossing, no injury shall be done to the works of the company hereby incorporated; and the State reserves the right to construct any canal or rail-road on the west side of the Maumee river, without interruption or charges by said company.

Sec. 18.   If the Legislature of this State shall, after the expiration of thirty-five years from the passage of this act, make provision by law for the repayment to said company of all moneys expended in the construction of said road, and for all moneys expended for necessary permanent fixtures at the time of purchase, with an advance of fifteen per cent. thereon, the said road and fixtures shall vest in and become the property of the State of Ohio.

Sec. 19. Whenever the dividends of said company shall exceed the rate of six per cent. per annum, the Legislature of this State may impose such reasonable taxes on the amount of such dividends as may be received from other rail-road companies.

WILLIAM MEDILL,
Speaker pro tem. of the House of Representatives.

ELIJAH VANCE,
Speaker of the Senate.

March 4, 1836.

AN ACT

To incorporate the Ohio, Miami and Wabash Rail-road Company.

Sec. 1. *Be it enacted by the General Assembly of the State of Ohio,* That Gustus Gale and Duthan Northrop, of the county of Portage; Joseph Harris, Timothy Burr, Allen Pardee and Henry Hosmer, of the county of Medina; Sylvanus Parmerly, Alexander Porter, Asa H. Baird, John Tanner, Joseph Sage and Ira Tillotson, of the county of Lorain; Richard Sailsbury, Daniel Beach, Daniel W. Brown, Benjamin Kniffin, Abijah Ives and Asahel Beach, of the county of Huron; and John Park and Abel Rawson, of the county of Seneca; together with such other persons as may thereafter become associated with them, in the manner hereinafter prescribed, their successors and assigns, be, and they are hereby created a body corporate and politic, by the name of "The Ohio, Miami and Wabash Rail-road Company;" and by that name shall be, and are hereby made capable in law to have, hold, purchase, receive, and possess, enjoy and retain, to them and their successors, all such lands, tenements, and hereditaments, with their appurtenances, as shall be necessary, or in any wise convenient, for the transaction of their business, and such as may in good faith be conveyed to them, by way of security, or in payment of debts, and the same to sell, grant, rent, or in any manner dispose of; to contract and be contracted with, sue and be sued, implead and be impleaded, answer and be answered, defend and be defended, in courts of record, or in any other place whatsoever; and also to make, have and use a common seal, and the same to alter, break or renew at pleasure; and they shall be and are hereby invested with all the powers and privileges which are by law incident to corporations of a similar nature, and which are necessary to carry into effect the objects of this association; and if either of the persons named in this section shall die, or neglect to exercise the powers and discharge the duties hereby created, it shall be the duty of the remaining persons hereinbefore named, or a majority of them, to appoint some suitable person or persons to fill such vacancy or vacancies, so often as the same shall occur.

Sec. 2. That said corporation are hereby empowered to cause such examinations and surveys to be made, between Akron, in the county of Portage, and some place at or near Fort Defiance, in the county of Williams, passing through the intermediate points of Harrisville, in the county of Medina; Sullivan, in the county of Lorain; Greenwich and New Haven villages, in the county of Huron; and Tiffin, in the county of Seneca, as shall be necessary to ascertain the most advantageous route whereon to construct a rail-road; and the said corporation are hereby invested with the right to construct a double or single rail-road or way along the said route, and with the right to take, transport, to carry, persons and property upon said road when constructed, by the force of steam, animals, mechanical or other power, or any combination of them, which the said corporation may choose to employ.

Sec. 3. That the capital stock of said corporation shall be one million dollars, and shall be divided into shares of fifty dollars each; and five dollars on each share shall be paid at the time of subscribing.

Sec. 4. That the above named persons, or a majority of them, or the survivors of them, are authorized to open books, for receiving subscriptions to the capital stock of such company, and shall prescribe the form of such subscriptions; which books shall be opened within one year from the passing of this act, at such place or places as they may deem expedient, giving twenty [days] notice in some newspaper printed in each of said counties of Portage, Medina, Lorain, Huron and Seneca, and in such other place or places as may be thought advisable, of the time and place, or times and places, of opening said books: *Provided, however*, That if the publisher of any newspaper printed in either of said counties, shall neglect or refuse to print such notice, then the required notice shall be published, by affixing the same to the door of the court house in said county, at least twenty days previous to the opening of said books; and said books shall be kept open at least ten days.

Sec. 5. That as soon as said stock, or one hundred thousand dollars thereof shall have been subscribed, the above named persons, or the same number thereof as shall have given the notice above required, shall give like notice for a meeting of the stockholders to choose directors, at some time at least twenty days thereafter, and at some place within the said counties of Portage and Medina, Lorain, Huron and Seneca; and if, at such time and place, the holders of one half or more of said capital stock shall attend, either in person or by lawful proxy, they shall proceed to choose from the stockholders, by ballot, twelve directors, each share of capital stock entitling the owner to one vote; and at such election the persons named in the first section of this act, or those appointed by its provisions to fill vacancies which may have occurred, or any three of them, if no more be present, shall be inspectors of such election, and shall certify in writing, signed by them, or a majority of them, what persons are elected directors; and if two or more have an equal number of votes, said inspectors shall determine, by lot, which of them shall be director or directors, to complete the number required, and shall certify the same in like manner; and said inspectors shall appoint the time and place of holding the first meeting of directors, at which meeting seven shall form a board competent to transact all business of the company; and thereafter a new election of directors shall be made annually, at such time and place as the stockholders at their first meeting shall appoint; and if the stockholders shall, at their first meeting, fail to appoint the day of such election, then it shall be holden in the succeeding year, on the same day of the same month on which said first election was holden, unless the same should be the first day of the week, in which case it shall be holden on the day next succeeding; and if no election be had on the day appointed, said company shall not be dissolved, but such election may be made at any time appointed by the by-laws of said company; and the directors chosen at any election shall remain directors until others are chosen; and directors chosen at any election shall, as soon thereafter as may be, choose of their number one person to be president, another to be treasurer of such company, and another to be secretary of said company, and from time to time may choose such other officers as by their by-laws they may designate as necessary, provided that no person shall be a director of such company, who is not a citizen of the State of Ohio.

Sec. 6. That the directors may require payment of subscriptions to the capital stock, at such times, in such proportion, and on such conditions as they shall deem fit, under penalty of forfeiture of all previous payments thereon, or otherwise, provided they shall never require the payment to be made at any place out of the counties through which said road shall pass; and said directors shall, at least thirty days previous to the appointed time of such required payment, give notice thereof in the manner provided in the fourth section of this act, for giving notice of the opening of books of subscription for the stock of said company.

Sec. 7. That the directors of said company shall have power to make, from time to time, all needful rules, regulations, and by-laws, not inconsistent with the constitution and laws of this State, or of the United States, touching the business of said company, and to determine the number of tracks or rail ways upon said road, and the width thereof, and the description of carriages which may be used thereon; to regulate the time and manner in which passengers or goods shall be transported thereon, and manner of collecting tolls for such transportation; and to fix penalties for the breach of any such rule, regulation, or by-law, and direct the mode and condition of transferring the stock of said company; and penalties provided for by said by-laws may be sued for by any person or persons authorized thereto, in the name of said company, and recovered in an action of debt, before any court having jurisdicton of the amount; and said company may erect and maintain toll houses, and such other buildings and fixtures for the accommodation of those using said road, and of themselves, as they may deem in any way necessary for their interest and convenience.

Sec. 8. That said company shall have a right to enter upon any lands, to survey and lay down said road, not exceeding one hundred feet in width, and to take any materials necessary for the construction of said road; and whenever any lands or materials shall be taken for the construction of said road, and the same shall not be given or granted to said company, and the owners thereof do not agree with said company as to the compensation to be paid therefor, the person or persons claiming compensation as aforesaid, or if the owner or owners thereof are minors, in sane persons, or married women, then the guardian or guardians of said minor or minors and insane persons, and the husbands of such married women may select for themselves an arbitrator, and the said company shall select one arbitrator, and the two thus selected shall take to themselves a third, who shall be sworn and paid as arbitrators in other cases; and the three, or a majority of them, shall award as arbitrators between the parties, and render copies of their award to each of the parties, in writing, from which award either party may appeal to the court of common pleas, in the county wherein such lands and materials may have been situated; and in all cases where compensation shall in any manner be claimed for lands, it shall be the duty of the arbitrators and the court to estimate any advantage which the location and construction of said road may be to the claimant for such compensation, and the value of such advantage, if any, shall be set off against the compensation so claimed of said company; and appeals in such cases shall, when taken, be in all respects proceeded in as appeals in other cases to said court, and be brought into said court by filing the award with the clerk of said court, whose duty it shall be to enter the same on the docket of said court, setting down the claimant or claimants as plaintiffs and said company as defendants; and when the valuation so ascertained shall be paid, or tendered by said company, said company shall have the same right to retain, own, hold and possess said personal property, and the use and occupation of said landed property for the purposes of said road, as fully and absolutely as if the same had been granted and conveyed to said company by deed.

Sec. 9. That the said company shall construct the said rail-road across or upon any public road, highway, stream of water or water course, if the same shall be necessary; but the said company shall restore such road, highway, stream of water or water course to its former state, or in a sufficient manner not to impair the usefulness of such road, highway, water or water course to the owner or public, without delay.

Sec. 10. That any rail-way company, now or yet to be chartered by law of this State, shall have power join and unite with the road hereby incorporated, at any point which the directors of such company may think advisable, on such terms as the directors of such companies may respectively agree; and in case of disagreement, then upon such terms as the supreme court in chancery may determine.

Sec. 11. That full right and privilege is hereby reserved to the State or citizens, or to any company incorporated by law of this State, to cross the road hereby incorporated: *Provided,* That in so crossing no injury shall be done to the works of the company hereby incorporated.

Sec. 12. That said company may demand and receive for tolls upon, and the transportation of persons, goods, produce, merchandize or property of any kind whatsoever, transported by them along said rail-way, any sum not exceeding the following rates: on all goods, merchandize, or property of any description whatsoever, transported by them, a sum not exceeding one and a half cents per mile, for toll, and five cents on a ton per mile, for transportation, on all goods, produce, merchandize or property of any description whatsoever, transported by them or their agents; and for the transportation of passengers, not exceeding three cents for each passenger.

33—L

Sec. 13. That all persons, paying the toll aforesaid, may. with suitable and proper carriages, use, and travel upon said rail-road; always subject, however, to such rules and regulations as said company are authorized to make, by the seventh section of this act.

Sec. 14. That if proceedings be not had, under this act, within three years from the taking effect thereof, and if said road be not completed within ten years thereafter, then the same to be void and of no effect.

Sec. 15. That so soon as the amount of tolls accruing and received for the use of said road, or of any part, according to the provisions of this act, shall exceed five per cent. on the amount of capital stock paid in, after deducting therefrom the expenses and liabilities of said company, the directors of said company shall make a dividend of such nett profits among the stockholders in proportion to their respective shares; and no contingent or accumulating fund, exceeding one per centum of the profits of said company, shall remain undivided more than six months.

Sec. 16. That if any person or persons shall wilfully obstruct, or in any way spoil, injure or destroy said road, or either of its branches, or any thing belonging or incident thereto, or any materials to be used in the construction thereof, or any buildings, fixtures, or carriages, erected or constructed for the use or convenience thereof, such person or persons shall each be liable for every such offence to treble the damages sustained thereby, to be recovered by action of debt, in any court having jurisdiction of that amount.

Sec. 17. That the State shall have the right, after the expiration of thirty-five years from the passage of this act, to purchase the Ohio, Miami and Wabash rail-road, and the necessary permanent fixtures, at the time of purchase, and the same to hold for the use of the State, at a price not exceeding the original cost, and fifteen per centum thereon; of which cost an accurate account shall be kept and submitted to the General Assembly, duly attested by the oath of the officers of said company.

Sec. 18. Whenever the dividends of said company shall exceed the rate of six per cent. per annum, the Legislature of this State may impose such reasonable taxes on the amount of such dividends as may be received from other rail-road companies.

WILLIAM MEDILL,
Speaker pro tem. of the House of Representatives.
ELIJAH VANCE,
Speaker of the Senate.

March 4, 1836.

AN ACT

To incorporate the town of Lithopolis, in the county of Fairfield.

Sec. 1. *Be it enacted by the General Assembly of the State of Ohio,* That so much of the township of Bloom, in the county of Fairfield, as is included within the bounds of the town plat of the town of Lithopolis, formerly called Centerville, in said county of Fairfield, as the said town plat now stands on record in the office of the recorder of said county, and such plats of additions to said town as may be hereafter recorded, be, and the same are hereby erected into, and constituted a town corporate, by the name of the Town of Lithopolis.

Sec. 2. That for the order and good government of said town and the inhabitants thereof, it shall be lawful for the white male inhabitants who have resided in said town for the space of six months next preceding said election, having the qualifications of electors of members of the General Assembly, to meet at the school house in said town of Lithopolis, on the first Tuesday of April next, and on the first Tuesday of April annaully thereafter, and then and there proceed, by a plurality of votes, to elect by ballot, one mayor, one recorder, and five trustees, who shall be householders in said town; who shall hold their respective offices for the term of one year, and until their successors are elected and qualified; such mayor, recorder, and trustees, being so elected and qualified, shall constitute a Town Council, any five of whom shall constitute a quorum for the transaction of any business pertaining to their duties; but any less number shall have no power other than to adjourn from time to time until a quorum shall have convened.

Sec. 3. That at the first election to be held under this act, there shall be chosen, *viva voce*, by the electors present, two judges and a clerk of such election; who shall each take an oath or affirmation faithfully to discharge the duties required of him by this act; and at all subsequent elections, the trustees, or any two of them, shall be judges, and the recorder, or in case of his absence, some person appointed by the judges, shall be clerk; the polls shall be opened between the hours of one and two, and close at four o'clock, P. M. of said day; and at the close of the polls the votes shall be counted and a true statement thereof proclaimed to the electors present, by one of the judges, and the clerk shall make a true record thereof; and within five days thereafter said clerk shall give notice to the persons, so elected, of their election; and it shall be the duty of such town council, at least ten days before each and every annual election, to give notice of the same by setting up advertisements at three of the most public places of said town.

Sec. 4. That it shall be the duty of the mayor, and in case of his absence or disability to serve, the recorder, to preside at all meetings of the town council; and it shall also be the duty of the recorder to attend all such meetings, and to keep a fair and accurate record of their proceedings.

Sec. 5. That the town council shall have power to fill all vacancies which may happen in said board, from the householders who are qualified electors in said town, whose appointment shall continue until the next annual election, and until their successors are duly elected and qualified; and whenever it may happen that neither the mayor or recorder is present at any such meeting, the trustees shall have the power to appoint one of their number to perform the duty of such mayor or recorder, or both, as the case may be, which appointment shall be *pro tem*.

Sec. 6. That the said mayor, recorder, and trustees of said town shall be a body politic and corporate, with perpetual succession, to be known and distinguished by the name and title of "The Town Council of the Town of Lithopolis;" and shall be capable in law, in their corporate name, to acquire property, real, personal, and mixed, for the use of said town, with power to sell and convey the same; may have a common seal, which they may alter, break and renew at pleasure, and may sue and be sued, plead and be impleaded, defend and be defended, in any court of competent jurisdiction, whether of law or chancery; and when any suit shall be commenced against said corporation, the first process shall be by summons, an attested copy of which shall be left with the recorder, or at his usual place of residence, at least ten days before the return day thereof.

Sec. 7. That each member of said town council shall, before entering upon the duties of his office, take an oath or affirmation to support the constitution of the United States and of the State of Ohio, and also an oath of office.

Sec. 8. That the said town council shall have power to ordain and establish by-laws, rules and regulations for the government of said town, and the same to alter, amend or repeal at pleasure; to provide in said by-laws for the election of a treasurer, town marshal, and all such subordinate officers as may be deemed necessary for the good government and well being of the inhabitants of said town; to prescribe their duties, and determine the period of their appointment, and the fees they shall be entitled to receive for their services; and to require of them to take the usual oath or affirmation, and to give such security as may be deemed proper, previous to their entering upon the duties of their respective offices; the town council shall also have power to affix to the violation of the by-laws and ordinances of the corporation such reasonable fines and penalties as they may deem proper to enforce obedience to the same, and to provide for the disposition or appropriation of said fines and penalties: *Provided*, Such by-laws and ordinances be not inconsistent with the constitution and laws of the United States and of this State: *And provided also*, That no by-law or ordinance of said corporation shall take effect or be in force until the same shall have been posted up for two weeks in one of the most public places within said corporation.

Sec. 9. That the said town council shall, at the expiration of each and every year, cause to be made out and posted up as aforesaid, the receipts and expenditures of the preceding year.

Sec. 10. That the town council shall have power to regulate and improve the streets, lanes and alleys, and determine the width of side-walks; they shall have power to remove all nuisances and obstructions from the streets and commons of said town, or to provide for the removal of the same; and to do all things which corporations of a similar nature can do, to secure the peace, health, and good order of the inhabitants of said town.

Sec. 11. That for the purpose of more effectually enabling said town council to carry into effect the provisions of this act, they are hereby authorized and empowered to levy a tax on all personal and real property, subject to taxation, within the bounds of said corporation, as the same has been or shall be appraised and returned on the grand levy of the State: *Provided*, That said tax shall not exceed in any one year, one half of one per centum on the aggregate amount of all such taxable property within the limits of said corporation; and the said town council shall, between the first Tuesday in April and the first Tuesday in July, determine the amount of tax to be assessed and collected for the current year.

Sec. 12. That it shall be the duty of the recorder of said corporation to make out duplicates of taxes, charging each individual within said corporation an amount of tax in proportion to the aggregate value of the taxable property belonging to said individual within the limits of said corporation, as the same appears from the auditor's books of Fairfield county; and the said auditor shall, at all reasonable office hours, lay open to the inspection of the recorder, any books which may be in his office, affording such information; and the recorder shall be allowed to take such abstracts or memorandums or transcripts therefrom, free of expense, to enable him to make out such duplicates; which duplicates shall be certified by the mayor and recorder; and one of said duplicates shall be delivered to the marshal or to such other person as shall be appointed collector, whose duty it shall be to collect said tax, in the same manner and under the same regulations as the collectors of state and county taxes are required by law to collect the state and county taxes; and the said marshal or collector so appointed, shall, immediately after collecting said tax, pay the same over to the treasurer of said corporation, and take his receipt therefor; and the said marshal or other collector shall have the same power to sell both real and personal property as is given by law to county treasurers; and when necessary, the recorder shall have power to make deeds for real estate so sold, in the same manner that county auditors are by law empowered to do, for lands sold by the county treasurer; and the marshal or other collector shall receive for his fees such sum as the town council may direct, not exceeding six per centum on all moneys so by him collected, to be paid by the treasurer on the order of the recorder.

Sec. 13. That the said town council shall have full power to appropriate any money remaining in the corporation treasury to the improvement of the streets and alleys and side walks of said town, when they may deem it necessary so to do, and to make all other improvements of a public nature which may conduce to the convenience and prosperity of the inhabitants of said town.

Sec. 14. That the mayor of said corporation shall be conservator of the peace throughout said town, and shall, within the same, have all the powers and jurisdiction of a justice of the peace, in all matters, either civil or criminal, arising under the by-laws and ordinances of said corporation, to all intents and purposes whatsoever; the said mayor shall perform all the duties required of him by the laws and ordinances of said corporation; and appeals may be taken from the decisions of of said mayor in all cases where appeals are allowed from the decisions of justices of the peace, and in the same manner.

Sec. 15. That the marshal shall be the principal ministerial officer of said town, and shall have the same powers that constables have by law; and his jurisdiction in criminal cases shall be co-extensive with the county of Fairfield, and he shall execute the process of the mayor, and receive the same fees for his services that constables are allowed in similar cases for like services.

Sec. 16. That the mayor shall receive the same fees that justices of the peace are entitled to in like cases; and the recorder such fees for his services, as the by-laws and ordinances of said corporation shall prescribe; but the residue of said town council shall receive no pecuniary compensation.

Sec. 17. That if no election should be held by the electors of said town, on the first Tuesday of April next, it shall be lawful for any ten householders of said town to call a meeting of the electors, by giving twelve days notice in three of the most public places therein; which notice shall state the time and place, and object of the meeting, and shall be signed by said householders; and if a majority of the electors of said town shall attend at the time and place mentioned in said notice, it shall be lawful for them to proceed to the election of officers in the same manner as though the meeting had taken place on the first Tuesday of April; and the officers so elected shall hold their offices until the first Tuesday of April following, and until their successors are duly elected and qualified.

Sec. 18. That said corporation shall be allowed the use of the jail of said county, for the imprisonment of such persons as may be liable to imprisonment under the by-laws and ordinances of said town council; and all persons so imprisoned shall be under the charge of the sheriff or jailor, as in other cases.

Sec. 19. That any future Legislature may have the power to alter, amend, or repeal this act, not thereby affecting, however, in any manner, the rights of individual citizens.

WILLIAM MEDILL,
Speaker pro tem. of the House of Representatives.

ELIJAH VANCE,
Speaker of the Senate.

March 4, 1836.

AN ACT

To declare a part of the Clear Fork of Stillwater creek, in the county of Tuscarawas, a public highway.

Sec. 1. *Be it enacted by the General Assembly of the State of Ohio,* That the Clear fork of Stillwater creek, from its confluence with Big Stillwater creek, up to the mill now owned by Samuel Osborn, in the county of Tuscarawas, be, and the same is hereby declared a public highway.

Sec. 2. That if any person shall fell, or put, or cause to be felled or put, any tree, log, timber, brush, stone, or other obstruction, into, or over that part of said creek, hereby declared a public highway, to the obstruction or injury of the navigation of the same, every person so offending, shall forfeit and pay, for every such offence, a sum not less than five, nor more than one hundred dollars; to be recovered before any court having jurisdiction thereof, in the name of the State of Ohio, upon the complaint of any person; which money, when collected, shall be paid into the treasury of the township where such offence shall have been committed, and be applied by the trustees of said township, in improving said highway.

Sec. 3. That any person offending against the provisions of this act, shall also be liable to the action of any person or persons, for such damages as he, she, or they, may have sustained, by or in consequence of the commission of such offence, to be recovered before any court having jurisdiction thereof.

WILLIAM MEDILL,
Speaker pro tem. of the House of Representatives.
ELIJAH VANCE,
Speaker of the Senate.

March 4, 1836.

AN ACT

To change the name of Truxville to that of Ganges.

Sec. 1. *Be it enacted by the General Assembly of the State of Ohio,* That the name of Truxville, in the county of Richland, be, and the same is hereby changed to that of Ganges.

WILLIAM MEDILL,
Speaker pro tem. of the House of Repeesentatives.
ELIJAH VANCE,
Speaker of the Senate.

March 4, 1836.

AN ACT

For the relief of the heirs of Marcus Heylin.

WHEREAS, Marcus Heylin, late of Champaign county, Ohio, departed this life, owning the section No. 26, in town 4, south of range 5, E. situated in the county of Allen, the taxes on which have not been regularly paid by the guardians of his minor heirs, and the proper amount actually due thereon, cannot now be actually known: Therefore,

Sec. 1. *Be it enacted by the General Assembly of the State of Ohio,* That the auditor of State is hereby authorized to settle with the owners of said land for all taxes due thereon, as well as the same can be known; and on the payment into the treasury of the sum agreed on, to release the said land from the forfeiture incurred by the non-payment of such taxes

WILLIAM MEDILL,
Speaker pro tem. of the House of Representatives.
ELIJAH VANCE,
Speaker of the Senate.

March 4, 1836.

AN ACT

To incorporate the Ohio Commercial and Manufacturing Company.

Sec. 1. *Be it enacted by the General Assembly of the State of Ohio,* That Allen Farquhar, Joshua V. Roberts)n, George Corwin, and their associates, be, and they are hereby created a body politic and corporate, in perpetual succession, by the name and style of the Ohio Commercial and Manufacturing Company; and may acquire, hold, use, transfer, and convey all such property, real, personal, and mixed, as may be convenient and necessary for the prosecution of their business, and the use and convenience of said company; and may make and execute, alter and repeal all such by-laws and regulatiqns, for the government of the company, and the management of their business and proceedings, and for the control of their property, real, personal and mixed, as they may deem expedient: *Provided,* That each and every stockholder shall be liable in his individual capacity, for any debt or debts of the corporation, to the full amount of his, her, or their stock subscribed: *Provided, always,* That the joint funds and other property of the corporation, shall be first subjected to the payment of such debts, before the individual property of any stockholder shall be seized in execution, or other proceedings be had to subject the same to the payment of such debts.

Sec. 2. That the capital stock of said company shall consist of two hundred and fifty thousand dollars, divided into two thousand five hundred shares, of one hundred dollars each; and the stock, property and business of said company shall be managed, conducted, and controlled in such manner, and by such officers, agents, or other persons, as the said company shall by their by-laws, rules, and regulations prescribe.

Sec. 3. That the said corporation shall have full power and authority to survey, locate, and construct a navigable canal, of such dimensions as the said company may deem proper, from the Ohio Canal, near Bear creek, to cross the Scioto river by a dam, and other works, and to terminate in a basin near the bank of the Ohio river, on the east side of the Scioto river, within the corporation bounds of the town of Portsmouth, and shall have the right to connect such canal with the Ohio canal, at such convenient place near the mouth of Bear creek, as the canal commissioners may designate, by means of a lock or locks, to be erected upon such place and in such manner as said canal commissioners, or the acting commissioner on said Ohio canal, shall deem best calculated to secure the Ohio canal from injury, and to prevent an expenditure of water beyond what is necessary for the passage of boats or floats, through said lock or locks: *Provided, however,* That if, in the opinion of the acting commissioner, engineer, or superintendent, having charge of that part of the Ohio canal, said company shall at any time suffer said lock or locks, or other work appertaining to said connexion, to be so far out of repair as to endanger the safety of the Ohio canal, or cause an unnecessary expenditure of water, such acting commissioner, engineer, or superintendent, shall have the right of closing the connexion between said canal, by a bank of earth, dam, or otherwise, and continuing the same until such repairs shall be made as will, in his opinion,

render it safe, to open or renew such connexion; and said company shall
pay the expenses of the said bank, dam, or other closing, and the removal
of the same, as often as the same may occur, as provided for in this section, without delay, on the certificate of the acting commissioner, engineer
or superintendent.

Sec. 4. That said company shall have the right to draw from the Scioto river, at the place of crossing the same, so much water as they may
deem expedient, for hydraulic purposes, or for purposes of navigation: *Provided*, Nothing in this section shall be so construed as to authorize said
company to interfere with the rights of individuals who may own lands
adjoining said river, at any place below said place of crossing, without the
consent of such individuals.

Sec. 5. That the said company shall have the exclusive right to construct such additional basins, to be connected with the said canal, as they
may think proper; and shall have the right to the use, and control of all
the water that the said canal and basins may be capable of containing, and
may make any application or disposition of the same, that they may think
proper; and shall have the right to charge such rates of toll and wharfage,
on the said canal and basins, as may be just and equitable: *Provided*,
The company shall not charge less tolls on said canal than are now, or may
hereafter be charged on the corresponding portion of the Ohio canal, between the mouth of Bear creek and the Ohio river.

Sec. 6. That the three persons named in the first section of this act,
be, and they are hereby appointed commissioners, under the direction of
a majority of whom books may be opened, at such times and places as may
be deemed proper, for the purpose of receiving subscriptions to the capital stock of said company; and it is hereby made the duty of said commissioners to give at least thirty days notice in one or more newspapers printed in the vicinity of the place where said books are intended to be opened,
of the times and places of opening said books; and the said commissioners
shall keep the books open for the subscriptions to the capital stock of said
company, at least four days from the time specified in said notice.

Sec. 7. That it shall be lawful for the said company to commence the
construction of said canal, basins, and other works mentioned in this act,
as soon as the sum of one hundred thousand dollars shall have been subscribed to the capital stock of said company, if within two years from the
passage of this act.

Sec. 8. That if more than two thousand five hundred shares shall have
been subscribed to the capital stock of said company, the said commissioners shall reduce the number to two thousand five hundred, by striking from
the largest number of shares in succession, until reduced to the proper
number.

Sec. 9. That each subscriber to the capital stock of said company, shall
for each share subscribed, pay such instalments, and at such times, as the
president and directors of said company may require: *Provided*, That no
instalment shall be required unless upon thirty days notice; and if any subscriber, upon notice being given as aforesaid, shall neglect or refuse to pay
any instalment, or part thereof, said president and directors may sell the
stock of such subscriber, being delinquent as aforesaid, in such manner as
may be prescribed in the by-laws of said company.

34—L

Sec. 10. That if the sum of one hundred thousand dollars shall have been subscribed to the capital stock of said company, within the term of two years from the passage of this act, the said commissioners shall call a general meeting of the stockholders, at such time and place as they may deem proper, giving at least thirty days notice thereof, in some newspaper published in the town of Portsmouth; and at such meeting the said commissioners shall lay the books before the subscribers, or a majority of them, shall proceed to elect by ballot, seven directors, being stockholders, to manage and conduct the business and affairs of the said company; and the said seven directors shall, within ten days thereafter, elect from their own number, a president of said company, whose duty shall be prescribed in their by-laws; and in said election, as in all others where the votes of the stockholders are taken, each stockholder shall be allowed one vote for every share under ten, one vote for every two shares over ten. and under twenty, one vote for every three shares over twenty and under fifty, and one vote for every four shares over fifty; and each stockholder may depute any other stockholder or person to vote in his or her behalf, in such manner as the by-laws may prescribe; and the said commissioners, or either of them, shall act as judges of the first election of officers of said company.

Sec. 11. That to continue the succession of the president and directors of said company, they shall be elected annually, on the first Monday of October, at the place of holding the annual meetings of the stockholders; and if any vacancy shall occur, by death, resignation, or otherwise, of any president or director, before the expiration of the term for which he was elected, a person to fill such vacancy, for the residue of the year, shall be appointed by the directors; and the said president and directors shall hold their offices, and exercise the duties thereof, until others are duly elected and qualified; and any election fixed upon a particular day and not held, may be held at any time within six months thereafter, upon thirty days notice of such election being given by the president of said company.

Sec. 12. That a general meeting of the stockholders shall be held annually, at the time and place of holding the election for directiors; or may be called at any time, if in the opinion of the president and directors, or a majority of the stockholders in value, that the interests of the company should require such meeting: it shall then be the duty of the president of said company to give at least thirty days notice of the time of holding it.

Sec. 13. That at the regular meetings of the stockholders it shall be the duty of the president and directors in office the preceding year, to exhibit a clear and distinct statement of the affairs and business of the company; and at any called meeting of stockholders, a majority of those present or by proxy, may require a similar statement of the president and directors; and at all general meetings of the stockholders, a majority in value of two-thirds present or by proxy, may remove any president or director from office, at which time an election to fill such vacancy for the residue of the year shall be held.

Sec. 14. That every president and director shall, previous to commencing the duties of his office, swear or affirm that he will faithfully perform the duties of his office, according to his best skill and judgment.

Sec. 15. That whenever it may become necessary for said company to have or use any materials or other property, in the construction or repair of the said canal or basins, the president and directors of said company, their agents, or those contracting with them, for constructing or repairing the same, may immediately take and use the said materials or other property; having first caused the same to be examined by three disinterested freeholders of Scioto county, to be appointed by the associate judges of said county, who shall make out a statement, in writing, of the value of such materials or other property: the amount of which assessment the company shall pay to the owner or owners of said property.

Sec. 16. That when the said canal shall have been completed, according to the provisions of this act, all persons, through whose lands said canal may pass, feeling themselves injured by reason thereof, and claiming damage, shall have such damage assessed, upon the same principles as are prescribed in the law authorizing the construction of the Ohio canal, upon the oath of three disinterested freeholders, to be appointed as prescribed in the fifteenth section of this act; which damages shall be paid by the company, to the persons entitled thereto, on demand.

Sec. 17. That whenever it may become necessary for the said canal, or basins, to cross any established road or way, the said company shall construct, within a reasonable time, and keep the same in repair, such bridges and other conveniences as may be necessary, in order that persons and property may pass with safety, and the ordinary transaction of business on said road or way shall not be obstructed thereby.

Sec. 18. That the said company shall have the exclusive right to construct and use such boats, and other machinery, as they may deem proper and convenient, for the purpose of conveying canal boats and other craft across the Scioto river, at the place where said canal may cross said river, and shall have the right to charge such rates of ferriage, as may hereafter be prescribed by the court of common pleas for Scioto county, and shall have the right to use said boats, and other machinery, for the common purposes of a ferry.

Sec. 19. That the said commissioners named in the first section of this act, or a majority of them, shall appoint a competent engineer, to survey and locate the canal and basin, authorized to be constructed by this act, at such time as they may deem proper, previous to opening books for subscription to the capital stock of said company; and the said commissioners shall require of the said engineer an accurate statement of the amount of each kind of work necessary to be done, in the construction of the said canal and basin, together with the probable cost of the same; and the said engineer shall plant stakes at such distances apart, as may be necessary to designate the location of the said canal line, and shall also make out an accurate plat of the line of the said canal and basin, together with such plans and estimates of the work, as the said commissioners may think necessary, for the use of the company; and the said commissioners shall have the plat of said location recorded in the office of the recorder of Scioto county; which location, thus established, shall be adopted by the company, in the construction of said canal and basin.

Sec. 20. That if the canal authorized to be constructed by this act, shall not be commenced within three years, and be completed within five years from the commencement thereof, then this act shall be null and void.

Sec. 21. That at the expiration of fifteen years from the completion of the said canal, the State shall have the right to charge tolls on said canal, and make such other regulations respecting its navigation, as will place it in the same situation as any other portion of the Ohio canal, with respect to its navigation and tolls; and shall be kept in repair by the State, as a part of the Ohio canal.

WILLIAM MEDILL,
Speaker pro tem. of the House of Representatives.
ELIJAH VANCE,
Speaker of the Senate.

March 4, 1836.

AN ACT

Authorising a review of a State road in the counties of Muskingum, Morgan, and Washington.

Sec. 1. *Be it enacted by the General Assembly of the State of Ohio,* That Samuel Beach, of the county of Washington; Benjamin Thorla, of the county of Morgan; and Samuel Chandler, of the county of Muskingum, be, and they are hereby appointed commissioners to review so much of a state road, leading from Marietta, in Washington county, to Zanesville, in Muskingum county, as lies between Coal run, in Washington county, and Chandlersville, in Muskingum county; beginning at Coal run, and make thereon such alterations and locations as they shall deem just and proper for the benefit of said road.

Sec. 2. That said road, when reviewed and altered as aforesaid, shall in no case exceed an angle of six degrees with the horizon; and the commissioners aforesaid shall in all cases be governed by the act defining the mode of laying out and establishing state roads, passed March 14th, 1831.

Sec. 3. That should either of the commissioners die, or remove out of the county, or refuse to serve, the commissioners of the county in which such vacancy shall happen shall forthwith, on being notified of such vacancy, appoint some suitable person to fill the same as often as it may occur.

WILLIAM MEDILL,
Speaker pro tem. of the House of Representatives.
ELIJAH VANCE,
Speaker of the Senate.

March 4, 1836.

AN ACT

To permit and authorise the State of Indiana to construct a part of the Whitewater canal within the territory of Ohio.

Sec. 1. *Be it enacted by the General Assembly of the State of Ohio,* That the State of Indiana be, and is hereby permitted to construct so much of the Whitewater canal in the State of Ohio, as may be found necessary for the purpose of terminating said canal at or near Lawrenceburgh, in the State of Indiana: *Provided*, Said canal be located and constructed on such plan as will, in the opinion of the acting commissioner on the Miami canal, afford every reasonable facility to this State, to connect with and extend a branch canal from said Whitewater canal, to the lower plane of the city of Cincinnati; and that the said branch shall be supplied from said canal, with all the water that shall be necessary for the navigation of the branch: *Provided, also*, That previous to the final location of a canal, a survey shall be made on each side of the Whitewater, from Brookville to the mouth of said river, and also west of the village of Elizabethtown; and in determining the location and plan of the canal, reference shall be had to the general interests and convenience of the neighborhoods through which said canal may pass, so far as may be practicable and expedient, without increasing materially the cost of the work.

Sec. 2. That all the laws now in force, or which may hereafter be enacted for the construction and protection of the Ohio canals, and the works connected therewith, be, and are hereby [extended] to the construction and protection of so much of said Whitewater canal, and the necessary works connected therewith, as may be located in the State of Ohio.

Sec. 3. That the State of Indiana shall have the right of collecting tolls on said *part* of the Whitewater canal, at the same rates which may be charged on said canal in other parts of it: *Provided*, That no greater rates of toll shall be charged on property passing on the said Whitewater canal, which [property] may pass on any branch of said canal that may be made by the State of Ohio, than is charged on property passing entirely on the said Whitewater canal.

Sec. 4. That all claims for damages on account of injuries sustained by private individuals for the construction of, or in the repairing and securing said canal within this State, shall be submitted by the proper officers of the Whitewater canal, to the acting commissioner on the Miami canal; whose duty it shall be to appoint a board of appraisers, consisting either of the board of appraisers for the Miami canal, or of other three disinterested freeholders, citizens of this State; which board, or a majority of them shall examine and decide on all such claims, when submitted to them by the said acting commissioners, in accordance with and agreeably to the laws of this State, relating to assessments of damages on the Ohio canals, and report the same to the proper authority of Indiana; which assessment so made shall be paid to the State of Indiana, and shall be final: *Provided*, That the appraisers shall be paid for their services by the State of Indiana, at the rate that the appraisers, for similar purposes, are paid in this State.

Sec. 5. That whenever in the construction of said part of said canal, it shall be necessary to cross any established road or way, it shall be the duty of the State of Indiana so to construct the said canal, as not to impede the passage or transportation of persons or property along the same; and shall construct good and substantial bridges over said part of said canal for said roads, and shall keep the same in repair, and reconstruct the same whenever necessary.

WILLIAM MEDILL,
Speaker pro tem. of the House of Representatives.
ELIJAH VANCE,
Speaker of the Senate.

March 4, 1836.

AN ACT

To vacate a part of the State road from Columbus, in Franklin county, to Waldo, in Delaware county.

Sec. 1. *Be it enacted by the General Assembly of the State of Ohio,* That so much of the State road from Columbus, in Franklin county, to Waldo, in Delaware county, as lies north of the town of Delaware, in Delaware county, to Waldo, in said county, inclusive, be, and the same is hereby vacated.

WILLIAM MEDILL,
Speaker pro tem. of the House of Representatives.
ELIJAH VANCE,
Speaker of the Senate.

March 4, 1836.

AN ACT

To incorporate the German Lutheran and Reformed Presbyterian Congregation of New Lisbon, in the town of New-Lisbon, Columbiana county.

Sec. 1. *Be it enacted by the General Assembly of the State of Ohio,* That George Crowl, William Helman, Jacob Coblentz, and Peter Brinker, and their associates, together with those that may hereafter be associated with them, be, and they are hereby created a body corporate and politic, by the name of the "German Lutheran and Reformed Presbyterian Congregation of the German Church of New Lisbon," in the town of New Lisbon, Columbiana county, and as such shall remain and have perpetual succession.

Sec. 2. That the said corporation shall be capable in law, by the name aforesaid, of suing and being sued, pleading and being impleaded, in any action or suit, in any court having competent jurisdiction; and they may have a common seal, which may be altered, changed or renewed at pleasure.

Sec. 3. That said corporation, by the name aforesaid, shall be capable in law and equity, of holding, receiving, having and acquiring, either by gift, grant, devise or purchase, any estate, real or personal, for the use of said corporation, not exceeding six thousand dollars.

Sec. 4. That the trustees of said corporation may at any time after the passage of this act, borrow money, to the amount of any sum not exceeding five hundred dollars, for the use and benefit of said corporation: *Provided, however,* That a majority of the members of said corporation first assent thereto.

Sec. 5. That the trustees of said corporation shall be capable in law of selling any estate, real or personal, belonging to said corporation, for its use and benefit, by the concurrence of a majority of its members.

Sec. 6. That the trustees aforesaid, and their associates shall meet on the first Saturday in May, in the year of our Lord, one thousand eight hundred and thirty seven, and thereafter on the first Saturday of May, annually; but in case of any failure or vacancy in office, the trustees may call a meeting at such time and place as they may deem proper, and elect by ballot three trustees, and such other officers as the said corporation may deem necessary; and may adopt and establish such by-laws and ordinances as may be thought proper, for the good government of said corporation: *Provided,* They are not inconsistent with the constitution already formed by the members of said German Lutheran and Reformed Presbyterian Congregation: *And provided, also,* They are and shall be compatible with constitution and laws of the United States, and of this State.

Sec. 7. That George Crowl, William Helman, Jacob Coblentz, and Peter Brinker, be, and they are hereby appointed trustees until the first Saturday in May, eighteen hundred and thirty-seven, and until their successors are chosen, under the provisions of this act.

Sec. 8. That any future Legislature shall have power to alter, amend or repeal this act: *Provided,* Such modification or repeal shall not affect the title to any real or personal estate, acquired or conveyed under its provisions, or divert the same to any other purpose than originally intended.

WILLIAM MEDILL,
Speaker pro tem. of the House of Representatives.

ELIJAH VANCE,
Speaker of the Senate.

March 5, 1836.

AN ACT

To incorporate the city of Cleveland.

Sec. 1. *Be it enacted by the General Assembly of the State of Ohio,* That so much of the county of Cuyahoga as is contained within the following bounds, to wit: beginning at low water mark, on the shore of Lake Erie, at the most north-eastwardly corner of Cleveland ten acre lot, number one hundred and thirty-nine, and running thence on the dividing line between lots number one hundred and thirty-nine, and one hundred and forty, numbers one hundred and seven and one hundred and eight, numbers eighty and eighty-one, numbers fifty-five and fifty-six, numbers thirty-one and thirty-two, and numbers six and seven of the ten acre lots, to the south line of ten acre lots; thence on the south line of the ten acre lots, to the Cuyahoga river; thence to the centre of the Cuyahoga river; thence down the same to the extreme point of the west pier of the harbor; thence to the township line between Brooklyn and Cleveland; thence on that line northwardly to the county line; thence eastwardly with said line to a point due north of the place of beginning; thence south to the place of beginning; shall be, and is hereby declared to be a city; and the inhabitants thereof are created a body corporate and politic, by the name and style of the City of Cleveland; and by that name shall be capable of contracting and being contracted with, of suing and being sued, pleading and being impleaded, answering and being answered unto, in all courts and places, and in all matters whatsoever; with power of purchasing, receiving, holding, occupying and conveying real and personal estate; and may use a corporate seal, and change the same at pleasure; and shall be competent to have and exercise all the rights and privileges, and be subject to all the duties and obligations appertaining to a municipal corporation.

Sec. 2. That the government of said city, and the exercise of its corporate powers, and the management of its fiscal; prudential and municipal concerns shall be vested in a mayor and council, which council shall consist of three members from each ward, actually residing therein, and as many aldermen as there may be wards, to be chosen from the city at large, no two of which shall reside in any one ward, and shall be denominated the city council; and also such other officers as are hereinafter mentioned and provided for.

Sec. 3. That the said city, until the city council see fit to increase, alter or change the same, be divided into three wards, in the manner following, to wit: the first ward shall comprise all the territory lying easterly of the centre of the Cuyahoga river, and southerly of the centre of Superior lane, and Superior street to Ontario street, and of a line thence to the centre of Euclid street, and of said last mentioned centre; the second ward shall comprise all the territory not included in the first ward, lying easterly of the centre of Seneca street; the third ward shall include all the territory westerly of the centre of Seneca street, easterly of the westerly boundary of the city, and northerly of the centre of Superior street and Superior lane.

Sec. 4. That the mayor, aldermen, councilmen, marshal and treasurer of said city shall be elected by the qualified voters thereof, at the annual election of said city, to be held on the first Monday in March, and shall hold their respective offices for one year, and until their successors are chosen and qualified; it shall be the duty of the mayor to keep the seal of said city, sign all commissions, licenses and permits, which may be granted by the city council; to take care that the laws of the State and the ordinances of the city council be faithfully executed; to exercise a constant supervision and control over the conduct of all subordinate officers, and to receive and to examine into all complaints against them, for neglect of duty; to preside at the meetings of the city council, when other duties shall permit; to recommend to said city council such measures as he may deem expedient; to expedite all such as shall be resolved upon by them; and in general to maintain the peace and good order, and advance the prosperity of the city; as a judicial officer, he shall have exclusive original jurisdiction of all cases, for the violation of any ordinance of said city; and in criminal cases, he is hereby vested with powers co-equal with justices of the peace within the county of Cuyahoga, and shall be entitled to like fees; and he shall award all such process, and issue all such writs as may be necessary to enforce the due administration of right and justice throughout said city, and for the lawful exercise of his jurisdiction, agreeably to the usages and principles of law; and when presiding at the meetings of the city council, he shall have a casting vote, when the votes of the members are equal.

Sec. 5. The members of the city council shall, on the second Monday after each annual election, assemble at the council chamber, or some other suitable place in said city, and elect from their own body a president, to preside in their meetings, in the absence of the mayor; and a majority of all the members shall be a quorum for the transaction of business: the city council shall determine the rules of their proceedings, and keep a journal thereof, which shall be open to the inspection of every citizen; may compel the attendance of absent members, under such penalties and in such manner as they may think fit to prescribe; and shall prescribe the place and fix the time of holding their meetings, which shall at all times be open to the public; and said council may adopt any by-laws for their own government, not inconsistent with the provisions of this act; and in case of the absence or inability of both the mayor and president of the city council, the senior alderman present, shall, for the time being, discharge the duties of either the mayor or president of the city council, as the case may require.

Sec. 6. That the city council shall have the custody and control of all the real and personal estate, and other corporate property belonging to said city, its public buildings, rights and interests; and may make such orders, regulations and provisions, for the maintenance and preservation thereof, as they shall deem expedient; it shall be their duty to regulate the police of the city, preserve the peace, prevent riots, disturbances and disorderly assemblages; they shall have authority to appoint watchmen, and prescribe their powers and duties, and to prescribe fines and penalties for their delinquencies; to restrain vagrants or other persons soliciting alms or subscriptions; to suppress and restrain disorderly and gaming houses, billiard tables, and other devices and instruments of gaming; to prevent the vending of liquors to be drank on any canal boat, or other place not duly licensed; to prevent and punish immoderate driving in any street or other highway of said city; to abate and remove nuisances; to prohibit bathing in any public water within the city; to prevent the encumbering of any of the streets or highways of the city, in any manner whatever; to provide for clearing the Cuyahoga river of drift wood and other obstructions, and to prevent encroachments of any kind thereon, within said city; to regulate the keeping and carrying of gunpowder and other combustible materials; to establish, alter and regulate markets; to regulate the vending of meats, vegetables and fruits, pickled and other fish, and the time and place of selling the same; weighing and selling hay, measuring coal, cord wood and other fuel, and lumber, and shingles; weighing and measuring salt, lime, fish, iron, and any other commodity exposed, or intended to be exposed, for sale in said city; to provide for, and regulate the guaging of all casks, and other vessels containing liquids, sold, or intended to be sold in said city; to regulate
35—L

cartmen and cartage, porters, hacking carriages and their drivers, and
limit their fees and compensation; and to regulate pawn-brokers; to
light the streets of the city; to regulate or restrain the running at large of
horses, cattle, dogs, and swine; and to establish and regulate one or more
pounds; and to impose a tax on the owners of dogs; to estabish and preserve public wells and cisterns. and to prevent the waste of water; to
regulate the burial of the dead, and to compel the keeping and return of
bills of mortality; to regulate all taverns and porter houses, and places
where spirituous liquors are bought and sold by less quantity than one
quart; all houses or places of public entertainment; all exhibitions and
public shows; with exclusive power to grant or refuse licenses thereto, or
to revoke the same, and to exact such sum or sums therefor, as they may
deem expedient; to establish and settle the boundaries of all streets or
highways of all kinds within the city, and prevent or remove encroachments thereon; to prescribe the bonds and securities to be given by the
officers of the city, for the discharge of their duties, where no provision
is otherwise made by law; and further to have power and authority, and
it is hereby made their duty, to make and publish from time to time all
such laws and ordinances, as to them may seem necessary to suppress
vice, provide for the safety, preserve the health, promote the prosperity,
improve the order comfort and convenience of said city and its inhabitants, and to benefit the trade and commerce thereof, as are not repugnant
to the general laws of the State; and likewise they shall have power to
regulate wharves and the mooring of vessels in the harbor; to appoint a
harbor master, with the usual powers, and to prevent fishing lights; and
for the violation of any ordinance by them made by the authority of this
act, the said city council may prescribe any penalty not exceeding one
hundred dollars, and provide for the prosecution, recovery and collection
thereof, or for the imprisonment of the offender, in case of the non-payment of such penalty.

Sec. 7. That for the purpose of guarding against the calamities of fire,
the city council may from time to time, by ordinance, designate such portions and parts of the city as they shall deem proper, within which no
buildings of wood shall be erected; and may regulate and direct the erections of buildings within such portions and parts, the size and materials,
and the size of the chimneys therein; and every person who shall violate
such ordinance or regulation shall forfeit to said city the sum of one hundred dollars; and every building erected contrary to such ordinance, is
hereby declared to be a common nuisance, and may be abated and removed as such by the city council; and the city council may by ordinance require the owners and occupants of houses and other buildings to have
scuttles on the roofs of such houses and buildings, and stairs or ladders
leading to the same; and whenever any penalty shall have been recovered
against the owner or occupant of any house or other building for not complying with such ordinance, the city council may, at the expiration of
twenty days after such recovery, cause such scuttles and stairs or ladders
to be constructed, and may recover the expense thereof, with ten per cent.
in addition, of the owner or occupant, whose duty it was to comply with
such ordinance; and for the purpose of arresting the progress of any fire,
the mayor and council, or any three members thereof, may direct any

building or buildings to be torn down, removed or blown up with gun powder.

Sec. 8. That the city council shall have power, on petition, signed by at least twelve freeholders of said city, and notice given for six consecutive weeks in one or more of the newspapers of said city, to lay out and establish, vacate, change or alter, any street or streets, alley or alleys, lane or lanes in said city; and if any person shall claim damages by reason of the laying out or vacating, changing or altering thereof, and shall file his notice of such claim, in writing, with the city clerk, within thirty days after the order for laying out, vacating, changing or altering, shall have been published, which said order said city council shall cause to be published in some newspaper in said city, for four weeks in succession; the city council shall cause the damage, if any, over and above the benefit accruing thereby to such claimant, to be assessed by the oaths of three disinterested judicious freeholders of said city, by them appointed for that purpose; and the amount so assessed, shall be paid within three months after the return of such assessment, either by the petitioners, or out of the city treasury, as said council shall determine; or in default thereof, the order for laying out, vacating, changing or altering, shall be null and void; the city council shall have power to cause all the streets, highways, commons and market places of said city to be kept in repair, and may cause the same to be graded, paved or otherwise improved, as the interest of said city may seem to require; and shall have exclusive power of appointing supervisors and officers of streets and other highways within said city, and prescribing their several duties; and the city council shall cause the public streets, roads, lanes, alleys and highways, and the public squares, and other public grounds that now exists within the limits of said city, to be, by the surveyor of the county of Cuyahoga, or some other competent surveyor, to be surveyed, described and permanently marked, and a plat thereof recorded by the city clerk, in a book to be provided for that purpose, in which book shall also be recorded a plat of any new street which may hereafter be established by said council, under the provisions of this act; and also of any change or alterations in any of the streets or highways of the city; and such survey and record shall be thereafter conclusive evidence of the position and limits of such street, lane, alley, highway, square or public ground, subject, however, to such alterations as may be made therein, agreeably to the provisions of this act; all persons residing within said city, who by law are liable to work on the roads, shall perform such work under the direction of the supervisors, to he appointed by the city council, and shall be liable for delinquencies in the same manner, and all fines and forfeitures incurred for delinquencies shall be collected in the manner pointed out by the laws of this State regulating roads and highways; and when collected, shall be paid over to the city treasurer, to be expended as other road taxes are; and the road tax levied by law on property within said city shall be collected in money by the treasurer of Cuyahoga county; and when collected shall be by him paid over to the city treasurer, and which shall be expended in the improvement of the roads and streets of said city under the direction of the city council.

Sec. 9. That the city council shall have power to levy a special tax to defray the expense of grading, paving, or otherwise improving any road, street, alley, lane, square, market place or common within said city, by a discriminating assessment upon the land and ground bounding and abutting on such road, street, alley, lane, market place, square or common, or near thereto, in proportion to the benefit accruing therefrom to such land or ground; and the city council shall appoint a committee of three disinterested judicious freeholders of said city to estimate the cost of any such projected improvement, and to assess the expense on the land and ground as aforesaid; and it shall be the duty of the city council to provide by ordinance for the correction and equalization of such assessment; and the city council shall give notice in one or more of the newspapers published in said city for six consecutive weeks, of the improvement to be made, in order that any one, damaged by reason of such improvement, may file his claim in writing in the office of the city clerk within ten days after the expiration of the said six weeks notice; and the said committee shall assess the damages, if any, of such claimants, and shall add the same to the cost of the improvement as a part of the expense thereof to be assessed as aforesaid; and said committee, within twelve days after the time shall have expired for filing claims for damages, (unless for good cause the council shall grant them further time) shall make return to the office of the city clerk, setting forth the ultimate cost of such projected improvement, including the damages awarded by them to the claimants, together with the names of such claimants and ground of claim, with the amount awarded them severally set opposite their respective names; and also a brief description of the lands and grounds upon which they shall have assessed the expense of the improvement, with the names of the owners or persons liable to pay the assessment respectively annexed, and the amount thereon assessed, set opposite their respective names; and if the name of the person owning, or liable for the tax, is unknown, the fact shall be stated by writing "unknown owner," in place of the name; and the city council, if they order and direct the improvement to be made, shall direct the city clerk, whose duty it shall be to annex a duplicate of taxes, so assessed, to the annual assessment roll hereinafter specified, and to deliver it therewith, on or before the first Monday in July following, to the city collector, to be by him collected at the same time and in the same manner as the annual taxes, and the proceedings of said collector shall in all respects be the same as in the collection of the annual taxes of said city, and he shall in like manner pay the same into the city treasury; and in case of any tax being returned unpaid and delinquent, the proceedings shall in all respects be the same as in cases of delinquency in the payment of the annual taxes, with the addition of like interest and penalty; and when the improvement so ordered shall be completed, each claimant shall be entitled to receive from the city treasury the amount of damages so, by the return of said committee, awarded him.

Sec. 10.   That the city council shall appoint a city clerk and any other agents or officers necessary for the interest of said city, not herein provided for, and prescribe the duties and compensation of the same, and to remove the same at pleasure; and when the office of any person *appointed* under the provisions of this act shall become vacant, the city council shall fill such vacancy; and the person appointed to fill such vacancy shall continue in office the remainder of the term of his predecessor; and when the office of any person elected under the provisions of this act by the qualified voters of the city or any ward thereof, shall become vacant, the mayor, by order of the city council, shall issue an order for a special election to fill such vacancy; and the person elected shall continue in office during the remainder of the term of his predecessor: and in case of vacancy in the office of mayor, the president of the city council shall give notice for holding a special election to fill such vacancy, and until the same is filled, shall have power and authority to do and perform all the duties appertaining to the office of mayor; and in case of the absence or inability, at any time, of the mayor, he shall have like power and authority; and all the officers elected or appointed under the provisions of this act, shall, before entering upon the duties of their respective offices, take an oath or affirmation faithfully and impartially to perform the several duties of the office to which such person is respectively elected or appointed; and when required shall give bond with good and sufficient security, to said city, in such sum or sums, and with such conditions thereto, as the city council may from time to time determine; and in all cases not in this act provided for, shall receive such fees and compensation for their services, and be liable to such fines, penalties and forfeitures, for negligence, carelessness, misconduct in office, and positive violations of duty, as the said city council shall by ordinance order and determine; and the city council may grant to the mayor such compensation as shall be approved by the concurring vote of two-thirds of all the members, and to members of their own body such sum not exceeding one dollar per day to each member, for his attendance at any regular or special meeting of the board, as by a like vote shall be approved; and in all cases when a vacancy shall happen in the office of any officer elected by the provisions of this act, the city council shall, by appointment, fill such vacancy; and the person so appointed shall hold such office until a person shall be elected and qualified to execute the duties thereof.

Sec. 11. That it shall be the duty of the marshal to execute and return all writs and process, to him directed by the mayor; and when necessary in criminal cases, or for a violation of any ordinance of said city, he may serve the same in any part of Cuyahoga county: it shall be his duty to suppress all riots, disturbances, and breaches of the peace; to apprehend all disorderly persons in said city, and to pursue and arrest any person fleeing from justice in any part of the State of Ohio; to apprehend any person in the act of committing any offence against the laws of the State, or ordinances of the city, and forthwith to bring such person or persons before competent authority, for examination; and to do and perform all such duties as may lawfully be enjoined on him by the ordinances of said city; and he shall have power to appoint one or more deputies, to be approved by the city council, but for whose official acts he shall be responsible, and of whom he may require bail for the faithful performance of their duties.

Sec. 12. That the treasurer of said city shall perform such duties, and exercise such powers, as may be lawfully required of him by the ordinances of said city; all moneys raised, received, recovered and collected, by means of any tax, license, penalty, fine, forfeiture or otherwise, under the authority of this act, or which may belong to said city, shall be paid into the city treasury, and shall not be drawn therefrom except by a written order, under the authority of the city council, specifying the object of the appropriation; and it shall be the duty of the city council to settle all claims and demands against said city, and publish accounts of the receipts and expenditures of said city, annually, for public information.

Sec. 13. That the city council shall, when the public good may require it, erect a city prison, and regulate the police and internal government thereof; may authorize solitary confinement, or hard labor therein, for a violation of any of the ordinances of said city, punishable by imprisonment; and until such prison is prepared for the reception of prisoners, the said city shall be allowed the use of the jail of Cuyahoga county, for the confinement of all persons convicted by the mayor, and sentenced under any of the laws of this State, or ordinances of said city; and all persons so imprisoned, shall be under the charge of the sheriff of said county, who shall receive and discharge such prisoners in and from jail, in such manner as shall be prescribed by the ordinances of said city, or otherwise by due course of law: the city council shall also erect an almshouse, when the public good may require, and such other buildings as may be necessary for the convenience of the city.

Sec. 14. That the city council shall have power to borrow money for the discharge and liquidation of any debt of the city, either present or prospective, and to provide for the redemption of any loan by them made, and the payment of the interest thereon; and to pledge the revenues and property of the city therefor, in such manner, and upon such terms and conditions as said council may by ordinance prescribe; and any ordinance for obtaining a loan of money, shall be considered and adopted by a vote of said city council, two-thirds of all the members concurring, by yeas and nays, and be entered at large on their journal; the proceedings shall then be postponed, for at least two weeks, to a subsequent meeting of said council, and shall then be passed by a like majority concurring, and the vote thereon shall be entered as aforesaid.

Sec. 15. That for the discharge of any debt against said city, or expenditure authorized by the city council, under the provisions of this act, or any ordinance of said city, or to defray the current expenses of the city, the city council shall have power, annually, to levy and collect taxes on all the real and personal property, or capital of any kind, within said city, subject to taxation by the laws for levying the taxes of this State, for the time being; which property shall be listed and assessed annually, for taxation, by assessors appointed by the city council, one from each ward, who shall make return of their assessment roll to the office of the city clerk, at such time and in such form as the city council shall, by ordinance, direct; and it shall be the duty of the city council to make provision, by ordinance, for the listing and ascertaining the property to be assessed, for the valuation of such portions thereof, as by the laws levying the taxes of this State, shall, for the time being, be required to be valued, and for the correction and equalization of such assessment; and the city council, on or before the first Monday in June, annually, shall levy upon the whole amount of such assessment as corrected and equalized, such per centage, as by the concurring vote of two-thirds of all the members, shall be deemed necessary; and it shall be the duty of the city clerk, on or before the first Monday in July, annually, to deliver to the city collector, a duplicate of the assessment roll, with the amount of taxes therein specified to be paid by each individual, with a warrant annexed thereto, under the hand of said clerk, and the mayor of said city, commanding such collector to collect from the several persons named in said assessment roll, the several sums set opposite their respective names; and in case such persons shall refuse or neglect to pay such tax, then to levy the same by distress and sale of the goods and chattels of such person, in the same manner as constables are required to do on execution, and the collector shall tax and collect, in such cases, the like fees; and it shall be the duty of such collector, and by said warrant he shall be directed, to make return on the first Monday in October thereafter, to the office of the city clerk, of his proceedings thereon, and to pay into the city treasury the amount by him collected, after deducting therefrom such amount as the city council, by ordinance, shall allow, him as compensation; and when any tax, imposed by the city council pursuant to law, shall be returned as unpaid, or shall not be paid within the time required by law, the said city council may maintain an action therefor, in the name of the city, against any person liable for the payment of the same, as owner of the real estate, or as owner of the personal property charged with said tax, in any court having cognizance thereof, with interest from the time such tax was returned unpaid, and costs of suit; and when any tax, charged upon any real estate within the city, shall be returned as unpaid, by the officer authorized to collect the same, the city council may direct the city treasurer to advertise and sell such real estate, as hereinafter provided: the city treasurer shall cause a notice to be published in a newspaper of the said city, for six successive weeks, describing the real estate charged with such tax remaining unpaid, notifying all persons concerned, that unless the said tax, with interest, and twenty-five per cent. penalty thereon, shall be paid before the time of sale in such notice specified, he will, on a day and place therein to be stated, expose the said real estate to sale at public auction; if such tax, with the interest and penalty thereon, be not paid by the time of sale; the said treasurer shall proceed to sell the same, for the shortest time any bidder will take the said premises, and pay the said tax, and interest and penalty thereon; and on such sale, he shall execute to the bidder a certificate of sale, in which the property purchased shall be described, the amount for which it was sold, and the time for which the premises were purchased, shall be specified: also, the time when the purchaser will be entitled to receive the lease hereinafter mentioned; and said treasurer shall cause a copy of said certificate, to be filed in the office of the city clerk; the grantee in such certificate, shall, at the expiration of one year after such sale, be entitled to a lease of such premises, for the time he so bid off the same, which term shall commence at the day of the date of said lease; said lease shall be given by the mayor of said city, under the corporate seal of said city, and shall be presumptive evidence in all courts and places, that such tax and assessment were legally imposed, and that the proceedings touching such sale were correct; and such grantee may obtain possession thereof in the manner prescribed by law, in cases of forcible detainer; and shall hold, and enjoy the said premises during the term for which the same were granted to him, free and clear from all claim and demands of any other owner or occupant of the same, but subject to any tax that may be charged thereon, during said term; and at the expiration of said term, such grantee, his heirs or assigns, may remove any building or fixture that may have been erected on the said premises, during the said term; any owner or claimant of the premises so sold, may, within one year after such sale, redeem the same, by paying to such grantee, his heirs or assigns, or into the city treasury, for his or their benefit, the amount paid by such purchaser, with the addition of twenty-five per cent. on the amount; and on such payment being made, the title of such grantee shall absolutely cease and determine: the mayor, by direction of the city council, may renew any warrants that may be lawfully issued for the collection of any tax, from time to time, as often as any tax shall be returned uncollected, or may issue a new warrant for the collection of such tax, and in such warrant shall specify the time when the same shall be returned; and the same proceedings shall, in all respects, be had on such renewed warrants, as are herein authorized upon the first warrant.

Sec. 16. That every law or ordinance of said city, before it shall be of any force or validity, shall be ordered to be engrossed for its final passage, by a majority of all the members of the city council concurring; it shall then be reconsidered by the city council, and if at its final passage, it shall be adopted by a majority of all the members concurring, it shall become a law for said city; and all questions on the engrossment or final passage of any law or ordinance, or on the appointment of any officer of said city, shall be decided by yeas and nays; an I the names of the persons voting for or against the same, shall be entered in the journals of said council; and all laws or ordinances passed as aforesaid, shall be signed by the presiding officer of the council and the city clerk, and forthwith published in one or more newspapers of said city.

Sec. 17. That all qualified electors for members of the General Assembly of this State, who have resided within the bounds of said city one year next preceding the election, shall be deemed qualified voters of said city, and shall be entitled to vote in the ward in which they respectively reside, for any officer in the city required by this act to be elected by the qualified voters of said city; and in all elections for city officers, after the organization of said city government under this act, the mayor shall issue his proclamation to the qualified voters of said city, setting forth the time of such election, the place or places where the same is to be held in the several wards, and the several officers to be chosen; and said proclamation shall be published in one or more newspapers, printed, or in general circulation in said city, for at least ten days previous to said election; and after the organization of the city government under this act, it shall be the duty of the city council to provide the place or places of holding all elections in said city for said city officers, the hour of the day the same shall be opened, the time the same shall continue open, to appoint the judges thereof, provide for the making and directing the returns of elections, the time and manner of opening the returns and of making an abstract thereof, and of keeping a journal of the same; and may make such other arrangements respecting said elections, as may be lawful and convenient for the citizens of the several wards; and the person or persons having the highest number of votes, shall be declared duly elected.

Sec. 18. That in all cases brought before the mayor, for the violation of any of the ordinances of the city, when the defendant is adjudged to pay a fine or penalty, the defendant shall have a right, within ten days, to appeal to the court of common pleas of Cuyahoga county, upon giving bond with such security as the mayor shall approve, in double the amount of the debt and costs; and if double the amount of such judgment do not amount to fifty dollars. such bond shall be fifty dollars, conditioned to pay the judgment and costs which may be rendered against him, her or them, in said court of common pleas; and in all cases appealed under the provisions of this act, the prosecution may be by action of debt or by indictment, as the case may require, and may proceed in the same manner as offences against the laws of this State are prosecuted; and the prosecution shall be managed and conducted by such counsel as for that purpose shall be authorized by the city council; and all fines imposed or penalties recovered shall, when collected, be paid into the city treasury; and whenever bail for an appeal as aforesaid, shall have been perfected as above provided, the mayor shall recall any execution which may have issued on any judgment as aforesaid.

Sec. 19. That the city council be, and they are hereby authorized, at the expense of said city, to provide for the support of common schools therein; and for that purpose each of the wards of said city shall constitute a school district, until such time as the city council may divide each ward into two or more school districts, which they are hereby authorized to do, in such manner as they may deem most convenient, having due regard to present and future population; and they are hereby authorized to purchase in fee simple, or to receive as a donation for the use of the city, a suitable lot of ground in each school district, as a site for a school house therein; and they are hereby authorized to erect in each district a good and substantial school house, of such dimensions as shall be convenient for the use of common schools in said city, and to defray the necessary expenses of the building and constructing such school houses, and also to pay the purchase money for the lots of land on which the same shall be erected: it shall be lawful for the city council, annually, to levy, in addition to the other taxes in said city, a tax, not exceeding one mill on the dollar, upon all property in the city subject to the payment of annual taxes by the provisions of this act, until a sufficient sum shall be raised and collected from such tax to meet all the expenses which shall be incurred, for the purchase of lots of land and the erection of the school houses aforesaid: *Provided*, It shall be lawful for said city to borrow such sum or sums of money as may be sufficient and necessary for purchasing or building as aforesaid, and to refund or pay the same as the tax aforesaid shall be collected; and the said tax is hereby made a special fund to be appropriated to no other purpose.

Sec. 20. That for the support of common schools in said city, and to secure the benefits of education to all the white children therein, it shall be the duty of the city council annually, to levy and collect a tax not exceeding one mill on the dollar, upon all the property in said city subject to the payment of annual taxes by the provisions of this act, which shall be collected at the same time and in the same manner as is provided for the collection of the annual taxes; which tax, together with such as may be

36—L

collected by the county treasurer for school purposes, within such part of the county of Cuyahoga as is within the limits of said city, shall be exclusively appropriated to defray the expense of instructors and fuel for said schools. and for no other purpose whatever; which schools shall be accessible to all white children, not under four years of age, who may reside in said city, subject only to such regulations for their government and instruction, as the board of managers hereinafter mentioned, may from time to time prescribe.

Sec. 21. That the city council shall annually, select one judicious and competent person from each school district in the city as a manager of common schools in said city, which managers shall constitute and be denominated " The Board of Managers of Common Schools in the city of Cleveland;" who shall hold their office for one year, and until their successors are appointed and qualified, and shall fill all vacancies which may occur in their own body, during the time for which they shall be appointed.

Sec. 22. That the said board of managers shall have the general superintendence of all common schools in said city, and from time to time shall make such regulations for the government and instruction of the white children therein, as to them shall appear proper and expedient, and shall examine and employ instructors for the same; and shall cause a school to be kept in each district for at least six months in each year, and shall cause an accurate census to be taken annually, in each district, of all the white children therein, between the ages of four and twenty-one years; and require of the several instructors thereof, to keep a record of the names and ages of all persons by them respectivly instructed, and the time each shall · have attended said schools, and return a copy of such record to the board of managers, at the close of each and every current year; and said board shall certify to the city council the correctness of all accounts for expenses incurred in support of said schools, and give certificates thereof to the persons entitled to receive the same: they shall, at the close of every current year, report to the city council the state and condition of the several common schools in said city, as well the fiscal as the other concerns in relation thereto, and a particular account of their administration thereof; and they shall do and perform all other matters and things pertaining to the duties of their said offices, which may be necessary and proper to be done, to promote the education and morals of the children instructed in said schools, or which may be required of them by the ordinances of said city, not inconsistent with the provisions of this act: *Provided,* That no person shall be employed as an instructor in any of said schools, who has not been first examined by the board of managers, and received a certificate of qualifications, as to his or her competency and moral character.

Sec. 23. That all moneys which shall belong to the village of Cleveland, or which said village shall be entitled to at the time said city shall be organized under this act, for the use of common schools therein, shall be paid over to and held by the city treasurer, and all moneys hereafter levied and collected within the limits of said city, for the support of common schools, and also all other moneys appropriated by law for the use of common schools therein, shall be paid into the city treasury as a separate and distinct fund, and shall not be applied, under any pretence whatever, to any other use than that for which it is levied and collected; and a separate and particular account of the receipts and expenditures thereof, shall be kept by the treasurer, in a book to be provided for that purpose; and the said treasurer shall not be entitled to receive any per centage, premium or compensation, for receiving or paying out said fund, or for keeping the accounts thereof.

Sec. 24. That the city council shall fix by ordinance, the commencement and termination of the current year of said common schools, and determine the time and duration of all vacancies thereof; which shall be the same throughout said city; and said city council may at their discretion, at any time previous to the erection of the school houses provided for in this act, lease on such terms and conditions as they may deem proper in the several school districts of said city, and for such times as they shall think necessary, convenient buildings for the use of common schools therein, to be occupied only till such school houses shall be erected and prepared for the reception of such schools: *Provided*, That the property of black or mulatto persons shall be exempted from taxation for school purposes under this act.

Sec. 25. That any person to be eligible for any office under the provisions of this act, shall be a qualified voter of the city.

Sec. 26. That the president, recorder, and trustees, and all other officers of the corporation of the village of Cleveland now in office therein, shall remain in their respective offices and perform the several duties thereof, until the mayor and city council are elected and qualified under this act; and all laws ordinances, and resolutions passed and adopted by the corporate authorities of said village, shall be and remain in full force until altered or repealed by the city council established by this act.

Sec. 27. That the said city of Cleveland shall be, and is hereby invested as the lawful owner and proprietor of all the real and personal estate, and all the rights and privileges thereof belonging to the corporation of the village of Cleveland; together with all the property, funds and revenues, and all moneys, debts and demands, due and owing to said village of Cleveland, or to the president, recorder and trustees thereof, as a corporate body, which by or under any former acts, ordinances, grants, donations, gifts, or purchases, have been acquired, vested, or in any manner belonging to said corporation, and the same are hereby transferred to the corporate body created by this act; and all suits pending and judgments recovered by or in favor of or against said village of Cleveland, and all rights, claims and demands, in favor of, or against the same, may be continued, prosecuted, completed, defended, and collected, in the same manner as though this act had never been passed; and the said city shall be accountable for all debts and liabilities of said village corporation.

Sec. 28. The president and trustees, or a majority of them, of the corporation of Cleveland village, shall designate such time in the month of April, 1836, for holding the first election, as to them shall seem expedient, and they shall appoint three suitable persons in each ward of said city, to be judges of the first election under the provisions of this act, also two suitable persons to be clerks thereof, in each ward, and shall notify the several persons so appointed; and shall publish in one or more of the newspapers in said city, at least ten days before said election, the several places designated for holding the same, and to procure a suitable place in each ward for holding the elections; which said first election shall be opened between the hours of nine and eleven o'clock in the forenoon, and shall continue open till five o'clock in the afternoon; and said election shall be conducted agreeably to the laws regulating township elections; and it shall be the duty of the judges of said elections in the several wards within two days thereafter, to make and direct the return thereof to the president of said village corporation at his office, in the same manner that election returns are required to be made to the clerk of the court of common pleas, by the act entitled, "An act to regulate elections;" and the said president, or person acting as such, shall, within three days after such election, open the returns which shall have been made to him as aforesaid, and make an abstract thereof, and immediately notify in writing the persons elected as aforesaid of their several elections under this act.

Sec. 29.   That the act entitled "An act to incorporate the village of Cleveland," passed December 22, 1814, and the several acts amendatory thereto, and all acts or parts of acts inconsistent with this act, be, and the same are hereby repealed, saving and excepting as is herein above excepted.

WILLIAM MEDILL,
Speaker pro tem. of the House of Representatives.
ELIJAH VANCE,
Speaker of the Senate.

March 5, 1836.

AN ACT

To incorporate the town of Cuyahoga Falls, in the county of Portage.

Sec. 1.   *Be it enacted by the General Assembly of the State of Ohio,* That so much of the townships of Talmadge and Stow, as is comprised within the following limits, to wit: Beginning at the north-west corner of the township of Talmadge, and running south, on the west line of said township, two hundred and forty rods; thence east two hundred and forty rods; thence north to the north line of lots number one and two, in said Stow; thence west two hundred and forty rods; thence south to the place of beginning; and any addition thereto that may be hereafter platted and recorded, be hereby constituted a town corporate, by the name of Cuyahoga Falls.

Sec. 2.   That for the government of said town, there shall be elected a mayor, a recorder, and five trustees, who shall be a body corporate and politic, with perpetual succession, to be known by the name of " The Town Council of Cuyahoga Falls;" a majority of whom, including the mayor or recorder, shall, in all cases, constitute a quorum; and they and their successors in office may use a common seal, and the same to alter at discretion; may acquire any estate, real or personal, and manage or dispose of the same, in such manner, as a majority of them shall deem expedient: they shall also be capable of suing and being sued, pleading and being impleaded, answering and being answered, in any suit or action, and in any court of law or equity in this State; and when any suit shall be commenced against said corporation, the first process shall be a summons; a certified copy of which shall be left with the recorder, and in his absence, with the mayor, at least ten days previous to the return day thereof.

Sec. 3. That the qualified electors for members of the General Assembly, who shall have been residents of said town one year previous to the day of election, shall meet at the school house in said town, on the first Monday in July, eighteen hundred and thirty-six, and on the first Monday in May, annually, thereafter, at such place as the town council may direct, between the hours of one and five o'clock, P. M. and then and there proceed to elect, by ballot, from the said qualified electors, who shall also be freeholders or householders in said town, the mayor, recorder, and trustees aforesaid, who shall hold their offices until the next annual election, and until their successors are duly elected and qualified.

Sec. 4. That at the first election, to be holden under this act, two judges and a clerk shall be chosen *viva voce*, by the electors present, and at all subsequent elections the town council, or any two of them, shall be judges, and the recorder clerk of elections: the result of the elections to be publicly declared, and a record thereof made by the clerk, who shall also notify the person elected of the same, within six days after the election; and the persons so elected, before entering upon the duties of their respective offices, shall take the proper oath or affirmation of office, and to support the constitution of the United States, and of this State.

Sec. 5. That the town council shall make all such by-laws, not inconsistent with the laws of the United States, and of this State, as they may deem necessary for the interest of said town, and the same to alter or repeal; audit and settle the accounts of the town, and draw and appropriate the money that may at any time be in the treasury; and may adopt measures proper to secure the town against injuries by fire; and for this purpose may organize one or more fire companies, and establish rules for the same; may open streets, or alter those already opened, under the liability to pay a fair compensation to the person or persons, if any there be, aggrieved thereby; may fill all vacancies occurring in any offices, herein named; and may provide for the election or appointment of a treasurer, a town marshal, and such other subordinate officers, as they may find necessary; to prescribe their duties, and fees, and take security for the faithful performance of their respective duties; and to do all things which corporations of a similar nature can do, to secure the peace, health, and good order of said town: *Provided*, Said council shall have no power to grant license, in any case whatever to sell spirituous liquors.

Sec. 6. That the town council shall have power to levy and collect a tax, annually, for town and corporation purposes, not exceeding five mills on the dollar, on all property within said town, subject to taxation for State or county purposes, as the same may be found valued on the books of the auditor of the county of Portage, for the current year; and they shall have power, also, when it is deemed necessary, for the opening or repairing any street in said town, to levy and collect a tax, not exceeding five mills on the dollar, on the value of any lot or part thereof, with improvements thereon, on said street, not otherwise subject to taxation; the value of the same to be assessed by the marshal, who shall make return of the valuation so made, to the recorder, on or before the first Monday in June, of the year in which said levy shall be made; and the town council shall meet on the said second Monday in June, annually, and hear and determine on all complaints that may be made respecting said valuation, and equalize the same as nearly as possible; and at the same meeting they shall fix upon and determine the amount of taxes to be raised for the current year: *Provided*, Property situate within the limits of the corporation, and not within the town plat, shall be exempted from the payment of the corporation tax.

Sec. 7. That it shall be the duty of the recorder of said corporation to (make duplicates of taxes assessed, agreeably to this act; which duplicates shall be certified by the mayor and recorder; and one of said duplicates shall be delivered to the marshal, whose duty it shall be to collect said tax, in the same manner and under the same regulations as the collector of State and county tax is required to collect State and county taxes; and the marshal shall, immediately after collecting said tax, pay the same over to the treasurer of said corporation, and take his receipt therefor: and the said marshal shall have the same power to sell both real and personal property, as is given by law to county treasurers; and when necessary, the recorder shall have power to make deeds for real estate so sold, and in the same manner that county auditors are by law empowered to do, for lands sold by the county treasurer.

Sec. 8. That the mayor of said corporation shall be conservator of the peace throughout said town, shall give bond and security in like manner as justices of the peace are required to do, and shall, within the same, have all the powers and jurisdiction of a justice of the peace, in all matters, either civil or criminal, arising under the laws of this [State,] and receive the same fees as justices are allowed: appeals to be taken from the decisions of of said mayor in all cases where appeals are allowed from the decisions of justices of the peace, and in the same manner.

Sec. 9. That the marshal shall be the principal ministerial officer of said town, and shall have the same powers as constables have by law; and his jurisdiction in criminal cases shall be co-extensive with the county of Portage; and he shall execute the process of the mayor, and receive the same fees for his services that constables are allowed for like services.

Sec. 10. That the corporation [shall] be entitled to the use of the jail of Portage county, for the confinement or imprisonment of such persons as may be liable thereto, under this act, or under the laws of said town council: and all persons so imprisoned shall be under the charge of the sheriff of said county.

Sec. 11. That any future Legislature may alter, amend, or repeal this act, *Provided*, That such alteration, amendment or repeal shall not divert the property of said corporation from the purposes expressed in this act.

WILLIAM MEDILL,
Speaker pro tem. of the House of Representatives.
ELIJAH VANCE,
Speaker of the Senate.

March 5, 1836.

AN ACT

To authorize the county commissioners of Champaign county to subscribe to the capital stock of the Mad river and Lake Erie Rail-road Company.

Sec. 1. *Be it enacted by the General Assembly of the State of Ohio,* That if the county commissioners of Champaign county shall consider it to be for the general interest of said county, and desired by the inhabitants thereof, they are hereby authorized to subscribe, on behalf of the people of said county, for six hundred shares of the capital stock of the Mad river and Lake Erie Rail-road Company; and to pay the instalments thereon as they shall be required by the president and directors of said company.

Sec. 2. If the board of commissioners shall subscribe for the said shares of stock, as above provided, they are further authorized to borrow, on the credit of said county of Champaign, any sum of money not exceeding thirty thousand dollars; and, for the final payment of the principal and of the interest thereon, to pledge the faith of said county; and they shall levy and collect, annually, such taxes as, together with the tolls arising from the stock of said road, will suffice to pay the interest of such loan, and other incidental charges and liabilities connected therewith.

Sec. 3. The said commissioners shall have power to hypothecate the said stock as a security for the loan they may make, and to sell the same, and apply the proceeds to the payment of the loan, and the premiums obtained thereon shall be paid into the county treasury; and they shall also be empowered to make such arrangements for the payment of interest on said loan, or the saving of interest thereon, as the good of the people of Champaign county may require.

WILLIAM MEDILL,
Speaker pro tem. of the House of Representatives.
ELIJAH VANCE,
Speaker of the Senate.

March 5, 1836.

AN ACT

To authorize the Clerk of the Court of Common Pleas of Hamilton county to appoint an additional deputy clerk.

Sec. 1. *Be it enacted by the General Assembly of the State of Ohio,* That the present clerk of the court of common pleas of Hamilton county, be, and he is hereby authorized to appoint an additional deputy clerk, subject to the approval of the court of common pleas of said county, agreeably to the provisions of an act, entitled "An act for the appointment of certain officers therein named," passed February 17th, 1831.

WILLIAM MEDILL,
Speaker pro tem. of the House of Repeesentatives.
ELIJAH VANCE,
Speaker of the Senate.

March 5, 1836.

AN ACT

Making further provision for the erection of a Lunatic Asylum for the State of Ohio.

Sec. 1. *Be it enacted by the General Assembly of the State of Ohio,* That there shall be erected, on the lands recently purchased for the State, by the directors of the Lunatic Asylum of Ohio, suitable buildings for the reception and medieal treatment of insane persons, to be constructed in such manner and on such a scale as shall, in the opinion of said directors, be best calculated to promote the object in view, and not exceed, in expense, the amount stated in their report to the present General Assembly.

Sec. 2. That the said board of directors shall appoint a suitable person to superintend the erection of said buildings, who shall hold his appointment during the pleasure of said board, or until the said buildings are completed, who shall execute a bond to the State of Ohio, in the penal sum of 10,000 dollars, with two sufficient securities, to be approved of by said board, conditioned for the faithful performance of all duties which may from time to time be required of him; who shall, under the direction and advice of said board, contract for and procure all the materials which may be necessary and proper for the erection of said buildings, and make contracts for the workmanship and labor necessary for the erection and completion of the same, and superintend the work during the progress of construction.

Sec. 3. That the directors and warden of the Ohio Penitentiary are hereby authorized and directed to cause to be employed in preparing materials and executing any part of the work hereby authorized to be done, so many of the convicts under their charge as they may deem safe and advantageous to the State, and under such rules and regulations as they shall prescribe; and the amount of labor thus performed by the convicts, if any, shall be reported by the said directors of the penitentiary to the General Assembly, in their annual report.

Sec. 4. That for the purchase of materials and the commencement of said buildings, there is hereby appropriated the sum of fifteen thousand dollars, to be paid out of any money in the treasury not otherwise appropriated; and all moneys to be drawn from the treasury for the purposes aforesaid, shall be drawn on the order of the superintendent, approved by a majority of the board of directors of the Lunatic Asylum, an accurate account of which, and the disbursements thereof, shall be annually reported to the General Assembly.

Sec. 5. The superintendent of said buildings shall receive as a compensation for the services required of him, such sum as the board of directors shall deem reasonable, not exceeding the rate of eight hundred dollars per annum, to be paid quarterly out of the State treasury, on the order of the board of directors.

WILLIAM MEDILL,
Speaker pro tem. of the House of Representatives.
ELIJAH VANCE,
Speaker of the Senate.

March 5, 1836.

AN ACT

To amend the "Act to incorporate the Cincinnati and Harrison Turnpike Company," passed
Dec. 20th; 1831.

Sec. 1. *Be it enacted by the General Assembly of the State of Ohio,* That the county commissioners of Hamilton county, be, and they are hereby authorized and empowered to receive in payment for the bridge over Mill creek, and the graded and improved road lying between said bridge and the corporation line of the city of Cincinnati, over and upon which the Cincinnati and Harrison turnpike road has been located, such an amount of stock in said company as may be agreed upon by the commissioners aforesaid and said turnpike company.

Sec. 2. That the ninth section of the act to which this is an amendment, be, and the same is hereby so amended, as that it shall be lawful for the said company, so soon as any extent of said road, not less than five continuous miles, shall be completed in the manner prescribed in the eighth section of said act, and shall so be reported in writing to the president of the company by an agent appointed for that purpose by the court of common pleas for Hamilton county, to erect a gate or gates for tolls, at which they may charge and collect toll at a rate per mile which shall not exceed in proportion the rate for any ten miles as prescribed in the tenth section of the same act: *Provided,* That no gate shall be put up on the road on the city side of the road leading up Lick run.

Sec. 3. That said company shall be allowed to charge for every head of sheep or hogs, over six months old, one half cent for every ten miles travel on said road, and in that proportion for a less number of miles.

Sec. 4. The county commissioners of Hamilton county shall, in person or by an agent specially appointed as their proxy, vote on said shares of stock at the election of president and directors of said company, and do all other acts at public meetings of the company which individual stockholders may do under the charter, and shall have power to sell and transfer said stock at any time, and appropriate the proceeds for county purposes.

WILLIAM MEDILL,
Speaker pro tem. of the House of Representatives.

ELIJAH VANCE,
Speaker of the Senate.

March 5, 1836.

AN ACT

To incorporate the Jefferson Literary Society of Franklin College, in the county of Harrison.

Sec. 1. *Be it enacted by the General Assembly of the State of Ohio,* That George C. Vincent, and Jacob Blickensderfer, jr. and their asso-

37—L

ciates, together with such other persons as may hereafter be associated with them, be, and they are hereby created a body corporate and politic, by the name and style of the Jefferson Literary Society of Franklin College, in the county of Harrison; and as such shall remain and have perpetual succession, and by their corporate name may contract and be contracted with, sue and be sued, plead and be impleaded, answer and be answered unto, defend and be defended, in any court of competent jurisdiction, in all manner of actions whatsoever; and may have a common seal, which they may break, alter or renew at pleasure.

Sec. 2. That the said corporation, by the name and style aforesaid, shall be capable in law of acquiring, holding, and conveying property, real, personal or mixed, either by purchase, donation, gift, grant, devise, deed or legacy: *Provided,* The annual income of such estate shall not exceed one thousand dollars: *And provided, also,* That no part of the stock of said corporation, or property owned by it, shall at any time be used or employed for any other than literary and scientific purposes; the purchase of books, maps, charts, pamphlets, newspapers, or other useful publications, lands, and buildings, necessary for the business of the society, and its other necessary expenses.

Sec. 3. That the members of the said corporation may, from time to time, elect such officers as may be deemed necessary, and in such manner as may be pointed out by the constitution or by-laws of said society; and make such by-laws, rules and regulations as they may deem necessary, for the good government of the same; and affix such pecuniary fines and penalties for breaches thereof, as they may deem reasonable and necessary to enforce the same.

Sec. 4. That any future Legislature may alter, amend or repeal this act, not thereby affecting the title to any property, real or personal, acquired or conveyed under its provisions.

WILLIAM MEDILL,
Speaker pro tem. of the House of Representatives.
ELIJAH VANCE,
Speaker of the Senate.

March 7, 1836.

AN ACT

To incorporate the First Presbyterian Church and Congregation in Norwalk, Huron county, Ohio.

Sec. 1. *Be it enacted by the General Assembly of the State of Ohio,* That Agar B. Hoyt, Cortland L. Lattimer, John Tifft, Thaddeus B. Sturges, William F. Griswold, Pickett Lattimer, John Miller, George Mygatt, Benjamin Bensen, David Higgins, Miner Lawrence, John Buckingham, Andrew Bishop, and Edward H. Mead, and their associates for the time being, be, and they are hereby created and declared a body corporate and politic, by the name and style of the "First Presbyterian Church and Congregation in Norwalk, Huron county, Ohio;" and as such shall remain and have perpetual succession, subject however to such regulations as the Legislature may hereafter think proper to make.

Sec. 2. That the said corporation shall be capable in law by the name aforesaid, of contracting and being contracted with, of suing and being sued, pleading and being impleaded, defending and being defended, in any action or suit, in any court of competent jurisdiction; may have a common seal for the use of the corporation, and alter the same at pleasure; may acquire and hold any estate, real or personal, by gift, grant, devise or purchase; may make and enforce all by-laws necessary for the regulation of said society: *Provided,* The annual income of such property shall not exceed two thousand dollars; and that such property shall be held in trust for the use of the said First Presbyterian Church and Congregation of Norwalk, to defray the expenses incident to their mode of worship, and in the support of a pastor, or any system of charity or education connected with said church.

Sec. 3. That the affairs of said corporation shall be managed by five trustees, who shall have power and authority to make all contracts in behalf of the corporation, and to manage all pecuniary and prudential matters, and other concerns pertaining to the good order, interest and welfare of the society, and to make such rules, regulations and by-laws as they may deem advisable from time to time, for their own government, and that of the corporation: *Provided, always,* That they shall make no by-laws, nor pass any order for the imposition of any tax on the sale of any property on account of the corporation, unless by the consent of said corporation, expressed by a majority of two thirds of the members present legally assembled.

Sec. 4. That the trustees shall be elected annually on the first Monday in January, and shall hold their offices for one year, and until their successors shall be duly elected: *Provided,* In the event of a failure to make an election on the day aforesaid, the trustees shall have power to appoint such other day for the election as they shall see fit.

Sec. 5. That all elections shall be by ballot, and determined by a majority of votes; each member of the corporation who shall have been a member of the congregation one year, or a member of the church, shall be entitled to vote at any election under such rules and regulations as the corporation shall adopt.

Sec. 6. Every person shall be considered a member of the congregation who contributes one dollar or more annually, for the support of a pastor of said church and congregation.

Sec. 7. That the trustees, or a majority of them, shall have power to call a meeting of the corporation, by giving to the society ten days previous notice of said meeting, either by anouncement immediately after service on the Sabbath, or by advertisement in a public newspaper published in Norwalk.

Sec. 8. That the trustees shall give bond with sufficient security to the corporation, conditioned for the faithful performance of the duties that may appertain to his office under the by-laws and regulations of the trustees and corporation; and original process against the corporation shall be by summons, and the service of the same shall be by leaving an attested copy thereof with the treasurer of the corporation, at least twenty days before the return of the same.

Sec. 9. That George Mygatt, Picket Lattimer, John Miller, William F. Griswold, and Thaddeus B. Sturges, are hereby appointed trustees until the annual election, and until others are elected in their place; and should any vacancy occur in the board of trustees previous to any annual election, the remaining trustees shall have power to fill the same.

Sec. 10. That any future Legislature shall have power to alter, amend or repeal this act.

WILLIAM MEDILL,
Speaker pro tem. of the House of Representatives.
ELIJAH VANCE,
Speaker of the Senate.

March 7, 1836.

AN ACT

To incorporate the First Presbyterian Church of New Lisbon.

Sec. 1. *Be it enacted by the General Assembly of the State of Ohio,* That George Lee, James M'Kaig, Joseph Hambleton, Samuel Martin, William Crow, Davidson Filson and John Armstrong, and their associates, together with such others as may hereafter be associated with them, be, and they are hereby created a body corporate and politic, by the name of the "First Presbyterian Church of New-Lisbon," and as such shall remain and have perpetual succession.

Sec. 2. That the said corporation, by the name and style aforesaid, shall be capable in law of holding property, real, personal, or mixed, either by purchase, gift, grant, devise or legacy, which may become the property of said corporation, to any amount not exceeding six thousand dollars: *Provided,* That such property shall be considered as held in trust under the management and at the disposal of said corporation for the purpose of promoting the interests of said society or congregation, defraying the expenses incident to their mode of worship, and maintaining or supporting any institution of charity or education connected therewith: *Provided further,* That when any money or other property shall be given, granted, bequeathed or devised to said congregation for any particular use or purpose, it shall be faithfully applied to such use or purpose, and that the property and other concerns of the corporation shall be under the management and control of trustees, to be appointed agreeable to the direction of the congregation.

Sec. 3. That on the first Monday of June, in the year one thousand eight hundred and thirty-six, and on the first Monday of June, in each and every year thereafter, the members of said society shall elect seven trustees and such other officers as they may deem necessary, who shall hold their offices for one year, and until their successors shall be elected: *Provided,* That in case of any failure to elect officers as aforesaid, the trustees may call a meeting at such time and place as they may think proper for the purpose of electing such officers.

Sec. 4. That the three first named persons in the first section of this act, be, and they are hereby appointed trustees until the first election, and until others are elected in their places.

Sec. 5. That the trustees, or any two of them, shall have power to call a meeting of the corporation, either for the election of officers, or for the transaction of other business of the society, by giving, or causing to be given to the society, immediately after public worship, ten days' previous notice, or causing notifications thereof to be put up in three or more public places within the limits of said congregation at least fifteen days before said meeting.

Sec. 6. That any meeting of the congregation duly assembled, may adopt and establish such by-laws and ordinances as may be deemed proper and necessary for the good government of said corporation.

Sec. 7. That original process against said corporation shall be by summons, which shall be served by leaving an attested copy with one or more of the trustees, at least ten days before the return day thereof.

Sec. 8. That any future Legislature shall have power to modify or repeal this act.

WILLIAM MEDILL,
Speaker pro tem. of the House of Representatives.
ELIJAH VANCE,
Speaker of the Senate.

March 7, 1836.

AN ACT

To incorporate the First Presbyterian Church in Olive township, in Morgan county.

Sec. 1. *Be it enacted by the General Assembly of the State of Ohio,* That Peter Eckley, Samuel Marquis, Allen Greenlee, John Lyons, Mickel Morrison, Joseph M. Marquis, Jonathan Lyons, and their associates for the time being, be, and they are hereby created a body corporate and politic, by the name of "The First Presbyterian Church of Olive;" and as such shall remain and have perpetual succession; subject, however, to such future regulations as the Legislature may think proper to make, touching matters of mere temporal concernment.

Sec. 2. That said corporation shall be capable in law, by the name aforesaid, of suing and being sued, pleading and being impleaded, in any action or suit in any court having competent jurisdiction.

Sec. 3. That the said corporation, by the name aforesaid, shall be capable in law, of having, receiving, acquiring and holding, either by trust, grant, devise or purchase, any estate, real, personal, or mixed, which may become the property of said corporation: *Provided,* The annual income of all such property shall not exceed the sum of two thousand dollars: *And provided also,* That all such property shall be considered as held in trust, under the management and at the disposal of said corporation, for the purpose of promoting the interest of said congregation, defraying the expenses incident to their mode of worship, and maintaining any institutions of charity or education that may therewith be connected: *Provided, moreover,* That when money or other property shall be given, granted, bequeathed or devised, to said congregation for any particutar use or purpose, it shall be fathfully applied to such end or purpose.

Sec. 4. That on the third Monday of October, one thousand eight hundred and thirty-six, and on the third Monday of October, in each and every year after the year eighteen hundred and thirty-six, there shall be elected five trustees and such other officers as the said congregation may deem necessary; who shall hold their offices for one year, and until their successors shall be elected: *Provided,* That a failure to make an election on the day appointed, shall not work a forfeiture of the privileges of the corporation; but in every such failure, from any cause, the. trustees, or any two of them, shall have power to appoint such other day for an election as they may judge fit.

Sec. 5. That all elections shall be by ballot, and shall be determined by a plurality of votes; each male supporter, by subscriptions, of said congregation, being entitled to one vote in this as in all other matters touching the interest of the corporation.

Sec. 6. That extra meetings of the congregation shall and may be called by the trustees, or any two of them, at any time, on their giving ten days previous notice, by advertisement in three public places in Olive, one of which shall be on the door of the house used by said congregation as a place of public worship.

Sec. 7. That the trustees, or a majority of them, may establish a common seal, which they may alter, change, or renew, at pleasure; and shall have power and authority to make all contracts, in behalf of the corporation, and to manage all pecuniary and prudential matters and other concerns pertaining to the good order, interest and welfare of the congregation; and to make such rules, regulations or by-laws, consistent with the constitution and laws of the United States, and of the State of Ohio, as they may deem advisable, from-time to time, for their own government and for that of the corporation: *Provided,* That they shall make no by-laws, or pass any order for the imposing or assessing of any tax, or for the sales of any property, on account of the corporation, unless by consent of said corporation, expressed by a majority of the male supporters of said congregation present, upon a day legally advertised for said purpose.

Se. 8. That original process against said corporation shall be served by leaving an attested copy with one or more of the trustees, at least ten days before the return day, and such service shall be deemed sufficient to bind said corporation.

Sec. 9. That Peter Eckley, Samuel Marquis, Allen Greenlee, John Lyons, and Mickel Morrison, be, and they are hereby constituted trustees of said congregation, with full power to act until the first annual election, and until their successors are chosen.

Sec. 10. That the trustees of said congregation shall have power to sell the lot whereon the house of worship now stands; providing they pay

to those who do not consent to the sale, the money they once donated towards the same.

WILLIAM MEDILL,
Speaker pro tem. of the House of Representatives.

ELIJAH VANCE,
Speaker of the Senate.

March 7, 1836.

AN ACT

To incorporate the Higginsport and Hillsborough Turnpike Company.

Sec. 1. *Be it enacted by the General Assembly of the State of Ohio,* That
Thomas L. Hamer, David Johnston, David Ammen, Peter L. Wilson,
James Loudon, Nathaniel Woods, Edward Thompson, Samuel Horne,
John J. Higgins, William Moore, William Davidson, Vincent Crabb,
George W. King, John H. Blair, James Clark, Thomas H. Linch, Jesse
Dugin, Benjamin F. Holden, John Wylie, Peter Spinkle, John Lindsey,
and Uriah Springer, of Brown county; and Joseph J. M'Dowell, Samuel
Bell, Henry Turner, Benjamin H. Johnston, David Miller, Allen Trimble,
John Smith, John W. Price, Joshua Woodrow, John Roads, Moses Patterson, George W. Barrere, and James Morrow, of Highland county, as
commissioners; and their associates, stockholders, as hereinafter provided,
their successors and assigns, be, and they are hereby created and declared
a body politic and corporate, perpetual, by the name and style of the Higginsport and Hillsborough Turnpike Company; to construct and keep in
repair a turnpike road, toll gates, and gate keepers houses; commencing
at a suitable point at Higginsport, in Brown county; thence by the most
eligible route, through Georgetown, in Brown county, to Hillsborough, in
Highland county; and by such corporate name and style, said company
is made and declared capable in law and equity, to contract, sue and be
sued, make by-laws, not contrary to the constitution or laws of the United States, or of this State; and to have and use a common seal, which
they may break, alter or renew at pleasure; and to acquire, have hold, sell,
transfer and convey property, real and personal, for their corporate use
and purposes, but for no other use or purpose whatsoever.

Sec. 2. That the capital stock of the company, hereby incorporated, shall
consist of one hundred thousand dollars, in shares of fifty dollars each,
and may be subscribed and held by individuals, companies or corporations,
and shall be appropriated and applied to the uses and purposes, in the
first section of the act set forth, and to no other use or purpose; and any
person desiring to discharge his subscription to the capital stock of said company, in labor or materials, on or for said roads, shall so specify, at the time
of subscribing; in which case, the labors to be performed by such subscriber, shall be assigned, and the value of the same estimated by the principal engineer, superintending the construction of the road; or if materials
be subscribed, the value thereof shall be estimated by such principal en-

gineer: *Provided*, That in all cases of subscription to the capital stock of said company, five dollars, in cash, shall be paid to the person or persons, under whose superintendence subscriptions may be received, on such share subscribers; and the residue of such capital stock, whether in cash, labor, or materials, shall be paid, discharged, performed and furnished, on the requisition of the directors, for the time being.

Sec. 3. That books for receiving subscriptions to the capital stock of said company, shall be opened on the tenth day of July next, at such places, and under the superintendence of such persons, as a majority of said commissioners, or a majority of such of them as may consent to act, may designate and appoint; it shall be the duty of said commissioners, or a majority of them, or a majority [of such] of them as consent to act, to give ten days' notice of the times, places, and persons, at which, and under whose superintendence, will be opened the books for receiving subscriptions to the capital stock of said company; which notice shall be published in some newspaper published, or in general circulation, in each of the counties of Highland, and Brown; and the books for receiving subscriptions, as aforesaid, shall be kept open as long as said directors shall see fit, unless said sum of one hundred thousand dollars, of said capital stock, shall be sooner subscribed.

Sec. 4. That as soon as it shall be ascertained, that twenty thousand dollars of the capital stock of said company has been subscribed, said commissioners, or a majority of them, or a majority of such of them as consent to act, shall give ten days notice, as provided in the third section of this act, of the time of holding an election, which shall be held at Georgetown, aforesaid, for seven directors. to manage and conduct the business and affairs of said company; and on the day thus specified, at Georgetown, aforesaid, the stockholders of said company shall proceed to the election, by ballot, of seven directors, stockholders, any five of whom shall constitute a quorum, for the transaction of the business and concerns of said company; the first election for directors, under this act, shall be conducted by two inspectors, who shall be appointed by a majority of such commissioners, as may consent to act; and such inspectors shall act under oath; none but stockholders shall vote for, or be elected directors; and the stockholders shall be entitled to one vote, which may be given in person, or by proxy, for each share of stock by him, her, or them owned and held, on the day of election; the seven directors, having the highest number of votes, shall be declared duly elected; but if an election of seven directors shall not be effected, by reason of an equal number of votes being given, in favor of two or more stockholders; in that case, the inspectors of the election shall determine, by lot, amongst the eight or more stockholders, having the highest and an equal number of votes, who shall be directors, to complete the number of seven: *Provided*, Such determination, by lot, shall not postpone as director, one stockholder having a higher, to another having a lower, number of votes; the directors first elected, under this act, shall hold their office until the first Monday of November next, after election, and until their successors are elected and qualified; and on the first Monday of November annually; after the first elections for directors, there shall be an election for directors of said company; annual elections for directors of said company shall be under the superintendence of the directors, for the time being; who shall designate a place, and shall give the like notice of the time of such annual election, as is required to be given by the commissioners, as aforesaid, of the time and place of holding the first election, under this act; and shall, in like manner, notify the persons elected, and designate a time and place for the persons elected directors, to meet and qualify; and the directors, annually elected, shall proceed, as required of the first directors.

Sec. 5. That within five days, after the first election of directors, under this act, the inspectors of the election shall give notice, in writing, to the seven stockholders, elected directors, of such their elections; and shall appoint a day, on which the directors so elected shall meet at Georgetown aforesaid, for organization; and on the day so appointed, which shall not be more than ten days from the day of election, or sooner, if the directors elected can agree, the directors so elected, shall meet at Georgetown, and severally take an oath faithfully and impartially, to discharge the several duties of director of the turnpike company, hereby incorporated; and being thus qualified, such directors shall appoint one of their body president of the board; they shall also appoint a treasurer, who shall not be a director, and they may require and take cf the treasurer, bond, in such sum, and with such security, as to them may appear reasonable and necessary, to secure said company; said directors shall also appoint a secretary, who shall keep a full and fair journal of the corporate acts of said company, and shall perform such other duties, as may be required of him by the directors.

Sec. 6. That the said company shall have a right to lay out, survey, and locate a turnpike road, as specified in the first section of this act, through any improved or unimproved lands; and to take from the lands, occupied by such road, when located as aforesaid, any stone, gravel, timber, or other materials, necessary to construct a good, secure, and substantial turnpike road, as contemplated by this act, and the necessary bridges connected therewith; and if any difference should arise between the owner or owners of any ground, on which said road may be located, or from which such materials are taken, as aforesaid, and the agents of the company, respecting damage, it shall be determined, by three disinterested freeholders, to be appointed by the commissioners of the county, in which the subject of difference lies; who, after being duly sworn, faithfully and impartially to perform the duties, required of them in this act, and taking it into consideration, whether the land be, really, rendered more or less valuable, by the road passing through it, shall make out their assessment in writing, of the damage, if any; a copy of which shall be given to the proprietor of the land, and another copy to the agent of the company; and said agent shall pay, or offer to pay, the owner of said land, the amount of such assessed damages, before he shall enter upon and take any such ground or materials, other than to survey the road; and all such assessment of damages, if any should be awarded, shall be paid by the company; but if no damage shall be awarded, then the expense shall be paid by the person who had claimed damages; and in case sufficient materials cannot be procured on the land so as aforesaid required for said road and bridges, said company, or their agents, shall have a right to, and they are hereby authorized, to enter upon any unimproved lands, adjoining or in the vicinity of said road,

38—L

and to dig, cut down, take, and carry away, so much stone, gravel, timber, or other materials, (not previously cut down, taken, approrpriated or prepared, by the owner for any particular use,) as may be necessary to enable said company to construct said road and the necessary bridges, toll gates, and gate keepers' houses; and in case of difference between the owners of any lands, from which materials may be taken, as last aforesaid, such difference shall be determined, and compensation made by said company, in manner provided by this section.

Sec. 7. That said company shall cause such turnpike road to be opened, not exceeding eighty feet wide; at least fifteen feet of which shall be made an artificial road, composed of stone, gravel, wood, or other suitable materials, well compacted together, in such a manner as to secure a good, firm, substantial and even road, rising in the middle, with a gradual arch or curve, with sufficient drains on each side, to carry the water therefrom, and shall keep the same in good repair; and in no case shall the ascent in such road be of greater elevation, than four degrees with the horizon.

Sec. 8. That so soon as said company shall have completed such roads, or the grading thereof, as aforesaid, or any part of such roads, not less than five continuous miles, and so from time to time, as often as five continuous miles thereof shall be completed, or completely graded, an agent, to be appointed for that purpose by the commissioners of the proper county, if not otherwise appointed by order, under the Legislature or its authority, shall, on application of said company, examine said road, or part thereof, as aforesaid, and report his opinion to the president of said company; and if such agent shall report said road, or any continuous five miles thereof, to be completed or completely graded, agreeable to the requisitions of this act, said company shall thereupon be entitled to erect a toll gate or gates, at suitable distances on said road, and to demand and receive of those travelling or using the same, the tolls allowed by this act.

Sec. 9. That the following shall be the rates of tolls demandable or receivable for each and every ten miles of said road, when completed, and in the same proportion for any greater or lesser distance, to wit: for every four wheeled carriage or wagon, drawn by one horse or ox, eighteen and three fourth cents; for every horse or ox in addition, six and one fourth cents; for every chaise, riding chair, cart, or gig, or other two wheeled carriage, of any kind, drawn by one horse or ox, twelve and a half cents; for every horse or ox in addition, six and one fourth cents; for every sled or sleigh, drawn by one horse or ox, twelve and a half cents; for every coach, chariot, or other four wheeled pleasure carriage, drawn by one horse, (driver included,) twenty-five cents; for every additional horse, six and one fourth cents; for every horse and driver, six and one fourth cents; for every horse, mule, or ass, led or driven, of six months old and upwards, two cents; for every head of neat cattle, six months old and upwards, three fourths of a cent; for every head of sheep or hogs, one fourth of a cent; and for equal distances and like objects, said company shall be entitled to demand and receive one half of the foregoing amount of tolls on said road, when completely graded as aforesaid, but not fully completed, as a turnpike road.

Sec. 10. That if any person or persons using said road shall, with intent to defraud said company, or to evade the payment of tolls, pass through any private gate, or bars, or other ground, except around cross-ways, authorized by law, near to any turnpike gate of said road, every person guilty of, or concerned in such fraudulent practices, shall, for every such offence, be liable to pay said company a sum not less than two dollars, nor more than ten dollars, to be recovered in action of debt, with cost of suits, before any justice of the peace of the county in which such offence may be committed; and from such judgments of the justice of the peace, an appeal may be taken to the court of common pleas of the proper county, but no stay of execution shall be allowed.

Sec. 11. That if said company shall fail for ten days in succession, to keep said road in good repair, and complaint thereof be made to a justice of the peace of the county in which said road may be out of repair, it shall be his duty forthwith to summons three disinterested freeholders of the county to examine the same, and he shall give notice to the toll gatherer, at the nearest gate, of the time when such freeholders will proceed to examine said road; and such freeholders, after taking an oath or affirmation to act impartially, shall proceed to examine said road; and if such free-holders shall find said road out of repair, they shall certify their finding to the justice of the peace, who shall immediately transmit a copy of such certificate to the toll gatherer nearest the defective part of said road; and from the time the toll gatherer's receiving such notice, no tolls shall be demanded or received for such part of the road, until the same shall be put into complete repair, under the penalty of five dollars for each offence, to be recovered of said company, with cost, on the complaint and for the use of the party aggrieved.

Sec. 12. That if any person shall, wilfully or wantonly, destroy or in any manner injure or obstruct any part of said road, or gate thereon, otherwise than in the just or lawful use thereof, every such person shall be liable to pay said company for every such offence a sum not less than five dollars, nor more than fifty dollars, to be recovered with cost before any justice of the peace of the county in which such offence may have been committed; from which judgment an appeal may be taken to the court of common pleas, but no stay of execution shall be allowed.

Sec. 13. That said company shall put a post or stone at the end of each mile, with the number of miles from Higginsport fairly cut or painted thereon; and also in a conspicuous place near each toll gate shall be placed a board, with the rates of tolls fairly printed thereon, with directions to keep to the right.

Sec. 14. That if any person shall wilfully deface or destroy any guide board, mile post or stone, or painted list or rate of tolls, erected on said road, he shall, on conviction thereof, before a justice of the peace of the proper county, forfeit and pay a sum, not less than five dollars, nor more than ten dollars, with cost of suit, in an action of debt, at the suit of said company; and from the judgment of the justice of the peace in such case, an appeal may be taken to the court of common pleas, but no stay of execution shall be allowed.

[Sec. 15.] That if any toll gatherer on said road shall unreasonably detain any person after payment or tender of the proper amount of toll, or shall demand or receive a greater amount than by this act is authorized, he shall for every such offence forfeit and pay a sum, not exceeding twenty dollars, to be recovered with cost of suit, before any justice of the peace of the proper county, in an action of debt, at the suit of the party aggrieved; and from the judgment of the justice, in such case, an appeal may be taken to the court of common pleas, but a stay of execution shall be allowed: *Provided*, That no action under this section shall be commenced after the expiration of twenty days from the accruing thereof.

Sec. 16. That there shall be kept a fair account of the whole expenses of making and repairing said road, with all incidental expenses; and also a fair account of the tolls received; and the State shall have a right to purchase the same, or any part of the stock thereof, on paying said company a sum of money which, together with tolls received, shall equal the cost and expenses of said road, as aforesaid, with ten per cent. interest per annum; and the books of said company shall always be open to the inspection of the agent of the State appointed for that purpose by the Legislature; and if the company shall neglect or refuse to exhibit their account agreeably to this section, when thereunto required, then all the rights and privileges granted by this act shall cease.

Sec. 17. That if said company shall not, within three years from the passage of this act, proceed to carry on the work, according to the true intent and meaning of this act, then in that case it shall be lawful for the Legislature to resume all the rights and privileges hereby granted.

Sec. 18. That said company shall be, and they are hereby authorized and entitled, to demand and receive the like toll from persons conveying the United States mail, as from other persons; and in case of neglect or refusal on the part of any person or persons engaged in the transportation of the mail, to pay the tolls by this act authorized to be demanded and received, said company may proceed to collect the same by action of debt; but shall not obstruct or delay the passage of the mail.

WILLIAM MEDILL,
Speaker pro. tem. of the House of Representatives.
ELIJAH VANCE,
Speaker of the Senate.

March 7, 1836.

<hr>

AN ACT

To incorporate the Chillicothe, Xenia and Dayton Turnpike Company.

Sec. 1. *Be it enacted by the General Assembly of the State of Ohio,* That David Adams, James T. Worthington, Strander McNeill, A. Heigler, Isaac Sperry, Erasmus Tulleys, Felix Wells, George J. Hardey and Martin Peterson, all of the county of Ross; Norman T. Jones, Benjamin Hinton, J. S. Williams, Thomas M. Garraugh, and Shepherd Berriman, of the county of Fayette; Mathias Winans, Noah Hixon, James Galloway, John Dodd, Adam Hains and John Heddleson, of the county of Green; and Robert Edgar and George Newcom, of the county of Montgomery, and their associates, be, and they are hereby incorporated as a body politic and corporate, by the name and title of the "Chillicothe, Xenia and Dayton Turnpike Company;" and by that name they and their successors shall have perpetual succession; and shall be capable of holding capital stock to the amount of one hundred and fifty thousand dollars, and the increase and profits thereof; and of enlarging the same, if they shall think proper, to an amount in all, not exceeding two hundred thousand dollars; and for taking, purchasing and holding to them, their successors and assigns, in fee simple, and for any less estate, any such lands, tenements, or hereditaments and estates, real, personal or mixed, as shall be necessary for them in the prosecution of their works; and shall be capable of suing and being sued, pleading and being impleaded; and have a common seal, and the same break, alter and renew at pleasure.

Sec. 2. That so soon as the company aforesaid shall have duly organized themselves, by written articles of association, recognizing this act, they may then proceed to open books for subscription to the capital stock of said company, at Chillicothe, Dayton, and at such other places as they may deem proper, to receive subscriptions to the stock of said company, in shares of twenty-five dollars each; which books shall be opened at such time and under such regulations as shall be directed by David Adams, and his associates aforesaid.

Sec. 3. That whenever twelve hundred shares shall have been subscribed, it shall be the duty of the commissioners, who may have received the subscriptions aforesaid, to call a meeting of the stockholders, by giving public notice thereof in some newspaper printed in Chillicothe and in Dayton, not less than fifteen, nor more than sixty days previous thereto, for the purpose of electing nine directors; at which elections, at least three of the commissioners shall preside; and all votes shall be by ballot, each stockholder having one vote for each and every share he may own; stockholders may also vote by proxy, under such regulations as may be prescribed in the by-laws of the company; and the directors thus elected, shall, on the same or the next day thereafter, qualify themselves by an oath or affirmation of office; and then immediately proceed to elect from their number, a president, whose duty it shall be to sign all obligations or contracts in the behalf of the company: all elections for directors, shall be on the first Monday in January, unless otherwise determined by the by-laws.

Sec. 4. That the president and directors shall hold their offices for one year, and until their successors are chosen and qualified: they shall in all cases manage the concerns of the company; appoint such other officers and agents as are necessary; fill all vacancies that may happen in their own body, until the next annual election; make by-laws for the government of the corporation: *Provided*, The same be not inconsistent with the constitution and laws of this State, or of the United States; and may require an oath or affirmation of any of the agents of said company, when they may think necessary; may call special meetings of the stockholders by giving notice as before mentioned; keep a record of their proceedings relative to the company, and do all other matters and things touching the concerns of the company, contemplated by this act.

Sec. 5. That if any stockholder shall neglect or refuse to pay any instalment, after sixty days notice of the time and place of payment, it shall be at the option of the directors to declare the stock of such delinquent forfeited to the company, or to collect the deficient instalment by suit, with costs and interest thereon, from the time said unpaid instalment had be come due; and no delinquent stockholder shall have a right to vote at any meeting of the company.

Sec. 6. That the said company shall have a right to lay out and survey their said road through any improved or unimproved lands, on the nearest and best route from the town of Chillicothe, through Frankfort, in Ross county, Washington, in Fayette county, Jamestown and Xenia, in Green county, to Dayton, in Montgomery county; and to take from the land occupied by said road when located and surveyed as aforesaid, any stone, gravel, timber or other materials, necessary to construct a good, secure and substantial road, as contemplated by this act; and in case sufficient materials cannot be procured on the land so as aforesaid, located for said road, said company, or their agents, shall have a right to enter upon any unimproved lands adjoining or in the vicinity of said road, and to dig, cut down, take and carry away so much stone, gravel, timber or other materials (not previously cut down, taken or appropriated by the owners to any particular use,) as may be necessary to enable said company to construct said road; and if any difference should arise between the owner or owners of any ground from which such materials are taken, as aforesaid, and the agents of the company, respecting damages, it shall be determined by three disinterested freeholders, to be appointed by the commissioners of the county in which the subject of difference lies; who, taking into consideration whether the land be really made more or less valueable by the road passing through it, shall make out their assessment in writing, of the damages, if any, a copy of which shall be given to the proprietor of the land, and another copy to the agent of the company; and said agent shall pay or offer to pay, the owner of said land the amount of such assessed damages, before he shall enter upon or take any such ground or materials, other than to survey the road; and all expenses of such assessment of damages, if any are awarded, shall be paid by the company.

Sec. 7. That the president and directors of the Chillicothe, Xenia and Dayton Turnpike Company, shall cause the said road to be opened, not exceeding ninety feet wide, at least eighteen of which shall be made an artificial road composed of stone, gravel, wood, or other suitale materials, well compacted together, in such manner as to secure a firm, substantial and even road, rising in the middle, with a gradual arch; and shall maintain and keep the same in good repair; and in no case shall the ascent in the road be of greater elevation than five degrees.

Sec. 8. That as soon as the said turnpike company shall have completed the road as aforesaid, from Chillicothe to Dayton, or any part thereof, not less than ten miles, measuring from the corporation line of Chillicothe aforesaid; and so, from time to time, as often as ten miles of said road shall be completed, always measuring from the town of Chillicothe aforesaid, an agent, to be appointed for that purpose by the Governor, if not otherwise appointed by the Legislature, shall, on application of the company, examine the same, and report his opinion, in writing, to the president of the company; and if such report shall state the road, or any ten miles thereof, to be completed agreeably to the provisions of this act, the company may then erect a gate or gates at suitable distances, and demand and receive of persons travelling the same, the tolls allowed by this act.

Sec. 9. That the following shall be the rates of toll for each and every ten miles of said road, and in the same proportion for a greater or less distance, to wit: for every four wheel carriage, drawn by two horses or oxen, twenty-five cents; for every horse or ox in addition, six and one-fourth cents; for every two wheeled carriage, drawn by two horses or oxen, eighteen and three-fourth cents; for every horse or ox in addition, six and one-fourth cents; for every sled or sleigh, drawn by two horses or oxen, twelve and a half cents; and for every horse or ox in addition, six and one-fourth cents; for every horse and rider, six and one-fourth cents; for every horse, mule or ass, led or driven, six months old or upwards, three cents; for neat cattle, six months old or upwards, twenty-five cents for every score, and a less number in proportion; for every score of sheep or hogs, twelve and a half cents; for every four wheeled pleasure carriage, drawn by two horses, thirty-seven and a half cents; for every horse in addition, twelve and a half cents; for every two wheeled pleasure carriage, drawn by one horse, twenty-five cents; for every horse in addition, twelve and a half cents; for every four wheeled carriage, drawn by one horse, eighteen and three-fourth cents: *Provided,* That all persons going to, or returning from public worship, on the Sabbath, and all militiamen going to, and from their respective muster grounds, and all persons having the qualifications of electors, going to and from the place of holding annual elections and presidential elections, shall pass free of toll: *Provided, also,* That the Legislature may, at any time after the expiration of ten years from the completion of said road, make any alteration in the rate of toll aforesaid.

Sec. 10. That if any person or persons using said road shall, with intent to defraud said company, or to evade the payment of toll, pass through any private gate or bars, or along any other ground near to any turnpike gate which shall be erected pursuant to this act, or shall practice any fraudulent means, with intent to evade or lessen the payment of such toll; or if any person shall take another person off of said road, with intent to defraud said turnpike company; each and every one concerned in such fraudulent practices shall, for every such offence, forfeit and pay to the company the sum of five dollars, without stay of execution, to be recovered with costs of suit, before any justice of the peace in any county through which said road may pass: *Provided,* That nothing in this act shall be so construed as to prevent persons using said road between the gates for common purposes.

Sec. 11. That if the said company shall fail to keep said road in good repair for ten days in succession, and complaint thereof be made to a justice of the peace in the county in which said road is out of repair, it shall be his duty forthwith to summon three disinterested freeholders to examine the same; and he shall give notice to the toll gatherer at the nearest gate, of the time when said freeholders will proceed to examine the same; and the said freeholders, after having taken an oath or affirmation to act impartially, shall proceed to examine said road; and if the same is out of repair, they shall certify it to the justice of the peace, who shall immediately transmit a copy of such certificate to the nearest toll gatherer where such defective part of the road lies; and from the time of receiving such notice no toll shall be demanded or received for such part of the road until the same shall be put in complete repair, under the penalty of five dollars for every such offence; to be recovered, with costs, of said company, on the complaint and for the use of the person aggrieved.

Sec. 12. That the said company shall put up a post or stone at the end of each mile, with the number of miles from the town of Chillicothe, fairly cut or painted thereon; and also, in a conspicuous place near each gate, shall be placed a board with the rates of toll painted thereon, and directions to keep to the right.

Sec. 13. That any person wilfully defacing or destroying any guide board, mile post or stone, or painted list of rates of tolls, erected on said road, shall, on conviction thereof before a justice of the peace, be fined not less than five nor exceeding fifty dollars, with costs of prosecution; to be recovered at the suit of any person, for the use of said company.

Sec. 14. That if any toll gatherer on said road shall unreasonably detain any passenger after the toll has been paid or offered to be paid, or shall demand or receive greater toll than is by this act allowed, he shall, for every such offence, forfeit and pay a sum not less than five nor exceeding fifty dollars, to be recovered with costs of suit, before any justice of the peace having competent jurisdiction thereof: *Provided, however,* That no suit or action shall be brought against any person or persons for any penalty incurred under this section, unless the same shall be commenced within three weeks from the time of incurring the same; and the defendant or defendants in such suit or action may plead the general issue, and give this act and the special matter in evidence.

Sec. 15. That if said company shall not, within five years from the passage of this act, proceed to carry on the work according to the true intent and meaning of this act, then and in that case, it shall be lawful for the Legislature to resume all the rights and privileges hereby granted.

Sec. 16. That if said company shall at any time use their funds for banking purposes, or any other purposes than that of making and keeping in repair said road, and dividing the profits arising therefrom amongst the stockholders thereof, then the privileges granted by this act shall cease and determine; and the stockholders shall be liable in their private and individual capacity for any debt contracted by such company.

WILLIAM MEDILL,
Speaker pro tem. of the House of Representatives.

ELIJAH VANCE,
Speaker of the Senate.

March 7, 1836.

AN ACT

To incorporate the Zanesville and Maysville Turnpike Road Company.

Sec. 1. *Be it enacted by the General Assembly of the State of Ohio,* That

Levi Whipple, Alva Buckingham, John Porter and Austin A. Guthrie, of the county of Muskingum; William Beard, Charles C. Hood, James Ritchey, George Brumer and Robert Martin, of the county of Perry; Samuel F. Maccracken, Philamon Beecher, David Ewing, William J. Reese, William Coulson and Joseph Stukey, of the county of Fairfield; Otis Ballard, John Herman, Thomas J. Winship and John Entriken, of the county of Pickaway; David Crouse, James T. Worthington, John Maderia, David Adams, William Ferguson and Joseph G. White, of the county of Ross; John Patterson, Isaac Aerl, Westley Lee, George Sample, Thomas Bowles and Elijah Leedorn, of the county of Adams; Evan Campbell, Thomas J. Larwell and William Carpenter, of the county of Brown; Allen Gulliford, John Pervil, John Palmer, William Head, Edward Eastand, of the county of Highland; and their associates, be, and they are hereby created a body politic and corporate, under the name of The Zanesville and Maysville Turnpike Road Company; for the purpose of constructing a road from the west bank of the Muskingum river, at its ford, in Putnam, through Union Town, Somerset, Rushville, West-Rushville, Lancaster, Tarlton, Kingston, Chillicothe, Bainbridge, Sinking Spring, Jacksonville, West Union, and Aberdeen, to the Ohio river; and by their said name the said company and their successors shall have perpetual succession, and all the privileges and immunities incident to a corporation; and may take, purchase, and hold, in fee simple, or for any less estate, any lands, tenements and hereditaments, and any personalty which may be necessary for the objects contemplated by this act; and shall be capable of suing and being sued, pleading and being impleaded, answering and being answered unto, in all courts of competent jurisdiction, and have and use a common seal, and the same to break, alter, or renew, at pleasure.

Sec. 2. That so soon as the above named persons, or any nine of them, having duly organized themselves, by written articles of association, recognizing this act, they may proceed to open books of subscription to the capital stock of said company, at such times and places as they may deem proper.

Sec. 3. That the capital stock shall consist of six hundred thousand dollars, to be divided into shares of twenty-five dollars each, which may be required to be paid in instalments of not exceeding ten per cent. to be called for by notice published in at least one of the newspapers of Zanesville, Somerset, Lancaster, Chillicothe, West Union, and Maysville, respectively, sixty days before the day of payment.

Sec. 4. That if any stockholder shall fail to pay any instalment so called for, it shall be the duty of the board of directors to collect the delinquent instalment, with interest, from the time the same become due, before some court of competent jurisdiction: and no delinquent stockholder shall have the right to vote upon any share for which he may be delinquent.

Sec. 5. That when the whole amount of capital stock shall have been subscribed, by good and substantial stockholders, it shall be the duty of the said persons who may have received the subscriptions, or a majority of them, to report the subscriptions to the Governor of this State, whose duty it shall be, if he is satisfied with the responsibility of the subscribers, immediately to call a meeting of the stockholders, at Chillicothe, in the

39—L

county of Ross, by giving thirty days notice thereof, in at least one of the newspapers of Zanesville, Somerset, Lancaster, Chillicothe, West Union, and Maysville, respectively, for the purpose of electing nine directors, who shall be stockholders; at which meeting at least three of said persons shall be present, and superintend the election: all votes for directors at that and subsequent elections, shall be by ballot, either in person or by proxy; and each stockholder shall be entitled to one vote for each share he may own; and the directors thus elected shall hold their offices until their successors shall be elected, and shall immediately proceed to the election of a president from their own body.

Sec. 6. That after the first election, all subsequent elections for directors shall be holden on the first Monday of January in each and every year, at such place as the directors may appoint; and the directors so elected shall hold their offices for one year, and until their successors are elected, and shall immediately elect a president from their own body; and if from any cause there should be a failure to hold the elections at the time prescribed in this section, the corporation shall not be thereby dissolved, but it shall be lawful to hold an election at any subsequent time, notice thereof being given, as is provided in the fifth section of this act.

Sec. 7. That the directors shall manage the affairs of the company; appoint all agents that may be necessary, to carry on its concerns; fill vacancies that may happen in their own body; and make such by-laws, rules, and regulations, not inconsistent with the constitution and laws of this State, and of the United States, as they may deem expedient.

Sec. 8. That when the whole amount of value of capital stock shall have been subscribed, and one half paid in and expended in the construction of said road, and the same certified to the Governor by the directors under oath, the corporation hereby created, is authorized to loan of any person or persons body corporate or politic for any period of time not exceeding thirty years, any sum or sums of money not exceeding three hundred thousand dollars, at a rate of interest not exceeding six per cent. per annum, to be expended in the constructing and keeping of said road; and in order to enable the said corporation to effect the loan upon reasonable terms, the State of Ohio hereby guarantees its payment, together with the interest thereon, according to any contract the board of directors may make: *Provided,* Said loan or loans shall not exceed the sum of three hundred thousand dollars: and the stock of individual subscribers in this corporation, together with the tolls or dividends thereon, are hereby pledged to the State of Ohio for its indemnity in consideration of the aforesaid guarantee: *Provided, also,* That the stockholders in this incorporation are hereby held liable in their individual capacity for the amount of stock subscribed by each; and if the said company shall at any time fail in the punctual payment of the interest on the sums advanced or in repaying the principal when redeemable by the State, the Governor shall be and he is hereby authorized on behalf of the State to take possession of the works of said company and place them under the charge of such officers or boards of commissioners as may by law be provided for the preservation or construction of public works, and to hold the same until by the tolls and profits thereof, or by a sale of the works, the State shall be fully reimbursed.

Sec. 9. That the said company shall have a right to lay out and survey the said road, through any improved or unimproved land, along the aforesaid route, and to take from the lands occupied by said road, when located and surveyed as aforesaid, any stone, gravel, timber, or other materials, necessary to construct the same; and in case sufficient materials cannot be had on the land so occupied, said company, or their agents, shall have a right to enter upon any lands adjoining or in the vicinity of said road, and take therefrom so much stone, gravel, timber, or other materials, not previously appropriated by the owner, to any particular use, as may be necessary to enable said company to construct the said road: and if any difference should arise between the owner of the land, on which the said road may be located, or from which materials may be required to be taken, and the company, respecting damages or compensation, it shall be determined by three disinterested freeholders to be appointed by the commissioners of the county in which the subject of difference lies, and who, after being duly sworn or affirmed faithfully and impartially to perform the duties required of them by this act, and taking into consideration whether the land be rendered more or less valuable by the road passing through or near it, shall, if in their opinion any damage has been sustained, make out an assessment of the amount in writing, and furnish a copy thereof to the owner of the land, and another copy to the agent of the company; and said agent shall pay or offer to pay the owner of the land the amount of such assessment, before he shall enter upon or take any such land or materials, other than to survey the road; and if any damages are awarded, the costs of the assessment shall be paid by the company; and if none are awarded, then by the owner of the land or materials.

Sec. 10. That the profits and tolls arising from said road shall first be applied to the payment of the interest of the loan secured on the credit of the State, and the residue not exceeding one half, shall be received by the directors and distributed and paid among the individual stockholders in proportion to the amount of stock owned by each and actually paid in, and the surplus, if any, shall be paid into the State Treasury to be kept as a sinking fund for the final redemption of such loan.

Sec. 11. That the said road shall be opened, not exceeding one hundred feet in width, at least sixteen feet of which shall be made an artificial road, of stone, gravel or other suitable materials; and so soon as ten continuous miles thereof shall be completed, and so from time to time as each continuous distance of ten miles on any part of said road thall be completed, it shall be lawful for the company to erect gates at suitable distances, and to demand and receive the rates of toll, prescribed by this act.

Sec. 12. The stock of this corporation shall be taken and deemed personal estate; and any stockholder, after he shall have procured the written assent of the Governor of this State, and file the same in the office of the secretary of the corporation, may transfer stock to such person or persons, as by this permission aforesaid he is authorized to do, in such manner as the by-laws of the corporation may direct.

Sec. 13. That the following shall be the rates of toll, for each ten miles of said road, and in the same proportion for a less distance, to wit: For every four-wheeled wagon, carriage, or vehicle, drawn by one horse or other animal, eighteen and three-fourth cents; for every horse or animal, in addition, six and one-fourth cents; for every cart, chaise, or other two wheeled vehicle, drawn by one horse or other animal, twelve and a half cents; for every horse or other animal in addition, six and one-fourth cents; for every sled or sleigh, drawn by one horse or other animal, twelve and a half cents; for every horse or other animal in addition thereto, six and one fourth cents; for every coach or other four-wheeled pleasure carriage, drawn by one horse or other animal, twenty-five cents; for every horse or other animal in addition thereto, twelve and a half cents; for every horse and rider, six and one fourth cents; for every horse, mule or ass, six months old and upwards, led or driven, three cents; for every head of neat cattle, six months old and upwards, one cent; and for every head of sheep and hogs, one half cent: *Provided*, That all persons going to, and returning from public worship, militia musters, or funerals, shall pass free from toll.

Sec. 14. That if any person using said road shall, with intent to evade the payment of toll, pass through any private gate or bars, or any other ground, except around cross-ways, authorized by law, near to any turn-pike gate, or if any person shall take another around any turnpike gate, with intent to evade the payment of toll, every person so offending, shall, for every such offence, forfeit and pay to the company the sum of five dollars, to be recovered with costs, in an action of debt, before a justice of the peace, in any county in which such offence may be committed: *Provided*, That nothing in this section shall be so construed as to prevent persons using said road between the gates.

Sec. 15. That if said company shall fail for ten days in succession to keep the said road in good repair, and complaint thereof be made to a justice of the peace of the county in which said road is out of repair, it shall be his duty, forthwith, to summon three disinterested freeholders to examine the same; and he shall give notice to the toll gatherer at the gate nearest to the part of the road complained of, of the time when the said freeholders will proceed to examine the same; and the said freehold-ers, after having taken an oath or affirmation to act impartially, shall make examination, and if they find the complaint well founded, and that the road is out of repair, they shall certify the fact to the justice, who shall immediately transmit a copy of such certificate to the same toll gatherer; and from the time of the receiving of such copy, no toll shall be demand-ed or received at the said gate nearest to the defective part of the road, until the same be put in repair, under the penalty of five dollars for each offence, to be recovered of the said company at the suit and for the use of the party aggrieved.

Sec. 16. That if any person shall wilfully destroy, or in any manner injure or obstruct any part of said road, or the fixtures belonging there-to, every such person shall, on conviction thereof in an action of debt, at the suit of the State of Ohio, before any justice of the peace having ju-risdiction, be liable to a fine of not more than fifty, nor less than five dol-lars and costs, the one half thereof to go to the county in which the of-fence is committed, and the other half to the informer; and shall more-over be liable to the company for all damages sustained by them in con-sequence of such injury or obstruction.

Sec. 17. That the said company shall put up a stone at the end of each mile, with the number of miles from Zanesville fairly painted or cut thereon, and shall also place in a conspicuous condition near each gate, a board, with the rates of toll fairly painted thereon, and directions to keep to the right.

Sec. 18. That if any toll gatherer on said road shall unreasonably detain any passenger after the toll has been paid or tendered, or shall demand or receive greater toll than is by this act allowed, he shall, for every such offence, forfeit and pay a sum not exceeding twenty dollars, to be recovered with costs, before any justice of the peace having jurisdiction thereof, at the suit of the party injured: *Provided, however*, That such suit shall be brought within twenty days from the commission of the offence.

Sec. 19. That there shall be kept an accurate account of the whole expense of making and repairing said road, with all incidental expenses, and also of the tolls received; and the State shall have the right to purchase the road by paying the company a sum of money which with the loans secured, shall equal the whole of said expenditures and interest thereon, at the rate of eight per cent. per annum; and the books of said company shall always be open for the inspection of the agent of the State, to be appointed by the Legislature.

WILLIAM MEDILL,
Speaker pro tem. of the House of Representatives.
ELIJAH VANCE,
Speaker of the Senate.

March 7, 1836.

AN ACT

To incorporate a Bridge Company at the Bear Rapids of the Maumee river.

Sec. 1. *Be it enacted by the General Assembly of the State of Ohio,* That all persons who shall become stockholders pursuant to this act, shall be, and they are hereby constituted a body corporate, by the name of "The Bear Rapids Toll-bridge Company."

Sec. 2. The capital stock of said company shall be divided into eight hundred shares, of twenty-five dollars each.

Sec. 3. Asa Gilbert, Samuel B. Campbell, Henry Bennet, and R. A. Forsyth, shall be commissioners to open books for receiving subscriptions to the capital stock of said corporation; the said books shall be opened on or before the first day of October next, and each of the said commissioners may receive subscriptions; and the stockholders on subscribing shall each pay on each share subscribed, one dollar.

Sec. 4. Whenever two hundred shares of the capital stock of said corporation shall be subscribed, the commisioners shall cause to be given to each stockholder at least ten days notice of the time and place of meeting of said stockholders; at the time and place appointed the stockholders, either in person or by proxy, shall choose five directors, being stockholders of said corporation, a quorum of whom shall be competent to transact business, a new election of directors shall be held annually at such time and place as the stockholders at their first or some subsequent meeting shall direct; the directors shall, at some other meetings choose out of their number one person to be president, and also appoint a secretary and treasurer.

Sec. 5. The directors may continue to receive subscriptions to the stock until eight hundred shares are subscribed.

Sec. 6. The directors may demand from the stockholders respectively all such sums of money by them subscribed, at such times and in such proportions as they may think proper, giving ten days notice, under penalty of forfeiting their respective shares and all previous payments; not impairing thereby the right of enforcing the payment of said subscriptions by powers of law, if the directors shall so elect.

Sec. 7. The said corporation shall erect a bridge over the Maumee river at or near the Bear rapids thereof, on such land as it may purchase for that purpose, which purchase it is hereby authorized to make; and may receive the following tolls for passing the same, that is to say: for every four wheeled pleasure carriage, hung on metal springs, drawn by two horses, fifty cents, and for every additional horse, ten cents; every four wheeled pleasure carriage, hung on metal springs, and drawn by one horse, twenty-five cents; every two wheeled pleasure carriage, drawn by one horse, fifteen cents, for every additional horse ten cents; every wagon, cart, or sleigh, drawn by two horses, oxen or mules, twenty cents, and for every additional horse, ox or mule, six cents; every one horse wagon, sleigh or cart, twelve and one half cents; every man and horse, eight cents; every foot passenger, six cents; for every score of horses, cattle or mules, sixty cents; for every score of sheep or swine, twenty cents; and in proportion for a less number.

Sec. 8. If any person shall wilfully impair or injure said bridge, he shall forfeit ten dollars, and treble the amount of damages sustained, to be recovered, the penalty in an action of debt, and the damage in trespass, with double costs; and if any person shall forcibly pass the gate without having paid the toll, he shall forfeit to said corporation eight times the amount of the toll, to be recovered in an action of debt, with costs.

Sec. 9. If the toll gatherer shall unreasonably delay any passenger, or demand more than the legal toll, he shall, for each offence, forfeit the sum of five dollars; to be recovered with costs, in the name and for the use of the person delayed or defrauded.

Sec. 10. The shares of stock in said corporation shall be considered personal estate, and be transferred as such.

Sec. 11. It shall not be lawful for any person to ride or drive over said bridge faster than on a walk, or to drive more than twenty head of cattle at a time on said bridge, on pain of forfeiting one dollar to said corporation for each offence; to be recovered in the name of the treasurer, with costs of suit, for the use of said corporation.

Sec. 12. That if said bridge shall not be constructed within five years from the passage of this act, or if the same is carried away or destroyed and not rebuilt in three years thereafter, the said corporation shall cease and be void.

Sec. 13. This act shall be deemed a public act, and shall continue in force, unless forfeited, for the period of fifty years; and shall be favorably construed both in law and equity.

WILLIAM MEDILL,
Speaker pro tem. of the House of Representatives.
ELIJAH VANCE,
Speaker of the Senate.

March 7, 1836.

AN ACT

To provide for the continuation of the Hocking Canal.

Sec. 1. *Be it enacted by the General Assembly of the State of Ohio,* That the canal commissioners or the board of public works of this State, be, and they are hereby empowered and directed, if, after a full examination, it be found practicable, and in the opinion of said board, it will yield, together with the consequent increase of tolls on the Ohio canal, a sufficient revenue to the State, when completed, to meet the interest on the cost of construction, to construct a navigable communication, from the termination of the lateral canal in the town of Lancaster, in Fairfield county, to the town of Athens, in Athens county, by canal and slack water navigation, as they may deem most for the interest of the State; with such locks and dams as may be necessary to secure the safe transit and convenient passage of canal boats of such dimensions and capacity as are permitted to navigate the Ohio canal; and to accomplish that object, the said commissioners or board of public works are hereby empowered to seize, dedicate, acquire, hold, use and occupy, for the use and benefit of the State, all such private and corporate estate and property as shall be necessary for the convenience of the construction of that improvement, and for hydraulic purposes thereon, as they have heretofore had power to do, in the construction and maintenance of the Ohio and Miami canals. *Provided,* That the owners and proprietors of any property, so seized and dedicated, shall have all the rights of indemnity and remedies of compensation as by law have been provided for in the construction of the Ohio and Miami canals; and when the said improvement shall be completed, or any part thereof, the said canal commissioners or board of public works, at their discretion, shall levy and assess such tolls thereon as may at the time be levied and assessed on the Ohio canal; and rent out the water power thereon on such terms and conditions as may seem right and just, having reference to, and in view of the interest of the State and the permanent prosperity of the Hocking Valley: *Provided,* That the canal commissioners or board of public works are hereby required to make the necessary examinations during the present season: *And provided, also,* That if said commissioners deem it for the interest of the State, the owners or proprietors of the lands contiguous to the location of such dams and locks as shall be constructed by the State along the line of the contemplated improvement, shall convey to the State on such terms and conditions as the said board shall deem just and equitable, so much of said lands as shall be necessary for the proper and convenient use of the water power which will thereby be created: *Provided further,* That nothing in this act shall take from the proprietors of water power now in use any more water than is necessary for the convenient navigation of the canal, or interfere with lands now occupied for the purpose of using such power, further than is necessary in the construction of said canal.

Sec. 2. That preparatory to the construction of said improvement, the canal commissioners or a board of public works may cause such further surveys and examinations to be made in relation thereto, as, in their judgment, may be considered proper for the successful prosecution of the work; and the accounts and documents of all expenses incurred, and disbursements

made, and the revenue or income received by or under the authority of this
act, shall be kept separate and distinct from those belonging to or connected with the other public works of this State.

Sec. 3. That for the purpose of carrying into effect the provisions of
this act, the commissioners of the canal fund be, and they are hereby authorized to borrow on the credit of the State, any sum not exceeding one
hundred thousand dollars, in the year eighteen hundred and thirty-six; one
hundred thousand dollars in the year eighteen hundred and thirty-seven;
and one hundred and fifty thousand dollars in the year eighteen hundred
and thirty-eight,—in all, three hundred and fifty thousand dollars; at a rate
of interest not exceeding six per centum per annum, payable semi-annually
at the city of New York or elsewhere; the principal thereof to be paid at
any time after the year eighteen hundred and fifty-six, at the pleasure of
the State, whose faith is hereby pledged for the payment of such loan and
the interest thereon, as above specified; and further, for the payment of the
interest of said loan and the ultimate redemption of the principal thereof,
there is hereby irrevocably pledged the proceeds of all tolls and water
rents, and all other revenue and income which may be received on said improvements, after deducting therefrom the annual expenses thereof, in keeping the same in repair, and other incidental charges of its superintendence
and police.

Sec. 4. That in [the] construction of this work, and in the management and superintendence thereof, the canal commissioners or board of
public works, and the commissioners of the canal fund, shall possess and exercise the same powers in all respects as to the appointment of engineers
and other officers and agents, and providing for a strict accountability of
all moneys expended, as they have heretofore possessed and exercised, or
may hereafter be granted, in the construction, maintenance and supervision
of the Ohio and Miami canals.

WILLIAM MEDILL,
Speaker pro tem. of the House of Representatives.
ELIJAH VANCE,
Speaker of the Senate.

March 7, 1836.

AN ACT

Authorizing the sale of a piece of land therein described.

Sec. 1. *Be it enacted by the General Assembly of the State of Ohio,*
That James Anderson, John Arnail, Thomas Savage, William Campbell,
and Samuel F. McKenney, trustees of the "Antrim Congregation of the
Associate Reformed Synod of the West," are hereby authorized to surrender to the treasurer of the county of Guernsey, the lease of "five acres of
land; being part of lot number thirteen, of the first range and third township, in the county of Guernsey; beginning at the south east corner of said
lot, running thence north twenty poles; thence west forty poles; thence

south twenty poles; thence east forty poles, to the place of beginning;" the same lease being a permanent lease of said land, for ninety-nine years, renewable forever, to the trustees of the same church, by the name of "The Trustees of the Miller's fork and Cross road Congregation of the Union body," for the purpose of a burial ground and meeting house, made by force of "An act providing for the appraisement and leasing of a tract of United States Military School land, lying in the county of Guernsey," passed January 29th, 1827; and that they be entitled to demand and receive from said treasurer a certificate of purchase, and a deed of conveyance thereof, in the same manner as if the same surrender had been made before the first day of February, 1830, any law to the contrary notwithstanding.

WILLIAM MEDILL,
Speaker pro tem. of the House of Representatives.

ELIJAH VANCE,
Speaker of the Senate.

March 7, 1836.

AN ACT

Providing for the sale of one-fourth part of section sixteen, in township fourteen, of range six, now Union township, in the county of Carroll.

Sec. 1. *Be it enacted by the General Assembly of the State of Ohio,* That George Davis, Samuel Semple, and Arnold Barker, sen., of the county of Carroll, are hereby appointed commissioners, who, having taken an oath or affirmation before some person authorized to administer the same, shall, at some time between the twenty-fifth day of May and the fifteenth day of June next, ensuing the passage of this act, proceed to view and appraise the one-fourth part of school section sixteen, now remaining unsold, in the original surveyed township fourteen, range six, now Union township, in said Carroll county, granted by Congress for the use of schools, at its true cash value, taking into consideration the improvements, if there be any made thereon, and appurtenances thereto; and make return thereof to the auditor of said Carroll county on or before the twenty-fifth day of June next.

Sec. 2. That previous to such appraisement as aforesaid, the assessor of Carroll county shall, between the first day of March and the twenty-fifth day of May next, either in person or by deputy, call on every person resident in said originally surveyed township fourteen, having the qualifications of an elector, and take his vote for or against the sale of said quarter of said section, in a book to be by him provided for that purpose, carefully noting in one column, those who voted in favor of, and in another and separate column, the names of those who voted against said sale; and make return of the vote so taken, to the commissioners and auditor of said county, on the first Monday of June next.

40—L

Sec. 3. That so soon as said assessor shall have made his return of the votes so taken, and it shall be found that a majority of the qualified electors of said township fourteen have voted in favor of such sale, it shall be the duty of the auditor of Carroll county, after having given thirty days previous notice thereof, by advertisement in some newspaper printed in said county; and if no newspaper be printed in said county, or if the publisher of any newspaper refuse to print the same, then the notice shall be given by affixing a written notice on the door of the court house of said county, and in five other public places in said county; three of which shall be in said township of Union, thirty days previous to such sale; which notices shall be posted up by one or more of the said commissioners named in the first section of this act, and the affidavit of one or more of the said commissioners, certifying the manner, time, and places of publishing such notices, shall be conclusive evidence of such fact, to offer said quarter of said section for sale, between the hours of ten o'clock A. M. and five o'clock P. M. on the day and at the place designated in such notices, and said auditor shall strike off and sell the same to the highest bidder: *Provided*, That said fourth part of said section shall not be sold for a sum less than its appraised cash value; one half of the purchase money to be paid at the time of such sale, and the remainder in two equal payments, payable annually thereafter, with interest payable annually thereon, to be computed from the day of such sale; and if on the day mentioned in said notices, no person bids the appraised value for said land, the sale thereof may be publicly adjourned from day to day, or to such other day as the auditor may think proper.

Sec. 4. That the auditor of said county, on the receipt of such purchase money, shall make a deed of such land to the purchaser or purchasers thereof, and from the avails thereof shall pay the necessary fees and expenses of said appraisement, advertisement, and sale, and for making and acknowledging such deed; and the residue of such purchase money he shall deposit in the common school fund, for the benefit of said township, in proportion to the number of white youth in the several school districts within the same.

Sec. 5. That should a majority of the electors in said township, vote against the sale of said land, and for the leasing thereof, the commissioners named in the first section of this act, shall proceed to lease the same, after the same has been appraised, as provided in the first section of this act, at public sale, to the highest bidder, for the term of ten years, and the person or persons leasing said land, shall give bond and security, to the acceptance of the commissioners of Carroll county, for the amount of the rent thereof, which rent shall be paid annually to the auditor of said county, and by him paid over for the benefit of schools in said township, in proportion to the enumeration of white youths in the several school districts, except so much as may be necessary for defraying the expenses of appraising and leasing said land: *Provided, however*, That said fourth of said section shall not be leased or rendered for a less sum than six per cent. per annum upon the appraised value thereof.

Sec. 6. That should either of the commissioners named in the first section of this act, die, refuse to serve, or remove out of the county, the commissioners of Carroll county, shall forthwith fill such vacancy by the appointment of some suitable person, as often as the same may occur.

WILLIAM MEDILL,
Speaker pro tem. of the House of Representatives.
ELIJAH VANCE,
Speaker of the Senate.

March 7, 1836.

AN ACT
Supplementary to "An act incorporating the Milford and Chillcotho Turnpike Company," passed February 14th, 1835.

Sec. 1. *Be it enacted by the General Assembly of the State of Ohio,* That in order to aid the Milford and Chillicothe Turnpike Company in the completion of said road, the president and directors of said company shall have power to grade said road to a level not exceeding the angular elevation required by their charter, and having completely graded the same, and erected permanent bridges thereon, or having graded and bridged any one continued portion thereof, of not less than ten miles; said company shall thereupon be authorized and empowered to erect toll gates, and exact such tolls as shall correspond with the tolls authorized by their charter, having reference to the different estimates of expense, which estimates shall be made by a skilful and competent engineer employed by said company; a copy of which estimate shall be forthwith filed in the office of the Secretary of State, and be subject to the order and correction of the Legislature: *Provided always,* That the partial tolls hereby authorized, shall cease within ten years, unless said road shall within that time have been completed: *Provided,* That so soon as said road shall be completed, or any ten miles thereof, said partial tolls shall cease upon such part of the road as shall be finished, and the full amount of tolls authorized by the charter of said company shall commence.

Sec. 2. That it shall be competent for the county commissioners of the several counties through which said road passes, and they are hereby authorized to subscribe for stock in said company, for the purpose of aiding in the construction of such bridges and other parts of said turnpike, as the public interest may more immediately require to be completed; and said commissioners and their successors shall be entitled by themselves or their agents to vote on the shares thus subscribed at all elections for directors of said company, and be entitled on behalf of their respective counties to the same proportion of dividends as other stockholders.

WILLIAM MEDILL,
Speaker pro tem. of the House of Representatives.
ELIJAH VANCE,
Speaker of the Senate.

March 7, 1836.

316

AN ACT

To incorporate the town of Albion, in the county of Cuyahoga.

Sec. 1. *Be it enacted by the General Assembly of the State of Ohio,* That so much of the township of Strongsville, in the county of Cuyahoga, as is included within the following bounds, to wit: beginning at the west line of lot number 53, at such a point that a line due east will strike the south end of the turnpike bridge; thence south from said point on the same course with the lot line 185 rods; thence east 120 rods; thence north to the point of intersection with the first mentioned due east line, by the south end of the bridge; thence west to the place of beginning; be, and the same are hereby created into and constituted a town corporate, by the name of the Town of Albion.

Sec. 2. That for the order and good government of said town, and inhabitants thereof, it shall be lawful for the white male inhabitants thereof, who have resided therein for the space of six months next preceding the day of election, having the qualifications of electors for members of the General Assembly, to meet at the school house in said town, on the first Saturday of April next, and on the first Saturday of April, annually, thereafter, and then and there proceed, by a plurality of votes, to elect by ballot, on mayor, one recorder, and five trustees, who shall be house-holders in said town, who shall hold their office until the next annual election, and until their successors are elected and qualified; and such mayor, recorder, and trustees, so being elected and qualified, shall constitute the town council of said town, any five of whom shall constitute a quorum for the transaction of business.

Sec. 3. That at the first election, to be holden under this act, there shall be chosen *viva voce*, by the electors present, two judges and a clerk of said election, who shall take an oath or affirmation faithfully to discharge the duties required of them by this act; and at all subsequent elections, the trustees, or any two of them, shall be judges, and the recorder, or in his absence, some other person, to be appointed by the judges, shall be clerk: the polls shall be opened between the hours of one and two o'clock, and closed at four o'clock, in the afternoon of said day; and at the close of the polls, the votes shall be counted, and a true statement thereof proclaimed to the voters present, by one of the judges; and the person having the highest number of votes, shall be declared duly elected; and the clerk shall make a true record thereof, and within five days thereafter, he shall give notice to the persons so elected of their election; and it shall be the duty of the town council, at least ten days before each and every annual election, to give notice thereof, by setting up advertisements at three of the most public places in said town.

Sec. 4. That the mayor, and in case of his absence, the recorder, shall preside at all such meetings; and the recorder shall attend all meetings of the town council, and make a fair and accurate record of all their proceedings.

Sec. 5. That the town council shall have power to fill all vacancies which may happen in said board, from the householders, who are qualified electors in said town, who shall hold their appointments until the next annual election, and until their successors are elected and qualified; and in the absence of the mayor and recorder from any meeting of the town council, the trustees shall have power to appoint any two of their number, to perform the duties of mayor and recorder, for the time being.

Sec. 6. That the mayor, recorder, and trustees of said town, shall be a body corporate and politic, with perpetual succession, to be known and distinguished by the name and style of the "Town Council of the town of Albion;" and shall be capable in law, by their corporate name, to acquire property, real, personal and mixed, for the use of said town, and may sell, and convey the same at pleasure; they may have a common seal, which they may break, alter, or renew at pleasure; they may sue and be sued, plead and be impleaded, defend and be defended, in all manner of actions, and in all courts of law and equity; and whenever any suit shall be commenced against said corporation, the first process shall be by summons, an attested copy of which shall be left with the recorder of said town, or at his usual place of residence, at least six days from the day of return, and said summons shall bear date not more than twelve days from the return day.

Sec. 7. That each member of said town council, before entering upon the duties of his office, shall take an oath, or affirmation, to support the constitution of the United States, and of this State, and also an oath of office.

Sec. 8. That the town council shall have power to make, ordain and establish by-laws, rules and regulations, for the government of said town, and to alter, or repeal, the same at pleasure; to provide for the appointment of a treasurer, town marshal, and such other subordinate officers, as they may think necessary; to prescribe their duties, and determine the period of their appointments, and to determine their fees; and the said treasurer, marshal, and other officers shall before entering upon their duties, take an oath of office, and shall respectively give bond with security, in such sums as shall be determined by the town council, payable to the State of Ohio, conditioned for the faithful performance of their respective duties: the town council shall also have power to fix reasonable fines and penalties for any violation of the laws and ordinances of the corporation, and to provide for the collection and disposition of the same: *Provided, also*, That no by-law, ordinance, rule or regulation shall take effect and be in force, until the same shall have been posted up for two weeks, in three of the most public places in said town corporate.

Sec. 9. That the town council shall, at the expiration of each and every year, cause to be made out and posted up as aforesaid, the receipts and expenditures of the preceding year.

Sec. 10. That the town council shall have power to regulate and improve the streets, lanes and alleys, and determine the width of the side walks in said town: they shall have power to remove all nuisances and obstructions from the streets and commons of said town, and to do all things which similar corporations have power to do, to provide for, and secure the cleanliness and good order of said town.

Sec. 11. That for the purpose of effectually enabling the said town council to carry into effect the provisions of this act, they are hereby authorized and empowered to levy a tax on all the real and personal property, subject on the grand levy to taxation, within the limits of said corporation, upon the appraisement which is now, or may hereafter be made and returned upon the said grand levy: *Provided*, That said tax, so levied by said town council, shall not in any one year exceed one quarter of one per centum, on the aggregate amount of all such taxable property within the limits of said corporation, until the first day of Janury, 1840; after which time said town council may increase the tax, as aforesaid; to any sum not exceeding one half of one per centum, as aforesaid, and the said town council shall, annually, between the first Saturday in April, and the first Saturday in July, in every year, determine the amount of tax to be levied and collected for the current year.

Sec. 12. That it shall be the duty of the recorder of said corporation, to make out duplicates of taxes, charging each individual, within said corporation, an amount of tax in proportion to the aggregate value of the taxable property belonging to such individual, within the limits of said corporation, as the same appears upon the books of the auditor of said county of Cuyahoga, and the said recorder shall have the privilege of inspecting the books of said auditor, and to take any minutes or transcripts therefrom, as may be necessary to aid him in the discharge of the duties hereby enjoined upon him, free of expense: and when said recorder shall have made out said duplicate, as aforesaid, he shall deliver one of such duplicates to the marshal of said town, or to such other person as shall be appointed collector, whose duty it shall be to proceed immediately to collect the taxes charged thereon, in the same manner and under the same regulations, as are now, or may hereafter be provided by law for collecting State and county taxes: and the marshal or collector, shall, immediately after collecting said taxes, pay the same over to the treasurer of said corporation, and take his receipt therefor; and the said marshal, or collector, shall have the same power to sell both real and personal property, as is given, by law, to county treasurers; and when necessary, the recorder shall have power to make deeds for real estate, so sold, in the same manner that county auditors are, by law, empowered to do, for lands sold by the county treasurer; and the marshal, or collector shall receive such fees for their services, under this act, as the town council may direct, not exceeding six per centum on all moneys so by him collected, to be paid by the treasurer, on the order of the recorder.

Sec. 13. That the said town council shall have power to appropriate any money remaining in the corporation treasury to the improvement of the streets, alleys, and side walks of said town, whenever they may deem it necessary; and to make any other improvement which may conduce to the health and comfort of said town.

Sec. 14. That the mayor of said town shall be a conservator of the peace within said town, and shall have therein all the powers and jurisdiction of a justice of the peace, in all matters, either civil or criminal, arising under the by-laws of said town, and shall give bond and security, as is required by law of justices of the peace; he shall perform all the duties enjoined upon him by the laws and ordinances of the corporation; and appeal may in all cases be taken from the decision of said mayor to the court of common pleas, in the same manner and under the same regulations as from the decision of justices of the peace in similar cases, and in the same manner: *Provided*, That the powers of the mayor shall not extend to the taking of depositions, or taking the acknowledgments of deeds, or other instruments of writings, but only to the concerns of the corporation.

Sec. 15. That the marshal shall be the principal ministerial officer in said town, and shall have the same power as constables have by law; and his authority in the execution of criminal process shall be co-extensive with the limits of said county of Cuyahoga; and he shall receive for his services such fees as are, or may be by law allowed to constables for similar services.

Sec. 16. That the mayor shall receive for his services such fees as are allowed by law to justices of the peace, for similar services, in like cases; the recorder shall receive such fees for his services, as shall be fixed by the laws and ordinances of the corporation.

Sec. 17. That it shall not be lawful for the town council to grant a license to any person or persons to keep a coffee house, or any other house of public entertainment or resort, either with or without spiritous liquors.

Sec. 18. That the said corporation shall be allowed the use of the county jail for the imprisonment of such persons as may be liable to imprisonment, under the laws and ordinances of said town; and all persons so imprisoned shall be under the charge of the sheriff or jailor, as in other cases.

Sec. 19. That any future Legislature shall have power to alter, amend or repeal this act: *Provided*, That any obligations or penalties incurred shall not, in any wise, be thereby cancelled or remitted.

WILLIAM MEDILL,
Speaker pro tem. of the House of Representatives.

ELIJAH VANCE,
Speaker of the Senate.

March 8, 1836.

AN ACT

To incorporate the Ohio Rail-road Company.

Sec. 1. *Be it enacted by the General Assembly of the State of Ohio,* That Robert Harper, Asbel Dart, Henry J. Rees, Eliphalet Austin and James Post, of the county of Ashtabula; Thomas Richman, Charles C. Paine, Henry Phelps and Rice Harper, of the county of Geauga; John W. Allen, George W. Card, Thomas M. Kelley and Peter W. Weddell, of the county of Cuyahoga; Heman Ely, John S. Matson, Eliphalet Redington and Edwin Byington, of the county of Lorain; Picket Larimer, Cyrus Butler, John G. Camp and James Hollister, of the county of Huron; Rhodolphus Dickinson, Sardis Burchard, Jaques Hulburd and Jesse S. Olmsted, of the county of Sandusky; John E. Hunt, Andrew Palmer, Platt Lard, and S. B. Comstock, of the county of Lucas, be, and they are hereby appointed commissioners, under the direction of a majority of whom, subscriptions may be received to the capital stock of the Ohio Rail-road Company, hereby incorporated; and they, or a majority of them may cause books to be opened at such times and places in the aforesaid counties and such other places as they may direct, and for the purpose of receiving subscriptions to the capital stock of said company, after having given notice of the time and place of opening the same, at least twenty days, by advertisement published in some newspaper printed in the said counties; and that upon the first opening of books, they shall be kept open for at least ten days in succession, from ten o'clock A. M. until two o'clock P. M.; and if at the expiration of that period, such a subscription to the capital stock of said company as is necessary to its incorporation, shall not have been obtained, then said commissioners, or a majority of them, may cause said books to be opened from time to time, after the expiration of said ten days, and for the space of three years thereafter; and if any of said commissioners shall die, resign or refuse to act during the continuance of the duties devolved upon them by this act, another or others may be appointed in his or their stead by the remaining commissioners or a majority of them.

Sec. 2. That the capital stock of said Ohio Rail-road Company, shall be four millions of dollars, and shall be divided into shares of one hundred dollars each; which shares may be subscribed for by individuals only; and it shall and may be lawful for the said corporation to commence the construction of said Rail-road or way, and enjoy all the powers and privileges conferred by this act, as soon as the sum of one thousand shares shall be subscribed to said stock.

Sec. 3. That all persons who shall become stockholders pursuant to this act, shall be, and they are hereby, created a body corporate, and shall be and remain a corporation for ever, under the name of the Ohio Rail-road Company; and by that name shall be capable in law, of purchasing, holding, selling, leasing and conveying estates real, personal or mixed, so far as the same shall be necessary for the purposes hereinafter mentioned, and no further; and shall have perpetual succession; and by said corporate name may contract and be contracted with, sue and be sued, and may have and use a common seal, which they shall have power to alter or renew at pleasure, and shall have, enjoy and exercise all the powers, rights and privileges which corporate bodies may lawfully do for the purposes mentioned in this act.

Sec. 4. That upon all subscriptions, there shall be paid, at the time of subscribing, to the said commissioners or their agents, appointed to receive such subscriptions, the sum of five dollars on every share subscribed; which sum, so paid to said commissioners, or their agents, shall be paid over by him or them to the treasurer of said company, as soon thereafter as a treasurer shall be appointed and qualified; and the residue of the stock subscribed, shall be paid in such instalments, and at such times as may be required by the president and directors of said company: *Provided,* That no payment, other than the first shall be demanded until at least thirty days public notice of such demand shall have been given, by said president and directors, in some newspaper of general circulation in the State of Ohio; and in some newspaper printed in the counties aforesaid; and if any stockholder shall fail or neglect to pay any instalment or part of said subscription thus demanded, for the space of thirty days after the same shall be due and payable, the said president and directors, upon giving at least thirty days previous notice thereof, in manner aforesaid, may, and they are hereby authorized to sell at public vendue; so many of the shares of said delinquent stockholder or stockholders, as shall be sufficient to pay such instalment, and expenses of advertising, sale, and transfer of the same share or shares, so sold to the purchaser; and the residue of the money arising from such sale, after paying such instalment and expenses, shall be paid to said stockholders on demand.

Sec. 5. That at the expiration of ten days from the time the books are first opened, if one thousand shares of said capital stock shall have been subscribed, or if not, as soon thereafter as the same shall be subscribed, if within three years after the first opening of said books, the said commissioners, or a majority of them, shall call a general meeting of the stockholders, at such places as they may appoint, and shall give at least thirty days previous notice thereof; and at such meeting, the said commissioners shall lay the subscription books before the stockholders then and there present; and thereupon the said stockholders, or a majority of them, shall elect thirteen directors, by ballot, a majority of whom shall be competent to manage the affairs of said company: said directors shall have the power of electing a president and a treasurer from among said directors, and of allowing to said president and treasurer, such compensation per annum as they may deem proper; and in all elections for officers, each stockholder shall be allowed one vote for each share of capital stock he may own in said company; and in all other cases where a vote of said company is to be taken, it shall be by stock, each share having one vote; and every stockholder may vote by himself or by proxy; and the commissioners aforesaid, or any three of them, shall be judges of election for the first election of said directors.

Sec. 6. That to continue the succession of the president and directors of said company, thirteen directors shall be chosen annually on the first Monday in May in every year, in the borough of Cleveland, and at such other place on the line of said Rail road, as a majority of the directors may appoint; and if any vacancy shall occur by death, resignation or otherwise, of any officer of said company, before the expiration of the year for which he was elected, such vacant places for the residue of the year, may be filled by appointment by the president and board for the time being, or a majority of them; and that the directors and officers of said company, after having been elected and qualified, shall hold their offices until others are elected and qualified.

Sec. 7. That a general meeting of the stockholders shall be held annually at their office, for the election of directors of said company; and that meetings may be called at any time during the interval between said annual meetings, by the president and directors, or a majority of them, or by the stockholders owning at least one half the stock subscribed, upon giving at least thirty days public notice in one or more newspapers printed and in general circulation in this State, and in some newspaper printed in the counties aforesaid, of the time of holding said meetings, and whenever such meetings are called by the stockholders, such notice shall specify the particular object of the call; and if at any such called meeting a majority of all the stock subscribed shall not be represented, such meeting may adjourn from day to day, for three days, without transacting any business; and if within said three days a majority of stock subscribed shall not be represented, such meeting shall be dissolved.

Sec. 8. That at the regular annual meeting of the stockholders of said company, it shall be the duty of the directors and officers of said company for the previous year, to exhibit a full, clear and distinct statement of the affairs of the company; and it shall be the duty of the treasurer to make out and exhibit to the board of directors, a full and perfect statement of all money by him received and paid out, for and on account of the said company, at least once in three months, and oftener if required by the president and directors; and all money drawn from the treasurer shall be drawn on the order of the president of said company, or in such manner as shall be pointed out by the by-laws of said company; and the board of directors, or a majority of them, shall have the power to remove the president, treasurer or other officer or agent of said company, at any time when ever they may judge the interest of the company requires such removal, and may appoint other officers in their stead.

Sec. 9. That the president, treasurer and directors of said company, before they enter upon the duties of their appointments as such, shall severally take an oath or affirmation that he will well and truly discharge the duties of his appointment, according to the best of his ability.

Sec. 10. That the said president and directors, or a majority of them, may appoint all such officers, engineers or agents as they may deem necessary for the transaction of the business of said company; that they, or a majority of them, shall have power to determine by contract, the compensation of all engineers, officers, and agents in the employ of the company; and to determine by their by-laws, the manner of adjusting and settling all accounts against the company; and also the manner and evidence of transfers of stock in said company; and they, or a majority of them, shall have power to pass all by-laws which they may deem necessary or proper for exercising all powers vested in the company hereby incorporated, and for carrying the object of this act into effect: *Provided*, That such by-laws shall not be contrary to the laws of this State or of the United States.

Sec. 11. That the said company shall be, and they are hereby vested with the right to construct a double or single Rail road or way from some suitable point to be selected on the east line of the State of Ohio, in the county of Ashtabula, from, at, or near the north-east corner of the county of Ashtabula, and to pass westwardly through the counties of Ashtabula, Geauga, Cuyahoga, Lorain, Huron, Sandusky, Wood and Lucas, to the Maumee river, and from thence to some point on the Wabash and Erie Canal, if the company deem it expedient, as the western termination of said Rail road: *Provided*, That said Rail road should cross Sandusky river below the lower rapids, it shall not obstruct the navigation of said river; and if it shall cross the Maumee river below the rapids, it shall not obstruct the navigation of that river or other navigable river.

Sec. 12. That the president and directors of said company shall be, and they are hereby invested with all the rights and powers necessary for the location, construction and repairs of said road not exceeding one hundred feet wide, with as many sets of tracks as said president and directors may deem necessary; and they and their agents, or those with whom they may contract for making any parts of said road, may enter upon and use, and excavate any lands which may be wanted for the site of said road, or for any other purpose necessary and useful in the construction or repairs of said road or its works; and that they may build bridges, fix scales and weights, lay rails, take and use any earth, timber, gravel, stone or other materials which may be necessary for the construction or repairs of said road or any of its works.

Sec. 13. That the president and directors of said company, or a majority of them, or any persons authorized by them, or a majority of them, may agree with the owner or owners of any land, earth, timber, stone or other materials, or any improvements which may be wanted for the construction or repairs of said road, or any of their works, for the purchase, use or occupation of the same; and if they cannot agree, or if the owner or owners, or any of'them, be a married woman under age, a person of unsound mind, or out of the county in which the property may lie when such lands and materials are wanted, application may be made to any justice of the peace of such county, who shall thereupon issue his warrant, under his hand and seal, directed to the sheriff of said county, or to some disinterested person, if the sheriff shall be interested, requiring him to summon a jury of twelve men, inhabitants of said county, having the qualifications of jurors, not related or in any wise interested, to meet on the lands or near the other property or materials to be valued, on a day named in said warrant, not less than five nor more than ten days after the issuing of the same; and if at the said time and place any of said persons summoned do not attend, the sheriff or summoner shall immediately summons as many persons having like qualifications as may be necessary, with the persons in attendance, to furnish a pannel of twelve jurors in attendance; and from them each party or their agents may strike off three jurors if he chooses; and in case no objections be made by either party to a juror, then the whole twelve shall sit as a jury of inquest of damages; and before they act as such the said sheriff or summoner shall administer to each of them an oath or affirmation, as the case may be, that they will faithfully and impartially value the damages which the owner or owners will sustain by the occupation or use of the same, as required by the said company; and the jury estimating the damages, if for ground occupied by said road shall take into the estimate the benefits resulting to said owner or owners, by reason of said road passing through or upon the land of such owner or owners, towards the extinguishment of such claim or damages; and that the said jury shall reduce their inquest to writing, and shall sign and seal the same; and it shall then be returned to the clerk of the court of common pleas for said county at its next session, and by such clerk filed in his office, and shall at the first term of said court be confirmed, unless sufficient cause to the contrary be shown to said court; and when the same shall be confirmed, the proceeding shall be recorded by the clerk at the expense of the company; but if set aside, the court may direct another inquisition to be taken by jurors, by them appointed, and to appraise the property taken, or to be used, and to describe the bounds of the lands so taken; and such valuation when paid or tendered to the party claiming damages, by bringing the money into court, the court of common pleas shall then and there order the money so paid to be retained for the claimant, and that said company shall be entitled to the use of the full right to such personal property and to the use and occupation of such landed property thus appraised and valued, and that their title to the same shall be as perfect in all respects as if the same had been conveyed or granted by the owner or owners; and that the proceedings aforesaid shall be recorded by the clerk of said court, and be a part of the records thereof, and shall be final between the parties; and the clerk, sheriff, magistrate and jurors, shall be entitled to receive the same fees from said company as are allowed by law for like services in cases of fixing the valuation of real estate previous to sale on execution at law.

Sec. 14. That whenever, in the construction of said rail-road, it shall be necessary to cross or intersect any established or public road, it shall be the duty of said company so to construct said rail-road as not to impede the passage or transportation of persons or property along such other road; or when it shall be necessary to pass through the lands of any individual or corporation, it shall be the duty of said company without delay, to provide for such individual or corporation proper wagon ways across said road; and that any other rail-road company may join and connect any rail-road with the road hereby contemplated, and run cars upon the same under the rules and regulations of the president and directors of the Ohio rail-road company, as to the construction and speed of said cars; and that full right and privileges is hereby reserved to the State or the citizens, or any company hereafter incorporated under the authority of the State, to connect with or cross the road hereby provided for, any rail-road leading from the main route to any other part or parts of the State: *Provided,* That in forming such connections or crossing said rail-road, no injury shall be done to the works of the company hereby incorporated.

Sec. 15. That if it shall be necessary for such company, in the selection of the road, by them to be laid and constructed, or any part of it, to connect the same with, or to use any turnpike road or bridge made or erected by any person or persons or body corporate, to contract and agree with any such other corporation or person for the right to use such road or bridge, or for the transfer of any of the corporate or other rights or privileges of such corporation.

Sec. 16. That the funds of said company shall be paid out on orders drawn on the treasurer in such manner as shall be pointed out by the by-laws of the company; and that all such orders for the payment of money so drawn shall, when presented to the treasurer at the office of said treasurer, be by him paid and redeemed; but in case the same are not paid when presented, then in that case, said company shall be liable to pay an interest of six per cent. thereon to the holder or holders, from and after the time the same were presented for payment.

Sec. 17. That the president and directors shall have power to charge tolls on passengers, goods, produce, merchandize, or property of any kind whatsoever, transported by them on said rail-way; and the shares of the capital stock of said company shall be deemed and considered personal property, transferable by assignment agreeably to the by-laws of said company: *Provided,* The tolls hereby authorized to charge shall never exceed the sum of fifteen per cent. per annum on the original cost of the work.

Sec. 18. That all persons complying with the rules and regulations pre scribed by said company, may with suitable and proper carriages, use and travel upon said road.

Sec. 19. That the president and directors shall semi-annually declare and make such dividend as they may deem proper of the nett profits arising from the resources of said company, deducting the amount of the outstanding debts due by said company and the necessary and probable contingent expenses; and that they shall divide the same among the stockholders of said company in proportion to their respective shares.

Sec. 20. That if any person or persons shall wilfully, by any means, whatsoever, injure, impair or destroy any part of said rail-road, constructed by said company under this act, or so offending, shall, for every such offence, forfeit and pay to the said company a sum not exceeding three fold the value of said property so damaged, to be recovered in the name of the president and directors of said company, by action of debt in any court having competent jurisdiction in the county wherein the offence shall be committed; and shall also be liable to be indicted, and upon conviction, shall be punished by fine and imprisonment, or either, at the discretion of the court.

Sec. 21. That it shall be lawful for the president and directors of said company, or a majority of them, to cause the books of said company to be opened for subscription to the capital stock of said company, at any time when they may think proper, until the whole amount of said stock shall be subscribed: *Provided*, That the right to subscribe for one-fourth of the capital stock of said company is reserved to the State of Ohio, or any less amount, if the same be subscribed before it is otherwise disposed of.

Sec. 22. That for and in consideration of the expenses said company will be at in constructing said rail-road, and in keeping the same in repair, the said rail-road, together with all tolls and rents and profits arising therefrom shall be, and the same are hereby vested in said corporation: *Provided*, That the State shall have the power at any time after the expiration of thirty-five years from the passage of this act, to purchase and hold the same for the use of the State, by paying to said corporation therefor the amount expended by them in the original locating and constructing the same, together with fifteen per centum thereon, of which amount so expended an accurate statement in writing shall be submitted to the General Assembly, duly attested by the oaths of the officers of said company, if the General Assembly shall require it.

Sec. 23. That if said road shall not be finished within fifteen years from the passage of this act, then this act to be null and void, and the said corporation dissolved.

Sec. 24. That this act is hereby declared to be a public act, and shall be so construed in all courts of justice and elsewhere.

WILLIAM MEDILL,
Speaker pro. tem. of the House of Representatives.

ELIJAH VANCE,
Speaker of the Senate.

March 8, 1836.

To incorporate the Westchester, Middletown and Winchester Turnpike Company.

Sec. 1. *Be it enacted by the General Assembly of the State of Ohio,* That Joseph Layman, Arthur W. Elliott, William Webster, Thomas Reed, Israel T. Gibson, John P. Reynolds, Jacob Kemp, and John C. Dum, of the county of Butler; James Deniston, George Debolt, Christian Neff, and Peter Shidler, of the county of Preble, as commissioners; and their associates, as stockholders, as hereinafter provided, their successors and assigns, be, and they are hereby created and declared a body politic and corporate, by the name and style of the "Westchester, Middletown and Winchester Turnpike Company;" to construct and keep in repair a turnpike road, toll gates, and gate keepers' houses; commencing at Westchester, in the county of Butler; thence the most eligible route, through Huntsville to Middletown, in said county; thence crossing the great Miami river; and thence the best route, to the town of Winchester, in the county of Preble; and thence the best and most eligible route and course, to intersect the great National Road: and by such corporate name and style, said company is hereby made and declared capable in law and equity, to contract, sue and be sued, make by-laws, not contrary to the constitution and laws of the United States, or of this State; and to have and use a common seal, which they may break, or renew at pleasure; and to acquire, have, hold, sell, transfer and convey property, real and personal, for their corporate use and purposes, but for no other use or purpose whatsoever.

Sec. 2. That the capital of the company, hereby incorporated, shall consist of one hundred and fifty thousand dollars, in shares of twenty-five dollars each, and be deemed personal property, and may be subscribed and held by individuals, companies or corporations, and shall be appropriated and applied to the uses and purposes, in the first section of this act set forth, and to no other use or purpose; and any person desiring to discharge his subscription to the capital of said company, in labor or materials, on or for said road, shall so specify, at the time of subscribing; in which case, the labors to be performed by such subscriber, shall be assigned, and the value of the same estimated by the principal engineer, superintending the construction of the road; or if materials be subscribed, the value thereof shall be estimated by such principal engineer: *Provided,* That in all cases of subscription to the capital stock of said company, five dollars, in cash, shall be paid to the person or persons, under whose superintendence subscriptions may be received, on each share subscribed; and the residue of such capital stock, whether in cash, labor, or materials, shall be paid, discharged, performed and furnished, on the requisition of the directors, for the time being.

Sec. 3. That the books for receiving subscriptions to the capital stock of said company, shall be opened, within one year from the passage of this act, at such places, and under the superintendence of such persons, as a majority of said commissioners, or a majority of such of them as may consent to act, may designate and appoint; it shall be the duty of said commissioners, or a majority of them, or a majority of such of them as consent to act, to give ten days' notice of the times, and places, and persons, at which, and under whose superintendence, will, be opened the books for receiving subscriptions to the capital stock of said company; which notice shall be published in some newspaper published, or in general circulation, in the counties of Preble and Butler.

Sec. 4. That as soon as it shall be ascertained, that ten thousand dollars of the capital stock of said company has been subscribed, said commissioners, or a majority of them, or a majority of such of them as consent to act, shall give fifteen days notice, as provided in the third section of this act, of the time of holding an election, which shall be held at Middletown, aforesaid, for seven directors, to manage and conduct the business and affairs of said company; and on the day thus specified, at Middletown, aforesaid, the stockholders of said company shall proceed to the election, by ballot, of seven directors, stockholders, any five of whom shall constitute a quorum, for the transaction of [the] business and concerns of said company; the first election for directors, under this act, shall be conducted by two inspectors, who shall be appointed by a majority of such said commissioners, as may consent to act; and such inspectors shall act under oath; none but stockholders shall vote for, or be elected directors; and the stockholders shall be entitled to one vote, which may be given in person, or by proxy, for each share of stock by him, her, or them owned and held, on the day of election; the seven directors, having the highest number of votes, shall be declared duly elected; but if an election of seven directors shall not be effected, by reason of an equal number of votes being given, in favor of two or more stockholders; in that case, the inspectors of the election shall determine, by lot, amongst the eight or more stockholders, having the highest and an equal number of votes, who shall be directors, to complete the number of seven: *Provided*, Such determination, by lot, shall not postpone as director, one stockholder having a higher, to another having a lower, number of votes; the directors first elected, under this act, shall hold their office until the first Saturday in January, thereafter, and until their successors are elected and qualified; and on the first Saturday of January, annually, after the first elections for directors, there shall be an election for directors of said company; annual elections for directors of said company shall be under the superintendence of the directors, for the time being; who shall designate a place, and shall give the like notice of the time of such annual election, as is required to be given by the commissioners, as aforesaid, of the time and place of holding the first election, under this act; and shall, in like manner, notify the persons elected, and designate a time and place for the persons elected directors, to meet and qualify; and the directors, annually elected, shall proceed, as required of the first directors.

Sec. 5. That within ten days, after the first election of directors, under this act, the inspectors of the election shall give notice, in writing, to the seven stockholders, elected directors, of such their elections; and shall appoint a day, on which the directors so elected shall meet at Middletown aforesaid, for organizing; and on the day so appointed, which shall not be more than ten days from the day of election, or sooner, if the directors elected can agree, the directors so elected, shall meet at Middletown, and severally take an oath faithfully and impartially, to discharge the several duties of director of the turnpike company, hereby incorporated; and being thus qualified, such directors shall appoint one of their body president of the board; they shall also appoint a treasurer, who shall not be a director, and they may require and take of the treasurer, bond, in such sum, and with such security, as to them may appear reasonable and necessary, to secure said company; said directors shall also appoint a secretary, who shall keep a full and fair journal of the corporate acts of said company, and shall perform such other duties of secretary, as may be required of him by the directors; and also, said directors shall have power to borrow, on behalf of said company, any sum or sums of money, not exceeding seventy-five thousand dollars, for any term not exceeding twenty-five years; said money, so borrowed, to be appropriated for the construction of said turnpike road, and for no other purpose whatever: and the individual property of all the stockholders, real and personal, to be liable to the payment of said money so borrowed, in proportion to their respective interests in said company.

Sec. 6. That the said company shall have a right to lay out, and survey, and locate a turnpike road, as specified in the first section of this act, through any improved or unimproved lands; and to take from the lands, occupied by such road, when located as aforesaid, any stone, gravel, timber, or other materials, necessary to construct a good, secure, and substantial turnpike road, as contemplated by this act, and the necessary bridges connected therewith; and if any difference should arise between the owner or owners of any ground, on which said road may be located, or from which such materials are taken, as aforesaid, and the agents of the company, respecting damage, it shall be determined, by three disinterested freeholders, to be appointed by the commissioners of the county, in which the subject of difference lies; who, after being duly sworn, faithfully and impartially to perform the duties, required of them in this act, and taking into consideration, whether the land be, really, rendered more or less valuable, by the roads passing through it, shall make out their assessment in writing, of the damages, if any; a copy of which shall be given to the proprietor of the land, and another copy to the agent of the company; and said agent shall pay, or offer to pay, the owner of said land, the amount of such assessed damages, before he shall enter upon and take any such ground or materials, other than to survey the road; and all such assessment of damages, if any should be awarded, shall be paid by the company; but if no damage shall be awarded, then the expense shall be paid by the person who had claimed damages; and in case sufficient materials cannot be procured on the land so as aforesaid required for said road and bridges, said company, or their agents, shall have a right to, and they are hereby authorized, to enter upon any unimproved lands, adjoining or in the vicinity of said road, and to dig, cut down, take, and carry away, so much stone, gravel, timber, or other materials, (not previously cut down, taken, appropriated or prepared, by the owner for any particular use,) as may be necessary to enable said company to construct said road and the necessary bridges, toll gates; and in case of difference between the owners of any lands, from which materials may be taken, as last aforesaid, such difference shall be determined, and compensation made by said company, in manner provided by the sixth section of this act.

Sec. 7. That in addition to the land necessary for the construction, use, and repair of said road, said company shall be entitled to, and authorized to acquire, in manner aforesaid, not exceeding one acre of land, at each toll gate, for the erection thereon, and convenient occupation of a gate keeper's house; and said company shall cause such turnpike road to be opened, not exceeding eighty feet wide; at least fifteen feet of which shall be made an artificial road, composed of stone, gravel, wood, or other suitable materials, well compacted together, in such a manner as to secure a good, firm, substantial and even road, rising in the middle, with a gradual arch or curve, with sufficient drains on each side, to carry the water therefrom, and shall keep the same in good repair; and [in] no case shall the ascent in such road be of greater elevation, than four degrees with the horizon.

Sec. 8. That so soon as said company shall have completed such roads, or the grading thereof, as aforesaid, or any part of such roads, not less than five continuous miles, and so from time to time, as often as five continuous miles thereof shall be completed, or completely graded, an agent, to be appointed for that purpose by the commissioners of the proper county, if not otherwise appointed by order, under the Legislature or its authority, shall, on application of said company, examine said road, or part thereof, as aforesaid, and report his opinion to the president of said company; and if such agent shall report said road, or any continuous five miles, thereof, to be completed or completely graded, agreeably to the requisitions of this act, said company shall thereupon be entitled to erect a toll gate or gates, at suitable distances on said road, and to demand [and] receive of those travelling or using the same, the tolls allowed by this act.

Sec. 9. That the following shall be the rates of tolls demandable or receivable for each and every ten miles of said road, when completed, and in the same proportion for any greater or less distance, to wit: for every four wheeled carriage or wagon, drawn by one horse or ox, eighteen and three fourth cents; for every horse or ox in addition, six and one fourth cents; for every chaise, riding chair, cart, or gig, or other two wheeled carriage, of any kind, drawn by one horse or ox, twelve and a half cents; for every horse or ox in addition, six and one fourth cents; for every sled or sleigh, drawn by one horse or ox, twelve and a half cents; for every coach, chariot, or other four wheeled pleasure carriage, drawn by one horse, (driver included,) twenty-five cents: for every additional horse, six and one fourth cents; for every horse and rider, six and one fourth cents; for every horse, mule, or ass, led or driven, six months old and upwards, two cents; for every head of neat cattle, six months old and upwards, three fourths of a cent; for every head of sheep or hogs, one fourth of a cent; and for equal distances and like objects, said company shall be entitled to demand and receive one half of the foregoing amount of tolls on said road, when completely graded as aforesaid, but not fully completed, as a turnpike road: *Provided*, That all persons going to and returning from public worship or funerals, and all militiamen necessarily going to and returning from their respective muster grounds, and all persons having the qualifications of electors at the annual election or presidential elections, shall pass free of toll.

Sec. 10. That if any person or persons using said road shall, with intent to defraud said company, or to evade the payment of tolls, pass through any private gate, or bars, or other ground, except around cross-ways, authorized by law, near to any turnpike gate of said road, every person guilty of, or concerned in such fraudulent practice, shall, for every such offence, be liable to pay to said company a sum not less than two dollars, nor more than ten dollars, to be recovered in action of debt, with cost of suit, before any justice of the peace of the county in which such offence may be committed; and from such judgment of the justice of the peace, an appeal may be taken to the court of common pleas of the proper county, but no stay of execution shall be allowed.

Sec. 11. That if said company shall fail for ten days in succession, to keep said road in good repair, and complaint thereof be made to a justice of the peace of the county in which said road may be out of repair, it shall be his duty forthwith to summon three disinterested freeholders of the county to examine the same, and he shall give notice to the toll gatherer, at the nearest gate, of the time when such freeholders will proceed to examine said road; and such freeholders, after taking an oath or affirmation to act impartially, shall proceed to examine said road; and if such freeholders shall find said road out of repair, they shall certify their finding to the justice of the peace, who shall immediately transmit a copy of such certificate to the toll gatherer nearest the defective part of said road; and from the time of the toll gatherer's receiving such notice, no tolls shall be demanded or received for such part of the road, until the same shall be put in complete repair, under the penalty of five dollars for each offence, to be recovered of said company, with cost, on the complaint and for the use of the party aggrieved.

Sec. 12. That if any person shall, wilfully or wantonly, destroy or in any manner injure or obstruct any part of said road, or any gate thereon, otherwise than in the just or lawful use thereof, every such person shall be liable to pay said company for every such offence a sum not less than five dollars, nor more than fifty dollars, and shall, moreover, be liable for all damages to the company, and for all injuries occurring to travellers in consequence of any such damage to, or obstruction of said road; all damages and costs awarded to the company, or to travellers, under this section, to be recovered with costs before any justice of the peace of the county in which such offence may have been committed; from which judgment an appeal may be taken to the court of common pleas, but no stay of execution shall be allowed.

Sec. 13. That said company shall put a post or stone at the end of each mile, with the number of miles from Westchester fairly cut or painted thereon; and also in a conspicuous place near each toll gate shall be placed a board, with the rates of toll fairly painted thereon, with directions to keep to the right.

Sec. 14. That if any person shall wilfully deface or destroy any guide board, mile post or stone, or painted list or rate of tolls, erected on said road, he shall, on conviction thereof, before a justice of the peace of the proper county, forfeit and pay a sum, not less than five dollars, nor more than ten dollars, with costs of suit, in an action of debt, at the suit of said company; and from the judgment of the justice of the peace in such case, an appeal may be taken to the court of common pleas, but no stay of execution shall be allowed.

Sec. 15. That if any toll gatherer on said road shall unreasonably detain any person after payment or tender of the proper amount of toll, or shall demand or receive a greater amount of toll than by this act is authorized, he shall, for any such offence, forfeit and pay a sum not exceeding twenty dollars, to be recovered with costs of suit, before any justice of the peace of the proper county, in an action of debt, at the suit of the party aggrieved; and from the judgment of the justice in such case, an appeal may be taken to the court of common pleas, but no stay of execution shall be allowed: *Provided*, That no action under this section shall be commenced after the expiration of twenty days from the accruing thereof.

Sec. 16. That there shall be kept a fair account of the whole expense of making and repairing said road, with all incidental expenses; and also a fair account of the tolls received; and the State shall have a right to purchase the same, or any part of the stock thereof, on paying said company a sum of money which, together with the tolls received, shall equal the cost and expense of said road, as aforesaid, with ten per centum thereon; and the books of said company shall always be open to the inspection of the agent of the State appointed for that purpose by the Legislature; and if the company shall neglect or refuse to exhibit their accounts agreeably to this section, when thereunto required, then all the rights and privileges granted by this act shall cease.

Sec. 17. That if said company shall not, within five years from the passage of this act, proceed to carry on the work, according to the true intent and meaning of this act, then in that case it shall be lawful for the Legislature to resume all the rights and privileges hereby granted.

Sec. 18. That said company shall be, and they are hereby authorized and entitled, to demand and receive the like toll from persons conveying the United States mail, as from other persons; and in case of neglect or refusal on the part of any person or persons engaged in the transportation of the mail, to pay the tolls by this act authorized to be demanded and received, said company may proceed to collect the same by action of debt; but shall not obstruct or delay the passage of the mail.

WILLIAM MEDILL,
Speaker pro tem. of the House of Representatives.
ELIJAH VANCE,
Speaker of the Senate.

March 8, 1836.

AN ACT

To provide for the extension and completion of the Miami Canal, north of Dayton.

Sec. 1. *Be it enacted by the General Assembly of the State of Ohio*, That the commissioners of the canal fund be, and they are hereby authorized to borrow, on the credit of the State, any sum not exceeding two hundred thousand dollars in the year eighteen hundred and thirty-six; two hundred thousand dollars in the year eighteen hundred and thirty-seven; two hundred thousand dollars in the year eighteen hundred and thirty-eight; and three hundred thousand dollars annually, for the next three years thereafter; in all fifteen hundred thousand dollars; at a rate of interest not exceeding six per centum per annum; for which moneys so to be borrowed, they shall issue transferrable certificates of stock, redeemable at the pleasure of the State, at any time between the years eighteen hundred and fifty, and eighteen hundred and sixty: *Provided,* That, at least two months previously to their entering into any contract for such loan, they shall give notice by publication in some newspaper in each of the cities of Philadelphia, New York and Cincinnati, having general circulation therein, inviting proposals to be made to them, at such place and at such time as they may designate, for a loan of such sums of money as they may then propose to borrow: *And provided, also,* That no greater sum shall at any time be borrowed than will, in the opinion of the commissioners of the canal fund, and the canal commissioners, or a majority of each board, be fully provided for in this act, without the contingency of having to resort to taxation to meet the payment of either the principal or interest.

Sec. 2. That if the said commissioners be of opinion, at any of the times specified in this act for making a regular loan, that the same cannot then be obtained on terms favorable to the State, they shall be, and are hereby authorized to borrow, in behalf of this State, of any individual or individuals, or body corporate, in this State or elsewhere, any sum of money not exceeding in any one year, fifty thousand dollars, on such terms as they deem expedient, at a rate of interest not exceeding six per cent. per annum; which money, so borrowed, shall be repaid by the said commissioners, with the first money they may obtain on any regular loan made in pursuance of this act.

Sec. 3. That the money borrowed according to the provisions of the first section of this act, shall be applied to the construction and completion of the Miami canal, north of Dayton, commonly called the extension of the Miami canal, under the same regulations and provisions prescribed and adopted in the application of the canal fund for the construction of the Ohio and Miami canals.

Sec. 4. That the lands, and the proceeds of the lands granted by Congress in aid of the construction of the Miami canal, north of Dayton, remaining unsold, or unexpended, when the canal shall have been completed, and paid for to the mouth of the Loramies creek, shall be, and are hereby appropriated exclusively to the payment of the interest of the debt, or any part of the debt, created under the first section of this act.

Sec. 5. That the nett proceeds of the tolls of the Miami canal, north of Dayton, and of the Wabash and Erie canal, and any surplus funds, arising from the sales of the lands granted by Congress for the construction of the Wabash and Erie canal, more than are required for the construction of that work, shall be, and are hereby created a fund, for the payment of the interest and debt, created by virtue of the first section of this act.

Sec. 6. That the canal commissioners be, and are hereby authorized and required, to substitute for reservoirs, feeders from living streams, in all cases where the same can be done at less expense to the State than by using such reservoirs; and if a feeder from Mad River be thus substituted, the same shall be made navigable: *Provided,* The additional expense

shall not exceed the probable advantages to be derived by the State, therefrom.

WILLIAM MEDILL,
Speaker pro tem. of the House of Representatives.
ELIJAH VANCE,
Speaker of the Senate.

March 8, 1836.

AN ACT

To incorporate the village of Richmond, in the county of Geauga.

Sec. 1. *Be it enacted by the General Assembly of the State of Ohio,*
That so much of the township of Painsville, in the county of Geauga, as is
comprised within the following limits, to wit: beginning at the north-west
corner of lot No. 20, on the west line of the township of Painsville and
the dividing line between that and the township of Mentor, in said county; thence running north along the dividing line between said townships,
to the south line of lot No. 26. of Abraham Skinner's survey; thence along
said south line to Grand river; thence southerly along said river to the
north line of lot number 19, in said township; thence westwardly, along
the north lines of lots numbers 19 and 20 and 21, to the place of beginning; excluding the lands belonging to Charles C. Paine, and to the heirs.
of Abraham Skinner, and to Nathan and Paulina Perry; be and the same
is hereby created a village corporate, and shall henceforth be known and
distinguished by the name of the "Village of Richmond."

Sec. 2. That for the good order and government of said village, it
shall be lawful for the white male inhabitants who have resided within the
aforesaid limits of said village for the space of three months next preceding the second Tuesday of April next, and who have the qualifications
of electors of members of the General Assembly, to meet at the school
house in said village, on the second Tuesday of April next, and on the second Tuesday of April, annually thereafter, at such place as the village
council may direct, which shall be determined by notices of the time and
place posted up in three of the most public places in said village, at least
ten days before the election, or published in some newspaper, published
in said village; which notice shall be signed by the mayor and recorder;
and then and there proceed by ballot to elect, by a plurality of votes, one
mayor, one recorder, and five trustees, who shall be freeholders residing
within the limits of said village, and who shall hold their respective offices
for one year, and until their successors are elected and qualified; such
mayor, recorder, and trustees being so elected and qualified, shall constitute a village council, any four of whom shall constitute a quorum for the
transaction of business.

Sec. 3. That at the first election to be holden under this act, there
shall be chosen *viva voce*, by the electors present, three judges and a clerk
of said election; and at all subsequent elections the trustees, or any two
of them, shall be judges, and the recorder clerk; and at all elections held

under the provisions of this act, the polls shall be opened between the hours of one and two and closed at four o'clock, P. M. of said day; and at the close of the polls the votes shall be counted, and a true statement thereof proclaimed by one of the judges, to the electors present; and the clerk shall make a true record thereof, who shall notify the persons elected to their respective offices, of their election, within five days; and the persons so elected and notified, shall, within five days thereafter, take an oath or affirmation to support the constitutions of the United States and of the State of Ohio, and an oath of office; which oath any one of the directors is hereby authorized to administer to the mayor or recorder, and they in turn to the directors: any person, elected as aforesaid, neglecting or refusing to qualify as aforesaid, shall forfeit and pay into the treasury of said village the sum of five dollars, to be recovered by an action of debt, before the mayor of said village; and the recorder shall in the name of said village, demand, receive, or sue for such forfeiture, and pay over the same, when collected, to the treasurer, taking his receipt therefor: *Provided,* That no person shall be compelled to serve in any office in said corporation two years in succession.

Sec. 4. That the mayor, recorder, and trustees of said village shall be a body politic and corporate, with perpetual succession, to be known and distinguished by the name of the Village Council of Richmond; and they and their successors in office shall be authorized to use a common seal, and the same to alter at pleasure; to receive, purchase, acquire, hold and convey any real estate, personal or mixed, and to manage and dispose of the same in such manner as they, or a majority of them may deem proper; they shall be capable, in the name aforesaid, of suing and being sued, pleading and being impleaded, answering and being answered, in any suit or action in any court of law or equity in this State; and when any suit or action shall be commenced against said corporation, the first process shall be by summons, a copy of which shall be left with the mayor, or in his absence, at his usual place of abode, at least five days before the return day thereof.

Sec. 5. That it shall be the duty of [the] mayor, and in his absence or disability to serve, the recorder, to preside at all meetings of the village council; it shall also be the duty of the recorder to attend all such meetings, and keep an accurate record of their proceedings, to be recorded in a book provided for that purpose; it shall moreover be the duty of the recorder to attend all elections under the provisions of this act; but in case of his absence or disability to serve as such, the trustees shall have power to appoint one of their number clerk of said election, *pro tempore.*

Sec. 6. That the village council shall have power to fill all vacancies which may occur in their body by death, resignation or otherwise, from among the electors in said village, whose appointment shall continue until the next annual election, and until their successors are elected and qualified; and whenever it may happen that neither the mayor or recorder is present at any meeting of said village council, the trustees shall have power to appoint one of their number to perform the duties of such mayor, recorder, or both, as the case may be, which appointment shall be *pro tempore;* and that the mayor, or a majority of the trustees, shall have power to call a meeting of the village council whenever in his or their opinion the public good of said corporation shall require it.

Sec. 7. That the mayor, recorder, and trustees, or a majority of them, whereof the mayor or recorder shall always be one, or in their absence, one of the taustees appointed to fill their vacancy, shall have power and authority to make, ordain and publish all such by-laws and ordinances, consistent with the constitution of the United States and of this State, as they may deem necessary and expedient for the regulations, interest, safety, health, cleanliness and convenience of said town, and the same to alter or repeal at pleasure; they shall have power to appoint a treasurer, village marshal, and such other subordinate officers as they may deem necessary; to prescribe their duties, and to require of them such security as they may deem necessary for the faithful performance of their duties; to remove them at pleasure; to fix and establish the fees of the officers of said corporation not established by this act, except the trustees, who shall receive no fees; said village council shall also have power to affix to the violation of the by-laws and ordinances of said corporation such reasonable fines and forfeitures as they may deem proper, and provide for the collection and disposition of the same; they shall have power to lay out, regulate the lots, streets, lanes, alleys and public ground; to lay out and determine the width of side walks, and regulate the same; they shall also have power to remove or cause to be removed all nuisances and obstructions, and do all things which a corporation of a similar nature can do, to secure the health, peace and good order of the inhabitants of said town: *Provided*, *always*, That they shall not take or use any persons land without giving an equivalent therefor, the value of which and kind of equivalent shall be fixed by three disinterested persons, one of which shall be chosen by each party, and the third by them.

Sec. 8. That for the purpose of more effectually enabling the village council to carry into effect the provisions of this act, they are hereby authorized and empowered to assess for corporation purposes an amount of tax on all property within said village, made taxable by the laws of this State, for State and county purposes, not exceeding in any one year one per cent. on the value thereof, which value shall be ascertained by an assessor to be appointed by said village council for that purpose; they shall also have power to equalize any injudicious assessments thus made, on complaint of the owner or owners, his, her, or their agents so aggrieved; that in addition to the taxes herein provided for, the said corporation shall have power to assess such other tax as may be found necessary to purchase a good fire engine, for the use and safety of said village; and also to purchase a suitable piece of ground for a cemetery: *Provided*, That no greater sum shall be assessed in one year than will be sufficient to make one of the above purchases.

Sec. 9. That it shall be the duty of the village council to make out, or cause to be made out by the recorder, a duplicate of taxes, charging each individual therein an amount of tax in proportion to the property of such individual assessed as aforesaid within said town: which duplicate shall be signed by the mayor and recorder, and delivered to the marshal or such other person as shall be appointed collector, whose duty it shall be to collect the same within such time and in such manner as the by-laws shall direct; and the said collector shall have power to sell both real and personal estate for the non-payment of taxes within said town, and shall be governed therein by the same laws and regulations as the collectors of State and county taxes; and in case of the sale of any real estate, the recorder shall have power to make and execute deeds therefor, in the same manner that county auditors are by law, empowered to do for lands sold by the county treasurer; and the said collector shall, within ten days after collecting said taxes, pay the same over to the treasurer of said corporation, taking his receipt therefor: and who shall receive for his fees such sum as the town council may direct, not exceeding six per cent. on all moneys so by him collected and paid over; said fees to be paid by the treasurer, on the order of the recorder: and further, the said village council shall have power to assess, as above, one fourth part of one per cent. in addition to, and in the same manner as above, for the purpose and to be applied to the purchase of a library for said village, which library shall be regulated by the laws of said corporation. •

Sec. 10. That the by-laws and ordinances of said village, shall be posted up in two or more of the most public places within said village, or published in some newspaper published in said village, at least ten days before the taking effect thereof; and the certificate of the recorder upon the village record shall be considered sufficient evidence of the same having been done.

Sec. 11. That the village council shall, at the expiration of each year, cause to be made out and posted up in one or more of the most public places in said village, or published in some newspaper published in said village, an exhibit of the receipts and expenditures of the preceding year; which statement shall be certified by the recorder of said village.

Sec. 12. That the mayor of said corporation shall be a conservator of the peace throughout said village, and shall have all the powers and jurisdiction of a justice of the peace in all matters of a criminal nature arising under the laws of this State, to all intents and purposes whatever; he shall give bond and security as is required by law of justices of the peace; and the said mayor shall perform all the duties required of him by the by-laws and ordinances of said corporation, and appeals may be taken in all cases from the decisions of said mayor in the same manner as from the decisions of justices of the peace: he shall keep a docket, wherein he shall keep a fair record of all matters of difference tried before him, and shall be allowed and receive the same fees that justices of the peace are or may be entitled to in similar cases.

Sec. 13. That the marshal shall be the principal ministerial officer of said village, and shall have the same powers as constables have by law; and his jurisdiction in criminal cases shall be co-extensive with the county of Geauga, and in civil cases with the township of Painesville; he shall execute the process of the mayor, and receive the same fees for his services that constables are allowed in similar cases.

Sec. 14. That said corporation shall be allowed the use of the jail of the county of Geauga, for the imprisonment of such persons as may be liable to imprisonment under the by-laws and ordinances of said corporation; and all persons so imprisoned shall be under the charge of the sheriff of the county of Geauga, as in other cases.

Sec. 15. That the mayor, recorder, trustees, and other officers of said corporation, shall, on demand, deliver to their successors in office all such books and papers as may appertain in any wise to their office.

Sec. 16. That any future Legislature shall have power to alter, amend or repeal this act: *Provided,* That such alteration, amendment, or repeal shall not divert the property of said corporation from the purpose expressed in this act.

WILLIAM MEDILL,
Speaker pro tem. of the House of Representatives.
ELIJAH VANCE,
Speaker of the Senate.

March 8, 1836.

AN ACT

To lay out and establish a State road along the north line of Richland county.

Sec. 1. *Be it enacted by the General Assembly of the State of Ohio,* That Thomas Haney and Joseph Marshall, of the county of Richland, and Aldrich Carver, of the county of Huron, be, and they are hereby appointed commissioners, and Michael Runer, of the county of Richland, surveyor, to lay out and establish a state road, commencing at the place where the Ashland and Norwalk road crosses the line between Richland and Huron counties, to run east along said line, to the north-west corner of Wayne county.

Sec. 2. That the said road commissioners shall, in all respects, be governed by, and the expenses of laying out and establishing said road to be paid in accordance with the provisions of the act entitled "An act defining the mode of laying out and establishing state roads," passed March 14th, 1831, except the appointment of surveyor, which is provided for in the first section of this act.

Sec. 3. Should any vacancy at any time occur, in said board of commissioners, or surveyor, by any cause, it shall be the duty of the commissioners of the county in which such vacancy may happen, to fill the same from time to time, as often as the same may occur, by the aopointment of such persons as they may deem suitable without unreasonable delay.

WILLIAM MEDILL,
Speaker pro tem. of the House of Representatives.
ELIJAH VANCE,
Speaker of the Senate.

March 8, 1836.

AN ACT

To incorporate the First Universalist Society in Fredericktown, Knox county.

Sec. 1. *Be it enacted by the General Assembly of the State of Ohio,* That Alvin Corbin, James Martin, and William Allen, and their associates, together with those that may hereafter be associated with them, be, and they are hereby called a body corporate and politic, by the name of the "First Universalist Society of the county of Knox;" and as such shall re-main and have perpetual succession, subject to such regulations and alter-ations as the Legislature may from time to time think proper to make.

Sec. 2. That the said corporation shall be capable in law, by the name aforesaid, of suing and being sued, pleading and being impleaded, in any action or suit in any court having competent jurisdiction; and they may have a common seal, which they may alter, change or renew at pleasure.

Sec. 3. That the said corporation, by the name aforesaid, shall be ca-paple in law and equity, of holding, receiving, having and acquiring, either by gift, grant, or purchase, any estate, real, personal or mixed, for the use of said corportion: *Provided,* That the annual income of all such property shall not exceed the amount of two thousand dollars.

Sec. 4. That the members of said corporation and their associates, shall meet on the first Monday of September annually; but in case of any failure, the trustees may call a meeting at such time and place as they may think proper, and elect by ballot three trustees and such other officers as the said society may deem necessary, and make such other rules, regula-tions and by-laws as they may deem advisable: *Provided,* They be con-sistent with the constituion and laws of the United States, and of this State.

Sec. 5. That Alvin Corbin, James Martin and William Allen, be, and they are hereby appointed trustees, until the first election, and until their successors are chosen under the provisions of this act.

WILLIAM MEDILL,
Speaker pro tem. of the House of Representatives.
ELIJAH VANCE,
Speaker of the Senate.

March 8, 1836.

AN ACT

To incorporate the Hanging Rock and Lawrence Furnace Rail Road Company.

Sec. 1. *Be it enacted by the General Assembly of the State of Ohio,* That Robert Hamilton, Reuben Kelley, James Rodgers, Thomas W. Means and William Ellison, of the county of Lawrence, and Daniel Young and Wm. McColm, of the county of Scioto, be, and they are hereby appointed, com-missioners, under the direction of a majority of whom subscriptions may be received to the capital stock of the "Hanging Rock and Lawrence Furnace Rail road Company," hereby incorporated; and they, or a ma-jority of them, may cause books to be opened, within the county aforesaid, at such times and places as they may direct, for the purpose of receiving subscriptions to the capital stock of said company, after giving thirty days notice of the time and place of opening the same, as they may deem pro-per; and that upon the first opening of said books, they shall be kept open for at least five successive days, from ten o'clock, A. M., to two o'clock, P. M., of each day; and if at the expiration of that time, such subscription to the capital stock of said company, as is necessary to its incorporation, shall not have been obtained, the said commissioners, or a majority of them, may cause the said books to be opened from time to time, after the expiration of said five days, for the space of three years thereafter; and if any of the said commissioners shall die, resign, or refuse to act, others may be appointed by the remaining commissioners, or a majority of them.

Sec. 2. That the capital stock of the Hanging Rock and Lawrence Furnace Rail road Company, shall be fifty thousand dollars, divided into shares of twenty dollars each; and that as soon as five thousand dollars of said stock shall be subscribed, the subscribers of said stock, their successors and assigns, shall be, and they are hereby declared, a body politic and corporate, by the name and style of the " Hanging Rock and Lawrence Furnace Rail road Company," with perpetual succession; and by that name shall be capable in law of purchasing, holding, selling, leasing and conveying estate, either real, or personal, or mixed, so far as the same may be necessary for the purposes hereinafter mentioned; and in their corporate name may sue and be sued; may have a common seal, which they may alter and renew at pleasure.

Sec. 3. That at the expiration of five days, for which the books are to be opened at first, if two hundred and fifty shares of said stock shall have been subscribed, or if not, as soon thereafter as the same shall be subscribed, the said commissioners, or a majority of them, shall call a meeting of the subscribers, at such time and place as they may appoint; and at such meeting, the said commissioners shall lay the subscription books before the subscribers then and there present; and thereupon, the said subscribers, or a majority of them, shall elect seven directors, by ballot, to manage the affairs of the company; and these seven directors, or a majority of them, shall have power of electing a president of said company, either from among the directors or stockholders of said company; and in said election, and on all other occasions wherein a vote of the stockholders of said company is to be taken, each share shall be entitled to one vote, either by the holder thereof, or by proxy; and the commissioners aforesaid, or a majority of them, shall be judges of the first election of directors.

Sec. 4. That the directors may require payment of subscriptions to the capital stock, at such times, and in such proportions, and on such conditions, as they shall deem fit, under a forfeiture of all previous payments thereon; and the payments then required, shall be made as the work progresses, and as the engineers of the company may require; and thirty days previous notice shall be given to each stockholder, of the amount of payment required at each instalment.

Sec. 5. That said company be, and they are hereby authorized to cause such examinations and surveys to be made by their agents, surveyors and engineers, of the ground lying between Hanging Rock and Lawrence Furnace, as shall be necessary to determine the most eligible and advantageous route whereon to construct said Rail road; and it shall also be lawful for said company, by themselves or agents, to enter upon and take possion of all such lands, as may be necessary for the construction and maintenance of said Rail road: but all lands or real estate thus entered upon, which' are not donated, shall be purchased by said company, of the owner or owners thereof, at a price to be mutually agreed upon between them; and in case of a disagreement as to the price, it shall be the duty of the county commissioners of Lawrence county, to appoint three disinterested persons of such county, appraisers, to determine the damage which the owner or owners of the land so entered upon by said company, has or have sustained by the occupation of the same; and upon payment by the said company of such damages, to the person or persons to whom the same be awarded as aforesaid, then the said company shall be deemed to be, and stand, seized and possessed of the use and occupation of all such lands and real estate for the purposes of said road as shall have been appraised by said appraisers; and it shall be the duty of the said appraisers, to deliver to the said company, a written statement, signed by them, or a majority of them, of the awards they make, containing a description of the lands or real estate appraised; to be recorded by said company in the commissioners' office in said county: *Provided*, That either party shall have the power of appealing from the decision of the appraisers, to the court of common pleas of said county, at any time within thirty days after the return of the award of the appraisers shall have been made, as aforesaid; and the said court shall proceed thereon, as in cases of appeals for damages in laying out and constructing State roads.

Sec. 6. That said company shall have power to determine the width and dimensions of said Rail road, not exceeding one hundred feet wide; whether it shall be a double or single track; to regulate the time and manner of collecting tolls, and transportation of goods or passengers thereon; and to erect and keep toll houses, or other buildings, for the accommodation of the business, or as the directors may deem advisable for their interest.

Sec. 7. That the company may demand and receive of all persons, using or travelling on said Rail road, the following rates of toll, to wit: For every ton weight of goods, or freight of any kind or description, five cents per mile for every mile the same shall pass upon the said road, and at a rateable proportion for any greater or less quantity; and all persons paying the toll aforesaid, may, with suitable and proper carriages, use and travel upon the said Rail road, subject to such rules and regulations as the company shall, by their by-laws, establish.

Sec. 8. That the president and directors, or a majority of them, may appoint all such officers, engineers, agents or servants, as they may deem necessary for the transaction of the business of the company, and may remove them at pleasure; that they, or a majority of them, shall have power to determine, by contract, the compensation of all persons, in whatever capacity they may be employed by said company; and to determine, by their by-laws, the manner of adjusting and settling all accounts against the company, and also the manner and evidence of the transfers of stock in said company; and that they, or a majority of them, shall have power to pass all by-laws, which they may deem necessary and proper, for exercising all the powers vested in the company hereby incorporated, and for carrying the objects of this act into effect: *Provided*, Such by-laws shall not be contrary to the constitution and laws of this State, or of the United States.

Sec. 9. That whenever, in the construction of said road, it shall be necessary to cross or intersect any established road, it shall be the duty of the said president and directors of the said company, so to construct the said Rail road across such established road, as not to impede the transportation of persons or property along the same.

Sec. 10. That the president and directors shall have power to purchase, with the funds of the company, and place on said road, all machines, wagons, locomotive steam engines or carriages of any description whatsoever, which they may deem necessary or proper for the purpose of transportation on said Rail road; and that they may charge freight, in addition to the tolls, at a rate not to exceed five cents per mile per ton, for all goods or other freight conveyed on said Rail road, or in that proportion for a greater or less amount.

Sec. 11. That the president and directors, or other officers of said company, before they act as such, shall severally take an oath or affirmation, that they will well and truly discharge the duties of their several offices, to the best of their skill and judgment.

Sec. 12. That to continue the succession of the president and directors of said company, seven directors shall be chosen, annually, on the first Monday in January, in every year, at the Hanging Rock; at which time and place, there shall be a general meeting of the stockholders of said company; and it shall be the duty of the president and directors in office, for the previous year, to exhibit a clear and distinct statement of the affairs of the company, to the stockholders at said meeting.

Sec. 13. That the said president and directors shall, semi annually, declare and make such dividend as they may deem proper, of the nett profits arising from the resources of the company, after deducting the necessary current contingent expenses; and that they shall divide the same among the stockholders of said company, in proper proportion to their respective shares.

Sec. 14. That if any person shall wilfully, by any means whatever, injure, impair or destroy, any part of said Rail road, or any of the necessary works, buildings, carriages, vehicles or machines of said company, such person or persons so offending, shall each of them, for every such offence, forfeit and pay to the said company, treble damages; which may be recovered in the name of said company, by an action of debt in any court having jurisdiction of the same; and also be subject to indictment in the court of Lawrence county, and upon conviction of such offence, shall be punished by fine and imprisonment, at the discretion of the court.

Sec. 15. That any other Rail road Company, now or hereafter to be chartered by law of this State, may join and connect any Rail road, with the road hereby contemplated, and run cars upon the same, subject to the rules and regulations of the directors of this company, as to the construction and speed of said cars, and full right and privilege is hereby reserved to the State or citizens, or any company incorporated by law of this State to cross this road: *Provided,* In so crossing no injury shall be done to the works of the company hereby incorporated.

Sec. 16. If the Legislature of this State shall, after the expiration of thirty-five years from the passage of this act, make provision by law, for the repayment to said company of the amount expended by them in the locations and constructions of said road, together with the amount expended for necessary permanent fixtures at the time of purchase for the use of said road, with an advance of fifteen per cent. thereon, then said road, with all fixtures, shall vest in and become the property of the State of Ohio.

Sec. 17. Whenever the dividends of said company shall exceed the rate of six per cent. per annum, the Legislature of this State may impose such reasonable taxes on the amount of said dividends as are received from other Rail road Companies.

Sec. 18. That any suit instituted against said company, the service of legal process on the president, or on any one of the directors, or on the treasurer or secretary of said company, shall be deemed and held, in all courts and places, a sufficient and valid service on said company.

Sec. 19. That this act shall be deemed a public act; and shall be favorably construed for the purposes therein expressed and declared, in all courts and places whatever.

WILLIAM MEDILL,
Speaker pro tem. of the House of Representatives.

ELIJAH VANCE,
Speaker of the Senate.

March 9, 1836.

AN ACT

To incorporate the Licking Valley Insurance Company.

Sec. 1. *Be it enacted by the General Assembly of the State of Ohio,* That John J. Brice, William Spencer, Franklin Fullerton, Daniel Duncan, Isaac Schmucker, George Baker, Albert Sherwood, Samuel H. Bancroft, Lucius Smith, Ezekiel S. Woods, Israel Dille, Samuel D. King, Saml. M. Browning, Joshua Mathiot, Asa Beckwith, Benjamin W. Brice, jr., and Corrington W. Searle, or such of them, and their associates, as shall become subscribers for stock of this association, and their successors, shall be, and they are hereby declared a body corporate and politic, by the name and style of "The Licking Valley Insurance Company;" and by that name shall have perpetual succession, and be capable in law to sue and be sued, plead and be impleaded, answer and be answered, defend and be defended, in all courts of law and equity, and elsewhere; with full power and authority to acquire, hold, possess, occupy, and enjoy, and the same to sell, convey and dispose of, all such real estate, as shall be necessary and convenient for the transaction of its business, or which may be conveyed to said company, for the security or in payment of any debt, which may become due and owing to the same, or in satisfaction of any judgment of a court in law, or any order or decree of a court of equity, in their favor; and to make and use a common seal, and the same to alter and renew, at their pleasure; and generally, to do and perform all things relative to the objects of this institution.

Sec. 2. That the capital stock of said company shall be one hundred thousand dollars, divided into shares of fifty dollars each.

Sec. 3. That, at the time of subscribing, there shall be paid on each share, ten dollars; and the balance due on the shares subscribed, shall be subjected to the call of the directors; and the directors for the time being, shall have the power, at any time, for good cause, to require any stockholder to give additional security, reasonably sufficient to secure the payment of the arrears due on his stock, as the same may be called for.

Sec. 4. That so soon as one thousand shares are subscribed, and the first instalment thereon paid, and the residue secured, as provided in the preceding section, the company shall be competent to transact all kinds of business for which it is established.

Sec. 5. That the affairs of said company shall be managed by nine directors; a majority of whom shall be a quorum to transact any business of the company; who shall be chosen from the stockholders, as follows: there shall be a meeting of the stockholders convened, pursuant to a notice to be given for that purpose, by the commissioners hereinafter named, within one month after one thousand shares of the stock shall have been subscribed; at which meeting the stockholders present shall proceed by ballot, to elect a board of directors, who shall contiue in office until their successors are chosen; at which election, as well as at all other elections thereafter to be holden, each stockholder shall have one vote for each share of stock which he may hold, not exceeding five shares; and one vote for every three shares over five shares, and not exceeding eleven shares; and one vote for every share over eleven.

Sec. 6. That there shall be an an election for directors holden on the first Monday of June, in each and every year, next after the organization of the company; and the directors, at their first meeting after their election, shall choose by ballot, from among themselves, a president, to serve until the next election of directors; but in case of the death or inability of the president, they shall fill the vacancy, by ballot, as before; and in case of a vacancy in the board of directors, it shall be filled by the directors from the stockholders.

Sec. 7. That if it shall, at any time happen, from any cause, that no election shall be held on the first Monday of June, the directors may order an election at any time thereafter: *Provided*, That it shall be the duty of the directors to give at least two weeks notice, by publication in some newspaper printed in the town of Newark, of the time and place at which any stated or special election shall be holden.

Sec. 8. That the corporation hereby created, shall have full power and lawful authority, to insure all kinds of property against loss or damage by fire, or other casualty; to make all kinds of insurances upon life or lives; to cause themselves to be insured against any loss or risk which they may incur in the course of their business; and generally, to do and perform all other matters and things connected with, and proper to promote those objects: and it shall be lawful for said company to use and employ its capital stock, or other funds, in the purchase of any stock, or in the stock of any other incorporated company or association, and any such stock to sell again at pleasure; and they may loan their stock, money, or other funds, or any part thereof, to individuals or corporations, on real or personal security, for such periods of time as the directors shall deem prudent, for the interest and safety of the company: *Provided,* That it shall not be lawful for said company to employ any part of their capital stock, money, or other funds, in merchandizing; nor shall said company issue or emit any bills of credit, to be used as a circulating medium; nor shall said company, in any manner, engage in the business of banking, otherwise than to purchase and make sale of stocks, as hereinbefore provided, or receive on money or loans, a rate of interest greater than at the rate of six per cent. per annum: *Provided,* That nothing in this act contained, shall be so construed as to authorize said corporation to borrow money, in any case whatever, unless such borrowing shall be necessary to meet any loss, which said corporation shall have sustained upon its insurances.

Sec. 9. That the president and directors shall declare such dividends of profits, as the business of said company, as shall not impair, or in anywise lessen, the capital stock of the same; which dividends shall be declared half-yearly, on the first Monday in May and November, shall be paid to the stockholders at any time after ten days thereafter; but no dividend shall be paid to any stockholder who is delinquent to the company.

Sec. 10. That any house or building, insured by this company, which shall be destroyed by fire, from the first floor upwards, shall be deemed demolished; and the directors, in such case, shall order the money insured thereon, to be paid in sixty days after due notice is given of the loss, in such manner that shall be required and specified in the policy, or the conditions annexed thereto.

Sec. 11. That the president and directors, shall have power and authority to appoint such officers under them, as shall be necessary to transact the business of the company, and to prescribe the duties of such officers and may allow them such salaries as they shall judge reasonable: to ordain such by-laws, ordinances and regulations, as shall appear to them necessary, for regulating and conducting the concerns of said company, consistent with the constitution and laws of this State, and of the United States; and they shall keep full, fair, and accurate entries of their transactions, which shall, at all times, be open to the inspection of the stockholders.

Sec. 12. That the stock of this company, may be assigned and transferred on the books of the company, by any stockholder, or by his attorney duly constituted, agreeably to the rules of the company: but no stockholder shall be permitted, whilst indebted to the company, to assign his stock, or any part thereof, until such indebtedness is discharged, or secured, to the satisfaction of the directors.

Sec. 13. That all policies or contracts of insurance, or other contracts made by the company, or their authorized agents, shall be signed by the president and attested by the clerk or secretary of the board of directors; and any contract, thus attested, which may afterwards be filled up by any agent of the company, authorized to contract in behalf of the company, shall be obligatory and binding on the company.

Sec. 14. That the president and directors of the company, shall transact the business of said company, at Newark, in the county of Licking: but they shall have power and authority to appoint agents at other places, to make surveys of property, and to fill up and deliver policies, executed as aforesaid.

Sec. 15. That in all suits, prosecuted against said company, the process may be served by a copy thereof being delivered to the president, or any one of the directors, by any officer authorized to serve such process; at least ten days before the return day thereof; and the person thus served with process, shall, at the next meeting of the board of the board of direct. ors, report the fact, and lay before the board the copy of the process so served.

Sec. 16. That William Spencer, Benjamin W. Brice, jr., Franklin Fullerton, Isaac Schmucker, Israel Dille, Corrington W. Searle and Samuel M. Browning, or any four of them, are hereby appointed commissioners to open books for the subscription of stock, and to superintend the business of the subscribers, until a board of directors shall be elected; which books shall be opened in the town of Newark, on the first Monday of May next, and shall be kept open every day, (Sundays excepted,) between the hours of nine in the morning and five in the afternoon, for twenty days, or at least until one thousand shares of the stock be subscribed for; and if there shall be a failure to open books as aforesaid, or if there shall be a failure to subscribe one thousand shares of the capital stock as aforesaid, within one year from the passage of this act, then this act shall become null and void and of no effect.

Sec. 17. That this act shall be taken and received in all courts of justice, and by all public officers, as a public act; and all printed copies thereof, printed under the authority of the General Assembly of this State, shall be admitted as good evidence thereof, without any other proof whatever.

Sec. 18. That this act shall continue and be in force, for the term of twenty years from the passage thereof: *Provided,* That any future Legislature shall have power to alter, amend, or modify this act.

WILLIAM MEDILL,
Speaker pro tem. of the House of Representatives.
ELIJAH VANCE,
Speaker of the Senate.

March 9, 1836.

AN ACT

To incorporate the Hudson Steam Mill Company, in the county of Portage.

Sec. 1. *Be it enacted by the General Assembly of the State of Ohio,* That Van R. Humphrey, Owen Brown, Heman Oviatt, Augustus Baldwin, John B. Clark, Israel Town and Moses Thompson, and such other persons as may hereafter be associated with them, for the purpose of driving machinery by steam, in the township of Hudson, in the county of Portage, be, and they are hereby created a body corporate and politic, by and under the name and style of the "Hudson Steam Mill Company;" and by that name and style, shall have perpetual succession, and be capable of suing and be-

44—L

ing sued, contracting and being contracted with, answering and being answered unto, in any court having jurisdiction of the same; and may have a common seal, and the same break, alter or renew at pleasure; and shall be capable of holding and disposing of at pleasure, all kinds of property, real, personal or mixed, to the amount of the capital stock of said company, necessary for the object and purposes of said corporation: *Provided,* The junds thereof shall never be used for banking purposes.

Sec. 2. That the capital stock of said corporation shall not exceed fifty thousand dollars, to be divided into shares of fifty dollars each; and the persons named in the first section of this act, or a majority of them, are hereby authorized and appointed commissioners to open books of subscription to the stock of said company, at such place and times, and under such regulations as they shall deem proper.

Sec. 3. That said corporation shall have power to make such by-laws and rules for its government and regulation as may be thought necessary and proper.

Sec. 4. That the private property of each stockholder of said corporation shall be liable for the debts of the same in proportion to the amount of stock by them held and owned respectively: *Provided always,* That the joint assets and funds of the corporation shall first be subject to the payment of said debts before the individual property of any stockholder shall be seized in execution, or other proceedings taken to subject the same to the payment of such debts.

Sec. 5. That any future Legislature shall have power to alter, amend or repeal this act.

WILLIAM MEDILL,
Speaker pro tem. of the House of Representatives.
ELIJAH VANCE,
Speaker of the Senate.

March 9, 1836.

AN ACT

To improve the navigation of the Muskingum river by Slack-water Navigation.

Sec. 1. *Be it enacted by the General Assembly of the State of Ohio,* That the canal commissioners of the State be, and they are hereby empowered and directed to improve the navigation of the Muskingum river, by slack-water navigation, from its mouth to such point thereon at or near the town of Zanesville, as has not already been dedicated and appropriated by the State for such object, in such manner and with such locks and dams as may be necessary to secure the safe transit and convenient passage of steamboats of such dimensions and capacity as the said commissioners may prescribe: *Provided,* The said commissioners shall not commence said work unless, in their opinion, the work when finished will not lessen business upon the Ohio canal, and the tolls and water rents to be derived therefrom will pay the interest annually on the cost of construction; and to accomplish that object, the said commissioners are hereby empowered to seize, dedicate, acquire, hold, use and occupy, for the use and benefit of the State, all such private and corporate estate and property as shall be necessary for the convenience of the construction of that improvement, and for hydraulic purposes thereon, as they have heretofore had power to do, in the construction and maintenance of the Ohio and Miami canals: *Provided*, That the owners and proprietors of any property, so seized and dedicated, shall have all the rights of indemnity and remedies of compensation as by law have been provided for in the construction of the Ohio and Miami canals; and when the said improvement shall be completed, or any part thereof, the said canal commissioners, at their discretion, shall levy and assess such tolls thereon, and rent out the water power thereof, on such terms and conditions as may seem right and just, having reference to, and in view of the interest of the State and the permanent prosperity of the Muskingum Valley: *And provided further*, That said commissioners shall not be required to execute said work until the owners or proprietors of the lands contiguous to the places where the dams are to be located on said river, shall convey to the State upon such terms and conditions as said board shall deem just and equitable, a sufficient quantity of such land as will be necessary for the convenient and proper use of the water power which will be thereby created.

Sec. 2. That preparatory to the construction of said improvement, the canal commissioners may cause such further surveys and examinations to be made in relation thereto, as, in their judgment, may be considered proper for the successful prosecution of the work; and the accounts and documents of all expenses incurred, and disbursements made, and the revenue or income received by or under the authority of this act, shall be kept separate and distinct from those belonging to or connected with the other public works of this State.

Sec. 3. That for the purpose of carrying into effect the provisions of this act, the commissioners of the canal fund are hereby authorized and empowered to borrow on the credit of the State, any sum or sums of money, not exceeding four hundred thousand dollars, at a rate of interest not exceeding five per centum per annum, payable semi-annually at the city of New York or elsewhere; the principal thereof to be paid at any time after the year eighteen hundred and fifty-six, at the pleasure of the State, whose faith is hereby pledged for the payment of such loan and the interest thereon, as above specified; and further, for the payment of the interest of said loan and the ultimate redemption of the principal thereof, there is hereby irrevocably pledged and appropriated the proceeds of all tolls and water rents, and all other revenues and income which may be received on said improvement, after deducting therefrom the annual expenses thereof, in keeping the same in repair, and other incidental charges of its superintendence and police.

Sec. 4. That in the construction of this work, and in the management and superintendence thereof, the canal commissioners and the commissioners of the canal fund, shall possess and exercise the same powers in all respects as to the appointment of engineers and other officers and agents, and providing for a strict accountability of all moneys expended, as they

have heretofore possessed and exercised, in the construction, maintenance
and supervision of the Ohio and Miami canals.

WILLIAM MEDILL,
Speaker pro tem. of the House of Representatives.
ELIJAH VANCE,
Speaker of the Senate.

March 9, 1836.

AN ACT

To incorporate the Chippeway Canal Company.

Sec. 1. *Be it enacted by the General Assembly of the State of Ohio,* That
Stephen Oviatt, and Thomas M'Elhany, of Wayne county, and Nathaniel
Bell, and Edward G. Dawson, of Medina county, and their associates, be,
and they are hereby constituted and declared a body politic and corporate,
by the name and style of the Chippeway Canal Company, for the purpose
of making a canal from Clinton, in Stark county, on the Ohio canal, to
the Chippeway lake, in Medina county, or improving the navigation of
the Chippeway creek, by slackwater navigation, canal, or otherwise, with
leave to improve the surplus water, for hydraulic purposes; and the said
company is hereby authorized and empowered to have and receive, purchase, possess, enjoy, and retain lands, rents, goods, chattels and effects
of any kind, and to any amount, necessary to carry into effect the plans
and objects of the corporation; and the same to use, sell, alien, and di-
pose of, at pleasure; to sue and be sued, defend and be defended, in all
courts having competent jurisdiction; and to have and use a common seal,
and the same to break and alter at pleasure; to ordain and establish such rules,
regulations and by-laws, as may be necessary for the well ordering and
governing the corporation; subject, however, to the restrictions, provisions, and limitations, contained in this act.

Sec. 2. That the capital stock of said company shall consist of one
hundred thousand dollars, which shall be divided into shares of fifty dollars
each, and shall be transferable in entire shares, in such manner as the rules
of the corporation shall prescribe.

Sec. 3. That the persons named in the first section of this act, shall
be commissioners to receive subscriptions; and also, to do and perform all
necessary acts, to organize the company; and they are hereby authorized
and empowered to cause books to be opened, at such times, and in such
places as a majority of them shall direct, to receive subscriptions to the
capital stock of said company: the commissioners shall require five per
centum upon each share to be paid, at the time it is subscribed; and each
subscriber shall be bound to pay, from time to time such instalments on
his stock, as the directors, or a majority of them, shall require.

Sec. 4. That whenever one hundred shares are subscribed, the commissioners shall call a meeting of the stockholders, by causing notice of
the time and place of such meeting to be published in some newspaper of

the county, for three successive weeks, in which the books shall have been opened, and the stock subscribed; and on such notice being given, the stockholders shall meet at the time and place appointed; and when so assembled, may proceed to elect from three to seven directors, and adopt such rules and regulations for the government of the corporation, as are lawful and expedient; the stockholders may vote by person or proxy, and for each share such stockholder may possess he shall be entitled to one vote.

Sec. 5. That the affairs of the company shall be managed by the directors, or a majority of them, who shall be elected by the stockholders, and hold their office until others shall be elected in their stead, according to the constitution and by-laws of said company; each director shall be a stockholder at the time of his election; whenever he ceases to be a stockholder, he shall cease to be a director.

Sec. 6. That the directors so elected or appointed, shall, at their first meeting after said election, choose one person from their own number, who shall serve as president of the board for and during the time for which he shall have been elected a director; the president and directors, previous to their entering on the duties of their office, shall severally take an oath or affirmation faithfully and impartially to discharge the duties appertaining to said office, by virtue of the provisions of this act, and rules of the corporation; they shall appoint a treasurer, who shall give bond, with security, for the faithful performance of the trust committed to him; the directors shall order and direct the time and place when the stockholders shall pay in their instalments, and determine the amount of such instalment; and give notice thereof in some newspaper in general circulation in the county where such stock was subscribed, for at least three successive weeks; neither shall any stockholder be bound to pay more than fifteen per centum on the amount of his stock, at any one time, nor more than fifty per centum in any one year.

Sec. 7. That it shall be lawful for said company, their agents, engineers, superintendents, or workmen, to enter upon and take possession of lands, waters, or streams, necessary to make said canal, under the provisions of this act, and enter upon the lands contiguous and near to said canal, and take therefrom earth, sand, gravel, stone and timber, necessary to make the improvements contemplated by this act, doing no unnecessary injury or damage, by paying therefor a fair valuable consideration; if the parties cannot mutually agree upon the damages, or value of the land and materials so taken by said company, in that case either of the parties may apply to any president or associate judge of the district or county (not being a stockholder,) in which said land is situated, who shall appoint five disinterested freeholders in said county, as appraisers, who shall examine and appraise the damages, the value of the land, and materials necessary to construct and finish the improvements contemplated by this act; nevertheless taking into consideration, as an off-set, the benefits which such person, proprietor or proprietors will derive from the location and construction of said canal, or improvement, by the creation of hydraulic power, &c., the appraisers so appointed, who, after being duly sworn or affirmed faithfully and impartially to discharge their appointed duties, shall make a certificate of such appraisement, with a particular description of the premises; to which certificate, a majority of them shall sign their names, and deliver to each party one copy; and immediately thereafter, if no damages are assessed, or on payment, or tender of the money, to the amount of damages assessed, to the person or persons injured, his guardian, agent or attorney, the said company, as aforesaid, may proceed to enter upon and occupy such lands, streams, or waters, and a complete title to the premises, to the extent, and for the purposes set forth in or contemplated by this act, shall thereby be vested, and forever remain in the said company: *Provided, however*, That if either party shall consider himself aggrieved by the decision of the appraisers, so aforesaid made, such party may appeal to the court of common pleas of the proper county, at the succeeding term of said court, and such decision shall be final and determinate between the parties; but the pendency of any such appeal shall not in the mean time hinder the progress of the work: *And provided, also*, That this act shall not be so construed as to authorize the taking or diverting from their course any streams or waters, probably necessary, to feed or supply the Ohio canal, without permission first obtained from the board of canal commissioners: *Provided, further*, That nothing in this act shall be so construed as to authorize the company hereby incorporated to take or use the waters of the Chippeway lake, or take and use any waters or streams that may be necessary for the construction of the Lake Erie and Muskingum Road and Canal Company, passed March 3d, 1834.

Sec. 8. That when the whole, or any part of said canal, or improvement, is completed, the president and directors of said company shall have power, if deemed by them advisable, to ordain and establish a rate of tolls, which shall be paid on vessels, rafts, boats, or other property, passing on such part, or whole of said canal or improvement, that is navigable; and for the collection of said tolls, the president and directors may appoint a collector, and establish a toll house, at some suitable place; and may ask, demand, and receive on all boats, rafts, vessels, or other property, passing or navigating on said [canal] or improvements, such toll or tolls as shall be established by said company, under the provisions of this act.

Sec. 9. That the president and directors shall, annually or semi-annually, declare and make a dividend of the profits arising from tolls, or any other source, reserving such sum or sums as will defray the necessary current and probable contingent expenses; which dividend shall be paid or passed to the credit of the stockholders severally, in proportion to the shares each may hold in the stock of said company.

Sec. 10. That the company shall be entitled to the benefit of all laws which are, or hereafter shall be in force, for the collection of tolls or rents, or for the protection of any canals constructed by the State, so far as such law or laws are necessary to insure the collection of tolls, or rents, or for the protection of the canal, its appendages or other property, which the company may lawfully hold, in order to carry into effect the provisions of this act.

Sec. 11. That nothing in this act contained shall be so construed as to authorize said company to employ its funds for banking purposes.

WILLIAM MEDILL,
Speaker pro tem. of the House of Representatives.
ELIJAH VANCE,
Speaker of the Senate.

March 9, 1836.

AN ACT

To incorporate the Akron and Perrysburg Rail-road Company.

Sec. 1. *Be it enacted by the General Assembly of the State of Ohio,* That Picket Lattimer, John Whyler, Moses Kimble, and John Tift, of Huron county; Daniel J. Johns, Harvey Grant and William Andrews, of the county of Lorain; Jesse S. Olmsted, James Justice and N. B. Eddy, of Sandusky county; David King, William H. Canfield, William King, Uriel H. Peak and Joel Tiffany, of Medina county; John Hollister, David Ladd, John C. Sprink, Daniel Wheeler and Jessup W. Scott, of Wood county; John E. Hunt, Robert A. Forsythe, Horatio Counout, of Lucas county; Richard Howe, R. K. Dubois, H. McCune, E. Crosby, J. W. Phillips and S. A. Wheeler, of Portage county; be, and they are hereby appointed commissioners, under the direction of a majority of whom, subscriptions may be received to the capital stock of the Akron and Perrysburg Rail-road Company, hereby incorporated; and they, or a majority of them, may cause books to be opened at such times and places as they may direct, in the counties through which said road passes, for the purpose of receiving subscriptions to the capital stock of said company, after having given at least thirty days notice of the time and place of opening the same, and that upon the first opening of said books, they shall be kept open for at least ten days in succession, from ten o'clock A. M. until two o'clock P. M.; and if at the expiration of that period, such a subscription to the capital stock of said company as is necessary to its incorporation, shall not have been obtained, then said commissioners, or a majority of them, may cause said books to be opened from time to time, after the expiration of said ten days, and for the space of three years thereafter, or until the sum necessary to the incorporation of the company shall be subscribed; and if any of said commissioners shall die, resign or refuse to act during the continuance of the duties devolved upon them by this act, another or others may be appointed in his or their stead by the remaining commissioners or a majority of them.

Sec. 2. That the capital stock of the Akron and Perrysburg Rail-road Company shall be nine hundred thousand dollars, and shall be divided into shares of fifty dollars each; which shares may be subscribed for by individuals only; and it shall and may be lawful for the said corporation to commence the construction of the said rail-road or way, and enjoy all the powers and privileges conferred by this act, as soon as the sum of fifty thousand dollars shall be subscribed to said stock.

Sec. 3. That all persons who shall become stockholders pursuant to this act, shall be, and they are hereby, created a body corporate, and shall be and remain a corporation forever, under the name of the Akron and Perrysburgh Rail-road Company; and by that name, shall be capable in law, of purchasing, holding, selling, leasing and conveying estates real, personal or mixed, so far as the same shall be necessary for the purposes hereinafter mentioned, and no further; and shall have perpetual succession; and by said corporate name may contract and be contracted with, sue and be sued, and may have and use a common seal, which they shall have power to alter or renew at their pleasure; and shall have, enjoy and may exercise all the powers, rights and privileges which corporate bodies may lawfully do for the purposes mentioned in this act.

Sec. 4. That upon all subscriptions, there shall be paid, at the time of subscribing, to the said commissioners or their agents, appointed to receive such subscriptions, the sum of five dollars on every share subscribed; and the residue thereof shall be paid in such instalments, and at such times as may be required by the president and directors of said company: *Provided*, No payment, other than the first shall be demanded until at least thirty days public notice of such demand shall have been given, by said president and directors, in some newspaper of general circulation in the State of Ohio, and in some newspaper printed in the counties through which said road passes; and if any stockholder shall fail or neglect to pay any instalment or part of said subscription thus demanded, for the space of sixty days next after the time the same shall be due and payable, the said president and directors, upon giving at least thirty days previous notice thereof in manner aforesaid, may, and they are hereby authorized to sell at public vendue so many of the shares of the said delinquent stockholder or stockholders as shall be necessary to pay such instalment, and the expenses of advertising and sale, and transfer the shares so sold to the purchasers; and the residue of the money arising from such sale, after paying such instalments and expenses, shall be paid to said stockholder on demand.

Sec. 5. That at the expiration of ten days, for which the books are first opened, if two hundred shares of said capital stock shall have been subscribed; or, if not, as soon thereafter as the same shall be subscribed, if within three years after the first opening of the books; the said commissioners, or a majority of them, shall call a general meeting of the stockholders at such time and place as they may appoint, and shall give at least sixty days previous notice thereof; and at such meeting the said commissioners shall lay the subscription books before the stockholders then and there present; and thereupon the said stockholders, or a majority of them, shall elect twelve directors by ballot, a majority of whom shall be competent to manage the affairs of said company; they shall have the power of electing a president of said company, either from among said directors or others, and of allowing him such compensation as they may deem proper; and in said election, and on all other occasions wherein a vote of the stockholders of said company is to be taken, each stockholder shall be allowed one vote for every share owned by him or her; and every stockholder may depute any other person to vote and act for him or her, as his or their proxy; and the commissioners aforesaid, or any three of them, shall be judges of the first election of said directors.

Sec. 6. That to continue the succession of the president and directors of said company, twelve directors shall be chosen annually on the third Monday of October in every year, in the town of Norwalk, or at such other place as a majority of the directors shall appoint; and if any vacancy shall occur by death, resignation, or otherwise, of any president or director, before the year for which he was elected had expired, a person to fill such vacant place for the residue of the year may be appointed by the president and directors of said company, or a majority of them; and that the president and directors of said company shall hold and exercise their offices until a new election of president and directors; and that all elections which are by this act or the by-laws of the company, to be made on a particular day or at a particular time, if not made on such day or time, may be made at any time within thirty days thereafter.

Sec. 7. That a general meeting of the stockholders shall be held annually at the time and place appointed for the election of president and directors of said company; that meetings may be called at any time during the interval between the said annual meetings, by the president and directors, or a majority of them, or by the stockholders owning at least one-fourth of the stock subscribed, upon giving at least thirty days public notice of the time and place of holding the same; and when any such meetings are called by the stockholders, such notice shall specify the particular object of the call; and if at any such called meeting a majority in value of the stockholders of said company are not present in person or by proxy, such meeting shall be adjourned from day to day without transacting any business, for any time not exceeding three days; and if, within said three days, stockholders holding a majority in value of the stock subscribed, do not thus attend, such meeting shall be dissolved.

Sec. 8. That at the regular meetings of the stockholders of said company, it shall be the duty of the president and directors in office for the previous year, to exhibit a clear and distinct statement of the affairs of the company; that at any called meeting of the stockholders, a majority of those present in person or by proxy may require similar statements from the president and directors, whose duty it shall be to furnish them when thus required; and that at all general meetings of the stockholders, a majority in value of all the stockholders of said company may remove from office any president or any of the directors of said company, and may appoint officers in their stead.

Sec. 9. That any president and director of said company, before he acts as such, shall swear or affirm, as the case may be, that he will well and truly discharge the duties of his said office to the best of his skill and judgment.

Sec. 10. That the said president and directors, or a majority of them, may appoint all such officers, engineers, agents whatsoever, as they may deem necessary for the transaction of the business of the company, and may remove any of them at their pleasure; that they, or a majority of them, shall have power to determine by contract, the compensation of all engineers, officers, agents, in the employ of said company, and to determine by their by-laws the manner of adjusting and settling all accounts against the said company; and also, the manner and evidence of transfers of stock in said company; and they, or a majority of them, shall have power to pass all by-laws which they may deem necessary or proper for exercising all the powers vested in the company hereby incorporated, and for carrying the objects of this act into effect: *Provided only*, That such by-laws shall not be contrary to the constitution and laws of this State and of the United States.

Sec. 11. That the said corporation shall be, and they are hereby vested with the right to construct a double or single rail-road or way from Akron, in the county of Portage, through the villages of Medina, Wellington, Norwalk, and Lower Sandusky, to Perrysburg, in Wood county, to transport, take and carry property and persons upon the same by the power

45—L

and force of steam, of animals, or of any mechanical or other power, or of any combination of them, which the said corporation may choose to employ.

Sec. 12. That the president and directors of said company shall be and are hereby invested with all rights and powers necessary for the location, construction, and repair of said road, not exceeding one hundred feet wide, with as many sets of tracks as the said president and directors may deem necessary; and they may cause to be made, contract with others for making said rail-road or any part of it; and they, or their agents, or those with whom they may contract for making any part of the same, may enter upon and use and excavate any land which may be wanted for the site of said road, or for any other purpose necessary and useful in the construction or in the repair of said road or its works; and that they may build bridges, may fix scales and weights, may lay rails, may take and use any earth, timber, gravel, stone or other materials which may be wanted for the construction or repair of any part of said road or any of its works; and may make and construct all works whatsoever, which may be necessary in the construction or repair of said road.

Sec. 13. That the president and directors of said company, or a majority of them, or any persons authorized by them, or a majority of them, may agree with the owner or owners of any lands, earth, timber, gravel or stone or other materials, or any improvements which may be wanted for the construction or repairs of said road, or any of their works, for the purchase, or use or occupation of the same; and if they cannot agree, and if the owner or owners, or any of them, be a married woman, insane person, or idiot, or out of the county in which the property wanted may lie when such lands and materials may be wanted, application may be made to any justice of the peace of such county, who shall thereupon issue his warrant, under his hand and seal, directed to the sheriff of said county, or to some disinterested person, if the sheriff shall be interested, requiring him to summon a jury of twelve men, inhabitants of said county, not related or in any wise interested, to meet on the lands or near to the other property or materials to be valued, on a day named in said warrant, not less than ten nor more than twenty days after the issuing of the same; and if at the said time and place any of said persons summoned do not attend, the said sheriff or summoner shall immediately summons as many persons as may be necessary, with the persons in attendance, to furnish a pannel of twelve jurors in attendance; and from them each party or his, or her or their agents, the sheriff or summoner, for him, her or them, may strike off three jurors, and the remaining six shall act as a jury of inquest of damages; and before they act as such the said summoner or sheriff shall administer to each of them an oath or affirmation, as the case may be, that they will faithfully and impartially value the damages which the owner or owners will sustain by the use or occupation of the same, required by said company; and the jury estimating the damages, if for the ground occupied by said road, shall take into the estimate the benefits resulting to said owner or owners, by reason of said road passing through or upon the land of such owner or owners, towards the extinguishment of such claim of damages; and the said jury shall reduce their inquisition to writing, and shall sign and seal the same; and it shall then be returned to the clerk of the court of common pleas for said county, and by such clerk filed in his office, and shall be confirmed by said court at its next session, if no sufficient cause to the contrary be shown; and when confirmed, shall be recorded by said clerk at the expense of said company; but if set aside, the court may direct another inquisition to be taken in the manner above described; and such inquisition shall describe the property taken, or the bounds of the land condemned; and such valuation when paid or tendered to the owner or owners of said property, or his, her or their legal representatives, shall entitle said company to the right and interest in such personal property and the use and occupation of such real property for the purposes of said road, thus valued, as fully as if it had been conveyed by the owner or owners of the same; and the valuation, if not received when tendered, may at any time hereafter be received from the company without cost, by the owner or owners, his, her or their legal representative or representatives; and that such sheriff or summoner, and jurors, shall be entitled to demand and receive from the said company the same fees as are allowed for like services in cases of fixing the valuation of real estate previous to sale under execution.

Sec. 14.   That whenever, in the construction of such road, it shall be necessary to cross or intersect any established road or way, it shall be the duty of the said president and directors of said company so to construct the said rail-road across such established road or way, as not to impede the passage or transportation of persons or property along the same; or when it shall be necessary to pass through the land of any individual, it shall also be their duty to provide for such individual proper wagon ways across said road, from one part of his land to another, without delay.

Sec. 15.   That if said company should neglect to provide proper wagon ways across said road, as required by the fourteenth section of this act, it shall be lawful for any individual to sue said company, and to be entitled to such damages as a jury may think him or her entitled to, for such neglect on the part of said company.

Sec. 16.   That if it shall be necessary for such company, in the selection of the route or construction of the road to be by them laid out and constructed, or any part of it, to connect the same with, or to use any turnpike road or bridge, made or erected by any company or persons incorporated, or authorized by any law of this State; it shall be lawful for the said president and directors, and they are hereby authorized to contract or agree with any such corporations or persons, for the right to use such road or bridge, or for the transfer of any of the corporate or other rights or privileges of such corporation or persons, to the said company hereby incorporated: and every such other incorporation, or persons incorporated by, or acting under the laws of this State, is, and are hereby authorized to make such an agreement, contract or transfer, by and through the agency of the person authorized by their respective acts of incorporation, to exercise their corporate powers, or by such persons as by any law of this State, are intrusted with the management and direction of said turnpike, road or bridge, or any of the rights and privileges aforesaid; and any contract, agreement or transfer, made in pursuance of the power and authority hereby granted, when executed by the several parties under their respective corporate seals, or otherwise legally authenticated, shall vest in the company hereby incorporated, all such road, part of road, rights and privileges, and the right to use and enjoy the same as fully to all intents and purposes as they now are or might be used and exercised by the corporation or persons in whom they are now vested.

Sec. 17. That the president and directors shall have power to purchase, with the funds of the company, and place on any rail-road constructed by them under this act, all machines, wagons, vehicles or carriages of any description whatsoever, which they may deem necessary or proper for the purposes of transportation on said road; and that they shall have power to charge for tolls, and the transportation of persons, goods, produce, merchandize or property of any kind whatsoever, transported by them along said rail way, any sum not exceeding the following rates on all goods, merchandize, or property of any description whatsoever transported by them, a sum not exceeding one and one half cents per mile for toll, and five cents on a ton per mile for transportation on all goods, produce, merchandize or property of any description whatsoever transported by them or their agents; and for the transportation of passengers, not exceeding three cents per mile for each passenger; and the said road, with all their works, improvements and profits, and all machinery on said road for transportation, are hereby vested in said company, incorporated by this act, and their successors forever, and the shares of the capital stock of said company shall be deemed and considered personal property, transferable by assignment, agreeable to the by-laws of said company.

Sec. 18. That any other rail road company may join and connect any rail road with the road hereby contemplated, and run cars upon the same under the rules and regulations of the president and directors of the Perrysburg and Akron Rail road Company, as to the construction and speed of said cars, and that full right and privilege is hereby reserved to the State or the citizens, or any company incorporated under the authority of the State to cross the rail road hereby incorporated: *Provided*, That in so crossing, no injury shall be done to the works of the company hereby incorporated.

Sec. 19. That the said president and directors shall, semi-annually, declare and make such dividend as they may deem proper, of the nett profits arising from the resources of said company, deducting the necessary current and probable contingent expenses, and that they shall divide the sum amongst the stockholders of said company in proportion to their respective shares.

Sec. 20. That if any person or persons shall wilfully, by any means whatsoever, injure, impair or destroy any part of said rail road, constructed by said company, under this act, or any of the works, buildings or machinery of said company, such person or persons, so offending, shall, each of them, for every such offence, forfeit and pay to the said company, any sum not exceeding three fold the damages, which may be recovered in the name of the company, by an action of debt in the court of common pleas for the county wherein the offence shall be committed, and shall also be subject to an indictment in said court, and upon conviction of such offence, shall be punished by fine and imprisonment, at the discretion of the court.

Sec. 21. If the Legislature of this State at any time after the expiration of thirty-five years from the passage of this act make provision by law for the repayment to said company of the amount expended by them in the construction of the said rail road, and of the value of the necessary permanent fixtures thereto at the time, with an advance of fifteen per cent. thereon, then said road and fixtures shall vest in, and become the property of the State of Ohio.

Sec. 22. Whenever the dividends of said company shall exceed the rate of six per cent. per annum, the Legislature of this State may impose such reasonable taxes on the amount of such dividends, as may be received from other rail road companies.

Sec. 23. That if said rail road shall not be commenced in three years from the passage of this act, and shall not be finished within fifteen years from the time of the commencement thereof, then this act to be null and void.

Sec. 24. That this act is hereby declared to be a public act, and shall be so construed in all courts of justice and elsewhere.

WILLIAM MEDILL,
Speaker pro tem. of the House of Representatives.
ELIJAH VANCE,
Speaker of the Senate.

March 9, 1836.

AN ACT

To incorporate the New Haven and Monroeville Rail-road Company.

Sec. 1. *Be it enacted by the General Assembly of the State of Ohio,* That Abijah Ives, C. S. Elderkin, Elisha Steward, Isaac Mills, James Hollister, Martin Smith, John G. Camp, Samuel Spencer, James Hanmon, John M. Latimer, George Hollister, and Isaac A. Mills, together with such other persons as may thereafter become associated with them, in the manner hereinafter prescribed, their successors and assigns, be, and they are hereby created a body corporate, by the name of "The New Haven and Monroeville Rail-road Company;" and by that name shall be and are hereby made capable in law to purchase, hold, and enjoy, and retain to them and their successors, all such lands, tenements, and hereditaments, with their appurtenances, as shall be necessary or in any wise convenient for the transaction of their business, and such as may in good faith be conveyed to them, by way of security or payment of debts, and the same to sell, grant, rent, or in any wise dispose of; to contract and be contracted with, sue and be sued, implead and be impleaded, answer and be answered, defend and be defended; and also to make, have and use a common seal, and the same to alter, break or renew at pleasure; and they shall be, and are hereby vested with all the powers and privileges which are by law incident to corporations of a similar nature, and which are necessary to carry into effect the objects of this association; and if either of the persons named in this section shall die, refuse or neglect to exercise the powers and discharge the duties hereby created, it shall be the duty of the remaining persons hereinbefore named, or a majority of them, to appoint some suitable person or persons to fill such vacancy or vacancies, so often as the same may occur.

Sec. 2. That the said corporation are hereby empowered to cause such examinations and surveys to be made, between the southern termination of [the] Sandusky and Monroeville rail-road, and at a point within the village plat of New Haven, in the county of Huron, as shall be necessary to ascertain the most advantageous route whereon to construct a rail-road; and shall cause such an estimate to be made of the probable cost thereof, for each mile separately; and the said corporation shall be, and they are hereby invested with the right to construct a rail-road, with one or more rail-ways or tracks, from the village of New Haven, aforesaid, to intersect the southern termination of the Sandusky city and Monroeville rail-road.

Sec. 3. That the capital stock of said corporation shall be seventy-five thousand dollars, and shall be divided into shares of fifty dollars each.

Sec. 4. That the above named persons, or a majority of them, or the survivors of them, are authorized to open books, for receiving subscriptions to the capital stock of such company, and shall prescribe the form of such subscription; which books shall be opened within one year from the passing of this act, at such place or places as they may deem expedient, giving twenty days notice in some newspaper printed in the county of Huron, and in such other place or places as may be thought advisable, of the time and place, or times and places, of opening said books; and said books shall be kept open at least ten days.

Sec. 5. That so soon as said stock, or one hundred shares thereof, shall have been subscribed, the above named persons, or the same number thereof as shall have given the notice above required, shall give like notice for a meeting of the stockholders to choose directors, at some time at least thirty days thereafter, and at some place within the said county of Huron; and if, at such time and place, the holders of one half or more of said stock subscribed, shall attend, either in person or by lawful proxy, they shall proceed to choose from the stockholders, by ballot, nine directors, each share of capital stock entitling the owner to one vote; and at such election, the persons named in the first section of this act, or those appointed by its provisions to fill vacancies which may have occurred, or any three of them, if no more be present, shall be inspectors of such election, and shall certify in writing signed by them, or a majority of them, what persons are elected directors; and if two or more have an equal number of votes, such inspectors shall determine, by lot, which of them shall be director or directors, to complete the number required, and shall certify the same in like manner; and said inspectors shall appoint the time and place of holding the first meeting of directors, at which meeting a majority shall form a board competent to transact all business of the company; and thereafter a new election of directors shall be made annually, at such time and place as the stockholders, at their first meeting shall appoint; and if the stockholders shall, at their first meeting, fail to appoint the day of such election, then it shall be holden in the succeeding year, on the same day of the same month on which said first election was holden, unless the same should be on the first day of the week, in which case it shall be holden on the day next succeeding; and if no election be made on the day appointed, said company shall not be dissolved, but such election may be had at any time appointed by the by-laws of said company; and directors choosen at any election, shall remain directors until others are choosen; and directors, at any election shall, as soon thereafter as may be, choose, of their own number, one person to be president, and another to be treasurer of such company, and another to be secretary of said company, and from time to time may choose such other officers, as by their by-laws they may designate as necessary: *Provided,* No person shall be a director of such company, who is not a citizen of the State of Ohio.

Sec. 6. That upon every subscription, there shall be paid at the time of subscribing, to the persons named in the first section of this act, or their agents, the sum of five dollars on every share subscribed; and the residue shall be paid in such instalments, and at such times and places, after the commencement of the work, as may be required by the president and directors of said company: *Provided,* That notice of such demand shall have been given in one or more newspapers published in said county; and if any stockholder shall fail or neglect to pay any instalment, or part of said subscription thus demanded, for the space of sixty days after the same shall be due and payable, the president and directors of said company may sell at public vendue, so many shares of such delinquent stockholder, as may be necessary to pay said instalment, and all necessary expenses incurred in making said sale; and may transfer the shares so sold, to the purchaser; and shall pay the overplus, if any, to such delinquent stockholder.

Sec. 7. That the directors of said company shall have power to make, from time to time, all needful rules, regulations and by-laws, touching the business of said company, and to determine the number of tracks or rail-ways upon said road, and the width thereof, not exceeding one hundred feet wide; and the description of carriages which may be used thereon; to regulate the time and manner in which passengers and goods shall be transported thereon, and the manner of collecting tolls for such transportation; and to fix penalties for the breach of any such rule, regulation or by-law, and to direct the mode and condition of transferring the stock of said company; and penalties provided for by said by-laws, may be sued for by any person or persons authorized thereto, in the name of said company, and recovered in an action of debt, before any court having jurisdiction to that amount; and said company may erect and maintain toll houses, and such other buildings and fixtures, for the accommodation of those using said road, and of themselves, as they may deem in any way necessary for their interest or convenience.

Sec. 8. That said company shall have a right to enter upon any lands, to survey and lay down said road, not exceeding one hundred feet in width, and to take any materials necessary for the construction of said road; and whenever any lands or materials shall be taken for the construction of said road, and the same shall not be given or granted to said company, and the owners thereof do not agree with said company, as to the compensation to be paid therefor, the person or persons claiming compensation as aforesaid, or if the owner or owners thereof are minors, insane persons, or married women, then the guardian or guardians of such minor or minors and insane persons, and the husbands of such married women, may select for themselves an arbitrator, and the said company shall select one arbitrator, and the two thus selected, shall take to themselves a third, who shall be sworn and paid, as arbitrators in other cases; and the three, or a majority of them, shall award as arbitrators between the parties, and render copies of their award to each of the parties, in writing, from which award either party may appeal to the court of common pleas for the county in which such lands or materials may have been situated; and in all cases where compensation shall, in any manner, be claimed, for lands, it shall be the duty of the arbitrators and the court, to estimate any advantage which the location and construction of said road may be to the claimant for such compensation, and the value of such advantage, if any, shall be set off against the compensation so claimed of said company; and appeals in such cases shall, when taken, [be] in all respects proceeded in as appeals in other cases to said court, and be brought into said court, by filing the award with the clerk of said court, whose duty it shall be to enter the same on the docket of said court, setting down the claimant, or claimants, as plaintiffs, and said company as defendants; and when the valuation, so ascertained, shall be paid, or tendered, by said company, said company shall have the same right to retain, own, hold and possess said materials, use and occupation of said land, for the purposes of said road, as fully and absolutely, as if the same had been granted and conveyed to said company by-deed.

Sec. 9. That the said company may construct the said road, across or upon any lands, public road, highway, stream of water or water course, if the same shall be necessary; but the said company shall restore such lands, road, highway, stream of water or water course, to its former state, or in a manner so as not to impair the usefulness of such lands, road, highway, [stream of] water or water course, to the owner or the public, without unnecessary delay.

Sec. 10. That any rail-way company, now, or yet to be chartered by law of this State, shall have power to join and unite with the road hereby incorporated, at any point which the directors of such company may think advisable, on such terms as the directors of such companies may respectively agree; and in case of disagreement, then upon such terms as the supreme court may in chancery determine.

Sec. 11. That said company may demand and receive for tolls upon, and the transportation of persons, goods, produce, merchandize or property of any description whatsoever, transported by them along said rail-way, any sum not exceeding the following rates: on all goods, merchandize or property of any description whatsoever, transported by them, a sum not exceeding two cents per mile, for toll; eight cents on a ton per mile, for transportation, on all goods, produce, merchandize or property of any description whatsoever, transported by them or their agents; and for passengers, one cent per mile, for toll, and four cents per mile, for transportation for each passenger.

Sec. 12. That all persons paying the toll aforesaid, may, with suitable and proper carriages, use and travel upon the said rail-road, always subject, however, to such rules and regulations, as said company are authorized to make, by the seventh section of this act.

Sec. 13. That full right and privilege is hereby reserved to the State, or citizens, or any company chartered by law of this State, to cross this road: *Provided,* That in so crossing, no injury shall be done to the works of the company hereby incorporated.

Sec. 14. That if proceedings be not had, under this act, within two years from the taking effect thereof, and if said road be not completed within five years thereafter, then the same to be void and of no effect.

Sec. 15. That so soon as the amount of tolls, accruing and received for the use of said road, or any part thereof, according to the provisions of this act, shall exceed five per cent. on the amount of capital stock paid in, after deducting therefrom the expenses and liabilities of said company, the directors of said company shall make a dividend of such nett profits, among the stockholders, in proportion to their respective shares; and no contingent or accumulating fund, exceeding one per centum of the profits of said company, shall remain undivided more than six months.

Sec. 16. That if any person or persons shall wilfully obstruct, or in any way spoil, injure or destroy said road, or either of its branches, or any thing belonging or incident thereto, or any materials to be used in the construction thereof, or any buildings, fixtures, or carriages, erected or constructed for the use or convenience thereof, such person or persons shall each be liable for every such offence to treble damages sustained thereby, to be recovered by action of debt, in any court having competent jurisdiction of that amount.

Sec. 17. That the State shall have power, at any time after the expiration of thirty-five years from and after the passage of this act, to purchase and hold the same for the use of the State, at a price not exceeding the original cost for the construction of said rail-road, and the necessary permanent fixtures, at the time of purchase, and fifteen per centum thereon; of which cost an accurate account shall be kept and submitted to the General Assembly, duly attested by the oath of the officers of said company, whenever the General Assembly shall require the same; and the right to alter or amend this act, when the Legislature shall deem the same expedient and proper, is hereby reserved to the State.

Sec. 18. Whenever the dividends of the said company shall exceed the rate of six per cent. per annum, the Legislature of this State may impose such reasonable tax on the amount of such dividends as may be received from other rail-road companies.

Sec. 19. This act is hereby declared to be a public act, and shall be so construed in all courts of justice, and elsewhere.

WILLIAM MEDILL,
Speaker pro tem. of the House of Representatives.
ELIJAH VANCE,
Speaker of the Senate.

March 9, 1836.

AN ACT

To incorporate the Aberdeen and Redoak Turnpike Company.

Sec. 1. *Be it enacted by the General Assembly of the State of Ohio,* That John M'Clure, of Aberdeen; William Riggs, William M'Dowell, Elie

46—L

Davidson, John Cochran, Francis Cobourn, Jacob Shepherd, Calvin Shaw, Samuel K. Stivers, Robert B. Tomb, and William Smith, of Brown county, as commissioners, and their associates, stockholders, as hereinafter provided, their successors and assigns, be, and they are hereby created and declared a body politic and corporate, perpetual, by the name and style of the Aberdeen and Redoak Ohio Turnpike Company; to construct and keep in repair a turnpike road, toll gates, and gate keepers' houses, commencing at a suitable point of junction with the Ripley and Hillsborough turnpike company, at or near the Redoak Meeting House, in Brown county, the most eligible route from Redoak Meeting House to Aberdeen, in said county of Brown; and by such corporate name and style, said company is hereby made and declared capable in law and equity to contract, sue and be sued, plead and be impleaded, defend and be defended in all manner of actions, and in all courts of law and equity, and make by-laws, not contrary to the constitution and laws of the United States or of this State; and to have and use a common seal, which they may break or renew at pleasure; and acquire, have, hold, sell, transfer and convey property, real and personal, for their corporate use and purposes, but for no other use or purpose whatever.

Sec. 2. That the capital stock of the company, hereby incorporated, shall consist of one hundred thousand dollars, in shares of fifty dollars each, and may be subscribed and held by individuals, companies or corporations, and shall be appropriated and applied to the uses and purposes, in the first section of this act set forth, and to no other use or purpose; and any person desiring to discharge his subscription to the capital of said company, in labor or materials, on or for said road, shall so specify, at the time of subscribing; in which case, the labor to be performed by such subscriber, shall be assigned, and the value of the same estimated by the principal engineer, superintending the construction of the road; or if materials be subscribed, the value thereof shall be estimated by such principal engineer: *Provided,* That in all cases of subscription to the capital stock of said company, five dollars, in cash, shall be paid to the person or persons, under whose superintendence subscriptions may be received, on each share subscribed; and the residue of such capital stock, whether in cash, labor, or materials, shall be paid, discharged, performed and furnished, on the requisition of the directors, for the time being.

Sec. 3. The books for receiving subscriptions to the capital stock of said company, shall be opened on the tenth day of June next, at such places, and under the superintendence of such persons, as a majority of said commissioners, or a majority of such of them as may consent to act, may designate and appoint; it shall be the duty of said commissioners, or a majority of them, or a majority of such of them as consent to act, to give ten days' notice of the time, places, and persons, at which, and under whose superintendence, will be opened the books for receiving subscriptions to the capital stock of said company; which notice shall be published in some newspaper published, or in general circulation, in the county of Brown; and the books for receiving subscriptions as aforesaid, shall be kept open as long as said directors shall see fit, unless said sum of one hundred thousand dollars of said capital stock shall be sooner subscribed.

Sec. 4. That as soon as it shall be ascertained, that ten thousand dollars of the capital stock of said company has been subscribed, said commissioners, or a majority of them, or a majority of such of them as consent to act, shall give ten days notice, as provided in the third section of this act, of the time of holding an election, which shall be held at Redoak Meeting House aforesaid, for seven directors, to manage and conduct the business and affairs of said company; and on the day thus specified, at Redoak Meeting House aforesaid, the stockholders of said company shall proceed to the election, by ballot, of seven directors, stockholders, any five of whom shall constitute a quorum, for the transaction of the business and concerns of said company; the first election for directors, under this act, shall be conducted by two inspectors, who shall be appointed by a majority of such said commissioners, as may consent to act; and such inspectors shall act under oath; none but stockholders shall vote for, or be elected directors; and the stockholders shall be entitled to one vote, which may be given in person, or by proxy, for each share of stock by him, her, or them owned and held, on the day of election; the seven directors, having the highest number of votes, shall be declared duly elected; but if an election of seven directors shall not be effected, by reason of an equal number of votes being given, in favor of two or more stockholders; in that case, the inspectors of the election shall determine, by lot, amongst the eight or more stockholders, having the highest an equal number of votes, who shall be directors, to complete the number of seven: *Provided*, Such determination, by lot, shall not postpone as director, one stockholder having a higher, to another having a lower, number of votes; the directors first elected, under this act, shall hold their office for one year next after their election, and until their successors are elected and qualified; and after the first elections for directors, there shall be an election for directors of said company annually thereafter; annual elections for directors of said company shall be under the superintendence of the directors, for the time being; who shall designate a place, and shall give the like notice of the time of such annual election, as is required to be given by the commissioners, as aforesaid, of the time and place of holding the first election, under this act; and shall, in like manner, notify the persons elected, and designate a time and place for the persons elected directors, to meet and qualify; and the directors, annually elected, shall proceed, as required of the first directors.

Sec. 5. That within five days, after the first election of directors, under this act, the inspectors of the election shall give notice, in writing, to the seven stockholders, elected directors, of such their election; shall appoint a day, on which the directors so elected shall meet at Redoak Meeting House aforesaid, for organization; and on the day so appointed, which shall not be more than ten days from the day of election, or sooner, if the directors elected can agree, the directors so elected, shall meet at Redoak Meeting House, and severally take an oath faithfully and impartially, to discharge the several duties of director of the turnpike company, hereby incorporated; and being thus qualified, such directors shall appoint one of their body president of the board; they shall also appoint a treasurer, who shall not be a director, and they may require and take of the treasurer,

bond, in such sum, and with such security, as to them may appear reasonable and necessary, to secure said company; said directors shall also appoint a
secretary, who shall keep a full and fair journal of the corporate acts of said
company, and shall perform such other duties of secretary, as may be required of him by the directors.

Sec. 6. That the said company shall have a right to lay out, survey, and locate a turnpike road, as specified in the first section of this act,
through any improved or unimproved lands; and to take from the lands,
occupied by such road, when located as aforesaid, any stone, gravel, timber, or other materials, necessary to construct a good, secure, and substantial turnpike road, as contemplated by this act, and the necessary bridges
connected therewith; and if any difference should arise between the owner or owners of any ground, on which the said road may be located, or from
which such materials are taken, as aforesaid, and the agents of the company, respecting damage, it shall be determined, by three disinterested freeholders, to be appointed by the commissioners of the county, in which the
subject of difference lies; who, after being duly sworn, faithfully and impartially to perform the duties, required of them in this act, and taking into
consideration, whether the land be, really, rendered more or less valuable,
by the road passing through it, shall make out their assessment in writing,
of the damage, if any; a copy of which shall be given to the proprietor of
the land, and another copy to the agent of the company; and said agent
shall pay, or offer to pay, to the owner of said land, the amount of such assessed damages, before he shall enter upon and take any such ground or
materials, other than to survey the road; and all such assessment of damages, if any should be awarded, shall be paid by the company; but if no
damage shall be awarded, then the expense shall be paid by the person who
had claimed damages; and in case sufficient materials cannot be procured
on the land so as aforesaid acquired for said road and bridges, said company, or their agents, shall have a right to, and they are hereby authorized, to
enter upon any unimproved lands, adjoining or in the vicinity of said road,
and to dig, cut down, take, and carry away, so much stone, gravel, timber,
or other materials, (not previously cut down, taken, appropriated or prepared, by the owner for any particular use,) as may be necessary to enable
said company to construct said road and the necessary bridges, toll gates,
and gate keepers' houses; and in case of difference between the owner of
any lands, from which materials may be taken, as last aforesaid, such difference shall be determined, and compensation made by said company, in
manner provided by the sixth section of this act.

Sec. 7. That in addition to the land necessary for the construction,
use, and repair of said road, said company shall be entitled to, and authorized to acquire, in manner aforesaid, not exceeding one acre of land, at
each toll gate, for the erection thereon, and convenient occupation of a
gate keeper's house; and said company shall cause such turnpike road to be
opened, not exceeding eighty feet wide; at least fifteen feet of which
shall be made an artificial road, composed of stone, gravel, wood, or other
suitable materials, well compacted together, in such a manner as to secure a
good, firm, substantial and even road, rising in the middle, with a gradual
arch or curve, with sufficient drains on each side, to carry the water therefrom, and shall keep the same in good repair; and in no case shall the as-

cent in such road be of greater elevation, than four degrees with the horizon.

Sec. 8. That so soon as said company shall have completed such road, or the grading thereof, as aforesaid, or any part of such road, not less than five continuous miles, and so from time to time, as often as five continuous miles thereof shall be completed, or completely graded, an agent, to be appointed for that purpose by the commissioners of the proper county, if not otherwise appointed by or under the Legislature or its authority, shall, on application of said company, examine said road, or part thereof, as aforesaid, and report his opinion to the president of said company; and if such agent shall report said road, or any continuous five miles, thereof, to be completed or completely. graded, agreeable to the requisitions of this act, said company shall thereupon be entitled to erect a toll gate or gates, at' suitable distances on said road, and to demand and receive of those travelling or using the same, the tolls allowed by this act.

Sec. 9. That the following shall be the rates of toll demandable and receivable for each and every ten miles of said road, when completed, and in the same proportion for any greater or less distance, to wit: for every four wheeled carriage or wagon, drawn by one horse or ox, eighteen and three fourth cents; for every horse or ox in addition, six and one fourth cents; for every chaise, riding chair, cart, or gig, or other two wheeled carriage, of any kind, drawn by one horse or ox, twelve and a half cents; for every horse or ox in addition, six and one fourth cents; for every sled or sleigh, drawn by one horse or ox, twelve and a half cents; for every coach, chariot, or other four wheeled pleasure carriage, drawn by one horse, (driver included,) twenty-five cents; for every additional horse, six and one fourth cents; for every horse and rider, six and one fourth cents; for every horse, mule, or ass, led or driven, six months old and upwards, two cents; for every head of neat cattle, six months old and upwards, three fourths of a cent; for every head of sheep or hogs, one fourth of a cent; and for equal distances and like objects, said company shall be entitled to demand and receive one half of the foregoing amounts of tolls on said road when completely graded as aforesaid, but not fully completed, as a turnpike road.

Sec. 10. That if any person or persons using said road shall, with intent to defraud said company, or to evade the payment of tolls, pass through any private gate, or bars, or other ground, except around crossways, authorized by law, near to any turnpike gate of said road, every person guilty of, or concerned in such fraudulent practice, shall, for every such offence, be liable to pay to said company a sum not less than two dollars, nor more than ten dollars, to be recovered in an action of debt, with costs of suit, before any justice of the peace of the county in which such offence may be committed; and from such judgment of the justice of the peace, an appeal may be taken to the court of common pleas of the proper county, but no stay of execution shall be allowed.

Sec. 11. That if said company shall fail for ten days in succession, to keep said road in good repair, and complaint thereof be made to a justice of the peace of the county in which said road may be out of repair, it shall be his duty forthwith to summon three disinterested freeholders of the county to examine the same, and he shall give notice to the toll gatherer, at the nearest gate, of the time when such freeholders will proceed to examine said road; and such freeholder, after taking an oath or affirmation to act impartially, shall proceed to examine said road; and if such freeholders shall find said road out of repair, they shall certify their finding to the justice of the peace, who shall immediately transmit a copy of such certificate to the toll gatherer nearest the defective part of said [road]; and from the time of the toll gatherer's receiving such notice, no tolls shall be demanded or received for such part of the road, until the same shall be put in complete repair, under the penalty of five dollars for each offence, to be recovered of said company, with costs, on the complaint and for the use of the party aggrieved.

Sec. 12.   That if any person shall, wilfully or wantonly, destroy or [in] any manner injure or obstruct any part of said road, or any gate thereon, otherwise than in the just or lawful use thereof, every such person shall be liable to pay said company for every such offence a sum not less than five dollars, nor more than fifty dollars, to be recovered with costs before any justice of the peace of the county in which such offence may have been committed; from which judgment an appeal may be taken to the court of common pleas, but no stay of execution shall be allowed.

Sec. 13.   The said company shall put up a post or stone at the end of each mile, with the number of miles from Aberdeen fairly cut or painted thereon; and also in a conspicuous place near each toll gate shall be placed a board, with the rates of toll fairly painted thereon, with directions to keep to the right.

Sec. 14.   That if any person shall wilfully deface or destroy any guide board, mile post or stone, or painted list or rate of tolls, erected on said road, he shall, on conviction thereof, before a justice of the peace of the proper county, forfeit and pay a sum, not less than five dollars, nor more than ten dollars, with costs of suit, in an action of debt, at the suit of said company; and from the judgment of the justice of the peace in such case, an appeal may be taken to the court of common pleas, but no stay of execution shall be allowed.

Sec. 15.   That if any toll gatherer on said road shall unreasonably detain any person after payment or tender of the proper amount of toll, or shall demand or receive a greater amount of toll than by this act is authorized, he shall, for any such offence, forfeit and pay a sum not exceeding twenty dollars, to be recovered with costs of suit, before any justice of the peace of the proper county, in an action of debt, at the suit of the party aggrieved; and from the judgment of the justice in such case, an appeal may be taken to the court of common pleas, but no stay of execution shall be allowed: *Provided,* That no action under this section shall be commenced after the expiration of twenty days from the accruing thereof.

Sec. 16.   That there shall be kept a fair account of the whole expense of making said road; and the State shall have the right, after the expiration of thirty-five years from the passage of this act, to purchase the same for the use of the State, paying said company the cost of making said road, together with fifteen per cent. thereon; and the books of said company shall always be open to the inspection of the agent of the State, appointed for that purpose by the Legislature; and if the company shall neglect or refuse to exhibit their accounts agreeably to this section, when thereunto required, then all the rights and privileges granted by this act shall cease.

Sec. 17. That if said company shall not, within three years from the passage of this act, proceed to carry on the work, according to the true intent and meaning of this act, then in that case it shall be lawful for the Legislature to resume all the rights and privileges hereby granted.

Sec. 18. That said company shall be, and they are hereby authorized and entitled, to demand and receive the like toll from persons conveying the United States mail, as from other persons; and in case of neglect or refusal on the part of any person or persons engaged in the transportation of the mail, to pay the tolls by this act authorized to be demanded and received, said company may proceed to collect the same by action of debt; but shall not obstruct or delay the passage of the mail.

WILLIAM MEDILL,
Speaker [pro tem.] of the House of Representatives.

ELIJAH VANCE,
Speaker of the Senate.

March 9, 1836.

To incorporate the Melmore and Republic Rail Road Company.

Sec. 1. *Be it enacted by the General Assembly of the State of Ohio,* That Buckley Hutchins, Philip J. Price, Case Brown, Micajah Heaton, Seldin Graves, Thomas J. Baker, William Patterson, Isaac J. Halsey, William Cornell, Timothy P. Roberts, Samuel Waggoner, Calvin Bradley, and Hamilton McCollester, of the county of Seneca, be, and they are hereby appointed commissioners, under the direction of a majority of whom, subscriptions may be received to the capital stock of the Melmore and Republic Rail road Company, hereby incorporated; and they, or a majority of them, may cause books to be opened at such times and places as they may direct, and for the purpose of receiving subscriptions to the capital stock of said company, after giving such notice of the time and place of opening the same, by publication in a newspaper printed nearest the place of opening the books for at least thirty days; and that, upon the first opening of said books, they shall be kept open for at least five days in succession, from ten o'clock, A. M. until two o'clock P, M.; and if, at the expiration of that period, such a subscription to the capital stock of said company, as is necessary to its incorporation, shall not have been obtained, then said commissioners, or a majority of them, may cause said books, by giving notice as aforesaid, to be opened from time to time, after the expiration of said ten days, for the space of three years thereafter: and if any of said commissioners shall die, resign, or refuse to act, during the continuance of the duties devolved upon them by this act, another or others may be appointed in his or their stead, by the remaining commissioners, or a majority of them.

Sec. 2. That the capital stock of the Melmore and Republic Rail road Company, shall be fifty thousand dollars, and shall be divided into shares of fifty dollars each; which shares may be subscribed for by individuals only; and it shall and may be lawful for said corporation, to commence the construction of the said Rail road or way, and enjoy all the powers and privileges conferred by this act, as soon as the sum of five thousand dollars shall be subscribed to said stock.

Sec. 3. That all persons who shall become stockholders pursuant to this act, shall be, and they are hereby created a body corporate, and shall be and remain a corporation forever, under the name of the Melmore and Republic Rail road Company; and by that name shall be capable in law of purchasing, holding, selling, leasing, and conveying estates, real, personal and mixed, so far as the same shall be necessary for the purposes hereinafter mentioned, and no further; and shall have; perpetual succession; and by said corporate name may contract and be contracted with, sue and be sued, and may have and use a common seal, which they shall have power to alter or renew at their pleasure; and shall have, enjoy, and may exercise, all the powers, rights and privileges, which corporate bodies may lawfully do, for the purposes mentioned in this act.

Sec. 4. That upon all subscriptions, there shall be paid at the time of subscribing to the said commissioners or their agents, appointed to receive such subscriptions, the sum of five dollars on every share subscribed; and the residue thereof shall be paid in such instalments, and at such times, as may be required by the president and directors of said company: *Provided*, No payment other than the' first shall be demanded, until at least thirty days public notice of such demand shall have been given by said president and directors in some newspaper of general circulation in the State of Ohio: and if any stockholder shall fail or neglect to pay any instalment or part of said subscription thus demanded, for the space of sixty days next after the time the same shall be due and payable, the said president and directors, upon giving at least thirty days previous notice thereof, in manner aforesaid, may, and they are hereby authorized to sell at public vendue, so many of the shares of the said delinquent stockholder or stockholders, as shall be necessary to pay such instalment, and the expenses of advertising and sale, and transfer the shares so sold to the purchaser or purchasers; and the residue of the money arising from such sale, after paying such instalment and expense, shall be paid to said stockholders on demand.

Sec. 5. That at the expiration of ten days for which the books are first opened, if one hundred shares of said capital stock shall have been subscribed, or if not, as soon thereafter as the same shall be subscribed, if within three years after the first opening of the books, the said commissioners, or a majority of them, shall call a general meeting of the stockholders, at such places as they may appoint, and shall give at least sixty days previous notice thereof; and at such meeting, the said commissioners shall lay the subscription books before the stockholders then and there present; and thereupon the said stockholders, or a majority of them, shall elect twelve directors, by ballot, a majority of whom shall be competent to manage the affairs of said company: they shall have the power of electing a president of said company, from among the directors, and of allowing him such compensation as they may deem proper; and in said election, and on all other occasions wherein a vote of the stockholders of said company shall be taken, each stockholder shall be allowed one vote for every share owned by it, him, or her; and every stockholder may depute any other person to vote, and act for it, him, or her, as its, his or their, proxy; and the commissioners aforesaid, or any three of them, shall be judges of the first election of said directors.

Sec. 6. That to continue the succession of the president and directors of said company, thirteen directors shall be chosen annually on the third Monday of October in every year, in the town of Melmore, or at such other place as a majority of the directors shall appoint; and if any vacancy shall occur by death, resignation or otherwise, of any president or director, before the year for which he was elected, had expired, a person to fill such vacant place for the residue of the year may be appointed by the president and directors of said company or a majority of them; and that the president and directors of said company shall hold and exercise their offices until a new election of president and directors; and that all elections which are by this act, or the by-laws of the company, to be made, on a particular day or at a particular time, if not made on such day or time, may be made at any time within thirty days thereafter.

Sec. 7. That a general meeting of the stockholders shall be held annually at the time and place appointed for the election of president and directors of said company; that meetings may be called at any time during the interval between the said annual meetings, by the president and directors, or a majority of them, or by the stockholders owning at least one fourth of the stock subscribed, upon giving at least thirty days public notice of the time and place of holding the same; and when any such meetings are called by the stockholders, such notice shall specify the particular object of the call; and if at any such called meeting, a majority in value of the stockholders of said company are not present, in person or by proxy, such meeting shall be adjourned from day to day without transacting any business, for any time not exceeding three days; and if, within three days, stockholders holding a majority in value of the stock subscribed, do not thus attend, such meeting shall be dissolved.

Sec. 8. That at the regular annual meetings of the stockholders of said company, it shall be the duty of the president and directors in office for the previous year, to exhibit a clear and distinct statement of the affairs of the company; that at any called meeting of the stockholders, a majority of those present, in person or by proxy, may require similar statements from the president and directors, whose duty it shall be to furnish them when thus required; and that at all general meetings of the stockholders, a majority in value of all the stockholders of said company, may remove from office any president or any of the directors of said company, and may appoint officers in their stead.

Sec. 9. That any president and director of said company, before he acts as such, shall take an oath or affirmation that he will well and truly discharge the duties of his said office to the best of his skill and judgment.

Sec. 10. That the said president and directors, or a majority of them,

47—L

may appoint all such officers, engineers, agents or servants whatsoever, as they may deem necessary for the transaction of the business of the company, and may remove any of them at their pleasure: that they, or a majority of them, shall have power to determine by contract the compensation of all engineers, officers, agents or servants, in the employ of said company, and to determine by their by-laws the manner of adjusting and settling all accounts against the said company, and, also, the manner and evidence of transfers of stock in said company: and they, or a majority of them, shall have power to pass all by-laws which they may deem necessary or proper for exercising all the powers vested in the company hereby incorporated, and for carrying the objects of this act into effect: *Provided*, Such by-laws shall not be contrary to the laws of this State or of the United States.

Sec. 11. That the said corporation shall be, and they are hereby vested, with the right to construct a double or single Rail road or way, from the town of Melmore, in Seneca county, to connect with the Mad River and Lake Erie Rail road, to the town of Republic, in said county; to transport, take, and carry property and persons upon the same, by the power and force of steam, of animals, or of any mechanical or other power, or of any combination of them, which the said corporation may choose to employ: *Provided*, That any future Legislature shall have power to alter the point of commencement or termination of said road so as to commence at or near Melmore, and terminate at or near Republic, in said county of Seneca.

Sec. 12. That the president and directors of said company shall be, and are hereby invested with all rights and powers necessary for the location, construction and repairs of said road not exceeding one hundred feet wide, with as many sets of tracks as said president and directors may deem necessary, and that they may cause to made; contract with others for making said rail road, or any part of it: and they or their agents, or those with whom they may contract for making any part of the same, may enter upon and use, and excavate any land which may be wanted for the site of said road, or for any other purpose necessary and useful in the construction or in the repair of said road or its works; and that they may build bridges, may fix scales and weights, may lay rails, may take and use any earth, timber, gravel, stone or other materials which may be wanted for the construction or repair of any part of said road or any of its works; and may make and construct all works whatsoever, which may be necessary in the construction or repair of said road.

Sec. 13. That the president and directors of said company, or a majority of them, or any persons authorized by them, or a majority of them, may agree with the owner or owners of any lands, earth, timber, gravel, or stone or other materials, or any improvements which may be wanted, for the construction or repair of said road, or any of their works, for the purchase, use, or occupation of the same: and if they cannot agree, or if the owner or owners, or any of them, be a married woman, under age, insane person, or out of the county in which the property wanted may lie, when such lands and materials may be wanted, application may be made to any justice of the peace of said county, who shall thereupon issue his warrant, under his hand and seal, directed to the sheriff of said county, or to some disinterested person, if the sheriff shall be interested, requiring him to summon a jury of twelve men, inhabitants of said county, not related, or in any wise interested, to meet on the land or near to the other property or materials to be valued, on a day named in said warrant, not less than ten nor more than twenty days after the issuing of the same: and if, at the said time and place, any of said persons summoned do not attend, the said sheriff, or summoner, shall immediately summon as many persons as may be necessary, with the persons in attendance, to furnish a pannel of twelve jurors in attendance, and from them, each party, or its, his, her, or their agent, the sheriff or summoner, for him, her, it, or them, may strike off three jurors, and the remaining six shall act as a jury of inquest of damages; and before they act as such, the said summoner or sheriff, shall administer to each of them, an oath or affirmation, that they will faithfully and impartially value the damages which the owner or owners will sustain, by use or occupation of the same, required by said company: and the jury estimating the damages, if for the ground occupied by said road, shall take into the estimate the benefits resulting to said owner or owners, by reason of said road passing through or upon the land of such owner or owners, towards the extinguishment of such claim for damages; and the said jury shall reduce their valuation to writing, and shall sign and seal the same; and it shall then be returned to the clerk of the court of common pleas for said county, and by such clerk filed in his office; and shall be confirmed by the said court at its next session, if no sufficient cause to the contrary be shown; and when confirmed, shall be recorded by said clerk, at the expense of said company: but if set aside, the court may direct another inquisition to be taken in the manner above prescribed; and such inquisition shall describe the property taken, or the bounds of the land condemned; and such valuation when paid, or tendered to the owner or owners of said property, or his, her, or their legal representatives, shall entitle said company to the estate and interest in said materials, and the use and occupation of said lands for the purposes of said road thus valued, as fully as if it had been conveyed by the owner or owners of the same; and the valuation, if not received when tendered, may at any time thereafter be received from the company without cost, by the owner or owners, his, her, or their legal representative or representatives: and that such sheriff or summoner, and jurors, shall be entitled to [demand,] and receive from the said company the same fees, as are allowed for like services in cases of fixing the valuation of real estate previous to the sale under execution.

Sec. 14. That whenever, in the construction of said road, it shall be necessary to intersect or unite with any established road or high way, it shall be the duty of the said president and directors of said company, so to construct the said Rail road across such established road or way, as not to impede the passage or transportation of persons or property along the same; or when it shall be necessary to pass through the land of any individual, it shall also be their duty to provide for such individual, proper wagon ways across said road, from one part of his land to another without delay.

Sec. 15. That if it shall be necessary for such company, in the selection of the route, or construction of the road to be by them laid out and constructed, or any part of it, to connect the same with, or to use any turnpike road or bridge, made or erected by any company or persons incorporated, or authorized by any law of this State; it shall be lawful for the said president and directors, and they are hereby authorized, to contract or agree with any such other corporation or persons, for the right to use such road or bridge, or for the transfer of any of the corporate or other rights or privileges of such corporation or persons, to the said company hereby incorporated: and every such other corporation, or persons incorporated by, or acting under the laws of this State, is, and are hereby authorized to make such an agreement, contract or transfer, by and through the agency of the person authorized by their respective acts of incorporation, to exercise their corporate powers, or by such persons as by any law of this State, are intrusted with the management and direction of said turnpike, road or bridge, or any of the rights and privileges aforesaid; and any contract, agreement or transfer, made in pursuance of the power and authority hereby granted, when executed by the several parties under their respective corporate seals, or otherwise legally authenticated, shall vest in the company hereby incorporated, all such road, part of road, rights and privileges, and the right to use and enjoy the same, as fully to all intents and purposes as they now are or might be used and exercised by the said corporation or persons in whom they are now vested.

Sec. 16. That the said president and directors shall have power to purchase, with the funds of the company, and place on any Rail road constructed by them under this act, all machines, wagons, vehicles or carriages of any description whatsoever, which they may deem necessary or proper for the purpose of transportation on said road; and that they shall have power to demand and receive for tolls upon, and transportation of goods, produce, merchandize or property of any kind whatsoever, transported by them along said Rail way, any sum not exceeding the following rates: on all goods, merchandize, or property of any description, transported by them or their agents a sum not exceeding one and a half cents per ton per mile for toll, five cents per ton per mile for transportation, and for the transportation of passengers, not exceeding three cents per mile for each passenger; and any company, person or persons, paying the tolls aforesaid, may with suitable and proper cars, transport persons or property on said road, subject to the rules and regulations of this company as to the construction and speed of said cars.

Sec. 17. That the president and directors shall, annually or semi-annually, declare and make such dividend as they may deem proper, of the nett profits arising from the resources of said company, deducting the necessary current and probable contingent expenses, and that they shall divide the same amongst the stockholders of said company in proportion to their respective shares.

Sec. 18. That any other rail-road company, now or hereafter to be chartered by law of this State, may join and connect any rail-road with the road hereby contemplated, and run cars upon the same, subject to the rules and regulations of this company as to the construction and speed of said cars; and full right and privilege is hereby reserved to the State, or individuals, or company incorporated by law of this State, to cross this road: *Provided,* That in so crossing no injury shall be done to the works of the company hereby incorporated.

Sec. 19. That the State shall have power at any time after the expiration of thirty-five years from the passage of this act, to purchase and hold said road for the use of the State, at a price not exceeding the original cost for the construction of the road and necessary permanent fixtures, at the time of purchase, and fifteen per cent. thereon; of which cost an accurate statement in writing shall be submitted to the the General Assembly, duly attested by the oath of the officers of said company, if the General Assembly shall require it.

Sec. 20. That if any person or persons shall wilfully, by any means whatsoever, injure, impair or destroy any part of said Rail road, constructed by said company, under this act, or any of the works, buildings or machinery of said company, such person or persons, so offending, shall, each of them, for every such offence, forfeit and pay to the said company, any sum not exceeding three fold the damages, which may be recovered in the name of the company, by an action of debt in the court of common pleas for the county wherein the offence shall be committed, and shall also be subject to an indictment in said court; and upon conviction of such offence, shall be punished by fine and imprisonment, at the discretion of the court.

Sec. 21. That if said Rail road shall not be commenced in three years from the passage of this act, and shall not be finished within ten years from the time of the commencement thereof, then this act shall be null and void.

Sec. 22. Whenever the dividends of said company shall exceed six per cent. per annum, the Legislature of this State may impose such reasonable tax on the amount of such dividends as may be received from other rail road companies.

Sec. 23. That this act is hereby declared to be a public act, and shall be so construed in all courts of justice and elsewhere.

WILLIAM MEDILL,
Speaker pro tem. of the House of Representatives.
ELIJAH VANCE,
Speaker of the Senate.

March 10, 1836.

AN ACT

To extend the time of making payment for certain school lands, in the county of Richland.

Sec. 1. *Be it enacted by the General Assembly of the State of Ohio,* That if any purchaser of school lands, in the Virginia Military District, and of the sections number sixteen, granted by Congress for the use of schools, in the county of Richland, or the assigns or legal representatives of such purchaser, shall pay to the proper officer, on or before the first day of June next ensuing the passage of this act, the full amount of interest which may then be due on any deferred payments for said lands, and shall also semi-annually thereafter pay the interest which may accrue on all payments which then or afterwards may become due therefor, then the times for making payment for such lands shall be extended to such purchasers, or the assigns or legal representatives of such purchasers, for the term of three years, in addition to the time by law allowed such purchasers, at the time of making the respective purchases.

WILLIAM MEDILL,
Speaker pro tem. of the House of Representatives.

ELIJAH VANCE,
Speaker of the Senate.

March 10, 1836.

AN ACT

For the relief of Robert Haines.

Whereas, Robert Haines, an associate judge of the county of Clermont, was appointed administrator of the estate of Thomas Speakman, deceased: *And whereas*, by a law of the State, an associate judge is disqualified to act as administrator, and consequently cannot settle with the court: Therefore,

Sec. 1. *Be it enacted by the General Assembly of the State of Ohio,* That Robert Haines, administrator of the estate of Thomas Speakman, deceased, be, and he is hereby authorized to settle the accounts of said deceased, in the same manner as he might have done had no legal disability existed.

WILLIAM MEDILL,
Speaker pro tem. of the House of Representatives.

ELIJAH VANCE,
Speaker of the Senate.

March 10, 1836.

AN ACT

To authorize the recorder and auditor of the county of Licking, to transcribe certain records in their respective offices, in said county.

Sec. 1. *Be it enacted by the General Assembly of the State of Ohio,* That the recorder of the county of Licking, be, and he is hereby authorized to transcribe books A, B, and C, now in his office, being part of the land records of said county, and such transcripts and certified copies thereof, as shall be received in all courts of justice in this State, and elsewhere, as *prima facie* evidence of the original records; and such original records shall be carefully preserved in the recorder's office in the county aforesaid.

Sec. 2. That the auditor of the county of Licking, be, and he is hereby authorized to transcribe so much of the records of said county, as was formerly kept by the clerk of the county commissioners from the year one thousand eight hundred and eight, up to the year one thousand eight hundred and twenty-one, and now constituting a part of the records in the office of the auditor of said county; and such transcripts and certified copies thereof shall be received in all courts of justice ·in this State, and elsewhere, as *prima facie* evidence of the original records; and such original records shall be carefully preserved in the office of the auditor of said county.

Sec. 3. That said recorder and auditor, for the performance of their duties required by this act, shall be entitled to receive such fees as they now are entitled to, by law, for similar services; which shall be allowed by the county commissioners, and paid out of the county treasury, on the order of the county auditor.

WILLIAM MEDILL,
Speaker pro tem. of the House of Representatives.

ELIJAH VANCE,
Speaker of the Senate.

March 10, 1836.

AN ACT

To incorporate the Canal Insurance Company.

Sec. 1. *Be it enacted by the General Assembly of the State of Ohio,* That there shall be, and hereby is established an insurance company, in the city of Cincinnati, with a capital stock of one hundred thousand dollars, to be divided into shares of twenty-five dollars each. and to be subscribed and paid for by individuals, companies, and corporations, in the manner hereinafter specified; which subscribers and stockholders, their successors and assigns shall be, and they are hereby created a body politic and corporate, by the name and style of the Canal Insurance Company, and shall so continue a body politic and corporate, with perpetual succession, and by that name shall be competent to contract and be contracted with, sue and be sued, plead and be impleaded, defend and be defended, in all courts and places, and in all matters whatsoever, with full powers to acquire, hold, possess, use, occupy, and enjoy, and the same to sell, convey and dispose of, all such real estate, goods, effects and chattles as shall be convenient for the transaction of its business, or which may be conveyed to said company as surety for any debts, or which may be received in discharge of any debt, or purchased in satisfaction of any judgment, or decree, in favor of said company, or in purchase of any property on which said company may have a lien; and said company may have and use a common seal, change, alter and renew the same at pleasure; and it may ordain and put in execution such by-laws, rules and regulations, as may be necessary for the good government of the company, and the prudent and efficient management of its affairs: *Provided,* They be not contrary to the constitution and laws of this State, or of the United States: *Provided, also,* That any future Legislature may alter, amend or repeal this act.

Sec. 2. That the corporation herein and hereby created, shall have full power and authority to insure all kinds of property against loss or damage, by fire, or any other cause or risk; to make all kinds of insurance upon life or lives; to make all kinds of insurance against loss or damage on goods or merchandize, in the course of transportation, whether on the land or on the water, on any vessels, or boats, wherever they may be; to lend money on bottomry, or respondentia; to cause themselves to be insured against any loss or risk they may incur in the course of their business.

Sec. 3. That it shall be lawful for said company to invest any part of their capital stock, moneys, funds, or other property, in any public stock, or funded debt, created, or to be created, by or under any law or laws of the United States, or of this or any other particular State, or in the stock of any chartered bank in this State, or of the United States, and the same to sell and transfer at pleasure, and again to invest the same, or any part thereof, in such stocks or funds whenever and so often as the exigencies of said corporation, or a due regard to the safety of its funds shall require, or they may loan the same, or any part thereof, to individuals, or public corporations, on real or personal security, at a rate of interest not exceeding six per cent. per annum, for such period of time, and under such restrictions and limitations as the directors, for the time being, may deem prudent and best for the interest of said company: *Provided*, That it shall not be lawful for said corporation to employ any part of their capital stock, money or other funds, in buying or selling goods, wares and merchandize, nor in the trade of exchange brokers, nor shall said company issue or emit any bills of credit as a circulating medium of trade or exchange, nor in any manner engage in the business or operations of banking, otherwise than in the purchase and sale of bank stock, as aforesaid, nor make any contracts in writing, except under the seal of said corporation, for the payment of money, other than such as may be contained in their policies of insurance.

Sec. 4. That all policies, or contracts of insurance, which may be entered into by the said corporation, shall be subscribed by the president, or president *pro tem.* or by such other officer as shall be designated for that purpose, by its by-laws, and attested by the secretary; and being so signed and attested, shall be binding and obligatory upon said corporation, without the seal thereof, according to the true intent and meaning of such policies or contracts; and all such policies or contracts may be so signed and attested, and the business of said corporation may be otherwise conducted and carried on, without the presence of the board of the directors, who, for that purpose shall divide themselves into committees of not less than two directors each, who shall attend at the office of said company, in weekly rotation, and who, with the president, shall have full power and authority to transact the current business of the corporation, subject always to the by-laws, ordinances, rules and regulations of the stockholders, and to the orders and instructions of the board directors: and the acts of such committee or committees shall be as binding and obligatory on said corporation as if done by the board of directors, to all lawful intents and purposes whatever; and the said directors shall, at any annual election, or other general meeting of the stockholders, lay before them a correct and particular statement of the condition and affairs of said company: *Provided*, That said directors, president, or any committee thereof, shall not be entitled to any pay, compensation, or emolument for their services, unless voted and allowed at some general and regular meeting of the stockholders.

Sec. 5. That the stock and affairs of said corporation shall be managed and conducted by eleven directors, who shall be stockholders of said company, and resident within this State; they shall, after the first election, be elected on the second Monday of June in each year, at such time and place, in the city of Cincinnati, as the board of directors shall appoint, and shall hold their offices for one year, and until others shall be chosen to supply their place, and no longer; and notice of such annual election shall be published for the space of three weeks, in two of the newspapers published in said city; and every such election shall be held under the inspection of three stockholders in said company, to be previously appointed by the directors for that purpose; and shall be made by ballot, by a plurality of votes of the stockholders present, allowing one vote for every share up to twenty shares; for every five shares over twenty shares and up to one hundred and twenty shares, one vote; and for every ten shares over one hundred and twenty shares, one vote; stockholders not personally attending may vote by proxy: *Provided*, Such proxy be a stockholder, and is granted directly to such person representing them at such election. In case it shall at any time happen that an election of directors shall not be made on any day, when, pursuant to this act, it ought to have been made, the said corporation shall not from that cause be deemed to be dissolved, but it shall and may be lawful on any other day, to hold and make an election of directors, as shall have been regulated by the by-laws and ordinances of said corporation.

Sec. 6. That the directors duly elected shall, as soon as may be, after every annual election, proceed to elect out of their body, a president, who shall preside until the next annual election, and in case of his death, resignation, or absence, the board shall appoint a president *pro tempore;* they shall fill all vacancies which may occur in their own body during the time for which they shall be elected; they shall appoint a secretary, and all such subordinate officers and agents of said corporation, as they may deem expedient, fix their compensation, define their powers, and prescribe their duties, who shall hold their several offices during the pleasure of the board, under such regulations, restrictions and limitations, not inconsistent with the provisions of this act, and the by-laws, ordinances, rules and regulations of said company; they shall hold stated meetings as often as once in every month, at such time and place as they from time to time shall appoint, and at such other times as the president thereof for the time being shall order and direct, and a majority of the whole number shall constitute a quorum, and shall be competent to the transaction of any business within the scope of their powers, and connected with their official duties; and all questions before the board shall be decided *viva voce*, by a majority of the directors present, any two of whom may require the yeas and nays to be taken on any proposition submitted, and entered and recorded in the journal of their proceedings; and no vote shall be reconsidered by a less number than were present and voted when the the original vote was taken; they shall have power, and it is hereby declared their duty, to make and declare such dividends of the profits resulting from the business of said

48—L

company, as shall not impair nor in any wise injure the capital stock of the same; to be paid to the stockholders thereof: *Provided*, That no such dividend shall be paid on any stock that has not been fully paid, but shall be passed to the credit of such stock, as part payment thereof.

Sec. 7. That the stock of said company shall be assigned and transferred on the books of the company, in person, or by power of attorney only; but no stockholder, indebted to the company, shall be permitted to make a transfer, or receive a dividend, until such debt is paid or secured, to the satisfaction of the president and board of directors.

Sec. 8. That the payments on said stock shall be made and completed by the subscribers respectively, at the times and in the manner following, to wit: at the time of subscribing, there shall be paid on each share two dollars; immediately after the first election of directors, and before the company shall go into operation, there shall be paid on each share the further sum of eight dollars, and the balance due on each share shall be subject to the call of the directors, and the said company shall not be authorized to make any policy or contract of insurance with any person, as insured, until the whole amount of shares subscribed for shall be paid, or satisfactorily secured, to be paid on demand by endorsed notes, hypothecated stocks or other property.

Sec. 9. That there shall be a general meeting of the stockholders, annually, at the time and place appointed for the election of directors, and any number of stockholders being the owners and proprietors of at least five hundred shares, may, at any other time, call a general meeting of the stockholders, on business interesting to the company, by giving at least three weeks previous notice of the time, place, and business of such meeting, in two newspapers printed in Cincinnati; and the stockholders present, or by proxy, at any such meeting, shall decide all questions proposed for consideration, by a plurality of votes; and may make and prescribe such by-laws, ordinances, rules and regulations, as to them shall appear needful and proper, in relation to the management of the stocks, money, estates, funds, property and effects of said company, or the disposition, or sale of the same, or the duties, powers and conduct of its officers, agents, and all things appertaining thereto, which shall not be inconsistent with the provisions of this act.

Sec. 10. That John H. Groesbeck, John C. Wright, William R. Morris, James Smith Armstrong, James Goodin, George W. Jones, jr. Samuel Devou, Robert T. Lytle, and Ransler W. Lee, or any three of them, be, and they are hereby authorized to open books in said city, for the capital stock of said company, at any time within three months after the passage of this act, and keep them open every day, between the hours of nine o'clock in the morning, and six o'clock in the afternoon, (Sundays excepted,) for twenty days, unless the whole amount should be sooner subscribed for; after which time it shall be lawful for the subscribers to meet, one weeks notice of the time and place of such meeting being first given in two newspapers, printed in said city, and choose the first board of directors, who shall continue in office until the next election: *Provided*, That if said company shall not go into operation by the first day of January, one thousand eight hundred and thirty-seven, then this act shall be null and void.

Sec. 11. That this act shall be taken and received in all courts, and by all judges, magistrates, and other public officers, as a public act, and all printed copies of the same which may be printed by and under the General Assembly, shall be admitted as good evidence thereof, without any further proof whatsoever.

WILLIAM MEDILL,
Speaker pro tem. of the House of Representatives.
ELIJAH VANCE,
Speaker of the Senate.

March 10, 1836.

AN ACT

To lay out and establish a State road from Sidney, in the county of Shelby, to Williamstown, in Hancock county.

Sec. 1. *Be it enacted by the General Assembly of the State of Ohio,* That L. D. Kennard, of the county of Shelby; John Moore, of the county of Hardin; and Reuben Hale, of the county of Hancock, be, and they hereby are appointed commissioners, and the county surveyor of the county of Hardin, by himself, or deputy surveyor, to lay out and establish a State road, commencing at Sidney, in Shelby county; thence to Roundheads-town, in the county of Hardin; thence, by way of Isaac Matthews', to Williamstown, in Hancock county.

Sec. 2. That should either of the commissioners die, refuse to serve, or remove out of the county, his place shall be supplied by the commissioners of the county where the vacancy shall happen, as often as it may occur.

Sec. 3. That the commissioners aforesaid, in all respects, shall be governed by the law defining the mode of laying out and establishing State roads, passed March 14th, A. D. 1831.

WILLIAM MEDILL,
Speaker pro tem. of the House of Representatives.
ELIJAH VANCE,
Speaker of the Senate.

March 10, 1836.

AN ACT

To incorporate the Wooster and Akron Turnpike Company.

Sec. 1. *Be it enacted by the General Assembly of the State of Ohio,* That J. S. Lake, J. H. Harris, John Plank, Joseph Springer, and Samuel K. Slanker, of Wayne county; Thos. Johnson, of Medina county; James W. Phillips, Elakine Crosby, and Simon Perkins, jr. of Portage county, and their associates, be, and they are hereby incorporated a body politic and corporate, by the name and style of the Wooster and Akron Turnpike Company, for the purpose of making a turnpike road from Wooster, through Doylestown, to Akron; with all the rights, privileges, and immunities, and subject to all the restrictions, limitations, provisions and disabilities prescribed in the act entitled an act passed January seventh, one thousand eight hundred and seventeen, and the acts amendatory thereto, "To provide for the regulation of Turnpike Companies."

Sec. 2. That the capital of said company shall consist of fifty thousand dollars; to be divided into shares of twenty-five dollars each.

Sec. 3. That the persons named in the first section of this act, shall be commissioners, for the purpose of receiving subscriptions to the capital stock of said company, and of performing all the duties required of them, or contemplated by the act to provide for the regulation of turnpike companies: books shall be opened for the purpose of receiving subscriptions to the capital stock of said company, on the first Monday of June next, at Wooster and Doylestown, in Wayne county, and Akron, in Portage county; and whenever ten thousand dollars shall be subscribed, it shall be lawful for the aforesaid commissioners to call a meeting of the stockholders, for the purpose of electing nine directors, who shall manage the concers of said company.

Sec. 4. That whenever said company shall have completed ten miles of said turnpike road, according to the provisions of the "Act to provide for the regulations of Turnpike Companies," they shall have a right to demand and receive from persons travelling the same, except soldiers of the revolution, and those who are exempt from the payment of toll by the above named act, the following rates of toll for every ten miles, and in the same proportion for a greater or less distance, to wit: for every four wheeled carriage, drawn by two horses or oxen, twenty-five cents; for every horse or ox in addition, six and one-fourth cents; for every two wheeled carriage, drawn by two horses or oxen, eighteen and three-fourths-cents; for every horse or ox in addition, six and one-fourth cents; for every sled or sleigh, drawn by two horses or oxen, twelve and one-half cents; for every horse or ox in addition, six and one-fourth cents; for every horse and rider, six and one-fourth cents; for every horse, mule, or ass, led or driven, six months old or upwards, three cents; for every head of neat cattle, six months old or upmards, two cents; at the same rate for a greater or less number; for every four wheeled pleasure carriage, drawn by two horses, thirty-seven and one-half cents; for every horse in addition twelve and one-half cents; for every pleasure two wheeled carriage, drawn by one horse, eighteen and three-fourths cents; for every horse in addition, twelve and one-half cents; for every four wheeled carriage, drawn by one horse, eighteen and three-fourths cents; for every two wheeled carriage, drawn by one horse or ox, twelve and one-half cents; for every sled or sleigh, drawn by one horse or ox, six and one-fourth cents: *Provided*, That no turnpike gate shall be erected within one mile of the court house, at Wooster, or village of Akron; and in the erection of each gate, a passage shall be left free, for foot passengers: *Provided*, That no part of the capital stock of this corporation shall be used for banking purposes, or any other purpose, not expressed in this act: *Provided, also,* That the Legislature may regulate the rates of toll herein fixed, after the year 1846.

Sec. 5. That if said turnpike company shall not commence making said road within two years from the passage of this act, and if the road shall not be completed within ten years thereafter, all the rights, privileges, and immunities granted to said company by this act, or by the act to provide for the regulation of turnpike companies, shall cease and determine.

WILLIAM MEDILL,
Speaker pro tem. of the House of Representatives.

ELIJAH VANCE,
Speaker of the Senate.

March 10, 1836.

AN ACT

To incorporate "The Calliopean Society," of the Granville Literary and Theological Institution, in the county of Licking.

Sec. 1. *Be it enacted by the General Assembly of the State of Ohio,* That J. G. Baker, S. C. Draper, John White, Charles Platt, John Kelly, Muncier Jones, W. S. Sherwood, L. S. Cary, George Quinby, Samuel White, James Hurst, E. T. Spelman, and their associates, students of the Granville Literary and Theological Institution, be, and they are hereby created a body corporate and politic, by the name of "The Calliopean Society," of said Granville Institution, with perpetual succession.

Sec. 2. That said corporation may purchase, receive, hold and convey any estate, real, personal, or mixed; the annual income of which shall not exceed five hundred dollars: *Provided,* That no part of the stock or property of [said] corporation shall, at any time, be used or employed for any other than literary and scientific purposes, the erection of the necessary buildings, the purchase of books, maps, charts, pamphlets, newspapers, or other useful publications, as they may deem expedient.

Sec. 3. That said corporation may form and adopt a constitution and by-laws, and provide for the election of all such officers as they may deem necessary; fix the period of time for which they may hold their offices: *Provided,* That such constitution or by-laws shall never be in force, until submitted to, and approved of by the faculty of said Granville Literary and Theological Institution: *Provided, also,* That any future Legislature may alter or repeal this act.

WILLIAM MEDILL,
Speaker pro tem. of the House of Representatives.

ELIJAH VANCE,
Speaker of the Senate.

March 10, 1836.

AN ACT

To incorporate the town of Fairfield, in the county of Columbiana.

Sec. 1. *Be it enacted by the General Assembly of the State of Ohio,* That so much of section number thirty-six, township number twelve, range number two, Columbiana county, as is comprised within the following described limits, including the town plat of the town of Fairfield, to wit: beginning at the north-east corner of Thomas Bradfield's land, and the south-east corner of a lot late the property of R. Craig, now of Sylvanus Fisher; running thence north on the township line thirty-three chains, to a post; thence west thirty-six chains, to a post; thence south nine chains, to a post; thence west thirteen chains, to a post; thence south nine chains to a post; thence west thirteen chains, to a post; thence south fifteen chains, to a post; thence east sixty-two chains to the place of beginning: together with all such additions as may hereafter be recorded thereto, be, and the same is hereby created a town corporate, and shall hereafter be known by the name of the "Town of Fairfield."

Sec. 2. That it shall be lawful for the white male inhabitants of said town included within said bounds, having the qualifications of electors of the General Assembly, to meet on the second Monday of April next, and on the second Monday of April annually thereafter, and elect, by ballot, one mayor, and recorder, and five trustees, who shall be freeholders, and shall hold their offices for one year, and until their successors are elected and qualified, and they shall constitute the Town Council.

Sec. 3. That at the first election under this act, the electors shall choose, *viva voce,* two judges and a clerk, who shall each take an oath or affirmation, faithfully to discharge the duties assigned them; and at all elections thereafter, the trustees, or any two of them, shall be judges, and the recorder, clerk; and at all such elections, the polls shall be opened between the hours of ten and eleven, A. M. and close at two P. M. of said day; and at the close of the polls, the votes shall be counted and proclaimed and the clerk shall deliver to each person elected, or leave at his usual place of abode, within three days after, a written notice of his election; and the person so notified, shall, within ten days thereafter, take an oath or affirmation to support the constitution of the United States, and also an oath of office.

Sec. 4. That the mayor, recorder, and trustees, shall be a body corporate and politic, with perpetual succession, by the name of the "Town of Fairfield;" shall be capable of acquiring and holding real and personal estate; may sell and convey the same; may have a common seal, and may alter the same; may sue and be sued, plead and be impleaded, answer and be answered unto, in any court of law and equity in this State or elsewhere; and when any suit is commenced against the corporation, the first process shall be a summons, an attested copy of which shall be left with the recorder, at least ten days before the return day thereof.

Sec. 5. That the mayor, recorder, and a majority of the trustees, shall have the power to make such by-laws and ordinances, and regulations, for the health and convenience of said town, as they may deem advisable: *Provided,* They be consistent with the constitution of the United States, and of this State: and they shall have power to fill all vacancies occasioned by death, removal or otherwise; to appoint a treasurer, town marshal, and such other subordinate officers as they may deem necessary; to prescribe their general duties, and to require such security as they may think necessary, to secure the faithful performance of their duties; to remove them at pleasure; to fix and establish the fees of offices not established by this act.

Sec. 6. The mayor shall be a conservator of the peace within the limits of said corporation, and shall have the jurisdiction of a justice of the peace; and shall receive the same fees as justices of the peace are entitled to for similar services; he shall give bond and security, as is required of justices of the peace; and an appeal may be had from the decisions of the mayor to the court of common pleas, in the same manner as appeals are taken from the decisions of justices of the peace.

Sec. 7. It shall be the duty of the recorder to keep a true record of the proceedings of the town council, which record shall, at all times be open for the inspection of the electors of said town; and the recorder shall preside at all meetings of the corporation in the absence of the mayor, and shall perform such other duties as may be required of him by the laws and ordinances of said corporation.

Sec. 8. That the town council shall have power to levy a tax annually, for corporation purposes, on the property within the limits of said town, returned on the grand levy, made subject to taxation by the laws of this State: *Provided*, That said tax shall not exceed in any one year, three mills on the dollar; and the recorder shall make out a duplicate thereof, charging thereon each individual, an amount of tax in proportion to his property, as assessed on the grand levy for taxation; which said duplicate shall be certified and signed by the mayor and recorder, and delivered to the marshal; who shall proceed to collect the same, in the same manner, and under the same regulations, as county treasurers are required by law to collect county and State taxes; and said marshal shall, as soon as collected, pay the same over to the treasurer of the corporation.

Sec. 9. That said town council may appropriate any money in the treasury, for the improvements of the streets and side-walks, or other improvements; and may have the use of the jail of the county, for the imprisonment of persons liable to imprisonment; and all persons so imprisoned, shall be under the care of the sheriff, as in other cases.

Sec. 10. The town council shall, under no circumstances, have power to license groceries.

Sec. 11. Any future Legislature may alter, amend or repeal this act.

WILLIAM MEDILL,
Speaker pro tem. of the House of Representatives.
ELIJAH VANCE,
Speaker of the Senate.

March 10, 1836.

AN ACT

To incorporate the Hopewell Library Company, in Muskingum county.

Sec. 1. *Be it enacted by the General Assembly of the State of Ohio,* That

Thomas Ijams, Jesse L. Manly, and Henry Woolf, of Hopewell, in the county of Muskingum, and their associates, together with such other persons as may be hereafter associated with them, are hereby created a body corporate, by the name of the "Hopewell Library Company," with perpetual succession; and by their corporate name, may contract, and prosecute and defend suits, and may hold, enjoy, and dispose of real and personal property, not exceeding the annual value of two thousand dollars, which shall be used solely for the puposes of a Library Company in Hopewell, aforesaid; and the corporation may appoint such officers, and make such regulations and by-laws for the government of its members, and the management of its affairs, as may be necessary and expedient.

Sec. 2. Any future Legislature may alter or repeal this act.

WILLIAM MEDILL,
Speaker pro tem. of the House of Representatives.
ELIJAH VANCE,
Speaker of the Senate.

March 10, 1836.

AN ACT

To amend the act entitled "An act to incorporate the town of Wooster, in the county of Wayne," passed Feb. 21st, 1834.

Sec. 1. *Be it enacted by the General Assembly of the State of Ohio,* That the president, recorder, and trustees of the town of Wooster, in Wayne county, Ohio, shall have power and authority to pass and publish all such by-laws and ordinances, as to them shall seem necessary, for making, constructing, and repairing sewers, along the streets and alleys of said town, for the purpose of carrying the waters from the cellars, streets and alleys of said town.

Sec. 2. They shall have power and authority to levy upon the lots of said towns, and collect from the owners of the same, by which lots said sewer or sewers may pass, such tax as they may direct; not exceeding such amount, as would be sufficient to construct said sewer or sewers, the length or breadth of the lot or lots which said sewers may pass; any thing in the twelfth section of the act to which this is an amendment, to the contrary notwithstanding.

Sec. 3. That in case of the neglect or refusal of any person or persons, owning lots in said town, and not residing therein, to pay any tax under or by virtue of this act, or any law or ordinance, passed in pursuance thereof, upon any lot or lots in said town, said tax on such lot shall be a lien upon the same, and collected in such manner, in all respects, as is provided for in the eighteenth section of the act, to which this is an amendment.

WILLIAM MEDILL,
Speaker pro tem. of the House of Representatives.
ELIJAH VANCE,
Speaker of the Senate.

March 10, 1836.

AN ACT

To lay out and establish a State road, commencing on the State road, one mile north of Truxville, in Richland county, to Milan, in Huron county.

Sec. 1. *Be it enacted by the General Assembly of the State of Ohio,* That John W. Tanner, and Abel A. Webster, of Richland county; John H. Rule, and Matthew McKelvy, of Huron county, be, and they are hereby appointed commissioners, and John S. Marshal, of Richland county, surveyor, to lay out and establish a state road, commencing on the state road leading from Truxville, in Richland county; from thence to the dwelling house of James Moss; from thence the nearest and best way to Milan, in Huron county.

Sec. 2. That the grade of said road shall not exceed an angle of five degrees with the horizon.

Sec. 3. That said road commissioners shall, in all respects, be governed by, and the expenses of laying out and establishing said road be paid, according to the provisions of the act entitled "An act defining the mode of laying out and establishing state roads," passed March 14th, 1831, except in the appointment of surveyor, which is provided for in the first section of this act.

Sec. 4. That should a vacancy at any time occur, in the foregoing appointments, by death, removal, refusal to serve, or otherwise, the county commissioners of the county in which such vacancy may happen, shall fill the same, as often as any such vacancy may occur, by the appointment of some suitable person, without delay.

WILLIAM MEDILL,
Speaker pro tem, of the House of Representatives.
ELIJAH VANCE,
Speaker of the Senate.

March 10, 1836.

AN ACT

To incorporate Mount Zion Chapel, in the town of Newark, in the county of Licking.

Sec. 1. *Be it enacted by the General Assembly of the State of Ohio,* That John Shennefelt, J. B. W. Haynes, John Gibson, James Hayes, Newton Trenary, and their associates, be, and they are hereby created a body corporate and politic, by the name and style of "Mount Zion Chapel of Newark;" and as such shall have perpetual succession, and shall be capable in law or equity, to have, receive, acquire, and hold, either by gift, grant, devise, or purchase, any estate, real, personal or mixed; and may lease, mortgage, sell and convey the same: *Provided,* That the value of all such property shall not exceed ten thousand dollars.

Sec. 2. That there shall be elected by ballot, on the first Monday of June next, and annually thereafter, five trustees, who shall have the entire control and management of the property and financial concerns of the

49—L

corporation; they shall have power to appoint a treasurer and clerk, and to fill all vacancies that may happen in their own body, until the next annual election thereafter; and make such by-laws, rules and regulations, as may be necessary for the prudent and efficient management of its pecuniary affairs.

Sec. 3. At all elections, held under the provisions of this act, each pew-holders, or member, above the age of twenty-one years, shall be entitled to vote; and a plurality of votes shall, in all instances, be deemed sufficient to elect; and the officers so elected shall hold their offices for one year, and until their successors shall be duly elected: *Provided*, That a failure to elect, on the day appointed, shall not be a forfeiture of the rights and privileges herein granted.

Sec. 4. That original process against said corporation shall be by summons; which shall be served by leaving an attested copy thereof with one of the trustees, at least ten days before the return day thereof.

Sec. 5. That John Shennefelt, J. B. W. Haynes, John Gibson, James Hayes, and Newton Trenary, named in the first section of this act, be, and they are hereby appointed trustees of said corporation, until the first annual election, and until others are elected in their places: *Provided*, Any future Legislature may alter or repeal this act.

WILLIAM MEDILL,
Speaker pro tem. of the House of Representatives.
ELIJAH VANCE,
Speaker of the Senate.

March 10, 1836.

AN ACT

To incorporate the Wooster Academy.

Sec. 1. *Be it enacted by the General Assembly of the State of Ohio,* That David Robison, Reasin Beall, William McComb, Edward Avery, Joseph S. Lake, John P. Coulter, Benjamin Bentley, David McConahay, and Joseph Stibbs, and their associates, be, and they are hereby declared a body corporate and politic, by the name of "The Wooster Academy;" and as such they shall have perpetual succession; by that name they shall sue and be sued, plead and be impleaded, defend and be defended, in any court of law or equity; they may have a common seal, and may alter or change the same at pleasure; they shall be capable in law, by the name aforesaid, to purchase, receive and dispose of, or sell any estate, real or personal: *Provided*, That the capital stock of said corporation shall not exceed twenty-five thousand dollars, to be divided into shares of five dollars each; no part of which capital shall ever be applied for banking purposes, or for any other but that of supporting said Academy.

Sec. 2. That the stockholders in said corporation, or so many of them as may think proper, shall meet in the township of Wooster, on the first Monday of April, annually, for the purpose of transacting the necessary business of the association, and shall then and there elect by ballot, from among the stockholders, the number of trustees hereinafter provided for, who shall serve until their successors are elected and qualified; and at all elections each stockholder shall be entitled to one vote for each share he or she may own; and the person who shall receive the highest number of votes, shall be elected; but if, by neglect or casualty, an election shall not have been held on the day hereby appointed, the corporation shall not thereby be dissolved, but an election may be held at any time thereafter; and for that purpose, a meeting of said corporation may be called, by a notice signed by any three of the stockholders, and posted up in three public places in said township, at least six days previous to the day of holding such election.

Sec. 3. That at the first election held under the provisions of this act, there shall be elected nine trustees, who shall divide themselves into three equal classes, by lot or otherwise; the first class shall hold their office three years; the second class, two years; and the third class, one year; after which there shall be annually elected three trustees, to fill the vacancies occasioned by this arrangement; who shall hold their offices for three years, and until their successors are elected and qualified.

Sec. 4. That the trustees of said corporation, any five of whom shall in all cases be a quorum, shall annually appoint from their own body, a president and secretary, and from among the other stockholders, a treasurer for said corporation; the president shall preside at all meetings of the stockholders, and of the board of trustees; he, or in his absence, either of the trustees, who may be agreed upon by said board, shall act as judge of all elections held under the provisions of this act, and shall direct at what place and hour the same shall be held; the president shall have power to call a meeting of the board of trustees, whenever he shall think it necessary, by giving personal or written notice to each; he shall also notify the stockholders of the time and place of holding the annual elections, at least six days previous to the day by this act appointed for holding such elections, by posting up a notice, attested by the secretary, in two public places in the said township of Wooster; the secretary shall faithfully record all proceedings of the board of trustees, and of the stockholders, when duly assembled; and when required, shall submit his records to the inspection of any of the stockholders; he shall also be clerk of all elections held under the provisions of this act, and shall perform such other duties as may from time to time be required of him by the board of trustees; the treasurer shall give bond to the president, with such penalty and security as the trustees shall require, conditioned for the faithful discharge of his duties as treasurer of said Academy, and shall collect and receive all moneys and other property that may be due to said corporation, and pay them out on the order of the trustees, attested by the secretary, and shall settle with the board of trustees as often as they may require.

Sec. 5. The board of trustees shall have power to make and establish such rules and by-laws consistent with the constitution and laws of the United States and of this State, as they may from time to time think expedient and necessary for the proper regulation of said corporation, and management of said academy; they shall have power to direct what branches of literature, and of the arts and sciences, shall be taught therein; to employ such professors and teachers, allow them such compensation, and continue them for such length of time, as they may judge proper; to regulate the admission and government of the students of said academy; to expel any disorderly student; to fill all vacancies which may be occasioned by the death, resignation, or removal of any officer of said corporation; to appoint a president and secretary, *pro tempore*, when the absence of these officers, or either of them shall make such appointment necessary; and to call a meeting of the stockholders of said corporation, whenever they may deem it expedient, by a notice for that purpose, attested by the secretary, and posted up in two public places in said township of Wooster, six days previous to the day of said meeting; they shall have the management and disposal of the funds and property of said corporation, and power to make all such purchases, sales, and contracts, as may, in their opinion, be expedient for the benefit of said institution: *Provided*, That no purchase or sale of real estate shall be made by the trustees without the consent of the stockholders, expressed by a vote equal to two thirds of all the shares in said corporation.

Sec. 6. That stock in said corporation may be transferred, new shares created, and new members admitted, upon such conditions and under such restrictions as the trustees shall think proper to prescribe, and not otherwise.

Sec. 7. That until the election shall take place under the provisions of this act, the persons named in the first section of this act shall be, and they are hereby vested with all the powers of trustees of the Wooster Academy, and shall so continue until their successors are elected and qualified.

Sec. 8. That this act shall be taken and received in all courts as a public act; all printed copies of the same which shall be printed by or under the authority of the General Assembly shall be admitted as good evidence thereof, without further proof whatever.

WILLIAM MEDILL,
Speaker pro tem. of the House of Representatives.
ELIJAH VANCE,
Speaker of the Senate.

March 11, 1836.

AN ACT

To incorporate the Second Ten-mile Baptist Church in the county of Clermont.

Sec. 1. *Be it enacted by the General Assembly of the State of Ohio,* That John Wheeler, jr. William Temple, and Andrew Coombs, and their associates, together with those that may hereafter be associated with them, be, and they are hereby called a body corporate and politic, by the name of the "Second Ten-mile Baptist Church, in the county of Clermont;" and as such shall remain and have perpetual succession: *Provided*, Said corporation shall not hold more real estate than is necessary for a meeting house, burying ground, and parsonage.

Sec. 2. That the members of said corporation, and their associates, shall meet on the first Monday in May, annually; but in case of any failure, the trustees may call a meeting, at such time and place as they may think proper, and elect by ballot three trustees, and such other officers as the said society may deem necessary, and make such other rules, regulations and by-laws, as they may deem advisable.

Sec. 3. That John Wheeler, jr. William Temple, and Andrew Coombs, be, and are hereby appointed trustees, until the next annual election, and until their successors are chosen under the provisions of this act.

Sec. 4. Any future Legislature shall have power to alter or repeal this act.

WILLIAM MEDILL,
Speaker pro tem. of the House of Representatives.
ELIJAH VANCE,
Speaker of the Senate.

March 11, 1836.

AN ACT

To incorporate the Wardens and Vestrymen of Christ's Church in Franklin, in the county of Portage.

Sec. 1. *Be it enacted by the General Assembly of the State of Ohio,* That Francis Furber, Asa Stanley, Edward Parsons, Levi Stodard, Lucas M. Latimer, George B. De Peyster, John Brown, Aaron Auter, David McBride, Thomas Cartright and Thomas Earl, their associates, and such other persons as may be hereafter associated with them, are hereby declared a body corporate and politic, with the name and style of the "Wardens and Vestrymen of Christ's Church in Franklin;" with perpetual succession, and capacity of contracting and being contracted with, of suing and being sued, answering and being answered, pleading and being impleaded, defending and being defended, in all courts of law and equity; and may have a common seal, which they may break, alter or renew at pleasure.

Sec. 2. That said church shall be capable in law, in their corporate capacity aforesaid, of having, receiving, acquiring and holding, either by gift, grant, devise or purchase, any estate, real, personal, or mixed, which may be necessary for a convenient meeting house or place of public worship, a grave yard, and dwelling for their preacher, and to defray the expenses incident to their mode of worship; and may also lease, mortgage, sell and convey the same; and property of whatsoever kind, shall be held in trust under the management and at the disposal of the trustees for the use and purposes aforesaid: *Provided,* That the annual income of all such property shall not exceed the sum of two thousand dollars: *And provided also,* That where money or other property shall be given, granted, devised or bequeathed, for purposes of charity, education, or any other purpose, it shall be faithfully applied to the purpose for which it may be intended.

Sec. 3. That this corporation shall have power to pass such by-laws for the election of their officers and the general regulation of their affairs as they may from time to time think proper: *Provided,* That the members of the corporation shall be entitled to vote in all elections and meetings of the corporation.

Sec. 4. That the persons named in the first section of this act, or a majority of them, shall be trustees until others are elected.

Sec. 5. That any future Legislature shall have power to alter, amend or repeal this act: *Provided,* That such alteration, amendment or repeal, shall not affect the title to any estate, real or personal, acquired or conveyed under its provisions.

WILLIAM MEDILL,
Speaker pro tem. of the House of Representatives.

ELIJAH VANCE,
Speaker of the Senate.

March 11, 1836.

AN ACT

To incorporate the "Akron and Middlebury Baptist Church and Society."

Sec. 1. *Be it enacted by the General Assembly of the State of Ohio,* That Nathan Dodge, Joseph Cole, Robert K. Du Bois, Smith Burton, Daniel B. Stewart and John Rhodes, their associates, and such other persons as may be hereafter associated with them, are hereby declared a body corporate and politic, with the name and style of the "Akron and Middlebury Baptist Church and Society;" with perpetual succession, and capacity of contracting and being contracted with, of suing and being sued, answering and being answered, pleading and being impleaded, defending and being defended, in all courts of law and equity; and may have a common seal, which they may break, alter or renew at pleasure.

Sec. 2. That said church shall be capable in law, in their corporate capacity aforesaid, of having, receiving, acquiring and holding, either by gift, grant, devise or purchase, any estate, real, personal or mixed, which may be necessary for a convenient meeting house or place of public worship, a grave yard, and dwelling for their preacher, and to defray the expenses incident to their mode of worship; and may also lease, mortgage, sell and convey the same; and all property of whatsoever kind, shall be held in trust under the management and at the disposal of the trustees, for the uses and purposes aforesaid: *Provided,* That the annual income of all such property shall not exceed the sum of two thousand dollars: *And provided also,* That where money or other property shall be given, granted, devised or bequeathed, for purposes of charity, education, or any other purpose, it shall be faithfully applied to the purpose for which it may be intended.

Sec. 3. That this corporation shall have power to pass such by-laws for the election of their officers and the general regulation of their affairs as they may from time to time think proper: *Provided,* That the members of the corporation shall be entitled to vote in all elections and meetings of the corporation.

Sec. 4. The persons named in the first section of this act, or a majority of them, shall be trustees until others are elected.

Sec. 5. That any future Legislature shall have power to alter, amend or repeal this act.

WILLIAM MEDILL,
Speaker pro tem. of the House of Representatives.
ELIJAH VANCE,
Speaker of the Senate.

March 11, 1836.

AN ACT

To incorporate the town of Christansburgh, in the county of Champaign.

Sec. 1. *Be it enacted by the General Assembly of the State of Ohio,* That so much of the township of Jackson, in the county of Champaign, as is comprised and designated as the town of Christiansburgh, such plats as have been, or may hereafter be recorded as additions thereto, be, and the same is hereby created a town corporate, and shall hereafter be known and distinguished by the name of the Town of Christiansburgh.

Sec. 2. That it shall be lawful for the white male inhabitants of the town, residing within the limits thereof, having the qualifications of electors of the General Assembly, to meet at some convenient place in said town, on the second Monday of June next, and on the first Monday of April annually thereafter, and then and there proceed to elect by ballot, one mayor, one recorder, and five trustees, who shall be householders; and the persons so elected shall hold their respective offices one year and until their successors are elected and qualified, and they shall constitute a Town Council: *Provided,* That the persons elected at the first election shall hold their offices until the next annual election.

Sec. 3. That at the first election to be holden under this act, two judges and a clerk shall be chosen *viva voce,* by the voters present, who shall take an oath or affirmation faithfully to discharge the duties required of them by this act, and at all subsequent elections the mayor and trustees, or any two of them, shall be judges, and the recorder clerk of the election; and at all such elections, the polls shall be opened between the hours of ten and eleven o'clock, A. M. and close at three, P. M. of the same day; and at the close of the polls the votes shall be counted, and a true statement thereof proclaimed; and the clerk shall deliver to each person elected, or leave at his usual place of abode, within three days from the day of election, a written notice of his election; and the person so elected and notified shall, within ten days from said election, take an oath or affirmation to support the constitution of the United States and State of Ohio, and also an oath of office.

Sec. 4. That the mayor, recorder and trustees of said town shall be a body corporate and politic, with perpetual succession, to be known and distinguished by the name of "The Town Council of the Town of Christiansburgh;" and shall be capable in law to acquire property, real and personal, for the use of said town, and sell and convey the same; may have a common seal, and alter the same at pleasure; may sue and be sued, plead and be impleaded, answer and be answered unto, in any court of law or equity in this State; and when any suit shall be commenced against said corporation, the first process shall be a summons; an attested copy of which shall be left with the recorder at least eight days before the return day thereof.

Sec. 5. That the mayor, recorder and trustees, or a majority of them, of whom the mayor or recorder shall always be one, shall have authority to make, ordain and publish all such by-laws and ordinances, consistent with the constitution and laws of the United States and of this State, as they shall deem necessary for the regulation, health, cleanliness and convenience of said town of Christiansburg; and they shall have power to fill all vacancies occasioned by death, resignation, removal or otherwise; to appoint a treasurer, town marshal, and such other subordinate officers as they may deem necessary; to prescribe their general duties; and to require of them such security as they shall deem necessary to secure the faithful performance of their duties; to remove them at pleasure; to fix and establish the fees of the officers of said corporation, not established by this act; to impose such fines, not exceeding two dollars, as they may deem just, for refusing to [accept] any office in said corporation: *Provided,* That no law or ordinance of said corporation shall ever subject horses, cattle, sheep or hogs owned by persons not residing in said town, to be taken up, sold, or abused, for coming within the limits of said corporation.

Sec. 6. That the mayor shall be a conservator of the peace within the limits of said corporation; and shall have the jurisdiction of a justice of the peace therein, both in criminal and civil cases; and in all his acts as justices of the peace, he shall be governed by the laws defining the duties of justices of the peace, and shall be entitled to the same fees as justices of the peace are entitled to receive for similar services; he shall give bond and security as is required by law of justices of the peace; he shall be authorized to hear and determine all cases arising under the laws and ordinances of the corporation, and to issue such process as may be necessary to carry into execution such laws and ordinances; and an appeal may be had in all cases from the decisions of the mayor to the court of common pleas of the county aforesaid, in the same manner that appeals are taken from the decision of justices of the peace.

Sec. 7. That it shall be the duty of the recorder to make out and keep a true record of the by-laws and ordinances made and ordained by the town council of said town, and all proceedings in their corporate capacity; which record shall at all times be open for the inspection of the electors of said town, and others interested therein: and the recorder shall preside at all meetings of the corporation in the absence of the mayor, and shall perform such other duties as may be required of him by the by-laws and ordinances of said corporation.

Sec. 8. That the town council shall have power to levy a tax annually for corporation purposes on the property within the limits of said town, returned on the grand levy, and made subject to taxation by the laws of this State: *Provided,* That said tax shall not exceed in any one year three mills on the dollar; the amount of said tax to be levied being determined by said town council; and it shall be the duty of the recorder to make out a duplicate thereof, charging therein each individual owning property in said town an amount of tax in proportion to the amount of his property, as assessed and returned on the grand levy for taxation; which duplicate shall be signed by the mayor and recorder, and delivered to the marshal, who shall proceed to levy and collect said tax in the same manner and under the same regulations as collectors of state and county tax are required by law to collect state and county tax; and the said marshal, immediately after collecting the said tax, pay the same over to the treasurer of said corporation and take his receipt therefor; and the said marshal shall have the same power to sell both real and personal estate, as is given by law to the county treasurer; and when necessary the said recorder shall have power to make deeds for real estate so sold in the same manner as county auditors are by law empowered to make deeds for real estate sold for taxes by the county treasurer; and the marshal receive for his fees in the collection aforesaid such sum as the town council may direct, not exceeding six per centum on all moneys by him collected, to be paid by the treasurer on the order of the recorder.

Sec. 9. That said town council shall have full power to appropriate any moneys remaining in the corporation treasury, to the improvement of the streets and side walks in said town; and when they may deem it necessary, to make any contract therefor.

Sec. 10. That said corporation shall be allowed to use the jail of said county for the imprisonment of such persons as may be liable to imprisonment under the laws and ordinances of said town; and all persons, so imprisoned, shall be under the charge of the sheriff of said county, as in other cases.

WILLIAM MEDILL,
Speaker pro tem. of the House of Representatives.
ELIJAH VANCE,
Speaker of the Senate.

March 11, 1836.

AN ACT

To repeal certain acts making appropriation for the improvement of the Muskingum river.

Sec. 1. *Be it enacted by the General Assembly of the State of Ohio,* That the act, entitled "An act making an appropriation for the improvement of the Muskingum river," and which was passed on the twenty-seventh day of February, one thousand eight hundred and thirty-four, and likewise an act amendatory thereto, entitled "An act to amend an act making an appropriation for the improvement of the navigation of the Muskingum river," and which was passed on the ninth day of March, one thousand eight hundred and thirty-five; be, and they are both hereby repealed.

Sec. 2. That the Auditor of State is hereby required to give notice to William Silvey, of Muskingum county, and Luther D. Barker, of Morgan county, the managers and superintendents of the said improvement of the repeal of the above recited act, and to demand and collect, by pro

50—L

cess of law or otherwise, such unexpended balance of the aforesaid appropriation as remains in their hands.

Sec, 3. That the said Auditor require a regular and detailed account of the expenditures, with the corresponding vouchers to sustain the report, which has been submitted to the General Assembly by the aforesaid William Silvey and Luther D. Barker.

Sec. 4. That the Auditor of State is hereby required to report his proceedings on the provisions of this act, to the next General Assembly, on the first Monday in December, one thousand eight hundred and thirty-six.

Sec. 5. That in case the said William Silvey and Luther D. Barker have, during the course of the last year, made any contracts for the improvements of the Muskingum river, and which improvement or improvements are only partially completed, the contractors shall be entitled to receive compensation in proportion to the amount of labor done thereon.

WILLIAM MEDILL,
Speaker pro tem. of the House of Representatives.
ELIJAH VANCE,
Speaker of the Senate.

March 11, 1836.

AN ACT

To incorporate the Newark and Lancaster Turnpike Company.

Sec. 1. *Be it enacted by the General Assembly of the State of Ohio,* That Jas. Parker, Daniel Duncan, Wm. Spencer, Israel Dille, and Rob't R. Clark, of Licking county; Henry Wilson, Jas. Culberson, John A. Peters, Moses D. Brook, and Peter Cool, of Perry county; John Paden, Hocking H. Hunter, Thomas M'Naughten, M. Z. Kreider, and Daniel Swayre, sen. of Fairfield county, as commisssoners, and their associates, stockholders, as hereinafter provided, their successors and assigns be, and they are hereby created and declared a body politic and corporate, perpetual, by the name and style of the Newark and Lancaster Turnpike Company; to construct and keep in repair a turnpike road, toll gates, and gate keeper's houses; commencing at Newark, in Licking county; thence by the most eligible route, through Jackson Town, Thornville, New Salem, and Pleasantville, to Lancaster, in Fairfield county; and by such corporate name and style said company is hereby made and declared capable, in law and equity, to contract, sue and be sued, make by-laws, not contrary to the constitution or laws of the United States or of this State; and to have and use a common seal, which they may break, alter, or renew at pleasure; and to acquire, have, hold, sell, transfer and convey property, real and personal, for their corporate use and purposes, but for no other uses or purposes whatsoever.

Sec. 2. That the capital stock of the company, hereby incorporated, shall consist of one hundred thousand dollars, in shares of twenty five dollars each, and may be subscribed and held by individuals, companies or corporations, and shall be appropriated and applied to the uses and purposes, in the first section of this act set forth, and to no other use or purpose; and any person desiring to discharge his subscription to the capital stock of said company, in labor or materials, on or for said road, shall so specify, at the time of subscribing; in which case, the labor to be performed by such subscriber, shall be assigned, and the value of the same estimated by the principal engineer, superintending the construction of the road; or if materials be subscribed, the value thereof shall be estimated by such principal engineer: *Provided*, That in all cases of subscription to the capital stock of said company, five dollars, in cash, shall be paid to the person or persons, under whose superintendence subscriptions may be received, on each share subscribed; and the residue of such capital stock, whether in cash, labor, or materials, shall be paid, discharged, performed and furnished, on the requisition of the directors, for the time being.

Sec. 3. That books for receiving subscriptions to the capital stock of said company, shall be opened on the fourth day of July next, at such places, and under the superintendence of such persons, as a majority of said commissioners, or a majority of such of them as consent to act, may designate and appoint; it shall be the duty of said commissioners, or a majority of them, or a majority of such of them as consent to act, to give ten days' notice of the time, places, and persons, at which, and under whose superintendence, will be opened the books for receiving subscriptions to the capital stock of said company; which notice shall be published in some newspaper printed, or in general circulation, in each of the counties of Licking and Fairfield; and the books for receiving subscriptions as aforesaid, shall be kept open as long as said directors shall see fit.

Sec. 4. That as soon as it shall be ascertained, that twenty thousand dollars of the capital stock of said company has been subscribed, said commissioners, or a majority of them, or a majority of such of them as consent to act, shall give thirty days notice, as provided in the third section of this act, of the time and place of holding an election, which shall be held at some convenient place, in some one of said counties, for the purpose of choosing seven directors, to manage and conduct the business and affairs of said company; and on the day and place thus specified, in said notice the stockholders of said company shall proceed to the election, by ballot, of seven directors, who shall be stockholders, any five of whom shall constitute a quorum, for the transaction of the business and concerns of said company; the first election for directors, under this act, shall be conducted by two inspectors, who shall be appointed by a majority of such of said commissioners, as may consent to act; and such inspectors shall act under oath; none but stockholders shall vote for directors; and the stockholders shall be entitled to one vote, which may be given in person, or by proxy, for each share of stock by him, her, or them owned and held, on the day of election; the seven directors, having the highest number of votes, shall be declared duly elected; but if an election of seven directors shall not be effected, by reason of an equal number of votes being given, in favor of two or more stockholders; in that case, the inspectors of the election shall determine, by lot, amongst the eight or more stockholders, having the highest and an equal number of votes, who shall be directors, to complete the number of seven: *Provided,* Such determination, by lot, shall not postpone as director, one stockholder having a higher, to another having a lower, number of votes; the directors first elected, under this act, shall hold their offices until the first Monday of July next after their election, and until their successors are elected and qualified; and on the first Monday of July, annually, after the first election for directors, there shall be an election for directors of said company; annual elections for directors of said company shall be under the superintendence of the directors, for the time being; who shall designate a place, and shall give the like notice of the time of such annual election, as is required to be given by the commissioners, as aforesaid, of the time and place of holding the first election, under this act; and shall, in like manner, notify the persons elected, and designate a time and place for the persons elected directors, to meet and qualify; and the directors, annually elected, shall proceed, as required of the first directors.

Sec. 5. That within ten days, after the first election of directors, under this act, the inspectors of the election shall give notice, in writing, to the seven stockholders, elected directors, of such their election; and shall appoint a day and place, on which the directors so elected shall meet for organization; and on the day and at the place so appointed, which shall not be more than fifteen days from the day of election, or sooner, if the directors elected can agree, the directors so elected, shall meet at said place, and severally take an oath, faithfully and impartially to discharge the several duties of directors of the turnpike company, hereby incorporated; and being thus qualified, such directors shall appoint one of their body president of the board; they shall also appoint a treasurer, who shall not be a director, and they may require and take of the treasurer, bond, in such sum, and with such security, as to them may appear reasonable and necessary, to secure said company; said directors shall also appoint a secretary, who shall keep a full and fair journal of the corporate acts of said company, and shall perform such other duties of secretary, as may be required of him by the directors.

Sec. 6. That the said company shall have a right to lay out, survey, and locate a turnpike road, as specified in the first section of this act, through any improved or unimproved lands; and to take from the lands, occupied by such road, when located as aforesaid, any stone, gravel, timber, or other materials, necessary to construct a good, secure, and substantial turnpike road, as contemplated by this act, and the necessary bridges connected therewith; and if any difference should arise between the owner or owners of any ground, on which such road may be located, or from which such materials are taken, as aforesaid, and the agents of the company, respecting damage, it shall be determined, by three disinterested freeholders, to be appointed by the commissioners of the county, in which the subject of difference lies; who, after being duly sworn, faithfully and impartially to perform the duties, required of them in this act, and taking into consideration, whether the land be, really, rendered more or less valuable, by the road passing through it, shall make out their assessment in writing, of the damages, if any; a copy of which shall be given to the proprietor of the land, and another copy to the agent of the company; and said agent shall pay, or offer to pay, the owner of said land, the amount of such assessed damages, before he shall enter upon and take any such ground or materials, other than to survey the road; and all such assessment of dama. ges, if any should be awarded, shall be paid by the company; but if no damages shall be awarded, then the expense shall be paid by the person who had claimed damages; and in case sufficient materials cannot be procured on the land so as aforesaid acquired for said road and bridges, said company, or their agents, shall have a right to, and they are hereby authorized, to enter upon any unimproved lands, adjoining or in the vicinity of said road, and to dig, cut down, take, and carry away, so much stone, gravel, timber, or other materials, (not previously cut down, taken, appropriated or pre. pared, by the owner for any particular use,) as may be necessary to enable said company to construct said road and the necessary bridges, toll gates, and gate keepers' houses; and in case of difference between the owners of any lands, from which materials may be taken, as last aforesaid, such dif. ference shall be determined, and compensation made by said company, in manner provided for the assessment of damages for the land on which said road may be laid.

Sec. 7. That in addition to the land necessary for the construction, use, and repair of said road, said company shall be entitled to, and author. ized [to] acquire, in manner aforesaid, not exceeding one acre of land, at each toll gate, for the erection thereon, and convenient occupation of a gate keeper's house; and said company shall cause such turnpike road to be opened, not exceeding eighty feet wide; at least fifteen feet of which shall be made an artificial road, composed of stone, gravel, wood, or other suitable materials, well compacted together, in such a manner as to secure a good, firm, substantial and even road, rising in the middle, with a gradual arch or curve, with sufficient drains on each side, to carry the water there. from, and shall keep the same in good repair; and in no case shall the as. cent in such road be of greater elevation, than four degrees with the hori. zon.

Sec. 8. That so soon as said company shall have completed such road, or the grading thereof, as aforesaid, or any part of such road, not less than five continuous miles, and so from time to time, as often as five continuous miles thereof shall be completed, or completely graded, an agent, to be appointed for that purpose by the commissioners of the proper coun. ty, if not otherwise appointed by or under the Legislature or its au. thority, shall, on application of said company, examine said road, or part thereof, as aforesaid, and report his opinion to the president of said com. pany; and if such agent shall report said road, or any continuous five miles, thereof, to be completed or completely graded, agreeable to the requisi. tions of this act, said company shall thereupon be entitled to erect a toll gate or gates, at suitable distances on said road, and to demand and re. ceive of those travelling or using the same, the tolls allowed by this act.

Sec. 9. That the following shall be the rates of toll demandable and receivable for each and every ten miles of said road, when so much thereof as will entitle said company to erect a gate shall be completed, and in the same proportion for any greater or less distance, to wit: for every four wheeled carriage or wagon, drawn by one horse or ox, eighteen and three fourth cents; for every horse or ox in addition, six and one fourth cents; for every chaise, riding chair, cart, or gig, or other two wheeled

AN ACT

Providing for the sale of section Sixteen, in the township of Lykins, in the county of Crawford.

Sec. 1. *Be it enacted by the General Assembly of the State of Ohio,* That it shall be the duty of the assessor of Crawford county, on or before the first day of April next, to provide himself with a suitable book for that purpose, and proceed to take the votes of all the white male inhabitants over the age of twenty-one years, residing in the bounds of original surveyed township number one, south of range sixteen, in the county of Crawford, aforesaid, who have resided therein for twelve months next preceding the first day of April aforesaid, whether such white male inhabitants be, or be not citizens of the United States; and it shall further be the duty of said assessor, between said first day of April and the twenty-fifth day of May next, to call upon all the white male inhabitants residing in the township aforesaid, and request any such inhabitants to give his vote for or against a sale of the school land aforesaid, by signing his name under the head of the proper columns; and if such inhabitant be unable to write, the assessor shall write the name of such inhabitant, to which he shall affix his mark of approbation; which said vote taken as aforesaid, shall be entered in said book by said assessor, in form following, to wit: The votes of the white male inhabitants over the age of twenty-one years, residing within the bounds of said original surveyed township, (there being twenty of said inhabitants within the same,) for and against the sale of section sixteen; it being the tract granted by Congress for the use of schools in said original surveyed township.

Names of those who voted in favor of a sale.	Names of those who voted against a sale.

Which said list of votes, taken as aforesaid, the assessor shall deliver to the county auditor of said Crawford county forthwith. after having taken the same as aforesaid; and if it shall appear, from said list, that a majority of the white male inhabitants aforesaid, have voted in favor of a sale, then a sale of said school section may be made, in the manner hereinafter prescribed.

Sec. 2. That J. E. Elliot, Robert Maze and Milton E. Waller, of the county of Crawford, be and they are hereby appointed commissioners, whose duty it shall be to view and appraise said school section sixteen, so soon as the assessor shall have performed the duties required of him by the first section of this act; they having first taken an oath or affirmation, before some person competent to administer the same, faithfully and impartially to appraise said land.

Sec. 3. That should either of the commissioners die, or refuse to perform the duties required by this act, or remove out of said county of Crawford, then the county commissioners of said county shall fill such vacancy so often as it may occur.

Sec. 4. That the commissioners appointed by virtue of this act, are hereby authorized, if they deem it expedient, to take to their assistance the surveyor of Crawford county, who under their direction shall make such surveys, divisions and maps thereof, as may be necessary for the performance of the duties required of them by this act; and said commissioners and surveyor shall each receive for his services, one dollar and fifty cents, for each day he may be employed in said service, to be paid from the treasury of said county of Crawford, which shall be refunded to said treasury in manner hereinafter provided.

Sec. 5. That so soon as said school section sixteen has been surveyed under the direction of said commissioners, and maps thereof made as provided in the fourth section of this act, the said commissioners shall cause to be delivered to the auditor of Crawford county, such surveys, and divisions and map thereof, and the separate appraisement of such lot laid off in said section, if the same shall have been divided into lots, and otherwise, the appraisement of the entire section so made under the requirements of this act; and it shall be the duty of such auditor, after having given thirty days previous notice thereof, by advertisement in some newspaper published in Crawford county, and if no newspaper be published in said county, or if the publisher of any newspaper in said county shall refuse to publish the same, then the notice shall be given by affixing such notice on the door of the court house in said county, and in five other public places in said county, three of which shall be in the township of Lykins, thirty days previous to such sale; and the affidavit of one or more such commissioners, certifying the manner, time, and places of publishing such notice, shall be conclusive evidence of such fact, to offer such section or such lot laid off in such section separately, for sale, between the hours of ten o'clock A. M. and five o'clock P. M. on the day designated in such notice, and shall sell the same, and each of the same, to the highest bidder: *Provided*, That neither said section, nor any part of said section, shall be sold for less than its appraised value, and that one fourth of the money, bid for the same, shall be paid at the time of sale; and the remaining three-fourths of the money so bid, shall be paid in three equal instalments, payable annually, and successively after the day of said sale, with interest at the rate of six per cent. per annum, on all moneys unpaid, to be computed from said day of sale: and said commissioners may continue said sale, by adjournment, from day to day, for three successive days, if any portion of such section shall remain unsold; the sale thereof may be adjourned for a time not exceeding three months; and said commissioners shall in like manner proceed giving like notice of each succeeding sale, until the whole be sold.

Sec. 6. That on the sale of said lands so made as aforesaid, the auditor of said county shall take a bond from each purchaser, with at least one sufficient surety conditional for the payment to the treasurer of Crawford county, of all the moneys due for said land, or any part thereof, with the interest thereon to become due or accruing, to be applied to the use of schools in said township of Lykins; and said auditor, on the final payment of said bond, according to the conditions thereof, shall make and execute a deed or deeds of said land, to the purchaser or purchasers thereof, his or their heirs or assigns in fee simple; and said purchase money, when received, shall be deposited in the common school fund, for the benefit of said township; *Provided*, That if any person or persons, who shall purchase any part of said school section, under the provisions of this act, shall be desirous of completing the payment for the same, within a less

51—L

time than that required by the obligation of the bond, he shall be allowed to complete payment for the same at any time, and shall be entitled to receive a deed, in fee simple, for said land, in the manner herein provided.

Sec. 7. That the auditor of said county shall be entitled to receive, for all conveyances he may be required to make by virtue of this act, twelve and a half cents for each hundred words contained therein, and in like proportion for any smaller number; and that the assessor be entitled to receive for his services performed under the provision of this act, the sum of one dollar and fifty cents per day, for each day he may be necessarily employed in said service.

Sec. 8. That the treasurer of said county shall, out of the first moneys that may come to his hands of the interest of said purchase money, or moneys, pay the said assessor, commissioners, surveyor, and auditor, the fees and compensation hereinbefore specified to be paid to said assessors, commissioners, surveyor, and auditor, as well as all necessary fees and expenses for acknowledging said deeds, and for publishing the advertisements, made necessary by the requirements of this act.

WILLIAM MEDILL,
Speaker pro tem. of the House of Representatives.

ELIJAH VANCE,
Speaker of the Senate.

March 11, 1836.

AN ACT

To incorporate the North Union School Association of Carroll county.

Sec. 1. *Be it enacted by the General Assembly of the State of Ohio,* That Jacob Everhart, Geo. Tope, Jonathan Kelley, Jacob Tope, Augustus Rigly, John Scott, jr., John Tope, and William Crow, together with such other persons as may hereafter be associated with them, be, and they are hereby created a body corporate and politic, by the name and style of the North Union School Association of Carroll county, with perpetual succesion, and by their corporate name may contract and be contracted with, sue and be sued, answer and be answered unto, plead and be impleaded, defend and be defended, in any court of competent jurisdiction, in all manner of action whatsoever, and may have a common seal, which they may change, alter, or renew at pleasure.

Sec. 2. That the said corporation, by the name and style aforesaid, shall be capable in law of holding real property, either by purchase, gift, grant devise or legacy, to the amount of one acre of land, together with a school house, and such other buildings as may be necessary for the accommodation of a teacher, and the same to dispose of, at pleasure; to receive any gift, grant, or donation, for the use and benefit of said society, and to make and establish such by-laws, rules and regulations, as they may deem necessary, for the good government of the same: *Provided, however,*

That the money and funds of the corporation shall be applied exclusively to the payment of a teacher, and furnishing fuel for the school, and to no other purpose whatever, except so much as may be necessary for the purchase of a lot, erection of a school house, and dwelling house for a teacher.

Sec. 3. That the business and concerns of the society shall be managed by a president, treasurer, clerk, and three trustees, who shall each hold their offices for the term of three years, if they so long continue to discharge the duties of their respective offices with fidelity, except the trustees first elected, who shall hold their offices for the term of one, two and three years, to be by them determined by lot, at their first meeting after their first election; so that one of said trustees shall be elected annually thereafter; and the president and trustees aforesaid shall have power to fill any vacancies that may happen in either of said offices, and the person or persons so appointed shall hold their offices until the next annual election, and until their successors are chosen.

Sec. 4. That the first meeting of the society shall be held on the first Saturday of April, A. D. 1836, and on the first Saturday of April annually, thereafter: and the members of said society, at their first meeting under this act, shall elect, *viva voce*, three judges and a clerk; and when thus organized, shall proceed to elect, by ballot, the officers specified in the third section of this act; and if from any cause there should not be an election held on the day above specified, the corporation shall not thereby be dissolved, but it shall be lawful for said society to elect their officers at any other time, by giving ten days previous notice thereof, by advertisement posted up in three of the most public places in the bounds of. said society.

WILLIAM MEDILL,
Speaker pro tem. of the House of Representatives.
ELIJAH VANCE,
Speaker of the Senate.

March 11, 1836.

AN ACT

To lay out and establish a State road from Lima, in Allen county, to intersect the road from St. Mary's in a direction to Fort Wayne.

Sec. 1. *Be it enacted by the General Assembly of the State of Ohio*, That John Elliot, of Mercer county, Alexander Baity and Ezekiel Hoover, of Allen county, be, and they are hereby appointed commissioners, and Stephen Smith, of said county, surveyor, to lay out and establish a State road from Lima, in Allen county, by way of Hoover's mill, to the town of Armanda; thence to the line of the Miami canal; thence to intersect the road running from St. Mary's in a direction to Fort Wayne, in Indiana.

Sec. 2. That said road commissioners shall, in all respects, be governed by, and the expenses of laying out and establishing said road be paid, according to the provisions of the act entitled, "An act defining the mode of laying out and establishing State roads," passed March 14th, 1831.

Sec. 3. That should a vacancy at any time occur, in the foregoing appointments, by death, removal, refusal to serve, or otherwise, the county commissioners of the county in which such vacancy may happen, shall fill the same, as often as such vacancy may occur, by the appointment of some suitable persons without delay.

WILLIAM MEDILL,
Speaker pro tem. of the House of Representatives.

ELIJAH VANCE,
Speaker of the Senate.

March 1t, 1836.

- - -- --- -- - - - - - .. - -- --

AN ACT

To incorporate the Little Miami Rail-road Company.

Sec. 1. *Be it enacted by the General Assembly of the State of Ohio,* That all persons who shall become stockholders pursuant to this act, in the company hereby authorized, shall be, and are hereby made a body corporate, under the name of "The Little Miami Rail-road Company," with power to construct and maintain a rail-way, with a double or single track, with such appendages as may be deemed necessary for the convenient use of the same; commencing at any eligible point in, or near the town of Springfield, in Clark county; thence by the most practicable route, through the town of Xenia, or the suburbs thereof, and down the valley of the Little Miami river, and of the Ohio river, to the city of Cincinnati, and such points therein, as may be designated and agreed on by the city council of Cincinnati, and the directors of said rail-road company.

Sec. 2. The capital stock of said company shall be seven hundred and fifty thousand dollars, which shall be divided into shares of fifty dollars each, and be deemed personal property.

Sec. 3. Robert Buchanan, George W. Neff, Charles Shultz, William Lewis, and Mathias Kugler, of Hamilton county; John Emery, of Clermont county; Jeremiah Morrow, M. Roosa, Thomas Smith, John M. Hadden, and Allen Wright, of Warren county; John Hadley, of Clinton county; Jas. Galloway, jur. Robert D. Forsman, Bennet Lewis, John Hivling and Joseph Kyle, of Green county; Peter A. Sprigman, James Bogle, Charles Anthony, John T. Stewart, and Roland Brown, of Clark county; shall be commissioners for receiving subscriptions to the capital stock of the corporation agreeably to the provisions of this act.

Sec. 4. It shall be the duty of said commissioners, within six months after the passage of this act, to give notice, once in a week, for three weeks in succession, in some newspaper printed in Xenia, and one other paper printed in Cincinnati, of the time of opening books for the subscription to said stock; and they shall open books at Cincinnati, Xenia, Clifton, Springfield, and such other places as they may deem fit; at each of which places one or more of said commissioners shall attend on the day fixed, and for three days successively, and during at least six hours of each day, shall continue to receive subscriptions to the capital stock of said corporation, from all persons or companies, who will subscribe thereto, in conformity with the provisions of this act.

Sec. 5. Each subscriber, at the time he subscribes, shall pay to the commissioners five dollars on each share of the stock subscribed by him.

Sec. 6. If, at the expiration of the time mentioned in the fourth section of this act, it shall appear that more than the requisite number of shares have been subscribed, it shall be the duty of the commissioners to distribute the same among the subscribers, deducting the excess from the largest sums subscribed; and if, at the expiration of said time, the amount subscribed be less than two hundred thousand dollars, the commissioners shall take further measures to fill the subscriptions to that amount, when the books shall again be closed.

Sec. 7. As soon as may be after the closing of the books, the commissioners shall give notice of the time and place at which a meeting of of the stockholders will be held for the choice of directors; such notice shall be published in one or more newspapers of general circulation along the route of said road: at the time and place appointed for such election, the commissioners, or some of them, shall attend, and the stockholders, or their proxies, duly appointed in writing, shall proceed to elect, by ballot, twelve directors; the commissioners present shall preside at the election, and certify the result in writing, and their certificate recorded in the books of the corporation, shall be evidence of the election of the directors therein named: all subsequent elections shall be conducted in the manner prescribed by the by-laws of said corporation.

Sec. 8. Each stockholder shall be allowed as many votes as he owns shares of stock at the commencement of any election of directors, and a plurality of votes shall determine the choice.

Sec. 9. The directors shall hold their offices for one year, and until others shall be elected in their stead; they shall appoint one of their own number president, and some suitable person as secretary of the corporation; they shall moreover appoint all such officers and agents as the convenience of the company may require.

Sec. 10. The directors shall have power to cause such examinations and surveys of the route for said rail-road to be made as may be necessary to the selection, by them, of the most advantageous line, course or way for said road; and the board of directors shall, as soon thereafter as practicable, select the route on which said road shall be constructed.

Sec. 11. The corporation is hereby empowered to purchase, receive, and hold such real estate as may be necessary and convenient in accomplishing the object for which the corporation is granted: and may, by their agents, engineers, and surveyors, enter upon such route, place or places selected, as aforesaid, by the directors, as the line whereon to construct the said rail-road; and it shall be lawful for the said corporation to enter upon, and take possession of, and use all such lands and real estate, as may be indispensable for the construction and maintenance of said rail-road, and the accommodations requisite to and appertaining unto them; and may also receive, hold, and take all such voluntary grants and donations of land, and real estate, as may be made to said corporation to aid in the construction, maintenance, or accommodation of said road or ways; but all lands or real estate thus entered upon and used by said corporation, and all earth, timber, gravel, and other materials needed by said company, shall be purchased of the owners thereof, at a price to be mutually agreed upon between them; and in case of disagreement of the owner as to the price of any lands or materials so required, for said road, or if the owners are under any disability in law, to contract, or are absent from the county, application may be made, either by said owners, or by said corporation, to any judge of the court of common pleas within which said lands or materials may lie, specifying the lands or materials so required, or already appropriated; and thereupon said judge shall issue his warrant in writing, directed to the sheriff of the county, requiring him to summon an inquest of three freeholders of the county, who shall not be stockholders, nor interested therein, to appear at, or near said land, or materials, to be valued on a day named in said warrant, not less than five, nor more than ten days after issuing the same; and if any of the persons do not attend, the said sheriff shall forthwith summon as many as may be necessary to fill said inquest, and the persons so empannelled, shall, on their oaths or affirmations, value the damages which the several owners will sustain by the use or occupation of the lands, or materials, or property required by said company, having due regard to the benefit such owners may derive from the location and structure of said road; and said inquest shall reduce their valuation to writing; and such valuation, when paid, or tendered to said owners, or deposited in any bank, to their credit, or their proper representatives, shall entitle said company to the materials, use and occupation of said lands, for the purposes of said road, and all estate and interest therein, as fully as if it had been conveyed by the owners of the same: and every sheriff, and freeholder, so acting, shall receive one dollar per day, for his services, to be paid by said company; either party may, within ten days after such valuation is made, appeal from the same, to the court of common pleas of the county, by giving notice thereof to the opposite party, or by filing in the clerk's office, a copy of such valuation, with notice thereto annexed; and said court may, for good cause shown, order a new valuation, and on final hearing, the court shall award costs according to equity.

Sec. 12. Whenever it shall be necessary for the construction of the rail-road, to intersect or cross any stream of water, or water course, or any road or highway, lying in or across the route of said road, it shall be lawful for the corporation to construct the said rail-way across or upon the same; but the corporation shall restore the stream, or water course, or road or highway, thus intersected, to its former state, or in a sufficient manner not to impair its usefulness: and if said corporation, after having selected a route for said rail-way, find any obstacle to continuing said location, either by the difficulty of construction, or procuring right of way at reasonable cost, or whenever a better and cheaper route can be had, it shall have authority to vary the route, and change the location.

Sec. 13. The said corporation shall have power to locate and construct branched roads from the main route, to other towns, or places, in the several counties through which said road may pass.

Sec. 14. It shall be lawful for the directors to require payment of the sums to be subscribed to the capital stock, at such time, and in such instalments, as they shall see fit; and if the instalments remain unpaid for sixty days after the time'of payment has elapsed, the board may collect the same by suit, or shall have power to sell the stock at public auction, for the instalments then due, giving twenty days notice of the time and place of sale, by advertisement in some newspaper in general circulation in the county where such sale is to be made; and the costs of making said sale, and the residue of the price obtained, shall be paid over to the former owner.

Sec. 15. That said company may demand and receive for tolls upon, and transportation of goods, produce, merchandize, or property of any kind whatsoever, transported by them along said rail way, any sum not exceeding the following rates: on all goods, merchandize, or property of any description, transported by them, a sum not exceeding one and a half cents per mile, for toll, five cents per ton per mile, for transportation; and for the transportation of passengers, not exceeding three cents per mile, for each passenger: and all persons paying the tolls aforesaid, may, with suitable and proper cars, transport persons and property on said rail-road; subject to the rules and regulations of said company, as to the construction and speed of said cars, and the regulation of the motive power.

Sec. 16. It shall be lawful for said corporation to make any contract with the Mad river and Lake Erie rail-road company, either to unite in the construction of such parts of a road, as may with propriety be common to both, or to provide for the joint transportation of burdens and passengers, over their respective roads; and to apportion the receipts and tolls among the stockholders of their respective companies, in such manner as the boards of directors may agree and determine; and if the company hereby created, shall join their road with the Mad river and Lake Erie rail-road, they shall receive and transport over the road hereby authorized, the cars of said Mad river and Lake Erie rail-road company, furnishing the motive power for drawing the same, without unlading, and charging therefor, the same rates of toll as shall be charged by the Mad river and Lake Erie. rail-road company, on their own road, north of Springfield.

Sec. 17. That the State shall have the right at any time after the expiration of thirty-five years from the passage of this act, to purchase and hold said rail-road for the use of the State, at a price not exceeding the original cost for the construction of the road, and the necessary permanent fixtures thereto, at the time of purchase, and fifteen per centum thereon; of which cost an accurate statement, in writing, shall be submitted to the General Assembly, duly attested by the oath of the officers of said company, if required by the General Assembly.

Sec. 18. If the subscribers to the company hereby created, shall not become so far organized as to elect a board of directors within eighteen months from the passage of this act, and within one year thereafter, make *bona fide* contracts for the construction of at least one fourth of said road, the privileges of said corporation shall cease, and this act to be void; and if said company shall not complete said road, within seven years, the further privilege of constructing the same, shall also cease, and revert to the State.

Sec. 19. Whenever the dividends of said company shall exceed the rate of six per cent., the Legislature of this State may impose such reasonable taxes on the amount of such dividends, as may 'be reserved from other rail road companies.

Sec. 20. That any other rail-road company, which has been, or may hereafter be chartered by law of this State, may join and connect any rail-road with the road hereby contemplated, and full right and privilege is hereby reserved to the State, or individuals, or any company incorporated by law of this State, to cross this road: *Provided,* That in so crossing no injury shall be done to the works of the company hereby incorporated, on such terms as the said companies may agree, and on payment of proper tolls, to have their cars drawn on the road hereby authorized, by the Little Miami rail-road company, without delay, and without unlading; the said Little Miami rail-road company furnishing the motive power, at a reasonable price.

Sec. 21. The directors of said company shall semi-annually make and declare a dividend of the profits arising from the business of the company, after deducting their present liabilities, and the current and probable contingent expenses, and divide the same among the stockholders, in proportion to the number of their respective shares.

Sec. 22. If any person or persons, shall wilfully and maliciously injure the said road, or any building, machine, or other works of the said corporation, appertaining thereto, the person or persons so offending, shall forfeit and pay to the said corporation, double the amount of damages sustained by means of such offence, injury, or obstruction; to be recovered in the name of said corporation, with costs of suit, in any court having cognizance thereof: and shall also be subject to indictment in the court of common pleas, in the county where the offence was committed, and upon conviction, shall be punished by fine, not exceeding two hundred dollars, or imprisonment, not exceeding thirty days, or both, at the discretion of the court.

WILLIAM MEDILL,
Speaker pro tem. of the House of Representatives.
ELIJAH VANCE,
Speaker of the Senate.

March 11, 1836.

--- --- --- --- ---

AN ACT

To incorporate the Shaw Academy, in the county of Cuyahoga

WHEREAS, John Shaw, late of Euclid, Cuyahoga county, Ohio, deceased, by his last will and testament, devised certain lands therein described, to William Adams, Thomas Crosby, and Andrew Cozzard, their heirs and assigns, in trust that, the rents and profits thereof should be appropriated to the support of a professor or professors, or other teachers of an academy, which might thereafter be established in the township of Euclid: *Provided,* That the building to be erected, should, with the apparatus, be worth at least two thousand dollars; be erected on a designated portion of the devised premises; and be called and named "The

Shaw Academy;" and that the character of the institution should be purely literary and scientific, and be governed upon principles of Christian morality: Therefore,

Sec. 1. *Be it enacted by the General Assembly of the State of Ohio*, That there shall be an academy established in Euclid, in the county of Cuyahoga, by the name of "The Shaw Academy;" and that Clifford Belden, Alvin Hollister, Wm. M. Camp, J. H. Camp, S. E. Smith, P. P. Candit, Joseph Newell, Moses Mash, Jas. P. Bannel, Horatio N. Parks, Curtis Burton, M. S. McIlrath, Theron Parks, S. Currier, E. Burton, M. Wimple, Darius Adams, George W. Williams, John West, jr., F. Jared, Ira Sawtell, M. Linley, Rowland H. Lee, Isaac Page, H. B. Burton, Benjamin Houghland, Adaniram Peck, Henry L. Porter, H. Foote, Wm. Adams, S. B. Meeker, William Nott, Denis Cooper, David Bannel, Cornelius Thorp, Ezekiel Adams, John Adams, Garret Tharp, 2d, Samuel McIlrath, Sheldon Parks, Hiram McIlrath, Luther Dille, Ezra M. Dille, Peter Thorp, Abijah, Abner and Thos. D. Crosby, Lyman Crosby, Ithamee Bonnel, Thomas McIlrath, jr. John Welch, Stephen R. Stebbins, Josephus Hendershot, John Perkins, Samuel Ruple, Chauncey Hendershot, Lebbeus S. Dille, Jedutham Actum, H. G. Campton, Charles S. Ellarmey, C. Kingsbury, Albert Stebbins, Casper Hendershot, L. C. Ruple, Jacob Compton, Andrew McIlrath, jr., Samuel Eddy, Richard Curtis, Smith Meeker, Wm. B. Lucas, J. D. Crocker, who have subscribed stock, and associated themselves together for the purpose of establishing such academy, together with such other persons as may hereafter subscribe stock in said academy, their successors and assigns, shall be, and they are hereby created a body coporate and politic, by the name and style of "The Shaw Academy;" by that name they shall have perpetual succession, and shall have power to acquire, purchase, receive and possess, hold, retain, and enjoy to themselves and their successors, property, both real, and personal, and mixed; and the same to sell, grant, and convey, rent and dispose of; to sue and be sued, plead and be impleaded, answer and be answered unto, defend and be defended, contract and be contracted with; and also to have and use a common seal, and the same to alter and renew at their pleasure.

Sec. 2. That the stock of said academy shall consist of shares of ten dollars each; shall be deemed personal property, and shall be transferable on the books of said corporation, in such manner, and under such rules as may be prescribed by the board of trustees: *Provided*, That the property of said corporation shall not exceed twenty thousand dollars, nor its annual income two thousand dollars.

Sec. 3. That the corporate concerns of said academy shall be managed by a board of trustees, consisting of nine members, one of whom they shall elect their president, any five of whom shall constitute a quorum to do business; they shall be elected by the stockholders on the first Monday of March, annually, and shall hold their offices for one year, and until their successors are elected: the election of trustees shall be by ballot; each stockholder shall be entitled to one vote for each share by him or her owned, to the amount of ten shares; above this number one vote for every four shares, and may in writing appoint another stockholder his or her proxy, to vote in his or her stead; and the trustees elected as aforesaid, shall constitute said board of trustees, and the said trustees shall have power to fill all vacancies in their own body, by appointment, and the persons appointed as aforesaid, shall continue in office until the next regular election; and if any election should not be made on the day pointed out by this act, such election, as aforesaid, may be made on any other day, by giving ten days notice of the time and place of holding such election.

Sec. 4. That the board of trustees shall have power to make, pass, ordain and establish all such ordinances, by-laws, rules and regulations as they may deem necessary and convenient for the good government of said academy, its officers and servants, and for the management of the property and affairs of the said corporation to the best advantage.

Sec. 5. The board of trustees shall from time to time appoint such professors or instructors, or teachers for said academy, as they may deem necessary, with such salaries or compensation as in their opinion shall be reasonable, and may remove them, or any of them at pleasure, and may prescribe and direct the course of study in said academy to be pursued.

Sec. 6. That the said trustees shall faithfully apply all funds or property by them collected or received, or the proceeds of the same, according to their best judgment, and as nearly according to the intentions and directions of the subscribers, or donors, as the nature of the case will admit, either in erecting or repairing suitable buildings, or in supporting professors or teachers, or in procuring suitable books, maps, or apparatus for said academy, and generally to advance the interest and prosperity of said institution.

Sec. 7. The said board of trustees shall appoint a treasurer, secretary, and such other agents or servants as may be necessary, and prescribe the term of service, and duties of their respective offices; the treasurer, before entering on the duties of his office, shall give bond to the said corporation, with such securities and in such sum as the trustees shall require and approve; and they may require bond and security from any other officer by them appointed, when they deem it necessary; all process against said institution shall be by summons, which shall be served by leaving an attested copy, by the proper officer, with the president or treasurer, at least ten days before the return day thereof.

Sec. 8. That all deeds of conveyance shall be made by order of the trustees, signed by the president, and be under the seal of said corporation, and be acknowledged by the president in his official capacity.

Sec. 9. That the object of creating this corporation is to afford greater facilities for the instruction of youth in literature and science, and for the inculcating of good morals, upon christian principles, and to these purposes shall its funds and energies be exerted: *Provided*, That any future Legislature shall have power to alter or amend this act.

WILLIAM MEDILL,
Speaker pro tem. of the House of Representatives.

ELIJAH VANCE,
Speaker of the Senate.

March 12, 1836.

411

AN ACT

To incorporate the Rome Academical Company, in the county of Ashtabula.

Sec. 1. *Be it enacted by the General Assembly of the State of Ohio,* That Erastus Chester, Albert H. Marrion, Levi Crosby, Richard Tinan, Elijah Croply, Sebre Champion, Richard Miller, Travers A. Miller, Cyrus Richmond, Reuben Saunders, Joseph Tinan, and Eliel Croply, together with such other persons as may hereafter be associated with them for academical purposes, are hereby created a body politic and corporate, with perpetual succession, by the name of the "Rome Academical Company;" and by that name shall be competent to contract and be contracted with, sue and be sued, to answer and be answered unto, in all courts of law and equity; and to acquire, possess, and enjoy, sell, convey and dispose of property, both real and personal; and shall have a common seal, which they may alter at pleasure: *Provided,* That the value of such property shall not exceed ten thousand dollars.

Sec. 2. That Erastus Chester, Albert H. Marvin and Levi Crosby, are hereby constituted trustees; Richard Miller, treasurer; and Travers A. Miller, secretary, until their successors are chosen: *Provided,* That any three of the persons named in the first section of this act shall have power to call a meeting, by giving ten days previous notice thereof, by advertisements set up at three of the most public places in the town of Rome.

Sec. 3. That said corporation shall have power to form a constitution, and adopt by-laws for its government; to prescribe the number and title of its officers, and define their powers and duties; to prescribe the manner in which members may be admitted and dismissed, and all other powers necessary to the efficient management of its corporate concerns: *Provided,* That the constitution, by-laws and regulations of the corporation be consistent with the constitution and laws of the United States and of this State.

Sec. 4. That any future Legislature may modify or repeal this act: *Provided,* That the title to any property, real or personal, acquired or conveyed, under its provisions, shall not be thereby affected.

WILLIAM MEDILL,
Speaker pro tem. of the House of Representatives.

ELIJAH VANCE,
Speaker of the Senate.

March 12, 1836.

AN ACT

To incorporate the First Congregational Society of Dover, in the county of Cuyahoga.

Sec. 1. *Be it enacted by the General Assembly of the State of Ohio,* That Wells Porter, Nathan Basset, H. W. Howard, Joseph Stocking, Jonathan

Oaks, and Andrew Ford, and their associates, that now are, or may be hereafter associated with them, be, and they are hereby created a body politic and corporate, by the name and style of "The First Congregational Society of Dover," and as such shall have perpetual succession, and be capable in law of suing and being sued, answering and being answered unto, in any court of law or equity.

Sec. 2. That said corporation, by the name aforesaid, shall be capable in law and equity, to have and receive, acquire and hold, either by gift, grant, devise or purchase, any estate, real, personal or mixed, and may have, mortgage, sell and convey the same: *Provided*, That the annual income of all such property shall not exceed two thousand dollars.

Sec. 3. That there shall be elected by ballot, on the first Tuesday of May, annually, a president, secretary, treasurer, and three trustees, who shall have the entire control and management of the property and financial concerns of the corporation, and may fill all vacancies that may happen in their own body, until the next annual election, and make such written by-laws, rules and regulations, as may be necessary for the prudent and efficient management of its pecuniary and ecclesiastical affairs.

Sec. 4. That the unfinished house for public worship erected in said society, by individuals belonging to said society, and avails of a donation made by Nehemiah Hubbard, of Middletown, Connecticut, shall belong to said society; and all members of said society who have, or may hereafter contribute the sum of ten dollars towards the completion of said house, or shall own at least one third part of some one of the slips in said house, shall be entitled to vote in all matters relating to said house, which shall forever be appropriated as a place of public worship, exercise and business of said society: *Provided*, The church in said society shall retain substantially the same confession of faith that was adopted by the said church, October first, 1832; but said house shall never be permanently appropriated to the use of any church which shall adopt a confession of faith substantially different from the one above referred to.

Sec. 5. That all meeting of the corporations in their corporate capacity, shall, be called by the trustees; who shall cause notice of the time and place of such meeting to be posted up on the door of said meeting house, at least ten days before such meeting.

Sec. 6. That Wells Porter shall be president; H. W. Howard, secretary; Nathan Bassett, treasurer; Joseph Stocking, Jonathan Oaks, and Andrew Ford, trustees of said corporation, until the first annual election, and until others are elected in their places.

Sec. 7. That any future Legislature may alter, amend or repeal this act: *Provided*, Such alteration, amendment or repeal shall not affect the title of any property acquired or conveyed under its provisions.

WILLIAM MEDILL,
Speaker pro tem. of the House of Representatives.

ELIJAH VANCE,
Speaker of the Senate.

March 12, 1836.

413

AN ACT

To incorporate the First Congregational Society of Sharon, in the county of Medina.

Sec. 1. *Be it enacted by the General Assembly of the State of Ohio,* That Luther Fitch, Cyrus M. Johnston, Barnabas Crane, Samuel Castner, William Johnston, Christian Hackett, Porter Smith and Homer Johnston, and their associates that now are or may hereafter be associated with them, be, and they are hereby created a body politic and corporate by the name and style of " The First Congregational Society of Sharon;" and as such shall have perpetual succession, and be capable in law, to sue and be sued, plead and be impleaded, answer and be answered, defend and be defended, in any court of law or equity; and may have a common seal, which they may alter, change, or renew at pleasure.

Sec. 2. That said corporation, by the name aforesaid, shall be capable in law and equity to have, receive, acquire and hold, either by gift, grant, devise, or purchase, any estate, real, personal and mixed, and may lease, mortgage, sell and convey the same: *Provided,* That the annual income of all such property shall not exceed two thousand dollars.

Sec. 3. That there shall be elected, by ballot, on the first Monday in November, annually, three trustess, who shall have the entire control and management of the property and financial concerns of the corporation; they shall have power to appoint a clerk and treasurer, to fill all vacancies that may happen in their own body, until the next annual election thereafter; and make such written by-laws, rules and regulations, as may be necessary for the prudent and efficient management of its pecuniary affairs: *Provided,* The same be not inconsistent with the laws of the United States, and of this State.

Sec. 4. That [at] all elections, held under the provisions of this act, each member, above the age of twenty-one years, shall be entitled to vote; and a plurality of votes shall, in all instances, be deemed sufficient to elect; and the officers so elected shall hold their offices until their succesors shall have been duly elected: *Provided,* That a failure to hold an election shall not be a forfeiture of the rights and privileges herein granted.

Sec. 5. That all meetings of the corporation, in their corporate capacity, either for the election of officers, or other purposes, shall be called by the trustees; who shall cause notice of the time and place of such meeting to be given, in any manner they may deem most suitable.

Sec. 6. That original process against the corporation shall be served by leaving an attested copy thereof, with any one of the trustees, at least ten days before the return day therein mentioned.

Sec. 7. That Luther Fitch, Barnabas Crane and Porter Smith, be, and they are hereby appointed trustees of said corporation, until the first annual election, and until others are elected in their places.

Sec. 8. That any future Legislature may alter or repeal this act: *Provided,* That such alteration or repeal shall not affect the title of any property acquired or conveyed under its provisions.

WILLIAM MEDILL,
Speaker pro tem. of the House of Representatives.
ELIJAH VANCE,
Speaker of the Senate.

March 12, 1836.

AN ACT

To incorporate the Methodist Protestant Church of the town of Lancaster, in Fairfield county.

Sec. 1. *Be it enacted by the General Assembly of the State of Ohio,* That Jacob Myers, Benjamin Connell, George Myers, Salmon Shaw, George Hood, and their associates, who are, or shall be hereafter connected with them, be, and they are hereby created a body politic and corporate, by the name and style of " The Methodist Protestant Church of Lancaster;" and as such shall have perpetual succession; and by their corporate name may contract and be contracted with, sue and be sued, plead and be impleaded, answer and be answered, defend and be defended, in any court of law and equity; may have a common seal, and alter the same at pleasure.

Sec. 2. That said corporation shall have power to purchase, receive, hold and enjoy, any estate, real, personal and mixed; the annual income of which shall not exceed one thousand dollars, for church purposes, and such other expenses as may be incident to the support of public worship.

Sec. 3. That for the better management of the affairs of said congregation, there shall be elected, by ballot, on the first Monday of May, one thousand eight hundred and thirty six, and on the first Monday of May in each and every year thereafter, by the male members of said church, who are in full connection, above the age of twenty-one years, five trustees, and such other officers, as the said corporation may deem necessary; who shall hold their officers for one year, and until their successors shall be elected.

Sec. 4. That said trustees, any three of whom shall be a quorum to transact business, shall have the entire management and control of all the property of the corporation; erect suitable buildings for public worship, and hold all the property of the congregation in trust for the benefit of the members thereof forever; and shall have power to do any act, or acts, in relation to the same, as in their opinion, may be necessary to advance the interest of the corporation.

Sec. 5. That said trustees shall have power to adopt and establish such by-laws and ordinance as may be deemed necessary for the good government of the corporation: *Provided,* That the same be not contrary to the constitution and laws of the United States, and the State of Ohio; and they shall have farther power to fill any vacancies that may happen in their own body, until the next annual election thereafter: *Provided,* That a failure to meet, and hold any election required by this act, shall not be considered a forfeiture of this charter; but the officers previously chosen, shall serve until their successors are elected; which election may be held at any meeting duly notified by them for that purpose.

Sec. 6. That until the first annual election, required to be held under the provisions of this act, Jacob Myers, Benjamin Connell, George Myers, Salmon Shaw and George Hood, be, and the same are hereby appointed trustees, to take charge of and manage the property and affairs of said corporation.

Sec. 7. That original process against the said corporation, shall be served by leaving an attested copy with one or more of the trustees, at least ten days before the return day; and such service shall be deemed sufficient to bind said corporation.

Sec. 8. That any future Legislature shall have power to modify or repeal this act: *Provided*, That such modification or repeal shall not affect the title to any real estate, or personal, acquired or conveyed under its provisions.

WILLIAM MEDILL,
Speaker pro tem. of the House of Representatives.
ELIJAH VANCE,
Speaker of the Senate.

March 12, 1836.

AN ACT

To incorporate the Cuyahoga Falls Branch Rail-road Company.

Sec. 1. *Be it enacted by the General Assembly of the State of Ohio,* That Samuel A. Wheeler, Henry Newberry, Elisha N. Sill, Ogden Wetmore, Birdseye Booth, Alanson Baldwin and Van R. Humphrey, of the county of Portage; together with such other persons as may hereafter become associated with them, in the manner hereinafter prescribed, their successors and assigns, be, and they are hereby created a body corporate and politic, by the name of "The Cuyahoga Falls Branch Rail-road Company;" and by that name, shall be and are hereby made capable in law to have, hold, purchase, receive and possess, enjoy and retain to them and their successors, all such lands, tenements and hereditaments, with their appurtenances, as shall be necessary or in anywise convenient for the transaction of their business, and such as may in good faith be conveyed to them by way of security or in payment of debts; and the same to sell, grant, rent, or in any manner dispose of; to sue and be sued, plead and be impleaded, answer and be answered, defend and be defended; and also to have and use a common seal, and the same to alter, break or renew at pleasure; and if either of the persons named in this section shall die, or refuse or neglect to exercise the powers and discharge the duties hereby created, it shall be the duty of the remaining persons hereinbefore named, or majority of them, to appoint some suitable person or persons to fill such vacancy or vacancies so often as the same shall occur.

Sec. 2. That the said corporation shall be and is hereby vested with the right to construct a rail-road, with one or more tracks or ways, from some point in Cuyahoga Falls, in the county of Portage, to unite with the Cleveland and Warren rail-road, in the township of Aurora, or at such other point of said rail-road as shall be found expedient, and also from said point in Cuyahoga Falls, to unite with the Akron and Perrysburgh rail-road at Akron, or any part thereof; and to transport, to take and carry persons and property upon the same by the power and force of animals, or of any mechanical or other power, or any combination of them, which said corporation may choose to employ.

Sec. 3. That the capital stock of said company shall be divided into shares of fifty dollars each.

Sec. 4. That the said corporation shall be, and is hereby authorized to raise, of capital stock, sufficient funds for the accomplishment of the objects aforesaid; and for that purpose, the persons named in the first section of this act, or a majority of them, so soon after the taking effect of this act as they shall judge proper, shall cause books to be opened at such times and places as they shall think fit, giving thirty days notice thereof in some newspaper printed in said county, under the management of such persons as they shall appoint, for receiving the subscriptions to the capital stock of said company, and shall keep the same open at least ten days; and each subscriber shall be a member of said corporation for all purposes; and the above named persons, or a majority of them, may prescribe the form of said subscription; and whenever the sum of ten thousand dollars, or a greater part of said stock, shall have been subscribed, it shall be the duty of said persons, or a majority of them, to call a meeting of the stockholders, by causing notice to be published in one or more newspapers in general circulation in the respective places in which such stock shall have been subscribed, at least thirty days previous thereto, of the time and place of holding said meeting, which place shall be at some convenient point on or near the route of said railroad; at which meeting the stockholders who shall attend for that purpose, either in person or by lawful proxy, shall elect by ballot, five directors, who shall hold their offices during one year, and until others are chosen and qualified in their places; and the persons named in the first section, or a majority of them, shall be inspectors of the first election of directors of the said corporation, and shall certify under their hands the names of those duly elected; and shall deliver over to them the said certificates and subscription books; and at said election, and at all other elections, or voting of any description, every member shall have a right of voting by himself, or proxy duly authorized in writing; and each share shall entitle the holder to one vote; and the management of the concerns of said corporation shall be entrusted to five directors, to be elected annually by the stockholders, by ballot; and the directors first chosen, and such directors as shall thereafter be chosen at any subsequent election, shall immediately thereafter meet and elect one of their number, who shall be president thereof, until another election; and also elect a treasurer and secretary, who may be removed at the pleasure of the said president and directors, and others elected in their places; and a majority of said directors shall constitute a board for every purpose within the provisions of this act.

Sec. 5. That in case it should at any time happen that the election of directors shall not be made on any day when, pursuant to this act, it ought to be made, the said corporation shall not for that cause be deemed to be dissolved, but such election may be held at any other time, directed by the by-laws of said corporation.

Sec. 6. That the books of subscription shall remain open as long as the president and directors of said company shall see fit; and each subscriber shall be bound to pay from time to time such instalments on his stock as the said president and directors may lawfully require, they giving at least thirty days previous notice of the time and place of making the payments required, in at least one newspaper in general circulation where the road may pass; but no assessment shall ever be made so as to render any subscriber liable to pay more than fifty dollars for a share; if, however, after the closing of said books, or at any time, it shall appear that sufficient funds have not been raised, the president and directors of said company, or its officers duly authorized for that purpose, may at any time, and from time to time, raise the necessary funds by creating and selling additional shares, in such manner and upon such terms as the said president and directors shall prescribe; and the holders of such additional shares shall thenceforward be members of said corporation for all purposes.

Sec. 7. That if any subscriber shall neglect to pay his subscription, or any portion thereof, for the space of thirty days after he is required so to do by the said president and directors, notice having been given as required in this act, the treasurer of said corporation, or other officers duly authorized for that purpose, may make sale of such share or shares at public auction to the highest bidder, giving at least thirty days notice thereof in some newspaper in general circulation at the place of sale; and the same shall be transferred by the treasurer to the purchaser; and such delinquent subscriber shall be held personally accountable to the corporation for the balance, if his share or shares shall be sold for less than the amount remaining due thereon, and shall be entitled to the overplus, if the same be sold for more than the amount so remaining due, after deducting the costs of sale.

Sec. 8. That the said corporation be, and they are hereby authorized to cause such examinations and surveys to be made by their agents, surveyors and engineers, of the ground lying in the vicinity of said route, as shall be necessary to determine the most eligible and expedient route whereon to construct said rail-road; and the examination being made, and the route determined, it shall be lawful for said corporation, by themselves or lawful agents, to enter upon and take possession of all such lands, materials and real estate, as may be indispensable for the construction and maintenance of said rail-road, and the examination requisite and appertaining thereto; but all lands, materials or real estate thus entered upon, used or occupied, which are not donations, shall be purchased by the corporation, of the owner or owners thereof, at a price to be mutually agreed upon between them; and in case of disagreement as to the price, it shall be the duty of the commissioners of the proper county, upon a notice to be given them by either party, in writing, and making satisfactory proof that the opposite party has had at least three days notice of the intended application, to appoint three disinterested freeholders of the proper county, to determine the damages which the owner or owners of the lands, materials or real estate so entered upon or used by the said corporation, has or have sustained by the occupation or use of the same; and upon payment by the said corporation of such damages to the person or persons to whom the same may be awarded as aforesaid, then the said corporation shall be deemed to be, and stand seized and possessed of the use, for the purpose of said road, of all such lands, materials or real estate, as shall have been appraised; and it shall be the duty of said appraisers to deliver to the said corporation a written statement, signed by them or a majority of them, of the award they shall make, containing a description of the land, materials or real estate appraised; to be recorded by the said corporation in the commissioners office in said county: *Provided*, That either party shall have power, except in cases only where materials are

53—L

used, to appeal from the decision of the said appraisers to the court of common pleas of the proper county, at any time within twenty days after the appraisers shall have made their return as aforesaid, and said court shall proceed thereon as in cases of appeals on application for damages in laying out and establishing county roads.

Sec. 9. That the appraisers, authorized by the foregoing section of this act, before they proceed to estimate damages, shall severally take an oath or affirmation, faithfully, impartially and honestly to discharge their said duty, by returning the true amount of damages, over and above the benefits arising from said road, estimated in cash; and the said appraisers shall severally be entitled to receive from said corporation one dollar per day for every day they may be necessarily employed: *Provided, however,* That if said applicant or applicants shall not obtain an award of damages, then, and in such case, said applicant or applicants shall pay all costs.

Sec. 10. That the said corporation shall have power to determine the width and dimensions of said rail-road, not exceeding one hundred feet; whether it shall be a double or single track; to regulate the time and manner in which property and passengers shall be transported thereon; and the manner of collecting tolls for transportation; and to erect and maintain buildings for the accommodation of the business of the corporation, as they may deem advisable or for their interest.

Sec. 11. That said corporation may construct the rail-road across any road, canal, highway, stream of water or water course, if the same shall be necessary; but the said corporation shall restore said road, highway, stream of water or water course, thus intersected or crossed, to its former state of usefulness, or in such a manner as not to impair its convenience, usefulness or value, to the owners or the public.

Sec. 12. That said corporation may demand and receive for tolls and transportation on said rail-road, such amount as may be fixed by the by-laws of said company: *Provided,* That the amount shall not exceed that charged in like cases upon the rail-roads with which said branch may be connected; and any person or persons paying the tolls may place cars upon said road, and transport and carry persons and property on the same; subject to the rules and regulations of said company as to the construction and speed of said cars.

Sec. 13. That at the regular annual meeting of the stockholders of said company, it shall be the duty of the president and directors in office for the previous year, to exhibit a clear and distinct statement of the affairs of the company; and the president and directors shall annually or semi-annually declare and make such dividend as they may deem proper of the nett profits arising from the resources of said company, deducting the necessary current and probable contingent expenses, and they shall divide the same among the stockholders of said company in proportion to their respective shares in the stock paid in to the company.

Sec. 14. That the said president and directors, or a majority of them, may appoint all such officers, engineers, agents or servants whatsoever, as they may deem necessary for the transaction of the business of the company, and may remove any of them at their pleasure; and they, or a majority of them, shall have power to determine the compensation of all such engineers, officers, agents or servants, and to contract with them for their respective services; and to determine by their by-laws the manner of adjusting and settling all accounts against the said company; and also, the manner and evidence of the transfers of stock in said company; and they, or a majority of them, shall have power to pass all by-laws which they may deem necessary or proper for exercising all the powers vested in the company hereby incorporated, and for carrying into effect the objects of this act; such by-laws not being inconsistent with the constitution and laws of Ohio and of the United States.

Sec. 15. The State shall have the power, at any time after the expiration of twenty years from the completion of the road, to purchase and hold the same for the use of the State, by paying to the corporation therefor the amount expended by them in locating and constructing the same, and the necessary permanent fixtures at the time of purchase, with fifteen per cent. thereon: *Provided*, That the sum to be paid by the State for the said road and appurtenances shall not be less in the aggregate than the amount expended in the construction thereof, and six per cent. per annum thereon, after deducting the dividend received by the stockholders.

Sec. 16. That in any suit instituted against said corporation, service of process made upon any one of the directors, not less than ten days before the return day of said process, shall, in all courts and places be deemed and held a sufficient and valid service on the said corporation.

Sec. 17. That when the said rail-road shall be completed, the president and directors of said company shall make out a minute, full and detailed statement, in writing, of the expenses incurred by said corporation in locating, exploring of routes, and constructing said rail-road; which report shall be verified by the oaths of said president and directors, and filed by them in the office of the Secretary of State; and if, after the first location of the route of said rail-road, or the completion of the same, as aforesaid, any alteration shall be made in the course thereof, or in any of its branches or connections, the said president and directors shall, in like manner, from time to time, make out and file statements of the expenses incurred by such alterations, branches or connections, as aforesaid.

Sec. 18. That any rail-road company, now or hereafter to be chartered or created by law of this State, shall have power to join and unite with the road hereby incorporated, at any point which the directors of said company may think advisable; and any cars, carriage or other vehicle, used on either road, joined or intersected, may run, pass and occupy the intersected or united road, without re-loading, or change of cargo or passengers; subject, however, to the rules and regulations, and to the tolls and charges, common on the road so used and occupied.

Sec. 19. That if any person shall wilfully obstruct, or in any way spoil, injure, or destroy said road, or any part thereof, or either of its branches, or any part thereof, or any thing belonging or incident thereto, or any materials to be used in the construction thereof, or any building, fixture or carriage, erected or constituted for the use or convenience thereof, or used thereon, such person or persons shall each be liable for every such offence in treble the damages sustained thereby, to be recovered by action of debt in any court having jurisdiction thereof; and shall also be subject to an indictment in the court of common pleas of the county where such offence was committed; and upon conviction thereof, shall be punished by fine, not exceeding one hundred dollars, and imprisonment in the county jail, not exceeding twenty days.

Sec. 20. Whenever the dividends of said company shall exceed six per cent. per annum, the Legislature of this State may impose such reasonable tax on such dividends as shall be received from other rail-road companies.

WILLIAM MEDILL,
Speaker pro tem. of the House of Representatives.
ELIJAH VANCE,
Speaker of the Senate.

March 12, 1836.

AN ACT

To incorporate the Bridgeport, Cadiz and Sandusky Rail-road Company.

Sec. 1. *Be it enacted by the General Assembly of the State of Ohio,* That Ebenezer Martin, David Allen, and Moses Roads, of Belmont county; John B. Bayless, John W. Gill, Joseph Updergraff, Rhodes R. Dilworth, of Jefferson county; John S. Lacey, Daniel Kilgore, Samuel Osborn, Thos. Bingham, and Thomas Hogg, of Harrison county; Jacob Blickensderfer, John Coventry, C. Deardorff, James Boyd, and Peter Williams, of Tuscarawas county; Samuel S. Henry, and William R. Sapp, of Holmes county; Luther L. Pratt, and Francis Graham, of Richland county; Edward Avery, John Walter, and Thomas Robinson, of Wayne county; Platt Bendict, and John V. Budenburg, of Huron county; Jesse S. Olmsted, and John Bell, of Sandusky county; together with such other persons as may thereafter become associated with them, in the manner hereinafter prescribed, their successors and and assigns, be, and they are hereby created a body corporate and politic, by the name of "The Bridgeport, Cadiz and Sandusky Rail-road Company;" and by that name shall be and are hereby made capable in law to have, hold, purchase, receive and possess, enjoy and retain to them and their successors, all such lands, tenements, and hereditaments, with their appurtenances, as shall be necessary or convenient for the transaction of their business, and such as may, in good faith, be conveyed to them, by way of security, or in payment of debts, and the same to sell, grant, rent, or in any manner dispose of; to sue and be sued, implead and be impleaded, answer and be answered, defend and be defended, in courts of record, or in any other place whatever; and also to make, have and use a common seal, and the same to alter, break or renew at pleasure; and they shall be, and are hereby invested with all the powers and privileges which are by law incident to corporations of a similar nature, and which are necessary to carry into effect the objects of this association; and if either of the persons named in this section shall die, refuse or neglect to exercise the powers and discharge the duties hereby created, it shall be the duty of the remaining persons hereinbefore named, or a majority of them, to appoint some suitable person or persons to fill such vacancy or vacancies, so often as the same shall occur.

Sec. 2. That said corporation shall be, and they are hereby vested with the right to construct a single or double rail-way or road, from Bridgeport, in Belmont county, or other point on the Ohio river, by the valley of Short creek, through Cadiz, in Harrison county; New Philadelphia and Dover, in Tuscarawas county; thence (passing through Millersburgh, in Holmes county, if the same, in the opinion of said company, can be done without injury to the best interest of said company) by such route and other intermediate points, as said company may think best, to the town of Lower Sandusky, in Sandusky county, with privilege of extending said road to the Maumee river, or the Maumee bay; and the said company shall have the right to carry persons and property on said road when constructed, by the force of steam, animal, or mechanical, or other power, or any combination of them which the company may choose to employ.

Sec. 3. That the capital stock of said corporation shall be two millions of dollars, and shall be divided into shares of fifty dollars each; and five dollars on each share shall be paid at the time of subscribing.

Sec. 4. That the above named persons, or majority of them, are authorized to open books, for receiving subscriptions to the capital stock of such company, and shall prescribe the form of such subscriptions; which books shall be opened within one year from the passing of this act, at such place or places as they may deem expedient, giving thirty days notice in one or more newspapers in each county, through which the said road will pass, of the time and place, or times and places, of opening said books; and said books shall be kept open at least ten days.

Sec. 5. That as soon as said stock, or fifty thousand dollars thereof, shall have been subscribed, the above named persons, or a majority of them, shall give like notice for a meeting of the stockholders to choose directors, at some time and place at least twenty days thereafter; and if, at such time and place, the holders of one half or more of said stock subscribed, shall attend, either in person or by lawful proxy, they shall proceed to choose from the stockholders, by ballot, twelve directors, each share of capital stock entitling the owner to one vote; and at such election, the persons named in the first section of this act, or those appointed by its provisions to fill vacancies which may have occurred, or any three of them, if no more be present, shall be inspectors of such election, and shall certify in writing, signed by them, or a majority of them, what persons are elected as directors; and if two or more have an equal number of votes, such directors shall determine, by lot, which of them shall be director or directors, to complete the number required, and shall certify the same in like manner; and said inspectors shall appoint the time and place of holding the first meeting of directors, at which meeting seven shall form a board competent to transact all business of the company; and thereafter a new election of directors shall be made annually, at such time and place as the directors shall appoint, by giving thirty days previous notice, in manner aforesaid; and if no election be made on the day appointed, said company shall not be dissolved, but such election may be made at any time appointed by the by-laws of said company; and directors chosen at any election, shall remain directors until others are chosen; and directors chosen at any election shall, as soon thereafter as may be, choose, of their own number, one person to be president, and another to be treasurer of such company, and another to be secretary of said company; and from time to time

Sec. 15. That as soon as the amount of money received for tolls and transportion on said road, or any part thereof, according to the provisions of this act, shall exceed four per cent. on the amount of capital stock paid in, after deducting therefrom the expenses and liabilities of said company, the directors of said company shall make a dividend of such nett profits, among the stockholders, in proportion to their respective shares; and no contingent or accumulating fund, exceeding one per centum of the profits of said company, shall remain undivided for more than six moths.

Sec, 16. That full right and privilege is hereby reserved to the State, or individuals, or any company incorporated by law of this State, to cross this road: *Provided*, That in so crossing, no injury shall be done to the works of the company hereby incorporated.

Sec. 17. That the State shall have the power, at any time after the expiration of thirty-five years from the passage of this act, to purchase and hold the same for the use of the State, at a price not exceeding the original cost for the location and construction of said rail-road, and necessary permanent fixtures at the time of purchase, and fifteen per cent. thereon; of which cost [an] accurate statement in writing, shall be submitted to the General Assembly, duly attested by the oaths of the officers of said company, if the General Assembly shall require it.

Sec. 18. Whenever the dividends of said company shall exceed the rate of six per cent. per annum, the Legislature of this State may impose such reasonable taxes on the amount of such dividends as are received from other Rail road Companies.

Sec. 19. The said corporation shall have power to locate and construct branched roads from the main route, to other towns, or places, in the several counties through which said road may pass.

Sec. 20. That if said rail road shall not be commenced in three years from the passage of this act, and shall not be completed within fifteen years thereafter, then this act to be null and void, and of no effect.

Sec. 21. That this act is hereby declared to be a public act, and shall be so construed in all courts of justice and elsewhere.

WILLIAM MEDILL,
Speaker pro tem. of the House of Representatives.
ELIJAH VANCE,
Speaker of the Senate.

March 12, 1836.

AN ACT

To incorporate the Newark and Mount Vernon Rail-road Company.

Sec. 1. *Be it enacted by the General Assembly of the State of Ohio,* That Daniel Duncan, Isaac Schmucker, Israel Dille, Calvin K. Warner, and Benjamin W. Brice, jr. of the county of Licking; and Benjamin S. Brown, Eli Miller, and Daniel S. Norton, of the county of Knox, together with such other persons as may hereafter become associated with them, in manner herereinafter prescribed, their successors and assigns, be, and they are hereby created a body corporate and politic, by the name of the Newark and Mount Vernon Rail road Company:" and by that name shall be and are hereby made capable in law to purchase, hold, enjoy, and retain to them and their successors, all such lands, tenements, and hereditaments, as shall be necessary for the purposes contemplated by this act, and the same to sell, grant, rent, or in any manner dispose of; and to contract and be contracted with; and if either of the persons named in this section shall die, refuse or neglect to exercise the powers and discharge the duties hereby created, it shall be the duty of the remaining persons hereinbefore named, or a majority of them, to appoint some suitable person or persons to fill such vacancy or vacancies, so often as the same shall occur.

Sec. 2. That said corporation are hereby empowered to cause such examinations and surveys to be made between the town of Newark and Mount Vernon, in the counties of Licking and Knox, as shall be necessary to ascertain the most advantageous route whereon to construct a rail-road, and shall cause an estimate to be made of the probable cost thereof, for each mile separately; and the said corporation shall be and they are hereby invested with the right to construct a rail-road, with one or more railways, or tracks, from the Ohio canal, at the town of Newark, to Mount Vernon aforesaid.

Sec. 3. That the capital stock of said corporation shall be one hundred and fifty thousand dollars, and shall be divided into shares of fifty dollars each; and five dollars on each share shall be paid at the time of subscribing.

Sec. 4. That the above named persons, or a majority of them, or the survivors of them, are authorized to open books for receiving subscriptions to the capital stock of said company, and shall prescribe the form of such subscription; which books shall be opened within two years from the passing of this act, at such place or places as they may deem expedient, giving twenty days notice in some newspaper printed in the counties of Licking and Knox, and in such other place or places as may be thought advisable, of the time and place, or times and places of opening said books; and they shall be kept open at least ten days.

Sec. 5. That as soon as said stock, or one hundred shares thereof, shall have been subscribed, the above named persons, or the same number thereof as shall have given the notice above required, shall give like notice for a meeting of the stockholders to choose directors, at some time, at least thirty days thereafter; and at some place within the said county of Licking; and if at such time and place, the holders of one half or more of said stock subscribed shall attend, either in person or by lawful proxy, they shall proceed to choose from the stockholders, by ballot, nine directors, each share of capital stock entitling the owner to one vote; and at such election, the persons named in the first section of this act, or those appointed by its provisions to fill vacancies which may have occurred, or any three of them, if no more be present, shall be inspectors of such election, and shall certify in writing, signed by them, or a majority of them, what persons are elected directors; and if two or more have an equal number of votes, such inspectors shall determine by lot, which of them shall be director or directors, to complete the number required, and shall certify the same in like manner; and said inspectors shall appoint the time and place of holding the first meeting of directors, at which meeting a majority shall form a board competent to transact all business of the company; and thereafter a new election of directors shall be made annually, at such time and place as the stockholders at their first meeting shall appoint; and if the stockholders shall, at their first meeting, fail to appoint the day of such election, then it shall be holden in the succeeding year, on the same day of the month on which said first election was holden, unless the same should be the first day of the week, in which case it shall be holden on the day next succeeding: and if no election be made on the day appointed, said company shall not be dissolved, but such election may be made at any time appointed by the by-laws of said company; and directors chosen at any election shall remain directors until others are chosen; and directors chosen at any election shall, as soon thereafter as may be, choose of their own number one person to be president, and another to be treasurer of such company, and another to be secretary of said company; and from time to time may choose such other officers as by their by-laws they may designate as necessary: *Provided*, No person shall be a director of said company, who is not a citizen of the State of Ohio.

Sec. 6. That the president and directors of said company may require payment of the subscription to the capital stock, at such times and places, and in such proportions, and on such conditions as they shall think expedient: *Provided*, That notice of such requisition shall be first given in some newspaper printed and in general circulation in the counties in which said road may be located; and if any stockholder shall fail or neglect to pay his subscription to the capital stock, or such part thereof as shall be thus required, for the space of sixty days after the time appointed by said notice for the payment thereof, the president and directors of said company may sell at public vendue so many shares of such delinquent stockholder, as may be necessary to pay such requisition, and all necessary expenses incurred in making said sale; and the share or shares so sold shall be transferred to the purchaser, paying the overplus, if any, to said delinquent, on demand.

Sec. 7. That the directors of said company shall have power to make, from time to time, all needful regulations and by-laws, not inconsistent with the constitution and laws of this State, or of the United States, touching the business of said company, and to determine the number of tracks or rail-ways upon said road, and the width thereof, and the description of carriages which may be used thereon; to regulate the time and manner in which passengers or goods shall be transported thereon, and the manner of collecting tolls for such transportation; and to fix penalties for the breach of any such rule, regulation or by-law, and to direct the mode and condition of transferring the stock of said company; and penalties provided for by said by-laws, may be sued for by any person or persons authorized thereto, in the name of said company, and recovered in an action of debt, before any court having jurisdiction of the amount; and said company may erect and maintain toll houses, and such other buildings and fixtures, for the accommodation of those using said road, and of themselves, as they may deem in any way necessary for their interest or convenience.

Sec. 8. That said company shall have a right to enter upon and lands, to survey and lay down said road, not exceeding one hundred feet in width, and to take any materials necessary for the construction of said road; and whenever any lands or materials shall be taken for the construction of said road, and the same shall not be given or granted to said company, and the owners thereof do not agree with said company, as to the compensation to be paid therefor, the person or persons claiming compensation to be paid as aforesaid, or if the owner or owners thereof are not residents of said county, or minors, insane persons, or married women, then the agents of such non-residents, guardian or guardians of such minor or minors, and insane persons, and the husbands of such married women, may select for themselves an arbitrator, and the said company shall select one arbitrator, and the two thus selected shall take to themselves a third, who shall be sworn and paid, as arbitrators in other cases; and the three, or a majority of them, shall award as arbitrators between the parties, and render copies of their award to each of the parties, in writing, from which award either party may appeal to the court of common pleas for the county in which such lands or materials may have been situate; and in all cases where compensation shall in any manner be claimed for lands, it shall be the duty of the arbitrators and the court to estimate any advantage which the location and construction of said road may be to the claimed for such compensation, and the value of such advantage, if any, shall be set off against the compensation so claimed by said company: and appeals in such cases shall, when taken, be in all respects proceeded in as appeals in other cases to said court, and be brought into said court, by filing the award with the clerk of said court, whose duty it shall be to enter the same on the docket of said court, setting down the claimant or claimants as plaintiff, and said company as defendant; and when the valuation, so ascertained, shall be paid or tendered by said company, said company shall have the same right to retain, own, hold and possess said lands and materials, as fully and absolutely, as if the same had been granted and conveyed to said company by deed, so long as the same shall be used for the purposes of said road.

Sec. 9. That said company may construct the said rail-road across or upon any lands, public road, highway, stream of water or water course, if the same shall be necessary; but the said company shall restore such lands, road, highway, stream of water or water course, to its former state, or in a sufficient manner so as not to impair the usefulness of such road, highway, water or water course, to the owner or the public, without unnecessary delay.

Sec. 10. That any rail-way company, now, or yet to be chartered by law of this State, shall have power to join and unite with the road hereby incorporated, at any point which the directors of such company may think advisable, on such terms as the directors of such companies may respectively agree; and in case of disagreement, then upon such terms as the supreme court may in chancery determine.

Sec. 11. That said company may demand and receive for tolls upon, and the transportation of persons, goods, produce, merchandize, or property of any kind whatsoever, transported by them along said rail-way, any sum not exceeding the following rates: on all goods, merchandize or property of any description whatsoever, transported by them, a sum not exceeding three cents per mile, for toll; ten cents on a ton per mile, for transportation, on all goods, produce, merchandize or property of any description whatsoever, transported by them or their agents; and for the transportation of passengers, not exceeding three cents per mile for each passenger.

Sec. 12. That all persons paying the toll aforesaid, may, with suitable and proper carriages, use and travel upon the said rail-road; always subject, however, to such rules and regulations, as said company are authorized to make, by the seventh section of this act.

Sec. 13. That if proceedings be not had, under this act, within three years from the taking effect thereof, and if said road be not completed within ten years thereafter, then the same to be void and of no effect.

Sec. 14. That so soon as the amount of tolls accruing and received for the use of said road, or any part thereof, according to the provisions of this act, shall exceed five per cent. on the amount of capital stock paid in, after deducting therefrom the expenses and liabilities of said company, the directors of said company shall make a dividend of such nett profit, among the stockholders, in proportion to their respective shares; and no contingent or accumulating fund, exceeding one per centum of the profits of said company, shall remain undivided for more than six months.

Sec. 15. If any person or persons shall wilfully obstruct, or in any way spoil, injure or destroy said road, or either of its branches, or any thing belonging or incident thereto, or any materials to be used in the construction thereof, or any buildings, fixtures or carriages, erected or constructed for the use or convenience thereof, such person or persons shall each be liable for every such offence, to treble the damages sustained thereby; to be recovered by action of debt, in any court having jurisdiction of that amount.

Sec. 16. That the Legislature shall, after the expiration of thirty-five years from the passage of this act, make provision by law for the repayment to said company of the amount expended by them in the construction of said rail-road, and of the necessary permanent fixtures thereto, at the time, with an addition of fifteen per cent. thereon, of which an accurate statement in writing, attested by the oath or affirmation of the officers of said company, shall be submitted to the General Assembly, if required, then said road shall vest in, and become the property of the State.

Sec. 17. That whenever the dividends of said company shall amount to any sum exceeding six per cent. per annum, upon the cost of said road, and the necessary expenses of the same, the Legislature may impose such reasonable taxes upon the amount of such dividend, as may be imposed on other rail-road companies.

WILLIAM MEDILL,
Speaker pro tem. of the House of Representatives.

ELIJAH VANCE,
Speaker of the Senate.

March 12, 1836.

AN ACT

To incorporate the Columbus, London, and Springfield Rail Road Company.

Sec. 1. *Be it enacted by the General Assembly of the State of Ohio,* That all persons who may become stockholders, pursuant to this act, in the company hereby authorized, are hereby made a body corporate, under the name of "The Columbus, London, and Springfield Rail road Company," with power to construct and maintain a rail-way, with a double or single track, with such appendages as may be deemed necessary for the convenient use of the same; commencing at any eligible point, in the city of Columbus; thence, by the most practicable route, through the town of London, or the suburbs thereof; thence through the town of South Charleston, or the suburbs thereof, to Springfield, in Clark county.

Sec. 2. The capital stock of said company, shall be two hundred thousand dollars, which shall be divided into shares of fifty dollars each, and be deemed personal property.

Sec. 3. Gustavus Swan, and William Sullivant, of Franklin county, John Moore, and Aquilla Tolland, of Madison county; and Timothy Lyon, Absalom Mattox, and Rowland Brown, of Clark county, shall be commissioners for receiving subscriptions to the capital stock of the corporation, agreeably to the provisions of this act.

Sec. 4. It shall be the duty of said commissioners, within six months after the passage of this act, to give notice, once in each week, for three weeks in succession, in the newspapers printed in Columbus and Springfield, of the time of opening books for the subscription to the capital stock; and they shall open books at Columbus, London, South Charleston, and Springfield, and such other places as they may deem fit; at each of which places, one or more of said commissioners shall attend on the day fixed, and for three days successively; and, during at least six hours in each day, shall continue to receive subscriptions to the capital stock of said corporation, from all persons or companies, who will subscribe thereto, in conformity with the provisions of this act.

Sec. 5. Each subscriber, at the time he subscribes, shall pay to the commissioners five dollars on each share of the stock subscribed by him.

Sec. 6. If, at the expiration of the time mentioned in the fourth section of this act, it shall appear that more than the requisite number of shares have been subscribed, it shall be the duty of the commissioners to distribute the same among the subscribers, deducting the excess from the largest sums subscribed; and if, at the expiration of said time, the amount subscribed be less than fifty thousand dollars, the commissioners shall take further measures to fill the subscriptions to that amount, when the books shall again be closed.

Sec. 7. As soon as may be, after the closing of the books, the commissioners shall give notice of the time and place at which a meeting of the stockholders will be held, for the choice of directors; such notice shall be published in one or more newspapers, of general circulation, along the route of said road: at the time and place appointed for such election, the commissioners, or some of them, shall attend; and the stockholders, or their proxies, duly appointed in writing, shall proceed to elect, by ballot, ten directors; the commissioners present shall preside at the election, and certify the result in writing, and their certificate recorded in the books of the corporation, shall be evidence of the election of the directors therein named; all subsequent elections shall be conducted in the manner prescribed by the by-laws of said corporation.

Sec. 8. Each stockholder shall be allowed as many votes as he owns shares of stock, at the commencement of any election of directors; and a plurality of votes shall determine the choice.

Sec. 9. The directors, shall hold their offices for one year, and until others shall be elected in their stead; they shall appoint one of their own number president, and some suitable person as secretary of the corporation; they shall moreover appoint all such officers and agents as the convenience of the company may require.

Sec. 10. The directors shall have power to cause such examinations and surveys of the route for said rail-road to be made, as may be necessary to the selection, by them, of the most advantageous line, course or way, for said road; and the board of directors shall, as soon thereafter as practicable, select the route not exceeding one hundred feet in width on which said road shall be constructed.

Sec. 11. The corporation is empowered to purchase, receive, and hold, such real estate, as may be necessary and convenient for the construction and use of said road: and may, by their agents, engineers, and surveyors, enter upon such route, place or places selected, as aforesaid, by the directors, as the line whereon to construct the rail road; and it shall be lawful for the said corporation to enter upon, and take possession of, and use all such lands and real estate, as may be indispensable for the construction and maintenance of said rail road, and the accommodations requisite and appertaining unto them; and may also receive, hold, and take, all such voluntary grants and donations of land, and real estate, as may be made to said corporation, to aid in the construction, maintenance, or accommodation, of said road or ways; but all lands or real estate thus entered upon and used by said corporation, and all earth, timber, gravel, and other materials needed by said company, shall be purchased of the owners thereof, at a price to be mutually agreed upon between them; and, in case of disagreement of the owner as to the price of any lands or materials so required, for said road, or if the owners are under any disability in law, to contract, or are absent from the country, application may be made, either by said owners, or by said corporation, to any judge of the court of common pleas within which said lands or materials may lie, specifying the lands or materials so required, or already appropriated, and, thereupon, said judge shall issue his warrant in writing, directed to the sheriff of the county, requiring him to summon an inquest of five freeholders of the county, who shall not be stockholders, nor interested therein, to appear at, or near said land, or materials, to be valued, on a day named in said warrant, not less than five, nor more than ten days after issuing the same; and if any of the persons do not attend, the said sheriff shall forthwith summon as many as may be necessary to fill said inquest, and the persons so impannelled, shall, on their oaths or affirmations, value the damages which the several owners will sustain by the use or occupation of the lands, or materials, or property required by said company, having due regard to the benefit such owners may derive from the location and structure of said [road;] and said inquest shall reduce their valuation to writing; and such valuation, when paid, or tendered to said owners, or deposited in any bank, to their credit, or their proper representatives, shall entitle said company to the land and materials, and all estate and interest therein, whilst used for the purpose of said road, as fully as if it had been conveyed by the owners of the same: and every sheriff, and freeholder, so acting, shall receive one dollar per day, for his services, to be paid by said company; either party may, within ten days after such valuation is made, appeal from the same, to the court of common pleas of the proper county, by giving notice thereof to the opposite party, or by filing in the clerk's office, a copy of such valuation, with notice thereunto annexed; and said court may, for good cause shown, order a new valuation, and, on final hearing, the court shall award costs according to equity.

Sec. 12. Whenever it shall be necessary for the construction of the rail road, to intersect or cross any stream of water, or water course, or any road or highway, lying in or across the route of said road, it shall be lawful for the corporation to construct the said rail-way across or upon the same; but the corporation shall restore the stream, or water course, or road, or highway thus intersected, to its former state, or in a sufficient manner not to impair its usefulness; and if said corporation, after having selected a route for said rail-way, find any obstacle to continuing said location, either by the difficulty of construction, or procuring right of way at reasonable cost, or whenever a better and cheaper route can be had, it shall have authority to vary the route, and change location, and when it shall be necessary to pass through the lands of any individual, it shall be the duty of said company to provide for such individual proper wagon ways across said road from one part of his land to another without unnecessary delay.

Sec. 13. It shall be lawful for the directors to require payment of the sums to be subscribed to the capital stock, at such time, and in such instalments, as they shall see fit; and if the instalments remain unpaid for sixty days after the time of payment has elapsed, the board may collect the same by suit, or shall have power to sell the stock at public auction, for the instalments then due, and the costs of making such sale, and the residue of the price obtained, shall be paid over to the former owner.

Sec. 14. That said company may demand and receive for tolls upon, and transportation of goods, produce, merchandize, or property of any kind whatsoever, transported by them along said rail-way, any sum not exceeding the following rates: on all goods, merchandize, or property of any description, transported by them a sum not exceeding one and a half cents per mile, for toll; five cents per ton per mile, for transportation; and for the transportation of passengers, not exceeding three cents per mile for each passenger.

Sec. 15. That all persons paying the tolls aforesaid, may, with suitable and proper carriages, transport persons or property on said rail road, subject to the by-laws of said company.

Sec. 16. That any other rail road company now or hereafter to be chartered by law of this State, may join and connect any rail road with the road hereby contemplated, and run cars upon the same, subject to the rules and regulations of this company, as to the construction and speed of said cars, and full right and privilege is hereby reserved to the State or individuals, or any company incorporated by law of this State, to cross this road: *Provided*, That in so crossing, no injury shall be done to the works of the company hereby incorporated.

Sec. 17. That so soon as the money received for tolls and transportation on said road, or of any part thereof, according to the provisions of this act, shall exceed four per cent. on the amount of capital stock paid in after deducting therefrom the expenses and liabilities of said company: the directors of said company shall make a dividend of such nett profits among the stockholders, in proportion to their respective shares: and no contingent or accumulating fund exceeding one per centum of the profits of said company shall remain undivided for more than six months.

Sec. 18. That the State shall have power at any time after the expiration of thirty-five years from the passage of this act to purchase and hold said road for the use of the State at a price not exceeding the original cost for the construction of the road and the necessary permanent fixtures at the time of purchase, and fifteen per cent. thereon; of which cost an accurate statement in writing shall be submitted to the General Assembly, duly attested by the oaths of the officers of said company, if the General Assembly require it.

Sec. 19. If any person or persons shall wilfully and maliciously, injure the said road, or any building, machine or other works of the said corporation, appertaining thereto, the person so offending shall forfeit and pay to said corporation, double the amount of damage, sustained by means of such offence, injury or obstruction, to be recovered in the name of said corporation, with costs of suit, in any court having cognizance thereof, and shall also be subject to indictment in the court of common pleas in the county where the offence was committed, and upon conviction, shall be punished by fine not exceeding two hundred dollars, or imprisonment not exceeding thirty days, or both at the discretion of the court.

Sec. 20. If the subscribers to the company hereby created, shall not become so far organized as to elect a board of directors, within two years from the passage of this act, and within one year thereafter, make *bona fide* contracts for the construction of at least one fourth of said road, the privileges of said corporation shall cease, and this act be void; and if said company shall not complete said road within fifteen years, the further privileges of constructing the same, shall also cease, and revert to the State.

Sec. 21. Whenever the dividends of said company shall exceed the rate of six per cent., the Legislature of this State may impose such reasonable taxes on the amount of such dividends, as may be received from other rail road companies.

WILLIAM MEDILL,
Speaker pro tem. of the House of Representatives.

ELIJAH VANCE,
Speaker of the Senate.

March 12, 1836.

AN ACT

To incorporate the town of Akron, in the county of Portage.

Sec. 1. *Be it enacted by the General Assembly of the State of Ohio,* That so much of the townships of Portage and Coventry, in the county of Portage, as is comprised within the following limits, to wit: beginning on the south line of tract number eight, in said township of Coventry, and at a point in said line, which is three fourths of a mile east of the south-east corner of the south town plat of Akron, as surveyed by John Henshaw; thence north to a line running due east and west, drawn ten rods north of lock sixteen, of the Ohio canal; thence west, along 'such east and west line, one and a half miles; thence south, to the south line of tract number eight, aforesaid; thence east, along said south line, to the place of beginning; be, and the same is hereby created a town corporate, and shall henceforth be known and distinguished by the name of "The Town of Akron."

Sec. 2. That for the good order and government of said town, it shall be lawful for the white male inhabitants, who have resided within the aforesaid limits of said town, for the space of six months next preceding the second Tuesday of June next, and who have the qualifications of electors of members of the General Assembly, to meet at the usual place of holding elections in said township of Portage, on the said second Tuesday of June next, and on the first Tuesday of June, annually, thereafter, at such place as the town council may direct, which shall be determined by notices of the time and place, posted up in three of the most public places in said town, at least ten days before the election, which notice shall be signed by the mayor and recorder, and then and there proceed, by ballot, to elect, by a' plurality of votes, one mayor, one recorder, and five trustees, who shall be either householders or freeholders, residing within the limits of said town, and who shall hold their respective offices for one year, and until their successors are elected and qualified; such mayor, recorder and trustees being so elected and qualified, shall constitute a Town Council, any five of whom shall constitute a quorum for the transaction of business.

Sec. 3. That at the first election to be holden under this act, there shall be chosen *viva voce,* by the electors present, three judges and a clerk of said election, who shall each take an oath or affirmation faithfully to discharge the duties required of them by this act; and at all subsequent elections the trustees, or any two of them, shall be judges, and the recorder clerk; and at all elections held under the provisions of this act, the polls shall be opened between the hours of nine and ten. A. M. and closed at four o'clock, P. M. of said day; and at the close of the polls, the votes shall be counted, and a true statement thereof proclaimed by one of the judges, to the electors present; and the clerk shall make a true record thereof, who shall notify the persons elected to their respective offices, of their election, within five days; and the persons so elected and notified, shall, within five days thereafter, take an oath or affirmation to support the constitution of the United States and of the State of Ohio, and an oath of office: any person elected as aforesaid, neglecting or refusing to qualify

55—L

as aforesaid, shall forfeit and pay into the treasury of said town, the sum of five dollars, to be recovered by an action of debt, before the mayor of said town; and the recorder shall, in the name of said town, demand, receive or sue for such forfeiture, and pay over the same, when collected, to the treasurer, taking his receipt therefor: *Provided,* That no person shall be compelled to serve in any office in said corporation two years in succession.

Sec. 4. That the mayor, recorder and trustees of said town shall be a body politic and corporate, with perpetual succession, to be known and distinguished by the name of the Town Council of Akron; and they and their successors in office shall be authorized to use a common seal, and the same to alter at pleasure; to receive, purchase, acquire, hold and convey any estate, real, personal, or mixed; and to manage and dispose of the same, in such manner as they, or a majority of them, may deem proper: they shall be capable, in the name aforesaid, of suing and being sued, pleading and being impleaded, answering and being answered, in any suit or action, in any court of law and equity in this State; and when any suit or action shall be commenced against said corporation, the first process shall be by summons, a copy of which shall be left with the mayor, or in his absence, at his usual place of abode, at least five days before the return day thereof.

Sec. 5. That it shall be the duty of the mayor, and in his absence or disability to serve, the recorder, to preside at all meetings of the town council; and it shall also be the duty of the recorder to attend all such meetings, and keep an accurate record of their proceedings, to be recorded in a book provided for that purpose: it shall moreover be the duty of the recorder to attend all elections under the provisions of this act; but in case of his absence or disability to serve as such, the trustees shall have power to appoint one of their own number clerk of said election, *pro tem.*

Sec. 6. That the town council shall have power to fill all vacancies which may occur in their body by death, resignation, or otherwise, from among the electors in said town, whose appointment shall continue until the next annual election, and until their successors are elected and qualified; and whenever it may happen that neither the mayor or recorder is present at any meeting of said town council, the trustees shall have power to appoint one of their number to perform the duties of such mayor or recorder, or both, as the case may be, which appointment shall be *pro tempore,* and that the mayor, or a majority of the trustees, shall have power to call a meeting of the town council whenever in his or their opinion the public good of said corporation shall require it.

Sec. 7. That the mayor, recorder, and trustees, or a majority of them, whereof the mayor or recorder shall always be one, or in case of their absence, one of the trustees appointed to fill their vacancy, shall have power and authority to make, ordain and publish all such by-laws, and ordinances, consistent with the constitution of the United States and of this State, as they may deem necessary and expedient for the regulation, interest, safety, health, cleanliness, and convenience of said town, and the same to alter or repeal at pleasure: they shall have power to license groceries, and to provide reasonable penalties for the establishment of the same without such license, within the corporate limits, and shall also be entitled to license the exhibition of public shows within their limits, in the same manner as county auditors are now by law authorized and required to do, and all money so acquired shall be paid into the township treasury, and be appropriated to the support of common schools, within said town: they shall have power to appoint a treasurer, town marshal, and such other subordinate officers as they may deem necessary; to prescribe their duties, and to require of them such security as they may deem necessary for the faithful performance of their duties; to remove them at pleasure; to fix and establish the fees of the officers of said corporation not established by this act, except the trustees, who shall receive no fees: said town council shall also have power to affix to the violation of the by-laws and ordinances of said corporation such reasonable fines and forfeitures as they may deem proper, and provide for the collection and disposition of the same: and they shall have power to lay out and regulate the lots, streets, lanes, alleys, and public grounds; to lay out and determine the width of the side-walks, and regulate the same; to establish and regulate markets: they also shall have power to remove, or cause to be removed, all nuisances and obstructions, and do all things which a corporation of a similar nature can do, to secure the health, peace, and good order of the inhabitants of said town.

Sec. 8. That for the purpose of more effectually enabling the town council to carry into effect the provisions of this act, they are hereby authorized and empowered to assess, for corporation purposes an amount of tax on all property within said town, made taxable by the laws of this State, for State and county purposes, not exceeding in 1836 and 1837, one per cent. and in any one year thereafter, one half of one per cent. on the value thereof, as the same may be found valued on the books of the auditor of the county of Portage, for the current year; the town council shall also have power to organize and establish a fire department, and to promote this object they shall have power, if thereto authorized, by a vote of of the inhabitants of the town, assembled for that purpose, in public meeting, ten days notice of the same being previously given, to raise, by tax, a sum of money, not exceeding five hundred dollars, for the years 1836 and 1837; which sum shall be appropriated to the purchase or repairs of engines, hose, hooks, ladders, and other implements of use, in the arrest and extinguishment of fire.

Sec. 9. That it shall be the duty of the town council to make out, or cause to be made out, by the recorder, a duplicate of taxes, charging each individual therein assessed as aforesaid, within said town; which duplicate shall be signed by the mayor and recorder, and delivered to the marshal, or such other person as shall be appointed collector, whose duty it shall be to collect the same within such time, and in such manner, as the by-laws shall direct; and the said collector shall have power to sell both real and personal estate for the non-payment of taxes within said town, and shall be governed therein by the same laws and regulations as the collectors of State and county taxes; and in case of the sale of any real estate, the recorder shall have power to make and execute deeds therefor, in the same manner that county auditors are by law empowered to do, for lands sold by the county treasurer; and the said collector shall, within ten days after collecting said taxes, pay the same over to treasurer of said corporation, taking his receipt therefor, and who shall receive for his fees such sum as the town council may direct, not exceeding six per cent. on all moneys so by him collected and paid over; said fees to be paid by the treasurer, on the order of the recorder.

Sec. 10. That the by-laws and ordinances of said town shall be posted up in two or more of the most public places within said town, at least ten days before the taking effect thereof, and the certificate of the recorder upon the town record shall be considered sufficient evidence of the same having been done.

Sec. 11. That the town council shall, at the expiration of each year, cause to be made out and posted up in one or more of the most public places in said town, or published in some newspaper, printed in or nearest to said town, an exhibit of the receipts and expenditures of the preceding year; which statement shall be certified by the recorder of said town.

Sec. 12. That the mayor of said corporation shall be a conservator of the peace throughout said town, and shall have within the same, all the powers and jurisdiction of a justice of the peace, in all matters, civil or criminal, arising under the laws of this State, to all intents and purposes whatever: he shall give bond and security, as is required by law of justices of the peace; and the said mayor shall perform all the duties required of him by the by-laws and ordinances of said corporation; and appeals may be taken in all cases from the decisions of said mayor, in the same manner as from the decisions of justices of the peace: he shall keep a docket wherein he shall keep a fair record of all matters of difference tried before him, and shall be allowed and receive the same fees that justices of the peace are or may be entitled to in similar cases.

Sec. 13. That the marshal shall be the principal ministerial officer of said town, and shall have the same powers as constables have by law; and his jurisdiction in criminal cases shall be co-extensive with the county of Portage: he shall execute the process of the mayor, and receive the same fees for his services that constables are allowed in similar cases.

Sec. 14. That said corporation shall be allowed the use of the jail of the county of Portage, for the imprisonment of such persons as may be liable to imprisonment under the by-laws and ordinances of said corporation, and all persons so imprisoned shall be under the charge of the sheriff of the county of Portage, as in other cases.

Sec. 15. That the mayor, recorder, trustees, and other officers of said corporation shall on demand deliver to their successors in office all such books and papers as appertain in anywise to their office.

Sec. 16. That any future Legislature shall have power to alter, amend or repeal this act: *Provided,* That such alteration, amendment or repeal shall not divert the property of said corporation from the purposes expressed in this act.

WILLIAM MEDILL,

Speaker pro tem. of the House of Representatives.

ELIJAH VANCE,

Speaker of the Senate.

March 12, 1836.

To incorporate the town of Taylorsville, in the county of Muskingum.

Sec. 1. *Be it enacted by the General Assembly of the State of Ohio,* That so much of the township of Saltcreek, in the county of Muskingum, as is comprised within the town plat of Taylorsville, together with all such additions as may hereafter be recorded thereto, be, and the same is hereby created a town corporate, and shall hereafter be known by the name of the "Town of Taylorsville."

Sec. 2. That it shall be lawful for the white male inhabitants of said town, having the qualifications of electors of the General Assembly, to meet on the second Monday of April next, and on the second Monday of April annually thereafter, and elect by ballot one mayor, one recorder, and five trustees, who shall be householders, and shall hold their offices for one year, and until their successors are elected and qualified, and they shall constitute the Town Council.

Sec. 3. That at the first election under this act, the electors shall choose, *viva voce,* two judges and a clerk, who shall each take an oath or affirmation, faithfully to discharge the duties assigned them; and at all elections thereafter, the trustees, or any two of them, shall be judges, and the recorder, clerk; and at all such elections, the polls shall be opened between the hours of ten and eleven, A. M. and close at three o'clock, P. M. of said day; and at the close of the polls, the votes shall be counted and proclaimed, and the clerk shall deliver to each person elected, or leave at his usual place of abode, within three days after, a written notice of his election; and the person so notified, shall within ten days thereafter, take an oath or affirmation to support the constitution of the United States, and of this State, and also an oath of office.

Sec. 4. That the mayor, recorder, and trustees, shall be a body corporate and politic, with perpetual succession, by the name of the "Town of Taylorsville;" shall be capable of acquiring and holding real and personal estate; may sell and convey the same; may have a common seal, and may alter the same; may sue and be sued, plead and be impleaded, answer and be answered unto, in any court of law or equity, in this State or elsewhere; and when any suit is commenced against the corporation, the first process shall be a summons, an attested copy of which shall be left with the recorder, at least ten days before the return day thereof.

Sec. 5. That the mayor, recorder, and a majority of the trustees, shall have the power to make such by-laws and ordinances, and regulations, for the health and convenience of said town, as they may deem advisable; and they shall have power to fill all vacancies occasioned by death, removal, or otherwise; to appoint a treasurer, town marshal, and such other subordinate officers, as they may deem necessary; to prescribe their general duties, and to require such security as they may think necessary, to secure the faithful performance of their duties; to remove them at pleasure; to fix and establish the fees of officers not established by this act.

Sec. 6. The mayor shall be a conservator of the peace within the limits of said corporation, and shall have the jurisdiction of a justice of the peace therein, in criminal and civil cases, and shall receive the same fees as justices of the peace are entitled to for similar services; he shall give bond and security, as is required of justices of the peace; and an appeal may be had from the decision of the mayor to the Court of Common Pleas, in the same manner as appeals are taken from the decisions of justices of the peace.

Sec. 7. It shall be the duty of the recorder, to keep a true record of the proceedings of the town council, which record shall, at all times, be open for the inspection of the electors of said town; and the recorder shall preside at all meetings of the corporation in the absence of the mayor, and shall perform such other duties as may be required of him by the by-laws and ordinances of said corporation.

Sec. 8. The town council shall have power to levy a tax annually, for corporation purposes, on the property within the limits of said town, returned on the grand levy, made subject to taxation by the laws of this State: *Provided,* That said tax shall not exceed in any one year, three mills on the dollar; and the recorder shall make out a duplicate thereof, charging thereon each individual, an amount of tax in proportion to his property, as assessed on the grand levy for taxation; which said duplicate shall be certified and signed by the mayor and recorder, and delivered to the marshal; who shall proceed to collect the same, in the same manner, and under the same regulations, as county treasurers are required by law to collect county and State taxes; and said marshal shall, as soon as collected, pay the same over to the treasurer of the corporation.

Sec. 9. That said town council may appropriate any money in the treasury, for the improvement of the streets and side-walks, or other improvements; and may have the use of the jail of the county, for the imprisonment of persons liable to imprisonment; and all persons so imprisoned, shall be under the care of the sheriff, as in other cases.

Sec. 10. That any future Legislature may alter, amend, or repeal this act.

WILLIAM MEDILL,
Speaker pro tem. of the House of Representatives.

ELIJAH VANCE,
Speaker of the Senate.

March 12, 1836.

AN ACT

To incorporate the town of Hanover, in the county of Columbiana.

Sec. 1. *Be it enacted by the General Assembly of the State of Ohio,* That so much of the township of Hanover, in the county of Columbiana, known as the town of Hanover, as is included in the original recorded plat of said town of Hanover, and any addition made thereto and recorded, and such plats of additions to said town, as may be hereafter recorded; be, and the same are hereby created and constituted a town corporate, by the name of the "Town of Hanover."

Sec, 2. That the qualified electors for members of the General Assembly, residing within the limits of said corporation, shall meet at some convenient place within the bounds of said corporation, on the first Saturday of April, eighteen hundred and thirty-six, and on the first Saturday of April annually thereafter, at such place as the town council may direct, and then and there proceed by a plurality of votes, to elect by ballot, a mayor, recorder, and five trustees, who shall have the qualifications of electors, and shall reside within the limits of said corporation; and the persons so elected shall hold their offices one year and until their successors are elected and qualified: *Provided*, That a failure to elect on said day, shall not forfeit the charter of said corporation.

Sec. 3. That at the first election to be holden under this act, two judges and a clerk shall be chosen *viva voce*, by the electors present, and shall take an oath or affirmation faithfully to discharge the duties required of them by this act, and at all subsequent elections the mayor, or any two of them, shall be judges, and the recorder clerk of the election; and at all such elections, the polls shall be opened between the hours of ten and eleven in the forenoon, and closed at three in the afternoon of said day; and at the close of the polls the votes shall be counted, and a statement thereof proclaimed at the door of the house in which the election shall be held; and the persons elected shall, within ten days after the election, take an oath or affirmation to support the constitution of the United States and of this State, and an oath of office; a certificate of which shall be deposited with the recorder, and be by him preserved.

Sec. 4. That the mayor, recorder and trustees of said town shall be a body politic and corporate, with perpetual succession, to be known and distinguished by the name of "The Town Council of the Town of Hanover;" and shall be capable in law to acquire, receive, hold, any estate, real or personal, for the use of said town; and may have a common seal, and alter the same at their discretion; may sue and be sued, plead and be impleaded, answer and be answered, in any court of law or equity in this State; and when any suit shall be commenced against said corporation, the first process shall be by summons; an attested copy of which shall be left with the recorder, or at his usual place of residence, at least ten days before the return day thereof.

Sec. 5. That the mayor, recorder and trustees, or a majority of them, whereof the mayor or recorder shall always be one, shall have authority to make, ordain and publish all such by-laws and ordinances, consistent with the constitution and laws of the United States and of this State, as they may deem necessary for the regulation, interest, safety, health, cleanliness and convenience of said town and the inhabitants thereof; they shall have power to fill all vacancies that may happen by resignation, death, or removal, in any of the different offices herein named; they shall also have power to appoint a treasurer, town marshal, and such other subordinate officers as they may deem necessary; to prescribe their duties; and to require of them such security as they may deem necessary to secure the performance; to remove them at pleasure; to fix and establish the fees of the officers of said corporation, not established by this act; to impose such fines, not exceeding three dollars, as they may deem just, for refusing to accept any office in said corporation, or for neglect or misconduct therein; they shall have power to audit and settle the accounts of the town; to appropriate and draw out the money in the hands of the treasurer; to establish and regulate markets; to establish and erect wharves and docks, and to regulate the landing of canal boats, and other crafts and rafts: *Provided,* That no tax shall be collected of any boat, or other craft or raft, landing in said town; the council shall have power to regulate, to license or prohibit, all shows, public exhibitions, or coffee houses and groceries: *Provided,* That no person shall be compelled to serve two years in succession in any office of said corporation.

Sec. 6. That the mayor shall be a conservator of the peace within the limits of said corporation; and shall have all the powers of a justice of the peace therein, both in civil and criminal cases; who shall give bond as required by justices of the peace; and in all his acts as justice of the peace, he shall be governed by the laws defining the duties of justices of the peace, and shall be entitled to the same fees as justices of the peace are entitled to receive for similar services; and an appeal may be had from any final decisions or judgments of the said mayor of said corporation, to the court of common pleas of the county of Columbiana, in the same manner as from that of a justice of the peace.

Sec. 7. That it shall be the duty of the recorder to make and keep an accurate record of all laws and ordinances made and ordained by the town council of said town. and of all proceedings in their corporate capacity; which record shall at all times be open to the inspection of the electors of said town; and the recorder shall preside at all meetings of the corporation, and of the town council, in the absence of the mayor, and shall perform such other duties as may be required of him by the by-laws of said corporation.

Sec. 8. That all process issued by the mayor, shall be directed to the marshal of said town, and in the service and execution thereof, the marshal shall have the same power as is or may be given to constables; and shall be entitled to receive the same fees as are or may be given or allowed to constables for similar services.

Sec. 9. That the town council shall have power to assess, for corporation purposes, an annual tax on all property in said town, made subject to taxation by the laws of this State for state and county purposes, not exceeding in any one year one per cent. on the value of such property; which value shall be ascertained by an assessor, to be appointed by the town council for that purpose; a duplicate of which shall be made out and signed by the recorder, and delivered to the collector; they shall have the power of equalizing any injudicious assessment, thus made, on complaint of the person or persons aggrieved.

Sec. 10. That the town marshal shall be collector of any tax assessed, and he is hereby authorized and required by distress and sale of property. as constables on executions, to collect and pay over said tax to the treasurer, within three months of the time of receiving the duplicate thereof, and the treasurer's receipt shall be his voucher; the town marshal shall make personal demand of every resident charged with tax, and shall give ten days notice by advertisement in three of the most public places within the corporation, of any tax; and if the tax on any lot or part of a lot on which no personal property can be found, shall remain unpaid three months after the expiration of the time by this act allowed the collector for the collection of the tax, then the said town marshal shall give notice, by written or printed handbills, stating the amount of such tax, and the number of the lot on which it is due, and that the same will be sold to discharge such tax unless the payment thereof be made within three months from the date of such advertisements; and if such tax be not paid within that time, the town marshal, after having given thirty days notice of the time and place of sale at three of the most public places in said town, shall proceed to sell at public auction, so much of said lot or part of a lot as will discharge said tax and the accruing costs, taking the part so sold in such a manner as will include the same distance on the back line of the lot or part of lot, as on the front line; and the said town marshal is hereby authorized and required to make and execute to the purchaser or purchasers a deed in fee simple, conveying all the right, title and interest which the owner and owners had in and to said lot or part of a lot so sold as aforesaid: *Provided*, That any such owner or owners, who shall appear at any time within two years after such sale, and pay the purchase money, with interest, and twenty per cent. penalty thereon, shall be entitled to the right of redemption, and to receive a conveyance of said lot or part of a lot, so sold, from the purchaser or purchasers: *And provided also*, That nothing in this section contained shall affect the rights of minor. in law or equity, to the benefit of the right of redemption, when they shall arrive at full age.

Sec. 11. That said corporation shall be allowed the use of the county jail of said county for the confinement of such persons as may be liable to imprisonment under the laws and ordinances of said corporation, and also for the confinement of such persons as may be arrested, or be in custody, either in civil or criminal cases; and all persons so imprisoned shall be under the charge of the sheriff of said county, as in other cases.

Sec. 12. That any future Legislature shall have power to alter, amend or repeal this act.

WILLIAM MEDILL,
Speaker pro tem, of the House of Representatives.

ELIJAH VANCE,
Speaker of the Senate.

March 12, 1836.

AN ACT

To incorporate the Zanesville Insurance Company.

Sec. 1. *Be it enacted by the General Assembly of the State of Ohio,* That Solomon Sturges, Levi Whipple, James Raguet, Samuel Sullivan, Charles B. Goddard, George Reeve, Gordius A. Hall, Charles G. Wilson, Moses D. Wheeler, John S. Ligget, Bernard Van Horne, James Doster, Daniel Convers, William Galligher and Wyllys Buell, or such of them and their associates, as shall become subscribers for stock of this association, and their successors, shall be, and they are hereby declared to be a body

56—L

politic and corporate, by the name and style of "The Zanesville Insurance Company;" and by that name to have corporate succession, and be capable in law, to sue and be sued, plead and be impleaded, answer and be answered, defend and be defended, in all courts of law and equity, and elsewhere, with full power and authority to acquire, hold, possess, use, employ, sell, convey and dispose of, all such real estate as shall be necessary and convenient for the transaction of its business. or which may be conveyed to said company for the security, or in the payment of any debt which may become due and owing to the same, or in satisfaction of any judgment of a court of law, or any order or decree of a court of equity in their favor; and to make and use a common seal, and generally, to do and perform all things relative to the objects of this institution.

Sec. 2. That the capital stock of this company shall be two hundred thousand dollars, divided into shares of twenty-five dollars each.

Sec. 3. That at the time of subscribing, there shall be paid on each share, five dollars, and the balance due on the shares subscribed, shall be subject to the call of the directors, and shall be secured to be paid accordingly, by the notes of the stockholders well secured, or by other adequate security, to the satisfaction of the directors; and the directors for the time being, shall have the power, at any time, for good cause, to require any stockholder to give additional and reasonable sufficient security.

Sec. 4. That so soon as two thousand shares are subscribed, and the first instalment thereon paid, and the residue secured, as provided in the preceding section, the company shall be competent to transact all kinds of business for which it is established.

Sec. 5. That the affairs of said company shall be managed by nine directors, a majority of whom shall be a quorum to transact any business of the company, who shall be chosen from the stockholders, as follows: a meeting of the stockholders shall be convened, pursuant to a notice for that purpose, given by the commissioners hereinafter named, within one month after two thousand shares of stock shall have been subscribed; at which meeting the stockholders present shall proceed by ballot to elect a board of directors, who shall continue in office until their successors shall be chosen; at which election, as well as at all elections thereafter, each stockholder shall have one vote for each share of stock, not exceeding five shares; and one vote for every three shares over five, not exceeding eleven shares; and one vote for each five shares over eleven.

Sec· 6. That there shall be an election for directors held on the first Monday in June in each year, after the organization of the company; and the directors, at their first meeting after the election shall, by ballot, choose from among themselves, a president, to serve until the next election of directors; but in case of death or disability of the president, they shall fill the vacancy by ballot, as before; and in case of a vacancy in the board of directors, it shall, by the directors, be filled from the stockholders.

Sec. 7. That if it shall at any time, from any cause, happen that no election shall be held on said first Monday of June, the directors may order an election at any time thereafter: *Provided*, That it shall be the duty of the directors to give at least two weeks notice, in some newspaper printed in the town of Zanesville, of the time and place at which any stated or special election will be held.

Sec. 8. That the corporation hereby created shall have power and authority to insure all kinds of property against loss or damage by fire; to to make all kinds of insurance on life or lives, and against loss or damage on goods, wares and merchandize, in the course of transportation, whether on land or water; and on any vessel or other water craft; and also to cause themselves to be insured against any loss or risk in the course of their business; and generally to do and perform all other matters and things connected with, and proper to promote these objects; and it shall be lawful for said company to use and employ its capital stock, money, or other funds, in the purchase of any public stocks, or in the stock of any other incorpoted company or association; and any such stock to sell again at pleasure: and they may loan their stock, money, or other funds, or any part thereof, to individuals or corporations, on real or personal security, for such period of time as the directors shall deem prudent for the interest and safety of the company: *Provided*, Thal it shall not be lawful for said company to employ any part of their capital stock, money, or other funds, in merchandizing; nor shall said company emit any bills of credit, to be used as a circulating medium; nor shall said company, in any manner, engage in the business of banking, otherwise than to purchase and make sale of stocks, as hereinbefore provided; or receive on money or loans, a greater interest than at the rate of six per centum per annum: *Provided*, That nothing in this act contained shall be so construed as to authorize said corporation to borrow money, in any case whatever, unless such borrowing shall be necessary to meet losses which said corporation shall have sustained upon its insurances.

Sec. 9. That the president and directors shall declare such dividends of the profits of the business of said company, as shall not impair or lessen the capital stock of the same, which dividend shall be declared on the first Monday of May, and November, in each year; and shall be paid to the stockholders at any time after ten days thereafter; but no dividend shall be paid to any stockholder, who is delinquent to the company.

Sec. 10. That any house or building insured by this company, which should be destroyed by fire, from the first floor upwards, shall be deemed demolished; and the directors, in such case, shall order the money insured thereon to be paid in sixty days, after due notice is given of the loss, in such manner as shall be required and specified in the policy or conditions annexed thereto; and in case of partial loss by fire, one of the conditions shall be, that the loss shall be determined by assessors, appointed as follows: the person whose property is insured, shall have the privilege of selecting one disinterested person; the board of directors shall select another; should these two disagree in their valuation of the loss, they shall select a third disinterested person, and their award shall be final.

Sec. 11. That the president and directors shall have power and authority to appoint such officers under them as shall be necessary to transact the business of the company, to fix their salaries, and prescribe their duties; to ordain such by-laws, ordinances and regulations, as shall appear to them necessary for conducting the concerns of said company, not inconsistent with the constitution and laws of Ohio, and of the United States; and they shall keep full and fair entries of their transactions, which shall, at all times, be open to the inspection of the stockholders.

Sec. 12. That the stock of this company may be assigned and transferred on the books of the company, by any stockholder, or by his attorney duly constituted, agreeably to the rules of the company; but no stockholder shall be permitted, whilst indebted to the company, to assign his stock, or any part thereof, until such indebtedness be discharged or secured to the satisfaction of the directors.

Sec. 13. That all policies, or contracts of insurance, or other contracts, made by the company or their authorized agents, shall be signed by the president, or such other person as the directors, agreeably to their by-laws, shall appoint, and attested by the acting clerk, or secretary of the board of directors; and any contract thus signed and attested, which may afterwards be filled up by any agent of the company, authorized to contract in behalf of the company, shall be obligatory and binding on the company.

Sec. 14. That the business of said company shall be transacted at Zanesville, in Muskingum county; but they shall have power and authority to appoint agents at other places, to make and receive surveys of property, and to fill up and deliver policies, executed as aforesaid.

Sec. 15. That in all suits prosecuted against said company, the process may be served by a copy thereof being delivered to the president, by any officer, authorized to serve such process; and the president shall, at the next meeting of the board, report the fact.

Sec. 16. That Charles B. Goddard, Solomon Sturges, George Reeve, Gordius A. Hall, James Raguet, Charles G. Wilson, Moses D. Wheeler, John S. Ligget and Bernard Van Horn, or any five of them, are hereby appointed commissioners to open books for the subscription of stock, and to superintend the business of the subscribers, until a board of directors shall be elected; which books shall be opened in Zanesville, on the first Monday of May next; and, with the exception of Sundays, shall be kept open every day, between the hours of nine in the morning, and five in the afternoon, for twenty days, inclusive, or until at least two thousand shares of the stock shall be subscribed for; and if there should be a failure to open the books as aforesaid, or if there should be a failure to subscribe two thousand shares of the capital as aforesaid, within one year from the passage of this act, then this act shall become void and of no effect: *Provided, however,* That in case more than the capital stock shall be subscribed, in the said twenty days, it shall be the duty of said commissioners to make such equal deduction upon each and every share so subscribed, as shall leave the total amount of the remainder of said shares so subscribed equal to the capital stock of said company; and no demand shall ever thereafter be made of the subscribers, by the board of directors, of any greater sum than the remainder on the shares, by each person subscribed, after such deduction shall have been made.

Sec. 17. That this act shall be taken and received in all courts of justice, and by all public officers as a public act; and all copies, printed under the authority of the General Assembly of this State, shall be admitted as good and sufficient evidence thereof.

Sec. 18. That this act shall continue and be in force for the term of twenty years from the passage thereof: *Provided,* That any future Legislature shall have power to amend or modify the same: *Provided,* Such

445

amendment or modification shall not divért the funds of said corporation from the purposes herein and hereby intended.

WILLIAM MEDILL,
Speaker pro tem. of the House of Representatives.
ELIJAH VANCE,
Speaker of the Senate.

March 12. 1836.

AN ACTAN ACT

To incorporate the Cincinnati Fultonian Association, in Hamilton county.

SEC. 1. *Be it enacted by the General Assembly of the State of Ohio,* That John Perry, G. E. Clements, Thomas Fawcett, Gerret Meldrum, Alexander H. North, Tilford Empsom, Hugh A. M'Lean, Joseph Bennet, and Jenkins S. Jenkins, artists, with their associates, who have associated together, in establishing a society, in the county of Hamilton, for the purpose of improving themselves in their several callings, and rendering the same more generally useful and beneficial to the community; and for the further purpose of more conveniently and effectually affording relief to distressed members of said society; and all such persons as now are, or hereafter may become members of the same, shall be, and hereby are created a body corporate and politic, by and under the name and style of " The Cincinnati Fultonian Association;" to have perpetual succession, and by their corporate name may contract and be contracted with, sue and be sued, plead and be impleaded, answer and be answered, defend and be defended, in any court of competent jurisdiction in this State, and elsewhere; may have a common seal, and alter or renew the same, at pleasure; shall be capable of holding personal and real estate, by purchase, gift, devise, or otherwise; and may sell, dispose of, and convey the same; may grant certificates or evidences to its members of improvements in their several branches of industry; and shall have power to form and ratify a constitution, and enact and adopt by-laws for the government of said association, the management and regulation of its fiscal concerns, the admission and expulsion of its members, the appointment of its officers, together with all other powers necessary for the corporate existence, and the proper and efficient management of its concerns: *Provided,* That said constitution and by-laws be not inconsistent with the laws of this State, or of the United States: *And provided, also,* That the funds of said association shall not be applied to any other purpose than that contemplated in this act.

SEC. 2. That any future Legislature may alter or repeal this act: *Provided,* Such alteration or repeal shall not affect the title to any estate, real or personal, acquired or conveyed under its provisions, or divert the same to any other use than originally intended.

WILLIAM MEDILL,
Speaker pro tem. of the House of Representatives.
ELIJAH VANCE,
Speaker of the Senate.

March 12, 1836.

AN ACT

For the removal of the State Land Office from Piqua.

Sec. 1. *Be it enacted by the General Assembly of the State of Ohio,* That the State land office, now at Piqua, shall be moved, on or before the first day of May next, to Lima, in Allen county; and the officers of said office are hereby required to remove said office to Lima; and, should the United States' land office, now at Lima, be removed to a point within this State west or north of Lima, said State officers are hereby required to move the State office with it, and that the register and receiver heretofore appointed for said office, and who are now discharging the duties thereof as such, shall be entitled to hold their respective places until the said first day of May next, and until their successors are appointed, as is provided for in this act, and no longer.

Sec. 2. That there shall be appointed by joint ballot of both branches of this General Assembly, one register and one receiver for said office, who shall succeed the present officers thereof, and who shall hold their offices for and during the term of three years from and after the said first day of May next, and until their successors are appointed and qualified, who shall each before he enters upon the discharge of the duties of his office, enter into a bond to the State of Ohio, with surety to be approved by the Governor, in the sum of ten thousand dollars, conditioned for the faithful discharge of the duties of his office.

Sec. 3. That said register and receiver shall, as a compensation for their services, under this act, and other acts in relation to the sale of lands belonging to this State, receive each one per centum on the amount of all moneys received at said office in payment for lands subject to sale at that office.

Sec. 4. That so much of each and every act heretofore passed on this subject, or on the subject of the sale of the lands belonging to this State, as is contrary to the provisions of this act, be, and the same is hereby repealed.

WILLIAM MEDILL,
Speaker pro tem. of the House of Representatives.

ELIJAH VANCE,
Speaker of the Senate.

March 12, 1836.

AN ACT

To authorize the trustees of Washington township, Dark county, to appropriate a certain amount of money in the treasury of said township, to promote Common Schools.

Sec. 1. *Be it enacted by the General Assembly of the State of Ohio,* That the trustees of the township of Washington, in the county of Dark, are hereby authorized to appropriate all money that may be in said township treasury, not needed for the usual purposes of the township, to the use of common schools in the said township.

Sec. 2. That the said trustees shall distribute the money aforesaid, among the several school districts, in proportion to the number of children in each district, as returned to the auditor of the county, by the clerk of the district.

WILLIAM MEDILL,
Speaker [pro tem.] of the House of Representatives.
ELIJAH VANCE,
Speaker of the Senate.

March 12, 1836.

AN ACT

Extending the times of payment for certain School Lands in Logan county.

Sec. 1. *Be it enacted by the General Assembly of the State of Ohio,* That if the purchaser of any part of school section sixteen, in township number one, in range number eight, now Miami township, in Logan county; or if the heirs or assigns of any such purchaser, shall pay to the treasurer of said county, one tenth part of the money by him, her or them due for any portion of said section, with the interest due on the whole purchase money, on or before the first day of October next ensuing the passage of this act; and the remaining nine parts, in nine equal instalments, annually thereafter, with interest thereon, year by year, as the same becomes due; then each purchaser, complying with the provisions of this act, his or her heirs or assigns, shall be entitled to receive a deed or deeds of said land or lands, in the same manner as if the original terms of sale had been strictly complied with: *Provided,* That if any such purchaser, his or her heirs or assigns, shall sell or destroy any timber growing upon said land, except such as may be unavoidably destroyed in the ordinary mode of clearing wood lands, and for the necessary buildings and fences on said lands, and for their fuel, without first obtaining, in writing, the consent of a majority of the trustees of said township, then all the privileges granted by this act shall cease.

WILLIAM MEDILL,
Speaker pro tem. of the House of Representatives.
ELIJAH VANCE,
Speaker of the Senate

March 12, 1836.

AN ACT

Extending to Thomas Edgington the time of payment for a certain school lot in Richland county.

Sec. 1. *Be it enacted by the General Assembly of the State of Ohio,*

That if Thomas Edgington, his heirs or assigns, shall pay to the Register of the Virginia Military District, one third part of the purchase money from said Thomas Edgington, to become due for lot number two hundred and seven, in the town of Mansfield, in Richland county, on or before the first day of October next ensuing the passage of this act, with the interest due on the whole purchase money, and the remaining two parts, in two equal instalments annually thereafter, with interest thereon, year by year; then the said Thomas Edgington, his heirs and assigns, shall be entitled to receive a deed of said lands, in the same manner as if the original terms of the sale of said lot had been strictly complied with.

WILLIAM MEDILL,
Speaker pro tem. of the House of Representatives.
ELIJAH VANCE,
Speaker of the Senate.

March 12, 1836.

AN ACT

Further to amend the several acts relative to the incorporation of the town of Rossville, in the county of Butler.

Sec. 1. *Be it enacted by the General Assembly of the State of Ohio,* That the officers of the town of Rossville, known and designated by the name and style of "The President and Trustees of the Town of Rossville," shall hereafter be distinguished and known by the name and style of "The Mayor and Council of the Town of Rossville;" and the president and trustees of said town, now in office, shall continue to perform the duties of their respective offices, by the name and style of "The Mayor and Council of the Town of Rossville," during the time for which they were elected, and shall have power to appoint another member of their board.

Sec. 2. That the qualified voters, within said corporation, shall meet on the first Saturday of May, eighteen hundred and thirty-seven, and biennally, thereafter, on the first Saturday of May, at such time and place within said corporation, as may be designated by the time and place of holding said election, to be put up by the recorder, in three public places in said corporation, at least ten days previous to the day of election, and then and there proceed to elect by ballot, and by a plurality of votes, one mayor and six councilmen, to serve for the term of two years, and until their successors are elected and qualified; said mayor and councilmen shall, at their first meeting after their election, appoint one of said councilmen, recorder; and four of said councilmen, with the mayor or recorder, shall be a quorum for the transaction of business; and said mayor, councilmen, and recorder, are hereby vested with the same powers, and bound to the performance of the same duties, prescribed to the president and trustees by the act to which this is an amendment, and shall be governed by the provisions thereof, not inconsistent with this act.

Sec. 3. That the mayor and council of said corporation shall have power to appoint a supervisor of streets and highways within said corporation, who shall hold his office for the term of one year, and until his successor shall be appointed and qualified; and the said supervisor is hereby authorized and empowered to require all persons within the limits of said corporation, who are, or may be liable, by an act defining the duties of supervisors of roads and highways, passed the seventh of March, eighteen hundred and thirty-one, to labor on the public roads and highways, to perform two days labor under said supervisor, to be appointed as aforesaid, upon the streets and highways within the limits of said corporation: *Provided*, That the two days labor herein required, shall be in lieu of the two days labor required under the general law.

Sec. 4. That said supervisor, appointed as aforesaid, shall be subject to the direction and control of said mayor and council; and shall account and settle with them in the same manner that supervisors are required by said act, to settle with the trustees of townships; and shall be liable to said mayor and council, for neglecting or refusing to discharge his said duties, in the same manner that supervisors are to the trustees of townships.

Sec. 5. That all persons within the limits of said corporation, who are, or may be liable to perform labor on the public roads, who shall have been legally notified by said supervisor, and who shall fail within the time prescribed by said statute, to perform the same, shall be liable to the same penalties prescribed in said act; and which may be recovered in the name of said corporation of the town of Rossville, agreeably to the provisions of said act.

Sec. 6. That said mayor and council shall, prior to the first Monday of June, in each year, determine the per centum to be levied for the current year, for corporation purposes, upon the assessed value of the property in said town, subject to taxation for State and county purposes; and it shall be the duty of the recorder, forthwith to make out and deliver to the auditor of said county, at his office, a certificate of the per centum to be levied for the use of said corporation; and the auditor shall charge to the proper person, the tax so assessed upon the amount of taxable property held by such person, in a separate column, to be ruled for that purpose, on the duplicate of taxes assessed for State and county purposes; said tax to be collected in such manner as said mayor and council shall prescribe: *Provided*, That no law or ordinance of said corporation, shall ever subject cattle, horses, sheep, or hogs, owned by any persons not residing in said town, to be taxed, taken up, or sold, or abused, for coming within the limits of said corporation.

Sec. 7. That the collector, or such other officer as may hereafter be authorized by law, to collect or receive the State and county taxes of said county, shall also be the collector of the taxes assessed for corporation purposes; and in the collection of said taxes, he shall be governed, in all respects, by the laws which shall then be in force for the collection of State and county taxes; and he shall be entitled to receive, on settlement with the county auditor, the same fees, to be paid out of the corporation taxes, so collected, as he may be allowed for the collection of the amount of other taxes.

57—L

Sec. 8. That the same penalties shall accrue, and the same proceedings be had for the collection of corporation taxes on town lots, and other property returned delinquent by the collector, as in the case of other taxes which may be due on said lots, or other property; and when any town lot, or other property, shall be liable to sale for arrearages of State and county county taxes, the arrears of taxes assessed for corporation purposes, shall be added thereto, and collected therewith, whenever such sale shall take place.

Sec. 9. That it shall be the duty of the county auditor, at the time of settlement with the collector, to make out and deliver to said collector, a certificate of the amount collected for corporation purposes, after deducting fees, as provided for in the seventh section of this act; and it shall be the duty of the collector, within five days after such settlement, to pay over the full amount of the money, as specified in said certificate, to the treasurer of the corporation, and take duplicate receipts therefor, one of which he shall forthwith deliver to the recorder, to be filed in his office, and the other he shall retain for his voucher; and the said mayor and council shall allow the county auditor, for his services rendered under this act, the same fees which may be allowed by law, for like services in similar cases, to be paid out of the funds of the corporation.

Sec. 10. That so much of the several acts relative to the town of Rossville, in the county of Butler, as are inconsistent with the provisions of this act, shall be, and they hereby are repealed. This act shall be in force from and after the passage thereof.

WILLIAM MEDILL,
Speaker pro tem. of the House of Representatives.

ELIJAH VANCE,
Speaker of the Senate.

March 12, 1836.

AN ACT

To lay out and establish a State road, from a point at or near where the State road from Lima to Perrysburgh, crosses Sugar creek, to the mouth of Riley's creek.

Sec. 1. *Be it enacted by the General Assembly of the State of Ohio,* That Joseph Hoover, and Samuel Watt, of Allen county, and Christian Huber, of Putnam county, be, and they are hereby appointed commissioners, and John Jackson, of Allen county, surveyor, to lay out and establish a state road, from a point at or near where the road from Lima, in Allen county, to Perrysburgh, in Wood county, crosses Sugar creek; from thence to the centre post of section thirteen, town two, and range seven, east; thence to Rileysville, in Putnam county; thence to run so as to intersect the county road from Finley to Defiance, at or near the mouth of Riley's creek.

Sec. 2. That said road commissioners shall, in all respects, be governed by, and the expenses of laying out and establishing said road be paid, according to the provisions of the act entitled "An act defining the mode of laying out and establishing state roads," passed March 14th, 1831.

Sec. 3. That should a vacancy occur, in the foregoing appointments, by death, removal, refusal to serve, or otherwise the county commissioners of the county in which such vacancy may happen, shall fill the same, as often as any such vacancy may occur, by the appointment of some suitable person, without delay.

WILLIAM MEDILL,
Speaker pro tem. of the House of Representatives.
ELIJAH VANCE,
Speaker of the Senate.

March 12, 1836.

AN ACT

To amend the act, entitled "An act to incorporate the Lake Erie and Muskingum Road and Canal Company," passed March 3d, 1834.

Sec. 1. *Be it enacted by the General Assembly of the State of Ohio,* That "The Lake Erie and Muskingum Road and Canal Company," shall have the power, and they are hereby authorized to connect and terminate the canal with the Ohio canal, at or near the town of Roscoe, or any state work hereafter constructed at or near the mouth of Killbuck, in the county of Coshocton; any thing in the act to which this is an amendment, to the contrary notwithstanding.

Sec. 2. That the said company shall have the privilege of charging the same amount of tolls from Roscoe to the mouth of Black river, as may from time to time, be charged on the Ohio canal from Roscoe to Cleveland.

Sec. 3. That so much of the act to which this is an amendment, as is contrary to the provisions of this act, shall be, and the same is hereby repealed.

WILLIAM MEDILL,
Speaker pro tem. of the House of Representatives.
ELIJAH VANCE,
Speaker of the Senate.

March 12, 1836.

AN ACT

To amend the act, entitled "An act to incorporate the town of Springfield, in the county of Clark.

Sec. 1. *Be it enacted by the General Assembly of the State of Ohio,* That the corporate limits of the town of Springfield, in the county of Clark, shall be included within the following boundaries, to wit: Beginning at the north-west corner of Dement's western, or new town plat, and running thence east with the north boundary thereof, to Plumb street; thence north to the north shore of Buck creek; thence up that stream, with the meanders thereof, to the line dividing sections numbered thirty-five und twenty-nine; thence south to the north-east corner of section thirty-four, it being the corner of sections thirty-four and thirty-five, twenty-eight and twenty-nine; thence south with the line dividing sections numbered thirty-four and twenty-eight, one hundred and eighty-five poles; thence west to the line dividing section four, township four and range nine, and continuing west of said line about one hundred and twenty-five poles, to a point in the line with the western boundary of the above named town plat; thence north from the said point to the south-west corner of the said plat, and continuing north with the western boundary of said plat, to the place of beginning.

Sec. 2. All mills, situated upon streams of water within the foregoing limits, driven by the force of such streams, shall be exempt from a corporation tax.

Sec. 3. The corporate authorities of said town shall have power to borrow money for corporation purposes, in such sums and at such times as may by them be deemed expedient.

Sec. 4. The president of said town shall, before entering upon the duties of his office, give bond, with two sufficient sureties, to the State, to be approved by the trustees of said town, in any sum not exceeding three thousand dollars, nor less than three hundred dollars, for the faithful discharge of his duties; the said corporation shall be considered a road district, and no person residing therein shall be compelled to work on the roads beyond the limits thereof.

Sec. 5. All acts or parts of acts inconsistent with this act, are hereby repealed.

WILLIAM MEDILL,
Speaker pro tem. of the House of Representatives.
ELIJAH VANCE,
Speaker of the Senate.

March 12, 1836.

AN ACT

To incorporate the Mansfield and New Haven Rail-road Company.

Sec. 1. *Be it enacted by the General Assembly of the State of Ohio,* That Thomas W. Bartley, Robert McComb, John Pugh, Baldwin Bently, Mathias Crall, Harvey Westfall, John W. Tanner, Matthew McCelvy, Samuel Ralston, William Bets, James N. Ayres, Eli Wilson, and Uriah Mattson, together with such other persons as may thereafter become associated with them, in the manner hereinafter prescribed, their successors and assigns, be, and are hereby created a body corporate, by the name of "The Mansfield and New Haven Rail-road Company;" and by that name shall be, and are hereby made capable in law to purchase, hold, and enjoy, and retain to them and their successors, all lands, tenements, and hereditaments, necessary for the purposes contemplated in this act, and the same to sell, grant, rent, or in any manner dispose of; to contract and be contracted with, sue and be sued, implead and be impleaded, answer and be answered, defend and be defended; and also to make, have and use a common seal, and the same to alter, break or renew at pleasure; and they shall be, and are hereby invested with all the powers and privileges which are by law incident to corporations of a similar nature, and which are necessary to carry into effect the objects of this association; and if either of the persons named in this section shall die, or refuse or neglect to exercise the powers and discharge the duties hereby created, it shall be the duty of the remaining persons hereinbefore named, or majority of them, to appoint some suitable person or persons to fill such vacancy or vacancies as often as the same shall occur.

Sec. 2. That said corporation are hereby empowered to cause such examinations and surveys to be made between the southern termination of the New Haven and Monroeville Rail-road, in the village of New Haven, and at a point at or near Mansfield, in the county of Richland, as shall be necessary to ascertain the most advantageous route whereon to construct a rail-road, and shall cause an estimate to be made of the probable cost thereof, for each mile separately; and the said corporation shall be, and they are hereby invested with a right to construct a rail-road, with one or more rail-ways, or tracks, from the town of Mansfield aforesaid, to intersect the New Haven and Monroeville Rail-road.

Sec. 3. That the capital stock of said corporation shall be one hundred thousand dollars, and shall be divided into shares of fifty dollars each.

Sec. 4. That the above named persons, or a majority of them, or the survivors of them, are authorized to open books for receiving subscriptions to the capital stock of said company, and shall prescribe the form of such subscription; which books shall be opened within one year from the passing of this act, in the county aforesaid, at such place or places as they may deem expedient, giving twenty days notice in some newspaper printed in the county of Richland, and such other place or places as may be thought advisable, of the time and place, or times and places of opening said books; *Provided, however*, That if the publisher of any newspaper printed in said county, shall neglect or refuse to print such notice, then the required notice shall be published by affixing the same to the door of the court house in said county, at least twenty days previous to the opening of said books; and said books shall be kept open at the discretion of the person opening the same.

Sec. 5. That as soon as the said stock, or fifty thousand dollars thereof, shall have been subscribed, the above named persons, or the same number thereof as shall have given the notice above required, shall give like notice for a meeting of the stockholders to choose directors, at some time, at least thirty days thereafter; and at some place within the said county of Richland; and if at such time and place, the holders of one half or more of said stock subscribed shall attend, either in person or by lawful proxy, they shall proceed to choose from the stockholders, by ballot, nine directors, each share of capital stock entitling the owner to one vote; and at such election, the persons named in the first section of this act, or those appointed by its provisions to fill vacancies which may have occurred, or any three of them, if no more be present, shall be inspectors of such election, and shall certify in writing, signed by them, or a majority of them, what persons are elected directors; and if two or more have an equal number of votes, such inspectors shall .determine by lot, which of them shall be director or directors, to complete the number required, and shall certify the same in like manner; and said inspectors shall appoint the time and place of holding the first meeting of directors, at which meeting a majority shall form a board competent to transact all business of the company; and thereafter a new election of directors shall be made annually, at such time and place. as the stockholders at their first meeting shall appoint; and if the stockholders shall, at their first meeting, fail to appoint the day of such election, then it shall be holden in the succeeding year, on the same day of the same month on which said first election was holden, unless the same should be the first day of the week, in which case it shall be holden on the day next succeeding: and if no election be made on the day appointed, said company shall not be dissolved, but such election may be made at any time appointed by the by-laws of said company; and directors chosen at any election shall remain directors until others are chosen; and directors chosen at any election shall, as soon thereafter as may be, choose of their own number one person to be president, and another to be treasurer of such company, and another to be secretary of said company; and from time to time may choose such other officers as by their by-laws they may designate as necessary: *Provided,* No person shall be a director of such company, who is not a citizen of the State of Ohio.

Sec. 6. That upon every subscription, there shall be paid at the time of subscribing, to the persons named in the first section of this act, or their agents, the sum of five dollars on every share subscribed; and the residue shall be paid in such instalments, and at such times and places, after the commencement of the work, as may be required by the president and directors of said company: *Provided,* That notice of such demand shall have been given in one or more of the newspapers published in said county; and if any stockholder shall fail or neglect to pay any instalment or part of said subscription thus demanded, for the space of sixty days after the same shall be due and payable, the president and directors of said company may sell at public vendue, so many shares of such delinquent stockholder, as may be necessary to pay said instalment, and all necessary expenses incurred in making said sale; and may transfer the shares so sold to the purchaser; and shall pay the overplus, if any, to such delinquent stockholder.

Sec. 7. That the directors of said company shall have power to make, from time to time, all needful rules, regulations and by-laws, touching the business of said company, and to determine the number of tracks or rail-ways upon said road, and the width thereof, and the description of carriages which may be used thereon; to regulate the time and manner in which passengers or goods shall be transported thereon, and the manner of collecting tolls for such transportation; and to fix penalties for the breach of any such rule, regulation or by-law, and to direct the mode and condition of transferring the stock of said company; and penalties provided for by said by-laws, may be sued for by any person or persons authorized thereto, in the name of said company, and recovered in an action of debt, before any court having jurisdiction of the amount; and said company may erect and maintain toll houses, and such other buildings and fixtures, for the accommodation of those using said road, and of themselves, as they may deem in any way necessary for their interest or convenience.

Sec. 8. That said company shall have a right to enter upon any lands, to survey and lay down said road, not exceeding one hundred feet in width, and to take any materials necessary for the construction of said road; and whenever any lands or materials shall be taken for the construction of said road, and the same shall not be given or granted to said company, and the owners thereof do not agree with said company, as to the compensation to be paid therefor, the person or persons claiming compensation as aforesaid, and if the owner or owners thereof are minors, insane persons, or married women, then the guardian· or guardians of of said minor or minors, and insane persons, and the husbands of such married women, may select for themselves an arbitrator, and the said company shall select one arbitrator, and the two thus selected shall take to themselves a third, who shall be sworn and paid, as arbitrators in other cases; and the three, or a majority of them, shall award as arbitrators between the parties, and render copies of their award to each of the parties, in writing, from which award either party may appeal to the court of common pleas for the county in which such lands or materials may have been situated; and in all cases where compensation shall in any manner be claimed for lands, it shall be the duty of the arbitrators and the court to estimate any advantage which the location and construction of said road may be to the claimant for such compensation, and the value of such advantage, if any, shall be set off against the compensation so claimed of said company: and appeals in such cases shall, when taken, be in all respects proceeded in as appeals in other cases to said court, and be brought into said court, by filing the award with the clerk of said court, whose duty it shall be to enter the same on the docket of said court, setting down the claimant or claimants as plaintiff, and said company as defendants; and when the valuation, so ascertained, shall be paid or tendered by said company, said company shall have the same right to retain, own, hold and possess· said materials, and the use and occupation of said lands, for the purposes of said road, as fully and absolutely, as if the same had been granted and conveyed to said company by deed.

Sec. 9. That the said company may construct the said rail-road across or upon any lands, public road, highway, stream of water or water course, if the same shall be necessary; but the said company shall restore such lands, road, highway, stream of water or water course, to its former state, or in a manner so as not to impair the usefulness of such lands, road, highway, water or water course, to the owner or the public, without unnecessary delay.

Sec. 10. That any rail-way company, now, or yet to be chartered by law of this State, shall have power to join and unite with the road hereby incorporated, on such point which the directors of said company may think advisable, on such terms as the directors of such company may respectively agree; and in case of disagreement, then upon such terms as the supreme court may in chancery determine.

Sec. 11. That said company may demand and receive for tolls upon, and the transportation of persons, goods, produce, merchandize, or property of any kind whatsoever, transported by them along said rail-way, any sum not exceeding the following rates: on all goods, merchandize or property of any description whatsoever, transported by them, a sum not exceeding one and a half cents per mile, for toll; five cents on a ton per mile, for transportation, on all goods, produce, merchandize or property of any description whatsoever, transported by them or their agents; and for passengers, one cent per mile, for toll, and not exceeding three cents for the transportation on each passenger.

Sec. 12. That all persons paying the toll aforesaid, may, with suitable and proper carriages, use and travel upon the said rail-road; always subject, however, to such rules and regulations, as said company are authorized to make, by the seventh section of this act.

Sec. 13. That if proceedings be not had, under this act, within four years from the taking effect thereof, and if said road be not completed within ten years thereafter, then the same to be void and of no effect.

Sec. 14. That so soon as the amount of tolls accruing and received for the use of said road, or any part thereof, according to the provisions of this act, shall exceed five per cent. on the amount of capital stock paid in, after deducting therefrom the expenses and liabilities of said company, the directors of said company shall make a dividend of such nett profits, among the stockholders, in proportion to their respective shares; and no contingent or accumulating fund, exceeding one per centum of the profits of said company, shall remain undivided for more than six months.

Sec. 15. That full right and privilege is hereby reserved to the State, or individuals, or any company incorporated by law of this State, to cross this road: *Provided*, That in so crossing, no injury shall be done to the works of the company hereby incorporated.

Sec. 16. That if any person or persons shall wilfully obstruct, or in any way spoil, injure or destroy said road, or either of its branches, or any thing belonging or incident thereto, or any materials to be used in the construction thereof, or any buildings, fixtures or carriages, erected or constructed for the use or convenience thereof, such person or persons shall each be liable for every such offence, to treble the damages sustained thereby; to be recovered by an action of debt, in any court having jurisdiction of the amount.

Sec. 17. That the State shall have power, at any time after the expiration of thirty years, from and after the passage of this act, to purchase and hold the same for the use of the State, at a price not exceeding the original costs for the construction, repairs and fixtures of said rail-road, and fifteen per centum thereon; of which cost, an accurate account shall be kept and submitted to the General Assembly, duly attested by the oath of the officers of the said company, whenever the General Assembly shall require the same.

Sec. 18. [That] whenever the dividends of this company shall exceed the rate of six per cent. per annum, the Legislature of this State may impose such reasonable taxes on the amount of such dividends, as shall be received from other rail-road companies.

Sec. 19. This act is hereby declared to be a public act, and shall be so construed in all courts of justice, and elsewhere.

WILLIAM MEDILL,
Speaker pro tem. of the House of Representatives.
ELIJAH VANCE,
Speaker of the Senate.

March 12, 1836.

To lay out and establish a graded state road in the counties of Tuscarawas and Guernsey

Sec. 1. *Be it enacted by the General Assembly of the State of Ohio,* That William Allen, of the county of Guernsey, and James McCue and Charles Hagen, of the county of Tuscarawas, be, and they are hereby appointed commissioners, and Otho Brasheans, of the county of Guernsey, surveyor, to lay out and establish a graded state road, commencing at Antrim, Guernsey county; thence, the nearest and best route to Shanesville, in Tuscarawas county, crossing the Ohio canal at Fort Washington.

Sec. 2. That the ascent and descent of said road, when completed, shall not exceed an angle of five degrees with the horizon.

Sec. 3. That the commissioners aforesaid, shall be governed, in all respects, by the law now in force, defining the mode of laying out and establishing state roads, passed March the fourteenth, eighteen hundred and thirty-one.

Sec. 4. That should a vacancy happen in any of the foregoing appointments, by death, removal, or otherwise, the commissioners of the county in which the vacancy occurs, shall forthwith fill such vacancy, on being notified of the same.

WILLIAM MEDILL,
Speaker pro tem. of the House of Representatives.
ELIJAH VANCE,
March 14, 1836.   *Speaker of the Senate.*

AN ACT

To lay out and establish a graded State road in the counties of Tuscarawas, Coshocton, Guernsey and Muskingum.

Sec. 1. *Be it enacted by the General Assembly of the State of Ohio,* That Ephraim Sears and Andrew Creter, of Tuscarawas county, and Isaac M. Lanning, of Guernsey county, be, and they are hereby apppointed commissioners, and William G. Williams, of Coshocton county, surveyor, to lay out and establish a graded state road, beginning at the town of New Philadelphia, in the county of Tuscarawas; thence to Lockport; thence to Collin C. Duling's; thence through Newcomerstown, to Mulvane's fording; thence to John Malatt's, in Guernsey county; thence to Martin Richardson's saw mill, in Monroe township, Muskingum county.

Sec. 2. That the said road shall in no case exceed an angle of five degrees with the horizon; and the commissioners aforesaid, shall in all respects be governed by the "Act defining the mode of laying out and establishing state roads," passed March 14th, 1831, except in the appointment of surveyor, which is provided for in the first section of this act.

Sec. 3. That should either of the commissioners or surveyor die, remove out of the county, or refuse to serve, the commissioners of the county in which such vacancy shall happen, shall forthwith, on being notified thereof, appoint some suitable person to fill the same, as often as] it may occur.

WILLIAM MEDILL,
Speaker pro tem. of the House of Representatives.

ELIJAH VANCE,
Speaker of the Senate.

March 14, 1836.

AN ACT

To incorporate the Academy of Sylvania, in the county of Lucas.

Sec. 1. *Be it enacted by the General Assembly of the State of Ohio,* That William Willson, James Woolcott, Horatio Conant, Eli Hubbard, Andrew Palmer, John Baldwin, Platt Card, Cyrus Holloway, Stephen B. Comstock, and their associates, be, and they are hereby declared a body corporate and politic, by the name of " The Academy of Sylvania;" and, as such they shall have perpetual succession; by that name, they shall sue and be sued, plead and be impleaded, defend and be defended, in any court of law or equity; they may have a common seal, and may alter or change the same at pleasure; they shall be capable in law, by the name aforesaid, to purchase, receive, and dispose of, or sell any estate, real or personal: *Provided,* That the capital stock of said corporation shall not exceed twenty-five thousand dollars, to be divided into shares of five dollars each; no part of which capital shall ever be applied for banking purposes, or for any other but that of supporting said Academy.

Sec. 2. That the stockholders in said corporation, or so many of them as may think proper, shall meet in the township of Sylvania, on the first Monday of April, annually, for the purpose of transacting the necessary business of the association, and shall then and there elect by ballot, from among the stockholders, the number of trustees hereinafter provided for, who shall serve until their successors are elected and qualified; and at all elections each stockholder shall be entitled to one vote for each share he or she may own, and the person who shall receive the highest number of votes shall be elected; but if, by neglect or casualty, an election shall not have been held on the day hereby appointed, the corporation shall not thereby be dissolved, but an election may be held at any time thereafter; and, for that purpose, a meeting of said corporation may be called, by a notice signed by any three of the stockholders, and posted up in three public places in said township, at least six days previous to the day of holding such election.

Sec. 3. That, at the first election held under the provisions of this act, there shall be elected nine trustees, who shall divide themselves into three equal classes, by lot or otherwise; the first class shall hold their office three years; the second class, two years; and the third class, one year; after which there shall be annually elected, three trustees, to fill the vacancies occasioned by the arrangement; who shall hold their offices for three years, and until their successors are elected and qualified.

Sec. 4. That the trustees of said corporation, any five of whom shall in all cases be a quorum, shall annually appoint, from their own body, a president and secretary, and from among the other stockholders, a treasurer, for said corporation; the president shall preside at all meetings of the stockholders, and of the board of trustees; he, or in his absence, either of the trustees, who may be agreed upon by said board, shall act as judge of all elections held under the provisions of this act, and shall direct at what place and hour the same shall be held; the president shall have power to call a meeting of the board of trustees, whenever he shall think it necessary, by giving personal or written notice to each; he shall also notify the stockholders of the time and place of holding the annual elections, at least six days previous to the day by this act appointed for holding such elections, by posting up a notice, attested by the secretary, in two public places in the said township of Sylvania; the secretary shall faithfully record all proceedings of the board of trustees, and of the stockholders, when duly assembled; and when required, shall submit his records to the inspection of any of the stockholders; he shall also be clerk of all elections held under the provisions of this act, and shall perform such other duties as may from time to time be required of him by the board of trustees; the treasurer shall give bond to the president, with such penalty and security as the trustees may require, conditioned for the faithful discharge of his duties as treasurer of said Academy, and shall collect and receive all moneys and other property that may be due to said corporation, and pay them out on the order of the trustees, attested by the secretary, and shall settle with the board of trustees as often as they may require.

Sec. 5. The board of trustees shall have power to make and establish such rules and by-laws, consistent with the constitution and laws of the United States and of this State, as they may from time to time think expedient and necessary for the proper regulation of said corporation, and management of said Academy; they shall have power to direct what branches of literature, and of the arts and sciences, shall be taught therein to employ such professors and teachers, allow them such compensation, and continue them for such length of time, as they may judge proper; to regulate the admission and government of the students of said Academy; to expel any disorderly student; to fill all vacancies which may be occasioned by the death, resignation, or removal of any officers of said corporation; to appoint a president and secretary, *pro tempore*, when the absence of these officers, or either of them, shall make such appointment necessary; and to call a meeting of the stockholders of said corporation, whenever they may deem it expedient, by a notice for that purpose, attested by the secretary, and posted up in two public places in said township of Sylvania, six days previous to the day of said meeting; they shall have the management and disposal of the funds and property of said corporation, and power to make all such purchases, sales, and contracts, as may, in their opinion, be expedient for the benefit of said institution; *Provided*, That no purchase or sale of real estate shall be made by the trustees without the consent of the stockholders, expressed by a vote equal to two-thirds of all the shares in said corporation.

Sec. 6. That stock in said corporation may be transferred, new shares created, and new members admitted, upon such restrictions as the trustees shall think proper to prescribe, and not otherwise.

Sec. 7. That, until the election shall take place under the provisions of this act, the persons named in the first section of this act shall be, and they are hereby vested with all the powers of trustees of "The Academy of Sylvania," and shall so continue until their successors are elected and qualified.

Sec. 8. That this act shall be taken and received in all courts as a public act; all printed copies of the same, which shall be printed by or under the authority of the General Assembly, shall be admitted as good evidence thereof without further proof whatever.

WILLIAM MEDILL,

Speaker pro tem. of the House of Representatives.

ELIJAH VANCE,

Speaker of the Senate.

March 14, 1836.

AN ACT

To incorporate the Granville Academy.

Sec. 1. *Be it enacted by the General Assembly of the State of Ohio,* That there shall be, and hereby is, established in the town of Granville, in the county of Licking, an institution for the education of youth in the various branches of useful knowledge, by the name of the Granville Academy; and that, Rev. Jacob Little, Samuel Bancroft, Spencer Wright, Knowles Lennel, Leonard Bushnell, William Smedley, Timothy M. Rose, Henry L. Bancroft, Ebenezer Crawford, Edwin C. Wright, and William W. Bancroft, and their successors, be, and they hereby are appointed trustees of said institution, and made a body corporate and politic, with perpetual succession, to be known by the name and style of "The Trustees of the Granville Academy."

Sec. 2. That said trustees by the name aforesaid, shall be competent to sue and be sued, plead and be impleaded, in all courts of law or equity; may have a seal, and alter the same at pleasure; and shall have power to fill all vacancies in their own body, occasioned by death, resignation, or neglect, for more than one year, to attend to the duties of the trust.

Sec. 3. That the trustees or a majority of them, shall constitute a board, and have power to appoint a president, secretary and treasurer, and such other officers and agents as they may deem necessary, and prescribe their duties; to make, ordain and establish such by-laws, rules and regulations, for managing the affairs of the corporation, as they may think necessary: *Provided,* They are not repugnant to the constitution or laws of the United States, or of this State.

Sec. 4. That the trustees, in their corporate capacity, shall be capable of receiving and holding, by deed or otherwise, property, real, personal, or mixed, to be used for the purposes of the trust: *Provided,* The annual income of the real property of said corporation shall not exceed five thousand dollars, and that the funds of the institution shall never be used for banking purposes.

Sec. 5. That the trustees shall have power to appoint such officers and teachers as may be necessary for the government and instruction of the institution, and prescribe their duties.

Sec. 6. That the trustees shall have power to elect honorary members, who shall have seats in the board of trustees, and be admitted to take part in the discussions therein, but not to vote.

Sec. 7. That any future Legislature may alter or amend this act, so far as may be necessary to restrict the corporation to the powers hereby intended to be conferred: *Provided,* That the funds of the corporation, or the management thereof, shall not thereby be changed from the purposes intended by the donors.

WILLIAM MEDILL,
Speaker pro tem. of the House of Representatives.

ELIJAH VANCE,
Speaker of the Senate.

March 14, 1836.

AN ACT

To incorporate the town of Bridgeport and its additions, in Belmont county.

Sec. 1. *Be it enacted by the General Assembly of the State of Ohio,* That so much of the township of Pens, in the county of Belmont, as lies within the following boundaries, (including all the lots in the original town plat of the town of New Canton, now called Bridgeport, together with all the lots in Zane's and Allen's addition to the said town,) be, and the same is hereby created into and constituted a town corporate, by the name of Bridgeport.

Sec. 2. That for the good government of said town, and the inhabitants thereof, it shall be lawful for the white male inhabitants, who have resided in said town for the space of six months next preceding any election to be held under this act, having the qualifications of electors of members of the General Assembly, to meet at some convenient place for holding an election in said town, on the first Saturday of April next, and on the first Saturday of April annually thereafter, and then and there proceed by a plurality of votes, to elect, by ballot, one mayor, one recorder, and five trustees, who shall be householders, and shall hold their respective offices for one year, and until their successors are chosen and qualified; such mayor, recorder, and trustees, so elected and qualified, shall constitute a town council, any five of whom shall constitute a quorum for the transaction of any business pertaining to their duties; but any less number shall have no power, other than to adjourn from time to time, until a quorum shall have been convened.

Sec. 3. That at the first election to be held under this act there shall be chosen, *viva voce,* by the electors present, two judges and a clerk of said election, who shall each take an oath or affirmation, faithfully to discharge the duties required of them by this act; and at all subsequent elections, the trustees, or any two of them, shall be judges, and the recorder shall be clerk of said election; and at all elections to be held under this act, the polls shall be opened between the hours of one and two, and closed at four o'clock, P. M. of said day; and at the close of the polls, the votes shall be counted, and a true statement thereof shall be proclaimed to the electors present, by one of the judges; and the clerk shall give notice to the persons so elected, of their election; and it shall be the duty of the said town council, at least ten days before each and every annual election, to give notice of the same, by setting up advertisements in three of the most public places in said town.

Sec. 4. That it shall be the duty of the mayor, or in case of his absence or inability to serve, the recorder, to preside at all meetings of the town council; and it shall also be the duty of the recorder to attend all such meetings, and keep a fair and accurate record of all their proceedings.

Sec. 5. That the town council shall have power to fill all vacancies which may happen in said board, from the householders, who are qualified electors in said town, whose appointment shall continue until the next annual election, and until their successors are duly elected and qualified; and whenever it may happen that neither the mayor or recorder is present at any such meeting, the trustees shall have power to appoint one of their number, to perform the duties of such mayor, recorder, or both, as the case may be; which appointment shall be *pro tempore.*

Sec. 6. That the said mayor, recorder, and trustees of said town, shall be a body corporate and politic, with perpetual succession, to be known and designated by the name and style of "The Town Council of the Town of Bridgeport;" and shall be capable in law, in their corporate name, to acquire property, real, personal and mixed, for the use of said town, with power to sell and convey the same; may have a common seal, which they may alter or amend at pleasure; may sue and be sued, plead and be impleaded, defend and be defended, in any court of competent jurisdiction, whether of law or in chancery; and when any suit shall be commenced against said corporation, the first process shall be by summons; an attested copy of which shall be left with the recorder, or at his usual place of abode, at least five days before the return day thereof.

Sec. 7. That each member of said town council shall, before he enters upon the duties of his office, take an oath or affirmation to support the constitution of the United States, and the State of Ohio, and also an oath [of] office.

Sec. 8. That the said town council shall have power to ordain and establish by-laws, rules and regulations, for the government of said town, and the same to alter, amend or repeal, at pleasure; to provide in such by-laws for the appointment or election of a treasurer, town marshal, and all the subordinate officers which they may think necessary for the good government and well being of the inhabitants of said town; to prescribe their duties, and determine the period of their appointments, and the fees they shall be entitled to receive for their services; and to require of them to take an oath of office, previous to their entering upon the duties of their respective offices; and may further require of them a bond, with security, conditioned for the faithful performance of their respective offices, as an officer of the said corporation; the town council shall also have power to affix to the violations of the by-laws and ordinances of the corporation, such reasonable fines and penalties, as they may deem proper to enforce obedience to the same, and provide for the disposition and appropriations of said fines and penalties: *Provided,* That such by-laws and ordinances be not inconsistent with the constitution and laws of the United States, and of this State: *And provided, also,* That no by-laws or ordinances of said corporation shall take effect or be in force until the same shall have been posted up, at least ten days, in one of the most public places within said town, unless it be a case of emergency; in which case, they shall be in force from and after the passage thereof.

Sec. 9. That the town council shall, at the end of each and every year, cause to be made out, and posted up as aforesaid, the receipt and expenditures of the preceding year.

Sec. 10. That the said town council shall have power to regulate and improve the lanes, streets, and alleys, and determine the width of the walks; they shall have power to remove all nuisances and obstructions from the streets, alleys, and commons, within said corporation; provide for the removal of the same, and to do all things which a corporation of a similar nature can do, to secure the peace, health, and good order of the inhabitants of the town.

Sec. 11. That for the purpose of more effectually enabling the town council to carry into effect the provisions of this act, they are hereby authorized to levy a tax on all the real estate and personal property, subject to taxation within the bounds of said corporation, as the same has been, or shall be appraised and returned, on the grand levy of the State: *Provided,* That said tax shall not exceed, in any one year, one half of one per centum, on the aggregate amount of all such taxable property within the limits of said corporation; and the said town council shall, between the first Saturday in April, and the first Saturday in July, determine the amount of tax to be assessed and collected for the current year.

Sec. 12. That it shall be the duty of the recorder of said corporation, to make out duplicates of taxes, charging each individual within said corporation, an amount of tax, in proportion to the aggregate value of taxable property belonging to said individual, within the limits of said corporation, as the same appears from the books of the auditor of Belmont county; and the recorder of said corporation shall, at all reasonable hours, have access to the county auditor's books, for the purpose of making out such duplicates, free of expense; and the duplicate, when made out, shall be certified by the mayor and recorder; and one of said duplicates shall be delivered to the marshal, or to such other person as shall be appointed collector, whose duty it shall be to collect said tax, in the same manner, and under the same regulations, as the collector of State and county taxes are required by law, to collect State and county taxes; and the said marshal or collector, so appointed, shall, immediately after collecting the said tax, pay the same over to the treasurer of said corporation, and take his receipt therefor; and the said marshal, or other collector, shall have the same power to sell both real and personal property, as is given by law to the county treasurer; and, when necessary, the recorder shall have power to make deeds for real estate, so sold, in the same manner that county auditors are, by law, empowered to do, for lands sold by the county treasurer; and the marshal, or other collector, shall receive for his fees, such sum as the town council may direct, not exceeding six per centum on all moneys so by him collected, to be paid by the treasurer, on the order of the recorder.

Sec. 13. That the town council shall have power to appropriate any money remaining in the corporation treasury, to the improvement of the streets, alleys and side walks of said town, when they may deem it necessary so to do, and to make wharves, and all other improvements of a public nature, which may conduce to the convenience and prosperity of the inhabitants of said town.

Sec. 14. That the mayor of said corporation, shall be a conservator of the peace throughout said town; and shall have, within the same, all the powers and jurisdiction of a justice of the peace, in all matters either civil or criminal, arising under the laws of this State, to all intents and purposes whatsoever; and shall give bond and security as by law is required of justices of the peace: and the said mayor shall perform all the duties required of him by the by-laws and ordinances of said corporation; and appeals may be taken from the decisions of said mayor, in all cases where appeals are allowed from the decisions of justices of the peace, and in the same manner.

Sec. 15. That the marshall shall be the principal ministerial officer of said town, and shall have the same powers as constables have by law; and his jurisdiction, in criminal cases, shall be co-extensive with the county of Belmont; and he shall execute the process of the mayor, and receive the same fees for his services, that constables are allowed in similar cases for like services.

Sec. 16. That the mayor shall receive the same fees that justices of the peace are, or may be entitled to, in like cases; and the recorder such fees for his services, as the by-laws and ordinances of such corporation shall prescribe.

Sec. 17. That if no election shall be held by the electors of said town, on the first Saturday of April next, it shall be lawful for any ten householders of said town, at any time thereafter, to call a meeting of the electors, by giving ten days notice in three of the most public places therein; which notice shall state the time, place, and objects of the meeting, and shall be signed by said householders; and if a majority of the electors of said town shall attend at the time and place named in said notice, it shall be lawful for them to proceed to the election of officers, in the same manner as though the meeting had taken place on the first Saturday of April, who shall hold their offices until their successors are duly elected and qualified.

Sec. 18. That said corporation shall be allowed the use of the jail of the county of Belmont, for the imprisonment of such persons as may be liable to imprisonment, under the laws and ordinances of said corporation; and all persons so imprisoned, shall be under the charge of the jailor of Belmont county, as in other cases.

Sec. 19. That the Legislature shall have power, at any time, to alter, amend or repeal this act; not thereby affecting, however, the right of any individual acquired under this act; and that the corporation shall be entitled to one copy of the local and general laws of the present session of the General Assembly.

WILLIAM MEDILL,
Speaker pro tem. of the House of Representatives.

ELIJAH VANCE,
Speaker of the Senate.

March 14, 1836.

AN ACT

To incorporate the town of Leesburg.

Sec. 1. *Be it enacted by the General Assembly of the State of Ohio,* That so much of the township of Orange, in the county of Carroll, as is comprised in the original town plat of the town of Leesburg and addition, together 'with all such additions as may hereafter be made thereto, and recorded, be, and the same is hereby created a town corporate, and shall hereafter be known by the name of the Town of Leesburg.

Sec. 2. That it shall be lawful for the white male inhabitants of said town, having the qualifications of electors of members of the General Assembly, to meet on the second Tuesday of April next, and on the second Tuesday of April, annually thereafter, and elect by ballot, one mayor, one recorder and five trustees, who shall be householders, and shall hold their offices for one year, and until their successors are elected and qualified, and they shall constitute the Town Council, any five of whom shall constitute a quorum for the transaction of business.

Sec. 3. That at all elections under this act, the electors shall choose, *viva voce,* two judges and a clerk, who shall each take an oath or affirmation, faithfully to discharge the duties required of them by this act; and at all subsequent elections the trustees, or any two of them, shall be judges, and the recorder, clerk; and at all such elections, the polls shall be opened between the hours of ten and eleven, A. M. and close at three o'clock, P. M. of said day; and at the close of the polls, the votes shall be counted and a true statement thereof proclaimed by one of the judges, to the electors present; and the clerk shall make a true record thereof; and deliver to each person elected, or leave at his usual place of residence, within five days after, a written notice of his election; and the person so notified, shall within five days thereafter, take an oath or affirmation to support the constitution of the United States, and of this State, and also an oath of office, a certificate of which shall be deposited with the recorder, and by him preserved.

Sec. 4. That the mayor, recorder, and trustees, shall be a body corporate and politic, with perpetual succession, by the name of the Corporation of the town of Leesburg; and shall be capable of acquiring and holding real and personal estate; may sell and convey the same in such manner as they, or a majority of them, may deem proper; they may have a common seal, and may alter the same at pleasure; may sue and be sued, plead and be impleaded, answer and be answered unto, in any court of law or equity, in this State; and when any suit or action shall be commenced

59—L

against said corporation, the first process shall be by summons, an attested copy of which shall be left with the recorder, or, in his absence, at his usual place of residence, at least ten days before the return day thereof.

Sec. 5. That the mayor, recorder, and a majority of the trustees, shall have the power to make such by-laws and enact such ordinances, as they may deem necessary for the health and convenience of said corporation; *Provided*, Such by-laws and ordinances are consistent with the laws of this State; may appoint a treasurer, town marshal, and such subordinate officers as they may deem necessary, and fill all vacancies that may occur in their own body; which officers so appointed, shall continue until the next annual election, and until their successors are elected and qualified; they may also prescribe their general duties, take bonds and security in such sums as they may deem proper, conditioned for the faithful performance of the several duties assigned them by this act, and the by-laws and ordinances under its provisions; and to remove them at pleasure; to fix and establish the fees of officers not established by this act, and to impose fines, not exceeding two dollars, for refusing to accept any office in said corporation; and whenever it may happen that neither the mayor or recorder is present at any meeting of said town council, the trustees shall have power to appoint one of their number to perform the duties of mayor or recorder, or both, as the case may be; which appointment shall be *pro tempore;* and that the mayor, or a majority of the trustees, shall have the power to call a meeting of the town council, whenever, in his or their opinion, the public good of said corporation shall require it.

Sec. 6. The mayor shall be conservator of the peace within the limits of said corporation, and shall therein have the jurisdiction of a justice of the peace in all civil and criminal cases, and shall receive the same fees as justices of the peace are entitled to for similar services; he shall give bond and security, as is required of justices of the peace; and an appeal may be had from the decisions of the mayor to the court of common pleas, in the same manner as appeals are taken from the decisions of justices of the peace.

Sec. 7. It shall be the duty of the recorder, to keep a true record of the proceedings of the town council, which record shall, at all times, be open for the inspection of the electors of said town; and the recorder shall preside at all meetings of the corporation in the absence of the mayor, and shall perform such other duties as may be required of [by] him by the laws and ordinances of said corporation.

Sec. 8. That the town council shall have power to levy a tax annually, for corporation purposes, on the property within the limits of said town, returned on the grand levy, made subject to taxation by the laws of this State: *Provided,* That said tax shall not exceed in any one year, three mills on the dollar; and the recorder shall make out a duplicate thereof, charging thereon each individual, an amount of tax in proportion to his property, as assessed on the grand levy for taxation; which said duplicate shall be certified and signed by the mayor and recorder, and delivered to the marshal; who shall proceed to collect the same, in the same manner, and under the same regulation, as county treasurers are required by law to collect county and State taxes; and said marshal shall, as soon as collected, pay the same over to the treasurer of the corporation: *Provided,*

That in the sale of real or personal property for taxes, and making deeds therefor, the same shall be conducted in the manner provided for by the act prescribing the duties of county auditors.

Sec. 9. That said town council may appropriate any money in the treasury, for the improvement of the streets and side-walks, or other improvements; and may have the use of the jail of the county, for the imprisonment of such persons as may be liable to imprisonment, under the by-laws and ordinances of said corporation; and all persons so imprisoned, shall be under the charge of the sheriff of the county, as in other cases.

Sec. 10. That the mayor, recorder, trustees, and other officers of said corporation shall, on demand, deliver to their successors in office all such books and papers as appertain in any wise to their office.

Sec. 11. That any future Legislature shall have power to alter or amend, this act: *Provided,* That such alteration or amenndment shall not divest the property of said corporation, from the purposes expressed in this act.

WILLIAM MEDILL,
Speaker pro tem. of the House of Representatives.
ELIJAH VANCE,
Speaker of the Senate.

March 14, 1836.

AN ACT

To incorporate the Westfield Library Society, in the township of Westfield, in the county of Medina.

Sec. 1. *Be it enacted by the General Assembly of the State of Ohio,* That Rufus Vaughan, Eber Mallary, Walker Cumber, Benjamin Jillit, Joseph J. Winstow and William F. Moore, and their associates, together with such others as may be hereafter associated with them, be, and they are hereby constituted a body politic and corporate, with perpetual succession, by the name and style of the Westfield Library Society; and by their corporate name, may contract and be contracted with, sue and be sued, plead and be impleaded, in all courts of law and equity in this State and elsewhere; may have a common seal, and alter the same at pleasure; shall be capable of holding personal and real estate by purchase, gift or devise, and may sell, dispose of and convey the same; and shall have power to form and ratify a constitution and adopt by-laws for the government of said association, the arrangement and regulation of its fiscal concerns, the admission of its members, and appointment of its officers, together with all other persons necessary for the corporate existence and the proper and efficient management of its concerns: *Provided,* That said constitution and by-laws be not inconsistent with the constitution and laws of the United States and of this State: *And provided, also,* That the funds of said association shall not be applied to any other purpose than the support of a library in said township of Westfield.

Sec. 2. That any future Legislature shall have power to alter or repeal this act: *Provided,* That such alteration or repeal shall not affect the title to any estate, real or personal, acquired or conveyed under its provisions, or divert the same to any use than originally intended.

WILLIAM MEDILL,
Speaker pro tem. of the House of Representatives.
ELIJAH VANCE,
Speaker of the Senate.

March 14, 1836.

AN ACT

To incorporate the Brooklyn Library Company, in Cuyahoga county.

Sec. 1. *Be it enacted by the General Assembly of the State of Ohio,* That Josiah Barber, Luke Risely, William Burten, G. W. Beebee and Richard Lord, and their associates, together with such other persons as may be hereafter associated with them, are hereby created a body corporate, by the name of the "Brooklyn Library Company," with perpetual succession; and by their corporate name, may make, contract, and prosecute and defend suits, and may hold, enjoy and dispose of real and personal property, not exceeding the annual value of two thousand dollars, which shall be used solely for the purposes of a Library company in Brooklyn aforesaid; and the corporation may appoint such officers and make such regulations and written by-laws for the government of its members, and the management of its affairs, as may be necessary and expedient.

Sec. 2. Any future Legislature may alter or repeal this act.

WILLIAM MEDILL,
Speaker pro tem. of the House of Representatives.
ELIJAH VANCE,
Speaker of the Senate.

March 14, 1836.

AN ACT

To incorporate the Greenville Library Association.

Sec. 1. *Be it enacted by the General Assembly of the State of Ohio,* That John Briggs, Abraham Scribner, Allen La Mott, Samuel Davis, Wm. M. Wilson, Hiram Potter, John Wharry and Isaac N. Gard, and their associates, together with those who may be hereafter associated with them, be, and they are hereby created a body politic and corporate, by the name of "The Greenville Library Association," with perpetual succession; and by their corporate name, may sue and be sued, plead and be impleaded, in all courts of law and equity in this State and elsewhere; may have a common seal, and the same alter at pleasure; shall be capable of holding personal and real estate, by purchase, gift or devise, and may sell, dispose of and convey the same; and they shall have power to form and ratify a constitution, and adopt by-laws for the government of said corporation, and the arrangement of its fiscal concerns, the admission of its members, and appointment of its officers; together with all powers necessary for the corporate existence, and proper and efficient management of its concerns: *Provided,* The funds of said society shall be applied to no other purpose than that of supporting a library in the town of Greenville.

WILLIAM MEDILL,
Speaker pro tem. of the House of Representatives.

ELIJAH VANCE,
Speaker of the Senate.

March 14, 1836.

AN ACT

To amend an act, entitled "An act for the distribution of the proceeds of the Virginia Military School Fund."

Sec. 1. *Be it enacted by the General Assembly of the State of Ohio,* That it shall be the duty of the county commissioners of the several counties lying wholly, or in part, within the Virginia Military district, between the first day of March, and the twenty-fifth day of May, in the year A. D. 1836, to cause to be surveyed, so as to ascertain the quantity of acres of land within these respective counties, or parts of counties, within said district, and make out a map of the same, and deliver to the county auditor of their county, on or before the 15th day of November next thereafter: *Provided,* That the county commissioners of any county composed wholly, or in part, of the lands in said Virginia Military District, may dispense with the survey, and be governed by the quantity of acres reported by the Auditor of State to this General Assembly.

Sec. 2. That immediately after the return of the survey, as required by the first section of this act, it shall be the duty of the county auditor to make out a correct copy of said survey, certified and signed by said auditor, and transmit the same to the Auditor of State; and the Auditor of State shall apportion and distribute the money in the State treasury, being the proceeds of the money or lands constituting the Virginia military district school fund, immediately after the first day of September annually, among the several counties and parts of counties within said district, according to territory, and shall inform the several county auditors of the amount so apportioned and due to these counties respectively; and the county auditors of the several counties lying wholly, or in part, within said district shall draw an order on the Auditor of State in favor of the county treasurer for the sum so apportioned and due to his county, and shall charge the county treasurer therewith; and the Auditor of State shall, on such order being presented to him, give an order on the Treasurer of State for the amount thereof.

Sec. 3. That any county commissioners or county auditor, who shall neglect or refuse to perform any of the duties required of them by this act, or who shall knowingly make a false return or certificate, in the duties assigned them by this act, shall, for such offence, forfeit and pay for the use of schools in such county a sum not exceeding five hundred dollars, which may be recovered by action of debt, in the name of the State of Ohio, in any court having competent jurisdiction.

Sec, 4. That in all cases where only a part of any county shall be situated within the Virginia Military District, the expenses to be incurred in making the surveys and returns required by this act. shall be paid by a tax to be assessed on the taxable property within that part of the county lying within said Military District.

Sec. 5. That so much of the act of February 13th, 1832, providing for the distribution of the proceeds of the Virginia military school fund, as comes within the provisions of this act, be, and the same is hereby repealed.

WILLIAM MEDILL,
Speaker pro tem. of the House of Representatives.

ELIJAH VANCE,
Speaker of the Senate.

March 14, 1836.

AN ACT

To amend the act entitled "An act to establish the county of Lucas," passed June 20th, 1835.

Sec. 1. *Be it enacted by the General Assembly of the State of Ohio,* That the following lines shall constitute the boundaries of the county of Lucas: Beginning at a point on Lake Erie, where the line commonly called "Fulton's line," intersects the same; thence due west with said Fulton's line, to the Maumee river; thence in n south-westerly direction, with the said river, to the east line of the county of Henry; thence north, on said line, to the northeast corner of township six, in range eight; thence west, on said township line, to the east line of the county of Williams; thence north, to the northern boundary line of the State, called the "Harris' line;" thence in an easterly direction, with said line, to Lake Erie; thence due east, until a line drawn due north, from the place of beginning, shall intersect the same.

WILLIAM MEDILL,
Speaker pro tem. of the House of Representatives.

ELIJAH VANCE,
Speaker of the Senate.

March 14, 1836.

AN ACT

To amend the act entitled "An act to incorporate the Batavia Turnpike and Miami Bridge Company," passed February 17, 1835.

Sec. 1. *Be it enacted by the General Assembly of the State of Ohio,* That the president and directors of the "Batavia Turnpike and Miami

Bridge Company," that now are, or may hereafter be elected by the stock-holders of said company, shall so far change the location of said turnpike road, as to make the point of commencement at the Union bridge, on the east bank of the Little Miami river, in the county of Hamilton; thence in an easterly direction, passing Newtown, *via* Whetstone's old tavern stand, to the town of Batavia, in Clermont county.

Sec. 2. That said company shall have power, whenever they deem it expedient, to extend the said turnpike road from the town of Ba-tavia, aforesaid, in an easterly direction, so as to intersect, at some point, the Milford and Chilicothe turnpike road.

Sec. 3. That so much of the act to which this is an amendment, as relates to the building of a bridge over the Little Miami river, at or near John Armstrong's mills, and so much of said act as is inconsistent with this act, is hereby repealed: *Provided, however,* That nothing in this act, or [the] act to which this is an amendment, shall be so construed as to pro-hibit the erection of toll gates, and the collection of tolls, when any ten miles of said road shall have been completed, and reported upon as pro-vided for in the eighth section of the act aforesaid.

WILLIAM MEDILL,
Speaker pro tem. of the House of Representatives.

ELIJAH VANCE,
Speaker of the Senate.

March 14, 1836.

AN ACT

To amend an act entitled "An act to incorporate the Cincinnati, Montgomery, Hepkinsville, Rochester, and Clarksville McAdamised Turnpike Company, passed March 3d, 1834.

Sec. 1. *Be it enacted by the General Assembly of the State of Ohio,* That the said company shall have the privilege of erecting a toll bridge over the Little Miami river, at the place where their said road is, or shall be located, to cross said river; and so soon as they shall have completed ten continuous miles of said road, between the city of Cincinnati, and the town of Montgomery, and shall have constructed their bridge over the Miami, as aforesaid, in a substantial manner, so as to afford a safe and convenient passage for all ordinary tavel, they then shall have the right to erect a gate and receive half the amount of toll that they are allowed to receive for ten miles of McAdamized road; and the said company shall also have the right to reduce the artificial part of their road to twenty feet in width, any thing in the act to which this is an amendment, to the contrary, notwithstand-ing: *Provided,* That if said company shall obtain a separate and sufficient subscribtion for the special purpose of erecting said bridge, then, and in that case, they may erect the same and receive toll in manner aforesaid, without reference to the completion of any part of their said McAdamized road.

Sec. 2. That so much of the above recited act of incorporation as gives to the said company a conditional right to occupy the road constructed by the commissioners of Hamilton county, so far as respects that part of the Montgomery road which lies between the intersection of the Madison road at the Walnut Hills and the corporation line of the city of Cincinnati, and so much of the said act as makes Sharpsburgh a point in said road, is hereby repealed.

WILLIAM MEDILL,
Speaker pro tem. of the House of Representatives.
ELIJAH VANCE,
Speaker of the Senate.

March 14, 1836.

AN ACT

Further to amend an act entitled "An act to incorporate the Sandy and Beaver Canal Company," passed January 11th, 1828, and for other purposes.

Sec. 1. *Be it enacted by the General Assembly of the State of Ohio,* That the stock of the Sandy and Beaver Canal Company shall be deemed personal property, and may be assigned and transferred on the books of said company, in person, or by power of attorney, in such manner as shall be directed by the president and directors of said company, any thing in the act to which this is an amendment, to the contrary, notwithstanding.

WILLIAM MEDILL,
Speaker pro tem. of the House of Representatives.
ELIJAH VANCE,
Speaker of the Senate.

March 14, 1836.

AN ACT

To amend an act entitled "An act to incorporate the One Leg Navigation Company."

Sec. 1. *Be it enacted by the General Assembly of the State of Ohio,* That the One Leg Navigation Company, be, and they are hereby authorized and empowered to improve the navigation of Knotton or One Leg creek, by locks, dams, side-cuts, either by the creation of slackwater navigation, or the construction of a canal, or in part by slackwater, and in part by canal, as they may deem expedient, commencing where the line between the sixth and seventh ranges crosses said creek, or at any point above that, where the said company may deem practicable; thence to intersect the Ohio canal at the Zoar feeder, or at some point between that and the town of Dover, in Tuscarawas county, where it may be done without taking water from the said Ohio canal; and they shall have power to use, sell, and dispose of all the surplus water of said creek, and for the purpose of assuring to the said corporation, all the lands, real estate and materials requisite for constructing and maintaining said locks, dams, side-cuts, canals, and the works connected therewith, incident and necessary to the improvement of the navigation of said creek, in manner aforesaid, that whenever said lands or materials shall not be obtained by voluntary donation, or fair purchase, it shall be lawful for said corporation, by any of its officers, and by each and every agent, superintendent, or engineer, by them employed, to enter upon, take possession of, and use all such real estate as shall be necessary for the purposes aforesaid; and also to enter upon, and take all necessary materials for the construction of said works, on whose land soever the same may be, doing thereby no unnecessary damage, they satisfying and paying all damages which may be occasioned thereby, to any person or persons, corporation or corporations, in the manner provided for in the act to which this act is an amendment.

Sec. 2. That upon every share subscribed to the capital stock of said company, there shall be paid, at the time of subscribing, to the commissioners, or to any other person or persons, lawfully authorized to receive such subscription, the sum of two dollars, and the residue thereof, at such times as may be required by the president and directors of said company: *Provided*, That not more than two dollars on each share, shall be demanded in any one year from the commencement of said work, nor any payment demanded until the notice, required in the fourth section of the act to which this is an amendment, shall have been given: *Provided*, That nothing contained in this section shall be so construed as to authorize the president and directors of said company, to demand in any one year more than one dollar, on each share subscribed previous to the passage of this act, except instalments already due under the act to which this is an amendment.

Sec. 3. That the said corporation be, and they are hereby authorized, in the construction of said locks, dams, side-cuts, and canals, to select such sites, as to them may seem most suitable.

Sec. 4. That the said company be allowed to demand and receive tolls for the passage of boats or other water craft, passing along or navigating said canal or slackwater navigation, and for the transportation of persons and property thereon, and to fix and regulate the amount thereof: *Provided*, That the amount thereof, shall in no case exceed the highest rate of tolls and duties, together with the charges of freight on the Ohio canal: *And provided*, That the distance for which tolls shall be paid, shall be the length of the said side-cuts, slackwater, or canals: and the said corporation, upon complying with the provisions of this act, and the act to which this is an amendment, shall be entitled to the benefit of all the laws which are or shall be in force for the collection of tolls, or for the protection of any canal constructed by this State, so far as such law or laws shall be necessary to insure the collection of tolls, or for the protection of the locks, dams, side-cuts, canals, or other works which the said company may construct, in order to carry into effect the provisions of this act, or the act to which this is an amendment.

Sec. 5. That if the president and directors of said company shall not proceed to carry on the said work within four years from the passage of this act, and shall not complete the same within eight years, according to the true intent and meaning of this act, then, and in either of these cases, all and singular, the rights, privileges and liberties, hereby granted to the said company by this act, and by the act to which this is an amendment, shall revert to the State of Ohio.

60—L

Sec. 6. That so much of the act, entitled "An act to incorporate the One Leg Navigation Company," passed on the thirteenth day of February, A. D. 1832, as may be contrary to the provisions of this act, be, and the same is hereby repealed.

WILLIAM MEDILL,
Speaker pro tem. of the House of Representatives.
ELIJAH VANCE,
Speaker of the Senate.

March 14, 1836.

AN ACT

Further to amend an act entitled "An act to incorporate the town of Painesville."

Sec. 1. *Be it enacted by the General Assembly of theState of Ohio,* That so much of the township of Painesville as included within the following boundaries, to wit: Beginning ten rods east of the house lately occupied by Asa Fifield, as a tavern, on the brow of the high bank of Grand river; thence north twenty-five rods; thence west twenty-five degrees south to the centre of the road leading from the road commonly called the Ingersoll road, a few rods west of the tavern of Joseph Rider, to the village of Richmond; thence southwardly along the centre of said mentioned road leading from the town of Painesville, to Cleveland; thence eastwardly along the south line of the road leading from the said Joseph Rider's, to the site of the old arched bridge over Grand river, to a stake and stones on the brow of the hill, near the orchard of David Matthews; thence north to the eastern bank of Grand river; thence down said river, on said eastern bank, seventy-five rods below tne Geauga grist-mill: thence in a direct line to the place of beginning; be, and the same is hereby created a town corporate, and shall hereafter be known by the name or title of the "Town of Painesville."

Sec. 2. That in all criminal cases, the jurisdiction of the mayor of said town shall be co-extensive with the county of Geauga; and the said mayor shall have custody of the seal of said town, and shall affix the seal of said town to all legal process; and he shall receive for his services the same fees fixed by law for justices of the peace in like cases.

Sec. 3. That the town council of said town shall have authority to regulate all exhibitions or public shows, with exclusive power to grant or refuse licenses thereto, and the same to revoke for good cause; and to exact such sums therefor, as the said council shall deem proper and expedient.

Sec. 4. That for the purpose of enabling the said town council to carry into effect the provisions of the act incorporating said town, and the act amendatory thereto, the said council is hereby authorized to levy a .tax on all the real and personal property, and capital of any kind within said town, subject to taxation for State, county, or township purposes; which property shall be assessed annually, for taxation, by an assessor appointed by said council; and said council shall provide, by an ordinance, for the correction and equalization of such annual assessment; and said council, on the first Monday of June, annually, shall levy on the whole amount of such assessment, corrected and equalized, such per centage as the members of said town council, by a concurring vote of two-thirds, shall deem necessary.

Sec. 5. That said town council shall have power to borrow money, for the discharge of any debt of the town, either present or prospective, and to provide for the redemption of any loan by them made, and the interest thereon; and may pledge the property of the town upon such conditions as shall be deemed expedient, by a concurring vote of two-thirds of the members of said council.

Sec. 6. That said town council shall, when the public good may require it, erect a prison for said town, and regulate the police and internal government thereof; and may authorize solitary confinement for a violation of any of the ordinances of said town, for a period of not more than five days, nor less than one day.

Sec. 7. That the seventh section of the act to which this is an amendment, be, and the same is hereby repealed.

WILLIAM MEDILL,
Speaker pro. tem. of the House of Representatives.

ELIJAH VANCE,
Speaker of the Senate.

March 14, 1836.

To revive an act entitled "An act to establish certain graded State roads therein named."

Sec. 1. *Be it enacted by the General Assembly of the State of Ohio,* That the second, third, fourth and fifth sections of the aforesaid act, to establish a certain graded State road therein named, passed January 29th, 1833, be, and the same is hereby revived.

Sec. 2. That John Crain, Henry Woolam, and William Bushong, commissioners named in said act, are hereby authorized and empowered to do and perform all the duties appertaining to said appointment, for and during the term of one year from the passage of this act, as in all respects as fully as though the term of said appointment had not expired.

WILLIAM MEDILL,
Speaker pro. tem. of the House of Representatives.

ELIJAH VANCE,
Speaker of the Senate.

March 14, 1836.

AN ACT

To continue in force an act to lay out and establish a State road from Winesburgh, in Holmes county, to intersect the State road leading from Carrolton, to the Steam Furnace, in Tuscarawas county.

Sec. 1. *Be it enacted by the General Assembly of the State of Ohio,* That the act entitled an act to lay out and establish a State road from Winesburg, in Holmes county, passed March 9th, 1835, to intersect the State road leading from Carrolton, to the Steam Furnace, in Tuscarawas county, be, and the same is hereby continued in force, and the time for laying out and establishing said road agreeably to the provisions of the above recited act, extended to the first day of July, one thousand eight hundred and thirty-six.

WILLIAM MEDILL,
Speaker pro. tem. of the House of Representatives.

ELIJAH VANCE,
Speaker of the Senate.

March 14, 1836.

AN ACT

To incorporate the first Methodist Episcopal Church in Monroe, in Ashtabula county.

Sec. 1. *Be it enacted by the General Assembly of the State of Ohio,* That William Ensign, Myran S. Hill, Eli G. Jewett, Samuel R. Parker, John E. Hill, and Josiah W. Blim, and their associates, together with such other persons as may hereafter be associated with them, be, and they are hereby declared a body corporate and politic, by and with the name and style of the "First Methodist Episcopal Church of Monroe;" with perpetual succession, and capacity of contracting and being contracted with, suing and being sued, answering and being answered, pleading and being impleaded, defending and being defended, in all courts of law and equity, and may also have a common seal, which they may break, alter or renew at pleasure.

Sec. 2. That they shall have power to make, pass, and enforce from time to time, such rules, by-laws and regulations, as they may deem proper for the good order and regulation of said association: *Provided,* That such rules, by-laws and regulations shall not be repugnant to the constitution or laws of this State and of the United States.

Sec. 3. That said association shall be capable in law of purchasing and holding any estate, real or personal, and of receiving any gift, grant, devise, donation or legacy made, or to be made, to said association; with full power to sell, dispose of, and convey the same: *Provided,* That the annual income of such property shall not exceed two thousand dollars.

Sec. 4. That William Ensign, Myran S. Hill, Eli G. Jewett, be, and they are hereby appointed trustees of said association, until others are appointed in corformity with the rules, by-laws, regulations made by said association.

Sec. 5. That any future Legislature shall have power to modify or repeal this act: *Provided,* That such modification or repeal shall not affect the title to any estate, real or personal, acquired or conveyed under its provisions.

WILLIAM MEDILL,
Speaker [pro tem.] of the House of Representatives.

ELIJAH VANCE,
Speaker of the Senate.

March 14, 1836.

AN ACT

To incorporate the Mount Carmel Regular Baptist Church, in Syeamore township, Hamilton county.

Sec. 1. *Be it enacted by the General Assembly of the State of Ohio,* That Solomon Ferris, Adam Lee, James Terwilliger, their associates, and such other persons as may hereafter become associated with them, be, and they are hereby declared to be a body corporate and politic, to be known by the name and style of "The Mount Carmel Baptist Church;" with perpetural succession, and by their corporate name may contract and be contracted with, sue and be sued, answer and be answered unto, plead and be impleaded, defend and be defended, in all courts of law and equity; and may have a common seal, which they may break, alter or renew at pleasure; and shall be capable in their corporate capacity of holding all property, real, personal, or mixed, either by purchase, gift, grant, donation, devise or legacy, which now belong, or may hereafter belong to said church: *Provided,* That the annual income of all such property shall not exceed five hundred dollars.

Sec. 2. That this association shall have power to make such rules and by-laws for the election of their officers, and the general regulation of their affairs, as they may from time to time deem proper; and at all business meetings for the election of officers, or the establishing of rules or by-laws for the government of said association, every member of the church over the age of twenty-one years, shall have a right to vote, and a majority shall govern: *Provided,* That such rules and by-laws shall not be incompatible with the constitution or laws of this State, and of the United States.

Sec. 3. That all property of whatsoever kind, belonging to the said church, shall be held in trust, under the management of the trustees, and shall be faithfully applied, agreeably to the by-laws and regulations of the church; and the persons named in the first section of this act, shall be trustees until others are elected or chosen, in conformity with the by-laws of the association.

Sec. 4. Any future Legislature may alter, amend, or repeal this act:

Provided, That the title to any property shall not be affected thereby.

WILLIAM MEDILL,
Speaker pro tem. of the House of Representatives.
ELIJAH VANCE,
Speaker of the Senate.

March 14, 1836.

AN ACT

To incorporate the "Free Will Baptist Society," in New Lyme, county of Ashtabula.

Sec. 1. *Be it enacted in the General Assembly of the State of Ohio,* That Nelson Hyde, Jeremiah Dodge, Jared Fuller, Eusibius Dodge, and Topher Gee, and their associates, together with such other persons as may hereafter be associated with them, be, and they are hereby created a body corporate and politic, by the name of the "Free Will Baptist Society in New Lyme," and as such such remain and have perpetual succession, and by their corporate name may contract and be contracted with, may sue and be sued, answer and be answered, plead and be impleaded, defend and be defended, in any court of competent jurisdiction, in all manner of actions, causes and complaints, whatsoever; and may have a common seal, which they may change or alter at pleasure.

Sec. 2. That said corporation shall be capable in law or equity, in their corporate name aforesaid, of having, receiving, acquiring and holding, by purchase, gift, grant devise or legacy, any estate, real, personal, or mixed, for the use of said corporation: *Provided,* That the annual income of such property shall not exceed the sum of one thousand dollars, and that all the property, of whatever kind, shall be considered as held in trust, under the management, and at the disposal of said corporation, for the purpose of promoting the interests of said society, defraying the expenses incident to their mode of worship, and maintaining any institution of charity or education, that may be therewith connected: *And provided, also,* That when money, or other property shall be given, granted, devised or bequeathed, for any particular use or purpose, it shall be faithfully applied to such use or purpose.

Sec. 3. That for the better managing of the affairs of said society, and promoting the interests thereof, there shall be elected, on the second Monday in March, one thousand eight hundred and thirty seven, and on the second Monday in March, in each succeeding year thereafter, three trustees, and such other officers as the company may deem necessary, who shall hold their offices for one year, and until their successors shall be elected: *Provided,* That if, from any cause, an election of officers should not be made [on] the day appointed for the annual election, the society may elect their officers at any meeting of the corporation duly assembled.

Sec. 4. That Nelson Hyde, Jeremiah Dodge, and Jared Fuller, named in the first section of this [act,] be, and they are hereby appointed trustees, until the first annual election, and until others are elected in their places.

Sec. 5. That all elections of the corporation shall be by ballot, and the person or persons having a majority of the votes given, for any office, shall be considered duly elected; each member shall have one vote, and all matters of the corporation shall be determined by a majority of the members present, at any meeting of the corporation duly assembled.

Sec. 6. That the trustees, a majority of whom shall be a quorum for the transaction of business, shall, under the direction of the society, have the management and control of the property and other concerns of the corporation; and they, or a majority of them, shall have power to call a meeting of the society, either for the election of officers, or for the transaction of any business of the society, by giving to said society, immediately after public worship, at least ten days previous notice of said meeting, or causing notification thereof to be put in three or more public places within the limits of said society, one of which shall be the usual place of holding public worship, at least fifteen days previous to such meeting.

Sec. 7. That any meeting of the society, duly assembled, may adopt and establish such by-laws and ordinances as may be deemed proper and necessary for the good government of said corporation: *Provided*, That such by-laws and ordinances shall be compatible with the constitution and laws of the United States, and of this State.

Sec. 9. That original process against the corporation shall be served by leaving an attested copy with one or more of the trustees, at least ten days before the return day thereof, and such service shall be deemed sufficient to bind the corporation.

Sec. 9. That any future Legislature shall have power to modify or repeal this act: *Provided*, That such modification or repeal shall not affect the title to any estate, real or personal, acquired or conveyed under its provisions.

WILLIAM MEDILL,
Speaker pro tem. of the House of Representatives.

ELIJAH VANCE,
Speaker of the Senate.

March 14, 1836.

AN ACT

To incorporate the Mount Vernon Lateral Canal Company.

Sec. 1. *Be it enacted by the General Assembly of the State of Ohio,* That Gilman Bryant, Daniel S. Norton, Jesse B. Thomas, Robert Giffin, George Browning, Isaac Hadley, Samuel J. Updegraff, Simon B. Kinton, William McCreary, William McWilliams, Marvin Tracy, Hosmer Curtis, Charles Sager, Alexander Elliott, Catharinus P. Buckingham, Benjamin S. Brown, Anthony Banning, John Hawn, Jonathan C. Hall, James E. Woodbridge, Timothy Colopy, Daniel Sapp, Thomas J. Humphrey, and also all other persons who shall become associated with them, by subscribing to the capital stock of said company, be, and they are hereby constituted and declared a body corporate and politic, with perpetual succession, by the name and style of "The Mount Vernon Lateral Canal Company;" for the purpose of making and constructing a navigable canal and slack water navigation, commencing at the town of Mount Vernon, in the county of Knox, and terminating at or near the juuction of the Mohican and Vernon rivers, in Coshocton county; and for this purpose, the said company is hereby authorized and empowered to have and receive, purchase, possess, enjoy and retain lands, rents, goods, chattels, rights and effects of any kind, and to any amount, necessary to carry into effect the objects of the institution; and the same to use, sell and dispose of at pleasure; to sue and be sued, defend and be defended, contract and be contracted with; to have and use a common seal, and the same to alter and renew at pleasure; to ordain and establish such regulations and by-laws as may be necessary for the well ordering and governing of the corporation; and generally to possess all the privileges, and perform all the acts necessary to a corporation; subject, however, to the restrictions contained in this act.

Sec. 2. That the capital of said company shall consist of two hundred thousand dollars; which stock shall be divided into shares of twenty-five dollars each, and shall be transferable in entire shares in such manner as the rules of the corporation shall prescribe.

Sec. 3. That the persons named in the first section of this act, or a majority of them, shall be commissioners to receive subscriptions; and also to do and perform all necessary acts to organize the company; and they are hereby authorized and empowered to cause books to be opened at such time and in such places, as a majority of them shall think proper, to receive subscriptions to constitute the capital stock of said company; said commissioners may require any sum not exceeding ten per centum of each subscription to be paid at the time it is subscribed; and each subscriber shall be bound to pay from time to time such instalments on his stock as the directors may lawfully require.

Sec. 4. That when two hundred shares shall have been subscribed, the commissioners shall call a meeting of subscribers, by causing notices of the time and place of such meeting to be published in some newspaper in general circulation in the places [in] which the books shall have been opened, and the stock subscribed, at least twenty days previous to such meeting; and on such notice having been given, the stockholders shall meet at the time and place appointed, and proceed to elect directors; in which election the stockholders may vote in person or by proxy; and for each share such stockholder may possess, he shall be entitled to one vote.

Sec. 5. That the affairs of said company shall be managed by five directors, or a majority of them; who shall be elected once in each year, unless a shorter period shall be ordained by the corporation; and each director shall be a stockholder at the time of his election, and shall cease to be a director if he cease to be a stockholder.

Sec. 6. That the directors so elected shall, at their first meeting after said election, choose one person from their number, who shall serve as president of the board for and during the time for which he has been elected a director; the president and directors, previous to entering on the duties of their office, shall severally take an oath or affirmation faithfully and impartially to discharge all the duties appertaining to said office; they shall appoint a treasurer, and cause him to give bond, with security, conditioned for the faithful performance of all duties appertaining to said office; they shall have power to determine the amount of any instalment, and the time when it shall be paid; but no stockholder shall be required to pay any instalment until after such order has been published in some newspaper which circulates where such stock was subscribed, at least sixty days before the time of payment; neither shall any stockholder be bound to pay more than twenty per centum on the amount of his stock at one time, nor more than fifty per cent. in any one year.

Sec. 7. That it shall be the treasurer's duty to keep the accounts and funds of the corporation, to receive and collect from the subscribers and others all moneys due the corporation, and on proper vouchers to pay out the same; he shall, as often as required, exhibit to the directors an account of all sums by him received and paid out; and the book accounts and vouchers thus kept shall at all times be subject to the inspection of the stockholders.

Sec. 8. That it shall and may be lawful for said directors to enter upon and take possession of any land, water and streams necessary to make said canal, or any of its appendages, such as feeders, dikes, locks, dams and other works; doing nevertheless no unnecessary damage; and in case any land, water, or streams, so wanted to be appropriated to any of the purposes aforesaid, shall not be given or granted to said corporation, and the proprietor or proprietors cannot or do not agree with the directors as to the amount of damages or compensation which ought to be allowed or paid for the same, and shall not mutually agree on some person or persons to appraise the damages, it shall be lawful for the directors aforesaid, to apply to any judge of the court of common pleas of the county in which the property may be situate, not a stockholder in said company, who shall appoint three disinterested freeholders to assess the damages, to whom the directors shall give notice of their appointment, and also to the adverse party or his guardian, agent or attorney; and it shall be the duty of the persons so appointed to attend at the time and place specified in the notice; who, after being duly sworn or affirmed, faithfully and impartially to discharge their duties, shall proceed, on actual view, to make a just estimate and appraisement of any damage such individual, owner or owners may sustain, taking into consideration the benefits which such proprietor or proprietors will derive from the location and making of said canal; and shall make a certificate of such appraisement, with a particular description of the premises; to which certificate they, or a majority of them, shall sign their names, and deliver to each party one copy; and immediately thereafter, if no damages are assessed, or on the payment or tender of money to the amount of damages assessed, to the person or persons injured, his guardian, agent or attorney, the said directors may proceed to enter and occupy such lands, streams, or water; and a complete title to the premises, to the extent and for the purposes set forth in or contemplated by this act, shall thereby be vested and forever remain in said company: *Provided, however,* That if either party shall consider himself aggrieved by the decision of the appraisers so as aforesaid made, such party may apply to the court of common pleas of the proper county, at the succeeding term of the court; or if there should not be a quorum of said court disinterested, then to the supreme court at their next session in said county, giving ten days notice of such intention to the adverse party; and on good cause shown, the said court shall appoint three disinterested freeholders, who shall, after being duly qualified, proceed to view and appraise the damages; and shall certify their proceedings in the same manner as the former appraiser; and their decision shall be final and determinate; but the pending of any such application to the court shall not in the meantime hinder the progress of the work.

Sec. 9. That it shall be the duty of the company hereby incorporated, to construct said canal and slack water, of such width and depth, with locks of such dimensions as will be most convenient for canal and slack water navigation; and it shall also be the duty of said company to construct a bridge over said canal, suitable for the passage of carriages, at each and every place where a state or county road crosses the same; and when the said canal is so made and completed, it shall forever thereafter be deemed and taken to be navigable as a public highway, free for the passage of boats, and for the transportation of all goods, commodities and produce whatsoever, on the payment of the tolls which may lawfully be required.

Sec. 10. That the State shall have power, at any time after the expiration of fifteen years from the time the said canal shall be completed, to purchase and hold the same for the use of the State, by paying to said company the original cost of said canal, with fifteen per centum thereon; of which cost an accurate account shall be kept and submitted to the General Assembly, duly attested by the oath of the officers of said company, whenever the General Assembly shall demand the same.

Sec. 11. That when the whole or any part of said canal and slack water is completed, according to the true intent and meaning of this act, the president and directors shall have power, and it is hereby made their duty, to ordain and establish a rate of tolls, which shall be paid upon vessels, boats, rafts, or other property, passing on such part or whole line of the canal that is navigable; and for the collection of such tolls, the president and directors shall appoint collectors, and establish toll houses, at all proper places, and may ask, demand and receive on all boats, rafts, vessels and other property, passing or navigated on said canal, such tolls as shall be established agreeably to the provisions of this act; and also, may rent, sell and dispose of any superabundant or waste of water of the canal: *Provided*, That after the lapse of twenty years from the completion of said canal, any subsequent Legislature may regulate the rate of tolls which said company may receive: *Provided, nevertheless*, That they do not reduce them to a lower rate than may be charged on the Ohio and Erie canal.

Sec. 12. That the president and directors shall annually or semi-annually declare a dividend of the nett profits arising from the tolls, or from any other source, reserving such sum or sums as will defray the necessary current and probable contingent expenses; which dividend shall be paid or passed to the credit of the stockholders severally, in proportion to the shares which each may hold in the stock of said company.

Sec. 13. That the company shall be entitled to the benefit of all laws which are or shall be in force for the collection of tolls, and for the protection of any canals constructed by this State, so far as such law or laws shall be necessary to insure the collection of tolls, and for the protection of the canal and other property, which the company may lawfully hold, in order to carry into effect the provisions of this act.

WILLIAM MEDILL,
Speaker pro tem. of the House of Representatives.
ELIJAH VANCE,
Speaker of the Senate.

March 14, 1836.

AN ACT

To incorporate the First Presbyterian Church of Clarksfield, in the county of Huron.

Sec. 1. *Be it enacted by the General Assembly of the State of Ohio,* That Benjamin Hill, Daniel Lee, Eleazer Hamlin, Albert W. Segar, Edward Husted, and their associates, be, and they are hereby created a body politic and corporate, by the name and style of "The First Presbyterian Church," in Clarksfield, in Huron county; with perpetual succession, and shall be capable, in their corporate capacity, to contract and be contracted with, to sue and be sued, plead and be impleaded, answer and be answered, defend and be defended, in any court of competent jurisdiction; to have a common seal; and to have power to ordain, pass, and enforce such by-laws and ordinances for the regulation and good government of said association, as they may deem necessary.

Sec. 2. That said association shall be capable in law of purchasing and holding any estate, real, or personal, and of receiving any gift, grant, donation, or legacy, made or given for the promotion of the objects of said association, and in their corporate capacity to sell and convey the same; and said association may from time to time, elect and appoint such trustees, or other officers, for the good government and management of its concerns, as may be deemed necessary and expedient: *Provided, however,* That the funds of said association shall not at any time exceed five thousand dollars; and also, that said funds shall never be used for any other purpose than for the purchase of suitable sites, and for the erection of suitable buildings for religious worship and public instruction.

Sec. 3. That the persons named in the first section of this act, be, and they are hereby appointed trustees of said association, until others are elected in conformity with the by-laws and ordinances made by said association.

Sec. 4. That any future Legislature may alter or repeal this [act.]

WILLIAM MEDILL,
Speaker pro tem. of the House of Representatives.
ELIJAH VANCE,
Speaker of the Senate.

March 14, 1836.

AN ACT

To incorporate the Presbyterian Church of Hebron, in the county of Licking.

Sec. 1. *Be it enacted by the General Assembly of the State of Ohio,*

That S. R. Cable, William Craig, Thomas Cully, Thomas Holmes, Alfred Pumphrey, and James Lyons, and their associates, shall be, and they are hereby declared to be a body politic and corporate, by the name and style of the "Presbyterian Church of Hebron, in the county of Licking," to have perpetual succession, and to be capable in their corporate capacity, to contract and be contracted with, to sue and be sued, plead and be impleaded, answer and be answered, defend and be defended, in any court of competent jurisdiction; to have a common seal, and the same to change at pleasure; and to have power to ordain, pass and enforce such by-laws, rules, regulations and ordinances, for the good government of said corporation, as they may deem necessary: *Provided,* That such by-laws and ordinances are not repugnant to, or incompatible with the constitution and laws of this State and of the United States.

Sec. 2. That said association shall be capable in law of purchasing and holding any estate, real or personal, and of receiving any gift, grant, donation, devise or legacy, made or given for the promotion of the objects of said incorporation, and in their corporate capacity, to sell and convey the same; and the members of the said church (or association) may from time to time, according to their own constitution or rules, elect and appoint such trustees or other officers for the good government and management of its concerns, as may be necessary or expedient, giving always due public notice of such election: *Provided, however,* That the annual income of all such property shall not exceed one thousand dollars, and that the funds of said association, or society, shall never be used for any other purpose than for the erection of a house or houses for religious worship and public instruction.

Sec. 3. That S. R. Cable, William Craig, Thomas Cully, Thomas Holmes, and Alfred Pumphrey, be, and they are hereby appointed trustees of said association, until others are elected in conformity with the provisions of this act, and their constitution.

Sec. 4. That any future Legislature may alter, amend or repeal this act: *Provided,* That such alteration or repeal shall not effect the title of any property, acquired or conveyed under its provisions; and that all contracts heretofore entered upon by the trustees, shall be binding upon the corporation.

WILLIAM MEDILL,
Speaker pro tem. of the House of Representatives.

ELIJAH VANCE,
Speaker of the Senate.

March 14, 1836.

--- --- --- --- --- ---

AN ACT

To incorporate the First Baptist Society of Fairfield and vicinity, in the county or Huron.

Sec. 1. *Be it enacted by the General Assembly of the State of Ohio,* That Henry Perry, Daniel S. Smith, Hocksey Fuller, Samuel Foot, Ebenezer Foot, Walter Holmes, Jonathan H. Smith, Issac Godfrey, Sampson Baker,

G. R. West, J. C. Campbell, Walter Branch, Aaron Abot, and their associates for the time being, be, and they are hereby created a body corporate and politic, by the name and style of the "First Baptist Society in Fairfield and vicinity;" and as such, shall have perpetual succession; and be capable in law of suing and being sued, pleading and being impleaded, defending and being defended, in all courts of law and equity; and to have a common seal, and to alter the same at pleasure; and the said corporation is hereby made capable of contracting and being contracted with, and of holding any estate, real or personal, and of acquiring the same by gift, grant, or legacy, devise or purchase; the annual income of said estate shall not exceed two thousand dollars, the management of which shall belong to the trustees of the society: *And provided, also,* That the funds of said corporation, shall be at their disposal, and shall be used exclusively for the support of public worship.

Sec. 2. That there shall be an annual meeting of the society, on the first Saturday in December, annually, at the place of holding public worship, and said meeting be adjourned, as occasion may require; at which meeting there shall be chosen a president of said corporation, together with five trustees, any three of whom shall be a quorum for the transaction of business, and a secretary; and all elections shall be by ballot; and such society shall make and constitute all such regulations and by-laws, as may be found necessary for the government thereof: *Provided,* Such by-laws be not contrary to the constitution and laws of the United States and of this State.

Sec. 3. That such members of the society who may be of the age of twenty-one years, shall be entitled to a vote in the meeting thereof.

Sec. 4. That a special meeting of said society may at any time be called by any three of the trustees, by giving ten days notice thereof, posted up in three of the most public places within the bounds of said society.

Sec. 5. That original process against said corporation shall be served by leaving an attested copy thereof with the secretary, and with one of the trustees, at least ten days before the return day thereof; and all suits instituted by said society, shall be brought in its corporate name.

Sec. 6. That the admission and dismission of members, shall be regulated by such laws as said corporation may adopt.

Sec. 7. That Ebenezer Foot, Samuel Foot, Walter Branch, Walter Holmes, and Henry Perry, be, and they are hereby constituted, trustees of said corporation, with full power to act as such, until the first annual meeting of said society.

Sec. 8. That any future Legislature may modify or repeal this act: *Provided,* That the title to any property, real or personal, acquired or conveyed under its provisions shall not be affected or diverted to any other purpose than that originally designed.

WILLIAM MEDILL,
Speaker pro tem. of the House of Representatives.

ELIJAH VANCE,
Speaker of the Senate.

March 14, 1836.

AN ACT

To incorporate the Wardens and Vestrymen of the Parish of All-Soul's, in the town of Springfield, in the county of Clark.

Sec. 1. *Be it enacted by the General Assembly of the State of Ohio,* That Joseph T. Thorp, Joseph Sprague, H. Vinal, P. A. Sprigman, E. C. Ross, Joseph Perine, J. C. Fletcher, George Mortimer, James Lykes, John Cook, D. Gwinne, C. T. Ward, and their associates, be, and they are here-by constituted a body corporate and politic, by the name of the "Wardens and Vestrymen of the Parish of All-Souls, in the town of Springfield, and county of Clark;" and by that name shall have perpetual succession; and be capable in law of suing and being sued, defending and being defended, in all courts and places, and in all manner of actions, causes and com-plaints whatsoever; and may have a common seal, and change the same at their discretion; and by that name and style, shall be capable in law or equity, of taking or holding by devise or otherwise, or of purchasing, hold-ing, and enjoying to them and their successors, any real estate, in fee sim-ple, or otherwise, and any goods, chattels, and personal estate, and of selling, leasing, mortgaging, or otherwise disposing of said real and personal estate, or any part thereof, as they may think proper: *Provided,* That the annual income of such real estate shall not exceed the sum of two thousand dollars.

Sec. 2. That the members of said corporation shall meet at such place as they may agree upon, in the town of Springfield, on the first Monday in April next; and shall have power, when so convened, or at any other time and place to which such meeting may be adjourned, to elect such officers as they may think necessary for carrying into effect the object of their in-corporation; to fix the time and place of future meetings, and to ordain and establish such by-laws and ordinances for the government of their of-ficers and members as they may think proper, not inconsistent with the constitution and laws of the United States, or of this State; and may alter, amend or repeal the same at pleasure.

Sec. 3. That any future Legislature shall have power to modify or repeal this act: *Provided,* Such modification or repeal shall not affect the title to any real or personal estate, acquired or conveyed under its pro-visions, or divert the same to any other use than originally intended.

WILLIAM MEDILL.
Speaker pro tem. of the House of Representatives.
ELIJAH VANCE,
Speaker of the Senate.

March 14, 1836.

AN ACT

To incorporate the First Episcopal Church and Society of Maumee and Miami City, in the county of Lucas.

Sec. 1. *Be it enacted by the General Assembly of the State of Ohio,*

That James Woolcot, Robert A. Forsyth, George S. Hagard, Nathan Rathborn, Amos Pratt, James H. Forsyth, F. E. Kirtland and George B. Knaggs, and their associates, together with such persons as may hereafter become associated with them, members of the Protestant Episcopal Church and Society of Maumee and Miami city, in Lucas county, be and they are created a body politic and corporate, with perpetual succession, by the name and style of the "Protestant Episcopal Church and Society of Maumee and Miami city, in Lucas county;" and by that name shall be capable in law, of contracting and being contracted with, of suing and being sued, of answering and being answered, of pleading and being impleaded, of defending and being defended, in all courts having competent jurisdiction; and may use a common seal, which they may alter at pleasure; with capacity to acquire, hold and enjoy, to sell, rent, convey and dispose of property, real, personal or mixed: *Provided,* That the annual income of all such property shall not exceed the sum of two thousand dollars: *And provided, also,* That said property shall be applied to the building of houses of public worship, procuring a parsonage, and to other objects incident to the support of public worship in said church and society, and the ordinances of the same, together with such institutions of learning and charity as may be connected therewith, and to no other purpose.

Sec. 2. That there shall be a meeting of the male members of such church and society, on Easter Monday of each and every year, at which time they shall elect two wardens, three or more vestrymen, a treasurer and secretary, and such other officers as they may deem necessary; and may also transact any other business of said church and society, not inconsistent with the limitations and restrictions of this act: *Provided,* That if at any time an election of officers should not be had on the day above appointed, the corporation shall not thereby be dissolved; but the officers previously chosen shall serve until their successors are elected; and said election may be held at any meeting duly notified and assembled for that purpose.

Sec. 3. That said corporation shall have power to adopt, establish and enforce such by-laws, ordinances, rules and regulations as may be deemed proper and necessary for its government, and the efficient management of its concerns: *Provided,* That such by-laws, ordinances, rules and regulations shall be consistent with the constitution and laws of the United States, and of this State.

Sec. 4. That mesne process against the corporation, shall be served by leaving an attested copy with one of the wardens or vestrymen, at least ten days before the return day thereof; and such service shall be deemed sufficient to bind the corporation.

Sec. 5. That any future Legislature shall have power to modify or repeal this act.

WILLIAM MEDILL,
Speaker pro tem. of the House of Representatives.
ELIJAH VANCE,
Speaker of the Senate.

March 14, 1836.

AN ACT

To incorporate the Port Washington Lyceum and Library Company, in the county of Tuscarawas.

Sec. 1. *Be it enacted by the General Assembly of the State of Ohio,* That Richard Hewitt, William Rankin, Thomas Taylor, John Knight, and B. L. Parsons, in the county of Tuscarawas, and their associates, and such other persons as may be hereafter associated with them, be, and they hereby are created a body corporate, by the name and style of the " Port Washington Lyceum and Library Company," with perpetual succession; and power to contract, prosecute, and defend suits; and by their corporate name, may hold, enjoy, and dispose of any estate; not exceeding the annual value of one thousand dollars; which shall be used for no other purpose than those of a literary or scientific character: they shall have power to form a constitution, appoint such officers, and adopt such by-laws for the regulation and management of the concerns of the company, and for the admission of members, as they may deem proper; and may have a common seal, which they may alter and renew at pleasure: any future Legislature may modify or repeal this act.

WILLIAM MEDILL,
Speaker pro tem. of the House of Representatives.

ELIJAH VANCE,
Speaker of the Senate.

March 14, 1836.

AN ACT

To incorporate the Rutland Library Association.

Sec. 1. *Be it enacted by the General Assembly of the State of Ohio,* That Jesse Hubbell, L. D. Hovey, Rodney Downing, Bartlet Paine, Jabez Benedict, and their associates, together with such as may hereafter be appointed with them, be, and they are hereby created a body corporate and politic, by the name of the " Rutland Library Association," with perpetual succession; and by their corporate name may sue and be sued, plead and be impleaded, in all courts of law and equity in this State and elsewhere; may have a common seal, and the same to alter at pleasure; shall be capable of holding personal and real estate, by gift, grant, or devise, and may sell, dispose of, and convey the same; and they shall have power to form and ratify a constitution, and adopt by-laws for the government of said corporation, the arrangement of, and regulation of its fiscal concerns, the admission of its members, and appointment of its officers: together with all power necessary for the corporate existence, and the proper and efficient management of its concerns: *Provided,* The funds of said society shall be applied to no other purpose than that of supporting a library in said town of Rutland.

Sec. 2. That Jesse Hubbell, L. D. Hovey, Rodney Downing, Bartler Paine and Jabez Benedict, be and they are hereby appointed trustees, with full power and authority to conduct all and singular the concerns of said association, until others shall be elected under this act.

Sec. 3. That any future Legislature shall have power to alter, modify or repeal this act: *Provided,* Such modification or repeal shall not affect the title to any real or personal estate acquired or conveyed under its provisions, or divert the same to any other use than originally intended.

WILLIAM MEDILL,

Speaker pro tem. of the House of Representatives.

ELIJAH VANCE,

Speaker of the Senate.

March 14, 1836.

AN ACT

To incorporate the Columbus and Marysville Rail-road Company.

Sec. 1. *Be it enacted by the General Assembly of the State of Ohio,* That Levi Phelps, Alexander Pollock, Samuel B. Johnson, Silas G. Strong, Cyprian Lee, Stephen M'Lain, and W. C. Lawrence, of Union county; Alexander Thompson, Eri Strong, and Obed Taylor, of the county of Hardin; and John M'Elvain, of the county of Franklin, together, with such other persons as may hereafter become associated with them, in the manner hereinafter prescribed, their successors and assigns, be, and are hereby created a body corporate and politic, by the name of "The Columbus and Marysville Rail-road Company;" and by that name shall be and are hereby made capable in law, to purchase, hold, enjoy, and retain to them, and their successors, such lands, tenements, and hereditaments, as may be necessary for the construction and use of said road, or such as may have been granted to the company by way of donation, to aid in the construction thereof, and the same to sell, grant, rent, or in any manner dispose of; and to contract and be contracted with; and if either of the persons named in this section shall die, or refuse or neglect to exercise the powers and discharge the duties hereby created, it shall be the duty of the remaining persons hereinbefore named, or majority of them, to appoint some suitable person or persons to fill such vacancy or vacancies so often as the same shall occur.

Sec. 2. That said corporation are hereby empowered to cause such examinations and surveys to be made between Columbus and Marysville, as shall be necessary to ascertain the most advantageous route whereon to construct a rail-road, and shall cause an estimate to be made of the probable cost thereof, for each mile separately; and the said corporation shall be, and they are hereby invested with a right to construct a rail-road, with one or more rail-ways or tracks, from the city of Columbus, to the town Marysville, and thence to the Mad river and Lake Erie Rail-road, at or near the Big Spring, in Logan county.

62—L

Sec. 3. That the capital stock of said corporation shall be three hundred and fifty thousand dollars, and shall be divided into shares of fifty dollars each; and five dollars on each share shall be paid at the time of subscribing.

Sec. 4. That the above named persons, or a majority of them, or the survivors of them, are authorized to open books for receiving subscriptions to the capital stock of said company, and shall prescribe the form of such subscriptions; which books shall be opened within two years from the passage of this act, at such place or places as they may deem expedient, giving twenty days notice in some newspaper in general circulation along the routes, of the time and place, or times and places of opening said books: and they shall be kept open at least ten days.

Sec. 5. That as soon as said stock, or fifty thousand dollars thereof, shall have been subscribed, the above named persons, or the same number thereof as shall have given the notice above required, shall give like notice for a meeting of the stockholders to choose directors, at some time, at least thirty days thereafter, and at some place within said county of Logan, and the county of Union; and if at such time and place, the holders of one half or more of said stock subscribed shall attend, either in person or by lawful proxy, they shall proceed to choose from the stockholders, by ballot, nine directors, each share of capital stock entitling the owner to one vote; and at such election, the persons named in the first section of this act, or those appointed by its provisions to fill vacancies which may have occurred, or any three of them, if no more be present, shall be inspectors of such election, and shall certify in writing, signed by them, or a majority of them, what persons are elected directors; and if two or more have an equal number of votes, such inspectors shall determine by lot, which of them shall be director or directors, to complete the number required, and shall certify the same in like manner; and said inspectors shall appoint the time and place of holding the first meeting of directors, at which meeting a majority shall form a board competent to transact all business of the company; and thereafter a new election of directors shall be made annually, at such time and place as the stockholders at their first meeting shall appoint; and if the stockholders shall, at their first meeting, fail to appoint the day of such election, then it shall be holden in the succeeding year, on the same day of the same month on which said first election was holden, unless the same should be the first day of the week, in which case it shall be holden on the day next succeeding: and if no election be made on the day appointed, said company shall not be dissolved, but such election may be made at any time appointed by the by-laws of said company; and directors chosen at any election shall remain directors until others are chosen; and directors chosen at any election shall, as soon thereafter as may be, choose of their own number one person to be president, and another to be treasurer of such company, and another to be secretary of said company; and from time to time may choose such other officers as by their by-laws they may designate as necessary: *Provided,* No person shall be a director of such company, who is not a citizen of the State of Ohio.

Sec. 6. That the president and directors of said company may require payment of the subscription of the capital stock, at such times and places, and in such proportions and on such conditions, as they may think expedient: *Provided,* That notice of such requisition shall be first given in some newspaper printed and in general circulation in the counties in which said road may be located; and if any stockholder shall fail or neglect to pay his subscription to the capital stock, or such part thereof as shall be thus required, for the space of sixty days after the time appointed by said notice for the payment thereof, the president and directors of said company may sell at public vendue so many shares of such delinquent stockholder, as may be necessary to pay such requisition, and all necessary expenses incurred in making said sale; and the share or shares so sold, shall be transferred to the purchaser; paying the overplus, if any, to said delinquent, on demand.

Sec. 7. That the directors of said company shall have power to make, from time to time, all needful rules, regulations and by-laws, touching the business of said company, and to determine the number of tracks or rail-ways upon said road, and the width thereof, and the description of carriages which may be used thereon; to regulate the time and manner in which passengers or goods shall be transported thereon, and the manner of collecting tolls for such transportation; and to fix penalties for the breach of any such rule, regulation or by-law, and to direct the mode and condition of transferring the stock of said company; and penalties provided for by said by-laws, may be sued for by any person or persons authorized thereto, in the name of said company, and recovered in an action of debt, before any court having jurisdiction of the amount; and said company may erect and maintain toll houses, and such other buildings and fixtures, for the accommodation of those using said road, and of themselves, as they may deem in any way necessary for their interest or convenience.

Sec. 8. That said company shall have a right to enter upon any lands, to survey and lay down said road, not exceeding one hundred feet in width, and to take any materials necessary for the construction of said road; and whenever any lands or materials shall be taken for the construction of said road, and the same shall not be given or granted to said company, and the owners thereof do not agree with said company, as to the compensation to be paid therefor, the person or persons claiming compensation as aforesaid, or the owner or owners thereof are not residents of said county, or minors, insane persons, or married women, then the agent of such non-residents, guardian or guardians of such minor or minors, and insane persons, and the husbands of such married women, may select for themselves an arbitrator, and the said company shall select one arbitrator, and the two thus selected shall take to themselves a third, who shall be sworn and paid, as arbitrators in other cases; and the three, or a majority of them, shall award as arbitrators between the parties, and render copies of their award to each of the parties, in writing, from which award either party may appeal to the court of common pleas for the county in which such lands or materials may have been situated; and in all cases where compensation shall in any manner be claimed for lands, it shall be the duty of the arbitrators and the court, to estimate any advantage which the location and construction of said road may be to the claimant for such compensation, and the value of such advantage, if any, shall be set off against the compensation so claimed of said company: and appeals in such cases shall, when taken, be in all respects proceeded in as appeals in other cases to said court, and be brought into said court, by filing the award with the clerk of said court, whose duty it shall be to enter the same on the docket of said court, setting down the claimant or claimants as plaintiff, and said company as defendants; and when the valuation, so ascertained, shall be paid or tendered by said company, said company shall have the same right to retain, own, hold and possess said lands and materials, as fully and absolutely, as if the same had been granted and conveyed to said company by deed, so long as the same may be used for the purpose of said road.

Sec. 9. That the said company may construct the said rail-road across or upon any lands, public road, highway, stream of water or water course, if the same shall be necessary; but the said company shall restore such lands, roads, highway, stream of water or water course, to its former state, or in sufficient manner so as not to impair the usefulness of such lands, road, highway, water or water course, to the owner or the public, without unnecessary delay; and whenever said road shall pass through the lanes of any individual, it shall be the duty of said company to provide for said individual proper wagon ways from one part of his land to the other, as soon as practicable.

Sec. 10. That any rail-way company, now, or yet to be chartered by law of this State, shall have power to join and unite with the road hereby incorporated, and any point which the directors of said company may think advisable, on such terms as the directors of such companies may respectively agree; and full right and privilege is hereby reserved to the State, or individuals, or any company incorporated by law of this State, to cross this road with any other road: *Provided*, That in so crossing, no injury shall be done to the works of the company hereby incorporated.

Sec. 11. That said company may demand and receive for tolls upon, and the transportation of persons, goods, produce, merchandize, or property of any kind whatsoever, transported by them along said rail-way, any sum not exceeding the following rates: on all goods, merchandize or property of any description whatsoever, transported by them, a sum not exceeding one and a half cents per mile, for toll; five cents on a ton per mile, for transportation, on all goods, produce, merchandize or property of any description whatsoever, transported by them or their agents; and for the transportation of passengers, not exceeding three cents per mile, for each passenger.

Sec. 12. That all persons paying toll aforesaid, may, with suitable and proper carriages, use and travel upon the said rail-road; always subject, however, to such rules and regulations, as said company are authorized to make, by the seventh section of this act.

Sec. 13. That if proceedings be not had, under this act, and at least one-fourth part of said road within three years from the taking effect thereof, and if said road be put under contract, and be not completed within ten years thereafter, then this act to be void and of no effect.

Sec. 14. That so soon as the amount of tolls accruing and received for the use of said road, or any part thereof, according to the provisions of this act, shall exceed five per cent. on the amount of capital stock paid in, after deducting therefrom the expenses and liabilities of said company, the directors of said company shall make a dividend of such nett profits, among the stockholders, in proportion to their respective shares; and no contingent or accumulating fund, exceeding one per centum of the profits of said company, shall remain undivided for more than six months.

Sec. 15. That if any person or persons shall wilfully obstruct, or in any way spoil, injure or destroy said road, or either of its branches, or any thing belonging or incident thereto, or any materials to be used in the construction thereof, or any buildings, fixtures or carriages, erected or constructed for the use or convenience thereof, such person or persons shall each be liable for every such offence, to treble the damages sustained thereby; to be recovered by an action of debt, in any court having jurisdiction of that amount.

Sec. 16. That if the Legislature of this State shall, after the expiration of thirty-five years from the passage of this act, make provision by law for the repayment to said company of the amount expended by them in the construction of said rail-road, and of the value of the necessary permanent fixtures thereto at the time, with an addition of fifteen per cent. thereon; of which expenditure an accurate statement, in writing, attested by the oaths or affirmations of the officers of said company, shall be submitted to the General Assembly, if required, then said road and fixtures shall vest in, and become the property of the State of Ohio.

Sec. 17. Whenever the dividends of said company shall exceed the rate of six per cent. per annum, the Legislature of this State may impose such reasonable tax on the amount of said dividend, as may be received from other rail-road companies.

WILLIAM MEDILL,
Speaker pro tem. of the House of Representatives.
ELIJAH VANCE,
Speaker of the Senate.

March 14, 1836.

AN ACT

To incorporate the Stillwater and Maumee Rail-road Company.

Sec. 1. *Be it enacted by the General Assembly of the State of Ohio,* That William B. Hubbard, William McMahon, Robert H. Miller, Daniel Peck, William C. Kirker, Doct. John Campbell, David Allen, John McCartney, Jacob Halloway, and Moses Rhodes, of the county of Belmont; William G. Smith, John Chalfant, Samuel Skinner, Samuel Calvin, Thomas P. Jenkins, William Shotwell and John Norris, of the county of Harrison; James McCue, Samuel Shane, Samuel Douglass, George Slingluff and Michael Urick, of the county of Tuscarawas; Joseph S. Lake and James Jacobs, of the county of Wayne; Allen G. Miller, John H. Culbertson, John Pugh, Christopher Lambertson, of the county of Richland; Matthew McKelvey and Abijah Ives, of the county of Huron; Willard Whitney and Johnson Ford, of the county of Seneca; Jaques Hulburd and Jesse L. Olmsted, of the county of Sandusky; Oscar White, William Kingsbury,

David Cook and F. E. Kirtland, of the county of Lucas; be, and they are hereby appointed commissioners, under the direction of a majority of whom, subscriptions may be received to the capital stock of the Stillwater and Maumee Rail-road Company, hereby incorporated; and they, or a majority of them, may cause books to be opened at such times and places as they may direct, for the purpose of receiving subscriptions to the capital stock of said company, after having given such notice of the times and places of opening the same, as they may deem proper; and that, upon the first opening of said books, they shall be kept open for at least fifteen successive days, from ten o'clock, A. M. until three o'clock, P. M.; and if, at the expiration of that period, such subscription to the capital stock of said company as is necessary to its incorporation, shall not have been obtained, then said commissioners, or a majority of them, may cause said books to be opened, from time to time, after the expiration of fifteen days, for the space of five years thereafter; and if any of the said commissioners shall die, resign, or refuse to act during the continuance of the duties devolving upon them by this act, another may be appointed in his stead by the remaining commissioners, or a majority of them.

Sec. 2. That the capital stock of the Stillwater and Maumee Rail-road Company, shall be fifteen hundred thousand dollars, and shall be divided into shares of one hundred dollars each; which shares may be subscribed for by individuals; and it shall and may be lawful for the said rail-road company to commence the construction of the said rail-road, or may exercise and enjoy all the powers and privileges conferred by this act, as soon as fifty thousand dollars shall be subscribed to said stock.

Sec. 3. That all persons who shall become stockholders pursuant to this act, shall be, and they are hereby created a body corporate, and shall be and remain a corporation forever, under the name of "The Stillwater and Maumee Rail-road Company;" and by that name, shall be capable in law of purchasing, holding, selling, leasing and conveying estates, real, personal and mixed, so far as the same shall be necessary for the purposes hereinafter mentioned, and no further; and shall have perpetual succession; and by said corporate name, may contract and be contracted with, sue and be sued, and have and use a common seal, which they shall have power to alter or renew at their pleasure.

Sec. 4. That upon every subscription there shall be paid at the time of subscribing, to the commissioners, or their agents appointed to receive such subscriptions, the sum of five dollars on every share subscribed; and the residue thereof shall be paid in such instalments, and at such times, as may be required by the president and directors of said company: *Provided,* That no payments other than the first shall be demanded, until at least thirty days public notice of such demand shall have been given by said president and directors, in at least three newspapers in general circulation in three of the counties through which said rail-road may run; and if any stockholder or stockholders shall fail or neglect to pay any instalment, or part of said subscription thus demanded, for the space of sixty days next after the time the same shall be due and payable, the said president and directors, upon giving at least thirty days notice thereof, in manner aforesaid, may, and they are hereby authorized to sell at public vendue so many of the shares of such delinquent stockholder or stockholders as shall be necessary to pay such instalment and the expense of advertising, and transfer the shares so sold to the purchaser; and the residue of the money arising from such sale, after paying such instalment and expense, shall be paid to such stockholder on demand.

Sec. 5.   That at the expiration of fourteen days, for which the books are first opened, if five hundred shares of said capital stock shall have been subscribed, or if not, as soon thereafter as the same shall be subscribed, if within three years after the first opening of the said books, the said commissioners, or a majority of them, shall call a general meeting of the stockholders at such time and place as they may appoint, and shall give at least thirty days previous notice thereof in three public newspapers printed in three of the counties through which said road may pass; and at such meeting, the said commissioners shall lay the subscription books before the stockholders then and there present; and thereupon the said stockholders, or a majority of them, shall elect nine directors by ballot; a majority of whom shall be competent to manage the affairs of said company; they shall have the power of electing a president of said company, either from among the directors or others of said stockholders, and of allowing him such compensation for his services as they may deem proper; and in said election, and on all other occasions wherein a vote of the stockholders of said company is to be taken, each stockholder is to be allowed one vote for every share owned by him or her; and every stockholder may depute any person or persons to vote and act for him or her, as his or her proxy; and the commissioners aforesaid, or any five of them, shall be judges of the election of said directors.

Sec. 6.   That to continue the succession of the president and directors of said company, nine directors shall be chosen annually, on the first Monday of October in every year, at such place as the majority of the directors shall appoint; and if any vacancy shall occur by death, resignation or otherwise, or if any president or director, before the year for which he was elected has expired, a person to fill such vacant place for the residue of the year may be appointed by the president and directors of said company, or a majority of them; and the president and directors of the company shall hold and exercise their offices until a new election of president and directors; and that all elections which are by this act, or the by-laws of the company, to be made on a particular day, or a particular time, if not made on such day or time, may be made at any time within thirty days thereafter.

Sec. 7.   That a general meeting of the stockholders of said company shall be held annually, at the time and place appointed for the election of the president and directors of said company; that they may be called at any time during the interval between the said annual meeting, by the president and directors, or a majority of them, or by the stockholders owning at least one-fourth of the stock subscribed, upon giving at least thirty days public notice in three of the counties through which said rail-road may pass, of the time and place of holding the same; and when any such meetings are called, by the stockholders, such notice shall specify the particular object of the call; and if, at any such called meeting, a majority (in value) of the stockholders of said company are not present in person or by proxy, such meeting shall be adjourned from day to day without transacting any business, for any time, not exceeding three days; and if, within said three days, stockholders, holding a majority in value of the stock subscribed, do not thus attend, such meeting shall be dissolved.

Sec. 8. That at the regular annual meeting of the stockholders of said company, it shall be the duty of the president and directors in office for the previous year, to exhibit a clear and distinct statement of the affairs of the company; that at any called meeting of the stockholders, a majority of those present in person or by proxy, may require similar statements from the president and directors, whose duty it shall be to furnish them when thus required; and at all general meetings of the stockholders, a majority in value of all the stockholders of said company may remove from office any president or any of the directors of said company, and may appoint officers in their stead.

Sec. 9. That any president and directors of said company, before he acts as such, shall take an oath or affirmation (as the case may be,) that he will well and truly discharge the duties of said office to the best of his skill and judgment.

Sec. 10. That the said president and directors, or a majority of them, may appoint all such officers, engineers, agents or servants whatsoever, as they may deem necessary for the transaction of the business of the company, and may remove any of them at their pleasure; that they, or a majority of them, shall have power to determine by contract, the compensation of all the engineers, officers, agents, or servants, in the employ of said company: and to determine by their by-laws the manner of adjusting and settling all accounts against the said company; and, also, the manner and evidence of transfer of stock in said company; and they, or a majority of them, shall have the power to pass all by-laws, which they may deem necessary or proper for exercising all the powers vested in the company hereby incorporated, and for carrying the objects of this act into effect: *Provided, only,* That such by-laws shall not be contrary to the laws of this State or of the United States.

Sec. 11. That if the capital stock of said company shall be deemed insufficient for the purposes of this act, it shall and may be lawful for the president and directors of said company, or a majority of them, from time to time, to increase the capital stock, by the addition of as many shares as they may deem necessary, not exceeding in amount the sum of five hundred thousand dollars, which they may, at their option cause to be subscribed, giving notice in the manner herein before prescribed; or may sell the same, for the benefit of the said company.

[Sec. 12.] That the said corporation shall be, and they are hereby vested with the right to construct a double or single rail-road, from a point on Stillwater, in the State of Ohio, where the Stillwater Navigation and Rail-road Company may make the point of termination for their rail-road on said Stillwater, to or near the mouth of Maumee river, so as to terminate at or near the termination of the Wabash and Erie canal; or to connect with the Ohio Rail-road at such point as said company shall deem expedient; making such other intermediate points as may hereafter be found necessary; to transport, take and carry property and persons upon the same, by the power and force of steam, of animals, or of any mechanical or other power, or of any combination of them, which the said corporation may choose to carry: *Provided, however*, That if the said Stillwater and Rail-road company should not fix the point of termination of their said rail-road on the said Stillwater, within two years from and after the passage of this act, then, and in that case, it shall be the duty of the president and directors of this company, or a majority of them, to fix the point of commencement for said rail-road somewhere on said Stillwater: *And provided, also*, That if the termination of the Wabash and Erie Canal should not be fixed in the State of Ohio, within two years after the passage of this act, then, and in that case, it shall be the duty of the president and directors of this company, or a majority of them, to fix the point of termination of said rail-road as before provided.

Sec. 13. That the president and directors of said company shall be, and they are hereby invested with all rights and powers necessary for the location, construction and repair of said road, not exceeding one hundred feet wide, with so many sets of tracks as the said president and directors may deem necessary, and they may cause to be made, or contract with others for making the said rail-road, or any part thereof; and they, or their agents, or those with whom they may contract for making any part of the same, may enter upon, and use and occupy any land which may be wanted for the site of said road, or for any other purpose necessary and useful in the construction, or in the repair of said road or its works, and that they may build bridges, may fix scales and weights, may lay rails, may take and use any earth, timber, gravel, stone or other materials which may be wanted for the construction or repair of any part of said road, or any of its works; and may make and construct all works whatsoever, which may be necessary in the construction of said road.

Sec. 14. That the president and directors of said company, or a majority of them, or any person or persons authorized by a majority of them, may agree with the owner or owners of any land or lands, earth, timber, gravel or stone, or other materials, or any improvements which may be wanted for the construction or repair of said road, or any of its works, for the purchase or use, or occupation of the same; and if they cannot agree, and if the owner or owners, or any of them, be a *feme covert*, under age, *non compos mentis*, or out of the county in which the property wanted may lie, when such land and materials may be wanted, application may be made to any justice of the peace in the township where such property may be, who shall thereupon issue his warrant, under his hand and seal, directed to the constable of said township, or the sheriff of the county in which said township may be situated, or some disinterested person if the constable or sheriff be interested, requiring him to summons a jury of twelve inhabitants of said county, not related or in any wise interested; to meet on the land, or near to the other property or materials, to be valued on a day named in the warrant, not less than ten nor more than twenty days after the issuing of the same, and if, at the said time and place, any of the persons summoned do not attend, the said constable, sheriff, or summoner shall immediately summons as many persons as may be necessary, with the persons in attendance, to furnish a pannel of twelve jurors in attendance; and from them each party, its, his, or her agent, if either be not present in person or by agent, the constable, sheriff, or other summoner, for him, her, it or them, may strike off three jurors, and the remaining nine shall act as

63—L

a jury of inquest of damages; and before they act as such, said constable, sheriff, or other summoner shall administer to each of them an oath, or affirmation, as the case may be, that they will justly and impartially value the damages which the owner or owners will sustain by the use or occupation of the same, required by said company; and the jury estimating the damages, if for the ground occupied by said road, shall take into the estimate the benefits resulting to said owner or owners, by reason of said road passing through or upon the lands of such owner or owners, towards the extinguishment of such claim for damages; and the said jury shall reduce their inquisition to writing, and shall sign and seal the same; and it shall then be returned to the clerk of the court of common pleas for said county, and by said clerk filed in his office, and shall be confirmed by said court at its next session, if no cause to the contrary be shown; and when confirmed, shall be recorded by said clerk, at the expense of said company; but if set aside, the said court may direct another inquisition to be taken in the manner above prescribed; and such inquisition shall describe the property taken, or the bounds of the lands condemned; and such valuation, when paid or tendered to the owner or owners of the property, or his, her, or their legal representatives, shall entitle said company to the estate and interest in the same, thus valued, as fully as if it had been conveyed by the owner or owners of the same, so long as the same shall be used for the purposes of said road; and the valuation, if not received when tendered, may, at any time thereafter, be received from the company without cost, by the owner or owners, his, her, or their legal representative or representatives; and that such constable, sheriff, or other summoner, and jurors, shall be entitled to demand and receive from the said company, the same fees, as are allowed for like services, in cases of fixing the valuation of real estate, previous to sale under execution.

Sec. 15. That whenever in the construction of such road, it shall be necessary to cross or intersect any established rail-road or way, it shall be the duty of said president and directors of said company so to construct the said rail-road across such established road or way, as not to impede the passage or transportation of persons or property along the same, or when it shall be necessary to pass through the land of any individual or individuals, it shall also be their duty to provide for such individual or individuals, proper wagon ways across said road, from one part of his land to another, without unnecessary delay.

Sec. 16. That if said company should neglect to provide proper wagon ways across said road, as required by the fifteenth section of this act, it shall be lawful for any individual or individuals to sue said company, and to be entitled to such damages, as a jury may think him, her, or them entitled to, for such neglect or refusal on the part of said company.

Sec. 17. That whenever it shall be necessary for said company to have, use or occupy any land, or materials, in the construction or repair of said road, or any part thereof, on their works or necessary buildings, the president and directors of the said company, or their agents, or those contracting with them for making or repairing the same, may immediately take and use the same; they having first caused the property wanted, to be viewed by a jury, (formed in the same manner hereinbefore prescribed,) and having tendered to the owner of the property the amount assessed, in those cases where the property is to be changed or altered, by admixture with other substances, before such alteration is made; and that it shall be necessary after such view, in order to the use or occupation of the same, to wait the issue of the proceedings upon such view, and the inquest of the jury, after confirmation, and after payment or tender of the valuation, shall be a bar to all actions for taking or using such property.

Sec. 18. That [if it] shall be necessary for the said rail road company, in the selection of the route, or construction of the road by them to be laid out and constructed, or any part of it, to connect the same with, or to use any turnpike, road or bridge, made or erected by any company or persons incorporated, or authorized by any law of this State, it shall be lawful for the said president and directors, and they are hereby authorized, to contract or agree with any such other corporation or persons, for the right to use such road or bridge, or for the transfer of any of the corporate or other rights or privileges of such corporation or persons, to the said company hereby incorporated; and every such other corporation, or persons incorporated by, or acting under the laws of this State, is, and are hereby authorized to make such an agreement, contract, or transfer, by and through the agency of the person authorized by their respective acts of incorporation, to exercise their corporate powers, or by such persons as by any law of this State, are entrusted with the management and direction of such turnpike, road or bridge, or of any of the rights and privileges aforesaid; and every contract, agreement or transfer, made in pursuance of the power and authority hereby granted, when executed, by the several parties under their respective corporate seals, or otherwise legally authenticated, shall vest in the company hereby incorporated, all such road, part of road, rights and privileges, and the right to use and enjoy the same, as fully, to all intents and purposes, as they now are, or might be used and exercised by the said corporation, or persons in whom they are now vested.

Sec. 19. That the president and directors shall have power to purchase with the funds of the company, and place on the rail-road constructed by them, under this act, all machines, wagons, vehicles, or carriages of any description whatsoever, which they may deem necessary or proper, for the purpose of transporting on said rail-road; and that they shall have full power to charge for tolls upon, and transportation of goods, produce, merchandize, or property of any kind whatsoever, transported by them along said rail way, any sum not exceeding the following rates: on all goods, merchandize, or property of any description, transported by them, a sum not exceeding one and a half cents per mile, for toll, five cents per ton per mile, for transportation; and for the transportation of passengers, not exceeding three cents per mile for each passenger; and all persons paying the tolls aforesaid, and furnishing suitable and proper cars to transport passengers or property shall be entitled to have the same drawn on said road, by the corporation hereby created, subject to their general rules as to the time of departure and speed of said cars.

Sec. 20. That the said president and directors shall, annually or semi-annually, declare and make such dividends as they may deem proper, of the nett profits arising from the resources of said company, deducting the necessary current and probable contingent expenses, and that they shall divide the same among the stockholders, of said company in proportion to their respective shares.

Sec. 21. That any other rail road company now or hereafter to be chartered by law of this State, may join and connect any rail road with the road hereby contemplated, and run cars upon the same, subject to the rules and regulations of this company, as to the construction and speed of said cars; and full right and privilege is hereby reserved to the State, or individuals, or any company incorporated by law of this State, to cross this road: *Provided*, That in so crossing, no injury shall be done to the works of the company hereby incorporated.

Sec. 22. That if any person or persons, shall wilfully, by any means whatsoever, injure, impair, or destroy any part of the rail road, constructed by said company under this act, or any of the necessary works, building, or machinery of said company, such person or persons so offending, shall, each of them, for every such offence, forfeit and pay to the said company a sum not exceeding three fold the damages which may be recovered in the name of said company, by an action of debt, in any court of common pleas, in the county wherein the offence shall be committed: and shall also be subject to indictment in said court and upon conviction of such offence shall be punished by fine, not exceeding one thousand dollars, and imprisonment, not exceeding thirty days, at the discretion of the court.

Sec. 23. That if the said rail road hereby authorized to be constructed, shall not be commenced within three years from the passage of this act, and finished within ten years thereafter, then and in that case, the the same shall be null and void.

Sec. 24. Whenever the dividends of said company shall exceed six per cent. per annum, the Legislature may impose such reasonable tax on the amount of such dividends as may be received from other rail road companies.

Sec. 25. That the State shall have power, at any time after the expiration of thirty-five years from the passage of this act, to purchase and hold said road for the use of the State, at a price not exceeding the original cost for the construction of the road, and the necessary permanent fixtures at the time of purchase, and fifteen per cent. thereon; of which cost an accurate statement in writing, shall be submitted to the General Assembly, duly attested by the oath of the officers of said company, if the General Assembly require it.

Sec. 26. That this act is hereby declared to be a public act, and shall be so construed in all courts of justice and elsewhere.

WILLIAM MEDILL,
Speaker pro tem. of the House of Representatives.
ELIJAH VANCE,
Speaker of the Senate.

March 14, 1836.

AN ACT

To incorporate the town of West Alexandria, in the county of Preble.

Sec. 1. *Be it enacted by the General Assembly of the State of Ohio,* That so much of the townships of Twin and Lanair, in the county of Preble, as is comprehended in the plat of the town of West Alexandria, together with such plats as have been, or may hereafter be recorded as additions thereto, be, and the same is hereby created and constituted a town corporate, by the name of "The Town of West Alexandria."

Sec. 2. That for the order and good government of said town, and the inhabitants thereof, it shall be lawful for the white male inhabitants, who have resided in said town for the space of six months next preceding said election, having the qualifications of electors of members of the General Assembly, to meet at some suitable place in said town of West Alexandria, on the third Monday of April next, and at such place as the town council may direct, and on the third Monday of April annually thereafter; and then and there proceed, by a plurality of votes, to elect, by ballot, one mayor, one recorder, and five trustees, who shall be householders, and shall hold their respective office for one year, and until their successors are elected and qualified; such mayor, recorder, and trustees, being so elected and qualified, shall constitute a town council, any five of whom shall constitute a quorum for the transaction of any business pertaining to their duties; but any less number shall have no power, other than to adjourn from time to time, until a quorum shall have been convened.

Sec. 3. That at the first election to be holden under this act there shall be chosen, *viva voce*, by the electors present, two judges and a clerk of said election, who shall each take an oath or affirmation, faithfully to discharge the duties required of them by this act; and at all subsequent elections, the trustees, or any two of them shall be judges, and the recorder clerk of said election; and at all elections to be holden under this act, the polls shall be opened between the hours of one and two, and close at four o'clock, P. M. of said day; and at the close of the polls, the votes shall be counted, and a true statement thereof proclaimed to the electors present, by one of the judges; and the clerk shall make out a true record thereof, and within five days thereafter, said clerk shall give notice to the persons so elected of their elections; and it shall be the duty of said town council, at least ten days before each and every annual election, to give notice of the same, by setting up advertisements at three of the most public places in said town.

Sec. 4. That it shall be the duty of the mayor, and in case of his absence or disability to serve, the recorder, to preside at all meetings of the town council; and it shall be the duty of the recorder to attend all such meetings, and keep a fair and accurate record of their proceedings.

Sec. 5. That the town council shall have power to fill all vacancies which may happen in said board, from the householders, who are qualified electors in said town; whose appointment shall continue until the next annual election, and until their successors are duly elected and qualified; and whenever it shall happen that neither the mayor or recorder is present at any such meeting, the trustees shall have power to appoint one of their own number, to perform the duties of such mayor, recorder, or both, as the case may be; which appointment shall be *pro tempore.*

Sec. 6. That the said mayor, recorder, and trustees of said town, shall be a body corporate and politic, with perpetual succession, to be known and distinguished by the name and title of "The Town Council of the town of West Alexandria;" and shall be capable in law, in their corporate name, to acquire property, real, personal and mixed, for the use of said town, with power to sell and convey the same; may have a common seal, which they may alter, break, and amend at pleasure; may sue and be sued, plead and be impleaded, defend and be defended, in any court of competent jurisdiction, whether of law or equity; and when any suit shall be commenced against said corporation, the first process shall be by summons; an attested copy of which shall be left with the recorder, at his usual place of abode, at least five days before the return thereof.

Sec. 7. That each member of said town council shall, before he enters upon the duties of his office, take an oath or affirmation to support the constitution of the United States, and of this State, and also an oath or affirmation of office.

Sec. 8. That the said town council shall have power to ordain and establish by-laws, rules and regulations, for the government of said town, and the same to alter, repeal or amend, at pleasure; to provide in said by-laws for the election of a treasurer, town marshal, and all the subordinate officers which may be thought necessary for the good government and well being of the inhabitants of said town; to prescribe their duties, and determine the periods of their appointment, and the fees they shall be entitled to receive for their services; and to require of them to qualify, previous to their entering upon the duties of their respective offices; and may further require of them a bond, with security, conditioned for the faithful discharge of their respective duties as officers of said corporation; the town council shall have power to affix to the violation of the by-laws and ordinances of the corporation, such reasonable fines and penalties as they may deem proper, to enforce obedience to the same, and to provide for the disposition or appropriation of said fines and penalties: *Provided,* Such by-laws and ordinances be not inconsistent with the constitution and laws of the United States and of this State: *And provided, also,* That no by-laws. or ordinance of said corporation shall take effect, or be in force, until the same shall have been posted up for two weeks, in one of the most public places in said corporation.

Sec. 9. That the town council shall, at the expiration of each and every year, cause to be made out and posted up as aforesaid, the receipts and expenditures of the preceding year.

Sec. 10. That the said town council shall have power to regulate and improve the lanes, streets and alleys, and to determine the width of the side walks; they shall have power to remove all nuisances and obstructions from the streets and commons of said town, or provide for the removal of the same, and to do all things which corporations of a similar nature can do, to secure the peace, health, and good order of the inhabitants of said town.

Sec. 11. That for the purpose of more effectually enabling said town council to carry into effect the provisions of this act, they are hereby authorized and empowered to levy a tax on all the real and personal property, subject to taxation within the bounds of said corporation, as the same has been, or shall be appraised and returned on the grand levy of the State: *Provided*, That said tax shall not exceed in any one year, one half of one per centum, on the aggregate amount of all such taxable property within the limits of said corporation; and the said town council shall, between the third Monday in April and the third Monday in July, determine the amount of tax to be assessed and collected for the current year.

Sec. 12. That it shall be the duty of the recorder of said corporation, to make out duplicates of taxes, charging each individual within said corporation, an amount of taxes, in proportion to the aggregate value of the taxable property belonging to said individual, within the limits of said corporation, as the same appears upon the auditor's books of Preble county, and the said auditor shall, at all reasonable office hours, lay open to the inspection of the recorder, any books which may be in his office affording such information; and the recorder shall be allowed to take abstracts, or memorandums, or transcripts therefrom, free of expense, to enable him to make out his duplicates, which duplicates shall be certified by the mayor and recorder, and one of said duplicates shall be delivered to the marshal, or to such other person as shall be appointed collector, whose duty it shall be to collect said tax, in the same manner and under the same regulations as collectors of State and county tax are required by law to collect State and county taxes; and the said marshal or collector so appointed, shall, immediately after collecting said tax, pay the same over to the treasurer of said corporation, and take his receipt therefor; and the said marshal or other collector shall have the same power to sell both real and personal property, as given by law to county treasurers; and when necessary, the recorder shall have power to make deeds for real estate so sold, in the same manner that county auditors are by law empowered to do, for lands sold by the county treasurer; and the marshal, or other collector, shall receive for his fees, such sum as the town council may direct, not exceeding six per centum on all moneys so by him collected, to be paid by the treasurer, on the order of the recorder.

Sec. 13. That said town council shall have no power, under any consideration whatever, to grant license to retailers of spirituous liquors.

Sec. 14. That said town council shall have full power to appropriate any money remaining in the corporation treasury, to the improvement of the streets, alleys and side walks of said town, when they may deem it necessary so to do, and to make all other improvements of a public nature, which may conduce to the convenience and prosperity of the inhabitants of said town.

Sec. 15. That the mayor of said corporation, shall be a conservator of the peace throughout said town; and shall, within the same, have all the powers and jurisdiction of a justice of the peace, in all matters either civil or criminal, arising under the laws of this State, to all intents and purposes whatsoever; the said mayor shall perform all the duties required of him by the by-laws and ordinances of said corporation; and appeals and writs of *certiorari* may be taken from the decision of the mayor, in all cases where appeals or writs of *certiorari* are allowed from the decision of justices of the peace, and in the same manner; said mayor shall give bond, as justices of the peace are required to do.

Sec. 16. That the marshal shall be the principal ministerial officer of said town, and shall have the same power as constables have by law; and his jurisdiction, in criminal cases, shall be co-extensive with the county of Preble, and he shall execute the process of the mayor, and receive the same fees for his services, that constables are allowed in similar cases for like services.

Sec. 17. That the mayor shall receive the same fees that justices of the peace are allowed in like cases; and the recorder such fees for his services, as the by-laws and ordinances of such corporation shall prescribe, but the residue of said town council shall receive no pecuniary compensation.

Sec. 18. That if no election should be held by the electors of said town, on the third Monday of April, it shall be lawful for any ten householders of said town, to call a meeting of the electors, by giving ten days notice in three of the most public places therein; which notice shall state the time, and place, and object of the meeting, and shall be signed by the said householders; and if a majority of the electors of said town shall attend at the time and place named in said notice, it shall be lawful for them to proceed to the election of officers, in the same manner as though the meeting had taken place on the third Monday of April; and the officers so elected shall hold their offices till the third Monday of April following, and until their successors be duly elected and qualified.

Sec. 19. That the said corporation shall be alloweld the use of the jail of said county, for the imprisonment of such persons as may be liable to imprisonment, under the laws and ordinances of said town, and all persons so imprisoned, shall be under the charge of the sheriff or jailor, as in other cases.

Sec. 20. That the Legislature may have power, at any time, to alter, amend or repeal this act; not thereby affecting, however, in any manner, the right of individual citizens.

WILLIAM MEDILL,
Speaker pro tem. of the House of Representatives.
ELIJAH VANCE,
Speaker of the Senate.

March 14, 1836.

AN ACT

To incorporate the Urbana and Columbus Rail-road Company.

Sec. 1. *Be it enacted by the General Assembly of the State of Ohio,* That John Reynolds, Joseph Vance, William Ward, Lemuel Weaver, Robert M. Woods, Israel Hamilton, Abram R. Colwell, Obed Hor, James Dallas, and such other persons and companies as shall, agreeably to the provisions of this act, become stockholders in the corporation hereby created, shall be a body corporate, under the name of "The Urbana and Columbus Rail-road Company."

Sec. 2. The capital stock of said corporation hereby created shall be three hundred thousand dollars, which shall be considered personal property, and be divided into shares of fifty dollars each.

Sec. 3. The persons named in the first section of this act, shall be commissioners for receiving subscriptions to the capital stock of said corporation, agreeably to the provisions of this act; and within twelve months from the date hereof, they shall give notice, for thirty days, in some newspaper of general circulation in the county of Champaign, of the time they will open books for subscription of said stock, in the town of Urbana, and such other places as they may deem fit; and shall continue the same open thirty days, and until the sum of thirty thousand dollars shall be subscribed.

Sec. 4. Each subscriber, at the time he subscribes, shall pay to the commissioners five dollars on each share of the stock subscribed by him.

Sec. 5. As soon as may be after the closing of the books, the commissioners shall give notice of the time and place at which a meeting of the stockholders will be held, for the choice of directors; and at the time and place appointed, the commissioners, or some of them, shall attend, and the stockholders, or their proxies, duly appointed in writing, shall proceed to elect, by ballot, nine directors, who shall serve until the next annual election, and until their successors are chosen and qualified; the commissioners present shall preside at the election, and certify the result in writing, and the certificate recorded in the books of the corporation, shall be evidence of the election of the directors therein named; all subsequent elections shall be conducted in the manner prescribed by the by-laws of said corporation.

Sec. 6. Each stockholder shall be allowed as many votes as he owns shares of stock at the commencement of any election of directors, and a plurality of votes shall determine the election.

Sec. 7. The directors shall hold their offices for one year, and until others shall be elected in their steads; they shall appoint one of their own number president, and some suitable person, secretary of the corporation; they shall moreover appoint all such officers and agents, as the convenience of the company may require, and allow them a suitable compensation; and they shall severally take an oath for the faithful performance of their duties.

Sec. 8. The corporation hereby created, shall have power to sue, complain, and defend, in all courts of law or equity; to have a common seal, and the same to alter at pleasure; to hold or purchase, and convey, real and personal estate, so far as the same may be necessary for the purposes contemplated by this act; and to make by-laws, not inconsistent with any existing law, for the management of its property, the regulation of its affairs, and the transfer of its stock.

Sec. 9. The said corporation shall have power to construct, maintain, and use a rail-way, not exceeding one hundred feet in width, with a double or single track, with such appendages as may be deemed necessary for the convenient use of the same; commencing at any eligible point in or near the town of Urbana, thence by the nearest and most eligible route to some point in or near the city of Columbus: and for that purpose the directors shall cause such examinations and surveys to be made, as may be necessary to the selection by them of the most advantageous line, course or way, of said road, and the board of directors shall, as soon thereafter as practicable, select the route on which said road shall be constructed.

Sec. 10. The said corporation may acquire title to the lands along the route of said road, by purchase or voluntary cession; in case the corporation shall not be able to acquire the title to such lands as may be requisite for the said rail-road, or the use thereof, by purchase, or voluntary cession, it may by its agents, engineers, and surveyors, enter upon such route, place or places selected, as aforesaid, by the directors, as a line whereon to construct the rail-road; and it shall be lawful for the said corporation to enter upon, and take possession of and use all such lands, real estate and materials, as may be indispensable for the construction and maintenance of said rail-road, and the accommodations requisite and appertaining thereto: and may also acquire, hold, and take such grants of land and real estate, as may be designed to aid in the construction, maintenance, or accommodation of said road or ways, with power to grant, pledge or lease the same for the benefit of said company; all lands or real estate entered upon and used by said corporation, and all earth, timber, gravel, and other materials, needed by said company, shall be purchased of the owners thereof, at a price to be mutually agreed upon between them; and in case of disagreement of the owners as to the price of any lands or materials, so required for said road, or if the owners are under any disability in law to contract, or are absent from the county, application may be made, either by said owners, or by said corporation, to any judge of the court of common pleas of the county within which said lands or materials may lie, specifying the lands or materials so required, or already appropriated; and thereupon the said judge shall issue his warrant in writing, directed to the sheriff of the county, requiring him to summon an inquest of five freeholders of the county, who shall not be stockholders, nor interested in said road, to appear at or near said land or materials to be valued, on a day named in said warrant, not less than five nor more than ten days after issuing the same; and if any of the persons summoned do not attend, the sheriff, or the person performing the duties of sheriff, shall forthwith summons as many as may be necessary to fill said inquest, and the persons so empannelled, shall, on their oaths or affirmations, value the damages which the several owners will sustain by the use or occupation of the land, materials, or property required by said company, having due regard to the benefit such owners may derive from the location and structure of said road; and said inquest shall reduce their valuation to writing, and such valuation when paid or tendered, to said owners, or deposited in any bank to their credit, or their proper representatives, if either be known, shall entitle said company to the lands and materials, and all estate and interest therein, as fully as if it had been conveyed by the owners of the same, so long as the same shall be used for the purposes of said road: and every sheriff and freeholder, so acting, shall receive one dollar per day for his services, to be paid by said company: either party may, within ten days after such valuation is made, appeal from the same, to the court of common pleas of the proper county, by giving notice thereof, to the opposite party, or by filing in the clerk's office, a copy of such valuation, with notice thereto annexed; and said court may, for good cause shown, order a new valuation, and on final hearing, the court shall award costs according to equity.

Sec. 11. The said corporation shall have power to locate and construct branch roads from the main route, to other towns, or to mills, quarries, and other places in the counties through which said road may pass.

Sec. 12. Whenever it shall be necessary for the construction of the rail-road, to intersect or cross any stream of water, or water course, or any road or highway, lying in or across the route of said road, it shall be lawful for the corporation to construct the said rail-way across or upon the same; but the corporation shall restore the stream, or water course, or road or highway thus intersected, to its former state, or in sufficient manner not to impair its usefulness, without unnecessary delay; and if said corporation, after having selected a route for said rail-way, find any obstacles to continuing said location, either by difficulty of construction, or procuring right of way at reasonable cost, or whenever a better and cheaper route can be had, it shall have authority to change the route and vary the location: and whenever said road shall pass through the land of any individual it shall be the duty of said company to provide for said individual proper wagon ways from one part of his land to the other.

Sec. 13. That said corporation shall also have power to locate and construct a navigable canal or basin, from the termination or depot of said rail-way, in or near the town of Urbana, to any proper point on Mad river, and to connect the same with any navigable feeder that may be constructed by the State from Mad river to the Miami canal, north of Dayton, and with consent of the owners, to use any streams of water necessary to feed the same; and to construct docks, wharves, dams, waste weirs, and reservoirs, at the termination thereof, or at any proper point on the canal, or on Mad river, convenient for the use of the same: *Provided,* Such canal shall not be so constructed as to draw off the water from such navigable feeder, as in any way to interfere with, or impair the usefulness of such feeder to the injury of the State, or any of the public works that the State may think proper to undertake.

Sec. 14. That the said corporation shall have the same powers to acquire title to lands along the route of said canal, and to procure right of way and materials, and in the manner pointed out in the tenth section of this act; but no stream of water already appropriated to mill purposes, nor the waters of Mad river, shall be diverted from any existing mill, or improved water power, without the consent of the owners, obtained by purchase or voluntary cession: and said corporation shall have power to make arrangement, with any mill owners on Mad river, to increase and maintain the water power on said river, and to contribute to the cost of such works, and to lease or dispose of any water power that may be available on the lands of said company.

Sec. 15. If the said canal shall be made across any existing public road, the said corporation shall, if required by the county commissioners, construct a suitable bridge at such crossing, to be maintained and repaired, as may be agreed with such county commissioners.

Sec. 16. It shall be lawful for the directors to require payment of the sums to be subscribed to the capital stock, at such time and in such instalments, as they shall see fit; and if the instalments remain unpaid for sixty days after the time of payment has elapsed, the board may collect the same by suit, or shall have power, on giving twenty days public notice, to sell the stock at public auction, for the instalments then due, and the cost of making such sale, and the residue of the price obtained, shall be paid over to the former owner.

Sec. 17. That any other rail-road company, now or hereafter to be chartered by law of this State, may join and connect with the road hereby incorporated, on such terms as the directors of said company may agree, and in case of a disagreement, then on such terms as the supreme court in chancery may determine; and full right and privilege is hereby reserved to the State, or individuals, or any company incorporated by law of this State, to cross this road with any other road: *Provided,* That in so crossing, no injury shall be done to the works of the company hereby incorporated.

Sec. 18. The said corporation shall be authorized to borrow, on the credit of said company, any amount of money not exceeding two-thirds of the capital stock, and to pledge the funds, tolls, lands, works, and rents of said company, for the payment of such loans, and of the interest thereon.

Sec. 19. That said corporation shall have power to fix the rate of tolls, and charges for transportation, and also such rates of wharfage as may be reasonable, on said road or canal; but said company shall not demand greater rate of tolls than at the rate of three cents per mile for each ton of merchandize or other freight, and four cents per mile for each passenger.

Sec. 20. The State of Ohio shall have power, at any time after the lapse of thirty-five years, to purchase of the said company, said rail-road and the fixtures thereof, by paying to the company the cost of such road and fixture, with fifteen per cent. profit thereon: *Provided,* That the said fifteen per cent, together with the annual profits of said road, shall not be less than an average annual dividend of six per cent.

Sec. 21. If the subscribers to said company shall not become so far organized as to elect a board of directors within two years from the passage of this act, and within two years thereafter to commence the construction of some part of said work, and finished within ten years thereafter, this act shall be void.

Sec. 22. Whenever the dividends of said company shall exceed the rate six per cent. per annum, the Legislature of this State may impose such reasonable tax on the amount of said dividends as may be received from other rail-road companies.

WILLIAM MEDILL,
Speaker pro tem. of the House of Representatives.

ELIJAH VANCE,
Speaker of the Senate.

March 14, 1836.

AN ACT

To incorporate the Cincinnati Western Rail-road Company.

Sec. 1. *Be it enacted by the General Assembly of the State of Ohio,* That for the purpose of establishing a communication by rail-road between the Miami canal and the Ohio river, in the western part of the city of Cincinnati, the formation of a company, to be styled the Cincinnati Western Rail-road Company, is hereby authorized, with a capital of one hundred thousand dollars, to be divided into shares of fifty dollars each, and subscribed and paid for by individuals, companies or corporations, in the manner hereinafter mentioned and specified; which subscribers and stockholders shall be and hereby are created a body corporate and politic, with perpetual succession, by the name and style of "The Cincinnati Western Rail-road Company;" and shall continue such body corporate and politic forever; and by that name, shall be competent to contract and be contracted with, to sue and be sued, plead and 'be impleaded, answer and be answered unto, defend and be defended, in all courts and places, and in all matters whatsoever; with full power and authority to acquire, hold and possess, use, occupy and enjoy, and the same to sell and convey, and dispose of, all such real estate as shall be necessary and convenient for the transaction of its business, or which may be conveyed to said company as collateral security, or received in payment of any debt which may become due or owing to the same, or in satisfaction of any judgment of a court of law, or by order or decree of a court of equity in their favor; and may have and use a common seal, and the same alter, change, break or renew at pleasure; and may also make, ordain and establish and put in execution, such by-laws, ordinances, rules and regulations, as may be necessary and proper for the good government of said company, and the prudent and efficient management of its affairs.

Sec. 2. That Jacob Burnet, Charles Tatem, Joseph Bonsall, William Price, George W. Jones, Nicholas Longworth, Stephen Burrows, John Whetstone, William Baird, William Crossman, Philip Grandin, David Loring, David Weaver, and John P. Foote, all of the city of Cincinnati, be, and are hereby appointed commissioners to open books and receive subscriptions for the capital stock of said company, and to superintend the election of the first board of directors thereof, any six of whom shall be competent to exercise the powers and perform the duties required of them by this act; they shall have power, and they are hereby authorized, at any time after the first day of April next, having given at least ten days previous notice thereof in two or more newspapers printed in said city, to open books of subscription, at some suitable place or places in Cincinnati, for the capital stock of said company, and to keep such books of subscription open from nine o'clock in the morning, until six o'clock in the evening, for ten days, exclusive of Sundays. and until at least five hundred shares thereof shall be subscribed, the said commissioners shall deduct the amount of such excess from the highest subscriptions, in such a manner that no subscription shall be reduced while any one remains larger, except so far as may be necessary to avoid the dividing of shares; and in case the full amount of two thousand shares shall not have been subscribed at the time of closing the books as aforesaid, the said books may be re-opened for subscriptions, under the superintendence of the board of directors, at such time and place as they may deem proper; the said directors causing at least ten days previous notice of the re-opening of such subscription books, to be published in at least two newspapers printed in said city of Cincinnati; and said commissioners, whenever five hundred shares or more shall have been subscribed, shall give public notice thereof in two newspapers as aforesaid; and by the same notice they shall appoint the day and place in said city, not less than six nor more than twenty days from the date of such notice, for the subscribers of said stock to meet and elect their first board of directors for said company, who shall continue in office until the first Monday in April, which will be in the year eighteen hundred and thirty-seven, and until their successors shall have been chosen; at which election the said commissioners, or a majority of them, shall act as judges and inspectors, and shall perform all the duties incident to judges and inspectors in like cases.

Sec. 3. The payment for shares of said capital stock shall be made and completed by the subscribers respectively, at the times, and in the manner following, to wit: at the time of subscribing there shall be paid on each share five dollars; immediately after the election of the first board of directors, the further sum of ten dollars shall be paid; and the remaining thirty-five dollars may be called for by the directors, in four equal instalments, at intervals of not less than sixty days; of which notice shall be given at least twenty days in some newspaper published in Cincinnati; and if any instalment so called for shall not be paid within thirty days after the same shall become due and payable, it shall be lawful for the board of directors, after thirty days notice thereof in some newspaper published in Cincinnati, to sell the share or shares on which payment shall not have been made, at public auction, to the highest bidder; and any surplus remaining after paying the instalment and the expense of sale, shall be paid over to the delinquen towner of such share or shares.

Sec. 4. The stock of said company may be transferred in such manner as may be directed by the by-laws of the company.

Sec. 5. The affairs of the said company shall be managed and directed by a board, to consist of thirteen directors, who shall be stockholders to the amount of not less than five shares each, and residents of the county of Hamilton; and after the first election, they shall be elected by the stockholders on the first Monday in April annually, at such time and at such place in Cincinnati, as the directors for the time being shall appoint; they shall hold their office for the term of one year, and until their successors shall be chosen; and notice of every such election shall be published for three weeks next preceding the same, in one or more of the newspapers printed in Cincinnati; and the election shall be by ballot, and plurality of votes, and under the direction of three stockholders, not directors at the time, to be previously appointed by the board of directors for that purpose; and at every such election, and at all other meetings of the stockholders, held under the provisions of this act, each stockholder shall be entitled to one vote for each share which he may hold in his own right; and after the first election no share shall confer a right of suffrage which shall not have been holden by the owner thereof at least three calendar months previous to the day of election; any stockholder not personally attending such election or other regular meeting of the stockholders, and having a right to vote, may vote by proxy, such proxy being a stockholder: *Provided,* That in case it shall so happen that an election of directors shall not be made on the day when, by this act, it ought to be made, this corporation shall not, for such cause, be deemed to be dissolved; but it shall and may be lawful for said stockholders to make an election of directors on any other day, in such manner as may be provided for by the by-laws and ordinances of said company.

Sec. 6. The directors duly chosen under the provisions of this act, shall, as soon as may be after their election, elect from their own body a president, who shall preside in the board until the next annual election; and in case of his death, resignation or absence, a new president shall be chosen; but in case of temporary absence, a president, *pro tempore,* shall be appointed; they shall fill all vacancies which may occur in their own body, during the time for which they shall be elected, and shall appoint a secretary, treasurer, or other officers, agents and servants of said company, fix their compensation, define their powers, and prescribe their duties, who shall give such bond, and in such penal sums, with such conditions, as the said directors shall prescribe, and hold their several offices during the pleasure of the board; they shall hold stated meetings on such days as they, from time to time, may appoint, and at such times as the president may direct, and a majority of the whole number shall constitute a quorum; they shall, on the first Mondays of January and July, annually, make and declare such dividends resulting from the profits of said company, as shall not impair, nor in anywise lessen the capital stock of the same, and cause the same to be paid, on demand, to the several stockholders thereof.

Sec. 7. The directors shall, once, at least, in every year, make a full report on the state of the affairs of the company to a general meeting of the stockholders; and shall have power to call a general meeting of the stockholders when they may deem it expedient.

Sec. 8. The said company shall have power, and they may proceed to construct, as speedily as their means will permit, a rail-road with one or more tracks, from the Ohio river, at the foot of Western Row, along said Western Row, to a point contiguous to a proposed basin, nearly opposite Eighth street, as recorded in the plan of the city of Cincinnati, together with such side-rails as may be found convenient and necessary: *Provided,* That the consent thereto of the city council shall first be obtained.

Sec. 9. That it shall be lawful for the said company, with the approbation and under the direction of the canal commissioners, to take a side-cut from the canal to the basin before mentioned.

Sec. 10. The city council of Cincinnati shall have the power at any time after twenty years from the passage of this act, to purchase and hold the property of this corporation for the use of the city by paying therefor to the corporation the amount expended by them in purchasing, locating, and constructing the same, with fifteen per centum thereon, and also of purchasing all such machines, fixtures, and other property, as the said company may then have on hand at their fair value in cash, to be assessed in case of disagreement by three disinterested persons, to be appointed in the following manner: one by the city council, one by the court of common pleas of Hamilton county, and one by the president and directors of said corporation: *Provided,* That the sum to be paid by the city for the said road and appurtenances shall not be less in the aggregate than the amount expended in the construction thereof, and six per cent. per annum thereon, after deducting the dividends received by the stockholders.

Sec. 11. In any suit instituted against said corporation, service of process made upon any one of the directors five days before the return day thereof shall, in all courts and places, be deemed and held a sufficient and valid service on the corporation.

Sec. 12. When the said basin and rail road shall be completed, the president and directors of said company shall make out a minute, full and detailed statement in writing of the expenses incurred by the said corporation in purchasing, locating, and constructing said basin, feeder and rail road, which report shall be verified by the oaths or affirmations of said president and directors, and filed by them in the office of the city clerk of Cincinnati, and if after the completion of the same as aforesaid, any alteration or extension thereof shall be made, the president and directors shall in like manner, from time to time, make out and file statements of the expenses incurred by such alteration or extensions as aforesaid, and also of the amount of all tolls collected.

Sec. 13. If any person shall wilfully or by gross negligence, injure or destroy the said road, or any track or part thereof, or any cars or other carriages used thereon, every such person shall be deemed guilty of a misdemeanor, and on conviction thereof before the court of common pleas, by indictment, shall be fined any sum, not exceeding one hundred dollars, or be imprisoned for any term, not exceeding three months, at the discretion of the court, and shall moreover be answerable to the said company for double damages, to be recovered in a civil suit of debt or trespass.

Sec. 14. That said company shall have the exclusive right of transportation or conveyance of persons, goods, merchandize and produce, over the said rail road and its branches, by them to be constructed: *Provided,* That the charge for transportation or conveyance shall not exceed fifty cents per ton on heavy articles, and twelve and a half cents per passenger, between the proposed basin and the Ohio river: *Provided, also,* That no steam locomotives shall be used on said rail road without the consent of the city council.

Sec. 15. The said company is hereby expressly prohibited from carrying on any banking operations.

Sec. 16. This act shall be taken and received in all courts, and by all judges, magistrates, and other public officers, as a public act; and all printed copies of the same, which shall be printed by or under the authority of the General Assembly, shall be admitted as good evidence thereof, without any other proof thereof whatever.

Sec. 17. Before any proceedings shall be had under this act, it shall receive the sanction of a majority of the legal voters of the citizens of Cincinnati, voting at an election to be held for that purpose on the first Monday in May next, of which election notice shall be given for thirty days in all the newspapers printed in said city.

WILLIAM MEDILL,
Speaker pro tem. of the House of Representatives.
ELIJAH VANCE,
Speaker of the Senate.

March 14, 1836.

To incorporate the Wardens and Vestrymen of St. Paul's Church, Norwalk, in the county of Huron.

Sec. 1. *Be it enacted by the General Assembly of the State of Ohio,* That Luke Keeler, Platt Benedict, Ebenezer Lane, Charles S. Bell, J. V. Vredenburgh, Eben Boalt, Amos Woodward, Eri Keeler, Daniel Mallon, and their associates, together with such other persons as may hereafter become associated with them, members of St. Paul's Church in Norwalk, be, and they are hereby created a body politic and corporate, with perpetual succession, by the name and style of "St. Paul's Church, Norwalk;" and by that name shall be capable in law of contracting and being contracted with, of suing and being sued, of answering and being answered, of pleading and being impleaded, of defending and being defended, in all courts having competent jurisdiction; and may use a common seal, with power to alter the same at pleasure; they shall have power to acquire, hold and enjoy, to sell, rent, convey and dispose of property, real, personal, and mixed: *Provided,* That the annual income of all such property shall not exceed the sum of two thousand dollars: *And provided, also,* That said property shall be applied to the building of a house of public worship, procuring a parsonage, and to other objects incident to the support of public worship in said church, and the ordinances of said church, together with such institutions of learning and charity as may be connected therewith, and to no other purpose.

Sec. 2. That there shall be a meeting of the male members of said church on Easter Monday of each and every year, at which time they shall elect two wardens, three or more vestrymen, a treasurer, and secretary, and such other officers as they may deem necessary; and may also transact any other business within the scope of the powers granted in this act: *Provided,* That if at any time an election of officers should not be held on the day above appointed, the corporation shall not thereby be dissolved; but the officers previously chosen shall serve until their successors are elected; and such election may be held at any meeting duly notified and assembled for that purpose.

Sec. 3. That said corporation shall have power to adopt, establish and enforce such by-laws, ordinances, rules and regulations, not inconsistent with the laws and constitution of this State, or of the United States, as may be deemed necessary and proper for its government, and the efficient management of its concerns; and shall have all other powers usually incident to such a corporation, and necessary to its existence.

Sec. 4. That any future Legislature may alter or repeal this act.

WILLIAM MEDILL,
Speaker pro tem. of the House of Representatives.
ELIJAH VANCE,
Speaker of the Senate.

March 14, 1836.
65—L

AN ACT

To incorporate the Sharon Academy, in the county of Medina.

Sec. 1. *Be it enacted by the General Assembly of the State of Ohio,* That Thomas Briggs, Edward Chandler, John Bridge, Jehial Squire, Cicero Phelps, and Norman Curtis, together with such other persons as may hereafter be associated with them, for the purpose of establishing an academy in the town of Sharon, in the county of Medina, be, and they are hereby created a body politic and corporate, with perpetual succession, by the name of the Sharon Academy; and by that name shall be competent to contract and be contracted with, to sue and be sued, to answer and be answered unto, in all courts of law and equity; and to acquire, posses, and enjoy, and to sell, convey, and dispose of property, both real and personal, and shall possess all the powers usually incident to such corporations: *Provided,* That the value of such property shall not exceed five thousand dollars; the proceeds of which shall be applied to the support of a school, and to no other purpose whatever.

Sec. 2. That any three of the above named persons shall have power to call a meeting, by giving ten days previous notice thereof, by advertisements set up at three of the most public places in the township of Sharon.

Sec. 3. That said corporation shall have power to form a constitution and adopt by-laws for its government, to prescribe the number and title of its officers, and define their powers and duties, to prescribe the manner in which members may be admitted and dismissed, and other powers necessary for the efficient mangement of its corporate concerns: *Provided,* That the constitution, by-laws and regulations of the corporation be consistent with the constitution and laws of the United States, and of this State.

Sec. 4. That any future Legislature may modify or repeal this act: *Provided,* That the title of any property, real or personal, acquired or conveyed under its provisions, shall not be thereby affected.

WILLIAM MEDILL,
Speaker pro tem. of the House of Representatives.
ELIJAH VANCE,
Speaker of the Senate.

March 14, 1836.

AN ACT

To secure to the poor children of the town of Zanesville, the benefits of the devise and donation of John M'Intire, deceased, and to incorporate "The McIntire Poor School."

WHEREAS, John McIntire, late of Zanesville, in the county of Muskingum, deceased, by his last will and testament, duly proved, and admitted to record in the court of common pleas of that county, on the fourth day of August, in the year of our Lord, eighteen hundred and fifteen, devised a large and valuable estate, and property, for the use and support of a poor school, to be established in the said town of Zanesville, for the use and benefit of the poor children therein; and appointed the president and directors of the Zanesville Canal and Manufacturing Company as trustees thereof: *And whereas*, It has been represented to this General Assembly that the said Canal and Manufacturing Company have ceased to exist, by that or any other corporate name, by means whereof no person or persons, or body corporate, are now competent in law, to perform and execute the duty, and exercise the authority required of said company, as trustees, aforesaid, and to carry into effect the said devise, according to the true intent and meaning of the testator: Therefore,

Sec. 1. *Be it enacted by the General Assembly of the State of Ohio*, That, for the purpose of securing to the poor children, and people of said town of Zanesville, the benefits and advantages of the aforesaid devise of the said John McIntire, deceased, according to the true intent and meaning thereof; and to carry into effect the same, for the uses and purposes in his last will and testament designated, there is hereby created and constituted, in the manner hereinafter provided, a board of five trustees, who shall reside in the town of Zanesville, and shall be a body politic and corporate, with perpetual succession, by the name and style of "The Trustees of the McIntire Poor School;" and by that name is hereby invested with full power and lawful authority by purchase, devise, or donation, to acquire, hold, possess, use, occupy and enjoy, and the same to sell, and convey, all such real and personal estate as may be necessary for the usefulness of said school, and for the proper management and good government of the same; and for such purposes, and all others, necessarily connected with the objects herein intended to be obtained and secured, shall be competent to contract and be contracted with, to sue and be sued, plead and be impleaded, answer and be answered unto, defend and be defended, in all courts and places, and in all lawful matters whatsoever; to have and use a common seal, and the same to alter, break and renew, at pleasure; with power to make, ordain, establish, and put in execution, and the same to alter, amend, and repeal, such by-laws, rules and regulations, not contrary to the constitution and laws of the United States, and of this State, as shall be necessary and proper for the good government of said corporation, and that of its officers, agents and servants, so as most effectually and beneficially to execute the charitable devise of the said John McIntire, deceased, hereinbefore mentioned.

Sec. 2. That the trustees of the McIntire Poor School, herein incorporated, shall be, and hereby is invested with all the property, estate, rights, credits, claims, demands, interest, power and authority, which by the last will and testament of the said John McIntire, deceased, was conferred on and vested in the President and Directors of the Zanesville Canal and Manufacturing Company; with all the privileges and appurtenances to the same belonging, and which have been vested in any other corporation or corporations, person or persons, so far as shall be necessary to all the objects, and secure to the poor children and people of said town of Zanesville, all the benefits intended by the devise of the said John McIntire, deceased: *Provided*, That nothing contained in this act shall be so construed as to affect the private or corporate rights of any person or persons, or to change the will of the said John McIntire, deceased; but on the contrary, to carry into effect the true intent and meaning thereof.

Sec. 3. That the estate, property, both real and personal, rights, credits, demands, and interests of the corporation hereby created, with the whole administration of its concerns, shall be under the control, direction, and management of said board of trustees, hereby incorporated, and their successors in trust, for the benefit and support of a poor school, in the town of Zanesville; which trustees shall hold their offices, respectively, for two years, and elected as hereinafter provided: they shall appoint a clerk, treasurer, and all such officers, teachers, agents, and servants, as they may deem necessary and convenient to the successful prosecution of the business, and the due and proper exercise of the corporate powers herein granted, who shall respectively give bond, with one or more sureties, and in such sum or sums, as a majority of the associate judges of Muskingum county may from time to time order, approve and direct: *Provided*, That the said board of trustees shall receive no compensation for the time employed by them, or either of them, in the discharge of their official duties, and shall not apply the funds of said corporation, in banking, nor for any other purpose, inconsistent with the provisions of this act; they shall report on or before the first day of January, annually, to the General Assembly of this State, a true and just account and statement of all the financial and prudential concerns of the McIntire Poor School, and a brief and general view of the administration of its affairs with the benefits resulting from this act; and any future General Assembly, on the consideration of such report, or on the neglect of making such report, may alter or amend this act, so as to secure all the benefits thereof.

Sec. 4. That all funds now in the State Treasury, with such as may hereafter be deposited therein, which of right and law may belong to the McIntire Poor School, shall be, and hereby is created an inconvertible fund, for the use and benefit of said school; the interest or income thereof, only, at the rate of six per centum per annum, shall be paid to the board of trustees aforesaid, so long as it shall be the pleasure of the General Assembly to retain the principal thereof; and it is hereby required of the said board of trustees to appropriate all the funds, interest, estate, and property, which they may from time to time receive from the estate of said John McIntire, deceased, under, or by virtue of his said last will and testament, or upon any body corporate, or person, or persons, to the same inconvertible fund, the income thereof only shall be expended for the support of said school.

Sec. 5. That for the purpose of carrying into immediate effect the provisions of this act, Samuel Sullivant, Peter Mills, Benard Van Horn, John A. Turner, and James Taylor, jr. are hereby appointed trustees of said McIntire School, to continue in office until the second Tuesday of May next, and until their successors shall have been elected and qualified; and that on the second Tuesday of May, biennially, commencing on the second Tuesday of May, in the year one thousand eight hundred and thirty-six, the qualified voters of the said town of Zanesville, shall, under the same regulations, in all respects, as are or may be prescribed by law for the election of township trustees, elect five trustees of said school, to serve

for the term of two years, and until their successors shall have been elected and qualified, three weeks notice of said election having been given in
the newspapers printed in the town and Zanesville, of the time and place
of holding it; and the said trustees shall fill all vacancies which may occur
in their own board, whether by death, resignation or otherwise, until the
next biennial election.

Sec. 6. That this act shall be taken and received in all courts and places, and by all judges, magistrates, and other public officers, as a public
act; and all printed copies of the same, which shall be printed by and under the authority of the General Assembly, shall be admitted as good evidence thereof, without any other proof whatever.

WILLIAM MEDILL,
Speaker pro tem. of the House of Representatives.
ELIJAH VANCE,
Speaker of the Senate.

March 14, 1836.

AN ACT

To incorporate the First Congregational Society of Morensi, in the county of Cuyahoga.

Sec. 1. *Be it enacted by the General Assembly of the State of Ohio,*
That Aaron Bliss, Thos. N. West, and Noah Graves, and their associates, be, and they are created a body politic and corporate, by the
name of "The First Congregational Society of Morensi, in the county
of Cuyahoga," with perpetual succession; and they shall be capable in
their corporate capacity, to contract, and sue, and defend; and shall have
power to pass and enforce such by-laws for the government of its members, as they may deem necessary.

Sec. 2. That said corporation may acquire, enjoy, and transfer real
or personal property, not exceeding the annual value of one thousand dollars, to be exclusively used for the support of religious worship and instruction; and the members may elect such officers, and under such rules
as they may think expedient; and all male members of the age of twenty-
one years, shall have the right to vote at all elections.

Sec. 3. Any future Legislature may repeal this act.

WILLIAM MEDILL,
Speaker pro tem. of the House of Representatives.
ELIJAH VANCE,
Speaker of the Senate.

March 14, 1836.

AN ACT

To lay out and establish a State road in the counties of Licking and Delaware.

Sec. 1. *Be it enacted by the General Assembly of the State of Ohio,*
That Jacob Baker, of the county of Licking, and Charles Day and Thomas

Perfect, of the county of Delaware, be, and they are hereby appointed commissioners, and Abram Boring, senr. of the county of Licking, surveyor, to lay out and establish a state road, to commence on the state road leading from Columbus to Johnstown, on the east line of Delaware county; from thence running north, on the county line, being the east line of said county, to the north-west corner of the county of Licking; thence north-east to intersect at a convenient point, the state road leading from Mt. Vernon to Sunbury, near Jacob Houk's.

Sec. 2. That the commissioners aforesaid, shall be governed, in all respects, by the law now in force, defining the mode of laying out and establishing state roads, passed March 14, 1831.

Sec. 3. That should a vacancy happen in any of the foregoing appointments by death, resignation, removal, or otherwise, the county commissioners of the county in which it shall happen, shall fill such vacancy as often as it may occur.

WILLIAM MEDILL,
Speaker pro tem. of the House of Representatives.

ELIJAH VANCE,
Speaker of the Senate.

March 14, 1836.

AN ACT

To lay out and establish a State road from Hanover, in Harrison county, to Harrisburgh in Carroll county.

Sec. 1. *Be it enacted by the General Assembly of the State of Ohio,* That John M'Donough, of Harrison county, and James Hooke, of Carroll county, be, and they are hereby appointed commissioners, and Van Brown, surveyor, to lay out and establish a graded state road, from the town of Hanover, in Harrison county, through Perrysville, and by Knapper's mill to Harrisburgh, in Carroll county.

Sec. 2. That the said road shall in no case exceed an angle of five degrees with the horizon; and the commissioners aforesaid, shall in all respects be governed by the act defining the mode of laying out and establishing state roads, passed March 14th, 1831, except in the appointment of surveyor, which is provided for in the first section of this act.

Sec. 3. That should either of the commissioners or surveyor die, remove out of the county, or refuse to serve, the commissioners of the county in which such vacancy shall happen, shall forthwith, on being notified thereof, appoint some suitable person to fill the same, as often as it may occur.

WILLIAM MEDILL,
Speaker pro tem. of the House of Representatives.

ELIJAH VANCE,
Speaker of the Senate.

March 14, 1836.

AN ACT

To lay out and establish a State road from Dublin, in Franklin county, to Pleasant Valley, in Madison county.

Sec. 1. *Be it enacted by the General Assembly of the State of Ohio,* That John Sells, of Franklin county; Thomas Parr, of Union county; and Isaac Bigalow, of Madison county, be, and they are hereby appointed, commissioners to lay out and establish a state road, commencing at the town of Dublin, in Franklin county; thence, the nearest and best route to Pleasant Valley, in Madison county.

Sec. 2. That the commissioners aforesaid, shall be governed, in all respects, by the law now in force, defining the mode of laying out and establishing state roads, passed March the fourteenth, eighteen hundred and thirty-one.

Sec. 3. That should a vacancy happen in any of the foregoing appointments, by death, removal, or otherwise, the commissioners of the county in which the vacancy occurs, shall forthwith fill such vacancies, on being notified of the same.

WILLIAM MEDILL,
Speaker pro tem. of the House of Representatives.

ELIJAH VANCE,
Speaker of the Senate.

March 14, 1836.

AN ACT

To lay out and establish a State road from Hillsborough, in Highland county, to Springfield, in Clark county.

Sec. 1. *Be it enacted by the General Assembly of the State of Ohio,* That David Carter, of Clinton county, and John T. Stewart, of Clark county, and Mathias Wynans, of Green county, are hereby appointed commissioners, and Jesse Barret, of Highland county, surveyor, to lay out and establish a state road, commencing at Hillsborough, in Highland county; thence to Daniel Hixon's, on the Urbana road; thence to New Lexington; thence the nearest and best way to David Carter's; thence to Daniel Parris', in Clinton county; thence to Jamestown, in Green county; thence to Springfield, in Clark county.

Sec. 2. That the commissioners aforesaid, shall be governed, in all respects, by the law now in force defining the mode of laying out and establishing state roads, passed March 14th, 1831, except in the appointment of surveyor, which is provided for in the first section of this act.

Sec. 3. That should a vacancy occur, in any of the foregoing appointments, by death, removal, or otherwise, the commissioners of the county in which such vacancy occurs, shall forthwith fill such vacancies, on being notified of the same, as often as such vacancy may occur.

WILLIAM MEDILL,
Speaker pro tem. of the House of Representatives.
ELIJAH VANCE,
Speaker of the Senate.

March 14, 1836.

AN ACT

To encourage the growth of Wool by taxing Dogs in the counties of Trumbull, Clark and Union.

Sec. 1. *Be it enacted by the General Assembly of the State of Ohio,* That the county commissioners within and for the counties of Trumbull, Clark and Union, are hereby authorized, if they deem it expedient, to levy a tax on all dogs owned by any person or persons within said counties, yearly, and every year, in manner following; which tax shall not be less than fifty cents, nor more than one dollar for the first dog, owned by any one person, nor less than seventy-five cents, nor more than one dollar and fifty cents for any dog in addition thereto, owned by any such persons.

Sec. 2. The county commissioners, if they should deem it necessary to levy such tax the present year, and may so determine at their June session, shall, within ten days thereafter, notify the clerk of each township within the county, whose duty it shall be to take a list of all the dogs owned in their respective townships, with the names of the owners, and the number owned by such persons, and may return the same to the county auditor of such county, before the first day of July following; for which service the township clerks shall each receive such compensation as the said commissioners may deem just and reasonable, and as shall have been fixed upon at said June session, to be paid out of the county treasury on the order of the county auditor.

Sec. 3. That whenever the county commissioners shall deem it necessary and expedient to assess any tax after the present year, they shall so determine at their December session previously thereto; and if they should so determine, they shall notify the county assessor of the county, previously to his taking a list of the taxable property; and it shall be his duty to take a list of such dogs so owned in said county, as is provided in the second section of this act, and return the same when he shall return the list of other taxable property.

Sec. 4. That the county auditor shall make out a separate duplicate of such tax, and deliver the same to the county treasurer when by law he is required to deliver the tax duplicate of chattel property for collection to said treasurer; and said treasurer shall collect the same in such manner as he is required to collect the tax on other chattel property, and shall be allowed the same per centage on collection and disbursement of said tax, as he is allowed on other taxes.

Sec. 5. That the tax so assessed and collected, after deducting the treasurer's per centage, shall be by the county auditor placed to the credit of the common school fund of the respective townships in said counties; and the same shall be applied to the support of common schools in the several school districts in such townships, in the same manner as other funds are applied.

WILLIAM MEDILL,
Speaker pro tem. of the House of Representatives.
ELIJAH VANCE,
Speaker of the Senate.

March 14, 1836.

AN ACT

To authorise the County Auditor of Perry county to make deeds to certain purchasers of lands and town lots heretofore sold for taxes.

Sec. 1. *Be it enacted by the General Assembly of the State of Ohio,* That the Auditor of Perry county be and is hereby authorized to make a deed to any purchaser or purchasers of lands or town lots heretofore sold for taxes by the treasurer, collector, or auditor, in said county, in all cases where the said officer or officers have neglected to give certificates to the purchaser or purchasers, if the whole tract or lot was sold, whenever demanded, or as soon as expedient: *Provided,* That the sale of such lands or lots shall have been entered on record in the books as required by law, and the auditor being satisfied that *bona fide* sales were actually made.

Sec. 2. That the Auditor shall, and is hereby empowered to make out and deliver to any purchaser or purchasers of any lands or lots, a certificate of purchase, either for the whole or a part of a tract of land or town lot heretofore sold for taxes, whenever thereto requested; and such certificate shall have the same force in law as is provided for in "An act prescribing the duties of county Auditors," passed March 14th, 1831.

WILLIAM MEDILL,
Speaker pro tem. of the House of Representatives.
ELIJAH VANCE,
Speaker of the Senate.

March 14, 1836.

AN ACT

To amend an act, entitled "An act authorising the sale of lands granted by Congress for the support of Religion within the Ohio Company's Purchase," passed March 3, 1834.

Sec. 1. *Be it enacted by the General Assembly of the State of Ohio,* That the several officers required to perform duties under the provisions of the act to which this is an amendment, shall be entitled to the following compensations: the county assessors shall be paid for all services rendered under the act which this act proposes to amend, out of their respective county treasuries, to be included in and paid, with his general account

66—L

of services rendered; and such county shall be refunded the sums so advanced, in manner following, viz: for taking the votes of the free white male inhabitants, two dollars for every hundred names found upon the book of votes; for appraising any lands which may be ordered by the Auditor of State, twenty-five cents for each half quarter section or smaller subdivisions thereof; and for all suitable and necessary books, furnished for the several officers, the price paid therefor; the account of which said advances shall be made out and certified by the proper county auditor, and paid out of the first rent or interest which shall be received into such treasury, and to be deducted from the dividend due the several townships in due proportion; the county audtor shall be paid by the purchaser for a certificate of sale and final certificate, each fifty cents; for a certificate to pay money to the county treasury, or for a receipt, six and one-fourth cents; for every sale of delinquent land, to be included in the amount to be paid by the bidder, two dollars, besides the printer's bills for advertising; and for transcribing the assessor's return of appraisement, and counting and certifying the votes, the said county auditor shall be allowed the same fees as for like services performed for such county, and to be paid out of such county treasury: the county treasurer shall be allowed one per cent. on the amount of money by him paid over to the state treasury, to be by him retained out of the money in his hands.

WILLIAM MEDILL,
Speaker pro tem. of the House of Representatives.
ELIJAH VANCE,
Speaker of the Senate.

March 14, 1836.

AN ACT

Authorizing the Commissioners of Fairfield and Scioto counties to comply with certain contracts for the purposes therein named.

WHEREAS, It was represented to the commissioners of Fairfield county, that the late return made by the assessor of said county, of the number of white male inhabitants residing therein, over the age of twenty-one years, was erroneous and deficient; *And whereas,* With a view of ascertaining that fact, and of correcting the same, the said commissioners caused a re-enumeration to be taken: Therefore,

Sec. 1. *Be it enacted by the General Assembly of the State of Ohio,* That the said commissioners be, and they are hereby authorized to pay the necessary expenses of taking or causing to be taken the said re-enumeration, out of the treasury of said county, in like manner as if the same had been previously authorized and imposed upon them by law.

Sec. 2. That the commissioners of Scioto county, in which the same deficiency and disability exists, be also authorized to pay the expenses of re-enumerating said county in the same manner as is provided in the preceding section of this act.

WILLIAM MEDILL,
Speaker pro tem. of the House of Representatives.
ELIJAH VANCE,
Speaker of the Senate.

March 14, 1836.

AN ACT

To authorize the appointment of a Special Assessor for Champaign county.

Sec. 1. *Be it enacted by the General Assembly of the State of Ohio,* That the county commissioners and the county auditor of Champaign county, are hereby authorized, if they consider it conducive to the public interest, and that the inequalities in the valuation of property in said county requires it, to appoint a special assessor, whose duty it shall be to list and restore to the duplicate all such lands liable to taxation that are now omitted, and affix to the same the proper values; and also to correct inequalities in the existing valuations of the property already listed and valued; and for this purpose, the said commissioners may at any time hold a meeting prior to the first Monday of May next: the assessor so appointed shall make return of his proceedings to the county board of equalization, at their annual session on the first Monday of June, or at such other day prior to the first Monday of July, that such board may appoint; and for the services of such assessor, the commissioners shall allow a proper compensation.

Sec. 2. When the assessor so appointed, shall have made return of his corrected valuation, the county board of equalization shall examine and equalize the same, together with all inequalites of valuation, on complaint of the owners or other persons, in the manner pointed out in the seventeenth section of the act to provide for the ro-valuation of real property in this State: *Provided,* That the aggregate amount of such valuation of property already assessed shall not be below what it now stands at.

WILLIAM MEDILL,
Speaker pro tem. of the House of Representatives.

ELIJAH VANCE,
Speaker of the Senate.

March 14, 1836.

AN ACT

Authorizing permanent leases to be given for section 26, in township 13, range 15, of the Ohio Company's Purchase.

Sec. 1. *Be it enacted by the General Assembly of the State of Ohio,* That the trustees of the original surveyed township number thirteen, in the sixteenth range, of the Ohio Company's Purchase, be, and they are hereby authorized and empowered to lease, by permanent leases, for ninety-nine years, renewable forever, subject to a re-valution every fifteen years, to the respective lessees, and their heirs and assigns, all or any part of the school section number twenty-six, lying in township thirteen, and range number fifteen, granted to said original surveyed township number thirteen, for the use of schools.

Sec. 2. That the trustees aforesaid are hereby authorized to cause such surveys to be made as they shall deem necessary and proper for the purpose of dividing and subdividing said school section into suitable sized lots; and may, if they think proper, cause the said section, or any part thereof, to be re-appraised: *Provided*, The same is not already leased.

Sec. 3. That the trustees aforesaid shall, in the management of said school section, be governed in all respects, by so much of the act, entitled "An act to incorporate the original surveyed townships," passed March 14, 1831, as is not inconsistent with this act.

WILLIAM MEDILL,
Speaker pro tem. of the House of Representatives.
ELIJAH VANCE,
Speaker of the Senate.

March 14, 1836.

AN ACT

To incorporate the Second Baptist Church and Society in Perry, in the county of Geauga.

Sec. 1. *Be it enacted by the General Assembly of the State of Ohio,* That Jocob Bailey, Jesse Hartwell, John Young, Ferdinand Haskell, Lovell D. Hartwell, Eli B. Haskell, Alpha Thorp, Benjamin Norris, and associates, together with such persons as may be hereafter associated with them, be, and they are hereby created a body corporate and politic, by the name of "The Second Baptist Church and Society in Perry;" and as such shall remain and have perpetual succession, and by their corporate name may contract and be contracted with, may sue and be sued, answer and be answered, plead and be impleaded, defend and be defended, in any court of competent jurisdiction, in all manner of actions, causes and complaints, whatsoever; and may have a common seal, which they may alter or change at pleasure.

Sec. 2. That said corporation shall be capable in law or equity, in their corporate name aforesaid, of having, receiving, acquiring and holding, by purchase, gift, grant devise or legacy, any estate, real, personal, or mixed, for the use of said corporation: *Provided*, That the annual income of such property shall not exceed the sum of one thousand dollars, and that all the property, of whatever kind, shall be considered as held in trust, under the management, and at the disposal of said corporation, for the purpose of promoting the interests of said society, defraying the expenses incident to their mode of worship, and maintaining any institution of charity or education, that may be therewith connected: *And provided, also,* That when money, or other property shall be given, granted, devised or bequeathed, for any particular use or purpose, it shall be faithfully applied to such use or purpose.

Sec. 3. That for the better managing of the affairs of said society, and promoting the interests thereof, there shall be elected, on the second Monday in March, one thousand eight hundred and thirty seven, and on the second Monday in March, in each succeeding year thereafter, three trustees, and such other officers as the corporation may deem necessary, who shall hold their offices for one year, and until their successors shall be elected: *Provided*, That if, from any cause, an election of officers should not be made on the day appointed for the annual election, the society may elect their officers at any meeting of the corporation duty assembled.

Sec. 4. That Jacob Baily, Jesse Hartwell and John Young, named in the first section of this act, be, and they are hereby appointed trustees, until the first annual election, and until others are elected in their places.

Sec. 5. That all elections of the corporation shall be by ballot, and the person or persons having a majority of the votes given, for any office, shall be considered duly elected; each member shall have one vote, and all matters of the corporation shall be determined by a majority of the members present, at any meeting of the corporation duly assembled.

Sec. 6. That the trustees, a majority of whom shall be a quorum for the transaction of business, shall, under the direction of the society, have the management and control of the property and other concerns of the corporation; and they, or a majority of them, shall have power to call a meeting of the society, either for the election of officers, or for the transaction of any other business of the society, by giving to said society, immediately after public worship, at least ten days previous notice of said meeting, or causing notifications thereof to be put up in three or more public places within the limits of said society, one of which shall be at the usual place of holding public worship, at least fifteen days previous to such meeting.

Sec. 7. That any meeting of the society, duly assembled, may adopt and establish such by-laws and ordinances may be deemed proper and necessary for the government of said corporation: *Provided*, That such by-laws and ordinances shall be compatible with the constitution and laws of the United States, and of this State.

Sec. 8. That original process against the corporation shall be served by leaving an attested copy with one or more of the trustees, at least ten days before the return day thereof, and such service shall be deemed sufficient to bind the corporation.

Sec. 9. That any future Legislature shall have power to modify or repeal this act: *Provided*, That such modification or repeal shall not affect the title to any estate, real or personal, acquired or conveyed under its provisions.

WILLIAM MEDILL,
Speaker pro tem. of the House of Representatives.

ELIJAH VANCE,
Speaker of the Senate.

March 14, 1836.

AN ACT

For the relief of certain contractors on the Miami Canal, north of Dayton.

Sec. 1. *Be it enacted by the General Assembly of the State of Ohio,* That the Canal Commissioners or board of Public Works be, and they are hereby authorized and required, under the restrictions and provisions hereinafter contained, to pay out of the fund appropriated for the extension of the Miami Canal, to each of the contractors on said canal, north of Dayton, a sum of money not exceeding twenty-five per centum, on the price of all the work done by him, subsequently to the twentieth day of May, in the year eighteen hundred and thirty-five, over and above the contract price: *Provided*, That in those cases where the work should, according to the terms of the contract, have been completed prior to the said twentieth day of May, in the year eighteen hundred and thirty-five, or where the contract has been abandoned, or abandoned and re-let, the said commissioners or board of public works shall examine into the circumstances of each case, and allow to either the original contractor or to the contractor to whom the work may have been re-let, so much as to the said commissioners, or board of public works, may seem just and reasonable: *Provided*, That the allowances so made as last aforesaid shall in no case exceed the amount of twenty-five per centum, as aforesaid.

Sec. 2. That said commissioners, or board of public works, be, and they are hereby further authorized and required to cause to be examined and ascertained all those contracts on said canal, in which losses have been sustained by the contractors, by reason of the expense or cost of excavation, or of procuring materials, proving greater than had been anticipated, both by the agent of the State, and the contractors; and to pay out of the said fund appropriated for the extension of the Miami Canal, to the contractors in such cases, such further sum, as to them may seem just and reasonable: *Provided*, That such future sum shall in no case exceed fifteen per centum on the contract price of the whole job.

Sec. 3. That the said commissioners, or board of public works, shall make all payments authorized by this act at such times and in such proportions as will best secure the completion of any unfinished jobs and shall withhold payment altogether in cases where the contractors refuse to finish any work he may have contracted to perform.

Sec. 4. That the said commissioners, or board of public works, shall cause notice to be given by advertisement, to be continued at least two weeks, in some newspapers in each of the counties of Montgomery, and Miami, notifying those persons to whom the contractors aforesaid are indebted for work or materials, done or furnished on said canal, to present their accounts to the acting canal commissioners, or board of public works, having charge of said work, at some suitable places on the line of said canal, and on some day or days within two months after the passage of this act; also notifying the said contractors to appear at the same time and place: and if the contractors against whom any such accounts may be presented shall admit the validity and correctness of said account, the said commissioners or board of public works is hereby authorized to discharge the same; and the amount so paid shall be deducted from any sum which may have been found due to said contractor, according to the provisions of this act: *Provided*, That if the amount of all such accounts against any contractor shall be found greater than the sum due said contractor, according to the provisions of this act, then the said commissioners or board of public works shall make a dividend thereof, and pay on each account in proportion to the amount thereof: *And provided, also*, That if any contractor shall dispute the correctness of any such account so presented against him, the said commissioners, or board of public works, believing the same to be correct, may retain so much of the money required by the provisions of this act, to be paid to any contractor, as will be equal to the amount of such disputed accounts, until the sums justly due thereon can be legally ascertained, or agreed upon between the parties.

Sec. 5. That nothing in this act shall be so construed as to allow any additional compensation to be made for work in cases when no price has been fixed by the contract and when the full value of the work has been allowed.

WILLIAM MEDILL,
Speaker pro tem. of the House of Representatives.
ELIJAH VANCE,
Speaker of the Senate.

March 14, 1836.

AN ACT

To authorize the County Commissioners of Hamilton county, to fund the debt due by said county.

Sec. 1. *Be it enacted by the General Assembly of the State of Ohio,* That the Commissioners of Hamilton county be, and are hereby authorized and empowered to fund the debt due by said county, at a rate of interest, not exceeding six per cent. per annum, and on such conditions that the whole debt, hereby authorized to be funded, shall be made redeemable, either in whole or by instalments, within five years, from and after the first day of January, eighteen hundred and thirty-seven: *Provided,* That the amount of debt hereby authorized to be funded, as aforesaid, shall not exceed the sum of fifteen thousand dollars.

WILLIAM MEDILL,
Speaker pro tem. of the House of Representatives.
ELIJAH VANCE,
Speaker of the Senate.

March 14, 1836.

AN ACT

To reduce the width of a part of a street, in the town of Dresden, in the county of Muskingum.

Sec. 1. *Be it enacted by the General Assembly of the State of Ohio,* That so much of North street, as is west of Main street, in the said town of Dresden, be, and the same is hereby reduced in width, six feet, to be stricken from the north side thereof, and extending from Main street to the west end of said North street; and that the same, (except so much as is included in a street and alley crossing the same,) be attached to the lots on the north side of, and adjoining said street.

WILLIAM MEDILL,
Speaker pro tem. of the House of Representatives.
ELIJAH VANCE,
Speaker of the Senate.

March 14, 1836.

AN ACT

For the appointment of six trustees of the Miami University.

Sec. 1. *Be it enacted by the General Assembly of the State of Ohio,* That James Galloway, jun., of the county of Green; John S. Galloway, of the county of Clark; Thomas J. S. Smith, of the county of Miami; William Mount, of the county of Hamilton; Jeremiah Morrow, of the county [of] Warren; and John B. Weller, of the county of Butler, be, and they are hereby appointed trustees of the Miami University, from and after the first day of March, one thousand eight hundred and thirty-six, for the term of three years.

WILLIAM MEDILL,
Speaker pro. tem. of the House of Representatives.

ELIJAH VANCE,
Speaker of the Senate.

March 14, 1836.

AN ACT

To lay out and establish a graded State road from Wooster, in Wayne county, to New Lisbon, in Columbiana county.

Sec. 1. *Be it enacted by the General Assembly of the State of Ohio,* That James Boyles, of Stark county, Samuel B. Miller, of Tuscarawas county, and Robert Filson, of the county of Columbiana, be, and they are hereby appointed commissioners, and John Lorance, of Wayne county, surveyor, to lay out and establish a graded state road, commencing at the town of Wooster, in Wayne county; thence the nearest and best way to Mount Eaton, in said county; thence to the town of Bolivar, in Tuscarawas county; thence to Sandyville, in said county; thence to Waynesburgh, in Stark county; thence to Minerva; thence to Hanover, in Columbiana county; thence to New-Lisbon, in said county.

Sec. 2. That said road shall in no case exceed an angle of three degrees with the horizon, when completed.

Sec. 3. That the commissioners aforesaid, shall in all respects be governed by the laws in force, defining the mode of laying out and establishing state roads; and should either of said commissioners or surveyor die, refuse to serve or remove out of the county, the commissioners of the county in which such vacancy may happen, are hereby authorized to fill the same as often as they may occur.

WILLIAM MEDILL,
Speaker pro. tem. of the House of Representatives.

ELIJAH VANCE,
Speaker of the Senate.

March 14, 1836.

To incorporate the Muskingum and Columbus Rail-road Company.

Sec. 1. *Be it enacted by the General Assembly of the State of Ohio*, That Elomas Wheaton, Solomon Wood, and Daniel Convers, of Muskingum county; William Spencer, J. Mathiot, and D. Marble, of Licking county; Joseph Ridgeway, jun. Alfred Kelly, and P. B. Wilcox, of Franklin county, together with such other persons as may hereafter become associated with them, in the manner hereinafter prescribed, their successors and assigns, be, and are hereby created a body corporate and politic, by the name of "The Muskingum and Columbus Rail-road Company;" and by that name shall be, and are hereby made capable in law to contract and be contracted with; and if either of the persons named in this section shall die, refuse or neglect to exercise the powers and discharge the duties hereby created, it shall be the duty of the remaining persons hereinbefore named, or a majority of them, to appoint some suitable person or persons to fill such vacancy or vacancies so often as the same shall occur.

Sec. 2. That said corporation are hereby empowered to cause such examinations and surveys to be made between the Muskingum river and the city of Columbus, by the route through the Licking valley, as shall be necessary to ascertain the most advantageous route whereon to construct a rail-road, and shall cause an estimate to be made of the probable cost thereof, for each mile separately; and the said corporation shall be, and they are hereby invested with the right to construct a rail-road, with one or more rail-ways or tracks, from the west bank of the Muskingum river, near the town of Zanesville, through said Licking valley, to the city of Columbus.

Sec. 3. That the capital stock of said corporation shall be four hundred thousand dollars, and shall be divided into shares of fifty dollars each; and five dollars on each share shall be paid at the time of subscribing.

Sec. 4. That the above named persons, or a majority of them, or the survivors of them, are authorized to open books for receiving subscriptions to the capital stock of said company, and shall prescribe the form of such subscription; which books shall be opened within two years from the passage of this act, at such place or places as they may deem expedient, giving twenty days notice in such newspapers printed in the counties of Muskingum, Licking, and Franklin, and in such other place or places, as may be thought advisable, of the time and place, or times and places of opening said books: and they shall be kept open at least ten days.

Sec. 5. That so soon as seventy-five thousand dollars of said stock shall have been subscribed, the above named persons, or the same number thereof as shall have given the notice above required, shall give like notice for a meeting of the stockholders to choose directors, at some time, at least thirty days thereafter, and at some place within the said county of Licking; and if at such time and place, the holders of one half or more of said stock subscribed shall attend, either in person or by lawful proxy, shall proceed to choose from the stockholders, by ballot, nine directors, each share of capital stock entitling the owner to one vote; and at

67—L

such election, the persons named in the first section of this act, or those appointed by its provisions to fill vacancies which may have occurred, or any three of them, if no more be present, shall be inspectors of such election, and shall certify in writing, signed by them, or a majority of them, what persons are elected directors; and if two or more have an equal number of votes, such inspectors shall determine by lot, which of them shall be director or directors, to complete the number required, and shall certify the same in like manner; and said inspectors shall appoint the time and place of holding the first meeting of directors, at which a majority shall form a board competent to transact all business of the company; and thereafter a new election of directors shall be made annually, at such time and place as the stockholders at their first meeting shall appoint; and if the stockholders shall, at their first meeting, fail to appoint the day of such election, then it shall be holden in the succeeding year, on the same day of the same month on which said first election was holden, unless the same should be the first day of the week, in which case it shall be holden on the day next succeeding: and if no election be made at any time appointed by the by-laws of said company, and directors chosen at any election shall remain directors until others are chosen; and directors chosen at any election shall, as soon thereafter as may be, choose of their own number one person to be president, and another to be treasurer of such company, and another to be secretary of said company; and from time to time may choose such other officers as by their by-laws they may designate as necessary: *Provided*, No person shall be a director of such company, who is not a citizen of the State of Ohio.

Sec. 6. That the president and directors of said company may require payment of the subscription to the capital stock, at such times and places, and in such proportions and on such conditions, as they may think expedient: *Provided*, That notice of such requisition shall be first given in some newspaper printed and in general circulation in the counties in which said road may be located; and if any stockholder shall fail or neglect to pay his subscription to the capital stock, or such part thereof as shall be thus required, for the space of sixty days after the time appointed by said notice for the payment thereof, the president and directors of said company may sell at public vendue so many shares of such delinquent stockholder, as may be necessary to pay such requisition, and all necessary expenses incurred in making said sale; and the share or shares so sold, shall be transferred to the purchaser; paying the overplus, if any, to said delinquent, on demand.

Sec. 7. That the directors of said company shall have power to make from time to time, all needful rules, regulations and by-laws, touching the business of said company, and to determine the number of tracks or rail-ways upon said road, and the width thereof, not exceeding one hundred feet, and the description of carriages which may be used thereon; to regulate the time and manner in which passengers or goods shall be transported thereon, and the manner of collecting tolls for such transportation; and to fix penalties for the breach of any such rule, regulation or by-law, and to direct the mode and condition of transferring the stock of said company; and penalties provided for by said by-laws, may be sued for by any person or persons authorized thereto, in the name of said company, and recovered in an action of debt, before any court having jurisdiction of the amount; and said com-- pany may erect and maintain toll houses, and such other buildings and fixtures, for the accommodation of those using said road, and of themselves, as they may deem in any way necessary for their interest or convenience.

Sec. 8. That said company shall have a right to enter upon any lands, to survey and lay down said road, not exceeding one hundred feet in width, and to take any materials necessary for the construction of said road; and whenever any lands or materials shall be taken for the construction of said road, and the same shall not be given or granted to said company, and the owners thereof do not agree with said company, as to the compensation to be paid therefor, the person or persons claiming compensation as aforesaid, or if the owner or owners thereof are not residents of said county, or minors, insane persons, or married women, then the agents of such non-residents, guardian or guardians of such minor or minors, and insane persons, and the husbands of such married women, may select for themselves an arbitrator, and the said company shall select one arbitrator, and the two thus selected shall take to themselves a third, who shall be sworn and paid, as arbitrators in other cases; and the three, or a majority of them, shall award as arbitrators between the parties, and render copies of their award to each of the parties, in writing, from which award either party may appeal to the court of common pleas for the county in which such lands or materials may have been situate; and in all cases where compensation shall in any manner be claimed for lands, it shall be the duty of the arbitrators and the court, to estimate any advantage which the location and construction of said road may be to the claimant for such compensation, and the value of such advantage, if any, shall be set off against the compensation so claimed of said company: and appeals in such cases shall, when taken, be in all respects proceeded in as appeals in other cases to said court, and be brought into said court, by filing the award with the clerk of said court, whose duty it shall be to enter the same on the docket of said court, setting down the claimant or claimants as plaintiff, and said company as defendant; and when the valuation, so ascertained, shall be paid or tendered by said company, said company shall have the same right to retain, own, hold and possess said materials, and to the use and occupation of said lands for the purposes of said road, as fully and absolutely, as if the same had been granted and conveyed to said company by deed.

Sec. 9. That said company may construct the said rail-road across or upon any lands, public road, highway, stream of water or water course, if the same shall be necessary; but the said company shall restore such lands, road, highway, stream of water or water course, to its former state, or in a sufficient manner as not to impair the usefulness of such road, highway, water or water course, to the owner or the public, without unnecessary delay; and whenever said road shall pass through the lands of any individual, it shall be the duty of said company to provide for said individual suitable wagon ways from one part of his land to the other, as soon as practicable.

Sec. 10. That any rail-way company, now, or yet to be chartered by law of this State, shall have power to join and unite with the road hereby incorporated, at any point which the directors of such company may think.

advisable, on such terms as the directors of such company may respectively agree; and in case of disagreement, then upon such terms as the Supreme Court may in chancery determine; and full right and privilege is hereby reserved to the State, or individuals, or any company incorporated by law of this State, to cross this road with any other road: *Provided,* That in so crossing, no injury shall be done to the works of the company hereby incorporated.

Sec. 11. That said company may demand and receive for tolls upon, and the transportation of persons, goods, produce, merchandize, or property of any kind whatever, transported by them along said rail-way, any sum not exceeding the following rates: on all goods, merchandize or property of any description whatever, transported by them, a sum not exceeding one and a half cents per mile, for toll; five cents on a ton per mile, for transportation, on all goods, produce, merchandize or property of any description whatever, transported by them or their agents; and for the transportation of passengers, not exceeding three cents per mile, for each passenger.

Sec. 12. That all persons paying the toll aforesaid, may, with suitable and proper carriages, use and travel upon said rail-road; always subject, however, to such rules and regulations, as said company are authorized to make, by the seventh section of this act.

Sec. 13. That if proceedings be not had, under this act, within three years from the taking effect thereof, and if said road be not completed within ten years thereafter, then the same to be void and of no effect.

Sec. 14. That if any person or persons shall wilfully obstruct, or in any way spoil, injure or destroy said road, or either of its branches, or any thing belonging or incident thereto, or any materials to be used in the construction thereof, or any buildings, fixtures or carriages, erected or constructed for the use or convenience thereof, such person or persons shall each be liable for every such offence, to treble the damages sustained thereby; to be recovered by an action of debt, in any court having jurisdiction of that amount.

Sec. 15. That the State shall have power at any time after thirty-five years from the passage of this act, to purchase and hold said road for the use of the State, at a price not exceeding the original cost for the construction of said road, and the necessary permanent fixtures at the time of purchase, and fifteen per cent. thereon; of which cost an accurate statement, in writing, shall be submitted to the General Assembly, attested by the oath of its officers of said company, if the General Assembly shall require it.

Sec. 16. Whenever the dividends of said company shall exceed the rate of six per cent. per annum, the Legislature of this State may impose such reasonable tax on the amount of such dividends, as may be received from other rail-road companies.

WILLIAM MEDILL,
Speaker pro tem. of the House of Representatives.
ELIJAH VANCE,
Speaker of the Senate.

March 14, 1836.

AN ACT

To incorporate the Cleveland, Columbus and Cincinnati Rail-road Company.

Sec. 1. *Be it enacted by the General Assembly of the State of Ohio,* That John H. Groesbeck, Oliver M. Spencer, John Kilgour, George Luckey, Griffin Taylor, Nicholas Longworth, and William Disney, of the county of Hamilton; Samuel Howell, of the county of Green; Charles Paist, of the county of Clark; Samuel N. Carr, of the county of Madison; Lyne Starling, William Neil, and John A. Bryan, of the county of Franklin; Hosea Williams, Milo D. Pettibone, Nathan Dustan, Charles Carpenter and James Eaton, of the county of Delaware; Allen G. Miller, William McLaughlin, Baldwin Bentley, John Rugler, James Purdy, and William McFaull, of the county of Richland; Richard Hargrave, Joseph McComb, John Ihrig, William Read, Thomas Robinson, and Joseph S. Lake, of the county of Wayne; Osmer Curtis, B. S. Brown, Alexander Elliott, D. S. Norton, and S. W. Hildreth, of Knox county; and John Miller, Isaac Bonnet, J. S. Irvine, and S. C. McDowell, of Holmes county; William Hadley, Samuel H. Hale, Isaiah Morris, and Thomas Palmer, for the county of Clinton; Stephen N. Sargeant, Abram Freese, Reuben Smith and Benjamin Durham, of the county of Medina; Herman Ely, Artemas Beebe, Edwin Byington, Samuel Crocker, and Eber W. Hubbard, of the county of Lorain; Josiah Barber, Reuben Wood, Richard Hilliard, Truman P. Handy, James S. Clarke, Samuel R. Hutchinson, Anson Hayden, and Silas Belden, of the county of Cuyahoga; and their associates, and such persons as may hereafter be associated with them, shall be, and they are hereby created a body politic and corporate, by the name of " The Cleveland, Columbus and Cincinnati Rail-road Company," for the purpose of constructing a rail-road from the city of Cleveland, through the city of Columbus, and the town of Wilmington, to the city of Cincinnati; and they are hereby invested with the powers and privileges which are by law incident to corporations of a similar character, and which are necessary to carry into effect the objects of the company; and if any of the persons above named, shall die, or neglect to exercise the powers and discharge the duties hereby created, it shall be the duty of the remaining persons, or a majority of them, to appoint suitable persons to fill such vacancies.

Sec. 2. The capital stock of said company shall be three millions of dollars, to be divided into shares of one hundred dollars; and the persons in the first section named, or a majority of them, shall cause books of subscription for said stock, to be opened, at such times and places, as they may appoint, under the direction of such individuals as they may designate, thirty days notice of which shall be given by advertisement in one or more newspapers printed in each of the cities above mentioned; and the books shall remain open ten days, and should it be necessary to open the books more than once, the like notice shall be given in each instance; and on every share subscribed for, five dollars shall be paid at the time of subscription.

Sec. 3. Whenever the sum of four hundred thousand dollars, or a greater part of said stock shall have been subscribed, it shall be the duty of said persons, or a majority of them, to call a meeting of the stockholders, by causing notice to be published in one or more newspapers in general circulation in the respective places in which stock shall have been subscribed, at least thirty days previous thereto, of the time and place of holding said meeting, which place shall be at some convenient point, on or near the route of said rail-road; at which meeting, the stockholders who shall attend for that purpose, either in person or by lawful proxy, shall elect by ballot, nine directors, who shall hold their offices during one year, and until others shall be chosen and qualified in their places; and the persons named in the first section, or any five of them, shall be inspectors of the first election of directors of said corporation, and shall certify, under their hands, the names of those duly elected; and shall deliver over to them the said certificates and subscription books; and at said election, and at all other elections, or voting of any description, every member shall have a right of voting, by himself, or by proxy duly authorized in writing; and each share shall entitle the holder to one vote; and the management of the concerns of said corporation shall be entrusted to nine directors, to be elected annually, by the stockholders, by ballot; and the directors first chosen, and such directors as shall thereafter be chosen, at any subsequent election, shall immediately thereafter, meet and elect one of their number, who shall be president thereof, until another election; and also elect a treasurer and secretary, who may be removed at the pleasure of said president and directors, and others elected in their stead; and a majority of said directors shall constitute a board, for every purpose within the provisions of this act.

Sec. 4. That in case it should at any time happen, that the election of directors shall not be made, on any day, when pursuant to this act it ought to be made, the said corporation shall not, for that cause, be deemed to be dissolved, but such election may be held at any other time, directed by the by-laws of said corporation.

Sec. 5. That the books of subscription shall remain open as long as the president and directors of said company shall see fit; and each subscriber shall be bound to pay, from time to time, such instalments on his stock, as the said president and directors may lawfully require, not exceeding ten dollars, every sixty days, on each share, by giving at least thirty days previous notice of the time and place of making the payments required, in at least one newspaper in general circulation in each of the counties through which the road may pass, if any stockholders reside therein.

Sec. 6. That if any subscriber shall neglect to pay his subscription, or any portion thereof, for the space of thirty days after he is required so to do, by the said president and directors, notice having been given, as required in this act, the treasurer of said corporation, or other officer duly authorized for that purpose, and may make sale of such share or shares, at public auction, to the highest bidder, giving at least thirty days notice thereof, in some newspaper in general circulation at the place of sale, and the same shall he transferred by the treasurer, to the purchaser; and such delinquent subscriber shall be held personally accountable to the corporation for the balance, if his share or shares shall be sold for less than the amount remaining due thereon, and shall be entitled to the overplus, if the same be sold for more than the amount so remaining due, after deducting the costs of sale.

·Sec. 7. That the said corporation be, and they are hereby authorized, to ˜cause such examinations and surveys to be made, by their agents, surveyors and engineers, of the ground lying in the vicinity of said route, as shall be necessary to determine the most eligible and expedient route, whereon to construct said rail-road; and the examination being made and the route determined, it shall be lawful for said corporation, by themselves or their lawful agents, to enter upon, and take possession of all such lands, materials, and real estate, as may be indispensable for the construction and maintenance of said rail-road, and the examination requisite and appertaining thereto; but all lands, materials, or real estate, thus entered upon, used or occupied, which are not donations, shall be purchased by the corporation, of the owner or owners, at a price to be mutually agreed between them; and in case of disagreement, as to the price, or if the owner be a married woman, infant, insane or an idiot, or non-resident of the county, it shall be the duty of the commissioners of the proper county, upon a notice to be given them by either party, in writing, and making satisfactory proof that the opposite party, if living in the county, or the husband of such married woman, or guardian of such infant, or insane person, if living in the county, has had at least three days notice of the intended application, to appoint three disinterested freeholders of the proper county, to determine the damages which the owner or owners of the lands, materials, or real estate so entered upon, or used by the said corporation, has or have sustained, by the occupation or use of the same; and upon payment, by the said corporation, of such damages, to the person or persons to whom the same may be awarded as aforesaid, then the said corporation shall be deemed to be, and stand seized and possessed of the use, for the purpose of said road, of all such lands, materials, or real estate, as shall have been appraised; and it shall be the duty of said appraisers, to deliver to the said corporation, a written statement, signed by them, or a majority of them, of the award they shall make, containing a description of the land, materials or real estate appraised; to be recorded by the said corporation, in the commissioners office in said county: *Provided*, That either party shall have power, except in cases only where materials are used, to appeal from the decision of the said appraisers, to the court of common pleas of the proper county, at any time within twenty days after the appraisers shall have made their return as aforesaid, and said court shall proceed thereon as in case of appeals, on application for damages in laying out and establishing county roads.

Sec. 8. That the appraisers, authorized by the foregoing section of this act, before they proceed to estimate damages, shall severally take an oath or affirmation, faithfully, impartially and honestly to discharge their said duty, by returning the true amount of damages, over and above the benefits arising from said road, estimated in cash; and the said appraisers shall, severally, be entitled to receive from said corporation, one dollar per day, for every day they may be necessarily employed: *Provided, however*, That if said applicant or applicants shall not obtain an award of damages, then, and in such case, said applicant or applicants shall pay all costs.

Sec. 9. That the said corporation shall have power to determine the width and dimensions of said rail-road, not exceeding one hundred feet in width; whether it shall be a double or single track: to regulate the time and manner in which passengers and property shall be transported thereon; and the manner of collecting tolls for such transportation; and to erect and maintain buildings for the accommodation of the business of the corporation, as they may deem advisable, or for their interest.

Sec. 10. That said corporation may construct the rail-road across, or upon any road, canal, highway, stream of water or water course, if the same shall be necessary; but the said corporation shall restore such road, canal, highway, stream of water or water course, thus intersected or crossed, to its former state of usefulness, or in such manner as not to impair its convenience, usefulness or value, to the owners or the public.

Sec. 11. That said company shall have the power to demand and receive for tolls upon, and the transportation of persons, goods, produce, merchandize or property of any kind whatsoever transported by them or their agents, along said rail way, any sum not exceeding the following rates: on all goods, merchandize, or property of any description whatsoever a sum not exceeding one and a half cents per ton per mile for tolls, five cents per ton per mile for transportation, and for the transportation of passengers not exceeding three cents per mile for each passenger; and any other company, person or persons, may, with suitable and proper cars, take, transport and carry persons and property on said road, subject to such by-laws as the company are by this act authorized to make.

Sec. 12. That at the regular annual meeting of the stockholders of said company, it shall be the duty of the president and directors in office for the previous year, to exhibit a clear and distinct statement of the affairs of the company; and the president and directors shall annually or semi-annually declare and make such dividend as they may deem proper, of the nett profits arising from the resources of said company, deducting the necessary current and probable contingent expenses; and they shall divide the same among the stockholners of said company in proportion to their respective shares in the stock paid into the company.

Sec. 13. That the said president and directors, or a majority of them, may appoint all such officers, engineers, agents and servants whatsoever, as they may deem necessary for the transaction of the business of the company, and may remove any of them at their pleasure; and they, or a majority of them, shall have power to determine the compensation of all such engineers, officers, agents or servants, and to contract with them for their respective services; and to determine by their by-laws the manner of adjusting and settling all accounts against the said company; and also, the manner and evidence of the transfers of stock in said company: and they, or a majority of them, shall have power to pass all by-laws which they may deem necessary or proper for exercising all the powers vested in the company hereby incorporated, and for carrying into effect the objects of this act.

Sec. 14. ·If the Legislature of this State shall, after the expiration of thirty-five years from the passage of this act, make provision by law for the repayment to said company of the amount expended by them in the construction of said road, together with all moneys expended by them for necessary permanent fixtures at the time of purchase for the use of the said road with an advance of fifteen per cent. thereon, then said road, with all fixtures and appurtenances, shall vest in and become the property of the

State of Ohio: *Provided*, That the sum to be paid by the State for the said road and appurtenances, shall not be less, in the aggregate, than the amount expended in the construction thereof, and six per cent. per annum thereon, after deducting the dividend received by the stockholders.

Sec. 15. That in any suit instituted against said corporation, service of process made upon any one of the directors, ten days before the return day thereof, shall, in all courts and places, be deemed and held, a sufficient and valid service on the said corporation.

Sec. 16. That when the said rail-road shall be completed, the president and directors of said company, shall make out a minute, full and detailed statement, in writing, of the expenses incurred by the said corporation, in locating, exploring of routes, and constructing said rail-road; which report shall be verified by the oaths of said president and directors, and filed by them in the office of the Secretary of this State; and if, after the first location of the route of said rail-road, or the completion of the same, as aforesaid, any alteration shall be made in the course thereof, or in any of its branches or connections, the said president and directors shall, in like manner, from time to time, make out and file statements of the expenses incurred by such alterations, branches or connections, as aforesaid.

Sec. 17. That any rail-road company, now or hereafter to be chartered or created by law of this State, shall have power to join and unite with the road hereby incorporated, at any point which the directors of said company may think advisable; and any cars, carriage, or other vehicle, used on either road, joined, or intersected, may run pass, and occupy the intersected or united road, without re-loading, or change of cargo or passengers; subject, however, to the rules and regulations, and to the tolls and charges, common on the road so used and occupied; and free right and privilege is hereby reserved to the State, or individuals, or any company incorporated by law of this State, to cross this road with any other road: *Provided*, That in so crossing, no injury shall be done to the works of the company hereby incorporated.

Sec. 18. That if any person shall wilfully obstruct, or in any way spoil, injure, or destroy said road, or any part thereof, or either of its branches, or any part thereof, or any thing belonging or incident thereto, or any materials to be used in the construction thereof, or any building, fixture or carriage, erected or constructed for the use or convenience thereof, so used thereon, such person or persons shall each be liable, for every such offence, in treble the damages sustained thereby, to be recovered by action of debt, in any court having jurisdiction thereof; and shall also be subject to an indictment in the court of common pleas of the county where such offence was committed; and upon conviction thereof, shall be punished by fine, not exceeding one hundred dollars, and imprisonment, in the county jail, not exceeding twenty days.

Sec. 19. That if said road shall not be commenced within three years from the passage of this act, and completed within ten years thereafter, then this act shall be void of no effect.

Sec. 22. Whenever the dividends of said company shall exceed the rate of six per cent. per annum, the Legislature of this State may impose

68—L

534

such reasonable taxes on the amount of such dividends as shall be received from other rail-road companies.

WILLIAM MEDILL,
Speaker pro tem. of the House of Representatives.

ELIJAH VANCE,
Speaker of the Senate.

March 14, 1836.

AN ACT

To incorporate the Muskingum and Ohio Rail-road Company.

Sec. 1. *Be it enacted by the General Assembly of the State of Ohio,* That David Ballantine, Charles G. Wilson, James Raguet, Richard Stillwell, James Taylor, jr., Gordius A. Hall, Bernard Van Horne and John T. Fracker, of Muskingum county; George Metcalf, Levi Rhinehart, William Skinner, William Allen, Thomas Hays, William Cowden, Buel Conmon and David Tullis, of Guernsey county; James Barnes, John McCartney, Hugh Rodgers, John Thompson, jr., William Dilworth, Thomas Thompson, Andrew Woods and Moses Roads, of Belmont county; be, and they are hereby appointed commissioners, under the direction of a majority of whom, subscriptions may be received to the capital stock of the Muskingum and Ohio Rail-road Company, hereby incorporated; and they, or a majority of them, may cause books to be opened, in the counties aforesaid, at such times and places as they may direct, for the purpose of receiving subscriptions to the capital stock of said company, after having given thirty days notice of the times and places of opening the same; and that, upon the first opening of the books, they shall be kept open for at least ten days in succession, from ten o'clock, A. M. until two o'clock, P. M.; and if, at the expiration of that period, such a subscription to the capital stock of said company as is necessary to its incorporation, shall not have been obtained, then said commissioners, or a majority of them, may cause said books to be opened, from time to time, after the expiration of said ten days, for the space of three years thereafter; and if any of the said commissioners shall die, resign, or refuse to act during the continuance of the duties devolving upon them by this act, another may be appointed in his stead by the remaining commissioners, or a majority of them.

Sec. 2. That the capital stock of the Muskingum and Ohio Rail-road Company, shall be one million of dollars, and shall be divided into shares of fifty dollars each; which shares may be subscribed for by individuals only; and it shall and may be lawful for said corporation to commence the construction of the said rail-road or way, and enjoy all the powers and privileges conferred by this act, as soon as the sum of fifty thousand dollars shall be subscribed to said stock.

Sec. 3. That all persons who shall become stockholders pursuant to this act, shall be, and they are hereby created a body corporate, and shall be and remain a corporation forever, under the name of the Muskingum and Ohio Rail-road Company; and by that name, shall be capable in law of purchasing, holding, selling, leasing and conveying estates, real, personal and mixed, so far as the same shall be necessary for the purpose hereinafter mentioned, and no further; and shall have perpetual succession; and by said corporate name, may contract and be contracted with, sue and be sued, and may have and use a common seal, which they shall have power to alter or renew at their pleasure; and shall have, enjoy, and may exercise all the powers, rights and privileges, which corporate bodies may lawfully do, for the purposes mentioned in this act.

Sec. 4. That if more than twenty thousand shares shall be subscribed to the capital stock of said company, said commissioners, or a majority of them, shall reduce the subscriptions to twenty thousand shares, by striking off from the largest number of shares in succession, until the subscriptions shall be reduced to twenty thousand shares, on the subscriptions to one share; and if there still be an excess, then lots shall be drawn by the commissioners, to determine who are to be excluded.

Sec. 5. That upon every such subscription there shall be paid at the time of subscribing, to the said commissioners, or their agents appointed to receive such subscriptions, the sum of five dollars on every share subscribed; and the residue thereof shall be paid in such instalments, and at such times, as may be required by the president and directors of said company: *Provided*, No payments other than the first shall be demanded, until at least thirty days public notice of such demand shall have been given by said president and directors, in some newspaper of general circulation in the State; and if any stockholder shall fail or neglect to pay any instalment, or part of said subscription thus demanded, for the space of ten days next after the time the same shall be due and payable, the said president and directors, upon giving at least ten days previous notice thereof, in manner aforesaid, may, and they are hereby authorized to sell at public vendue so many of the shares of such delinquent stockholders as shall be necessary to pay such instalment and the expenses of advertising and sale, and transfer the shares so sold to the purchaser; and the residue of the money arising from such sale, after paying such instalment and expense, shall be paid to such stockholder on demand.

Sec. 6. That at the expiration of ten days, for which the books are first opened, if five thousand shares of said capital stock shall have been subscribed, or if not, as soon thereafter as the same shall be subscribed, if within two years after the first opening of the books, the said commissioners, or a majority of them, shall call a general meeting of the stockholders at such time and place as they may appoint, and shall give at least sixty days previous notice thereof; and at such meeting, the said commissioners shall lay the subscription books before the stockholders then and there present; and thereupon the said stockholders, or a majority of them, shall elect twelve directors by ballot; a majority of whom shall be competent to manage the affairs of said company; they shall have the power of electing a president of said company, either from among the directors or others, and of allowing him such compensation for his services as they may deem proper; and in said election, and on all other occasions wherein a vote of the stockholders of said company is to be taken, each stockholder shall be allowed one vote for every share owned by him or her; and every stockholder may depute any other person to vote and act for him or her, as his or her proxy; and the commissioners aforesaid, or any three of them, shall be judges of the first election of said directors: *Provided*, That any president or director who shall cease to be a stockholder, shall cease to be a president or director.

Sec. 7. That to continue the succession of the president and directors of said company, twelve directors shall be chosen annually, on the first Monday in January, in every year, at such place as a majority of the directors shall appoint; and if any vacancy shall occur by death, resignation or otherwise, of any president or director, before the year for which he was elected has expired, a person to fill such vacant place for the residue of the year may be appointed by the president and directors of said company, or a majority of them; and that the president and directors of said company shall hold and exercise their offices until a new election of president and directors; and that all elections which are by this act, or the by-laws of the company, to be made on a particular day, or at a particular time, if not made on such day or time, may be made at any time within thirty days thereafter.

Sec. 8. That a general meeting of the stockholders of said company shall be held annually, at the time and place appointed for the election of president and directors of said company; that they may be called at any time during the interval between the said annual meetings, by the president and directors, or a majority of them, or by the stockholders owning at least one-fourth of the stock subscribed, upon giving at least thirty days public notice of the time and place of holding the same; and when any such meetings are called, by the stockholders, such notice shall specify the particular object of the call; and if, at any such called meeting, a majority in value of the stockholders of said company are not present in person or by proxy, such meeting shall be adjourned from day to day without transacting any business, for any time, not exceeding three days; and if, within said three days, stockholders, holding a majority in value of the stock subscribed, do not thus attend, such meeting shall be dissolved.

Sec. 9. That at the regular annual meeting of the stockholders of said company, it shall be the duty of the president and directors in office for the previous year, to exhibit a clear and distinct statement of the affairs of the company; and that at any called meeting of the stockholders, a majority of those present in person or by proxy, may require similar statements from the president and directors, whose duty it shall be to furnish them when thus required; and that at all general meetings of the stockholders, a majority in value of all the stockholders of said company may remove from office any president or any of the directors of said company, and may appoint officers in their stead.

Sec. 10. That every president and director of said company, before he acts as such, shall take an oath or affirmation (as the case may be,) that he will well and truly discharge the duties of his said office to the best of his skill and ability.

Sec. 11. That the said president and directors, or a majority of them, may appoint all such officers, engineers, agents or servants whatsoever, as they may deem necessary for the transaction of the business of the company, and may remove any of them at their pleasure; that they, or a majority of them, shall have the power to determine the compensation of all engineers, officers, agents, or servants, in the employ of said company: and to determine by their laws the manner of adjusting and settling all accounts against the said company; and, also, the manner and evidence of transfers of stock in said company; and they, or a majority of them, shall have the power to pass all by-laws, which they may deem necessary or proper for exercising all the powers vested in the company hereby incorporated, and for carrying the objects of this act into effect: *Provided, only,* That such by-laws shall not be contrary to the laws of this State or of the United States.

Sec. 12. That if the capital stock of said company shall be deemed insufficient for the purposes of this act, it shall and may be lawful for the president and directors of said company, or a majority of them, from time to time, to increase the capital stock, by the addition of as many shares as they may deem necessary, not exceeding in amount one million of dollars, for which they may, at their option, cause subscriptions to be received, giving notice in the manner hereinbefore prescribed; or may sell the same for the benefit of the company, on such terms as the stockholders at their annual meeting may direct.

Sec. 13. That the said corporation shall be, and they are hereby vested with the right to construct a double or single rail-road or way, from some point in the town of Zanesville, to some point on the Ohio river, in the county of Belmont; and also, to construct branches to the seat of justice of any county through which the road may be located; to transport, take and carry property and persons upon the same, by the power and force of steam, of animals, or of any mechanical or other powers, or of any combination of them, which the said corporation may choose to employ.

Sec. 14. That the president and directors of said company shall be, and they are hereby invested with all rights and powers necessary for the location, construction and repair of said road, not exceeding one hundred feet wide, with as many sets of tracks as the said president and directors may deem necessary, and they may cause to be made, contract with others for making the said rail-road, or any part of it; and they, or their agents, or those with whom they may contract for making any part of the same, and may enter upon and use and occupy any land which may be wanted for the site of said road, or for any other purpose necessary and useful in the construction, or in the repair of said road or its works, and that they may build bridges, may fix scales and weights, may lay rails, may take and use any earth, timber, gravel, stone or other materials which may be wanted for the construction or repair of any part of said road, or any of its works; and may make and construct all works whatsoever, which may be necessary in the construction of said road.

Sec. 15. That the president and directors of said company, or a majority of them, or any person or persons authorized by a majority of them, may agree with the owner or owners of any land, earth, timber, gravel or stone, or other materials, or any improvements which may be wanted for the construction or repair of said road, or any of their works, for the purchase or use, or occupation of the same; and if they cannot agree, and if the owner or owners, or any of them, be a *feme covert,* under age, *non compos mentis,* or out of the county in which the property wanted may lie, when such land and materials may be wanted, application may be made to any justice of the peace of such county, who shall thereupon issue his warrant, under his hand and seal, directed to the sheriff of said county or to some disinterested person if the sheriff shall be interested, requiring him to summon a jury of twelve inhabitants of said county, and not related or in any wise interested, to meet on the land, or near to the other property or materials, to be valued on a day named in said warrant, not less than ten nor more than twenty days after the issuing of the same, and if, at the said time and place, any of said persons summoned do not attend, the said sheriff, or summoner shall immediately summons as many persons as may be necessary, with the persons in attendance, to furnish a pannel of twelve jurors in attendance; and from them each party, or its, his, her or their agent, if either be not present in person or by agent, the sheriff, or summoner, for him, her, it or them, may strike off three jurors, and the remaining six shall act as a jury of damages; and before they act as such, the said sheriff, or summoner shall administer to each of them an oath, or affirmation, as the case may be, that they will justly and impartially value the damages which the owner or owners will sustain by the use or occupation of the same, required by said company; and the jury estimating the damages, if for the ground occupied by said road, shall take into the estimate the benefits resulting to said owner or owners, by reason of said road passing through or upon the lands of such owner or owners, towards the extinguishment of such claim for damages; and the said jury shall reduce their inquisition to writing, and shall sign and seal the same; and it shall then be returned to the clerk of the court of common pleas for said county, and by such clerk filed in his office, and shall be confirmed by said court at its next session, if no sufficient cause to the contrary be shown; and when confirmed, shall be recorded by said clerk, at the expense of said company; but if set aside, the said court may direct another inquisition to be taken in the manner above prescribed; and such inquisition shall describe the property taken, or the bounds of the lands condemned; and such valuation, when paid or tendered to the owner or owners of said property, or his, her, or their legal representatives, shall entitle said company to the full right to said personal property, and the use and occupation of said landed property, for the purposes of said road, thus valued, as fully as if it had been conveyed by the owner or owners of the same; and the valuation, if not received when tendered. may, at any time thereafter, be received from the company without cost, by the owner or owners, his, her, or their legal representative or representatives; and that such sheriff, or summoner, and jurors, shall be entitled to demand and receive from the said company, the same fees, as are allowed for like services, in cases of fixing the valuation of real estate, previous to sale under execution.

Sec. 16. That whenever in the construction of said road, it shall be necessary to cross or intersect any established road or way, it shall be the duty of said president and directors of said company so to construct the said rail-road across such established road or way, as not to impede the passage or transportation of persons or property along the same, or when it shall be necessary to pass through the land of any individual, it shall also be their duty to provide for such individual proper wagon ways across said road, or roads, from one part of his land to another, without delay.

Sec. 17. That if said company should neglect to provide proper wagon ways across said road, as required by the sixteenth section of this act, it shall be lawful for any individual to sue said company, and to be entitled to such damages, as a jury may think him, or her, entitled to, for such neglect or refusal on the part of said company.

Sec. 18. That whenever it shall be necessary for said company to have, use or occupy any land, or materials, in the construction or repair of said road or roads, or any part thereof, on their works or necessary buildings, the president and directors of said company, or their agents, or those contracting with them for making or repairing the same, may immediately take and use the same; they having first caused the property wanted, to be viewed by a jury, (formed in the same manner hereinbefore prescribed,) in those cases where the property is to be changed or altered, by admixture with other substances, before such alteration is made; and that it shall not be necessary after such view, in order to the use or occupation of the same, to wait the issue of the proceedings upon such view, and the inquest of the jury, after confirmation, and after payment or tender of the valuation, shall be a bar to all actions for taking or using such property.

Sec. 19. That if it shall be necessary for the said rail road company, in the selection of the route, or construction of the road by them to be laid out and constructed, or any part of it, to connect the same with, or to use any turnpike road, rail road or bridge, made or erected by any company or persons incorporated, or authorized by any law of this State, it shall be lawful for the said president and directors, and they are hereby authorized, to contract and agree with any such other corporation or persons, for the right to use such road or bridge, or for the transfer of any of the corporate or other rights or privileges of such corporation or persons, to the said company hereby incorporated; and every such other incorporation, or persons incorporated by, or acting under the laws of this State, is, and are hereby authorized to make such agreement, contract, or transfer, by and through the agency of the person authorized by their respective acts of incorporation, to exercise their corporate powers, or by such persons as by any law of this State, are entrusted with the management and direction of such turnpike road or bridge, or of any of the rights and privileges aforesaid; and any contract, or agreement or transfer, made in pursuance of the power and authority hereby granted, when executed, by the several parties under their respective corporate seals, or otherwise legally authenticated, shall vest in the company hereby incorporated, all such road, part of road, rights and privileges, and the right to use and enjoy the same, as fully, to all intents and purposes, as they now are, or might be used and exercised by the said corporation, or persons in whom they are now vested.

Sec. 20. That the said president and directors shall have power to purchase with the funds of the company, and place on any rail-road constructed by them, under this act, all machines, wagons, vehicles, or carriages of any description whatsoever, which they may deem necessary or proper, for the purpose of transportation on said road; and the said road or roads, with all their works, improvements, and profits, and all machinery used on said road for transportation owned by said company, are hereby vested in said company, incorporated by this act, and their successors forever;

and the shares of the capital stock of said company shall be deemed and considered personal property, transferable by assignment, agreeably to the by-laws of said company.

Sec. 21. That said company may demand and receive for tolls upon, and transportation of goods, produce, merchandize, or property of any kind whatsoever, transported by them along said rail way, any sum not exceeding the following rates: on all goods, merchandize, or property of any description, transported by them, a sum not exceeding one and a half cents per mile, for toll, five cents per ton per mile, for transportation; and for the transportation of passengers, not exceeding three cents per mile for each passenger; and all persons paying the tolls aforesaid may, with suitable and proper cars, transport persons or property on said road, subject to the rules and regulations of said company as to the construction and speed of said cars.

Sec. 22. That the said president and directors shall, semi-annually, declare and make such dividends as they may deem proper, of the nett profits arising from the resources of said company, deducting the necessary current and probable contingent expenses, and that they shall divide the sum among the stockholders, of said company in proportion to their respective shares.

Sec. 23. That any other rail road company now or hereafter *to be* created by law of this State, may join and connect any rail road with the road hereby contemplated, and run cars upon the same, subject *to* the rules and regulations of this company, as to the construction and speed of said cars; and full right and privilege is hereby reserved to the State, or individuals, or any company incorporated by law of this State, to cross this road: *Provided,* That in so crossing, no injury shall be done to the works of the company hereby incorporated.

Sec. 24. That if any person or persons, shall wilfully, by any means whatsoever, injure, impair, or destroy any part of any rail road, constructed by said company under this act, or any of the necessary work, buildings, or machinery of said company, such person or persons so offending, shall, each of them, for every such offence, forfeit and pay to the said company a sum not exceeding three fold the damages which may be recovered in the name of the company, by an action of debt, in the court of common pleas for the county wherein the offence shall be committed: and shall also be subject to an indictment in said court and upon conviction of such offence shall be punished by fine and imprisonment, at the discretion of the court.

Sec. 25. That if said rail road shall not be commenced in three years from the passage of this act, and shall not be finished within thirteen years from the time of the commencement thereof, then this act to be null and void.

Sec. 26. If the Legislature of this State shall, at any time after the expiration of thirty-five years from the passage of this act, make provision, by law, for the re-payment to said company of the amount expended by them in the construction of said road, together with all moneys expended by them for necessary permanent fixtures at the time purchased, for the use of said road, with an addition of fifteen per cent. thereon, the said road, with all fixtures and appurtenances, shall vest in and become the property of the State of Ohio.

Sec. 27. Whenever the dividends of said company shall exceed six per cent. per annum, the Legislature of this State may impose such reasonable tax on the amount of such dividends as may be received from other rail road companies.

Sec. 28. That this act is hereby declared to be a public act, and shall be so construed in all courts of justice and elsewhere.

WILLIAM MEDILL,
Speaker pro tem. of the House of Representatives.
ELIJAH VANCE,
Speaker of the Senate.

March 14, 1836.

AN ACT

To revive the act appointing commissioners to re-establish a certain State road, in the counties of Champaign, Miami, and Dark, passed March 5th, 1835.

Sec. 1. *Be it enacted by the General Assembly of the State of Ohio,* That the act, passed March 5th, 1835, to appoint commissioners to re-establish a certain state road, in the counties of Champaign, Miami and Dark, be, and the same is hereby revived; and the further time of one year allowed to carry its provisions into effect.

WILLIAM MEDILL,
Speaker pro tem. of the House of Representatives.
ELIJAH VANCE,
Speaker of the Senate.

March 14, 1836.

AN ACT

To incorporate the Medina Academy in the county of Medina.

Sec. 1. *Be it enacted by the General Assembly of the State of Ohio,* That U. H. Peak, R. Smith, Whitman Mead, Timothy Hudson, Israel Camp, William King, David King, S. N. Sargent, S. Humphreville, John L. Clark, James Carpenter, Charles Olcott, Julius G. Morse, George W. How, Joseph W. White, Earl Maulten, R. S. Chapman, Ansel Whitman, James Brown, Daniel Sanger, Barns Coon, William Root, O. B. Reed, J. A. Potter, A. L. Peak, J. Whaley, Samuel Lee, J. H. Lacey, J. Chadwick, B. C. Blair, Isaac Selleck, and Joshua Warner, together with such other persons as may hereafter be associated with them for the purpose of establishing an academy in the town of Medina, in the county of Medina, be, and they are hereby created a body politic and corporate, with perpetual succession, by the name of the Medina Academy; and by that name shall be competent to contract and be contracted with, to sue and be sued, to

69—L

answer and be answered unto, in all courts of law and equity; and to require, possess, and enjoy, and to sell, and convey, and dispose of property, both real and personal, and shall possess all the powers usually incident to such corporations: *Provided*, That the annual income of such property shall not exceed two thousand dollars.

Sec. 2. That any three of the above named persons shall have power to call a meeting by giving ten days previous notice thereof, by advertisements set up at three of the most public places in the town of Medina.

Sec. 3. That said corporation shall have power to form a constitution and adopt by-laws for its government, to prescribe the number and title of its officers, and define their powers and duties, to prescribe the manner in which members may be admitted and dismissed, and other powers necessary for the efficient management of its corporate concerns: *Provided*, That the constitution, by-laws and regulations of the corporation be consistent with the constitution and the laws of the United States, and of this State.

Sec. 4. That any future Legislature may modify or repeal this act: *Provided*, That the title of any property, real or personal, required or conveyed under its provisions, shall not be thereby affected or diverted to any other purpose than that originally designed.

WILLIAM MEDILL,

Speaker pro tem. of the House of Representatives.

ELIJAH VANCE,

Speaker of the Senate.

March 14, 1836.

AN ACT

To incorporate the Brooklyn Lyceum, in the county of Cuyahoga.

Sec. 1. *Be it enacted by the General Assembly of the State of Ohio,* That D. C. Tyler, Thomas Whelpley, H. H. Hulbert, George L. Chapman, C. L. Russell, W. H. Virts, and Luther M. Parsons, and their associates, together with such other persons as may become associated with them, are hereby constituted a body politic and corporate, with perpetual succession, by the name of the "Brooklyn Lyceum," to be located in the township of Brooklyn, in said county; by which name they may contract, and may prosecute and defend suits, and may acquire, hold, control, and dispose of real and personal property, not exceeding the annual value of one thousand dollars; which shall be applied to no other than literary purposes, the purchase of books, maps, charts, pamphlets and newspapers, and the expenses of the institution.

Sec. 2. They shall have power to form a constitution and by-laws, for the good government of the association, the regulations of its fiscal concerns, the admission of members, and the appointment of its officers, together with such other powers, as may be necessary to the corporate existence, and proper and efficient management of its affairs.

Sec. 3. Any future Legislature may alter or repeal this act.

WILLIAM MEDILL,
Speaker pro tem. of the House of Representatives.

ELIJAH VANCE,
Speaker of the Senate.

March 14, 1836.

AN ACT

To incorporate the Cleves Independent School, in the county of Hamilton.

WHEREAS, The law regulating common schools, does not sufficiently provide for schools, such as would suit the wishes and circumstances of the people in every section of the State; and that the citizens of the village of Cleves, and vicinity, may have a school where the different branches of education shall be taught, such as are not contemplated by the provisions of the general school law: Therefore,

Sec. 1. *Be it enacted by the General Assembly of the State of Ohio,* That Stephen Wood, Daniel G. Howel, Andrew Lind, Joseph M. Runyan, James S. Ogden, and their associates, the householders of school district, number two, Miami township, county of Hamilton, are created a body corporate and politic, with perpetual succession, by the name and style of "The Cleves Independent School;" and, in their corporate capacity, may contract and be contracted with, sue and be sued, plead and be impleaded, answer and be answered unto, in any court having competent jurisdiction.

Sec. 2. That said corporation shall be capable of receiving, acquiring, and holding, either by gift, grant, devise, or purchase, any estate, real, personal or mixed, and may sell, dispose of, and convey the same; and all the property of said corporation, real, personal or mixed, with the profits thereof, shall be appropriated to the use of paying teachers, either male or female, for building or repairing school house, or for the purpose of purchasing books, and other apparatus, for the use of said school, and no other purpose whatever.

Sec. 3. That for the better regulation and government of said school, there shall be elected, on the first Saturday in April, in the year eighteen hundred and thirty-six, and on the first Saturday in April, in each and every year thereafter, three trustees, one treasurer, and one secretary; and all powers, privileges, and trusts, vested by law in the directors of school district number two, aforesaid, are hereby transferred to the trustees of said "Cleves Independent School."

Sec. 4. That the directors of school district number two, in Miami township, and county aforesaid, shall be trustees of said school, till their successors are chosen: *Provided,* That if, from any cause, an election cannot be held, on the day named in the preceding section of this act, the said corporation shall not thereby be dissolved, but an election may be held on any other day by the trustees, or any householder, giving at least ten days notice thereof, by posting up advertisements in three of the most public places within the bounds of said corporation.

Sec. 5. That the trustees shall have power to fill all vacancies, in any of the offices herein named; and all officers, thus appointed, shall retain their respective appointments until the next annual election, and until their successors are elected.

Sec. 6. That the trustees shall have power to judge of the qualifications of the teachers to be employed in said school, and shall make arrangements for their compensation.

Sec. 7. That at any meeting of said corporation, two-thirds of the members being present, by-laws may be enacted for the government of the same, and the trustees shall have power to execute them: *Provided*, That the by-laws are not inconsistent with the constitution and laws of the United States, and this State.

Sec. 8. That said school shall be entitled to receive the same dividends of all moneys appropriated by law for the use and support of common schools, that school district number two, would be entitled to receive; and the secretary of said corporation shall, in making the annual return of the white youth within the bounds of said corporation, be governed by the provisions of the laws regulating common schools; and said school shall, at all times when the public funds are appropriated for the purpose of paying a teacher, or teachers, be free to all the white youth within the bounds of said corporation, under twenty-one years of age: *Provided*, That there shall be nothing in this act so construed, as to prohibit persons over twenty-one years of age, or youth not living in the bounds of said corporation, from attending said school, by obtaining the consent of the trustees thereof, and paying into the hands of the treasurer thereof, or securing to be paid, such sum, or sums, as may be required of them.

Sec. 9. That any future Legislature shall have power to alter, amend, or repeal this act: *Provided*, Such alteration, amendment, or repeal, shall not affect the title to any property, real or personal, acquired or conveyed under its provisions.

WILLIAM MEDILL,
Speaker pro tem. of the House of Representatives.
ELIJAH VANCE,
Speaker of the Senate.

March 14, 1836.

AN ACT

To amend an act entitled "An act to incorporate the town of Norwalk, in the county of Huron," passed February 11th, 1828.

Sec. 1. *Be it enacted by the General Assembly of the State of Ohio,* That it shall be lawful for the qualified electors of the town of Norwalk, in the county of Huron, at the time and place of electing mayor, recorder, and trustees, to elect an assessor, who shall, within five days after his election, take an oath of office before some competent authority; and it shall be the duty of said assessor, annually, in the month of May, to value and appraise all property situate within the limits of said corporation, whether lying in district lots or parcels, or in common and undivided with other lands within said corporation, which is made subject to taxation by by the laws of this State, for State and county purpose, or by the act to which this an amendment; and to make out, sign, certify, and return a true list of such valuation to the recorder of said town, on or before the first Monday in June annually; which list, when so returned, shall be open to the examination of any inhabitant of said town, or any other person interested.

[Sec. 2.] That the town council and assessor of said town shall have power to equalize said appraisement list, when they may believe justice requires it; after which they shall determine the amount of per cent. of tax to be levied on the amount of property so returned, not exceeding the amount of per centum per annum specified in the act to which this is an amendment.

[Sec. 3.] That when the town council shall have determined the amount of per cent. of tax to be levied, the recorder shall make a duplicate thereof, charging thereon each person owning property in said town an amount of tax in proportion to the amount of his or her property, assessed and returned on said appraisement list; a copy of which duplicate, certified and signed by the recorder, shall be delivered to the marshal for collection, who shall collect the same, agreeably to the provisions of the act to which this an amendment.

[Sec. 4.] That so much of the ninth section of the act to which this is an amendment, as relates to the mode of valuation, and the assessment of the tax, and the time of such valuation and assessment, as is inconsistent with, and contrary to this act, is hereby repealed.

WILLIAM MEDILL,
Speaker pro. tem. of the House of Representatives.
ELIJAH VANCE,
Speaker of the Senate.

March 14, 1836.

AN ACT.

To vacate part of a State road, in the county of Ross.

Sec. 1. *Be it enacted by the General Assembly of the State of Ohio,* That so much of the state road, known by the name of the Clouser and Benner road, leading from Frankfort to Benner's forge, as lies between Thomas Cox's and the widow Anderson's, in said county, be, and the same is hereby vacated.

WILLIAM MEDILL,
Speaker pro tem. of the House of Representatives.
ELIJAH VANCE,
Speaker of the Senate.

March 14, 1836.

AN ACT

To incorporate the First Presbyterian Church of Centre township, in Monroe county.

Sec. 1. *Be it enacted by the General Assembly of the State of Ohio,* That Robert Smyth, jr. James Kennedy, and Wm. Pickens, and their associates, together with such other persons as may hereafter be associated with them, be, and they are hereby declared a body corporate and politic, by and with the name and style of the "First Presbyterian Church of Centre township, in Monroe county;" with perpetual succession, and capacity of contracting and being contracted with, suing and being sued, answering and being answered, pleading and being impleaded, defending and being defended, in all courts of law and equity, and may also have a common seal, which they may break, alter or renew at pleasure.

Sec. 2. That they shall have power to make, pass, and enforce from time to time, such rules, by-laws and regulations, as they may deem proper for the good regulation of said association: *Provided,* That such rules, by-laws and regulations shall not be repugnant to the constitution and laws of this State and of the United States.

Sec. 3. That said association shall be capable in law of purchasing and holding any estate, real or personal, and of receiving any gift, grant, devise, donation or legacy made, or to be made, to said association; with full power to sell, dispose of, and convey the same: *Provided,* That the annual income of such property shall not exceed two thousand dollars.

Sec. 4. That Robert Smyth, jr. James Kennedy, and William Pickens, be, and they are hereby appointed trustees of said association, until others are appointed in conformity with the rules, by-laws, and regulations made by said association.

Sec. 5. That any future Legislature shall have power to modify, alter, or repeal this act: *Provided,* That such modification, alteration, or repeal shall not affect any estate, real or personal, acquired or conveyed under its provisions.

WILLIAM MEDILL,
Speaker pro tem. of the House of Representatives.
ELIJAH VANCE,
March 14, 1836.
Speaker of the Senate.

AN ACT

To incorporate the Wardens and Vestrymen of the Parish of St. John's, of the Protestant Episcopal Church, in Brooklyn, Cuyahoga county.

Sec. 1. *Be it enacted by the General Assembly of the State of Ohio,* That Josiah Barbee, Edwin Foote, N. C. Baldwin, Christopher E. Hill, F. A. Burrows, G. C. Huntington, H. Elldridge, and their associates and successors, be, and they are hereby constituted a body corporate and politic, by the name of the "Wardens and Vestrymen of St. John's Church," in Brooklyn, Cuyahoga county, in connection with the Protestant Episcopal Church, in the Diocese of Ohio; and by that name shall have perpetual succession; and may have a common seal, and change the same at discretion: and by that name and style shall be capable in law and equity of taking, holding, and enjoying, to them and their successors, any real and personal estate: *Provided,* The annual income of all such property shall not exceed the sum of two thousand dollars.

Sec. 2. That the members of said incorporation, and their associates, may meet on Easter Monday, and on that day annually, and when so convened, or at any other time to which such meeting may be adjourned, may select such officers as they may think necessary for carrying into effect the objects of their incorporation; fix the time and place for their future meetings; and ordain and establish such by-laws and ordinances, for the government of their officers and members, the employment and support of their minister, and for all the secular concerns of said parish, as they may deem expedient: *Provided,* That if, at any time, an election of officers shall not be had on the regular day, the corporation shall not thereby be dissolved, but the officers previously chosen shall serve until their successors are elected, which election may be held at any meeting duly notified and assembled for that purpose.

Sec. 3. That all male members of the corporation, of the age of twenty-one years and upwards, shall be entitled to vote at all meetings of said corporation.

Sec. 4. That original process against said corporation shall be by summons, which shall be served on one of the vestrymen or wardens, at least ten days before the return day thereof.

Sec. 5. Any future Legislature may alter or repeal this act.

WILLIAM MEDILL,
Speaker pro tem. of the House of Representatives.

ELIJAH VANCE,
Speaker of the Senate.

March 14, 1836.

AN ACT

To incorporate the town of Felicity, in the county of Clermont.

Sec. 1. *Be it enacted by the General Assembly of the State of Ohio,* That so much of the township of Franklyn, in the county of Clermont, as is comprised and designated in the town plat in the town of Felicity, together with such plat or plats, in addition thereto, as has been, or may hereafter be recorded in the recorder's office, in the county of Clermont, as additions thereto, be, and the same is hereby created into, and constituted a town corporate, by the name of the town of Felicity.

Sec. 2. That for the order and government of said town, and inhabitants thereof, it shall be lawful for the white male householders thereof, who have resided therein for the space of three months next preceding the day of election, having the qualifications of electors of members of the Gene-

ral Assembly, to meet at some convenient place in the said town of
Felicity, on the second Saturday of May next, and on the second Saturday of May annually thereafter; and there proceed, by a plurality
of votes, to elect, by ballot, one mayor, one recorder, and five trustees,
who shall be householders of said town, who shall hold their offices
until the next annual election, and until their successors are elected and
qualified; and such mayor, recorder, and trustees, so being elected and
qualified, shall constitute the town council of said town, any five of whom
shall constitute a quorum for the transaction of business pertaining to their
duties.

Sec. 3. That at the first election to be holden under this act there shall
be chosen, *viva voce*, by the electors present, two judges and a clerk of
said election, who shall each take an oath or affirmation, faithfully to discharge the duties required of them by this act; and [at] all subsequent elections, the trustees, or any two of them shall be judges, and the recorder,
or in his absence, some other person, to be appointed by the judges, shall
be clerk; the polls shall be opened between the hours of ten and eleven
o'clock in the forenoon, and closed at three o'clock, in the afternoon of
said day; and at the close of the polls, the votes shall be counted, and
a true statement thereof proclaimed to the voters present, by one of the
judges; and the clerk shall make a true copy thereof, and within five days
thereafter, he shall give notice to the persons so elected of their election;
and it shall be the duty of the town council, at least ten days before each
and every annual election, to give notice of the same, by setting up advertisements at three of the most public places in said town.

Sec. 4. That the mayor, and in case of his absence the recorder, shall
preside at all meetings of the town council; and the recorder shall attend
all meetings of the town council, and make a fair and accurate record of
all their proceedings.

Sec. 5. That the town council shall have power to fill all vacancies
which may happen in said board, from the householders, who are qualified
electors in said town; who shall hold their appointment until the next annual election, and until their successors are elected and qualified; and in
the absence of the mayor and recorder from any meeting of the town
council, the trustees shall have power to appoint any two of their number
to perform the duties of mayor and recorder, for the time being.

Sec. 6. That the mayor, recorder, and trustees of said town, shall
be a body corporate and politic, with perpetual succession, to be known
and distinguished by the name and style of "The Town Council of the town
of Felicity;" and shall be capable in law, by their corporate name, to acquire property, real, personal and mixed, for the use of said town, and may
sell and convey the same at pleasure; they may have a common seal, which
they may break, alter, or renew, at pleasure; they may sue and be sued,
plead and be impleaded, defend and be defended, in all manner of actions,
and in all courts of law and equity; and whenever any suit shall be commenced against said corporation, the process shall be served by copy,
which shall be left with the recorder, or at his usual place of residence,
at least five days before the return day thereof.

Sec. 7. That each member of said town council, before entering
upon the duties of his office, shall take an oath or affirmation to support

the constitution of the United States, and the constitution of this State, and also an oath of office.

Sec. 8. That the town council shall have power to make, ordain and establish by-laws, rules and regulations, for the government of said town, and to alter or repeal the same at pleasure; to provide for the appointment of a treasurer, town marshal, and such other subordinate officers as they may think necessary; to prescribe their duties, and determine the period of their appointment, and to fix the fees they shall be entitled to for their services; and the treasurer, marshal, and other officers, shall, before entering upon their duties, take an oath of office, and shall respectively give bond, with security, in such sums as shall be determined by the town council, payable to the State of Ohio, conditioned for the faithful performance of their respective duties: the town council shall also have power to fix reasonable fines and penalties for any violation of the laws and ordinances of the corporation, and to provide for the collection and disposition of the same: *Provided.* Such by-laws or ordinances, rules and regulations, be not inconsistent with the constitution and laws of the United States, and of this State: *And provided, also,* That no by-law, ordinance, rule or regulation, shall take effect, or be in force, until the same shall have been posted up for two weeks, in one or more of the most public places in said corporation.

Sec. 9. That the town council shall, at the expiration of each and every year, cause to be made out and posted up as aforesaid, the receipts and expenditures of the preceding year.

Sec. 10. That the town council shall have power to regulate and improve the streets, lanes, and alleys, and determine the width of the side walks in said town; they shall have power to remove all nuisances and obstructions from the streets and commons of said town, and to do all things which similar corporations have power to do.

Sec. 11. That for the purpose of more effectually enabling said town council to carry into effect the provisions of this act, they are hereby authorized and empowered to levy a tax on all the real and personal property, subject on the grand levy to taxation within the limits of said town, upon the appraisements made and returned upon said grand levy: *Provided,* That said tax, so levied by said town council, shall not, in any one year, exceed one half per centum, on the aggregate amount of all such taxable property within the limits of said town; and the said town council shall, annually, between the first day of April and the first day of July, determine the amount of tax to be assessed and collected for the current year.

Sec. 12. That it shall be the duty of the recorder of said corporation, to make out duplicates of taxes, charging each individual within said corporation, an amount of tax, in proportion to the aggregate value of the taxable property belonging to such individual, within the limits of said corporation, as the same appears upon the books of the auditor of said county of Clermont; and the said recorder shall have power of inspecting the books of said auditor, and to take any minutes or transcripts therefrom, as may be necessary to aid him in the discharge of his duties hereby enjoined upon him, free of expense: when said recorder shall have made out said duplicates, as aforesaid, he shall deliver one of such duplicates to the marshal

70—I'

of said town, or to such other person as may be appointed collector, whose duty it shall be to collect the taxes thereon, in the same manner and under the same regulations as are provided by law for the collection of State and county. taxes; and the said marshal or collector shall, immediately after collecting said taxes, pay the same over to the treasurer of said corporation, and take his receipt therefor; and the said marshal or collector shall have the same power to sell both real and personal property, as is given by law to county treasurers; and when necessary, the recorder shall have power to make deeds for real estate so sold, in the same manner that county auditors are by law empowered to do, for lands sold by the county treasurer; and the marshal, or collector, shall receive such fees for his service, as the town council may direct, not exceeding six per cent. on all moneys so by him collected, to be paid by the treasurer, on the order of the recorder.

Sec. 13. That the said town council shall have power to appropriate any money remaining in the corporation treasury, to the improvement of the streets, alleys and side walks of said town, whenever they may deem it nesary, and to make any other improvement, which may conduce to the health and comfort of said town.

Sec. 14. That the mayor of said town shall be a conservator of the peace within the limits of said corporation; and shall have therein, all the powers and jurisdiction of a justice of the peace, in all matters, either civil or criminal, arising under the laws of this State; he shall perform all the duties enjoined upon him by the laws and ordinances of the corporation, and shall give bond and security, in the same manner as justices of [the] peace are required to do; and appeals may be taken from the decision of the said mayor, in all cases where, by law, appeals are allowed from the decisions of the justices of the peace, and in the same manner.

Sec. 15. That the marshal shall be the principal ministerial officer in said corporation, and shall have the same power as constables have by law; and his authority, in the execution of criminal process shall be co-extensive with the limits of said county of Clermont, and he shall receive for his services, such fees as are allowed by law to constables, in similar cases, for like services.

Sec. 16. That the mayor shall receive for his services, such fees as are allowed by law to justices of the peace for similar services in like cases; the recorder shall receive such fees for his services, as shall be fixed by the by-laws and ordinances of the corporation.

Sec. 17. That if no election shall be held by the electors of said town, on the second Saturday in May next, it shall be lawful for any ten householders of said town, to call a meeting of the electors, by giving ten days notice thereof, in writing, to be posted up in one or more of the most public places in said town; which notice shall state the time, place, and object of said meeting, and shall be signed by the said householders; and if a majority of the qualified electors of said town shall attend at the time specified in said notice, it shall be lawful for them to proceed to the election of officers, in the same manner as hereinbefore provided for; and the officers so elected shall hold their offices until the second Saturday of May following, and until their successors are elected and qualified.

Sec. 18. That the said corporation shall be allowed the use of the county jail, for the imprisonment of such persons as may be liable to imprison-

ment, under the laws and ordinances of said town, and all persons so imprisoned, shall be under the charge of the sheriff or jailor, as in other
cases.

Sec. 19. That any future Legislature shall have power to alter, amend
or repeal this act.

WILLIAM MEDILL,
Speaker pro tem. of the House of Representatives.

ELIJAH VANCE,
Speaker of the Senate.

March 14, 1836.

AN ACT

To incorporate the First Baptist Church and Society in Madison, in the county of Geauga.

Sec. 1. *Be it enacted by the General Assembly of the State of Ohio,*
That Curtis A. Tisdale, Lester Brooks, Benjamin F. Fuller, Jos. Fuller,
Abner Hotchkiss, William Balch, Gwindal Rawson, John N. Mackin, and
their associates, together with such other persons as may be hereafter associated with them, be, and they are hereby created a body corporate and politic, by the name of "The First Baptist Church and Society in Madison;"
and as such shall remain and have perpetual succession, and by their corporate name may contract and be contracted with, may sue and be sued, answer and [be] answered, plead and be pleaded, defend and be defended,
in any court of competent jurisdiction, in all manner of actions, causes
and complaints, whatsoever; and may have a common seal, which they
may change or alter at pleasure.

Sec. 2. That said corporation shall be capable in law and equity, in
their corporate name aforesaid, of having, receiving, acquiring and holding, by purchase, gift, grant devise or legacy, any estate, real, personal,
or mixed, for the use of said corporation: *Provided,* That the annual income of all such property shall not exceed the sum of one thousand dollars;
and that all the property, of whatever kind, shall be considered as held in
trust, under the management, and at the disposal of said corporation, for
the purpose of promoting the interests of said society, defraying the expenses incident to their mode of worship, and maintaining any institutions
of charity or education, that may be therewith connected: *And provided,
also,* That when money, or other property shall be given, granted, devised
or bequeathed, for any particular use or purpose, it shall be faithfully applied to such use or purpose.

Sec. 3. That for the better managing of the affairs of said society, and
promoting the interests thereof, there shall be elected, on the second Monday in March, one thousand eight hundred and thirty seven, and on the
second Monday in March, in each succeeding year thereafter, three trustees, and such other officers as the corporation may deem necessary, who
shall hold their offices for one year, and until successors shall be elected: *Provided,* That if, from any cause, an election of officers should not

be made on the day appointed for the annual election, the society may elect their officers at any meeting of the corporation duty assembled.

Sec. 4. That Curtis A. Tisdale, Lester Brooks, and Benjamin F. Fuller, named in the first section of this act, be, and they are hereby appointed trustees, until the first annual election, and until others are elected in their place.

Sec. 5. That all elections of the corporation shall be by ballot, and the person or persons having a majority of the votes given, for any office, shall be considered duly elected; each member shall have one vote, and all matters of [the] corporation shall be determined by a majority of the members present, at any meeting of the corporation duly assembled.

Sec. 6. That the trustees, or a majority of them shall be a quorum for the transaction of business, shall, under the direction of the society, have the management and control of the property and other concerns of the corporation; and they, or a majority of them, shall have power to call a meeting of the society, either for the election of officers, or for the transaction of other business of the society, by giving to said society, immediately after public worship, at least ten days previous notice of said meeting, or causing notifications thereof to be put up in three or more public places within the limits of said society, one of which shall be at the usual place of holding public worship, at least fifteen days previous to such meeting.

Sec. 7. That any meeting of the society, duly assembled, may adopt and establish such by-laws and ordinances as may be deemed proper and necessary for the good government of said corporation: *Provided,* That such by-laws and ordinances shall be compatible with the constitution and laws of the United States, and of this State.

Sec. 8. That original process against the corporation shall be served by leaving an attested copy with one or more of the trustees, and such service shall be deemed sufficient to bind the corporation.

Sec. 9. That any future Legislature shall have power to modify or repeal this act: *Provided,* That such modification or repeal shall not affect the title to any estate, real or personal, acquired or conveyed under its provisions.

WILLIAM MEDILL,
Speaker pro tem. of the House of Representatives.
ELIJAH VANCE,
Speaker of the Senate.

March 14, 1836.

AN ACT

To incorporate the Fort Wayne and Piqua Rail-road Company.

Sec. 1. *Be it enacted by the General Assembly* of the State of Ohio, That Marshall S. Wines, William G. Ewing, Allen Hamilton, Dr. L. G. Thompson, Samuel Hamer and Francis Compant, of Fort Wayne, Indiana; Robert Young, Dr. John O'Ferrel, William Scott and James Alexander, of Piqua; John Pickrel and James W. Riley, of St. Mary's, Ohio; their associates and successors, be, and they are hereby constituted and made a body politic and corporate, and shall be and remain a corporation forever, under the name of "The Fort Wayne and Piqua Rail-Company;" and by that name, may sue and prosecute, and be sued and prosecuted to final judgment and execution in all courts having competent jurisdiction; and may have a common seal, and the same to alter and renew at pleasure; and shall be and hereby are invested with all the powers and privileges which are by law incident to corporations of a similar nature, and which are necessary for the purposes of constructing a single or double rail-road or way, from a point at or near the town of Fort Wayne, in the State of Indiana, by way of Shaw's Prairie and St. Mary's, to Piqua, in Ohio; to transport, take and carry property and persons upon the same, by the power and force of steam, of animals, or of any mechanical or other power, or of any combination of them, which the said corporation may choose to employ; and by that name, they and their successors shall be, and they are hereby vested with the right and privilege of constructing, erecting, building, making and using, a single or double rail-road or way, for the purposes aforesaid, from and to any point or place comprised within the limits aforesaid.

Sec. 2. That the capital stock of said company shall be one million of dollars, and shall be divided into shares of fifty dollars each; which shall be deemed personal property, and transferable in such manner as the by-laws of said corporation shall direct.

Sec. 3. That the persons named in the first section of this act, or any five or more of them, who may consent to act as such, shall be commissioners, whose duty it shall be, so soon after the taking effect of this act as a majority of them that will agree to act, will judge proper, to cause books to be opened at such times and places as they shall think fit, in the States of Indiana and Ohio, and elsewhere, under the management of such persons as they shall appoint for receiving subscriptions to the capital stock of said company, each subscriber to be a member of said corporation for all purposes; and public notice shall be given in such manner as may be deemed advisable by said commissioners, of the time and place of opening said books; and the said commissioners, or a majority ef them, may prescribe the form of said subscription; and when the sum of fifty thousand dollars have been subscribed, it shall be the duty of the said commissioners, or a majority of them, to call a meeting of the subscribers, by causing notice to be published in one or more newspapers in general circulation in the several places, or most contiguous thereto, in which the books may have been opened and stock subscribed, at least twenty days previous thereto, of the time and place of such meeting, which shall be at some convenient town or place near the route of the contemplated rail-road, at which meeting the stockholders who shall attend in person or by lawful proxy, shall elect by ballot, twelve directors, six of whom shall be residents of the State of Indiana, and the remaining six residents of the State of Ohio, who shall hold their offices until the expiration of one year and until others shall have been chosen in their places; and the said commissioners shall be inspectors of the first election of directors of the said corporation, and shall certify under their hands the names of those duly elected, and shall deliver over to them the said certificate and books of subscription.

Sec. 4. That each subscriber shall pay to the commissioners, or to the persons appointed by them to receive subscriptions to the capital stock of said company, at the time of subscribing, the sum of two dollars on each share for which he shall subscribe, and the same shall be deemed and taken as an instalment paid on account of the stock to which he shall become entitled by such subscription; and the commissioners shall pay over all moneys so paid, to the directors elected in pursuance of the provisions of the third section of this act.

Sec. 5. That the management of the concerns of said corporation shall be entrusted to twelve directors, to be elected annually by the stockholders by ballot, (at a time and place to be fixed on by the president and directors, of which due notice shall be given by them, as prescribed in the third section of this act,) and the directors first chosen, and such directors as shall thereafter be chosen at any subsequent election, shall immediately thereafter meet and elect one of their number, who shall be president thereof until superseded by another election, and also appoint a treasurer and secretary, who may be removed at the pleasure of said president and directors, and others appointed in their places; and a majority of said directors shall constitute a board for every purpose within the provisions of this act.

Sec. 6. That in case it should at any time happen that the election of directors should not be made, as agreeable to the provisions of the preceding section it ought to be made, the said corporation shall not for that cause be deemed to be dissolved, but such election may be held at any other time, on the notice before prescribed being given by the president and directors.

Sec. 7. That in the event of a sufficient amount of stock not being taken under the supervision of the commissioners, the president and directors are hereby authorized to re-open said books, and to continue them open so long as they shall see fit; and each subscriber shall be bound to pay, from time to time, such instalments on his or her, or their stock, as the said president and directors may lawfully require; they giving at least sixty days notice of the time and place of making the payments required, in such public newspapers in Indiana, Ohio, and elsewhere, as will be most likely to give information to the stockholders; but no assessment shall ever be made so as to render any stockholder liable to pay more than fifty dollars for a share: *Provided*, That not more than one-fifth part of the subscription shall be required to be paid within any time of six months after the commencement of the work; if, however, after the closing of said subscriptions for the stock, or at any time, it shall appear that sufficient funds have not been raised, the president and directors of said company, or their agents, duly authorized for that purpose, may at any time, and from time to time, raise the necessary funds, by selling additional shares, in such manner and upon such terms as the president and directors shall prescribe, for any sum not under their par value; and the holders of such shares shall thenceforward be members of said corporation for all purposes.

Sec. 8. That if any subscriber shall fail or neglect to pay any instalment, or any part of any subscription by him previously subscribed, for the space of sixty days after the same shall be due and payable, the stock shall be forfeited to the company, and may be sold by the president and directors for the benefit of said company, after thirty days notice given in some newspaper in general circulation; and if said shares so sold, shall not amount to a sufficient sum to discharge the balance due on said shares, the subscribers shall be personally liable for the balance still remaining due; and if said shares shall sell for a sum more than sufficient to pay said balance, the same shall be paid over to said subscribers, on demand being made for the same.

Sec. 9. That at all elections for directors, and at all general meetings of the stockholders, each stockholder shall be entitled to one vote for every share of stock owned by him or her; and every executor, administrator, trustee or guardian, shall be entitled to the privilege of voting on behalf of the estate, copartnership, corporation or society, of which he may be such executor, administrator, trustee or guardian: *Provided,* That no share shall confer the right of voting at the first election of said company, unless two dollars on such share shall have been fully paid, as directed by the fourth section of this act; at all subsequent elections no share or shares shall confer on the holder or holders thereof, the right of voting, unless all the instalments called for and then due, shall also have been fully paid, according to the seventh section of this act.

Sec. 10. That it shall and may be lawful for any State, or for the Government of the United States, to become subscribers for any number of shares of stock in said company, upon the same terms as other subscribers are authorized to take and subscribe for the same: *Provided,* That for every one thousand shares respectively owned by any State, or by the government of the United States, at the first election for directors of said company, and at all subsequent general elections for directors, such State, or government of the United States, may each appoint one additional director of said company, but shall not be permitted to vote upon their stock in the election for directors by the stockholders in general meetings: *And provided, also,* That no number of shares less than one thousand, owned by any State, or government of the United States, shall confer any right of voting for directors of said company, or at any meeting of the stockholders of said company.

Sec. 11. That if any vacancy shall occur by death, resignation, or refusal to act, of any president or directors, before the year for which he was elected to act shall have expired, a person to fill such vacant place for the residue of the year, may be appointed by the directors, or by the president and directors of said company, or a majority of them.

Sec. 12. That at the regular meetings of the stockholders of said company, it shall be the duty of the president and directors in office for the preceding year, to exhibit a clear and distinct statement of the affairs of said company; that at any general meeting of the stockholders, a majority (in value) of all the stockholders of said company, may remove from office the president or any of the directors of said company, and may appoint others in their stead.

Sec. 13. That every president and director of said company, before he act as such, shall take an oath or affirmation that he will well and truly discharge the duties of his said office to the best of his skill and judgment.

Sec. 14. That the said president and directors shall, annually or semiannually, declare and make such dividend as they may deem proper, of the nett profits arising from the resources of said company, after deducting the necessary current and probable contingent expenses, and that they shall divide the same amongst the proprietors of the stock of said company in proper proportion to their respective shares.

Sec. 15. That the president and directors of said company, or a majority of them, or any person or persons authorized by a majority of them, may agree with the owner or owners of any lands, earth, timber, gravel or stone, or other materials, for the purchase, use or occupation of the same; and if they cannot agree, and if the owner or owners, or any of them, be a *feme covert*, or under age, *non compos mentis*, or out of the county in which the property wanted, may be, when such land and materials may be wanted, application may be made to any justice of the peace in such county, who shall thereupon issue his warrant, under his hand and seal, directed to the sheriff of said county, or to some disinterested person, if the sheriff shall be interested, requiring him to summon a jury of twelve disinterested inhabitants of said county, to meet on the land or near to the other property or materials to be valued, on a day named in said warrant, not less than ten nor more than twenty days after the issuing of the same; and if, at the said time and place, any one of the said persons summoned, do not attend, the said sheriff or summoner shall immediately summons as many persons as may be necessary, with the persons in attendance, to furnish a pannel of twelve jurors, and from them each party, or its, his, her or their agent, or if either be not present in person or by agent, the sheriff or summoner, for it, him, her or them, may strike off three jurors, and the remaining six shall act as a jury of inquest of damages; and before they act as such, the said sheriff or summoner shall administer to each of them an oath or affirmation that they will justly and impartially value the damages which the owner or owners will sustain by use and occupation of such land or materials, or both, as may be required by the said company; and the said jury, in estimating the damages, in case it be for the land used for such road, shall take into the estimate the benefits resulting to said owner or owners, from conducting such rail-road through, along, or near the property of such owner or owners, in extinguishment of the claim for damages; and the said jury shall reduce their inquisition to writing, and shall sign the same; and it shall then be returned to the clerk of the court of the common pleas for the county, and by such clerk filed in his office; and shall be confirmed by said court at its next session, if no sufficient cause to the contrary be shown; and when confirmed, shall be recorded by said clerk, at the expense of said company; but if set aside, the said court may direct another inquisition to be taken in the manner before prescribed; and such inquisition shall describe the property taken, or the bounds of the land to be occupied; and the amount of such valuation, when paid or tendered to the owner or owners of said property, or his, her or their agent or legal representative, shall entitle said company to the said property, or the use and occupation of said land so long as the same shall be required for the use of said rail-road; and the valuation, if not received when tendered, may at any time thereafter be received from said company without cost, by said owner or owners, or their legal representatives; and that such sheriff or summoner, and jurors, shall be entitled to receive from said company the same fees as are allowed for like services in cases of appraisement of real estate previous to sale under execution.

Sec. 16. That the said corporation be, and they are hereby authorized to cause such examinations and surveys to be made by their agents, surveyors and engineers, of the ground lying between the aforementioned points as shall be necessary to determine the most eligible and advantageous route whereon to construct the rail-road: *Provided,* That if at any time after the examination aforesaid, or the location of said road, any unforeseen obstacles, impediments, or inconveniences, occur on the route located, the said corporation shall have power to deviate from the course marked out, so far and in such manner as will enable them to surmount, overcome or avoid such obstacles, impediments or inconveniencies; said corporation satisfying the damages that may be occasioned thereby, to be assessed in the manner provided by this act: and the said corporation may from time to time make such alterations in the course of said road, as may be necessary or expedient, satisfying all damages in manner aforesaid: *And provided, also,* That in all cases, it shall be competent for said company, and any corporation or corporations, person or persons injured by the location or construction thereof, to refer the question of damages to such arbitraters as they may agree upon, whose award, when made and returned to the court of common pleas within and for the county wherein the damages may have been sustained, and affirmed by said court, shall be final, and said court may enter judgment accordingly.

Sec. 17. That upon payment by the said company of such damages to the person or persons, corporation or corporations, to whom the same may have been assessed or awarded, as in this act before provided, then the said company shall be deemed to be seized and possessed of the use of all such lands or real estate, not exceeding one hundred feet in width, as shall have been assessed or appraised by commissioners or arbitrators, as hereinbefore provided, so long as the same shall be used for such road; and it shall be the duty of the commissioners and arbitrators so chosen, to embrace in their reports or awards, a description of the lands or real estate for which they shall assess damages as aforesaid.

Sec. 18. That in any suit instituted against the said incorporation, the service of legal process on the president or any one of the directors, or on the treasurer or secretary of said corporation, shall be deemed and held, in all courts and places, a sufficient and valid service on said corporation.

Sec. 19. That whenever, in the construction of said road or roads, it shall be necessary to cross or intersect any established road or way, it shall be the duty of the president and directors of said company, so to construct the rail-road across such established road or way, as not to impede the passage or transportation of persons or property along the same; or when it shall be necessary to pass through the land of any individual, it shall also be their duty to provide for such individual proper wagon ways across said road, from one part of his land to another.

Sec. 20. That the said president and directors, or a majority of them, shall have power to purchase, with the funds of the said company, and place on any rail-road constructed by them under this act, all machines, wagons, vehicles, or carriages of any description whatsoever, which they may deem necessary or proper for the transportation on said road; and they shall have power to charge for tolls upon, and the transportation of, persons, goods, produce merchandize, or property of any description what.

soever, transported by them along said rail-way, any sum not exceeding the following rates: on all goods, merchandize, or property of any description whatsoever, transported by them, one and half cents a ton, per mile, for toll, and five cents a ton, per mile, for transportation; and for the transportation of passengers not exceeding four cents per mile for each passenger: and that the said road or roads, with all their works, improvements, and profits, and all machinery for transportation, used on said road, and owned by them, are hereby vested in said company, incorporated by this act, and their successors forever.

Sec. 21. That any company, or person or persons, paying the tolls aforesaid, may, with suitable and proper cars, transport persons or property on said road, subject to the rules and regulations of said company as to the construction and speed of said cars.

Sec. 22. That if any person or persons shall wilfully, by any means whatsoever, injure, impair, or destroy any part of any rail-road, constructed by said company under this act, or any of the necessary works, buildings, carriages, vehicles, or machines of said company, such person or persons, so offending, shall each of them, for every such offence, forfeit and pay to the said company, treble damages, which may be recovered in the name of said company, by action of debt, in any court having jurisdiction of the same, and shall also be subject to indictment in the courts of the counties where such offence is committed, and upon conviction of such offence, shall be punished by fine and imprisonment, at the discretion of the court.

Sec. 23. That if the corporation hereby created, shall not, within three years from the passage of this act, commence, and within ten years thereafter, construct, finish, and put in operation, the single or double rail-road, or way, then the said corporation shall thenceforth cease, and this act be null and void.

Sec. 24. That any other rail-road company, now or hereafter to be chartered by law of this State, may join and connect any rail-road with the road hereby contemplated, and run cars on the same, subject to the rules and regulations of this company, as to the construction and speed of said cars; and full right and privilege is hereby reserved to the State, or individuals, or any company, incorporated by law of this State, to cross this road: *Provided*, That in so crossing, no injury shall be done to the works of the company hereby incorporated.

Sec. 25. That the State shall have the power, at any time after the expiration of thirty-five years from the passage of this act, to purchase and hold said road, for the use of the State, at a price not exceeding the original cost for the construction of said road, and the necessary permanent fixtures at the time of purchase, and fifteen per cent. thereon; of which costs an accurate statement in writing, shall be submitted to the General Assembly, duly attested by the oaths of the officers of said company, if the General Assembly shall require it.

Sec. 26. That whenever the Legislature of Indiana shall pass a law giving their assent to, and confirming the provisions of this act with such alterations and modifications as shall be necessary and applicable to that part of said rail-road, and other works, as aforesaid, lying within the limits of the State of Indiana, then this act shall take effect and be in force.

Sec. 27. This act shall be taken and received in all courts, and by all judges and magistrates, and other public officers, as a public act; and all printed copies of the same, which may be printed by or under the authority of the General Assembly, shall be admitted as good evidence thereof, without any proof whatever.

Sec. 28. Whenever the dividends of said company shall exceed the rate of six per cent. per annum, the Legislature of this State may impose such reasonable tax upon the amount of said dividends, as may be received from other rail-road companies.

WILLIAM MEDILL,
Speaker pro tem. of the House of Representatives.

ELIJAH VANCE,
Speaker of the Senate.

March 14, 1836.

AN ACT

To lay out and establish a State road in the counties of Meigs and Athens.

Sec. 1. *Be it enacted by the General Assembly of the State of Ohio,* That John McQuigg, William Green, of Meigs county, and Isaac B. Lotridge, of Athens county, be, and they are hereby appointed commissioners, and Arthur Leidle, jr. surveyor, to lay out and establish a state road, to commence at the state road at or near Entminger mill, in Rutland township, Meigs county; thence to pass by or near Braley's salt-works; thence to Amos Baker's, in Salem township; thence to William Green's, jr. in Columbia township; thence to cross Big Raccoon creek, at, or near the Sucford; thence the nearest and best way to M'Arthurstown, in Athens county.

Sec. 2. That should either of the commissioners die, refuse to serve, or remove out of the county, the commissioners of the county in which such commissioners may have lived, shall fill such vacancy as often [as] they may occur.

Sec. 3. That the commissioners shall, in locating and establishing said road, be in all things governed, and shall receive such compensation, and in such manner, as is provided in the act entitled "An act defining the mode of laying out and establishing state roads," passed March 14th, 1831.

WILLIAM MEDILL,
Speaker pro tem. of the House of Representatives.

ELIJAH VANCE,
Speaker of the Senate.

March 14, 1836.

AN ACT

To incorporate the First Methodist Episcopal Church in the town of Westfield, in the county of Medina.

Sec. 1. *Be it enacted by the General Assembly of the State of Ohio,* That Ansel Brainard, Joseph S. Winston, Shalor Brainard, Lambert E. Cook,

George Cook, John Morey, jr., Neil Brainard, Truman Eastman, Joel White, and Ansel Brainard, senr., and their associates, be, and they are hereby created a body corporate and politic, to be known by the name and style of the "First Methodist Episcopal Church of Westfield," and as such shall remain and have perpetual succession; and by the name and style aforesaid, shall be capable in law and equity, of having, receiving, acquiring and holding, either by gift, grant, devise, or purchase, any estate, real, personal, [or] mixed, for the use of said corporation, and of transferring the same at pleasure: *Provided*, That the annual income of all such property shall not exceed one thousand dollars.

Sec. 2. That said corporation shall be capable in law or equity, by the name aforesaid, of suing and being sued, pleading and being impleaded, in any action or suit, in any court having competent jurisdiction; and they may have a common seal which they may alter, change, or renew, at pleasure.

Sec. 3. That the said corporation shall, on the second Monday of June next, and annually thereafter, shall elect three trustees, a treasurer, and such other officers as the church may deem necessary, who shall hold their offices for one year, and until their successors shall be elected: *Provided*, That if, from any cause, the aforesaid officers shall not be elected on the day appointed for the annual election, the church may elect its officers at any meeting of the corporation duly assembled.

Sec. 4. That all the elections by said corporation shall be by ballot; and the person or persons having a plurality of votes given for any office, shall be considered duly elected; and each and every male member of twenty-one years of age or upwards, shall have equal suffrage; and all the temporal concerns of said church shall be determined by a majority of the members present, at any meeting of the corporation duly assembled.

Sec. 5. That all meetings of the corporation, either for the election of officers or for other other purposes, shall be called by the trustees, or a majority of them, who shall cause public notice of the time, place, and purpose, of such meeting, to be given at least ten days previous to any such meeting.

Sec. 6. That the trustees, or a majority of them, shall have power and authority to make all contracts on behalf of the church, and to manage all pecuniary and prudential matters, pertaining to the good order, interest, and welfare of the corporation; and to make such rules, regulations, and by-laws, consistent with the constitution of the United States, and of this State, as they may deem advisable, from time to time, for their own government, and that of the corporation: *Provided, always*, That they make no by-laws, [or] pass any order for the imposing of any tax on the corporation.

Sec. 7. That the treasurer shall give bond with security, to the trustees, and their successors in office, in such sum as they may deem sufficient, conditioned for the faithful performance of the duties that may pertain to his office by the regulations and by-laws of the corporation.

Sec. 8. That original process against said corporation shall be by summons, which shall be served [by leaving] an attested copy thereof with the treasurer of the corporation, five days before the return day mentioned therein; and such service shall be deemed sufficient in law to bind said corporation.

Sec. 9. That Ansel Brainard, Joseph S. Winston, and Joel White, be, and they ard hereby appointed trustees until the first annual election, and until others are elected and qualified.

Sec. 10. That any future Legislature may modify, amend, or repeal this act.

WILLIAM MEDILL,
Speaker pro tem. of the House of Representatives.

ELIJAH VANCE,
Speaker of the Senate.

March 14, 1836.

AN ACT

To incorporate the Troy, Carlisle and Springfield Turnpike Company.

Sec. 1. *Be it enacted by the General Assembly of the State of Ohio,* That H. W. Culbertson, Thos. W. Mansfield, Alanson Morris, John G. Telford, E. T. Harker, Asa Coleman, George Keifer, Zenus Hart, Stephen Dye, and William I. Thomas, of the county of Miami; and William G. Serviss, Churchill W. Philips,   Betts, Samson Mason, Charles Cavilier, and Wm. Werden, of the county of Clark, be, and they are hereby created a body politic and corporate, by the name and style of "The Troy, Carlisle, and Springfield Turnpike Company;" and by that name they and their successors shall have perpetual succession, and all the privileges and immunities incident to a corporation; and may hold capital stock to the amount of fifty thousand dollars, and the increase and profits thereof; and may increase the same, if they think proper, to an amount, in all, not exceeding two hundred thousand dollars; and they are hereby vested with full power and authority to take, purchase, use, hold, occupy, enjoy, sell, convey and dispose of any estate, real, personal or mixed, which may be necessary or convenient for the prosecution of their works, or the transaction of their business; to contract and be contracted with, to sue and be sued, plead and be impleaded, answer and be answered unto, in any court of competent jurisdiction; and to have and use a common seal, and the same to break, alter or renew, at pleasure.

Sec. 2. That so soon as the company aforesaid shall have duly organized themselves, by written articles of association, recognizing this act, they may then proceed to open books for subscriptions to the capital stock of said company, at Troy, in the county of Miami, New Carlisle, and Springfield, in the county of Clark, and at such other places as they may deem proper, to receive the subscriptions to the stock of said company, in shares of twenty-five dollars each; which books shall be opened at such time, and under such regulations as shall be directed by the persons named in the first section of this act, or a majority of them.

Sec. 3. That whenever three hundred shares shall have been subscribed, it shall be the duty of the persons who may have received the subscriptions aforesaid, to call a meeting of the stockholders, by giving public notice thereof in some newspapers having general circulation in each of the counties of Miami, and Clark, not less than fifteen, nor more than thirty days previous thereto, for the purpose of electing from their own number nine directors; at which election, at least three of the persons named in the first section of this act shall be present, one of whom shall preside; all votes for directors shall be [by] ballot; each stockholder shall be entitled to one vote for each share he may own, not exceeding ten; and for every two shares above ten, one vote; which vote he may cast by himself or by proxy, under such regulations as may be prescribed by the by-laws of the company; and the directors thus elected shall immediately proceed to elect from their own body a president, whose duty it shall be to sign all obligations or contracts in behalf of the company.

Sec. 4. That after the first election, all elections for directors shall be on the first Monday in January, unless otherwise determined by the by-laws of said company; and the president and directors shall hold their offices for one year, and until their successors are chosen; they shall, in all cases, manage the concerns of the company; appoint such officers and agents as are necessary, from whom they may require an oath or affirmation; fill all necessary vacancies that may happen in their own body, until the next annual election; call special meetings of the stockholders, by giving notice, as before mentioned; make by-laws for the government of the company, not inconsistent with the constitution or laws of the United States, or of this State; keep a record of their proceedings relative to the company; and do all matters and things touching the concerns of the company contemplated, by this act; which record shall, at all times, be open to the inspection of any person interested.

Sec. 5. That if any stockholder shall neglect or refuse to pay any instalment, after sixty days notice of the time and place of payment, by advertisement in some newspapers having general circulation in said counties of Miami and Clark, it shall be the duty of the directors to collect the deficient instalment by suit, with cost and interest thereon, from the time said unpaid instalment had become due; and no delinquent stockholder shall have a right to transfer nor to vote at any meeting of the company, on any share or shares of said stock, for which he may be delinquent.

Sec. 6. That the said company shall have a right to lay out and survey their said road through any improved or unimproved lands, on the nearest and best route from the town of Troy, in the county of Miami, through New Carlisle, in Clark county, to some point on the National road, east of Springfield, in the county of Clark; and to take from the land so occupied by said road, when located, and surveyed as aforesaid, any stone, gravel, timber, or other materials, necessary to construct a good, secure and substantial road, as contemplated by this act, and the necessary bridges connected therewith; and in case sufficient materials cannot be procured on the land so as aforesaid located for said road, said company, or their agents shall have a right to enter upon any unimproved lands adjoining or in the vicinity of said road, and to dig, cut down, take and carry away so much stone, gravel, timber, or other materials, (not previous, cut down, taken, or appropriated by the owners to any particular use,) as may be necessary to enable said company to construct said road, and the necessary bridges; and if any difference should arise between the owner or owners of any ground from which such materials are taken, as aforesaid, and the agents of the company, respecting damages, it shall be determined by three disinterested freeholders, to be appointed by the commissioners of the county in which the subject of difference lies; who, taking into consideration whether the land be made really more or less valuable by the road passing through it, shall make out their assessment in writing, of the damages, if any; a copy of which shall be given to the proprietors of the land, and another copy to the agent of the company; and said agent shall pay, or offer to pay the owner of said land the amount of such assessed damages, before he shall enter upon or take any such ground or materials, other than to survey the road; and all expenses of such assessment of damages, if any are awarded, shall be paid by the company; but if no damages shall be awarded, then the expenses shall be paid by the person who had claimed damages.

Sec. 7.   That the president and directors of the Troy, Carlisle, and and Springfield Turnpike Company, shall cause the said road to be opened, not exceeding ninety feet wide, at least eighteen of which shall be made an artificial road, composed of stone, gravel, wood, or other suitable materials, well compacted together, in such manner as to secure a firm, substantial, and even road, rising in the middle, with a gradual arch, and shall maintain and keep the same in good repair; and in no case shall the ascent in the road be of greater elevation than five degrees.

Sec. 8.   That as soon as the said turnpike company shall have completed the road, as aforesaid, or any part thereof, not less than five miles, measuring from the corporation line at Troy aforesaid, and so, from time to time, as often as five miles of said road shall be completed, always measuring from the town of Troy aforesaid, an agent, to be appointed for that purpose by the Governor, if not otherwise appointed by the Legislature, shall, on application of the company, examine the same, and report his opinion, in writing, to the president of the company; and if such report shall state the road, or any five miles thereof to be completed, agreeably to the provisions of this act, the company may then erect a gate or gates, at suitable distances, and demand and receive of persons travelling on the same, the tolls allowed by this act.

Sec. 9.   That the following shall be the highest rates of tolls for each and every ten miles of said road, and in the same proportion for a greater or less distance, to wit: for every four wheeled carriage, drawn by two horses or oxen, twenty-five cents; for every horse or ox in addition, six and one-fourth cents; for every two wheeled carriage, drawn by two horses or oxen, eighteen and three-fourth cents; for every horse or ox in addition, six and one-fourth cents; for every sled or sleigh, drawn by two horses or oxen, twelve and a half cents; and for every horse or ox in addition, six and one-fourth cents; for every horse and rider, six and one-fourth cents; for every horse, mule or ass, led or driven, six months old or upwards, three cents; for neat cattle, six months old or upwards, twenty-five cents twenty-five cents for every score, and for a less number in proportion; for every score of sheep or hogs, twelve and a half cents; for every four wheeled pleasure carriage, drawn by two horses, thirty-seven and a half cents; for every horse in addition, twelve and a half cents; for every two wheeled pleasure carriage, drawn by one horse, twenty-five cents; for every horse in addition, twelve and a half cents; for every four wheeled carriage, drawn by one horse, eighteen and three-fourth cents: *Provided,* That all persons going to or returning from public worship, and all militiamen going to and returning from their respective muster grounds, and all persons, having the qualifications of electors, in going to and returning from elections, shall pass free of tolls.

Sec. 10. That if any person or persons, using said roads, shall, with intent to defraud said company, or to avoid the payment of toll, pass through any private gate or bars, or along any other ground near to any turnpike gate which shall be erected pursuant to this act, with intent to evade or lessen the payment of such toll; or if any person shall take another person off of said road, with intent to defraud said turnpike company; each and every one concerned in such fraudulent practices, shall, for every such offence, forfeit and pay to the company the sum of five dollars, without stay of execution, to be recovered with costs of suit, before any justice of the peace in any county through which said road may pass: *Provided,* That nothing in this act shall be so construed as to prevent persons using said road between the gates for common purposes.

Sec. 11. That if the said company shall fail to keep said road in good repair for ten days in succession, and complaint thereof be made to a justice of the peace in the county in which said road is out of repair, it shall be his duty forthwith to summons three disinterested freeholders to examine the same; and he shall give notice to the toll-gatherer at the nearest gate, of the time when said freeholders will proceed to examine the same; and the said freeholders, after having taken an oath or affirmation to act impartially, shall proceed to examine said road; and if the same is out of repair, they shall certify it to the justice of the peace, who shall immediately transmit a copy of such certificate to the nearest toll gatherer where such defective part of the road lies; and from the time of receiving such notice, no toll shall be demanded or received for such part of the road, until the same shall be put in complete repair, under the penalty of five dollars for every such offence; to be recovered with costs, of said company, on the complaint and for the use of the person aggrieved.

Sec. 12. That if any person shall wantonly or wilfully destroy, or in any manner injure or obstruct any part of said road, or any gate thereon, otherwise than in the just and lawful use thereof, every such person shall, on conviction thereof, before any justice of the peace of the county, be liable to a fine of not more than fifty, nor less than five dollars, for every such offence, to be recovered in the proper form of action, at the suit of the State of Ohio, the one half thereof to go to the county in which such offence may have been committed, and the other half to the informer; and shall moreover be liable for all damages to the company, and for all injuries occasioned to other persons, in consequence of any such unlawful damage to, or obstruction of the said road; and all damages and costs awarded under this section, by a court of competent jurisdiction, shall be collected forthwith, without stay of execution.

Sec. 13. That the said company shall put up a post or stone at the end of each mile, with the number of miles from the town of Troy, fairly cut or painted thereon; and also in a conspicuous place near each gate, shall be placed a board, with the rates of toll painted thereon, and directions to keep to the right.

Sec. 14. That any person wilfully defacing or destroying any guide board, mile post or stone, or painted list of rates of toll, erected on said road, shall, on conviction thereof before a justice of the peace, be fined not less than five nor more than fifty dollars, with cost of prosecution, to be recovered at the suit of any person, for the use of said company.

Sec. 15. That if any toll-gatherer on said road shall unreasonably detain any passengers after the toll has been paid or offered to be paid, or shall demand or receive greater toll than is by this act allowed, he shall, for every such offence, forfeit and pay a sum not less than five nor exceeding fifty dollars; to be recovered with costs of suit, before any justice of the peace having competent jurisdiction thereof: *Provided, however,* That no suit or action shall be brought against any person or persons, for any penalty incurred under this section, unless the same shall be commenced within three weeks from the time of incurring the same; and the defendant or defendants in such suit or action, may plead the general issue, and give this act and the special matter of evidence.

Sec. 16. That if said company shall not, within three years from the passage of this act, proceed to carry on said road, according to the true intent and meaning of this act, then in that case, it shall be lawful for the Legislature to resume all the rights, liberties and privileges granted by this act.

Sec. 17. That if said company shall at any time use their funds for banking purposes, or any other purpose than that of making and keeping in repair said road, and dividing the profits arising therefrom amongst the stockholders thereof, then the privileges granted by this act shall cease and determine; and the stockholders shall be liable in their private and individual capacity for any debt contracted by such company.

WILLIAM MEDILL,
Speaker pro tem. of the House of Representatives.

ELIJAH VANCE,
Speaker of the Senate.

March 14, 1836.

AN ACT

To incorporate the First Universalist Society of Geneva, Harpersfield, Austinburg, and Saybrook, in Ashtabula county.

Sec. 1. *Be it enacted by the General Assembly of the State of Ohio,* That Anne Bond, Sailor Seymore, David Crosby, John M. Baldwin, George Turner, Aaron Wheeler, Philander Knapp, John B. Bartholomew, Orren Blakely, Gabriel C. Vanroper, and I. Thompson, and such other persons as may hereafter be associated with them, are, for the time being, hereby created a body corporate and politic, by the name and style of "The First Universalist Society of Geneva, Harpersfield, Austinburg, and Saybrook;" and as such shall remain and have perpetual succession.

72—L

Sec. 2. That said corporation, by the name and style aforesaid, shall be capable in law and equity, of having, receiving, acquiring and holding, either by gift, grant, devise or purchase, any estate, real, personal, or mixed, for the use of said corporation: *Provided*, That the annual income of such property shall not exceed six hundred dollars.

Sec. 3. That the members of said corporation, and their associates, shall meet on the first Monday of May, one thousand eight hundred and thirty-six, and on that day annually thereafter, for the purpose of electing three trustees, a secretary and treasurer; and of making such rules, regulations and by-laws for their government, and for that of the corporation, as they may deem advisable: *Provided*, That if at any time an election of officers shall not take place on the day herein above named, the corporation shall not thereby be dissolved; but the officers previously chosen, shall serve until their successors are elected: *And provided, also*, That such by-laws, rules and regulations be consistent with the laws and constitution of [the] United States and of this State.

Sec. 4. That the trustees, or a majority of them, may call a meeting of said society, at any time, by giving ten days previous thereof, by posting notice thereof in three of the most public places in Geneva, Harpersfield, Austinburg and Saybrook.

Sec. 5. That all elections shall be ballot, and determined by a majority of votes.

Sec. 6. That any future Legislature shall have power to amend or repeal this act: *Provided*, Such amendment or repeal, shall in no way, affect the title to any property acquired or conveyed under its provisions.

WILLIAM MEDILL,
Speaker pro tem. of the House of Representatives.

ELIJAH VANCE,
Speaker of the Senate.

March 14, 1836.

AN ACT

To authorize a loan of credit, by the State of Ohio, to the Mad River and Lake Erie Rail-Road Company.

Sec. 1. *Be it enacted by the General Assembly of the State of Ohio,* [That] the credit of the State of Ohio is hereby loaned and granted to the Mad River and Lake Erie Rail-road Company, for the sum of two hundred thousand dollars, which sum shall be delivered to the President and Directors of said Company, in bonds, or negotiable scrip of the State of Ohio, redeemable, at the pleasure of the State, after twenty years, and bearing an annual interest not exceeding six per cent.; and for the payment of said bonds, or scrip, with the annual interest thereon, the faith of the State is hereby pledged.

Sec. 2. It shall be the duty of the Commissioners of the Canal Fund, to prepare and deliver to the Mad River and Lake Erie Rail-road Company, the bonds or scrip, for the above sum, as the same may be needed for the purposes of said company, specifying therein the rate of interest, and where payable; and the said company shall be liable and bound to provide for the payment of said interest, at the times and the places so specified, and to repay the principal when the same shall be redeemable by the State: the receipt of said bonds, or any part thereof, by said railroad company, shall operate as a specific pledge of the capital stock, estate, tolls and profits of said rail-road company, to the State of Ohio, to secure the re-payment of the sum advanced in pursuance of this act; written evidence of such pledge, duly executed, shall be delivered to the Commissioners of the Canal Fund, accompanied with such security as they may approve, for the faithful expenditure of the principal, and the punctual payment of the interest thereon.

Sec. 3. Before delivering any part of the bonds above provided for, the Commissioners of the Canal Fund shall be satisfied that the said company has vested and expended a sufficient amount of their capital to make the State secure in the loan herein authorized, and the commissioners shall advance one hundred thousand dollars of the above sum, as soon as *bona fide* subscriptions to the amount of five hundred thousand dollars have been made, and two hundred and fifty thousand thereof actually expended and vested in the construction of said road, and the purchase of land for the same; and the remaining one hundred thousand dollars, so soon as capital stock to the amount of one million of dollars has been sold, and two hundred and fifty thousand dollars, in addition to the above mentioned two hundred and fifty thousand dollars paid in and expended from the resources of said company, upon said road, and the completion of the road from Lake Erie to Dayton thereby secured; and if the said company shall at any time fail in the punctual payment of the interest on the sums advanced, or in repaying the principal when redeemable, the Governor shall be authorized, on behalf of the State, to take possession of the works of the said company, and place them under the charge of such officers, or board of commissioners, as may, by law, be provided, for the promotion of public works, and to hold the same until, by the tolls and profits, or by a sale of the works, the State shall be fully reimbursed.

WILLIAM MEDILL,
Speaker pro tem. of the House of Representatives.

ELIJAH VANCE,
Speaker of the Senate.

March 14, 1836.

AN ACT

To incorporate the Circleville, Washington, Wilmington and Cincinnati Rail-road Company.

Sec. 1. *Be it enacted by the General Assembly of the State of Ohio,* That Andrew Huston, John L. Green, Joseph Doddridge, William Foresman, sen. George Radcliff, and George Tullman, of Pickaway county; James Carrothers, Wade Loofborough, Joseph Bell, James Shivers, Jacob Jamison, Norman F. Jones, of the county of Fayette; Samuel H. Hale,

Thomas Palmer, Wm. Hadley, Isaiah Morris, J. B. Posey, and Lawrence
Fitzhugh, of Clinton county; Arthur M. Neal, Jonathan H. Jackson, William
Sloan, Samuel Hill, Thomas Boyer, and Benjamin Brown, of Clermont
county; Jacob Strader, Levi Buckingham, jun. Timothy Day, jun.
Oliver Jones, Clayton Webb, and Moses Dawson, of Hamilton county, together
with such other persons as may thereafter become associated with
them, in the manner hereinafter prescribed, their successors and assigns,
be, and they are hereby enacted a body corporate and politic, by the name
of "The Circleville, Washington, Wilmington and Cincinnati Rail road
Company;" and by that name shall be and are hereby made capable in
law to have, hold, purchase, receive and possess, enjoy and retain, to them
and their successors, all such lands, tenements, and hereditaments, with
their appurtenances, as shall be necessary or in any wise convenient for
the transaction of their business, and such as may in good faith be conveyed
to them, by way of security, or in payment of debts, and the same to
sell, grant, rent, or in any manner dispose of; to sue and be sued, implead
and be impleaded, answer and be answered, defend and be defended, in
courts of record, or in any other place whatever; and also to make, have,
and use a common seal, and the same to alter, break or renew, at pleasure;
and they shall be, and are hereby invested with all the powers and
privileges which are by law incident to corporations of a similar nature,
and which are necessary to carry into effect the objects of this association;
and if either of the persons named in this section shall die, refuse
or neglect to exercise the powers and discharge the duties hereby created,
it shall be the duty of the remaining persons hereinbefore named, or
a majority of them, to appoint some suitable person to fill such vacancy
or vacancies so often as the same shall occur.

Sec. 2. That said corporation shall be, and they are hereby vested
with the right to construct a single or double rail-way or road, from Circleville,
in Pickaway county, by way of Washington, Fayette county, through
Wilmington, Clinton county, thence to the city of Cincinnati, in Hamilton
county, by such route and other intermediate points, as said company think
best; and the said company shall have the right to carry persons and property
on said road, when constructed, by the force of steam, animal or
mechanical, or other power, or any combination of them, which the company
may choose to employ.

Sec. 3. That the capital stock of said corporation shall be one million
of dollars, and shall be divided into shares of fifty dollars each; and
five dollars on each share shall be paid at the time of subscribing.

Sec. 4. That the above named persons, or a majority of them, are authorized
to open books for receiving subscriptions to the capital stock of
said company, and shall prescribe the form of such subscriptions; which
books shall be opened within one year from the passing of this act, at such
place or places as they may deem expedient, giving thirty days notice in
one or more newspapers in each county, through which said road
will pass, of the time and place, or times and places of opening said books:
and said books shall be kept open at least ten days.

Sec. 5. That so soon as said stock, or fifty thousand dollars thereof,
shall have been subscribed, the above named persons, or a majority of
them, shall give like notice for a meeting of the stockholders to choose di-

rectors, at some time and place, at least twenty days thereafter; and if, at such time and place, the holders of one half or more of said stock subscribed shall attend, in person or by lawful proxy, they shall proceed to choose from the stockholders, by ballot, twelve directors, each share of capital stock entitling the owner to one vote; and at such election, the persons named in the first section of this act, or those appointed by its provisions to fill vacancies which may have occurred, or any three of them, if no more be present, shall be inspectors of such election, and shall certify in writing, signed by them, or a majority of them, what persons are elected directors; and if two or more have an equal number of votes, such inspectors shall determine by lot, which of them shall be director or directors, to complete the number required, and shall certify the same in like manner; and said inspectors shall appoint the time and place of holding the first meeting of directors, at which meeting seven shall form a board competent to transact all business of the company; and thereafter a new election of directors shall be made annually, at such time and place as the directors shall appoint, by giving thirty days previous notice, in manner aforesaid; and if no election be made on the day appointed, said company shall not be dissolved, but such election may be made at any time appointed by the by-laws of said company; and directors chosen at any election shall remain directors until others are chosen; and directors chosen at any election shall, so soon thereafter as may be, choose of their own number one person to be president, and another to be treasurer of such company, and another to be secretary of said company; and from time to time may choose such other officers as by their by-laws they may designate as necessary: *Provided*, No person shall be a director of such company, who is not a citizen of the State of Ohio.

Sec. 6. That the directors may require payment on the subscription to the capital stock, at such times, in such proportions, and on such conditions, as they shall deem fit, under penalty of forfeiture of all previous payments thereon or otherwise: *Provided*, They shall never require the payment to be made at any place out of the counties, through which said road shall pass; and such directors shall, at least thirty days previous to the appointed time of such required payment, give notice thereof, in the manner provided in the fourth section of this act, for giving notice of the opening of the books of subscription for the stock of said company.

Sec. 7. That the directors of said company shall have power to make from time to time, all needful rules, regulations and by-laws, not inconsistent with the constitution and laws of the United States, or of this State, touching the business of said company, and to determine the number of tracks or rail-ways upon said road, and the width thereof, and the description of carriages which may be used thereon; to regulate the time and manner in which passengers or goods shall be transported thereon, and the manner of collecting tolls for such transportation; and to fix penalties for the breach of any such rule, regulation or by-law, and to direct the mode and condition of transferring the stock of said company; and penalties provided for by said by-laws, may be sued for by any person or persons authorized thereto, in the name of said company, and recovered in an action of debt, before any court having jurisdiction of the amount; and said company may erect and maintain toll houses, and such other buildings and fixtures, for the accommodation of those using said road, and of themselves, as they may deem in any wise necessary for their interest or convenience.

Sec. 8. That said company shall have a right to enter upon any lands, to survey and lay down said road, not exceeding one hundred feet wide, and to take any materials necessary for the construction of said road; and whenever any lands or materials shall be taken for the construction of said road, and the same shall not be given or granted to said company, and the owners thereof do not agree with said company, as to the compensation to be paid therefor, the person or persons claiming compensation as aforesaid, or if the owner or owners thereof are minors, insane persons, or married women, then the guardian or guardians of said minor or minors, and insane persons, and the husbands of such married women may select for themselves an arbitrator, and the said company shall select one arbitrator, and the two thus selected shall take to themselves a third, who shall be sworn and paid, as arbitrators in other cases; and the three, or a majority of them, shall award as arbitrators between the parties, and render copies of their award to each of the parties, in writing, from which award either party may appeal to the court of common pleas for the county in which such lands or materials may have been situate; and in all cases where compensation shall in any manner be claimed for lands, it shall be the duty of the arbitrators and the court, to estimate any advantage which the location and construction of said road may be to the claimant for such compensation, and the value of such advantage, if any, shall be set off against the compensation so claimed of said company: and appeals in such cases shall, when taken, be in all respects proceeded in as appeals in other cases to said court, and be brought into said court, by filing the award with the clerk of said court, whose duty it shall be to enter the same on the docket of said court, setting down the claimant or claimants as plaintiff, and said company as defendant; and when the valuation, so ascertained, shall be paid or tendered by said company, said company shall have the same right to retain, own, hold and possess said materials, and the use and occupation of said lands for the purposes of said road, as fully and absolutely, as if the same had been granted and conveyed to said company by deed.

Sec. 9. That the said company may construct the said rail-road across or upon any public road, highway, stream of water or water course, if the same shall be necessary; but the said company shall restore such lands, road, highway, stream of water or water course, to its former state, or in a sufficient manner so as not to impair the usefulness of such road, highway, water or water course, to the owner or to the public. without unnecessary delay; or when it shall be necessary to pass through the land of any individual, it shall also be their duty to provide for such individual proper wagon ways across said road, from one part of his land to another, without unnecessary delay.

Sec. 10. That if said company should neglect to provide proper wagon ways across said road, or to comply with the provisions of the preceding section of this act, it shall be lawful for any individual to sue said company, before any court having competent jurisdiction, and to be entitled to such damages as a jury may think him or her entitled to, for such neglect on the part of said company.

Sec. 11. That any rail-way company, now, or which may hereafter be chartered by law of this State, shall have power to join and unite with the road hereby incorporated, or any other rail-road branching from thence to any other part of the State, at any point which the directors of such company may think proper, on such terms as the directors of such companies may respectively agree; and in case of disagreement, then upon such terms as the Supreme Court may in chancery determine.

Sec. 12. That said company may demand and receive for tolls upon, and the transportation of persons, goods, produce, merchandize, or property of any kind whatsoever, transported by them along said rail-way, any sum not exceeding the following rates: on all goods, merchandize or property of any description whatsoever, transported by them, a sum not exceeding one and a half cents per mile, for toll; five cents on a ton per mile, for transportation; and for the transportation of passengers, not exceeding three cents per mile, for each passenger.

Sec. 12. That all persons paying the toll aforesaid, may, with suitable, and proper carriages, use and travel upon the said rail-road; always subject, however, to such rules and regulations, as said company are authorized to make, by the seventh section of this act.

Sec. 14. If any person or persons shall wilfully and maliciously injure the said rail-road, or any building, machine, or other work of the said corporation appertaining thereto, the person so offending shall forfeit and pay to the said corporation double the amount of damages sustained by means of such offence, injury or obstruction; to be recovered in the name of said corporation, with costs of suit, in any court having cognizance thereof.

Sec. 15. That so soon as the amount of money received for tolls and transportation on said road, or of any part thereof, according to the provisions of this act, shall exceed four per cent. on the amount of capital stock paid in, after deducting therefrom the expenses and liabilities of said company, the directors of said company shall make a dividend of such nett profits, among the stockholders, in proportion to their respective shares; and no contingent or accumulating fund, exceeding one per centum of the profits of said company, shall remain undivided for more than six months.

Sec. 16. That full right and privilege is hereby reserved to the State, or individuals, or any company incorporated by law of this State, to cross this road: *Provided,* That in crossing, no injury shall be done to the works of the company hereby incorporated.

Sec. 17. That the State shall have power at any time after the expiration of thirty-five years from the passage of this act, to purchase and hold the same for the use of the State, at a price not exceeding the original cost for the construction of said rail-road, and necessary permanent fixtures at the time of purchase, at fifteen per cent. thereon; of which cost an accurate statement, in writing, shall be submitted to the General Assembly, duly attested by the oath of the officers of said company, if the General Assembly shall require it.

Sec. 18. Whenever the dividends of said company shall exceed the rate of six per cent. per annum, the Legislature of this State may impose such reasonable taxes on the amount of such dividends, as may be received from other rail-road companies.

Sec. 19. That said corporation shall have power to locate and construct branch roads from the main route, to other towns, or places, in the several counties through which said road may pass.

Sec. 20. That if said rail road shall not be commenced within three years from the passage of this act, and shall not be completed within ten years thereafter, then this act to be void and of no effect.

Sec. 21. This act is hereby declared to be a public act, and shall be so construed in all courts of justice, and elsewhere.

W. MEDILL,
Speaker pro tem. of the House of Representatives.
ELIJAH VANCE,
Speaker of the Senate.

March 14, 1836.

AN ACT

To incorporate the Cleveland and Pittsburgh Rail-road Company.

Sec. 1. *Be it enacted by the General Assembly of the State of Ohio,* That Van R. Humphrey, Heman Oviatt, D. B. Bostwick, Darius Lyman, and Joseph De Wolf, of Portage county; Samuel Starkweather, Charles Whittlesey and John W. Willey, of Cuyahoga county; Robert Forbes, Isaac Wilson, James Robertson, John Wallis, George McCook and John Patrick, of Columbiana county, be, and they are hereby appointed commissioners, under the direction of a majority of whom, subscriptions may be received to the capital stock of the Cleveland and Pittsburgh Rail-road Company, hereby incorporated; and they, or a majority of them, may cause books to be opened in the counties of Cuyahoga, Portage and Columbiana, and at such other time and place as they may direct, for the purpose of receiving subscriptions to the capital stock of said company, after having given thirty days notice of the time and place of opening the same; and that, upon the first opening of the books, they shall be kept open for at least ten days in succession, from ten o'clock, A. M. until two o'clock, P. M.; and if, at the expiration of that period, such a subscription to the capital stock of said company as is necessary to its incorporation, shall not have been obtained, then said commissioners, or a majority of them, may cause said books to be opened, from time to time, after the expiration of said ten days, and for the space of three years thereafter; and if any of the said commissioners shall die, resign, or refuse to act during the continuance of the duties devolved upon them by this act, another or others may be appointed in his or their stead by the remaining commissioners, or a majority of them.

Sec. 2. That the capital stock of the Cleveland and Pittsburgh Railroad Company, shall be fifteen hundred thousand dollars, and shall be divided in shares of fifty dollars each; and it shall and may be lawful for said corporation to commence the construction of the said rail-road or way, and enjoy all the powers and privileges conferred by this act [as] soon [as] the sum of one hundred thousand dollars shall be subscribed to said stock.

Sec. 3. That all persons who shall become stockholders pursuant to this act, shall be, and they are hereby created a body corporate, and shall be and remain a corporation forever, under the name of the Cleveland and Pittsburgh Rail-road Company; and by that name, shall be capable in law of purchasing, holding, selling, leasing and conveying estates, real, personal and mixed, so far as the same shall be necessary for the purposes hereinafter mentioned, and no further; and shall have perpetual succession; and by said corporate name, may contract and be contracted with, sue and be sued, and may have and use a common seal, which they shall have power to alter or renew at their pleasure; and shall have, enjoy, and may exercise all the powers, rights and privileges, which corporate bodies may lawfully do, for the purposes mentioned in this act.

Sec. 4. That upon all subscriptions there shall be paid at the time of subscribing, to the said commissioners, or their agents appointed to receive such subscriptions, the sum of five dollars on every share subscribed; and the residue thereof shall be paid in such instalments, and at such times, as may be required by the president and directors of said company: *Provided*, No payment other than the first shall be demanded, until at least thirty days public notice of such demand shall have been given by said president and directors, in some newspaper of general circulation in the State of Ohio; and if any stockholder shall fail or neglect to pay any instalment, or part of said subscription thus demanded, for the space of sixty days next after the time the same shall be due and payable, the said president and directors, upon giving at least thirty days previous notice thereof, in manner aforesaid, may, and they are hereby authorized to sell at public vendue so many of the shares of the said delinquent stockholder or stockholders as shall be necessary to pay such instalment and the expenses of advertising and sale, and transfer the shares so sold to the purchasers; and the residue of the money arising from such sale, after paying such instalment and expense, shall be paid to said stockholders on demand.

Sec. 5. That at the expiration of ten days, for which the books are first opened, if seven hundred and fifty shares of said capital stock shall have been subscribed, or if not, as soon thereafter as the same shall be subscribed, if within three years after the first opening of the books, the said commissioners, or a majority of them, shall call a general meeting of the stockholders at such time and place as they may appoint, and shall give at least sixty days previous notice thereof; and at such meeting, the said commissioners shall lay the subscription books before the stockholders then and there present; and thereupon the said stockholders, or a majority of them, shall elect twelve directors by ballot; a majority of whom shall be competent to manage the affairs of said company; they shall have the power of electing a president of said company, either from among said directors or others, and of allowing him such compensation as they may deem proper; and in said election, and on all other occasions wherein a vote of the stockholders of said company is to be taken, each stockholder shall be allowed one vote for every share owned by it, him or her; and every stockholder may depute any other person to vote and act

73—L

for him or her, as his or their proxy; and the commissioners aforesaid, or any three of them, shall be judges of the first election of said directors.

Sec. 6. That to continue the succession of the president and directors of said company, twelve directors shall be chosen annually, on the third Monday in October, in every year, in the town of Ravenna, in the county of Portage, or at such other place as a majority of the directors shall appoint; and if any vacancy shall occur by death, resignation, or otherwise, of any president or director, before the year for which he was elected has expired, a person to fill such vacant place for the residue of the year may be appointed by the president and directors of said company, or [a] majority of them; and that the president and directors of said company shall hold and exercise their offices until a new election of president and directors; and that elections which are by this act, or the by-laws of the company, to be made on a particular day, or at a particular time, if not made on such a day or time, may be made at any time within thirty days thereafter.

Sec. 7. That a general meeting of the stockholders shall be held annually, at the time and place appointed for the election of president and directors of said company; that meetings may be called at any time during the interval between the said annual meetings, by the president and directors, or a majority of them, or by the stockholders owning at least one-fourth of the stock subscribed, upon giving at least thirty days public notice of the time and place of holding the same; and when any such meetings are called, by the stockholders, such notice shall specify the particular object of the call; and if, at any such called meeting, a majority in value of the stockholders of said company are not present in person or by proxy, such meeting shall be adjourned from day to day without transacting any business, for any time, not exceeding three days; and if, within said three days, stockholders, holding a majority in value of the stock subscribed, do not thus attend, such meeting shall be dissolved.

Sec. 8. That at the regular meetings of the stockholders of said company, it shall be the duty of the president and directors in office for the previous year, to exhibit a clear and distinct statement of the affairs of the company; that at any called meeting of the stockholders, a majority of those present in person or by proxy, may require similar statements from the president and directors, whose duty it shall be to furnish them when thus required; and that at all general meetings of the stockholders, a majority in value of all the stockholders of said company may remove from office any president or any of the directors of said company, and may appoint officers in their stead.

Sec. 9. That any president and director of said company, before he acts as such, shall swear or affirm, as the case may be, that he will well and truly discharge the duties of his said office to the best of his skill and judgment.

Sec. 10. That the said president and directors, or a majority of them, may appoint all such officers, engineers, agents or servants whatsoever, as they may deem necessary for the transaction of the business of the company, and may remove any of them at their pleasure; that they, or a majority of them, shall have the power to determine by contract the compensation of all engineers, officers, agents, or servants, in the employ of said company: and to determine by their by-laws the manner of adjusting and settling all accounts against the said company; and, also, the manner and evidence of transfers of stock in said company; and they, or a majority of them, shall have the power to pass all by-laws, which they may deem necessary or proper for exercising all the powers vested in the company hereby incorporated, and for carrying the objects of this act into effect: *Provided, only,* That such by-laws shall not be contrary to the laws of this State or of the United States.

Sec. 11. That the said corporation shall be, and they are hereby vested with the right to construct a double or single rail-road or way, from Cleveland, in the county of Cuyahoga, on the the most direct and least expensive route, to some point in the direction of Pittsburgh, on the State line between Ohio and Pensylvania, or on the Ohio river; to transport, take and carry property and persons upon the same, by the power and force and steam, of animals, or of any mechanical or other power, or of any combination of them, which the said corporation may choose to employ.

Sec. 12. That the president and directors of said company shall be, and they are hereby invested with all rights and powers necessary for the location, construction and repair of said road, not exceeding one hundred feet wide, with as many sets of tracks as the said president and directors may deem necessary, and they may cause to be made, contract with others for making the said rail-road, or any part of it; and they, or their agents, or those with whom they may contract for making any part of the same; may enter upon and use and excavate any land which may be wanted for the site of said road, or for any other purpose necessary and useful in the construction, or in the repair of said road or its works, and that they may build bridges, may fix scales and weights, may lay rails, may take and use any earth, timber, gravel, stone or other materials which may be wanted for the construction or repair of any part of said road, or any of its works; and may make and construct all works whatsoever, which may be necessary in the construction or repair of said road.

Sec. 13. That the president and directors of said company, or a majority of them, or any person authorized by them, or a majority of them, may agree with the owner or owners of any land, earth, timber, gravel or stone, or other materials, or any improvements which may be wanted for the construction or repair of said road, or any of their works, for the purchase or use, or occupation of the same; and if they cannot agree, or if the owner or owners, or any of them, be a married woman, insane person, or idiot, or out of the county in which the property wanted may lie, when such land and materials may be wanted, application may be made to any justice of the peace of such county, who shall thereupon issue his warrant, under his hand and seal, directed to the sheriff of said county or to some disinterested person if the sheriff shall be interested, requiring him to summon a jury of twelve men, inhabitants of said county, not related or in any wise interested, to meet on the land, or near to the other property or materials, to be valued on a day named in said warrant, not less than ten nor more than twenty days after the issuing of the same; and if, at the said time and place, any of said persons summoned do not attend, the said sheriff, or summoner shall immediately summon as many persons as may be necessary, with the persons in attendance, to furnish a pannel of twelve jurors in attendance; and from them, each party, or its, his or her, or their agent, the sheriff or summoner, for him, her, it or them, may strike off three jurors, and the remaining six shall act as a jury of inquest of damages; and before they act as such, the said summoner or sheriff shall administer to each of them an oath or affirmation, as the case may be, that they will faithfully and impartially value the damages which the owner or owners will sustain by use or occupation of the same, required by said company; and the jury estimating the damages, if for the ground occupied by said road, shall take into the estimate the benefits resulting to said owner or owners, by reason of said road passing through or upon the land of such owner or owners, towards the extinguishment of such claim for damages; and the said jury shall reduce their inquisition to writing, and shall sign and seal the same; and it shall then be returned to the clerk of the court of common pleas for said county, and by such clerk filed in his office, and shall be confirmed by the said court at its next session, if no sufficient cause to the contrary be shown; and when confirmed, shall be recorded by said clerk, at the expense of said company; but if set aside, the court may direct another inquisition to be taken in the manner above prescribed; and such inquisition shall describe the property taken, or the bounds of the land condemned; and such valuation, when paid or tendered to the owner or owners of said property, or his, her, or their legal representatives, shall entitle said company to the full right to said personal property, and the use and occupation of said landed property, for the purposes of said road, thus valued, as fully as if it had been conveyed by the owner or owners of the same; and the valuation, if not received when tendered, may, at any time thereafter, be received from the company without cost, by the owner or owners, his, her, or their legal representative or representatives; and that such sheriff, or summoner, and jurors, shall be entitled to demand and receive from the said company, the same fees, as are allowed for like services, in cases of fixing the valuation of real estate, previous to sale under execution.

Sec. 14. That whenever in the construction of said road, it shall be necessary to cross or intersect any established road or way, it shall be the duty of the said president and directors of said company so to construct the said rail-road across such established road or way, as not to impede the passage or transportation of persons or property along the same, or when it shall be necessary to pass through the land of any individual, it shall also be their duty to provide for such individual proper wagon ways across said road, from one part of his land to another, without delay.

Sec. 15. That if said company should neglect to provide proper wagon ways across said road, as required by the fourteenth section of this act, it shall be lawful for any individual to sue said company, and to be entitled to such damages, as a jury may think him, or her, entitled to, for such neglect on the part of said company.

Sec. 16. That if it shall be necessary for such company, in the selection of the route, or construction of the road to be by them laid out and constructed, or any part of it, to connect the same with, or to use any turnpike road, or bridge, made or erected by any company or persons incorporated, or authorized by any law of this State, it shall be lawful for the said president and directors, and they are hereby authorized, to contract or agree with any such other corporation or persons, for the right to use such road or bridge, or for the transfer of any of the corporate or other rights or privileges of such corporation or persons, to the said : company hereby incorporated; and every such other incorporation, or persons incorporated by, or acting under the laws of this State, is, and are hereby authorized to make such an agreement, contract, or transfer, by and through the agency of the person authorized by their respective acts of incorporation, to exercise their corporate powers, or by such persons as by any law of this State, are entrusted with the management and direction of said turnpike road or bridge, or of any of the rights and privileges aforesaid; and any contract, agreement or transfer, made in pursuance of the power and authority hereby granted, when executed, by the several parties under their respective corporate seals, or otherwise legally authenticated, shall vest in the company hereby incorporated, all such road, part of road, rights and privileges, and the right to use and enjoy the same, as fully, to all intents and purposes, as they now are, or might be used and exercised by the said corporation, or persons in whom they are now vested.

Sec. 17. That the said president and directors shall have power to purchase with the funds of the company, and place on any rail-road constructed by them, under this act, all machines, wagons, vehicles, or carriages of any description whatsoever, which they may deem necessary or proper, for the purpose of transportation on said road; and that they shall have power to charge for tolls upon, and the transportation of persons, goods, produce, merchandize, or property of every description whatsoever, transported by them along said rail-way, any sum not exceeding the following rates: on all goods, merchandize, or property of any description whatsoever, transported by them, a sum not exceeding one and a half cents per mile for toll, and five cents per mile per ton for transportation, on all goods, produce, merchandize, or property of any description whatsoever, transported by them or their agents; and for the transportation of passengers, not exceeding three cents per mile for each passenger; and it shall be lawful for any other company or any person or persons whatsoever, paying the tolls aforesaid, to transport any persons, merchandize, produce or property of any description whatsoever, along said road or any part thereof; and the said road, with all their works, improvements, and profits, and all machinery on said road for transportation are hereby vested in said company, incorporated by this act, and their successors forever; and the shares of the capital stock of said company shall be deemed and considered personal property, transferable by assignment, agreeably to the by-laws of said company.

Sec. 18. That any other rail road company now or hereafter to be chartered by law of this State, may join and connect said road with the road hereby contemplated, and run cars upon the same, under the rules and regulations of the Cleveland and Pittsburgh Rail-road Company, as to the construction and speed of said cars; and full right and privilege is hereby reserved to the State, or the citizens, or any company incorporated by authority of this State, to cross the rail-road hereby incorporated: *Provided,* That in so crossing, no injury shall be done to the works of the company hereby incorporated.

Sec. 19. That the said president and directors shall, semi-annually, declare and make such dividend as they may deem proper, of the nett profits arising from the resources of said company, deducting the probable amount of outstanding debts and the necessary current and contingent expenses, and that they shall divide the same amongst the stockholders of said company in proportion to their respective shares.

Sec. 20. That if any person or persons, shall wilfully, or by any means whatsoever, injure, impair, or destroy any part of said rail road, constructed by said company under this act, or any of the work, buildings, or machinery of said company, such person or persons so offending shall, each of them, for every such offence, forfeit and pay to the said company a sum not exceeding three fold the damages; which may be recovered in the name of the company, by an action of debt, in the court of common pleas for the county wherein the offence shall be committed: and shall also be subject to an indictment in said court, and upon conviction of such offence shall be punished by fine and imprisonment, at the discretion of the court.

Sec. 21. That if said rail road shall not be commenced in three years from the passage of this act, and shall not be finished within fifteen years from the time of the commencement thereof, then this act to be null and void.

Sec. 22. That if the Legislature of this State shall, after the expiration of thirty-five years from the passage of this act, make provision, by law, for the re-payment to said company of the amount expended by them in the construction of said rail-road, and the value of the necessary permanent fixtures thereto at the time, with an addition of fifteen per cent. thereon, together with interest on the cost of the road, at the rate of six per cent. per annum, unless the dividends shall have amounted to six per cent. per annum; of which expenditure an accurate statement in writing, attested by the oaths or affirmations of the officers of said company, shall be submitted to the General Assembly, if required; then said road and fixtures shall rest in and become the property of the State of Ohio.

Sec. 23. Whenever the dividends of said company shall amount to a sum not exceeding the amount of six per cent. per annum upon the cost of said road, and the necessary expenses of the same, the Legislature of this State may impose such reasonable taxes on the amount of such dividends as may be received from other rail-road companies.

WILLIAM MEDILL,
Speaker pro tem. of the House of Representatives.
ELIJAH VANCE,
Speaker of the Senate.

March 14, 1836.

AN ACT

To incorporate the First Presbyterian Church of Washington, in the county of Fayette.

Sec. 1. *Be it enacted by the General Assembly of the State of Ohio,* That Norman F. Jones, James N. Wilson, Ellis B. Stockdale, Robert Robinson, Thomas M. Garaugh, John Wilson, jr. James Pollock, and Isaac Templin, and their associates, are hereby constituted a body corporate and politic, in perpetual succession, by the name and style of the "First Presbyterian Church of Washington;" with full power to hold estate, real, personal, or mixed, by deed, grant, donation, or otherwise: *Provided,* The annual income shall not exceed two thousand dollars; may sue and be sued, plead and be impleaded, defend and be defended, in any court having competent jurisdiction, by the name and style aforesaid; to have a common seal, which they may alter at pleasure; to possess all power necessary to adopt by-laws, rules and regulations for the government of their corporate concerns: *Provided,* Said by-laws, rules and regulations be consistent with the laws and constitution of this State, and of the United States.

Sec. 2. That the corporation shall hold an election on the first Saturday of April annually, by giving ten days notice thereof by advertisement, at which time they shall elect three trustees, who shall manage the concerns of said corporation, and shall hold their offices for the term of one year. and until their successors are elected; and for, and on behalf of said church, said trustees shall receive titles to real estate, and sell and convey the same as the case may require; and shall keep a record of their proceedings, and render an account of the same when required so to do, by the session of said church.

Sec. 3. That Norman F. Jones, James N. Wilson, and Ellis B. Stockdale, the present deacons, of the said church of Washington, and such other deacons as said church may from time to time appoint and ordain, according to the directory of the Presbyterian church in the United States of America, shall manage the concerns of said corporation until the election.

Sec. 4. That original process against this corporation shall be served by summons, which shall be served by leaving an attested copy with one or more of the trustees, at least five days before the return day thereof; and such service shall be deemed sufficient in law to bind the corporation.

Sec. 5. That any future Legislature shall have power to modify or repeal this act: *Provided,* Such modification or repeal shall not affect any title to any estate, real or personal, acquired or conveyed under its provisions.

WILLIAM MEDILL,
Speaker pro tem. of the House of Representatives.

ELIJAH VANCE,
Speaker of the Senate.

March 14, 1836.

To incorporate the town of Fairport.

Sec. 1. *Be it enacted by the General Assembly of the State of Ohio,* That so much of the township of Painesville, in the county of Geauga, as is comprised in the original town plat of Grandon, including Grand river, up from the mouth, to the north line of the village of Richmond, and thence through the centre of said river, as far up as said town plat extends; together with all such additions, as shall hereafter be made thereto, by the owners of land, in its vicinity, and recorded, be, and the same is hereby created a town corporate, by the name of Fairport.

Sec. 2. That the white male inhabitants of said town, having the qualifications of electors of members of the General Assembly, may meet on the first, or any succeeding Tuesday of April next, at any place within the limits of said town, which may be designated by notices, signed by three or more electors of Fairport, and posted up in three conspicuous places in said town, at least five days before such election, and on the first Tuesday of April, annually, thereafter, unless some other day be named by the by-laws of the corporation; and elect, by ballot, one mayor, one recorder, and five councillors, who shall be freeholders, residing within the limits of said town, and who shall hold their offices for one year, and until their successors are chosen and qualified; and they shall constitute the "Town Council," any four of whom, including either the mayor or recorder, shall constitute a quòrum for the transaction of business.

Sec. 3. That at such election the electors shall choose *viva voce,* two judges and a clerk, who shall each take an oath faithfully to discharge the duties required of them by this act, and at all subsequent elections the councillors, or any two of them, shall be judges, and the recorder clerk; and at all such elections the polls shall be opened between the hours of ten and eleven o'clock A. M. and close at three o'clock P. M. of said day; and at the close of the polls the votes shall be publicly counted by the councillors present, and a true statement thereof by one of them proclaimed; and the clerk shall make a record thereof, and deliver to each person elected, or leave at his usual place of residence, within five days thereafter, a written notice of his election; and the person so notified, shall, within five thereafter, take an oath or affirmation to support the constitution of the United States, and of this State, and also an oath of office; a certificate of which shall be deposited with the recorder, and by him preserved.

Sec. 4. That the mayor, recorder, and councillors, shall be a body corporate and politic, with perpetual succession, by the name of "The Corporation of Fairport," and shall be capable of acquiring and holding estates and property, real, personal and mixed, which they may sell or dispose of, in such manner as they, or a majority of them, may deem proper; and they may have and use a common seal, which they may alter at pleasure; may sue and be sued, plead and be impleaded, answer and be answered, in any court of law or equity in this State; and when any action is commenced against them, it shall be by summons, an attested copy of which shall be left with the recorder, or in the absence, at his usual place of residence, at least ten days before the return day thereof.

Sec. 5. That the mayor, recorder, and a majority of the councillors, shall have power to make all by-laws and ordinances necessary for the health, safety, or comfort of said town or corporation; may appoint a treasurer, town marshal, health and fire officers, and watchmen, and all other subordinate officers necessary to execute their by-laws and regulations; and may remove said officers at pleasure; may prescribe their duties and define their powers; take such bonds, with surety, and for such amounts, as they may deem proper, to secure the faithful performance of the duties assigned them by this act, and the several by-laws and ordinances made under its provisions; may fix and establish the fees of such officers as are not established by this act; may impose fines, not exceeding two dollars, for refusing to accept any office in said corporation.

Sec. 6. That said corporation, or that a majority of them, mentioned in the previous section, shall have power to prescribe fines and penalties for the delinquencies of any officer or agent of the corporation; to restrain vagrants, or other persons soliciting alms, or subscriptions; to suppress and restrain all disorderly and gaming houses; to abate nuisances; to prevent and punish immoderate driving within the town; to regulate or prohibit public bathing in the town; to prevent and remove all and any obstructions in the streets, highways, or side-walks within the town; to provide for clearing Grand river of drift wood or other obstructions, and to prevent any filling up or encroachment thereon; to regulate the keeping and carrying of gun-powder, and any other highly combustible material; to establish, alter, and regulate markets; to regulate the vending of provisions, fuel, lumber, and other commodities in said town, and the weighing of such as should be weighed, and the measuring of such as should be measured; to designate the places where kilns of brick or lime may be burned, and where slaughter-houses may be kept, and regulate the latter; to regulate carters, porters, and coachmen, and the fees to be paid, and compensation to be received by them; to regulate or restrain the running at large of horses, cattle, swine, and dogs, and to impose a tax on the owners of the latter; to light the streets; to establish and preserve public wells and reservoirs of water, and to prevent the waste of water, and contract for a supply thereof; to regulate the burial of the dead, and compel the keeping and return of bills of mortality; to regulate all taverns, porter-houses, and places where spirituous liquors are sold by less quantities than one quart; and all houses or places of public entertainment, all exhibitions and public shows, with exclusive power to grant, refuse or revoke licenses therefor, and to fix the price of such licenses; to establish the boundaries of all streets within the corporate limits, and to pave or grade the same; and to levy such tax as may be necessary therefor, and to equalize such tax according to the benefits derived and injuries sustained by such grading; to prevent the firing of crackers, or other fire-works, and the discharge of fire arms in said town; to regulate wharves, wharfage, and the mooring of vessels in the harbor, and to remove all obstructions on the margin thereof; to appoint a harbor master, with the usual powers; to prevent fishing lights, and regulate fires on board of vessels and steam-boats; and for the violation of any by-laws, ordinances or regulations, by them made, under the authority of this act, the said corporation may prescribe any penalty, not exceeding one hundred dollars, and provide for the prosecution, recovery and collection thereof, and for the imprisonment of such

74—L

offender, in case of non-payment of the penalty: *Provided*, That no by-law, made under the provisions of this act, shall take effect until the smae shall have been posted up at three public places within the said town of Fairport; at least ten days of which posting, a recorded certificate of the officers, posting up the same shall be conclusive evidence.

Sec. 7. Whenever any vacancy shall occur in any office, either by death, resignation, legal disability to act, or removal beyond the limits of the corporation, the town council may fill such vacancy for the remainder of the term of the disqualified officer, from their own body or otherwise: *Provided*, The vacancy be filled by a person having the qualifications of an elector; and the person or persons so appointed shall become qualified to act in the same manner as is required of officers elected.

Sec. 8. That the mayor, or a majority of the councillors, may call a meeting of the town council, whenever in his or their opinion the same may be necessary.

Sec. 9. The mayor shall keep the seal of the corporation; shall be a conservator of the peace within the limits of the town, and shall therein have all the powers and jurisdiction of a justice of the peace, in civil cases, and in criminal matters his jurisdiction shall be co-extensive with the county, and process by him issued shall be directed to the marshal; he may take acknowledgment of deeds, solemnize marriages, and do and perform within said town, all acts which a justice of the peace may lawfully do; he shall receive the same fees as justices of the peace are entitled to receive for all similar services; he shall give bond with surety, as is required of a justice of the peace; and appeals may be had from his decisions to the court of common pleas, in the same manner as appeals are taken from the judgments of justices of the peace; and he shall keep a docket, and in all respects be governed by the laws allowing writs o' *certiorari* as a justice of the peace; and he shall be, *ex officio*, a notary public, with the right to demand the fees fixed by law for such officer.

Sec. 10. The marshal shall serve and return all process to him directd by the mayor, in the same manner as constables are required to serve and return process to them directed by justices of the peace; his power to execute civil process shall be limited to the bounds of Fairport, but in criminal matters his power shall be as extensive as that of a constable i: like cases; and before he enters upon the duties of his office, he shall giv bond to such amount and with such security, as shall be approved by the town council, conditioned for the faithful performace of his duties, and for the payment of all moneys which may come into his hands as mashal, for the benefit of the corporation or others.

Sec. 11. It shall be the duty of the recorder to keep an acurate record of all the proceedings of the town council; which record shall at all times be open to the inspection of the electors of said town, and the recorder shall preside at all meetings of the town council in ne absence of the mayor, and shall perform such other duties as shall be equired of him by the by-laws and ordinances of said corporation.

Sec. 12. That the town council may annually levy a tax, for corporation purposes, not otherwise provided for, on property within said town, returned on the grand levy, made subject to taxation oy the laws of this State: *Provided*, Said tax shall not exceed in any one year three mills on the dollar; and the recorder shall make out a duplicate thereof, charging thereon each individual an amount of tax, in proportion to his property, as assessed on the grand levy for taxation; which duplicate shall be certified by the mayor and recorder, and delivered to the marshal, who shall collect the same, in the same manner and under the same regulations as county treasurers are required by law to collect county taxes; and said marshal shall pay the same to the treasurer of said corporation as soon as collected, reserving therefrom such fees as the county treasurer might receive for similar services.

Sec. 13. The town council may appropriate any money in the treasury for the carrying into effect the provisions of this act; and may have the use of the jail of the county for the imprisonment of such persons as may be liable to imprisonment under the by-laws and ordinances of said corporation; and all persons so imprisoned shall be under the care of the sheriff, as in other cases.

Sec. 14. Three weeks before each annual election, the town council shall post up in some conspicuous place within said town an accurate account of the moneys received and expended by said corporation since the last annual election, with the sources from which the same were derived, and the objects on which they were expended.

Sec. 15. The officers of said corporation shall respectively deliver to their successors in office, on demand, all such books and papers as may in anywise appertain to their office.

Sec. 16. This shall be considered as a public act, and printed copies thereof be received accordingly; and any future legislature may alter or amend the same: *Provided*, Such alteration or amendment shall not divert the property of the corporation from the purposes herein expressed.

WILLIAM MEDILL,
Speaker pro tem. of the House of Representatives.
ELIJAH VANCE,
Speaker of the Senate.

March 14, 1836.

AN ACT

To incorporate the Baptist Church of Massillon.

Sec. 1. *Be it enacted by the General Assembly of the State of Ohio,* That William Field, William Cox, Ruplius Freeman, Andrew B. Cox, and O. N. Sage, and their associates, together with such other persons as may be hereafter associated with them, be, and they are hereby created a body corporate and politic, by the name of "The Baptist Church of Massillon;" and as such shall remain and have perpetual succession, and by their corporate name may contract and be contracted with, may sue and be sued, answer and be answered, plead and be impleaded, defend and be be defended, in any court of competent jurisdiction, in all manner of actions, causes and complaints, whatsoever; and may have a common seal, which they may change or alter at pleasure.

Sec. 2. That said corporation shall be capable in law and equity, in their corporate name aforesaid, of having, receiving, acquiring and holding, by purchase, gift, grant devise or legacy, any estate, real, personal, or mixed, for the use of said corporation: *Provided*, That the annual income of all such property shall not exceed the sum of one thousand dollars; and that all the property, of whatever kind, shall be considered as held in trust, under the management, and at the disposal of said corporation, for the purpose of promoting the interest of said corporation, defraying the expenses incident to their mode of worship, and maintaining any institutions of charity or education, that may be therewith connected: *And provided, also,* That when money, or other property shall be given, granted, devised or bequeathed, for any particular use or purpose, it shall be faithfully applied to such use or purpose.

Sec. 3. That for the better management of the affairs of said corporation, and promoting the interests thereof, there shall be elected, on the first Saturday in May, one thousand eight hundred and thirty six and on the first Saturday in May, in each succeeding year thereafter, three trustees, and such other officers as the corporation may deem necessary, who shall hold their offices one year, and until successors shall be elected: *Provided*, That if, from any cause, an election of officers should not be made on the day appointed for the annual election, the society may elect their officers at any meeting of the corporation duly assembled.

Sec. 4. That William Field, Rufus Freeman, and O. N. Sage, named in the first section of this act, be, and they are hereby appointed trustees, until the first annual election, and until others are elected in their places.

Sec. 5. That all elections of the corporation shall be by ballot, and the person or persons having a majority of the votes given, for any office, shall be considered duly elected; each member shall have one vote, and all matters of the corporation shall be determined by a majority of the members present, at any meeting of the corporation duly assembled.

Sec. 6. That the trustees, or a majority of whom shall be [a] quorum for the transaction of business, shall, under the direction of the society, have the management and control of the property and other concerns of the corporation; and they, or a majority of them, shall have power to call a meeting of the society, either for the election of officers, or for the transaction of any other business of said society, by giving to said society, immediately after public worship, at least ten days previous notice of said meeting, or causing notifications thereof to be put up in three or more public places within the limits of said society, one of which shall be at the usual place of holding public worship, at least fifteen days previous to such meeting.

Sec. 7. That any meeting of the corporation duly assembled, may adopt and establish such by-laws and ordinances as may be deemed proper and necessary for the good government of said corporation: *Provided*, That such by-laws shall be compatible with the constitution and laws of the United States, and of this State.

Sec. 8. That original process against the corporation shall be served by leaving an attested copy with one or more of the trustees, at least five days previous to the return thereof, and such service shall be deemed sufficient to bind the corporation.

Sec. 9. That any future [Legislature] shall have power to modify or repeal this act.

WILLIAM MEDILL,
Speaker pro tem. of the House of Representatives.
ELIJAH VANCE,
Speaker of the Senate.

March 14, 1836.

AN ACT

To authorize the Auditor of Gallia county to sell certain school lands therein named, for the benefit of fractional town number three, of range fourteen, of the Ohio Company's Purchase.

Sec. 1. *Be it enacted by the General Assembly of the State of Ohio,* That [the] auditor of Gallia county, be, and he is hereby authorized to sell the land granted and assigned in lieu of section number sixteen, to fractional town number three, in range number fourteen, of the Ohio Company's Purchase; it being the west half of the north-east quarter of section eight, town seven, range fifteen; and the west half of the south-east quarter of section eight, town. seven, range fifteen; and the west half of the north-east quarter of section eleven, town. six, range fifteen; and the east half of the south-west quarter of section eleven, town. four, and range fifteen, of the Ohio Company's Purchase; and to do all proper and necessary acts in relation to the sale and conveyance of the same, in the same manner and to the same effect, to all intents and purposes, according to the mode pointed out and prescribed in existing laws on that subject, as if the said lands were situated in the said fractional town number three; any thing contained in any law for the sale of section number sixteen, or lands granted in lieu thereof, to the contrary notwithstanding.

WILLIAM MEDILL,
Speaker pro tem. of the House of Representatives.
ELIJAH VANCE,
Speaker of the Senate.

March 14, 1836.

AN ACT

To incorporate the New Harbour Company.

WHEREAS, Richard Lord, of Brooklyn, Cuyahoga county, Ohio, owner and sole proprietor of that part of lot number fifty, original survey of said Brooklyn, bounded north by the old bed of the Cuyahoga river, east by the lot line, south by the centre of the road leading from Cleveland to Sandusky, and west by fifty acre tract, formerly owned by Alonzo Carter, containing eighty acres of land, more or less: *And whereas,* Said

Lord has divided said parcel of land into eighty shares, and sold several of those shares to sundry persons: Therefore,

Sec. 1. *Be it enacted by the General Assembly of the State of Ohio*, That Richard Lord, Luther M. Parsons, T. P. Handy, Ezekiel Fulsom, Asa Foot, Christopher E. Hill, Thomas Whelpley, Sherlock J. Andrews, John A. Foot, Francis A. Burrows, and their associates, be, and they are hereby created a body corporate and politic, with perpetual succession, by the name of the New Harbour Company, and by that name may contract and be contracted with, sue and be sued, answer and be answered, in all courts of justice and elsewhere; may receive a deed of eighty acres of land, mentioned in the preamble of this act, sell and dispose of the same, or any part thereof.

Sec. 2. That said corporation shall annually hold an election on the first Monday of April, for the purpose of electing one president, secretary and seven directors, who shall be residents of Cuyahoga county, and who shall hold their offices for one year, and until their successors are elected and qualified, according to the by-laws of said company: *Provided*, If said corporation shall neglect to elect officers for more than one year, then this act shall be void.

Sec. 3. That said corporation may make all such written by-laws for the government of said company, in regard to all improvements of said eighty acres of land, or any part thereof, as may promote the health of the citizens of said Brooklyn, or the interest of said company, and enforce the same, by such penalties as they may think proper, not inconsistent with the constitution and laws of this State, or of the United States.

Sec. 4. That if any vacancies shall occur in the offices of said corporation, within the year for which he or they were elected, the directors shall fill such vacancies by appointment; and the officers so appointed shall hold their office until the next annual election.

Sec. 5. That any future Legislature shall have power to alter or repeal this act.

WILLIAM MEDILL,
Speaker pro tem. of the House of Representatives.
ELIJAH VANCE,
Speaker of the Senate.

March 14, 1836.

AN ACT

To increase the capital stock of the Steubenville and Ohio Canal Rail-way Company.

Sec. 1. *Be it enacted by the General Assembly of the State of Ohio*, That the capital stock of the Steubenville and Ohio Canal Rail-way Company is hereby authorized to be increased to fifteen hundred thousand dollars.

WILLIAM MEDILL,
Speaker pro tem. of the House of Representatives.
ELIJAH VANCE,
Speaker of the Senate.

March 14, 1836.

AN ACT

To change the name of the Steubenville Insurance Company.

Sec. 1. *Be it enacted by the General Assembly of the State of Ohio,* That the act of February 18th, A. D. 1830, entitled "An act to incorporate the Steubenville Insurance Company," be amended, as to the name and style of said company, so that the said company shall hereafter be known and designated as the Jefferson Insurance Company, and that all legal obligations, heretofore incurred by or to said Steubenville Insurance Company, shall remain obligatory for or against said Jefferson Insuranc Company, as fully as though this change in the name and style of said company had not been made.

WILLIAM MEDILL,
Speaker pro tem. of the House of Representatives.
ELIJAH VANCE,
Speaker of the Senate.

March 14, 1836.

AN ACT

To legalize certain acts of the Town Council of Norwalk.

WHEREAS, The act entitled "An act to incorporate the town of Norwalk, in the county of Huron," requires that the town council of said incorporation, in the valuation of property within their limits, shall, in all respects, conform to and be governed by, the valuation of the county assessor, as returned to the auditor: *And whereas,* A portion of the land within the limits of the said corporation, lies in common ard undivided, in and with lots Nos. 1, 2, 3, 4, 5, 6, 7, 8, 24, 25, 26, 29, 30, 31, and 32, in the Star and Canfield tract, so called; the larger portion of which lots are not within said corporation: *And whereas,* The said council, at the sitting aforesaid, assessed a tax according to the valuation of the whole of said lots in the grand levy, in proportion to the part which lies within the said corporation; there being no such power deegated to them in their charter, to make such apportionment, differing from, and in alteration of, the return of the assessor: Therefore,

Sec. 1. *Be it enacted by the General Assembly of the State of Ohio,* That all the acts of the said town council, touching the aforesaid matter, are hereby made valid in law; and the tax thus levied upon said portions of said individuals lots, is hereby declared to be legally laid, and binding upon all person in interest, to all intents and purposes, as though the same had been done according to express words in their charter.

WILLIAM MEDILL,
Speaker pro tem. of the House of Representatives.
ELIJAH VANCE,
Speaker of the Senate.

March 14, 1836.

AN ACT

To incorporate the Washington Insurance Company of Cincinnati.

Sec. 1. *Be it enacted by the General Assembly of the State of Ohio,* That an insurance company shall be established in the city of Cincinnati, under the name and style of "The Washington Insurance Company," with a capital stock of one hundred and fifty thousand dollars, divided into shares of fifty dollars each, to be subscribed and paid for by individuals, companies or corporations, in the manner hereinafter specified.

Sec. 2. That O. M. Spencer. N. Hastings, S. G. Brown, O. Fairchild, H. Starr, H. H. Goodman, Jno. D. Jones, W. E. White, and J. R. Coram, or any three of them, be, and they are hereby authorized to open subscriptions in said city for the capital stock of said company, on the **second** Monday of April next, to and keep them open every day between the hours of ten o'clock A. M. and four o'clock P. M. for twenty days, (Sundays excepted,) when the same shall be closed; if, within the said tweny days, two thousand shares shall be subscribed for, the subscribers may meet at some suitable place in the city of Cincinnati, after fifteen days notice thereof shall have been given in two newspapers published in said city, and choose their directors, who may at any time, after having given thirty days notice in two of the newspapers of the city, cause the subscriptions to be reopened, and to continue open until the whole amont of stock shall be taken; if, however, within the said twenty days, more than three thousand shares shall be subscribed for, the said commissioners shall apportion the same among the applicants therefor.

Sec. 3. The payments of the subscriptions shall be made and completed by the subscribers respectively, at the times, and in the manner following: at the time of subscribing, there shall be paid on each share two dollars; after the election of directors, and before the company shall go into operation, five dolars; the balance due on each share, shall be subject to the call of the directrs; and the said company shall not be authorized to make any policy or contract of insurance with any person, until the whole amount of shares subsribed shall be actually paid, or satisfactorily secured to be paid on demand, by endorsed notes, hypothecated stocks, or by mortgages on real estate; *Provided,* That no person shall be an endorser for more than one hundred dollars.

Sec. 4. The subscribers to the said company, their associates, successors, and assigns, are hereby constituted a body corporate and politic, by the name and style of "The Washington Insurance Company;" and, by that name, they shall be capable in law, of pleading and being impleaded, answering and being answered unto, defending and being defended, in all courts and equity; and may have and use a common seal, and may change and alter the same at pleasure.

Sec. 5. The corporation hereby created, may insure on all kinds of property against loss or damage by fire; make all kinds of insurances against loss on goods and merchandize, in the course of transportation, whether on land or on water; and make such other insurances as the directors may judge expedient; they may lend money on bottomry and respondentia, and generally do and perform all necessary matters and things relating to, or connected with these objects, or with either of them; and they may also cause themselves to be insured against maritime risks upon the interest which they may have in any vessels, goods or merchandize, in virtue of any such loans on bottomry and respondentia.

Sec. 6. The stock and affairs of said corporation shall be managed and conducted by nine directors, who shall be stockholders and resident within this State; they shall, after the present year, be elected on the first Monday of May in each year, at such time of the day, and at such place in the city of Cincinnati, as the board of directors, for the time being, shall appoint; and shall hold offices for one year, and until others shall be chosen; and notice of such annual election shall be published for the space of three weeks in two of the newspapers printed in said city; and every such election shall be held under the inspection of three stockholders, not directors at the time, to be previously appointed by the board of directors for that purpose; and shall be made by ballot, by a plurality of votes of the stockholders present, allowing one vote for every share; and stockholders not personally attending, may vote by proxy, such proxy being granted directly to the person representing them at such election; in case it shall at any time happen that an election of directors shall not be made on any day when, pursuant to this act, it ought to have been made, the said corporation shall not, for that cause, be deemed to be dissolved; but it shall and may be lawful on any other day to hold an election of directors, in such manner as shall have been regulated by the by-laws and ordidances of said corporation.

Sec. 7. The directors regularly chosen by the stockholders of said corporation, shall, as soon as may be after every election, proceed to choose out of their body one person to be president, who shall preside until the next annual election; and in case of the death or resignation of the president, or of any director of the said corporation, such vacancy or vacancies may be filled by the board of directors; and in case of the absence of the president, the board shall have power to appoint a president *pro tempore*, who shall have and exercise such powers and functions as the by-laws of the said corporation may provide.

Sec. 8. The stock of the said company shall be assignable and transferable according to such rules and subject to such restrictions as the board of directors shall, from time to time, make and establish, and shall be considered personal property.

Sec. 9. The major part of the directors of the said company shall constitute a quorum, and be competent to the transaction of the business of the corporation; and they may, if done in pursuance of a by-law, appoint from their own body one or more persons to act or assist in the management of their business, with such salaries and allowances as they may think proper; also appoint a secretary, and so many clerks and servants for carrying on their business as they shall deem expedient; and they may also declare and make dividends of the profits resulting from the business of said company, and make and prescribe such by-laws, rules and regulations, as to them shall appear needful and proper, touching the management and disposition of the stock, property, estate and effects of the said company; the duties, powers, and conduct of its officers and servants, the election of directors, the transfer of shares, the management and conducting of its business, and all matters appertaining thereto.

75—L

Sec. 10. It shall be lawful for the said corporation to purchase and hold such and so much real estate as shall be necessary and convenient for the transaction of its business, not exceeding twenty thousand dollars in value; and also take and hold any real estate or securities, *bona fide* mortgage or pledged to the said corporation, either to secure the payment of any debts that may be due to it, or the payment of the shares of the capital stock, and also to purchase on sales made in their favor by virtue of any judgment at law, or any order or decree of a court of equity, or otherwise, to receive and take any real estate in payment, or towards satisfaction of any debt previously contracted and due to the said corporation, and to hold the same until they can conveniently sell and convert the same into money or other personal property, but not for a longer period than three years: *Provided, always,* That it shall not be lawful for the said corporation to use or employ any part of their stock, funds, or moneys, in buying or selling any goods, wares, merchandize, or commodities whatsoever, or in any banking operations or business, or in the trade or business of any exchange or stock broker, or in the purchase or sale of any stock or funded debt whatsoever, credit, or to be created by or under any act of the United States, or of any particular State, nor to emit any notes or bills, or make any contract for the payment of money, only except under the seal of said corporation; and all such notes and contracts shall, to all intents and purposes, be taken as specialties at law; but it shall, nevertheless, be lawful for the said corporation to purchase and hold any such stock or funded debt as last aforesaid, for the purpose of vesting any part of the capital stock, funds or moneys therein, instead of investing the same in and upon real security, and also to sell and transfer the same, and again invest the same or any part thereof, in the stock of funds, whenever, and as often as the exigencies of the said corporation, or due regard to the safety of its funds, shall require.

Sec. 11. All policies or contracts of insurance, which may be made or entered into by the said corporation, shall be subscribed by the president, or president *pro tem.*, or by such other officer as shall be designated for the purpose by its by-laws, and attested by the secretary; and, being so signed and attested, shall be binding and obligatory upon the said corporation, without the seal thereof, according to the tenor, intent and meaning of such policies or contracts; and all such policies or contracts may be so signed and attested, and the business of the said corporation may be otherwise conducted and carried on, without the presence of a board of directors, by assistants or committees, if done under, or in conformity to the by-laws of the said corporation; and the acts of such assistants or committees, shall be binding and obligatory upon said corporation, to all intents and purposes.

Sec. 12. This act shall be, and is hereby declared to be a public act; and the same shall be construed in all courts and places, favorably for every beneficial purpose herein intended: *Provided,* That any future Legislature may limit, amend, alter or repeal this act: this act shall take effect and be in force from and after its passage.

WILLIAM MEDILL,
Speaker pro tem. of the House of Representatives.
ELIJAH VANCE,
Speaker of the Senate.

March 14, 1836.

To incorporate the First Fire Engine Company of Painesville, in the county of Geauga.

Sec. 1. *Be it enacted by the General Assembly of the State of Ohio*, That William L. Perkins, Benjamin Adams, Storm Rosa, Peleg P. Sandford, Addison Hills, James H. Paine, and Reuben Hitchcock, and their associates, and those who may hereafter be associated with them, are hereby created a body politic and corporate, by the name of "The First Fire Engine Company of Painesville;" and by such name may contract, may sue and defend, in all courts of law and equity in this State; may acquire and receive, hold or dispose of property, real, personal, or mixed; and may make all necessary by-laws for their government, and amend or repeal the same, as they may deem proper; and said company may have a common seal, and alter the same at pleasure.

Sec. 2. The annual income of said company shall not exceed two thousand dollars; nor shall the funds of the same be used for any other purpose than to make said company efficient in the extinguishment of fires.

Sec. 3. Every person having been six months a member of said company, after the same has provided a fire engine, shall, while a member of said company, and a resident of said town, be exempt from militia duty, in time of peace.

Secr 4. Any future Legislature may amend or repeal this act, not thereby affecting the title to any property held or conveyed by said company.

Sec. 5. This act shall be received in all courts of this State as a public act.

WILLIAM MEDILL,
Speaker pro. tem. of the House of Representatives.

ELIJAH VANCE,
Speaker of the Senate.

March 14, 1836.

To incorporate the Tuscarawas Bridge Company.

Sec. 1. *Be it enacted by the General Assembly of the State of Ohio*, That Joseph Walton, and his associates, be, and they are hereby created a body politic and corporate, with perpetual succession, subject to the conditions hereinafter mentioned, under the name and style of the Tuscarawas Bridge Company, for the purpose of erecting, at their private expense, a toll bridge across the Tuscarawas river, in the county of Tuscarawas; and by their corporate name may contract and be contracted with, sue and be sued, answer and be answered, plead and be impleaded, defend and be defended, in any court of competent jurisdiction; and may have a common seal, which they may change or alter at pleasure.

Sec. 2. That said company be, and they are hereby authorized and vested with the right to erect a tóll bridge across the said river, at such place above the mouth of Big Stillwater creek, in said county, as they may deem suitable and proper; and shall be capable in law of acquiring and holding all property, real and personal, necessary for the construction and maintenance of said bridge; and shall have power to pass such by-laws, rules and regulations, not inconsistent with the constitution and laws of this State, as they shall deem necessary.

Sec. 3.   That if said company shall erect and complete said bridge in a substantial manner, of proper width, and in other respects of sufficient strength and dimensions, to admit of the safe passage of passengers, teams, and carriages, of the usual size, within three years from the passage of this act, then the said company may ask, demand and receive, from tavel-lers and others passing over said bridge, the following tolls, viz: for each foot passenger, three cents; for each horse, mule, or ass, one year old and upwards, four cents; for each horse and rider, twelve and a half cents; for each chaise, riding ·chair, or other two wheeled pleasure carriage, drawn by one horse, twenty-five cents; for every chariot, coach or other four wheeled pleasure carriage, if drawn by one horse, (driver included) thirty-one and a fourth cents; for the same, drawn by two horses, thirty-seven and a half cents; for every additional horse, six and a fourth cents; for every cart, drawn by one horse, mule, or ass, or ox, (driver included,) twelve and a half cents; for every additional horse, mule, ass, or ox, six and a fourth cents; for every wagon, drawn by one horse, mule ass or ox, (driver included,) eighteen and three fourth cents; for the same, drawn by two horses, mules, asses, or oxen, (driver included,) twenty-five cents; for the same, drawn by four horses, mules, asses, or oxen, (driver included,) fifty cents; and for every additional horse, mule, ass, or ox, six and a fourth cents; for each sled, drawn by one horse, mule, ass, or ox, (driver inclu-ded,) eighteen and three fourth cents; for each head of neat cattle, six months old and upwards, two cents; for each sheep or hog, one cent: *Pro-vided*, That all funeral processions, persons going to, and returning from public worship, children or teachers going to, or returning from school, all persons necessarily going to, or returning from elections or militia mus-ters, may pass said bridge free of toll; and it shall be the duty of said com-pany, previous to receiving any toll, to set, and keep up exposed to public view, near the end of said bridge, a board or canvass, on which shall be painted or printed, in legible characters, the rates of toll, (not exceeding those aforesaid,) which are demanded; and if the said company shall, at any time, demand and receive a greater toll than is herein allowed, they shall be liable, for each offence, to a fine of not exceeding five dollars, to be recovered before any court having jurisdiction.

Sec. 4.   That if any person or persons shall wilfully injure said bridge, or remove, or in any way spoil, injure or destroy any materials, or any thing belonging to said bridge, either in the building of said bridge, or for repairs thereof, such person or persons shall forfeit and pay to said corpo-ration treble the amount of damages sustained by means of such offence or injury, to be sued for and recovered with costs of suit, in action of debts, in any court having competent jurisdiction, by the treasurer of said cor-poration, or any person thereunto by said company authorized.

Sec. 5. That service of process on said company shall be by leaving a copy of the same with any officer or other member of said company.

Sec. 6. That whenever the amount of tolls received by said company, on said bridge, shall equal the amount of money expended by them, in the location, construction, repairs, maintenance and superintendence of said bridge, together with ten per cent. per annum thereon; or if, at any time after the completion of said bridge, the commissioners of said county shall pay to the said company the same, after deducting the amount of tolls received up to the time of such payment, then the said bridge and all property thereof shall vest in said county, and the said bridge shall thenceforth be a free bridge, and be open to all persons to pass the same free of toll; and said company shall cause to be filed with the auditor of said county, semi-annually, a true statement in writing of said receipts and expenditures.

WILLIAM MEDILL,
Speaker pro tem. of the House of Representatives.

ELIJAH VANCE,
Speaker of the Senate.

March 14, 1836.

AN ACT

To incorporate the "Chardon Steam Mill Company," in the county of Geauga.

Sec. 1. *Be it enacted by the General Assembly of the State of Ohio,* That Edward Paine, jr., Alfred Phelps, Edwin F. Phelps, Sylvester N. Hoyt, David D. Aikin, David T. Bruce, and Ralph Cowles, and such other persons as may hereafter become associated with them, for the purpose of building and conducting a grist mill, saw mill, and mills with other machinery, to be propelled by steam, in the town of Chardon, or its vicinity, in the county of Geauga, be, and they are hereby created a body corporate and politic, with perpetual succession, by the name and style of the "Chardon Steam Mill Company;" and by that name shall be capable of contracting and being contracted with, suing and being sued, answering and being answered, in any court of law or equity; and may have a common seal, and the same may break, alter, or renew at pleasure; and shall be capable of holding and disposing of all kinds of property, real, personal or mixed, to the amount of the capital stock of said company, and necessary for the objects and purposes of said corporation, as above expressed.

Sec. 2. That the capital stock of said corporation shall not exceed fifty thousand dollars, to be divided into shares of twenty-five dollars each; and the persons named in the first section of this act, or any five of them, are hereby empowered to open books of subscription to the stock of said company, at such times and places, and under such regulations as they shall deem proper; and when in their opinion a sufficient amount of stock has been subscribed, they shall give notice of the time and place of meeting, for the purpose of choosing directors of said company; which notice shall be given by publishing the same in some newspaper printed in the county, or by affixing the same to the door of the court-house in said Chardon, at least ten days previous to said election.

Sec. 3. That the concerns of said company shall be managed by seven directors, one of whom shall be president, who shall be elected by the stockholders, at such time and place, as may be designated under the second section of this act; and their successors shall be elected on the last Monday of May, in each year thereafter, in the town of Chardon, at such place as the by-laws and regulations of such company may prescribe; each member of said company being entitled one vote for each share of capital stock he may own, and may vote, either personally or by proxy; and the directors so elected shall hold their offices until their successors are regularly chosen and qualified; but if it should so happen that any election should not be bolden at the time appointed by the provisions of this act, the said corporation shall not thereby be dissolved; but said election may be holden at such other time as a majority of the directors for the time being may direct.

Sec. 4. That the said directors, or a majority of them, shall have power, from time to time, to make such by-laws, rules and regulations, for the government of said company, as they may deem fit, and may amend or repeal the same, at pleasure.

Sec. 5. That said company shall have no power to contract debts to an amount greater than their capital stock; and should the debts of said company at any time exceed said capital stock, the stockholders of said company shall be individually liable for such excess, in proportion to the amount of the stock by them subscribed for, or owned, at the time such debts were contracted: *Provided,* That the joint assets of said company shall be first exhausted in payment of the debts thereof, before resort be had to the individual property of any stockholder for that purpose.

Sec. 6. That no part of the funds of said company shall ever be applied to banking purposes: *Provided,* That any future Legislature may alter, amend or repeal this act.

WILLIAM MEDILL,
Speaker pro. tem. of the House of Representatives.

ELIJAH VANCE,
Speaker of the Senate.

March 14, 1836.

AN ACT

To incorporate "The Mt. Pleasant Silk Company."

Sec. 1. *Be it enacted by the General Assembly of the State of Ohio,* That John Fox, Robert Fox, Thomas White, Isaac Vail, Caleb Cope, Pinckney Lewis, and Henry Gurthy, of the county of Jefferson, and their associates, shall be, and they are hereby declared to be a body politic and corporate, by the name and style of "*The Mt. Pleasant Silk Company;*" and by that name shall have perpetual succession, and be capable in law to contract and be contracted with, to sue and be sued, plead and be impleaded, answer and be answered, defend and be defended, in courts of law and equity, and else-where; with full power and authority to acquire, hold, possess, use, occupy, and enjoy, and the same to sell, convey, and dispose of, all such real estate, and shall he necessary and convenient for the transaction of its business, or which may be conveyed to said company for to secure, or in payment of any debt which may become due and owing to said company, or in satisfaction of any judgment of any court of law, or decree of any court of equity, in their favor; and make and use a common seal, and the same to break, alter, and renew, at their pleasure; and generally to do and perform all things relative to the objects of this institution, which now is, or shall be lawful for any individual, or body politic or corporate to do.

Sec. 2. That the capital stock of said company shall be fifty thousand dollars, divided into shares of five hundred dollars each; that the said stock shall be deemed and considered personal estate, and be transferable under such rules and regulations as the said company may direct; that if the directors, or a majority of them, shall at any time deem it advisable to increase the capital stock of said company, they are hereby authorized to do so, until it shall amount to one hundred thousand-dollars.

Sec. 3. That the said stock, affairs, and concerns, of said company, shall be managed by seven directors, (one of whom shall preside as president,) being stockholders; who shall be elected on, and hold their offices from the first Monday in May, eighteen hundred and thirty-six, until the first Monday in January, eighteen hundred and thirty-seven, and until their successors in office are elected: that the directors shall call a meeting of the stockholders on the first Monday of January, annually, by an advertisement published in some newspapers having general circulation in said town of Mt. Pleasant, at least twenty days prior to the time of holding said election; that said election shall be made by such of the stockholders of said company as shall attend for that purpose, either in person or by proxy; that each share of stock shall be entitled to one vote, unless the holders thereof may have more than fifteen shares, but in no instance shall any stockholder be entitled to more than fifteen votes; that all elections shall be determined by ballot, and the seven persons who shall have the greatest number of votes shall be the directors the year ensuing; that if it shall happen, at any election, that two or [more] persons shall have an equal number of votes, the directors in office at the time of such election, or a majority of them, shall proceed by ballot, and by plurality of votes, to determine which of said persons so having an equal number of votes shall be director or directors of said company; that the stockholders shall then proceed, in like manner, to elect by ballot, a president from among the directors before elected; that if any vacancy should happen in the office of any of the officers of said company, by death, resignation, or otherwise, the vacancy shall be filled for the remainder of the year in which the same shall happen, by such person as the directors, or a majority of them, shall appoint; that in case of the absence of the president, the board of directors, or a majority of them, shall have power to appoint a president, *pro tem.*

Sec. 4. That the capital stock of said company being subscribed, shall be called in by such instalments, and in such manner as shall be provided for by the by-laws and regulations of said company: *Provided*, That the stockholders shall never be required to pay more than four cents on the dollar, until after the profits arising from the business shall enable the directors to declare a dividend; but when such dividend is declared, such portion thereof shall be retained as an instalment on the stock subscribed, as a majority of the directors may deem necessary: *Provided, also*, That John Fox, an experienced and skilful artist in the silk business, shall have five shares, free of cost, until a dividend is declared; that four per cent. on the said five shares shall be paid by the other stockholders in proportion to the stock they may severally hold.

Sec. 5. That a majority of the directors, or the president and directors, shall form a quorum for the transaction of business, and shall have power to make and subscribe such by-laws, rules and regulations, as to them shall appear needful and proper, touching the management and disposition of the stock, and payments which may be due thereon; the business, property, estate and effects of said company; and the duties and compensation of its officers, agents, clerks and workmen, employed by said company; and shall also have power to employ and appoint so many officers, clerks, servants, and agents, for carrying into effect the objects of said company, and with such salary or allowances as to them shall seem meet: *Provided*, That such by-laws, rules and regulations shall not be repugnant to the constitution and laws of the United States and of this State.

Sec. 6. No transfer of stock shall be valid or effectual unless it be made in conformity to the by-laws of the corporation hereby created, *being in all cases subject to the debts or demands due to the company at the time of making such transfer.*

Sec. 7. That John Fox, Robert Fox and Thomas White, persons named in the first section of this act, shall be the managers of the aforesaid company; and they or either of them shall have power to call a meeting of the stockholders on the first Monday in March next ensuing, for the purpose of electing the president and directors of said company, pursuant to the provisions of the third section of this act.

Sec. 8. That if the directors of the company shall at any time create a larger amount of debts than the sum actually paid in by the stockholders of said company, then the said directors shall be answerable in person, and their individual property shall be liable for the payment of such excess of debt or debts.

Sec. 9. That should it so happen from any cause whatsoever, that the annual election of directors should not take place in any year on the day hereinbefore mentioned, for that purpose, the company shall not for that cause or any other "non user," be deemed to be dissolved, but that it shall be lawful on any other day to hold an election for directors in such manner as shall be prescribed by the by-laws and ordinances of said corporation.

Sec. 10. That it shall not be lawful for the said corporation to engage in banking, or to discount any evidence of debt, or to issue any note or bond, or bill, for the purpose of loaning the same.

[Sec. 11.] That any future Legislature may modify, amend, or change this act: *Provided*, That such modification, amendment, or change, shall not in any way affect the right to any personal or real estate contracted for, or owned by said company, or in any way divert it from its original intention.

WILLIAM MEDILL,
Speaker pro tem. of the House of Representatives.
ELIJAH VANCE,
Speaker of the Senate.

March 14, 1836.

AN ACT

To incorporate the Ohio Silk Company.

Sec. 1. *Be it enacted by the General Assembly of the State of Ohio,* That Joseph Sullivant, Lyne Starling, jr., William A. Platt, Anthony S. Chew and Matthew J. Gilbert, of Franklin county, and the subscribers to the stock of this association, and their successors, shall be, and they are hereby declared to be a body politic and corporate, by the name and style of the "Ohio Silk Company;" and by that name, shall have perpetual succession, and be capable in law to contract and be contracted with, to sue and be sued, plead and be impleaded, answer and be answered, defend and be defended, in all courts of law and equity, and elsewhere; with full power and authority to acquire, hold, possess, use, occupy and enjoy, and the same to sell, convey and dispose of, all such real estate as shall be necessary and convenient for the transaction of its business, or which may be conveyed to said company for security; or in payment of any debt which may become due and owing to said company, or in satisfaction of any judgment of any court of law, or a decree of a court of equity in their favor; and to make and use a common seal, and the same to break, alter and renew at their pleasure.

Sec. 2. That the capital stock of said company shall be one hundred thousand dollars, which may be increased at the will of the stockholders, to two hundred thousand dollars, divided into one thousand share of one hundred dollars each; at the time of subscribing, there shall be paid on each share five dollars; and the balance on each shall be subject to the call of the directors in instalments of not less than five dollars on each share, payable upon notice of thirty days, by publication in any newspaper in the city of Columbus: *Provided,* That there shall be at least thirty days between the payment of any two instalments; and any stockholders failing to pay any instalment becoming due as above, shall forfeit all his interest in the company.

Sec. 3. Should any forfeiture occur, it shall, at any time within two years after such forfeitures, be remitted by the directors of said company, upon motion made for that purpose, and payment by the person incurring the forfeiture of the principal of said instalment and interest thereon, at the rate of five per cent. per annum from the time it became due, and the payment of all other instalments which may have become due, with interest at the above named rate.

76—L

Sec. 4. That so soon as five hundred shares of said stock are subscribed, and the first instalment of five dollars paid thereon, the company shall be competent to transact all business for which it is established.

Sec. 5. That transfer of the stock may be made by any stockholder or his legal representatives, subject to such restriction as the board of directors may from time to time make and establish.

Sec. 6. That the affairs of the company shall be managed by five directors, all of whom shall be stockholders, to be elected as follows: the stockholders comprising this association shall hold a meeting for the first election of directors within one month after the amount of five hundred shares of stock shall be subscribed for, and on the first Monday of December in each and every year thereafter, and choose by ballot five directors from among the stockholders; and each stockholder shall have one vote for each share of stock, not exceeding ten; and one vote for every five shares over ten, and not exceeding thirty; and one vote for every ten shares over thirty shares; and the directors so chosen shall serve until the first Monday of December, eighteen hundred and thirty-seven, and until others are chosen; their first meeting after every election the directors shall choose by ballot one of their number for president of said company; and in case of the death, disability or resignation of the president, the directors shall fill the vacancy by ballot as before; and in case of vacancies in the board of directors, it shall be filled by the directors from the stockholders for the remainder of the year.

Sec. 7. It shall be lawful for said company to purchase machinery for the manufacture of raw silk, and the necessary land and buildings for the same to lease, erect and own; to import raw silk for the purpose of manufacture; and to employ a part or the whole of their capital in the production of raw silk; and for that purpose to lease or purchase lands and such buildings upon the same as may be convenient and necessary to lease or erect.

Sec. 8. That the president and directors shall have power and authority to appoint a secretary and treasurer, and such other clerks and assistants as shall be necessary for transacting the business of said institution, and may allow them such salaries as they may judge reasonable; to ordain such by-laws, ordinances and regulations, as shall appear to them necessary for regulating and conducting the concerns of said institution, not being contrary to or inconsistent with this act, the constitution and laws of this State, and of the United States.

Sec. 9. That the stock of this institution may be assigned and transferred on the books of the company, in person or by power of attorney; but no stockholder indebted to the company shall be permitted to make any transfer or receive a dividend until such debt is paid or secured to the satisfaction of the president and board of directors.

Sec. 10. That the president and directors may call a general meeting of the stockholders for any purpose relative to the affairs of the institution, giving at least two weeks notice thereof in some newspaper printed in Columbus, or by written notice of ten days to each stockholder.

Sec. 11. That should it so happen, from any cause whatsoever, that the annual election of directors should not take place in any year on the day hereinbefore mentioned, for that purpose, this corporation shall not be, for that reason, dissolved; but such election may be lawfully held on such other convenient day within six months thereafter as may for that purpose be fixed on by the president and directors, they causing twenty days notice thereof to be given in one or more newspapers printed in Columbus.

Sec. 12. All contracts, under the seal of said company, signed by the president thereof, shall be binding and valid, and binding upon said company.

Sec. 13. That Joseph Sullivant, Lyne Starling, jr., and Anthony S. Chew, are hereby appointed commissioners to open books of subscription, and superintend the business of the subscribers, until a board of directors shall be elected; which books shall be opened in the city of Columbus, on or before the first day of January, one thousand eight hundred and thirty-seven, two weeks previous notice thereof having been given in any newspaper printed in Columbus.

WILLIAM MEDILL,
Speaker pro tem. of the House of Representatives.

ELIJAH VANCE,
Speaker of the Senate.

March 14, 1836.

AN ACT

Granting certain water privileges to Walter M. Blake.

Sec. 1. *Be it enacted by the General Assembly of the State of Ohio,* That there is hereby granted to Walter M. Blake, of Tuscarawas county, his heirs and assigns, the perpetual and exclusive right to use, for hydraulic purposes, the surplus water which it may be found necessary and safe to pass round lock number thirteen, on section number one hundred and four, south of the Portage summit: which said lock is erected and situate on the lands of said Blake, being lot number twenty-two, in the Schoenbrun tract, so called: *Provided,* Said Blake shall pay into the State Treasury the sum of one thousand dollars, to be paid in annual instalments of one hundred dollars each, commencing on the first day of April, A. D. one thousand eight hundred and forty: *Provided, however,* That the said Blake shall have the privilege of paying off said amount of one thousand dollars, at any time before the same becomes due: *And provided, also,* That if said Blake shall not make said payments in accordance with the provisions of this act, then it shall and may be lawful for the Board of Public Works, to commence suit, in the name of the State of Ohio, to enforce the collection of the same.

Sec. 2. That said grant or conveyance shall contain a condition or reservation, that the State shall have the right to resume the use of the water conveyed, under the provisions of this act, either in whole or in part, whenever the agents of the State, having charge of that part of the canal, shall deem such resumption necessary for the purpose of navigation upon the Ohio canal.

Sec. 3. That the grant made under the provisions of this act shall in
no wise abridge or interfere with the existing rights or privileges of any
person or persons, to the use of the water of Sugar creek.

Sec. 4. That the deed of grant or conveyance of the right to use the
water for hydraulic purposes, at said lock number thirteen, to said Blake,
to be made under the provisions of this act, shall contain a condition, that
said Blake, his heirs and assigns, shall erect, at their own proper expense,
under the direction of the engineers who, for the time being shall have
charge of that part of the canal, and agreeably to a plan to be furnished by
said engineer, the necessary weir, head and tail race, and other works and
devices, which said engineer may deem necessary, to prevent injury to the
canal, or impediments to the navigation thereof, and shall at all times keep
the same, and every part thereof, in a state of good order and repair; and
if said grantee, or his assigns, shall at any time neglect or refuse so to do,
such engineer, or other agent of the State, may cause the same to be done
at his expense; and that no saw-mill or other mill works, calculated to deposite or throw into the canal, saw dust, chips, barks, driftwood or rubbish
of any description, or to impede the navigation by the unequal flow, or vi-
olent action of the water, shall ever be erected for the purpose of using
said water power to be granted.

Sec. 5. The privileges herein granted, shall be considered in full for
any claim or claims, which the said Walter M. Blake may have for damages or losses by him sustained, in labour performed under contracts or otherwise, on the canals in this State.

WILLIAM MEDILL,
Speaker pro tem. of the House of Representatives.

ELIJAH VANCE,
Speaker of the Senate.

March 14, 1836.

AN ACT

To authorize the commissioners of Clark county to subscribe to the cap.tal stock of the
Mad River and Lake Erie Rail-road Company.

Sec. 1. *Be it enacted by the General Assembly of the State of Ohio,*
That if the commissioners of Clark county shall consider it to be for the
general interest of said county, and desired by the inhabitants thereof, they
are hereby authorized to subscribe, on behalf of the people of said county,
for not exceeding six hundred shares of the capital stock of the Mad River
and Lake Erie Rail-road Company; and to pay the instalments thereon
as they shall be required by the president and directors of said company.

Sec. 2. If the board of commissioners shall subscribe for the said stock,
as above provided, they are further authorized to borrow, on the credit of
said county of Clark, any sum of money not exceeding thirty thousand dollars; and, for the final payment of the principal sum, and of the interest

thereon, to pledge the faith of said county; and they shall levy and collect, annually, such taxes, as, together with the tolls arising from the stock in said road, will suffice to pay the interest of such loan, and other inciden.tal charges and liabilities connected therewith.

Sec. 3.. The said commissioners shall have power to hypothecate the said stock as a security for the loan they may make, and to sell the same, and apply the proceeds to the payment of the loan, and the premiums ob.tained thereon, shall be paid into the county treasury; and they shall also be empowered to make such arrangements for the payment of interests on said loan, or the saving of interest thereon, as the good of the people of Clark county may require.

WILLIAM MEDILL,
Speaker pro tem. of the House of Representatives.

ELIJAH VANCE,
Speaker of the Senate.

March 14, 1836.

AN ACT
To authorize the commissioners of the county of Huron to borrow money.

Sec. 1. *Be it enacted by the General Assembly of the State of Ohio,* That the county commissioners of the county of Huron, and their succes.sors in office, for the term of five [years] dollars, from and after the passage of this act, be, and they are hereby authorized to borrow, on the credit of said county, a sum of money not exceeding fifteen thousand dollars, at a rate of interest not exceeding seven per centum per annum; which mo.ney, when borrowed, under the provisions of this act, shall be applied by said commissioners, to the discharge of any debt or debts, which may be hereafter contracted by said commissioners, for the erection of a new court house and jail in said county, and to no other purposes whatever.

Sec. 2. That the commissioners of said county are hereby authorized to levy, annually, for the term aforesaid, a tax on all property entered upon the grand list of taxation, an amount, not exceeding two mills on the dollar, on the valuation thereof, in addition to the sum levied for county purposes; and the amount so levied and collected, is hereby pledged, and shall be applied by the commissioners aforesaid, to the discharge of any debt, or loan, which may be made under the provisions of this act.

Sec. 3. That the treasurer of said county shall be allowed, for his ser.vices, for receiving and paying out all such money, (when borrowed,) one per cent. on the amount so received and paid, to be settled by the county auditor.

WILLIAM MEDILL,
Speaker pro tem. of the House of Representatives.

ELIJAH VANCE,
Speaker of the Senate.

March 14, 1836.

AN ACT

To incorporate the Exchange Hotel Company, in the city of Columbus.

Sec. 1. *Be it enacted by the General Assembly of the State of Ohio,* That Robert W. McCoy, Joseph Ridgway; D. W. Deshler, Otis Crosby, John N. Champion, John Noble, Gustavus Swan, P. B. Wilcox, J. R. Swan, Noah H. Swayne, Demas Adams, John Patterson, Lincoln Goodale, Ira Grover, Bela Latham, William L. Sullivant, and John L. Gill, and others, who now are, or hereafter may become stockholders in the Exchange Hotel Company, of Columbus, with a capital not to exceed sixty thousand dollars, divided into shares of fifty dollars each, to be paid in the manner the directors may require, with powers to build and erect a hotel, in said city of Columbus, with such other buildings as the directors for the time being shall think proper, and to purchase, hold, and possess, all such real and personal estate as may be necessary to carry into effect the objects of this incorporation.

Sec. 2. That said corporation, by the name aforesaid, shall have power to contract and be contracted with, to sue and be sued, have and use a common seal, and the same to alter at pleasure: *Provided,* That it shall not be lawful for said corporation to ever engage in any banking operations whatsoever.

Sec. 3. That the stockholders of said corporation shall meet annually, on the first Monday of April, or at such other time as the directors for the time being may appoint, and elect from the body of stockholders nine directors, who shall have the management and control of all the business of said corporation, and shall serve until their successors are elected.

Sec. 4. That the directors shall choose from their own body a president, whose duty it shall be to preside at all meetings of the directors, and in his absence they shall choose a president *pro tempore;* the directors, five of whom shall be a quorum, shall have power to fill vacancies in their own body, to appoint a secretary, and all other needful officers and agents, for the management of the business of said corporation, and also, to make all necessary rules and regulations, by-laws and ordinances, for conducting the affairs of said corporation, and the same to alter or amend at pleasure.

Sec. 5. That the stock of said corporation may be transferred on the books of said company, under such rules and regulations as may be provided.

Sec. 6. That all elections for directors shall be by ballot, and each stockholder shall be entitled to as many votes as he has shares of stock.

Sec. 7. It shall be the duty of the directors, at such times as may be provided, to declare a division of the rents and profits of the property of the company, and to pay the same to the stockholders; and at each annual election they shall report to the stockholders the condition of the buildings, the amount of funds on hand, and the debts due to and from the company.

Sec. 8. It shall be the duty of the within named corporators, who are stockholders, so soon as the sum of thirty thousand dollars, in stock, is subscribed, to give notice of at least ten days, for the election of directors.

Sec. 9. This act shall be taken in all courts as a public act, and any copy thereof printed by the authority of the Legislature, shall be received in all courts as evidence thereof: *Provided*, That any future Legislature shall have power to alter, amend, or modify this act; but such modification or amendments shall not divert the property or funds of such corporation from the purposes hereby expressed.

Sec. 10. That the stockholders shall be liable, in their individual capacity, for all debts created by said corporation,

WILLIAM MEDILL,
Speaker pro tem. of the House of Representatives.

ELIJAH VANCE,
Speaker of the Senate.

March 14, 1836.

AN ACT

To revive an act entitled "An act to incorporate the Cincinnati Hotel Company.

Sec. 1. *Be it enacted by the General Assembly of the State of Ohio,* That the act entitled "An act to incorporate the Cincinnati Hotel Company," passed January 30th, 1834, be, an the same is hereby revived, and in force, from and after the passage of this act: *Provided,* That if the structure contemplated by the above recited act, shall not be commenced within eighteen months, and shall not be erected and completed within six years from the passage of this act, the corporate rights herein revived shall cease.

WILLIAM MEDILL,
Speaker pro tem. of the House of Representatives.

ELIJAH VANCE,
Speaker of the Senate.

March 14, 1836.

AN ACT

To incorporate the German Society of Cincinnati.

Sec. 1. *Be it enacted by the General Assembly of the State of Ohio,* That John Myers, Lewis Rehfuss, Charles Wolf, August Frank, Charles Remelen, citizens of Ohio, and their associate, together with such other persons as may be hereafter associated with them, be, and they are hereby created and declared a body corporate and politic, by the name and style of "The German Society of Cincinnati;" and as such shall remain and have perpetual succession, and by their corporate name may contract and be contracted with, sue and be sued, answer and be answered unto, plead and be impleaded, defend and be defended, in any court of competent jurisdiction, in all manner of actions whatsoever; and to have a common seal, which they may alter at pleasure.

Sec. 2. Said corporation, by the name and style aforesaid, shall be capable in law of holding property, real, personal, or mixed, either by purchase, gift, grant, devise or legacy, which may become the property of said corporation, and of transferring the same, at pleasure: *Provided*, The annual income thereof shall not exceed two thousand dollars.

Sec. 3. The society shall have power from time to time to ordain and establish such by-laws, rules and regulations, as shall be necessary and proper for the good government of said society, and the prudent and efficient management of its effects: *Provided*, Said by-laws, rules and regulations are not inconsistent with the constitution and laws of this State, and of the United States.

Sec. 4. The officers of the society shall consist of a president, two vice presidents, a treasurer and a secretary, who shall be elected annually, on the first Monday in May, in each year; and if it should at any time happen that the election is not held on that day, said corporation shall not for that cause be dissolved; and the officers may order an election on any subsequent day, by giving ten days notice of the time and place thereof.

Sec. 5. The real and personal estate, property, funds, revenue and prudential concerns of said society shall be managed by the officers thereof, under the direction of the society.

Sec. 6. The objects of the society are hereby declared to be the aid of the unfortunate and sick members thereof, in such sums of money, and in such manner, as may be stipulated in its by-laws, rules and regulations, and to perform such other offices of charity, as may be deemed expedient; to which objects, and no other, shall the money or income of said society ever be appropriated.

Sec. 7. That John Myers shall be the president; Lewis Rehfuss, and Charles Wolf, the vice-presidents; August Frank, treasurer; and Charles Remelin, secretary of said society, until the first election in May, eighteen hundred and thirty-six.

Sec. 8. That the right to alter, amend, or repeal this act, at any time the Legislature may think proper, is hereby reserved: *Provided*, Such alteration, amendment or repeal, shall not affect a title to any property acquired or transferred under its provisions, or divert the same to any other purpose than originally intended.

WILLIAM MEDILL,
Speaker pro tem. of the House of Representatives.

ELIJAH VANCE,
Speaker of the Senate.

March 14, 1836.

AN ACT

To incorporate the Erie Salt Company.

Sec. 1. *Be it enacted by the General Assembly of the State of Ohio*, That Samuel Wilson, Lucius Dunham, Nehemiah Allen, and such other persons as may hereafter be associated with them, and their successors, be, and they are hereby created a body corporate and politic, with perpetual succession, to be known by the name of the "Erie Salt Company;" and by that name may contract and be contracted with, sue and be sued, answer and be answered, in all courts and elsewhere, with full power to acquire, hold, sell, and convey, any real or personal property, which they may deem necessary, to carry on the business of boring for, manufacturing and disposing of salt.

Sec. 2. That the members of said corporation shall meet and organize under this act, by electing officers and adopting by-laws for their government, by or before the first day of July, 1836.

Sec. 3. Any future Legislature may amend or repeal this act.

WILLIAM MEDILL,
Speaker pro tem. of the House of Representatives.

ELIJAH VANCE,
Speaker of the Senate.

March 14, 1836.

AN ACT

To change the name of the town of West Liberty, in the county of Highland.

Sec. 1. *Be it enacted by the General Assembly of the State of Ohio,* That the town of West Liberty, in the county of Highland, shall henceforth be designated and known by the name of Marshall.

Sec. 2. That no right or title to any property, heretofore acquired, shall in any wise be affected by the passage of this act.

WILLIAM MEDILL,
Speaker pro. tem. of the House of Representatives.

ELIJAH VANCE,
Speaker of the Senate.

March 14, 1836.

AN ACT

Making a special appropriation of the three per cent. fund, within the counties of Union and Champaign.

Sec. 1. *Be it enacted by the General Assembly of the State of Ohio,* That fifty dollars of the three per cent fund, which is, or may hereafter become due to the county of Union, be expended under the direction of William Inskeep, senr., in improving that part of the road leading from Bellefontaine to Milford-centre, described as follows, to wit: commencing at the east line of Logan county, on the State road leading to Milford-centre, until it intersects the north line of Champaign county.

Sec. 2. That the following sums, to be paid out of the three per cent. fund, now due, or hereafter to be due to the following named counties,

77—L

shall be appropriated and expended on the Xenia and Sandusky road, under the superintendence of Cyrus T. Ward, to wit: from the county of Clark, fifty dollars; from the county of Champaign, fifty dollars; from the county of Logan, fifty dollars; from the county of Hardin, fifty dollars: the said superintendent shall make return of his proceedings to the county commissioners of Champaign, and settle his accounts with them; and the said county commissioners shall publish a statement of such settlement.

Sec. 3. That forty dollars of the three per cent. fund, which is, or may hereafter become due to the county of Champaign, be expended on the road named in the foregoing section, under the superintendence of William Andre, in improving so much of said road, as lies in the county of Champaign.

Sec. 4. That the above named commissioners account with the county commissioners of their respective counties, for the faithful application of the above appropriations.

WILLIAM MEDILL,
Speaker pro tem. of the House of Representatives.

ELIJAH VANCE,
Speaker of the Senate.

March 14, 1836.

AN ACT

Making an appropriation to Franklin College, in the county of Harrison, and Ripley College, in the county of Brown.

Sec. 1. *Be it enacted by the General Assembly of the State of Ohio,* That the sum of five hundred dollars, be, and the same is hereby appropriated to Franklin College, in the county of Harrison; and five hundred dollars to Ripley College, in the county of Brown; to be paid out of the literary fund now in the treasury, or out of the first moneys that may come into the treasury, belonging to said fund, on the order of the board of trustees of said institutions; to be applied for its benefit, in such manner as said boards shall direct.

WILLIAM MEDILL,
Speaker pro tem. of the House of Representatives.

ELIJAH VANCE,
Speaker of the Senate.

March 14, 1836.

AN ACT

Making a special appropriation of part of the three per cent. fund, in the counties of Logan and Shelby.

Sec. 1. *Be it enacted by the General Assembly of the State of Ohio,* That fifty dollars of the three per cent. fund, which now is, or may hereafter become due, to the counties of Logan and Shelby, one half of the sum from each county, be expended under the direction of John Means, of Logan county; and William Roberts of Shelby county, in the manner hereafter set forth.

Sec. 2. That so soon as there shall be a sum of money raised by subscription or otherwise, which, with the sum of fifty dollars as above appropriated, that in the opinion of said commissioners, shall be sufficient to erect a bridge across the Great Miami river, near Logansville, at a point where the state road leading from Bellefontaine to Sidney, crosses said river: said commissioners are hereby authorized to lay out and expend on said bridge the aforesaid sum of $50.

Sec. 3. That when the commissioners of the counties aforesaid, are satisfied that said sum of $50 has been faithfully appropriated as above directed, said commissioners shall direct the county auditors to issue their orders on the county treasurer of the proper county, for the aforesaid amount or amounts so due out of the three per cent. fund, which is now, or hereafter shall be in their hands from the State Treasury.

Sec. 4. That should either of the commissioners die, or remove from the county, the county commissioners of his proper county shall fill said vacancy, as often as the same may occur.

WILLIAM MEDILL,
Speaker pro tem. of the House of Representatives.

ELIJAH VANCE,
Speaker of the Senate.

March 14, 1836.

AN ACT

Making special appropriation of the three per cent. fund, in the county of Franklin, for the year 1836.

Sec. 1. *Be it enacted by the General Assembly of the State of Ohio,* That there shall be expended all of the three per cent. fund of the county of Franklin, under the superintendence of Henry Patch, Michael Neiswanger and John Hoover, for the erection of a good and permanent bridge across Alum creek, on the state road leading from Columbus, in Franklin, to Johnstown, in Licking county; and the said superintendents shall account to the commissioners of Franklin county for the faithful application of said appropriation: *Provided,* That should either of the superintendents die or refuse to serve, the commissioners of the county of Franklin, shall fill such vacancy, on being notified.

WILLIAM MEDILL,
Speaker pro tem. of the House of Representatives.

ELIJAH VANCE,
Speaker of the Senate.

March 14, 1836.

AN ACT

Making a special appropriation of part of the three per cent. fund, in the county of Trumbull.

Sec. 1. *Be it enacted by the General Assembly of the State of Ohio,* That one hundred and thirty dollars of the three per cent. fund, belonging to the county of Trumbull, be expended, under the direction of Walter Johnston, and Thadeas Bradley, of the township of Johnston, in said county, in opening and turnpiking a certain road, beginning near the centre of Johnston, from thence running to Warren, in said county.

Sec. 2. That when the commissioners of Trumbull county are satisfied that the said sum of one hundred and thirty dollars has been faithfully expended, according to the true intent and meaning of this act, they shall direct the auditor of said county to issue his order on the treasurer of said county for that amount of three per cent. fund, in his hands, if he should have that amount, if not, then out of the first dividend of the three per cent. fund he may receive from the Treasurer of State.

Sec. 3. That should the said Walter Johnston and Thadeas Bradley fail to perform the duties of the above appointment, the commissioners of said county may appoint others in their room to carry into effect this act.

WILLIAM MEDILL,
Speaker pro tem. of the House of Representatives.

ELIJAH VANCE,
Speaker of the Senate.

March 14, 1836.

AN ACT

For the relief of John Darrow.

Whereas, John Darrough, of Delaware county, on or about the first day of May, 1834, went upon the lands in the Piqua Land District, with the view of making an entry, and after selecting a lot to please him, obtained a description from a man residing near the lot selected, with which description, not knowing himself any thing about the division of a section, or manner of describing land, he applied for and and entered the west half of the south-east quarter of section thirty-six, township one, south, range six, east, Ohio canal land, containing eighty acres; and received a certificate therefor: *And whereas,* It now appears that he was deceived, and that the description given, did not embrace the lands that he intended to enter, but embraced lands that are not adapted to the purposes of cultivation, or to the wants and necessity of the purchaser: Therefore,

Sec. 1. *Be it enacted by the General Assembly of the State of Ohio,* That the Register and Receiver of the Ohio Canal Land Office for Piqua District, are hereby authorized and required to refund to John Dorrough, the sum of one hundred dollars, the amount paid by him for the west half of the south-east quarter of section thirty-six, township [one,] and south, of range six, east, Ohio canal land, containing eighty acres, upon his surrendering to them the final certificate, receipt, or other evidence of title to the same; and the said Register and Receiver are hereby authorized and required to cancel the said final certificate, receipt, or other evidence of title, and file the same in the office to which the same may properly belong, and also to cancel the said entry on their books, or balance the account on the same, and hold the said tract of land for sale, as though the same had not been sold.

WILLIAM MEDILL,

Speaker pro tem. of the House of Representatives.

ELIJAH VANCE,

Speaker of the Senate.

March 14, 1836.

AN ACT

To incorporate the Chillicothe and Cincinnati Rail-road Company.

Sec. 1. *Be it enacted by the General Assembly of the State of Ohio,* That Allen Latham, William Ross and John Madeira, of Ross county; John Ekin, Samuel Bell and James Young, of Highland county; Samuel Perin, William Curry and John M. Brown, of Clermont county; and Morgan Neville, George W. Holmes, Leonard Armstrong, of Hamiliton county, be, and they are hereby appointed commissioners, under the direction of a majority of whom, subscriptions may be received to the capital stock of the Chillicothe and Cincinnati Rail-road Company, hereby incorporated; and they, or a majority of them, may cause books to be opened at such times and places as they may direct, for the purpose of receiving subscriptions to the capital stock of said company, after giving thirty days notice of the time and place of opening the same, by publication in a newspaper printed nearest the place of opening the books, for at least thirty days; and that, upon the first opening of said books, they shall be kept open for at least ten days in succession, from ten o'clock, A. M. until two o'clock, P. M.; and if, at the expiration of that period, such a subscription to the capital stock of said company as is necessary to its incorporation, shall not have been obtained, then said commissioners, or a majority of them, may cause said books, by giving notice as aforesaid, to be opened from time to time, after the expiration of said ten days, and for the space of three years thereafter; and if any of said commissioners shall die, resign, or refuse to act, during the continuance of the duties devolved upon them by this act, another or others may be appointed in his or their stead by the remaining commissioners, or a majority of them.

Sec. 2. That the capital stock of the Chillicothe and Cincinnati Railroad Company, shall be eight hundred thousand dollars, and shall be divided in shares of fifty dollars each; which shares may be subscribed for by any corporation, or by individuals; and it shall and may be lawful for said corporation to commence the construction of the said rail-road or way, and enjoy all the powers and privileges conferred by this act as soon as the sum of eighty thousand dollars shall be subscribed to said stock.

Sec. 3. That all persons who shall become stockholders pursuant to this act, shall be, and they are hereby created a body corporate, and shall be and remain a corporation forever, under the name of the Chillicothe and Cincinnati Rail-road Company; and by that name, shall be capable in law of purchasing, holding, selling, leasing and conveying estates, real, personal and mixed, for the benefit of said company, so far as may be necessary for the purposes of said road; and shall have perpetual succession; and by said corporate name, may contract and be contracted with, sue and be sued, and may have and use a common seal, which they shall have power to alter or renew at their pleasure; and shall have, enjoy, and may exercise all the powers, rights and privileges, which corporate bodies may lawfully do, for the purposes mentioned in this act.

Sec. 4. That upon all subscriptions there shall be paid at the time of subscribing, to the said commissioners, or their agents appointed to receive such subscriptions, the sum of five dollars on every share subscribed; and the residue thereof shall be paid in such instalments, and at such times, as may be required by the president and directors of said company: *Provided*, No payment other than the first shall be demanded, until at least thirty days public notice of such demand shall have been given by said president and directors, in some newspaper of general circulation in the State of Ohio; and if any stockholder shall fail or neglect to pay any instalment, or part of said subscription thus demanded, for the space of sixty days next after the time the same shall be due and payable, the said president and directors, upon giving at least thirty days previous notice thereof, may, and they are hereby authorized to sell at public vendue so many of the shares of the said delinquent stockholder or stockholders as shall be necessary to pay such instalment and the expenses of advertising and sale, and transfer the shares so sold to the purchaser; and the residue of the money arising from such sale, after paying such instalment and expense, shall be paid to said stockholder on demand.

Sec. 5. That at the expiration of ten days, for which the books are first opened, if one hundred shares of said capital stock shall have been subscribed, or if not, as soon thereafter as the same shall be subscribed, if within three years after the opening of the books, the said commissioners, or a majority of them, shall call a general meeting of the stockholders at such time and place as they may appoint, and shall give at least sixty days previous notice thereof; and at such meeting, the said commissioners shall lay the subscription books before the stockholders then and there present; and thereupon the said stockholders, or a majority of them, shall elect thirteen directors by ballot; a majority of whom shall be competent to manage the affairs of said company; they shall have the power of electing a president of said company, from among the directors, and of allowing him such compensation as they may deem proper; and in said election, and on all other occasions wherein a vote of the stockholders of said company is to be taken, each stockholder shall be allowed one vote for every share owned by it, him or her; and every stockholder may depute any other person to vote and act for him or her, as his or their proxy; and the commissioners aforesaid, or any three of them, shall be judges of the first election of said directors.

Sec. 6. That to continue the succession of the president and directors of said company, thirteen directors shall be chosen annually on the third Monday of October, in every year, at such place as a majority of the directors shall appoint; and if any vacancy shall occur by death, resignation, or otherwise, of any president or director, before the year for which he was elected has expired, a person to fill such vacant place for the residue of the year may be appointed by the president and directors of said company, or a majority of them; and that the president and directors of said company shall hold and exercise their offices until a new election of president and directors; and that all elections which are by this act, or the by-laws of the company, to be made on a particular day, or at a particular time, if not made on such a day or time, may be made at any time within thirty days thereafter.

Sec. 7. That a general meeting of the stockholders shall be held annually, at the time and place appointed for the election of president and directors of said company; that meetings may be called at any time during the interval between the said annual meetings, by the president and directors, or a majority of them, or by the stockholders owning at least one-fourth of the stock subscribed, upon giving at least thirty days public notice of the time and place of holding the same; and when any such meetings are called, by the stockholders, such notice shall specify the particular object of the call; and if, at any such called meeting, a majority in value of the stockholders of said company are not present in person or by proxy, such meeting shall be adjourned from day to day without transacting any business, for any time, not exceeding three days; and if, within said three days, stockholders, holding a majority in value of the stock subscribed, do not thus attend, such meeting shall be dissolved.

Sec. 8. That at the regular meetings of the stockholders of said company, it shall be the duty of the president and directors in office for the previous year, to exhibit a clear and distinct statement of the affairs of the company; that at any called meeting of the stockholders, a majority of those present in person or by proxy, may require similar statements from the president and directors, whose duty it shall be to furnish them when thus required; and that at all general meetings of the stockholders, a majority in value of all the stockholders of said company may remove from office any president or any of the directors of said company, and may appoint others in their stead.

Sec. 9. That any president and director of said company, before he acts as such, shall take an oath or affirmation, as the case may be, that he will well and truly discharge the duties of his said office to the best of his skill and judgment.

Sec. 10. That the said president and directors, or a majority of them, may appoint all such officers, engineers, agents or servants whatsoever, as they may deem necessary for the transaction of the business of the company, and may remove any of them at their pleasure; that they, or a majority of them, shall have the power to determine by contract the compensation of all engineers, officers, agents, or servants, in the employ of said company: and to determine by their by-laws the manner of adjusting and settling all accounts against the company; and, also, the manner and evidence of transfers of stock in said company; and they, or a majority of them, shall have the power to pass all by-laws, which they may deem necessary or proper for exercising all the powers vested in the company hereby incorporated, and carrying the objects of this act into effect.

Sec. 11. That the said corporation shall be, and they are hereby vested with the right to construct a double or single rail-road or way, from Chillicothe, in the county of Ross, to Cincinnati, in the county of Hamilton; to transport, take and carry property and persons upon the same, by the power and force of steam, of animals, or of mechanical or other power, or of any combination of them, which the corporation may choose to employ.

Sec. 12. That the president and directors of said company shall be, and they are hereby invested with all rights and powers necessary for the location, construction and repair of said road, not exceeding one hundred feet wide, with as many sets of tracks as the said president and directors may deem necessary, and they may cause to be made, contract with others for making the said rail-road, or any part of it; and they, or their agents, or those with whom they may contract for making any part of the same, may enter upon and use and excavate any land which may be wanted for the site of said road, or for any other purpose necessary and useful in the construction, or in the repair of said road or its works, and that they may build bridges, may fix scales and weights, may lay rails, may take and use any earth, timber, gravel, stone or other materials which may be wanted for the construction or repair of any part of said road, or of any of its works; and may make and construct all works whatsoever, which may be necessary in the construction or repair of said road.

Sec. 13. That the president and directors of said company, or a majority of them, or any persons authorized by them, or a majority, may agree with the owner or owners of any lands, earth, timber, gravel or stone, or other materials, or any improvements which may be wanted for the construction or repair of said road, or any of their works, for the purchase, use, or occupation of the same; and, if they cannot agree, and if the owner or owners, or any of them, be a *feme covert*, under age, *non compos mentis*, or out of the county in which the property wanted may lie, when such lands and materials may be wanted, application may be made to any justice of the peace of such county, who shall thereupon issue his warrant, under his hand and seal, directed to the sheriff of said county, or to some disinterested person if the sheriff shall be interested, requiring him to summon a jury of twelve men, inhabitants of said county, not related, or in anywise interested, to meet on the land or near to the other property or materials to be valued, on a day named in said warrant, not less than ten nor more than twenty days after the issuing of the same; and if, at the said time and place, any of said persons summoned, do not attend, the said sheriff, or summoner shall immediately summon as many persons as may be necessary, with the persons in attendance, to furnish a pannel of twelve jurors in attendance; and from them, each party, or its, his or her, or their agent, the sheriff or summoner, for him, her, it or them, may strike off three jurors, and the remaining six shall act as a jury of inquest of damages; and before they act as such, the said summoner or sheriff shall administer to each of them an oath or affirmation, as the case may be, that they will faithfully and impartially value the damages which the owner or owners will sustain by use or occupation of the same, required by said company; and the jury estimating the damages, if for the ground occupied by said road, shall take into the estimate the benefits resulting to said owner or owners, by reason of said [road] passing through or upon the land of such owner or owners, towards the extinguishment of said claim for damages; and the said jury shall reduce their inquisition to writing, and shall sign and seal the same; and it shall then be returned to the clerk of the court of common pleas for said county, and by such clerk filed in his office, and shall be confirmed by the said court at its next session, if no sufficient cause to the contrary be shown; and when confirmed, shall be recorded by said clerk, at the expense of said company; and if set aside, the court may direct another inquisition to be taken in manner above prescribed; and such inquisition shall describe the property taken, or the bounds of the lands condemned; and such valuation, when paid or tendered to the owner or owners of said property, or his, her, or their legal representatives, shall entitle said company to the estate and interest in the same thus valued, as fully as if it had been conveyed by the owner or owners of the same, so long as the same shall be used for the purposes of said road; and the valuation, if not received when tendered, may, at any time thereafter, be received from the company without cost, by the owner or owners, his, her, or their legal representatives; and such sheriff, or summoner, and jurors, shall be entitled to demand and receive from the said company, the same fees, as are allowed for like services, in cases of fixing the valuation of real estate, previous to sale under execution.

Sec. 14. That whenever in the construction of said road, it shall be necessary to cross or intersect any established road or way, it shall be the duty of the said president and directors of said company so to construct said rail-road across such established road or way, as not to impede the passage or transportation of persons or property along the same, or when it shall be necessary to pass through the land of any individual, it shall also be their duty to provide for such individual proper wagon ways across said road, from one part of his land to another, without unnecessary delay.

Sec. 15. That if said company should neglect to provide proper wagon ways across said road, as required by the fourteenth section of this act, it shall be lawful for any individual to sue said company, and to be entitled to such damages, as a jury may think him, or her, entitled to, for such neglect on the part of said company.

Sec. 16. That [if] it shall be necessary for such company, in the selection of the route, or construction of the road to be by them laid out and constructed, or of any part of it, to connect the same with, or to use any turnpike road, or bridge, made or erected by any company or persons incorporated, or authorized by any law of this State, it shall be lawful for the said president and directors, and they are hereby authorized, to contract or agree with any such other corporation or persons, for the right to use said road or bridge, or for the transfer of any of the corporate or other rights or privileges of such corporation or persons, to the said company hereby incorporated; and every such other incorporaticn, or persons incorporated by, or acting under the laws of this State, is, and hereby are authorized to make such an agreement, contract, or transfer, by and through the agency of the person authorized by their respective acts of incorporation, to exercise their corporate powers, or by such [persons] as by any law of this State, are entrusted with the management and direction of said turnpike, road or bridge, or of any of the rights and privileges . aforesaid; and any contract, agreement or transfer, made in pursuance of the power and authority hereby granted, when executed, by the several parties under their respective corporate seals, or otherwise legally authenticated, shall vest in the company hereby incorporated, all such road, part of road, rights and privileges, and the right to use and enjoy the same, as fully, to all intents and purposes, as they now are, or might be used and exercised by the said corporation, or persons in whom they are now vested.

· Sec. 17. That the said president and directors shall have power to purchase with the funds of the company, and place on any rail-road constructed by them, under this act, all machines, wagons, vehicles, or carriages of any description whatsoever, which they may deem necessary or proper, for the purposes of transportation on said road; and that they shall have power to charge for tolls upon and transportation of goods, produce, merchandize, or property of any kind whatsoever, transported by them or their agents, along said rail-way, any sum not exceeding the following rates: on all goods, merchandize, or property of any description, transported by them, any sum not exceeding one and a half cents per ton per mile for toll, five cents per mile for transportation, and for the transportation of passengers, not exceeding three cents per mile for each passenger; and all persons paying the tolls aforesaid, may, with suitable and proper cars, take, transport and carry persons and property on the same, subject to the rules and regulations of said company as to the construction and speed of said cars; and the said road, with all their works, improvements, and profits, and all machinery owned by said company, and used on said road for transportation, are hereby vested in said company, incorporated by this act, and their successors forever; and the shares of the capital stock of said company shall be deemed and considered personal property, transferable by assignment, agreeably to the by-laws of said company.

Sec. 18. That the said president and directors shall, annually or semi-annually, declare and make such dividends as they may deem proper, of the nett profits arising from the resources of said company, deducting the necessary current and probable contingent expenses; and that they shall divide the same amongst the stockholders of said company in proportion to their respective shares.

Sec. 19. That any other rail road company now or hereafter to be chartered by law of this State, may join and connect said road with the roads hereby contemplated, and run cars upon the same, under the rules and regulations of this company, as to the construction and speed of said cars; and full right and privilege is hereby reserved to the State, or individuals, or any company incorporated by law of this State, to cross this road with any other road: *Provided,* That in so crossing, no injury be done to the works of the company hereby incorporated.

Sec. 20. That the State shall have power at any time after thirty-five years from the passage of this act, to purchase and hold said road, for the use of the State, at a price not exceeding the original cost for the construction of said road and the necessary permanent fixtures at the time of purchase, and fifteen per cent. thereon; of which cost an accurate statement in writing shall be submitted to the General Assembly, duly attested by the oath of the officers of said company, if the General Assembly shall require it.

Sec. 21. That if any person or persons, shall wilfully, or by any means whatsoever, injure, impair, or destroy any part of said rail road, constructed by said company under this act, or any of the works, buildings, or machinery of said company, such person or persons so offending, shall, each of them, for every such offence, forfeit and pay to the said company any sum not exceeding three fold the damages; which may be recovered in the name of the company, by an action of debt, in the court of common pleas for the county wherein the offence shall be committed: and shall also be subject to an indictment in said court, and upon conviction of such offence shall be punished by fine and imprisonment, at the discretion of the court.

Sec. 22. That if said rail road shall not be commenced in three years from the passage of this act, and shall not be finished within ten years from the time of the commencement thereof, then this act to be null and void.

Sec. 23. Whenever the dividends of said company shall exceed six per cent. per annum, the Legislature of this State may impose such reasonable taxes on the amount of said dividends as may be received from other rail-road companies.

WILLIAM MEDILL,
Speaker pro tem. of the House of Representatives.
ELIJAH VANCE,
Speaker of the Senate.

March 14, 1836.

AN ACT

For the relief of Archibald Cooper.

WHEREAS, It is reported to this General Assembly, that Archibald Cooper, of Fairfield county, did, on the twentieth day of December, A. D. 1831, purchase of the auditor of said county, one hundred acres of land, situated in range No. 20, township No. 16, S. C. No. 20, and purporting to be a part of the east half of lot No. 33, refugee lands, for the sum of $205 75, which he paid to said auditor, and received from him a certificate of purchase for said lands; which lands were so sold under the act of the 14th of March, 1831, as lands forfeited to the State for non-payment of taxes thereon, charged on the tax duplicate of said county, in the name of Hugh Flinn's heirs: *And whereas,* It has been satisfactorily ascertained that the whole of said lot No. 33, at the several times when said supposed taxes became due, was owned by other individuals than said Hugh Flinn's heirs, and the whole amount of taxes assessed thereon before the said supposed forfeiture and sale, regularly paid, by reason of which the said sale is void and of no effect: Therefore,

Sec. 1. *Be it enacted by the General Assembly of the State of Ohio,* That the State Treasurer be, and he is hereby authorized and required, upon the warrant of the auditor of State, to refund and pay to the said Archibald Cooper, the said sum of two hundred and five dollars and seventy-five cents, out of any moneys in the treasury of this State, not otherwise appropriated: that the commissioners of Fairfield county be, and they are hereby authorized and required, to refund and pay to the said Archibald Cooper, the amount of taxes by him paid on said land, since the 12th day of December, A. D. 1831, out of the treasury of said county.

WILLIAM MEDILL,
Speaker pro tem. of the House of Representatives.

ELIJAH VANCE,
Speaker of the Senate.

. March 14, 1836.

- - - - -- - - - -- - - - - - - - -

AN ACT

To improve the Navigation of the Walhonding and Mohican Waters.

Sec. 1. *Be it enacted by the General Assembly of the State of Ohio,* That the board of public works, of this State, be, and they are hereby, empowered and directed, to construct a navigable communication, commencing at the Ohio canal, near the mouth of the Walhonding river, in Coshocton county, up said stream as far as the board of public works shall deem to be for the best interests of the State; by canal and slack-water navigation, as they may deem most for the interest of the State; with such locks and dams, as may be necessary to secure the safe transit, and convenient passage of canal boats, of such dimensions and capacity as are permitted to navigate the Ohio canal; and to accomplish that object, the said board are hereby empowered to seize, dedicate, acquire, hold, use, and occupy, for the use and benefit of the State, all such private and corporate estate and property as shall ben ecessary for the convenience of the construction of that improvement, and for hydraulic purposes thereon, as they have heretofore had power to do, in the construction and maintenance of the Ohio and Miami canals: *Provided,* That the owners and proprietors of any property, so seized and dedicated, shall have all the rights of indemnity, and remedies of compensation, as by law have been provided for the construction of the Ohio and Miami canals; and when the said improvement shall be completed, or any part thereof, the said board of public works, at their discretion, shall levy and assess such tolls thereon as may, at any time, be levied and assessed on the Ohio canal; and rent out the water power thereon, on such terms and conditions, as may seem right and just, having reference to, and in view of the interest of the State, and the permanent prosperity of the country adjoining said waters: *Provided, also,* That no part of said work shall be put contract, until the owners of the land where any water power may be created by such part of the work, by locks, dams, or otherwise, shall first sell, or give and convey to the State, a sufficient quantity of such land for the convenient use of the water power so created.

Sec. 2.   That preparatory to the construction of said improvement, the board of public works may cause such further surveys and examinations to be made, in relation thereto, as in their judgment may be considered proper for the successful prosecution of the work; and the accounts and documents of all expenses incurred, and disbursements made, and the revenue or income received by, or under the authority of this act, shall be kept separate and distinct from those belonging to, or connected with, the other public works of the State.

Sec. 3.   That for the purpose of carrying into effect the provisions of this act, the commissioners of the canal fund be, and they are hereby authorized, to borrow, on the credit of the State, any sum not exceeding two hundred dollars, in the years eighteen hundred and thirty-six, and eighteen hundred and thirty-seven; at a rate of interest, not exceeding six per centum per annum, payable semi-annually, at the city of New York, or elsewhere; the principal thereof, to be paid at any time after the year eighteen hundred and fifty-six, at the pleasure of the State, whose faith is hereby pledged for the payment of such loan, and the interest thereon, as above specified; and further, for the payment of such loan, and the ultimate redemption of the principal thereof, there is, hereby, irrevocably pledged, the proceeds of all tolls and water rents; and all other revenues and incomes, which may be received on said improvements, after deducting therefrom the annual expenses thereof, in keeping the same in repair, and other incidental charges of its superintendence and police: *Provided,* That the loan herein authorized, shall not be made, nor the work herein authorized commenced, unless the board of public works shall be of opinion that said work would be conducive to the public interest, and yield a revenue to the State, sufficient to meet the interest on the costs of the improvement.

Sec. 4.   That in the construction of this work, and in the management and superintendence thereof, the board of public works, and the commissioners of the canal fund, shall possess and exercise the same powers, in all respects, as to the appointment of engineers, and other officers and agents, and providing for a strict accountability of all moneys expended, as they have heretofore possessed and exercised, in the construction, maintenance, and supervision of the Ohio and Miami canals.

Sec. 5.   That so much of the act to establish a board of commissioners for the purpose of improving the navigation of the Black Fork of Mohican and Walhonding river, passed March 7th, 1835, as interferes with the improvements contemplated in this act, be, and the same is hereby repealed.

WILLIAM MEDILL,

Speaker pro tem. of the House of Representatives.

ELIJAH VANCE,

Speaker of the Senate.

March 14, 1836.

AN ACT

Vesting the city council of the city of Cincinnati with powers to borrow money for the purpose of purchasing the Cincinnati Water Works, and to manage the same.

Sec. 1. *Be it enacted by the General Assembly of the State of Ohio*, That when the city council of the city of Cincinnati shall have submitted to the citizens a detailed proposition for the purchase of the "Cincinnati Water Works," and the qualified electors of said city shall have decided by a majority of their votes in favor of purchasing the same, the city council shall be, and they are hereby authorized to borrow, at a rate of interest not exceeding five per centum per annum, and for a period not exceeding fifty years, and a sum not exceeding the amount stated and specified in the proposition submitted to and accepted by the vote of the citizens, to provide for the payment of the interest thereon, and the final redemption of the debt, and to pledge the property and revenue of the city therefor, in such manner, terms and conditions, as may be necessary and proper to consummate the loan, and purchase of said water works, and to pass all such ordinances, not inconsistent with this act, as may be necessary to protect and manage the same.

Sec. 2. That so soon as the water works shall have become the property of the city, there shall be elected by the city council four judicious and competent freeholders, having other qualifications of members of council; and the four thus elected, together with the president of the city council, shall constitute and be denominated "The Board of Trustees of the Water Works;" and the term of service of the four trustees first elected, shall be so arranged by lot as that one of the four shall serve four years, one three years, one two years, and the other one year, from the second Monday of May, 1836; and there shall be one trustee elected on the first Wednesday in May, annually thereafter, to serve four years; and said trustees shall have the care, superintendence and management of said water works, and employ such officers, agents and laborers, and adopt such rules, and regulations as may be necessary to manage and conduct the same, and fix and determine their compensation; but no compensation shall be allowed to either of the trustees for their services.

Sec. 3. That it shall be the duty of said trustees to cause correct accounts to be kept of all transactions relating to the water works; to cause all accounts to be properly audited, certified and presented to the city council for allowance; and on the third Wednesday of March annually, a full detailed statement of all receipts and disbursements of the past year,

with an estimate of the amount necessary for the payment of the interest
and all other expenses for the ensuing year, shall be reported to the city
council; and it shall be their duty to levy and cause to be collected an
equitable water tax or rent from all that use the water furnished by the
water works; and in no case shall the rates of water tax or rent be so low
as not to insure a nett revenue at least equal to the payment of the interest on the loan, and all other disbursements necessary for the extending,
repairing and conducting of said water works; and if in any year the receipts should fall short of the necessary disbursements, the amount of such
deficiency shall be levied and collected in the succeeding year, in addition to the usual rates.

Sec. 4.   That all moneys received by the officers, agents or others, for
or on account of the water, shall be paid into the city treasury, and shall
be drawn out only by the order of the city council; but in no case shall
the funds belonging to the water works be drawn, appropriated or used
for any purpose whatever, except that of said works.

Sec. 5.   That it shall be the duty of said board of trustees to cause to
be faithfully executed, all ordinances of the city, not inconsistent with the
provisions of this act, made for the protection of the water works, waste
of water, collection of rents, and settlement and examination of accounts
with the officers and agents.

WILLIAM MEDILL,
Speaker pro tem. of the House of Representatives.
ELIJAH VANCE,
Speaker of the Senate.

March 14, 1836.

AN ACT

Making special appropriations of the three per cent. fund, in the county of Warren, for the
year 1836.

Sec. 1.   *Be it enacted by the General Assembly of the State of Ohio,*
That there shall be expended in the county of Warren, out of the three
per cent. fund belonging to said county, the sum of three hundred and
seventy-eight dollars, between the first day of April and the first day of
September, eighteen hundred and thirty-six, as follows: on the state road
from Phillips' mill, on the Little Miami, by Twenty Mile Stand, to Hamilton county line, the sum of ninety-seven dollars, under the superintendence of John Ross; on the state road from Lebanon, by Palmyra, to the
county line towards Cincinnati, the sum of ninety-nine dollars, under the
superintendence of John Randall; on the state road from Lebanon to Hamilton, between Lebanon and the county line, the sum of twenty-five dollars, under the superintendence of Micaijah Reeder; on the state road
from Lebanon to Dayton, the sum of thirty dollars, under the superintendence of Nathan Graham; on the state road from Lebanon to Wilmington,
between Lebanon and the Little Miami, the sum of twenty-seven dollars,
under the superintendence of Jeremiah Smith; on the state road from
Waynesville to Wilmington, to the county line, the sum of twenty-five
dollars, under the superintendence of Burwell Goode; and on the state

road from Lebanon, by Waynesville, to the county line towards Xenia, the sum of seventy-five dollars, under the superintendence of Samuel Rodgers: *Provided*, That the persons hereby authorized to make the expenditures aforesaid, shall account to the commissioners of Warren county, for the faithful application of the moneys hereby appropriated: *Provided, also*, That should any of the superintendents named in this act, die, remove out of the county, or refuse to serve, the commissioners of the county shall forthwith fill such vacancy, on being notified of the same.

WILLIAM MEDILL,
Speaker pro tem. of the House of Representatives.
ELIJAH VANCE,
Speaker of the Senate.

March 14, 1836.

AN ACT

To improve the navigation of Wills creek.

Sec. 1. *Be it enacted by the General Assembly of the State of Ohio,* That the Board of Public Works of this State be, and they are hereby empowered and directed, if, on a full examination, they shall deem it of public utility, and when completed that it will yield a revenue to the State, sufficient to meet the interest on its cost, taking into view the increased business it will introduce to the Ohio canal, to improve the navigation of Wills creek, from its mouth, at its junction with the Muskigum river, to the Seneca and Buffalo forks of the same, by means of dams, locks, towing paths, and such other improvements, as may be necessary to secure the safe transit, and convenient passage of canal and other boats, of such dimensions and capacity, as are permitted to navigate the Ohio canal, and, to accomplish that object, the said board of public works are hereby empowered to seize, dedicate, acquire, hold, use, and occupy, for the use and benefit of the State, all such private and corporate estate and property, as shall be necessary for the convenience of the construction of that improvement, and for hydraulic purposes thereon, as they have heretofore had power to do in the construction and maintenance of the Ohio and Miami canals: *Provided*, That the owners and proprietors of any property so seized and dedicated, shall have all the rights of indemity, and remedies of compensation, as by law have been provided for in the construction of the Ohio and Miami canals; and, when the the said improvement shall be completed, or any part thereof, the said board of public works, at their discretion, shall levy and assess such tolls thereon, as they may think the interest of the State may require, and rent out the water power thereon, on such terms and conditions, as may seem right and just, having reference to, and in view of the interest of the State, and permanent prosperity of the Wills creek valley: *Provided, however*, That the said board shall not be required to commence said improvement, until the owners or proprietors of the lands contiguous to the places where dams, or locks, shall be located and constructed by the State, shall convey to the State a sufficient quantity of such land, for the convenient use of the water power which will be created by such improvement, without any expense to the State.

Sec. 2. That preparatory to the construction of said improvement, the board of public works may cause such further surveys and examinations to be made in relation thereto, as in their judgment may be considered proper for the successful prosecution of the work; and the accounts and documents of all expenses incurred, and disbursements made, and the revenue or income received by, or under the authority of this act, shall be kept separate and distinct from those belonging to, or connected with, the other public works of the State.

Sec. 3. That for the purpose of carrying into effect the provisions of this act, the commissioners of the canal fund be, and they are hereby authorized to borrow, on the credit of the State, any sum not exceeding ninety thousand dollars, at the rate of interest not exceeding six per centum per annum, payable semi-annually, at the city of New York, or elsewhere, the principal thereof to be paid at any time after the year eighteen hundred and fifty six, at the pleasure of the State, whose faith is hereby pledged for the payment of such loan, and the interest thereon, as above specified; and further, for the payment of said loan, and the ultimate redemption of the principal thereof, there is hereby, irrevocably pledged, the proceeds of all tolls and water rents, and all other revenues and incomes which may be received on said improvement, after deducting therefrom the annual expenses thereof, in keeping the same in repair, and other incidental charges of its superintendence and police.

Sec. 4. That in the construction of this work, and in the management and superintendence thereof, the board of public works, and commissioners of the canal fund, shall possess and exercise the same powers in all respects, as to the appointment of engineers and other officers and agents, and providing for a strict accountability of all moneys expended, as they have heretofore possessed and exercised, in the construction, maintenance, and supervision of the Ohio and Miami canals.

Sec. 5. That no part of the improvement herein directed, shall be made until the sum of ten thousand dollars shall be raised by individual subscription, as a donation to the State, in aid of this work, and the payment thereof secured to the satisfaction of the board of public works, to be paid as follows, to wit: one-fourth thereof so soon as one-fourth of said work shall be completed; one-fourth so soon as one-half of said work shall be done; one-fourth so soon as three-fourths of said improvement shall be made; and the remainder so soon as the entire work shall be completed; and if, on the completion of the improvement herein contemplated, any portion of the funds herein directed to be expended thereon, should remain on hand, the canal commissioners are hereby directed to expend the same in improvement of the said Seneca and Buffalo forks, or either of them, at their discretion.

WILLIAM MEDILL,
Speaker pro tem. of the House of Representatives.
ELIJAH VANCE,
Speaker of the Senate.

March 14, 1836.
79—L

AN ACT

To incorporate the Bellville and Bolivar Canal Company.

Sec. 1. *Be it enacted by the General Assembly of the State of Ohio,* That Benjamin Jackson, Hugh Newel, William Morrow, John Markly, James Welch, Daniel Carpenter, Ira Babcock, Noble Calhoon, William McNaul, C. H. Rice, Jacob Armintrout, William Darling, Nathaniel Haskel, Thomas McMahen, Joseph White, Abel Strong, Esq., William C. Harrison, of the county of Richland; and Isaac Bonnett, Cornelius Quick, Seth Hunt, John Hall, George Snyder, Jacob Fry, and Peter Piersal, of the county of Holmes; and George W. Slingluff, John Patton, William Graham, Reason Pitchard, John Machar, and Amzi McNaul, of the county of Tuscarawas, their associates and successors, be, and they are hereby constituted and made a body politic and corporate, and shall be and remain a corporation forever, under the name and style of the Bellville and Bolivar Canal Company; and by that name may contract and be contracted with, plead and be impleaded, answer and be answered unto, and prosecute to final judgment, in all courts having competent jurisdiction; and may have a common seal, and the same to alter and renew at pleasure; and shall be, and hereby are vested with all the powers and privileges, which are necessary to carry into effect the objects of this association.

Sec. 2. That the said corporation be, and they are hereby authorized, to locate, make, construct, and forever maintain, a navigable canal, with all necessary locks, towing paths, basins, aqueducts, culverts, waste-weirs, dams, wharves, embankments, toll houses, and other necessary appendages; to commence in or near the town of Bellville, in the county of Richland; from thence to pass down the Clear Fork of Mohican, to Newville; from thence in a direction to Perrysville; from thence down the Black Fork of the Mohican, to Loudonville, in said county; from thence to Middletown, in Holmes county; from thence the most practicable route, until it shall intersect the Sandy and Beaver canal, at Bolivar, or some other suitable point on the Ohio canal, in the county of Tuscarawas; and that said corporation shall have the privilege and power of extending said canal from Bellville, in Richland county, under the provisions of this act, up the Clear Fork of Mohican, if it shall be found practicable, to the town of Lexington, in said county.

Sec. 3. That for the purpose of assuring to said corporation all the lands, real estate, waters and materials, requisite for most economically constructing and maintaining such navigation of the said canal, and the waters connected therewith, and incident and necessary to the navigation of the same, whenever the said lands, waters and materials, shall not be obtained by voluntary donation or fair purchase, it shall be lawful for said corporation, by any of their officers, and by each and every agent, superintendent, or engineer, by them employed, to enter upon, take possession of, and use all such lands and real estate, as shall be necessary for the purposes aforesaid; and also to enter upon and take all necessary materials for the construction of said canal, adjoining or near said canal, on whose lands soever the same may be, doing thereby no unnecessary damage; they satisfying and paying all damages which may be occasioned thereby, and any person or persons, incorporation or incorporations, in the manner hereinafter provided.

Sec. 4. That said corporation be, and hereby are authorized and empowered to purchase and hold, to them and their successors, forever, real and personal estate, to any amount necessary for constructing, maintaining and repairing said canal as aforesaid; and may receive, hold, and take all voluntary grants and donations of lands and real estates, which shall be made to aid the objects of said corporation.

Sec. 5. That a toll be, and hereby is granted and established, for the sole benefit of said corporation forever; and it shall be lawful for said corporation, from time to time, [to] fix, regulate and receive the tolls and charges by them to be received, for the transportation of property; or persons, on the canals authorized by this act: *Provided,* That the tolls and charges thus fixed, regulated and received by said corporation, shall at no time exceed the highest rate of tolls and duties, together with the charges of freight, to which property of a similar kind is subjected, as the costs of transportation on the Ohio canal during the same period of time.

Sec. 6. That the president and directors of said corporation shall have power, from time to time, to make and ordain such by-laws, rules, and regulations, as may be necessary, touching the premises; especially to fix upon and determine the size and form of boats, rafts, and all other vessels that shall be used for the purpose of navigating said canal; to determine the time and manner of their passing the locks, and what commodities shall not be transported during a want of water, should such an event happen, and also to regulate the mode of transferring the stock of said corporation: and the penalties imposed by said by-laws, rules and regulations, may be sued for and recovered by the treasurer of said corporation, or by any other person thereunto by said corporation authorized, to their own use and benefit, before any court having competent jurisdiction; which penalties shall in no case exceed the sum of ten dollars; and said corporation shall cause said by-laws, to the breach of which penalties are affixed, to be printed, and a copy thereof to be placed in some conspicuous situation at each toll house; and if any person or persons shall wilfully or maliciously mar, deface, or pull down any copy so set up, said corporation may sue for and recover to their own use, a sum not exceeding ten dollars, nor less than five dollars, of any such person or persons.

Sec. 7. That if any person or persons shall wilfully obstruct the water navigation, remove, or in any [way] spoil, injure or destroy said canal, or any part thereof, or any thing belonging thereto, or any materials to be used in the construction or repairs thereof, such person or persons shall forfeit and pay to said corporation, treble the amount of damages sustained by means of such offence or injury; to be sued for and recovered with costs of suit, in action of debt, in any court having competent jurisdiction, by the treasurer of said corporation, or by any person thereunto by said company authorized.

Sec. 8. That whenever any lands, waters, or materials, shall be taken and appropriated by said corporation for the location or construction of said canal navigation, or any work appertaining thereto, and the same shall not be given or granted to said corporation, and the proprietor or proprietors do not agree with the said corporation as to the amount of damages or compensations which ought to be allowed and paid therefor, and shall not mutually agree upon some person or persons to appraise the same, the damages shall be estimated and assessed by three commissioners, to be appointed by the court of common pleas for the county in which the damages complained of are sustained, in manner following: whenever said corporation shall have located said canal, or any part thereof, and shall have put the same under contract, or shall have used any water or materials for the construction thereof, any person or persons, corporation or corporations, injured thereby, may, at any time within twelve months thereafter, file his, her, or their claim for damages, in writing, particularly describing the premises, with some one of the said commissioners, or with the clerk of the court of common pleas for the county in which the damages complained of are sustained; and said commissioners, or any two of them, having been first duly sworn to a faithful and impartial discharge of their duties, within a reasonable time thereafter, (they themselves having had notice from the claimants, in case the claim is lodged with the clerk of the court of common pleas, that such claim has been filed,) having given previous notice to all parties interested, of the time and of the claims to be examined, by publishing an advertisement thereof three successive weeks in some newspaper printed in the counties in which said canal is located, in general circulation therein, in case one should be printed in the county, who shall meet and pass over the premises so used and appropriated by said corporation, for the purposes aforesaid; and after hearing the parties in interest, or such of them as desire to be heard, shall, according to the best of their skill and judgment, estimate all such damages as they shall think any person or persons, corporation or corporations, have sustaned, or will sustain by the opening of said canal navigation through his, her or their lands, or by the construction of any towing paths, basins, wharves, or other appendages, or for any materials used in the construction thereof, over and above the benefit and advantage which said commissioners shall adjudge may accrue to such person or persons, corporation or corporations, from opening said canal; and the said commissioners, or any two of them, shall make a report in writing, and, as soon as may be, file the same with the clerk of the court of common pleas for said county; and the same may be made the rule of said court at the next succeeding or any subsequent term thereof, as in the case of awards; and the report of said commissioners, when affirmed and recorded, shall forever be a bar to any action commenced, or to be commenced for damages against said corporation, on account of the injury for which such damages were awarded; and if the party, filing a claim for damages as aforesaid, shall fail to obtain damages in his favor, such party shall be liable for all costs arising from such application, and the court may enter judgment and issue execution therefor, as in other cases; and on all judgments against said corporation for damaged assessed as aforesaid, or for the costs thereof, execution may issue in the common form, *mutatis mutandis*, and may be levied on the goods and chattels, lands and tenements of said corporation; and said commissioners shall be allowed three dollars a day each for their services under the provisions of this act, to be paid by said corporation, except as hereinbefore provided.

Sec. 9. That the said corporation shall be, and is hereby authorized to raise sufficient funds for the accomplishment of the objects aforesaid; and, for that purpose, the persons named in the first section of this act, or a majority of them, shall be commissioners, whose duty it shall be, so soon after the taking effect of this act, as a majority of them shall judge proper, to cause books to opened at such times and places as they shall think fit, under the management of such persons as they shall appoint, for receiving subscriptions to the capital stock of said company; each share to be of the amount of fifty dollars, and each subscriber to be a member of said corporation for all purposes; and public notice shall be given in such manner as may be deemed advisable by said commissioners, of the times and places of opening said books; and the said commissioners, or a majority of them, may prescribe the form of said subscription; and whenever the sum of three hundred thousand dollars, or a greater part of the stock of said company shall have been subscribed, it shall be the duty of said commissioners, or a majority of them, to call a meeting of the stockholders, by causing notice to be published in one or more newspapers in general circulation in the respective places in which the books shall have been opened and stock subscribed, at least twenty days previous thereto, of the time and place of such meeting, which shall be at some convenient town or place near the route of the contemplated canal; at which meeting the stockholders, who shall attend for that purpose, either in person or by lawful proxy, shall elect by ballot seven directors, who shall hold their offices until the expiration of one year, and until others shall be chosen in their places; and the said commissioners shall be inspectors of the first election of directors of the said corporation, and shall certify, under their hands, the names of those duly elected, and shall deliver over to them the said certificates and subscription books; and at said election, and at all other elections or voting of any description, every member shall have a right to vote, by himself, or proxy duly authorized in writing; and each share shall entitle the holder to one vote; and the management of the concerns of the said corporation shall be entrusted to seven directors, to be elected annually by the stockholders by ballot; and that the directors first chosen, and such directors as shall thereafter be chosen at any subsequent election, shall immediately thereafter meet and elect one of their number, who shall be president thereof, until another election; and also elect a treasurer and secretary, who may be removed at the pleasure of the said president and directors, and others elected in their places; and that a majority of said directors shall constitute a board for every person [purpose] within the provisions of this act: *Provided, however*, In case it should at any time happen that the election of directors shall not be held on any day when, pursuant to this act, it ought to be held, the said corporation shall not, for that cause, be deemed to be dissolved; but such election may be held at any other time directed by the by-laws of said corporation.

Sec. 10. That the books of subscriptions shall remain open as long as the president and directors shall see fit; and each subscriber shall be bound to pay, from time to time, such amount of instalments on his stock, as the said president and directors may lawfully require; they giving at least thirty days previous notice of the time and place of making the payments required, in some newpapers having circulation in the county where said canal is located'; but no assessment shall ever be made so as to render any subscriber liable to pay more than fifty dollars for a share.

Sec. 11. That if any subscriber shall neglect to pay his subscription, or any part thereof, for the space of thirty days after he is required so to do by the said president and directors, notice having been given as required by this act, the treasurer of said corporation, or other officer duly authorized for that purpose, may make sale of such share or shares at public auction, to the highest bidder, giving at least thirty days notice thereof, in some newspaper in general circulation at the place of sale; and the same shall be transferred by the treasurer in the manner hereinafter provided, to the purchaser; and such delinquent subscriber shall be held accoutable to the corporation for the balance, if his share or shares be sold for less than the amount remaining due thereon, and shall be entitled to the overplus, if the same shall be sold for more than the amount so remaining due, after deducting the costs of sale.

Sec. 12. That when the land, or other property, belonging to any infant, *feme covert*, or insane person, shall be taken and appropriated for the use and purpose of said canal, as aforesaid, the husband of such *feme covert*, and the guardian of such infant, or insane person, respectively, may execute any deeds, enter into any contract, or to do any other matter or thing respecting such lands or other estate, to be taken and appropriated as aforesaid, as they might do if the same were by them holden in their own rights respectively.

Sec. 13. That for, and in consideration of the expenses the said company will be at in constructing said canal, and in keeping the same in repair, the said canal, together with all tolls and rents, and profits arising therefrom, shall be, and the same are hereby vested in said corporation: *Provided,* That the State shall have the power, at any time after the expiration of twenty-five years from the time of the completion of said work, to purchase and hold the same for the use of said State, by paying to the said corporation therefor, the amount expended by them in locating and constructing the same, together with fifteen per centum thereon.

Sec. 14. That the said corporation shall be entitled to the benefits of all laws which are, or shall be in force, for the collection of tolls, or for the protection of any canals constructed by this State; and in any suit instituted against the said corporation, the service of legal process on the president, any one of the directors, or on the treasurer or secretary of said corporation, shall be deemed and held, in all courts and places, a sufficient and valid service on the said corporation.

Sec. 15. That this act shall be deemed a public act, in all courts and places whatsoever.

WILLIAM MEDILL,
Speaker pro tem. of the House of Representatives.

ELIJAH VANCE,
Speaker of the Senate.

March 14, 1836.

RESOLUTIONS.

RESOLUTION

Appointing a Joint Select Committee, on the subject of the National Road.

Resolved, by the General Assembly of the State of Ohio, That so much of the message of His Excellency, the Governor, as relates to the ten and one half miles of the National Road, reported by Captain Brewerton, superintendent on the part of the United States, as finished and ready for delievery to the State, and so much of the report of the superintendent of repairs as relates to the same subject, be referred to a joint select committee of one member on the part of the Senate, and two members on the part of the House, and that said committee be instructed to make a personal inspection of the Road, and report the result to this General Assembly.

WM. SAWYER,
Speaker of the House of Representatives.
ELIJAH VANCE,
Speaker of the Senate.

14th Decr. 1835.

RESOLUTION

Adopting the Joint Rules of the last session, until others are adopted.

Resolved by the Senate and House of Representatives, That the Joint Rules adopted and in force for the government of both Houses, at their last session, be adopted for the government of both Heuses, at the present session, until others are adopted.

WM. SAWYER,
Speaker of the House of Representatives.
ELIJAH VANCE,
Speaker of the Senate.

15th Decr. 1835.

RESOLUTION

For printing two thousand copies of the Governor's Annual Message in the German Language.

Resolved, by the Senate and House of Representatives, That the State Printer be authorized to contract for the translation, and to print, two

thousand copies of His Excellency, the Governor's Annual Message in the
German language, for the use of the members of this General Assembly.

WM. SAWYER,
Speaker of the House of Representatives.
ELIJAH VANCE,
Speaker of the Senate.

5 Decr. 1835.

RESOLUTION

Authorizing the Clerks of both branches to employ Assistants.

Resolved by the General Assembly of the State of Ohio, That the clerks
of both branches of this Legislature, be authorized to employ one assistant
each, whose pay shall not exceed the sum of three dollars per day.

WM. SAWYER,
Speaker of the House of Representatives,
ELIJAH VANCE,
Speaker of the Senate.

January 2, 1836.

PREAMBLE AND RESOLUTIONS.

WHEREAS, The Senate of the United States did, on the 28th day of March,
1834, by resolution declare, "That the President, in the late Executive
proceedings in relation to the revenue, has assumed upon himself authority and power, not conferred by the constitution and laws, but in de-
rogation to both:" *And whereas,* The same was spread upon the journals
of the Senate, and now stands a part of the records of that body: *And
whereas,* That declaration was unauthorized by facts, and the adoption
of said resolution by the Senate of the United States, a manifest usurpation of the impeaching power of the House of Representatives, as well
as a dangerous invasion of the rights of the Executive, both as such, and
as a citizen of the Republic: *And whereas,* The President, on the passage of the resolution aforesaid, caused to be laid before the Senate his
protest against it, requesting the insertion thereof upon the journals of
that body: *And whereas,* The Senate did refuse compliance with such
just and reasonable request: *And whereas,* If the said act of the Senate
be permitted to pass uncensured, a precedent would thereby be established, founded in usurpation and injustice, and subversive of the first
first principle of a free government—the right of the vilest criminal to
meet his accusers, face to face, and be heard in his own defence: *And
whereas,* The people of the State of Ohio require and demand of their
Representatives in the Legislature assembled, a solemn and decided ex-
pression of disapprobation of the said act of the Senate: Therefore,

1st. *Resolved by the General Assembly of the State of Ohio,* That the
said resolution of the Senate, and the action had thereon by that body,

Were without precedent, gross "assumption of power, not conferred by the constitution and laws," but in violation of the spirit of both.

2d. *Resolved*, That the Senators representing in Congress this State, be, and they hereby are instructed and required to vote for the *expunging* of the resolution aforesaid from the journals of the Senate.

3d. *Resolved*, That we believe the right of instruction one of the fundamental principles of a Representative Government, and essentially necessary to the purity and stability of our republican institutions; and that in case the agents of the People are unable to obey the instructions of their respective constituents, it is their solemn duty to resign the power intrusted to them into the hands of those who gave it.

4th. *Resolved*, That the Governor of this State be requested to transmit to each of the Senators aforesaid, a copy of these resolutions; also a copy to the President and Vice-President of the United States.

5th. *Resolved*, That, in consideration of the distinguished relation in which the Honorable Thomas H. Benton, one of the Senators in Congress from the State of Missouri, stands to the subject of the foregoing resolutions, the Governor of this State be also requested to transmit a copy of these resolutions to that Senator.

WM. SAWYER,
Speaker of the House of Representatives.

ELIJAH VANCE,
Speaker of the Senate.

January 2, 1836.

PREAMBLE AND RESOLUTIONS

Relating to the National Road Bridge Company.

Whereas, The people of the State of Ohio feel a deep interest in the extension and completion of the *Cumberland Road*, and especially in the erection of a bridge across the Ohio river, at *Wheeling*, to connect the eastern section of said road, which now terminates at the eastern bank of said river, with the western section thereof, which commences at the western bank of said river, leaving a chasm in said road of nearly a mile, which is at times impassable: *And whereas*, It is believed by the General Assembly to be as much the duty of the government, resulting from its compacts with Ohio, and other western States, to erect such a bridge as it was to commence and construct said road: *And whereas*, The erection of a bridge at Wheeling, on a plan which will insure convenience, safety, and permanency, will be of immeasurable public and nation utility: Therefore,

Resolved by the Senate and House of Representatives of the General Assembly of the State of Ohio, That our Senators in Congress be instructed, and our Representatives be requested, to use their endeavors to procure further and more ample appropriations of the public money, for the continuation and more speedy construction and completion of the said Cum-

80—L

berland road, and for the purpose of erecting a permanent bridge across
the Ohio river, at *Wheeling, Virginia,* to connect the eastern with the
western section of said road.

Resolved, That the Governor be requested to forward duplicate copies
of the foregoing resolution and preamble to each of our Senators and Representatives in Congress, and also to the President and Vice-President of
the United States, to the Secretary of State, Secretary at War, Secretary
of the Navy, and the Post Master General.

WM. SAWYER,
Speaker of the House of Representatives.
ELIJAH VANCE,
Speaker of the Senate.

January 12, 1836.

RESOLUTION

To extend the time for the payment of taxes.

Resolved by the General Assembly of the State of Ohio, That the Auditor
and Treasurer of State, be, and they are hereby authorized to receive taxes on all lands and town lots not delinquent, and advertised for sale on the
last Monday of the current December; and also, on all lands and town
lots delinquent and advertised for sale, but not sold until the twentieth day of February, A. D. 1836, in the same manner that they are authorized by law to receive the same, if paid prior to the first day of January, 1836.

WM. SAWYER,
Speaker of the House of Representatives.
ELIJAH VANCE,
Speaker of the Senate.

January 13, 1836.

RESOLUTIONS

Relating to the Boundary line of Ohio and Indiana.

WHEREAS, There exist, at this time, doubts respecting the point on the Ohio
river at which the line between the States of Ohio and Indiana commences, and as differences of opinion exist between the citizens of the
two States as regards their respective boundaries:

Resolved by the General Assembly of the State of Ohio, That the Governor of the State of Ohio be, and is hereby authorized to appoint one commissioner on the part of the State of Ohio, who, in conjunction with one
to be appointed by the State of Indiana, shall meet in the town of Lawrenceburg, in the State of Indiana, on the first Monday in August, 1836, or

within fifteen days thereafter; and after having taken an oath or affirmation to faithfully and impartially discharge the duties required of them, shall take to their assistance a competent surveyor, who shall also take an oath or affirmation to faithfully and impartially discharge the duties' of surveyor; proceed to the mouth of the Great Miami, and then and there fix upon and determine the point on the north bank of the Ohio river where said line originally commenced, and at that point erect a monument or stone, with suitable monuments as witnesses thereto, and from thence run and mark the line to a point where it will intersect the State road leading from Elizabethtown, in the State of Ohio, to Lawrenceburg, in the State of Indiana, at which point they shall erect a monument or stone; and it shall be the duty of the Governor of the State of Ohio to procure from the Surveyor General and furnish said commissioners with a copy of the original field notes, and such other papers and instructions as may be necessary; and the said commissioners and surveyor shall make out three or more certified copies of the surveys made and directed; one copy of which shall be deposited with the Secretary of State of the State of Ohio, and one copy with the Surveyor General in Cincinnati, and the commissioner on the part of the State of Indiana, by him to be disposed of as the authorities of that State may direct; and the commissioner on the part of the State of Ohio, shall be entitled to the sum of three dollars per day for each day he may be employed in discharge of the duties herein required of him, and the surveyor shall receive the sum of one dollar and fifty cents for each day he may be employed as aforesaid, as being the half of his compensation; and the Governor of the State of Ohio is hereby authorized to pay the same out of the contingent fund; and further,

Resolved, That the Governor be directed to transmit a copy of these resolutions to the Governor of the State of Indiana, and request that they be laid before the Legislature of that State.

WM. SAWYER,
Speaker of the House of Representatives.

ELIJAH VANCE,
Speaker of the Senate.

January 15, 1836.

RESOLUTIONS

Relative to the Unavailable Funds in the Treasury.

Resolved by the General Assembly of the State of Ohio, That the Auditor and Treasurer of State, in presence of His Excellency the Governor, cancel the counterfeit bank notes and bills reported to be in the treasury on the 9th December, 1835, amounting to the sum of nine hundred and forty-nine dollars; and that the Auditor pass the amount thereof to the credit of the Treasurer, and furnish him with the necessary voucher.

Resolved, further, That the Treasurer be authorized to return to the Auditor four several drafts on the Commercial Bank of Cincinnati, heretofore drawn for 5 per cent. on the dividends of said bank, in all amounting to six thousand eight hundred and eighty-one dollars, eighty cents; and that the Audtor credit the Treasurer with the same, furnishing him with the proper voucher therefor; and that the Auditor draw anew on said bank, in favor of the Treasurer, for the amount due the State.

Resolved, further, That the Treasurer be, and he is hereby authorized and required to take such measures as, in his opinion, shall be most proper for the collection or final disposition of the claims on individuals, as reported, amounting to the sum of seventeen hundred and sixty dollars; also, the depreciated bills and paper on broken banks, amounting to four hundred and twenty-four dollars, and that he report the loss thereon, if any, to the Auditor, who shall pass such loss to the credit of the Treasurer, giving him the proper voucher therefor; and that the Treasurer report his proceedings under this resolution, to the next General Assembly.

WM. SAWYER,
Speaker of the House of Representatives.
ELIJAH VANCE,
Speaker of the Senate.

February 11, 1836.

RESOLUTION

Relative to the payment of taxes by certain corporations.

Resolved by the General Assembly of the State of Ohio, That the Auditor of State take measures to ascertain what corporations in the several counties of this State, are liable to the payment of taxes under the act to tax Banks, Insurance and Bridge Companies; and that he cause the provisions of said act to be duly enforced.

WM. SAWYER,
Speaker of the House of Representatives.
ELIJAH VANCE,
Speaker of the Senate.

Feb'y 11, 1836.

RESOLUTION

For the relief of Arthur Taggart.

Resolved by the General Assembly of the State of Ohio, That the Superintendent of the National Road be, and he is hereby directed to pay to Arthur Taggart, the sum of three hundred and sixty-six dollars and twenty-five cents, out of the National Road fund, which shall be in full of all quarry privileges and materials heretofore furnished by said Taggert on the National Road; and charge the same to said fund.

WM. SAWYER,
Speaker of the House of Representatives.
ELIJAH VANCE,
Speaker of the Senate.

February 11, 1836.

PREAMBLE AND RESOLUTIONS,

Relating to the French Indemnity.

Whereas, After more than twenty years unceasing endeavors on the part of the United States to obtain a fair compensation for accumulated injuries and aggressions committed on her commerce by the existing governments of France, between the years 1800 and 1817, France did at length bind herself by a treaty duly ratified, to pay to the Government of the United States a specific sum in satisfaction of said injuries, and aggressions: *And whereas,* France requires as a condition, precedent to the execution of said treaty, unconditionally ratified, and to the payment of a debt acknowledged by all the branches of her government to be justly due, that explanation shall be made of an annual communication of the President to Congress; a communication which the constitution of his country required him to make, and of which explanation she dictates the terms: *And whereas, further,* If such a requirement is persisted in by France, it must be considered as a deliberate refusal on her part to fulfil engagements binding by the laws of nations, and held sacred by the whole civilized world. If France feels exquisitively sensitive on points which only apparently affect her National Honor, how much more so ought Americans to feel on points which affect not only their National Honor, but likewise their National Independence? Attached to our country by every tie that can bind the affections and interests of civilized man to the blessings of a free and independent government, and reposing unlimited confidence in the patriotic energies of the American character, when compelled to enter into arduous competition with foreign nations, in defence of our rights and national honor, we will not submit to foreign dictation. The annals of our common country should not be tarnished with the foul reproach; and lest silence should, either at home or abroad, be considered as an acquiescence in the assumption of foreign powers to dictate or control the official communication between the co-ordinate branches of our government:

Be it therefore Resolved, That the Senate and House of Representatives of the State of Ohio, in Legislature assembled, consider it to be their duty to express their entire approbation of the dignified course pursued by the President, throughout the course of his negotiation with France, on this important question, and cordially respond to the just and enlightened views which he has presented thereon, in his late message to the Congress of the United States.

Resolved, That in the opinion of this General Assembly, France cannot rightfully demand, nor can the Executive of the United States, consistently with the Honor and National Independence of the American People, ever make the said required concessions.

Resolved, That we, the Representatives of the State of Ohio, are ready to sustain the General Government in all such measures as may be necessary to secure the rights, and preserve the honor and hitherto untarnished lustre of our national character.

Resolved, That the Governor be, and he is hereby requested to forward a copy of the foregoing Preamble and Resolutions to the President and Vice-President of the United States, and a copy to each of our Senators and Representatives in Congress.

WM. SAWYER,
Speaker of the House of Representatives.
ELIJAH VANCE,
Speaker of the Senate.

February 17, 1836.

RESOLUTION

Authorizing the payment of one hundred and fifty dollars to Two Stickney.

Resolved by the General Assembly of the State of Ohio, That the Governor be required to pay, out of his contingent fund, the sum of one hundred and fifty dollars to Two Stickney.

WM. SAWYER,
Speaker of the House of Representatives.
ELIJAH VANCE,
Speaker of the Senate.

February 16, 1836.

RESOLUTION

Relating to the Clear and Black fork of Mohican, in the county of Richland.

Resolved by the General Assembly of the State of Ohio, That the Board of Canal Commissioners be, and they are hereby authorized to cause the necessary survey and estimate to be made of a canal, commencing at or near Lexington, in Richland county; from thence down the valley of the Clear fork of the Mohican, to Bellville; from thence to Newville; from thence to Perrysville; thence down the valley of the Black fork of Mohican to Loudonville, in said county of Richland; from thence, the most practible route, terminating on the Ohio canal, at or near Bolivar; and report to the next Legislature, at their next session, the result of such survey and estimate, and also their opinion, as to the practicability of constructing such canal; and whether such improvement would be beneficial to the State generally, together with such other facts in relation to said route, as they may deem proper.

WM. SAWYER,
Speaker of the House of Representatives.
ELIJAH VANCE,
Speaker of the Senate.

February 18, 1836.

RESOLUTION

Appointing James Hedges, Register of the Virginia Military School Lands.

Resolved by the General Assembly of the State of Ohio, That James Hedges, of Richland county, be, and he is hereby appointed Register of the Virginia Military School Lands, for the term of three years, from and after the first day of April, eighteen hundred and thirty-six, whose term of service expires at that time.

WM. SAWYER,
Speaker of the House of Representatives.
ELIJAH VANCE,
Speaker of the Senate.

February 18, 1836.

RESOLUTION

Authorizing the payment of money to John Scatterday and William M'Mahen.

Resolved by the General Assembly of the State of Ohio, That the superintendent of the National Road, be authorized and required to pay out of the funds of said National Road, to John Scatterday and Willian M'Mahen, commissioners aforesaid, the sum of six dollars each, as a compensatoin for their services.

WILLIAM MEDILL,
Speaker pro tem. of the House of Representatives.
ELIJAH VANCE,
Speaker of the Senate.

February 29, 1836.

RESOLUTION

Providing certain Statutes for the counties of Logan, Hardin and Hancock.

Resolved by the General Assembly of the State of Ohio, That the Secretary of State, be instructed to forward to the county of Logan, ten coples of the revised code of laws of 1830, 1831; and to the counties of Hardin and Hancock, each fifteen copies of the same, to be forwarded to said counties with the laws and journals of the present session.

WILLIAM MEDILL,
Speaker pro tem. of the House of Representatives.

ELIJAH VANCE,
Speaker of the Senate.

March 1, 1836.

RESOLUTION

Authorizing the Governor to suspend the sales of Miami Canal Lands.

Resolved, by the General Assembly of the State of Ohio, That the Governor be, and is hereby authorized to cause to cause to be suspended, without delay, all further sales of the lands granted by Congress, to aid in the extension of the Miami canal, north of Dayton, until further ordered by the Legislature.

WM. SAWYER,
Speaker of the House of Representatives.

ELIJAH VANCE,
Speaker of the Senate.

February 29, 1836.

PREAMBLE AND RESOLUTIONS

Providing for the relief of John Smith, late sheriff of Green county.

WHEREAS, In the year eighteen hundred and twenty-one, one Jacob Funk, a fugitive from the State of Kentucky, charged with various felonies in that State, was apprehended on a warrant, issued by the Governor of the State of Ohio, on the requisition of the Governor of the State of Kentucky; and on the twelfth day of February, in the year aforesaid, was committed to jail in the county of Green, at which time John Smith was sheriff of said county, into whose custody the fugitive was delivered, and who sustained at his own expense said fugitive in said jail, for the term of one hundred and seventy-seven days: *And whereas,* By the laws of Ohio, there is no provision made for the paying to jailors or sheriffs their fees, or expenses incurred in keeping and maintaing persons in jail, in such cases as above named and described: *And whereas,* The said John Smith has not ever been paid his costs and charges by him laid out and expended, as above stated, although he has frequently applied therefor, both to the authority of Ohio and Kentucky: Therefore,

Resolved, That the Governor be, and is hereby authorized to pay out of his contingent fund the sum of eighty-six dollars and ninety-two cents, to John Smith, late sheriff of the county of Green, as a remuneration for his charges and expenses, in keeping and maintaining in the jail of the said county of Green, one Jacob Funk, a fugitive from justice, from the State of Kentucky, for the term of one hundred and seventy-seven days.

WILLIAM MEDILL,
Speaker pro tem. of the House of Representatives.
ELIJAH VANCE,
Speaker of the Senate.

March 14, 1836.

RESOLUTIONS

Relating to the election of President and Vice-President.

Be it resolved by the General Assembly of the State of Ohio, That our Senators in Congress be instructed, and our Representatives requested to use their exertions to procure an amendment of the Constitution of the United States, so as to prevent any future election of President of the United States by the House of Representatives, and of Vice-President of the United States by the Senate; and so that the election can in no case be taken from the people.

Be it further resolved, That His Excellency the Governor be requested to forward a copy of the foregoing resolution to each of our Senators and Representatives in Congress, and to each of the Governors, of the several States of this Union.

WILLIAM MEDILL,
Speaker pro tem. of the House of Representatives.
ELIJAH VANCE,
Speaker of the Senate.

February 29, 1836.

RESOLUTION

Appointing John Bell, Superintendent Western Reserve Road.

Resolved by the General Assembly of the State of Ohio, That John Bell, of Lower Sandusky, be, and he is hereby appointed superintendent of the Miami and Western Reserve Road, for the year one thousand eight hundred and thirty-six.

WILLIAM MEDILL,
Speaker pro tem. of the House of Representatives.
ELIJAH VANCE,
Speaker of the Senate.

February 29, 1836.
81—L

642

RESOLUTION
Relating to the National Road.

Resolved by the General Assembly of the State of Ohio, That a committee of one on the part of the Senate, and a committee of two on the part of the House of Representatives, be appointed to make a personal examination of so much of the Cumberland road, as included between the forty-third mile stone west of Zanesville, and the intersection of Friend and High streets, in the city of Columbus; and make report during the present session of this General Assembly, whether such portion of said road is constructed according to law, and whether the State of Ohio should take charge of the same.

WILLIAM MEDILL,
Speaker pro tem. of the House of Representatives.
ELIJAH VANCE,
Speaker of the Senate.

March 4, 1836.

RESOLUTION
Requesting the Governor to appoint a day of Thanksgiving.

Resolved by the General Assembly of the State of Ohio, That the Governor be, and he is hereby requested to issue, within the present year, his proclamation to the inhabitants of this State, recommending to them the observance of a day of Thanksgiving to Almighty God, for his blessings to us as a people; which day shall be selected at the discretion of the Governor, and designated in his proclamation.

WILLIAM MEDILL,
Speaker pro tem. of the House of Representatives.
ELIJAH VANCE,
Speaker of the Senate.

March 14, 1836.

RESOLUTION
Requesting the Governor to transmit to the Executive of Pennsylvania, an act therein named.

Resolved by the General Assembly of the State of Ohio, That His Excellency, the Governor, be requested to forward a certified copy of the Act to amend an act to incorporate the Pennsylvania and Ohio Canal Company, passed January 10th, 1827, and the Act amendatory thereof, passed February 10th, 1835, to the Executive of the State of Pennsylvania, with a request that the same be laid before the Legislature of that State for concurrence therein.

WILLIAM MEDILL,
Speaker pro tem. of the House of Representatives.
ELIJAH VANCE,
Speaker of the Senate.

March 4, 1836.

RESOLUTION

Relating to the Ohio University.

WHEREAS, By a resolution of the General Assembly, passed January 30th, 1827, it is made the duty of the President and Trustees of the Ohio University, annually, to report the condition, &c., of said institution: Therefore,

Resolved by the General Assembly of the State of Ohio, That the President and Trustees of the Ohio University, be, and they are hereby required to report to the Legislature, a statement of the situation of said University —amount of receipts and expenditures, and such other facts connected with the institution, as the said President and Trustees may deem expedient.

WILLIAM MEDILL,
Speaker pro tem. of the House of Representatives.
ELIJAH VANCE,
Speaker of the Senate.

March 7, 1836.

RESOLUTION

Appointing Trustees for the Deaf and Dumb Asylum.

Resolved by the General Assembly of the State of Ohio, That Noah H. Swayne, Asahel Chittenden, James Hoge, and P. H. Olmsted, be, and they are hereby appointed Trustees of the Deaf and Dumb Asylum, to serve for the term of three years, from and after the twentieth day of February, 1836.

WILLIAM MEDILL,
Speaker pro tem. of the House of Representatives.
ELIJAH VANCE,
Speaker of the Senate.

March 7, 1836.

RESOLUTION

Relating to certain Statutes for the county of Ashtabula.

Resolved by the General Assembly of the State of Ohio, That the Secretary of State be, and he is hereby required to forward to the Clerk of the Court of Common Pleas for Ashtabula county, ten copies of the 29th volume of the Revised Statutes, for the use of said county.

WILLIAM MEDILL,
Speaker pro tem. of the House of Representatives.

ELIJAH VANCE,
Speaker of the Senate.

March 7, 1836.

RESOLUTION

Providing for an examination of the Books of the Auditor and Treasurer of Perry county.

Resolved by the Senate and House of Representatives, That a Joint Select Committee be appointed, consisting of one member on the part of the Senate, and one member on the part of the House, and that said committee be authorized and empowered to examine the books and papers in the Auditor and Treasurer's office, in the county of Perry; and such persons as they may deem proper and expedient, so as to ascertain the amount of money paid into the treasury of Perry county, prior to the fourth day of July, 1835, on the sale of S. 15, T. 18, R. 17, and S. 15, T. 17, R. 16, granted to township 19, R. 17, and township 18, R. 16, in the Refugee Tract, for school purposes; and to examine the books and papers in the Auditor and Treasurer of State's office, to ascertain the amount paid to the Treasurer of State, and the amount retained in the hands of the late treasurer of Perry county, and after such examination is completed, to report to the Auditor of State, and such officers in the counties of Perry and Licking, as may be necessary and expedient, and on the report of the adjustment in relation to the said lands, and officers aforesaid, the Auditor of State shall proceed as is provided by law.

WILLIAM MEDILL,
Speaker pro tem. of the House of Representatives.

ELIJAH VANCE,
Speaker of the Senate.

March 7, 1836.

RESOLUTION

For paying money to Warren Jenkins.

Resolved by the General Assembly of the State of Ohio, That his Excellency the Governor, is hereby directed to pay out of his contingent fund, the

645

sum of twenty-five dollars to Warren Jenkins, as a compensation in full for his services in preparing an index to the journals of the last annual session General Assembly.

WILLIAM MEDILL,
Speaker pro tem. of the House of Representatives.
ELIJAH VANCE,
Speaker of the Senate.

March 8, 1836.

RESOLUTION

Authorizing a survey between Blanchard's Fork Creek and Fort Findley.

Resolved by the General Assembly of the State of Ohio, That the board of Public Works be, and they are hereby authorized and required, as soon as practicable, to examine and survey a line of canal and slack water navigation from the mouth of Blanchard's Fork creek to Fort Finnley, in Hancock county, and report to the General Assembly the estimate of the probable cost, together with their opinion as to the value and importance of such improvement.

WILLIAM MEDILL,
Speaker pro tem. of the House of Representatives.
ELIJAH VANCE,
Speaker of the Senate.

March 8, 1836.

RESOLUTION

Referring the claim of Jacob B. Sprague, to the Directors of the Penitentiary.

Resolved by the General Assembly of the State of Ohio, That the claim of Jacob B. Sprague, for losses sustained in a contract for furnishing stone for the erection of the new penitentiary, be referred, with the accompanying documents, to the directors of the penitentiary; and that said directors be directed to examine and settle the same on fair and equitable principles, and pay over the balance, if any they find due to said Jacob B. Sprague, and charge the same to the account of the penitentiary.

WILLIAM MEDILL,
Speaker pro tem. of the House of Representatives.
ELIJAH VANCE,
Speaker of the Senate.

March 8, 1836.

PREAMBLE AND RESOLUTIONS

On the subject of the Maumee and Western Reserve Road.

WHEREAS, By an act of Congress, passed February 28th, 1823, certain lands were granted to the State of Ohio, to enable her to lay out and construct a Road from the Lower Rapids of the Miami of Lake Erie to the Western boundary of the Connecticut Western Reserve, in such manner as the Legislature of said State should by law provide, with the approbation of the President of the United States, which road, when constructed, was to remain a public highway: *And whereas,* The proceeds of the sale of said lands have all been expended upon said road, together with the other funds which have been appropriated to that object by the State; and inasmuch as said road is in bad condition, and requires heavy expenditures to place and keep it in repair, for which no means have been provided: Therefore,

Resolved by the General Assembly of the State of Ohio, That our Senators and Representatives in Congress be requested to use their exertions to procure the passage of a law authorizing the State to make such regulations as she may deem advisable, in relation to said road, either by causing gates to be erected and tolls collected, or by authorizing a company to do so, after said road shall have been put in good repair.

Resolved, That His Excellency, the Governor, be requested to forward a copy of the foregoing Preamble and Resolutions to each of our Senators and Representatives in Congress.

WILLIAM MEDILL,
Speaker pro tem. of the House of Representatives.

ELIJAH VANCE,
Speaker of the Senate.

March 9, 1836.

RESOLUTION

Providing certain Statutes for Cuyahoga county.

Resolved by the General Assembly of the State of Ohio, That the Secretary of State be requested to forward to the Clerk of the Court of Common Pleas of Cuyahoga county, ten copies of the revised laws, vol. 29, ten copies of volume 31 of the general, and five copies of the local laws.

WILLIAM MEDILL,
Speaker pro tem. of the House of Representatives.

ELIJAH VANCE,
Speaker of the Senate.

March 10, 1836.

RESOLUTION

Providing for the distribution of the School Laws.

Resolved by the General Assembly of the State of Ohio, That the Secretary of State be, and he is hereby directed to procure the printing of a sufficient number of copies of the School law, in pamphlet form, to furnish each organized school district in this State with one copy, and forward the same to the several county auditors, as soon as practicable; and it shall be the duty of said auditors to deliver, or cause to be delivered, one copy of said law to the clerk of each school district in his county.

WILLIAM MEDILL,
Speaker pro tem. of the House of Representatives.
ELIJAH VANCE,
Speaker of the Senate.

March 11, 1836.

RESOLUTION

Authorizing the Board of Public Works to settle the claim of Samuel Reede.

Resolved by the General Assembly of the State of Ohio, That the board of Public Works are hereby authorized and required to settle, according to equity and justice, the claim of Samuel Reede, for labor performed on section, No. 199, south of the Licking summit, on the Ohio canal; and if any thing is found to be due to the said Reede, that the same be paid out of the canal fund.

WILLIAM MEDILL,
Speaker pro tem. of the House of Representatives.
ELIJAH VANCE,
Speaker of the Senate.

March 11, 1836.

RESOLUTION

For a survey from the Ohio canal, through Wooster, in Wayne county, and Mansfield, in Richland county, of a Canal or Rail-road.

Resolved by the General Assembly of the State of Ohio, That the board of Public Works be required to perform the duties under a resolution, passed June 16th, 1835, requiring the Canal Commissioners to cause a survey and estimate to be made of a canal or rail-road, commencing at or near where the Sandy and Beaver canal intersects the Ohio canal; thence westward through Wooster, in Wayne county; thence through Mansfield, in

Richland county; and that the time for making and reporting such survey and estimate to extend to the next General Assembly.

WILLIAM MEDILL,
Speaker pro tem. of the House of Representatives.
ELIJAH VANCE,
Speaker of the Senate.

February 11, 1836.

RESOLUTION

In regard to the appointment of trustees, for obtain'ng information on the subject of the instruction of the unfortunate blind of this State.

Resolved by the General Assembly of Ohio, That James Hoge, N. H. Swayne, and William M. Awl, be, and they are hereby appointed a board of trustees, for the purpose of obtaining information in relation to the instruction of the unfortunate blind of this State, in letters and mechanical arts; and that the said board be authorized and directed to submit a full report upon this subject, to the next General Assembly, together with the probable expense necessary for commencing a public school.

WILLIAM MEDILL,
Speaker pro tem. of the House of Representatives.
ELIJAH VANCE,
Speaker of the Senate.

March 11, 1836.

RESOLUTION

Relating to certain laws and journals.

Resolved by the General Assembly of the State of Ohio, That the Secretary of State shall hereafter prepare and deliver to the State Printer, to be printed at the end of the general laws, by their titles and dates only, a list of all the local acts, passed at the same session; and that he shall also prepare and cause to be affixed to each volume of local laws, a proper index to the acts and resolutions contained in the same, or so arrange the table of contents under general heads, as to serve as an index.

Be it further resolved, That the Secretary shall also annually cause to be half bound in cloth or leather, a sufficient number of the laws to furnish three copies to the United States, and to each State and Territory in the United States, and one copy to each member and officer of the General Assembly; and that he also cause to be bound in like manner, as many copies of the journals of each House, as will furnish one set to each member of the General Assembly.

Be it further resolved, That the Secretary shall prepare and report to the next General Assembly an estimate of the cost of having all the laws and journals hereafter published, stitched and trimmed, and done up in board or paper covers, with backs of cloth or leather.

WILLIAM MEDILL,
Speaker pro tem. of the House of Representatives.
ELIJAH VANCE,
Speaker of the Senate.

March 11, 1836.

RESOLUTION

In relation to the National Road.

Resolved by the General Assembly of the State of Ohio, That His Excellency the Governor be respectfully advised not to receive the road aforesaid, until it shall be completed in conformity with the law upon that subject; and that the committee be discharged from the further consideration of the subject.

WILLIAM MEDILL,
Speaker pro tem. of the House of Representatives.
ELIJAH VANCE,
Speaker of the Senate.

March 11, 1836.

RESOLUTION

Appointing trustees for the Ripley College, in the county of Brown.

Resolved by the General Assembly of the State of Ohio, That John Rankin, Thomas Kirker, Nathan Ellis, Francis Taylor, Rezin J. Bennet, John Johnson, and Robert Baird, be, and they are hereby appointed trustees of the College of Ripley, in the county of Brown, whose term of service shall expire on the first day of January, eighteen hundred and forty three; and that John D. Evans, be, and he is hereby appointed a trustee of said college, to supply the vacancy occasioned by the death of John W. Campbell; which appointment shall expire on the first day of January, eighteen hundred and thirty-seven; and that John Moore, William Humphrews, Asa Anderson, and Daniel P. Evans, be, and they are hereby appointed trestees of said institution, to fill the vacancies existing in the third class of said board, whose terms of service shall extend to the first day of January, eighteen hundred and forty.

WILLIAM MEDILL,
Speaker pro tem. of the House of Representatives.
ELIJAH VANCE,
Speaker of the Senate.

March 11, 1836.
82—L

650

RESOLUTION

Appointing Commissioners to fix upon a site for a seat of justice, for Paulding county.

Resolved by the General Assembly of the State of Ohio, That Thomas J. S. Smith, of Miami county; John Shelby, of Montgomery county; and John Blackburn, of Allen county, be, and they are hereby appointed commissioners to examine, determine, and fix the site for the seat of justice of Pauding county, agreeably to the act entitled "An act establishing seats of justice."

WILLIAM MEDILL,
Speaker pro. tem. of the House of Representatives.
ELIJAH VANCE,
Speaker of the Senate.

March 11, 1836.

RESOLUTION

In relation to a McAdamized road, from Steubenville to Cambridge.

Resolved by the General Assembly of the State of Ohio, That the Board of Public Works are hereby authorized and required to cause to be made a survey and estimates of a McAdamized road, from the town of Steubenville, in the county of Jefferson, through Cadiz, in Harrison county; thence to Cambridge, in Guernsey county; said survey and estimates to be made during the present season, and report thereof made to the next General Assembly, if practicable.

WILLIAM MEDILL,
Speaker pro. tem. of the House of Representatives.
ELIJAH VANCE,
Speaker of the Senate.

March 11, 1836.

RESOLUTION

In relation to the Zanesville and Maysville Turnpike road.

Resolved by the General Assembly of the State of Ohio, That the Board of Public Works be, and they are hereby directed to cause a survey, location, and estimate to be made of the Zanesville and Maysville Turnpike road, at the expense of the State, so soon as said company shall become organized, agreeably to the act passed by the present General Assembly, incorporating said company; and so soon as the said board shall be officially notified of such organization, and execute a plat of the same, to be returned to the General Assembly.

WILLIAM MEDILL,
Speaker pro tem. of the House of Representatives.
ELIJAH VANCE,
Speaker of the Senate.

March 11, 1836.

RESOLUTION

In relation to the Cincinnati and Whitewater Canal.

Resolved by the Senate and House of Representatives, That the Board of Public Works be, and they are hereby authorized and required to cause a survey to be made, at as early a period as practicable, of the route of a canal, proposed to be constructed between the city of Cincinnati, and the Whitewater canal, and report the same to the next General Assembly, together with their opinion of its cost, and the probable revenue therefrom: *Provided,* That before making said survey, the citizens of Hamilton county shall pay or secure to be paid to said board, the amount of the expense of the survey; which money shall appear charged against said board, in their annual report.

WILLIAM MEDILL,
Speaker pro tem. of the House of Representatives.
ELIJAH VANCE,
Speaker of the Senate.

March 11, 1836.

RESOLUTION

In relation to the South Fork Licking Feeder.

Resolved by the General Assembly of the State of Ohio, Tha the Board of Public Works are hereby authorized and required to examine the condition of the South Fork [of] Licking feeder, to the Licking summit of the the Ohio canal; and to clear the same of the fallen timber, in order to give a free passage to the water, if they think it expedient and proper to do the same.

WILLIAM MEDILL,
Speaker pro tem. of the House of Representatives.
ELIJAH VANCE,
Speaker of the Senate.

March 11, 1836.

RESOLUTION

Relating to postage.

Resolved by the General Assembly of the State of Ohio, That the Speakers of the respective branches, be, and they are hereby directed to audit for payment, the accounts for postage against the members and officers of the present General Assembly.

WILLIAM MEDILL,
Speaker pro tem. of the House of Representatives.
ELIJAH VANCE,
Speaker of the Senate.

March 11, 1836.

PREAMBLE AND RESOLUTIONS

In relation to the Waters of Lake Erie.

WHEREAS, This General Assembly have learned from various sources, which they think entitled to credit, that certain persons are using their name and influence to procure an appropriation by the United States, to extend the dam or travers pier, at Black Rock, in the State of New York: *And whereas,* It is believed that the dam or travers pier already erected at said Black Rock, has had a very injurious effect upon the shore or bank of Lake Erie, by raising the surface of said lake, so that the force of its waves are spent against, and tend to undermine the banks thereof: *And whereas,* It has been represented to this Legislature, that in many places the banks of said Lake have been undermined and washed away, to the distance of from ten to twenty rods, within the last ten years: Therefore,

Resolved by the General Assembly of the State of Ohio, That any further operations at Black Rock, in the State of New York, the tendency of which would be to raise the surface of Lake Erie, will, in the opinion of this Legislature, have an injurious effect upon many villages and farms, by undermining and washing them away, and of raising the water over many others, at the mouths of the rivers.

Resolved, That his Excellency the Governor, be requested to transmit a copy of the above preamble and resolutions to each of our Senators and Representatives in Congress.

WILLIAM MEDILL,
Speaker pro. tem. of the House of Representatives.
ELIJAH VANCE,
Speaker of the Senate.

March 12, 1836.

RESOLUTION

Requiring the Board of Public Works to make a survey and estimate of a Rail-road from Chillicothe to Cincinnati.

Resolved by the General Assembly of the State of Ohio, That the board of Public Works are hereby required to make a survey and estimate, of the route for the construction of a rail-road from Chillicothe to Cincinnati, and report said survey and estimate to the next General Assembly, or as soon thereafter as practicable.

WILLIAM MEDILL,
Speaker pro tem. of the House of Representatives.
ELIJAH VANCE,
Speaker of the Senate.

March 12, 1836.

RESOLUTION

Relative to certain surveys and estimates of a route for Canal or Slackwater Navigation from Columbus to Sandusky river.

Resolved by the General Assembly of the State of Ohio, That the board of Public Works be, and they are hereby authorized and required to examine and survey a line of canal or slackwater navigation, or such other plan of improvement as they may deem most practicable and useful or conducive to the public interest, from the Scioto river at the city of Columbus, to the foot of the rapids of the Sandusky river at Lower Sandusky, and report to the General Assembly as soon as practicable, estimates of the probable cost, together with their opinions as to the value and importance of such improvement.

WILLIAM MEDILL,
Speaker pro tem. of the House of Representatives.
ELIJAH VANCE,
Speaker of the Senate.

March 12, 1836.

RESOLUTION

Relating to certain bound Statutes for Lucas county.

Resolved by the General Assembly of the State of Ohio, That the Secretary of State is hereby authorized to forward to the Clerk of the Court of Lucas county, fifteen copies of the bound Statutes, and one copy of Chase's Ohio Laws, for the use of said county.

WILLIAM MEDILL,
Speaker pro tem. of the House of Representatives.
ELIJAH VANCE,
Speaker of the Senate.

March 12, 1836.

RESOLUTION

For the payment of certain claims

Resolved, by the General Assembly of the State of Ohio, That there is due to M'Coy, Work and M'Coy, the sum of fifty-two dollars and sixty cents: to Monroe Bell, the sum of one hundred sixty-five dollars twelve cents; to Lazell and Mattoon, the sum of twenty-two dollars and fifty cents; to Adin G. Hibbs, the sum of twelve dollars; and that the same be paid out of the moneys appropriated for that purpose, on the order of the Auditor of State.

WILLIAM MEDILL,
Speaker pro tem. of the House of Representatives.
ELIJAH VANCE,
Speaker of the Senate.

March 14, 1836.

Appointing a Committee to make certain Geological Observations and estimates of this State.

Resolved by the General Assembly of the State of Ohio, That Samuel P. Hildreth, of Marietta, John Locke and John L. Riddell, of Cincinnati, and I. A. Lapham, of Columbus, be, and they are hereby appointed a committee to report to the next Legislature, the best method of obtaining a complete Geoloical Survey of the State, and an estimate of the probable cost of the same.

WILLIAM MEDILL,
Speaker pro tem. of the House of Representatives.
ELIJAH VANCE,
Speaker of the Senate.

March 14, 1836.

RESOLUTION

Providing for a School District Manual.

Resolved by the General Assembly of the State of Ohio, That a committee of two persons, shall be appointed to prepare and report to the next General Assembly, a School District Manual, explaining the duties of all officers under the act regulating common schools, with proper forms of proceeding in levying taxes, holding meetings, conducting suits, and in all other matters relating to district schools; which manual shall when adopted, be printed in connection with the school laws, and distribuied to all the school districts in the State.

Resolved, That the said committee shall be appointed by the Governor, and he shall have authority to fill any vacancy that may be caused in said committee.

WILLIAM MEDILL,
Speaker pro tem. of the House of Representatives.
ELIJAH VANCE,
Speaker of the Senate.

March 11, 1836.

RESOLUTIONS

In relation to Public Instruction and Education.

Resolved by the General Assembly of the State of Ohio, That C. E. Stowe, Professor in one of the Literary Institutions of this State, be requested to collect, during the progress of his contemplated tour in Europe, such facts and information as he may deem useful to the State, in relation to the various systems of public instruction and education, which have been adopted in the several countries through which he may pass, and make report thereof, with such practicable observations as he may think proper, to the next General Assembly.

Resolved, That his Excellency, the Governor, be requested to transmit a certified copy of the foregoing proceedings to Professor Stowe.

WILLIAM MEDILL,
Speaker pro tem. of the House of Representatives.

ELIJAH VANCE,
Speaker of the Senate.

March 14, 1836.

A RESOLUTION

Appointing a Committee to examine the books and vouchers of the Canal Commissioners.

Resolved by the General Assembly of the State of Ohio, That a committee of two members be appointed on the part of the House, and one on the part of the Senate, to serve as a board of commissioners, whose duty, it shall be to examine the books and vouchers of the canal commissioners; also, the books and vouchers of the canal fund commissioners, and audit and adjust the same.

Resolved, That said board of commissioners shall meet at the city of Columbus, on the first Monday of May next, at which time and place the canal commissioners and the commissioners of the canal fund shall present their books and vouchers to the aforesaid board, for inspection and investigation.

Ressolved, That the aforesaid board of commissioners shall make out a report, in writing, which shall be signed by them, or a majority of them, and transmit the same to the Governor, on or before the first Monday of November next, stating, if practicable, the amount received by the canal fund commissioners, in each and every year since the year 1825, particularly stating what portion of the same was raised by taxation; also, what amount, if any, remains in the treasury, applicable to the canal sinking fund; which report the Governor shall lay before the General Assembly, at their next meeting.

Resolved, That a sense of justice to the canal commissioners, and the canal fund commissioners, the agents of the State employed in the management and superintendence of the great works of internal improvement in this State, and a sense of duty to the people require the auditing and adjusting of the books and vouchers aforesaid.

Resolved, That the Governor shall fill all vacancies which may happen in said board of commissioners, as often as the same may occur.

WILLIAM MEDILL,
Speaker pro tem. of the House of Representatives.

ELIJAH VANCE,
Speaker of the Senate.

March 14, 1836.

656

RESOLUTION

Requiring the Governor to make a deed to Joseph Twaddle, for lands therein described.

WHEREAS, Joseph Twaddle, of Logan county, purchased and paid for a lot of Ohio Canal Lands, lying in said county, being the west half of the south-east quarter of section twenty-eight, town four, and range thirteen, and obtained a deed for the same; the house was burned in which said deed was kept, and the deed consumed therein, before the owner had placed it on the record of said county of Logan: Therefore,

Be it resolved by the General Assembly of the State of Ohio, That the Governor be, and he is hereby required to make a deed to the said Joseph Twaddle, for the aforesaid west half of the south-east quarter of section twenty-eight, town four, of range thirteen, as aforesaid.

WILLIAM MEDILL,
Speaker pro tem. of the House of Representatives.
ELIJAH VANCE,
Speaker of the Senate.

March 14, 1836.

RESOLUTION

For the relief of Hampson & Parkinson.

Resolved by the General Assembly of the State of Ohio, That the Board of Public Works be, and they are hereby required to reinvestigate the claim of James Hampson, and John S. Parkinson, for compensation for work and labor done by them upon the Ohio canal: the investigation shall be made upon the principles prescribed in the act entitled "An act for the relief of James Hampson and John S. Parkinson," passed March 7, 1835; said board shall have power to send for persons and papers, and it shall be their duty carefully to re-examine all the books, papers, reports, and testimonials, relative to said claim. They shall ascertain the amount of labor done by the claimants, and make a fair estimate of the value thereof; they shall deduct from said estimate the amount already paid the claimants, and strike the balance, if any, due in equity and justice to said Hampson and Parkinson: they shall add to such balance, the interest rightfully due thereon; and certify the aggregate to the Canal Fund Commissioners: upon receiving such certificate, said Canal Fund Commissioners are hereby authorized and required, immediately to cause the amount so certified to be paid to said Hampson and Parkinson, out of the canal fund: it shall be the duty of said Board of Public Works, to perform the duties enjoined upon them by this resolution, prior to the next session of the General Assembly.

WILLIAM MEDILL,
Speaker pro tem. of the House of Representatives.
ELIJAH VANCE,
Speaker of the Senate.

March 14, 1836.

ABOLITION RESOLUTIONS.

Resolved by the General Assembly of the State of Ohio, That the State of Ohio has no power to legislate on the subject of slavery, and she disclaims the assertain of any power to interfere with it in other States.

Resolved, That no law can be passed to impair the freedom of speech, or the freedom of the press, except to provide remedy for the redress of private injury, or the breach of public peace resulting from the abuse of either.

Resolved, That a due regard to justice, and the comfort of others, should induce great forbearance in the discussion of subjects which prove disturbing in their nature, or injurious to the peace and quiet of the country.

Resolved, That the Governor be requested to transmit to the Governors of the several States, a copy of the foregoing report and resolutions, that the same be laid before their respective Legislatures.

WILLIAM MEDILL,

Speaker pro tem. of the House of Representatives.

ELIJAH VANCE,

Speaker of the Senate.

March 14, 1836.

RESOLUTION

In relation to the National Road.

Resolved by the General Assembly of the State of Ohio, That the Governor be respectfully advised not to receive and take charge of that part of the National Road, lying east of the city of Columbus, and west from the 43d mile stone.

WILLIAM MEDILL,

Speaker pro tem. of the House of Representatives.

ELIJAH VANCE,

Speaker of the Senate.

March 14, 1836.

RESOLUTION

Requiring the Board of Public Works to make a survey of Big Raccoon creek.

Resolved by the General Assembly of the State of Ohio, That the Board of Public Works be, and they are hereby instructed and required to cause a survey to be made [of] Big Raccoon creek, from Canney's Mills, in Lee township, Athens county, to the confluence of said creek with the Ohio river, in Gallia county; and that they cause the necessary estimates to be made of the probable cost of constructing a navigable communication from said mills, to the mouth of said creek, by slackwater, by dams, and

83—L

report to the Legislature as soon as practicable, the result of such examination, survey, and estimates, and also their opinion as to the practicability of constructing such navigable communication, and whether the same would be of general utility.

WILLIAM MEDILL,
Speaker pro tem. of the House of Representatives.
ELIJAH VANCE,
Speaker of the Senate.

March 14, 1836.

RESOLUTION

[Authorizing the Board of Public Works to reserve certain lands on the Wabash and Erie canals.]

Resolved, That should the Board of Public Works deem it advisable to reserve from sale a section of land, on the Ottowa reserve, at Wolf rapids, or at any other place between that point and the Indiana line, on the Wabash and Erie canal, where the water power will be used for the purpose of laying off a town; the lots of which shall be sold at public auction, at such time and place as said Board of Public Works may think most to the interest of the State, for the benefit of the State, in the construction of said canal; they are hereby authorized and empowered by this act to do so.

WILLIAM MEDILL,
Speaker of pro tem. the House of Representatives.
ELIJAH VANCE,
Speaker of the Senate.

March 14, 1836.

RESOLUTION

Appointing advisory members of the Board of Public Works.

Resolved by the General Assembly of the State of Ohio, That Alexander McConnel, of the first district, be, and he is hereby appointed advisory commissioner of the Board of Public Works for one year, from and after the fourth day of April next; and Timothy G. Bates, of the second district, is appointed advisory commissioner of said board, for two years, from and after the fourth day of April next; and Rodolphus Dickenson, of the third district, is appointed advisory commissioner of said board, for one year, from and after the fourth day of April next; and John Harris, of the fourth district, is appointed advisory commissioner of said board, for two years, from and after the fourth day of April next.

WILLIAM MEDILL,
Speaker pro tem. of the House of Representatives.
ELIJAH VANCE,
Speaker of the Senate.

March 14, 1836.

RESOLUTION

Appointing the Acting Members of the Board of Public Works.

Resolved by the General Assembly of the State of Ohio, That Leander Ransom be, and he is hereby appointed an Acting Commissioner of the board of Public Works, for two years, and William Wall, an Acting Commissioner of said board for one year, from and after the first day of April next.

WILLIAM MEDILL,
Speaker pro. tem. of the House of Representatives.
ELIJAH VANCE,
Speaker of the Senate.

March 14, 1836.

RESOLUTION

Requiring the Secretary of State to furnish copies of certain Acts to the Board of Public Works.

Resolved by the General Assembly of the State of Ohio, That the Secretary of State be, and he is hereby required to furnish the board of Public Works, at their first meeting in April next, with certified copies of the laws passed at the present session, providing for the construction of the Hocking canal, and the improvement of the navigation of the Muskingum river, and the Walhonding and Mohican canal; and also, the act for the extension and completion of the Miami canal; also the act for the adjustment and completion of the Warren county canal.

WILLIAM MEDILL,
Speaker pro tem. of the House of Representatives.
ELIJAH VANCE,
Speaker of the Senate.

March 14, 1836.

RESOLUTION

Requiring the Secretary of State to furnish the Board of Public Works with a certified copy of an Act.

Resolved by the General Assembly of the State of Ohio, That the Secretary of State be, and he is hereby required to transmit, without delay, a certified copy of the act to create a board of Public Works, passed at the present session, to each member of said board, together with a certified copy of the joint resolution by which they have been appointed.

WILLIAM MEDILL,
Speaker pro tem. of the House of Representatives.
ELIJAH VANCE,
Speaker of the Senate.

March 14, 1836.

RESOLUTION.

Resolved by the General Assembly of the State of Ohio, That the board of Public Works be required to cause to be made, at as early a day as practicable, a survey and estimate for a Canal or Slackwater Navigation, commencing at the Zoar dam, or the mouth of One Leg creek, in Tuscarawas county; thence up the valley of said creek, to the point where the state road crosses said creek, between Leesburg and New Hagerstown, in Carroll county; and make report to the President and Directors of the One Leg Navigation Company.

WILLIAM MEDILL,
Speaker pro tem. of the House of Representatives.
ELIJAH VANCE.
Speaker of the Senate.

March 14, 1836.

RESOLUTION

For the relief of Abner Enoch.

Resolved by the General Assembly of the State of Ohio, That the board of Public Works be, and they are hereby authorized and empowered to adjust and settle the claim of Abner Enoch, for damages, and for work and labor done, and materials furnished in the construction of the Canal Dam and Feeder near Middletown, in the county of Butler; and that said board is hereby vested with the same powers to settle and adjust said claim as were conferred on the Canal Commissioners, by an act for the relief of Abner Enoch, passed March 9, 1836; and in the same manner as is pointed out in the said law, to draw in favor of the said Enoch for such sum or sums as may be found due, upon a fair and equitable investigation of every matter pertaining to the same.

WILLIAM MEDILL,
Speaker pro tem. of the House of Representatives.
ELIJAH VANCE,
Speaker of the Senate.

March 14, 1836.

RESOLUTIONS

, For the Apportionment of the Laws and Journals.

Resolved by the General Assembly of the State of Ohio, That twelve thousand copies of all the Laws of a general nature, passed und ordered to be printed the present session; also, two thousand two hundred copies of the Laws of a local nature, together with the resolutions passed; also, sixteen hundred copies of the Journals of each branch of the General Assembly, for this session, shall be distributed by the Secretary of State, according to law, as follows:

Counties.	General Laws.	Local Laws.	Jour-nals.	Counties.	Gen. Laws.	Local Laws.	Jour-nas.
Adams	105	20	15	Guernsey	160	28	24
Allen	50	15	10	Harrison	160	24	20
Ashtabula	220	40	33	Hardin	60	15	10
Athens	170	40	33	Hancock	100	25	15
Belmont	168	28	23	Hamilton	190	34	25
Brown	125	25	20	Highland	130	24	18
Butler	156	30	23	Hocking	90	18	13
Crawford	110	30	18	Holmes	130	25	19
Carroll	120	23	16	Huron	235	38	30
Clermont	135	30	20	Tuscarawas	170	32	26
Coshocton	180	30	24	Union	90	18	30
Clark	120	24	16	Van Wert	60	15	10
Clinton	115	22	16	Warren	144	23	18
Cuyahoga	200	35	24	Henry	60	15	10
Columbiana	206	37	30	Jefferson	170	30	23
Champaign	130	24	19	Jackson	116	23	18
Delaware	200	32	24	Knox	200	33	27
Dark	110	20	14	Logan	145	36	20
Fairfield	164	30	24	Licking	200	33	27
Franklin	164	30	24	Lorain	160	28	22
Fayette	80	16	11	Lawrence	116	32	16
Green	100	20	15	Muskingum	200	35	30
Geauga	200	33	27	Madison	100	20	14
Gallia	145	26	20	Medina	160	35	22
Meigs	110	22	16	Ross	170	28	21
Mercer	70	15	10	Rickhland	235	36	30
Morgan	140	24	21	Sandusky	120	20	20
Montgomery	140	24	20	Seneca	130	25	25
Miami	120	22	16	Scioto	120	23	16
Marion	130	23	20	Shelby	100	20	16
Monroe	150	24	18	Stark	190	33	27
Paulding	60	15	10	Trumbull	280	46	36
Perry	130	23	16	Wayne	200	33	28
Pike	90	19	14	Washington	137	31	25
Portage	238	40	33	Williams	80	16	10
Preble	130	24	18	Wood	100	20	15
Pickaway	142	28	20	Lucas	60	16	10
Putnam	60	15	10				
	1710	318	242		1922	347	279

WILLIAM MEDILL,
Speaker pro tem. of the House of Representatives.
ELIJAH VANCE,
Speaker of the Senate.

March 14, 1836.

RESOLUTION

Directing the payment of eight dollars to Wm. Barker.

Resolved by the General Assembly of the State of Ohio, That the Superintendent of the National Road pay out of any moneys in his hands belonging to said road, to Maj. W. Barker, the sum of eight dollars.

WILLIAM MEDILL,
Speaker pro tem. of the House of Representatives.

ELIJAH VANCE,
Speaker of the Senate.

March 14, 1834.

RESOLUTION

For the relief of Nathan Carpenter.

Resolved by the General Assembly of the State of Ohio, That Nathan Carpenter be exonerated from the payment of the sum of three hundred and seventy-five dollars due by him to the Deaf and Dumb Asylum, for the education of one unfortunate daughter of his, of that description of persons.

WILLIAM MEDILL,
Speaker pro tem. of the House of Representatives.

ELIJAH VANCE,
Speaker of the Senate.

March 14, 1836.

RESOLUTION

In relation to the indexes to the journals.

Resolved by the General Assembly of the State of Ohio, That the clerks of both branches of the General Assembly be, and they are hereby authorized and required to make, or cause to be made, true and correct indexes to their respective journals, as far as may be practicable; for which services they shall be allowed such compensation as the Secretary of State shall deem just and reasonable, to be paid out of his contingent funds.

WILLIAM MEDILL,
Speaker pro tem. of the House of Representatives.

ELIJAH VANCE,
Speaker of the Senate.

March 14, 1636.

RESOLUTION

Appointing Commissioners under the act incorporating the Pennsylvania and Ohio Canal Company.

Resolved by the General Assembly of the State of Ohio, That Nehemiah Allen, of Cuyahoga county, Calvin Cone, of Trumbull county, and Owen Brown, of Portage county, be, and they are hereby appointed commissioners, to assess and estimate the damages, or compensation to be allowed to the owners or proprietors of lands, waters, streams, or materials, which may have been, or shall hereafter be taken or appropriated by the Pennsylvania and Ohio Canal Company, for the location or construction of the canal, or other works connected therewith, authorized by the provisions of the the the charter of said company, and to perform all the duties required of such commissioners, by the 9th section of the act to incorporate the Pennsylvania and Ohio Canal Company, passed January 10th, 1827.

WILLIAM MEDILL,
Speaker pro tem. of the House of Representatives.
ELIJAH VANCE,
Speaker of the Senate.

March 14, 1836.

RESOLUTION

Appointing a committee to examine the books of the Auditor and Secretary of State.

Resolved by the General Assembly of the State of Ohio, That Noah H. Swayne, of Columbus; John H. James, of Urbana, and William Allen, of Chillicothe, are hereby appointed a committee to examine the books and accounts in the Auditor and Treasurer of State's offices, and to seport to the next General Assembly what changes, if any, are necessary in the organization of said offices; and also to the propriety of establishing a comptroller's office, with any suggestions the said committee shall think proper to make on the foregoing subjects; and that in case any vacancy should occur in said committee, the Governor shall have power to fill the same.

WILLIAM MEDILL,
Speaker pro tem. of the House of Representatives,
ELIJAH VANCE,
Speaker of the Senate.

March 14, 1836.

RESOLUTION

Fixing the compensation of Assistant Door-keepers.

Resolved by the General Assembly of the State of Ohio, That the assistant Door-keepers of both branches of this General Assembly shall each be allowed the sum of three dollars per day, for their services, while attending as such.

WILLIAM MEDILL,
Speaker pro tem. of the House of Representatives.
ELIJAH VANCE,
Speaker of the Senate.

March 14, 1836.

RESOLUTION

Authorizing the payment of ten dollars to Anthony Barrett.

Resolved by the General Assembly of the State of Ohio, That the Governor is authorized to pay out of his contingent fund, to Anthony Barrett, the sum of ten dollars, for services rendered in taking care of the offices attached to the State House, during the present session.

WILLIAM MEDILL,
Speaker pro tem. of the House of Representatives.
ELIJAH VANCE,
Speaker of the Senate.

March 14, 1836.

RESOLUTIONS

Relative to the Baltimore and Ohio Rail Road.

Resolved by the General Assembly of the State of Ohio, That we deem the completion of the Baltimore and Ohio Rail road as of great importance to the Western States, and affecting in some measure, the interests of the whole Union; and therefore, that it be recommended to our Senators and Representatives in Congress, to use such means as they may deem expedient to procure aid from Congress towards the accomplishment, at an early period, of so desirable an object as the completion of the Baltimore and Ohio Rail road.

Resolved, That His Excellency the Governor be requested to forward a copy of the foregoing resolution to each of our Senators and Representatives in Congress.

WILLIAM MEDILL,
Speaker pro tem. of the House of Representatives.
ELIJAH VANCE,
Speaker of the Senate.

March 14, 1836,

To the Senate and House of Representatives of the United States in Congress assembled.

The Memorial of the General Assembly of the State of Ohio,
  Respectfully represents:

That this State having recently created a "Board of Public Works," and placed under its general superintendence the entire system of her internal improvements; and believing the principles upon which the Board is organized, to be such as will, in all respects, best promote the public interests; this General Assembly would suggest, that the future appropriations by Congress for the completion of the Cumberland Road, within this State, might, with the strictest regard to propriety, as well as to the policy of both this State and the Union, be placed under the control and direction of this Board, and the work hereafter prosecuted under its supervision, and by its agency: That the execution of the westward portion of this road has, within the last five years, advanced with a slothful tardiness, is a fact known not only to the people of the State, and to the traveling community of the whole country but is a fact which has been officially communicated to Congress in the late Report of the Secretary at War, and the appended documents.

It would not comport with the dignity of this General Assembly, and it is, therefore, not the object of this memorial, to ascribe this tardiness to any derilection in any department, or to the delinquency of any officer of the General Government. The Secretary's Repert discloses the numerical insufficiency of the Engineer Corps; and the appended documents attribute the dilatory execution of the work to other causes, which, doubtless, contributed much to the result. But it is believed, that there are still other causes existing in the very nature of the system pursued, and of the agency employed. It cannot be doubted, because the experience of all time has proven, that expenditures of public money are made with a severe economy, and that public agents in all the departments of service, discharge their duties with greater fidelity, when those expenditures are made, and the officers act, in the immediate presence of a vigilant people, who are to be affected by such economy, and to whom such agents are directly responsible. Distance impairs the force of responsibility, as it obscures those infinite details in the public service, in which are always to be found the effects of inattention and waste, and, consequently, shields delinquency from exposure.

The Cumberland Road is a national work, and the national faith stands pledged for its execution. The appropriations by Congress will be specific, and, therefore, the most fastidious expositor of constitutional powers will not question the authority of the Federal Government to place such appropriations, for such an object, under the control of a State, within whose limits the expenditure is to be made; as it is evident that, in such a case, there is a resort to no novel power; for the direction of the appropriation would remain unchanged, and no other consequence follow, than the substitution of one agency for another. Impressed itself with these considerations, this General Assembly respectfully suggest them to the just judgment of the National Legislature.

84—L

1st. *Resolved*, That our Senators in Congress be instructed, and our Representatives requsted, to use their influence and exertions to accomplish the object of the foregoing memorial.

2d. *Resolved*, That His Excellency, the Governor of this State, be requested to forward a copy of the foregoing memorial to the President of the Senate, the Speaker of the House of Representatives, and to each of the Senators and Representatives in Congress from this State.

WILLIAM MEDILL,
Speaker pro tem. of the House of Representatives.
ELIJAH VANCE,
Speaker of the Senate.

March 14, 1836.

RESOLUTION

Directing the Librarian to take charge of the State House.

Resolved by the General Assembly of the State of Ohio, That the State Librarian shall have charge of the State House, and furniture thereof, until the first Monday of December next; that he cause the same to be opened and aired, as often as once in two weeks, until that time; and immediately preceding the next session of the Legislature, to cause the rooms, windows, and carpets thereof, to be properly prepared for the reception of the members; and that immediately after the adjournment of the present session, he shall make an inventory of all furniture and property in the State House, and file a copy thereof with the Auditor of State.

WILLIAM MEDILL,
Speaker pro tem. of the House of Representatives.
ELIJAH VANCE,
Speaker of the Senate.

March 14, 1836.

STATE OF OHIO, SECRETARY'S OFFICE. } COLUMBUS, *May 9th, 1836.*

I certify that the foregoing Acts and Resolutions, are correct copies of the original rolls, remaining on file in this office.

C. B. HARLAN,
Secretary of State.

INDEX TO THE LOCAL LAWS.

85—L

ANNUAL REPORT

OF

THE AUDITOR OF STATE,

TO THE

𝕲𝖊𝖓𝖊𝖗𝖆𝖑 𝕬𝖘𝖘𝖊𝖒𝖇𝖑𝖞 𝖔𝖋 𝖙𝖍𝖊 𝕾𝖙𝖆𝖙𝖊 𝖔𝖋 𝕺𝖍𝖎𝖔;

DECEMBER 9, 1835.

𝕮𝖔𝖑𝖚𝖒𝖇𝖚𝖘:

JAMES B. GARDINER,
PRINTER TO THE STATE.

ANNUAL REPORT.

STATE OF OHIO,
Auditor of State's Office,
Columbus, Dec. 9, 1835.

To the Honorable the
General Assembly.

Gentlemen,

Herewith I transmit for your consideration my annual Report of the receipts and disbursements of the government for the current year. The finances of this State, as will be seen by the *exhibit* presented in the following pages, have increased in a rapid ratio since the organization of the government, and particularly since the year 1815. Accompanying this Report will be found a *comparative* statement of the financial resources of Ohio, from the first receipts into the Treasury to the present period. This statement will be found the more interesting to the General Assembly, and to the people, at this time, for the reason that a *revaluation of the real property of the State*, has recently been taken under a law of the Legislature created for that purpose. It will afford a general view of the different sources constituting our public Revenue, and the organization and success of our Financial System, under the superintending care of the Legislature.

I have found, from the little experience I have had in this department of the State Government, and from general observation, that the most plain and simple mode of making up the annual Report from this office, was to throw the whole Receipts and Expenditures of the Government into a *tabular form*, and to designate the respective items, either of monies received into the Treasury, or drawn from it, under the particular *fund* to which they appropriately belong. The following is a summary view of the condition of the General Revenue and Finances of the State, up to the close of the last fiscal year.

GENERAL REVENUE.

The amount of revenue collected and paid by County Treasurer's, the year ending Nov. 15, 1835,	$150,080	58 2
" paid into the Treasury through this office, the year ending Nov. 15, 1835,	11,224	44 0
" paid by Banks, Insurance, and Bridge Companies, the year ending November 15, 1835,	26,060	67 0
" paid by Lawyers and Physicians, Nov. 15, 1835,	1,598	47 0
" paid as license from Pedlers and Insurance,	924	46 0
" paid from the sale of Forfeited Lands,	1,713	48 4
" paid through this office, of taxes levied for 1835, prior to Nov. 15, 1835,	350	31 0
" paid into the Treasury, being the balance of interest on Forest Meeker's note, given to the State,	17	12 0
" paid into the Treasury by Benjamin Hinkson, Esq. for certain revised Statutes of Ohio,	8	00 0
" of H. Brown's receipt, in favor of B. Hinkson, Esq. for six dollars, error in a draft on the Auditor of State, drawn by the Secretary, in favor of Stow & Whitmore,	6	00 0
" of J. Whitehill, Esq'rs receipt, in favor H. Brown, for $173, being the difference between a judgment obtained by the State, against the German Bank of Wooster for $827, charged to said Brown, and a bond given for said judgment and interest by C. C. Paine and others for $1000,	173	00 0
" of arrears of taxes paid into the Treasury,	389	94 0
" J. Whitehill's receipt for wood sold N. Murray,	2	00 0
" paid on a judgment against James Hampson and others, as securities for Wm. Craige, late Collector for Muskingum county,	25	12 0
" paid G. W. Manypenny, (transferred)	1,022	00 0
" School Funds transferred to revenue,	8,170	90 8
	201,766	50 4

GENERAL DISBURSEMENTS.

By the amount of deficit for 1834,	$16,622 72 3
" of bills redeemed at the Treasury, the year ending Nov. 15, 1835,	182,905 55 0
" of interest paid on School Sec. 16, Nov. 15, 1835,	22,331 61 0
" of interest paid on Virginia Military School Fund, Nov. 15, 1835,	6,026 94 0
" interest paid on United States Military School Fund, Nov. 15, 1835,	4,743 14 1
" of Canal's proportion of revenue, after deducting the sum of $35,507 04 8; the amount of interest due to School Funds, after the 1st of January, 1835,	2,735 61 9
	235,365 58 3
From which deduct the amount of revenue as above,	201,766 50 4
Shewing a deficit in the revenue, of	$33,599 07 9

SCHOOL FUNDS.

VIRGINIA MILITARY SCHOOL.

The amount of said Fund loaned to Canal Commissioners, prior to the 15th Nov. 1834,	102,294 59 6
" paid in by the Register, the year ending Nov. 15, 1835,	7,642 74 1
	$109,937 33 7

UNITED STATES MILITARY SCHOOL.

The amount of said Fund loaned to Canal Fund Commissioners, prior to the 15th Nov. 1834,	$82,093 70 3
" paid in by Registers and Treasurers, the year ending Nov. 15th, 1815,	8,033 16 8
	$90,126 87 1

COMMON SCHOOL.

The amount of money arising from the sale of the Salt Reserve Lands, and loaned to the Canal

Fund Commissioners, prior to the 15th
day of Nov. 1834,   -   - $22,111 12 8
"   paid in by the agent of said lands, the
year ending Nov. 15, 1835,   -   1,068 27 0

$23,179 39 8

ATHENS UNIVERSITY.

The total amount of said Fund, arising from the sale
of College Lands, and loaned to the Ca-
nal Fund Commissioners, up to the 15th
Nov. 1835,   -   -   - $1,431 72 0

SCHOOL SECTION, No. 16.

The amount of said Fund loaned to the Canal Fund
Commissioners, prior to Nov. 15, 1834, $379,350 60 1
"   paid in during the year ending Nov, 15,
1835,   -   -   -   -   73,654 90 7

$453,005 50 8

CONNECTICUT WESTERN RESERVE SCHOOL.

The amount of said Fund loaned to Canal Fund Commissioners, prior to Nov. 15, 1864, $109,359 38 2
"   paid in the year ending Nov. 15, 1835,   16,398 92 3

$125,758 30 5

SCHOOL FUNDS, (SUBJECT TO DISTRIBUTION.)

VIRGINIA MILITARY SCHOOL.

The amount of said Fund remaining in the Treasury,
Nov. 15, 1834,   -   -   - $5,196 95 2
"   of rents paid in by the Register, for the
year ending Nov. 15, 1835,   -   4,157 92 0
"   of interest accruing on said Fund, in the
hands of the Canal Fund Commission-

ers, prior to January 1st, 1835, and deducted from the revenue, - 6,026 94 0

	$15,381 81 2

Deduct the amount paid out, the year ending Nov.
15, 1835, - - - 11,091 77 0

Amount remaining in the Treasury Nov. 15, 1835, **$4,290 04 2**

UNITED STATES MILITARY SCHOOL.

The amount of said fund in the Treasury, subject to
distribution, Nov. 15, 1834, - - $16,259 43 9
" of interest accruing on said fund in the
hands of the Canal Fund Commissioners, prior to January 1st, 1835, 4,743 14 1

$21,002 58 0

Deduct the amount paid out the year ending Nov. 15,
1835. . - - . - 11,367 26 0

$9,635 32 0

Estimated amount of interest on said fund on the
first day of January, 1836, 5,293 53 4

Amount remaining in the Treasury Nov. 15, 1835, **$14,928 85 4**

CANAL FUNDS.

MIAMI CANAL.

The total amount of money arising from the sale of
said lands, up to the 15th day of Nov.
1835, - - - - $310,178 74 0
" of said fund paid to the Canal Fund Commissioners,
up to the 15th day of
Nov. 1835, - - 301,896 04
" for selecting, commis-
sion, &c. - - - 7,640 31
refunded to purchasers,
as per act dated Feb. 3,
1834, - - - - 606 39 310,142 74 0

Amount remaining in the Treasury Nov. 15, 1835, **$36 00 0**

8

OHIO CANAL.

The amount of taxes collected for Canal purposes, in
     the year 1834, after deducting $35,507
     04 8, the amount of interest accruing on
     School Funds in the hands of the Canal
     Fund Commissioners, prior to the 1st of
     January, 1836, - - - - $2,735 61 9
Amount of money arising from the sale of Ohio
     Lands, the year ending Nov. 15, 1835,   64,549 84 7
     of money arising from tolls collected on
     the Miami Canal, - - -   51,134 25 0
     of money arising from tolls collected on
     the Ohio Canal, - - -   186,522 89 2
  " paid by A Kelly, Esq. on sale of State
     Lots, donations, &c. - - -   4,700 07 0
     arising from the sale of Virginia Mili-
     tary School lands, - - -   3,684 85 3
     arising from the sale of United States
     Military School lands, - - -   7,173 16 8
  " arising from the sale of Connecticut
     Western Reserve School lands,   13,045 90 3
  " arising from the sale of Salt Lands, for
     the use of Common Schools, . -   1,068 27 0
     arising from the sale of School Section,
     No. 16, - - - -   73,654 90 9
  " amount of said fund remaining in the
     Treasury on the 15th Nov. 1834,   101,052 59 4

                              $509,322 37 5

By amount paid Canal Fund Commis-
     sioners, the year ending
     Nov. 15, 1835, $413,946 84 2
     paid John Johnson, Esq.
     Canal Commissioner, as
     per act of last General
     Assembly, - -   2 79 00
     paid B. Tappan, Esq. Ca
     nal Commissioner, as per
     act of last General As-
     sembly, - -   108 00
     paid A. Kelley, Esq. Canal
     Commissioner, as per act
     of last General Assembly,   225 00
  " paid B. Tappan, Esq. Ca-
     nal Commissioner, for 5

days attendance at the
meeting of said Board, and
300 miles travel,   -   -   51 00
" paid B. Tappan, Esq. Ca-
nal Commissioner, as per
act, fixing the compensa-
tion of the Canal Commis-
sioners,   -   -   -   102 00
" paid A. Kelly, Esq. per
ditto,   -   -   -   69 00
" paid John Johnson, Esq.
per ditto,   -   -   -   48 00

	414,828 84 2
Amount remaining in the Treasury Nov. 15th, 1835,	$94,493 53 3

LITERARY FUND.

The amount of said Fund remaining in the Treasury Nov. 15, 1834, - - - -	$221 95 2
" paid in of said Fund, the year ending Nov. 15, 1835, - - - -	2,101 96 0
	$2,323 91 2
Deduct the amount paid out the year ending Nov. 15, 1835, - - - - - -	1,358 72 0
Amount remaining in the Treasury Nov. 15, 1835,	$965 19 2

ROAD FUNDS.

MIAMI AND WESTERN RESERVE ROAD.

The amount of money arising from the sale of said lands, and transferable to the general revenue, - - - - -	14,885 78 0

UNITED STATES ROAD.

The amount of said Fund remaining in the Treasury Nov. 15, 1834, - - - -	$4,313 71 6
" of tolls collected on said Road, the year ending Nov. 15, 1835, - - -	16,442 26 0
	20,755 97 6

2 A R

The amount drawn from the Treasury for said road,
by the Superintendent, the year ending
Nov. 15, 1835, - - - -   18,702 45 6

Amount remaining in the Treasury Nov. 15, 1835, $2,053 52 0

THREE PER CENT. FUND.

The amount of said Funds remaining in the Treasu-
ry Nov. 15, 1834, - - - $11,468 51 8
The total amount received from the United States,
which accumulated on land sold in this
State from the 1st day of January, to
December 31st, 1834, - - -   17,243 89 0

     28,712 40 8
Deduct the amount paid counties, the year ending
Nov. 15, 1835 - - - -   10,064 00 0

Total amount remaining in the Treasury Nov. 15,
1835, - - - - -   18,648 40 8
The following will exhibit the situation of said Fund,
on the first day of January, 1836:
Deduct the amount distributed and undrawn on the
15th day of Nov. 1835, - - -   1,392 17 6

Total amount subject to distribution on the 1st of January, 1836, - - - - $17,256 23 2

RECAPITULATION.

Balances remaining in the Treasury on the 15th day
of Nov. 1835, to wit:
     "   of the Virginia Military School Fund, $4,290 04 2
     "   of the United States Military School
         Fund, - - - - -   9,635 58 2
     "   of the Literary Fund, - -   965 19 3
     "   of the Miami and Western Reserve
         Road Fund, - - - -   14,885 78 0
     "   of the United States Road Fund, -   2,053 52 0
     "   of the Three per cent. Fund, - -   18,648 40 8
     "   of the Miami Canal Fund, - -   36 00 0

ITEMS OF EXPENDITURE.

Members, Clerks, and Door Keepers, of the General
Assembly, - - - - - - - $43,987 59 0

Officers of Government, - - - - -	20,828 43	0
W. W. Gault, Keeper of the Ohio Penitentiary, -	1,909 14	0
Ohio Penitentiary, - - - - -	46,050 67	0
State Printer, - - - - - -	12,243 89	0
Counties apportionment of taxes paid in through this Office, - - - - - - -	8,638 23	0
Paper for the use of the State, - - -	4,478 82	5
Wolf Scalp certificates, - - - -	2,824 00	0
Distributing, cleaning, and storage of public arms,	792 70	0
Adjutant and Quarter Master Generals, and Brigade Inspectors, - - - - - -	2,276 42	0
Double entries, - - - - - -	1,032 56	0
Contingent Fund for Governor, - - -	1,506 73	0
" for Auditor, - - - -	2,961 31	0
" for Treasurer, - - - -	324 32	0
" for Secretary, - - - -	730 93	0
Distributing Laws and Journals, - - -	2,013 93	0
Treasurers' mileage in making settlement with Auditor of State, - - - - - -	1,027 84	0
Registers and Receivers of Ohio Lands, - -	503 02	0
New entries from Land Offices, - - -	617 86	5
Librarian, (his salary.) - - - -	321 17	0
Court's Martial, - - - - - -	241 12	0
Deaf and Dumb Asylum, - - - -	5,700 00	0
Periodical Works, - - - - -	400 00	0
Interest paid Athens University, - - -	85 90	0
Bela Latham, postage on documents to Speakers, -	545 77	0
Redemption Fund, - - - - -	183 04	0
Northern Boundary, - - - - -	8,837 58	0
Lunatic Asylum, - - - - -	2,473 31	0
Selecting Maumee Canal Lands, - - -	621 95	0
Samuel Trowbridge, as per appropriation, -	10 00	0
J. J. Hawkins, - - - - - -	47 50	0
H. Kilbourn, as Deputy Sergeant-at-Arms, - -	16 50	0
Frederick Otstott, - - - - -	80 00	0
Adam Brotherlin, - - - - -	336 37	0
William Thomas, - - - - -	31 82	0
Charles Hammond, as reporter to Court in Bank, -	300 00	0
Isaac Cool, for sundry articles furnished Senate, -	4 50	0
Isaac N. Whiting, (paper furnished General Assembly.) - - - - - - -	252 08	0
McCoy & Work, do do do do	91,06	0
Potts & Turnbull, do do do do	64 18	0
Andrew McElvain, - - - - -	48 00	0
Dr. M. B. Wright, (addition to his salary as Physician to O. P.) - - - - - -	100 00	0
Brotherton & Kooken, - - - -	5 12	0
J. W. Yost, - - - - - -	75 00	0

N. H. Swayne, A. Kelly, and G. Swan, the Commit-

tee appoiuted to examine the Auditor and Treasu-
rer of States' Books, - - - - - 180 00 0
Conrad Heyl, (repairs done to the State House,) - 20 50 0
David and Milton Barrett, - - - - - 15 00 0
A. Pinney, (mending and laying down carpets in the
State House,) - - - - - - - 16 00 0
Corey & Fairbank's, for Ohio Reports, - - 300 00 0
Barker & Silvey, Special Commissioners for the
improvement of the navigation of the Muskingum
river, - . - - - - - 4,000 00 0
John A. Bryan, Esq. the amount appropriated to fur-
nish wood for the State House, - - - 500 00 0
Daniel Kerr, Agent to select the Connecticut School
Lands, - - - - - - - 201 64 0
Samuel Fosdick, for returning abstract of election
from Hamilton county, to fill the vacancy occasion-
ed by the resignation of the Hon. R. T. Lytle, - 17 60 0
Members and Clerks of the Board of Equalization, and
articles furnished said Board, - - - 1,960 37 0
United States Road, - - - - 1,022 00 0
W. W. McKaig, Paymaster General of the O. M. 2,000 00 0

Total, - - - $185,853 48 0

UNEXPENDED

Balances of appropriations on the 15th day of Nov.
1835, to wit:

Members, Clerks, and Door Keepers of the General
Assembly, - - - - - - - $10,977 63 0
Officers of Government, - - - . - 171 57 0
State Printer, - - - - - - 139 90 0
Double entries, - - - - - - 3,353 32 0
Adjutant and Quarter Master Generals, Brigade In-
spectors, and Courts Martial, - - - 694 78 0
Paper for the use of the State, - - - 3,628 73 5
Wolf Scalps, - - - - - 2,051 75 0
Distributing Laws and Journals, - - - 2,159 24 0
Contingent Fund for Governor, - - - 1,211 08 3
"   for Auditor, - - - - 115 69 0
"   for Treasurer, - - - - 09 0
"   for Secretary, - - - - 696 02 5
Distributing, cleaning, and storage of public arms, - 4,458 82 0
Ohio Penitentiary, - - - - - 4,016 33 0
Northern Boundary, - - - - - 291,162 42 0

ESTIMATED

Amount of revenue for the support of Government, for the year 1836, is composed of the following items, to wit:

Amount of taxes levied for State and Canal purposes the year 1835, - - - - - -		142,854 15 0
Deduct defalcations, - - -	4,200 00 0	
Treasurers' fees, - - -	6,428 43 0	
Canal's proportion of revenue, -	23,809 02 0	
Total, - -		34,457 45 8
Nett balance for revenue purposes, - -		$108,416 70 0
Add Miami and Western Reserve Road Fund transferrable to the revenue, - - - - -		14,885 78 0
Tax on Banks and Insurance Companies, -		27,000 00 0
Lawyers and Physicians, - - - - -		1,500 00 0
Total, - -		$151,802 48 0

Deduct the amount necessary for the

	Penitentiary, -	$40,000 00 0	
"	support of Government,	89,000 00 0	
"	deficit of revenue 15th Nov. 1835, - -	33,799 07 9	
	Total, - - - - -		162,599 07 9
Estimated deficit in the Treasury Nov. 15th, 1836,			$10,796 59 9

ESTIMATED

Amount of the several Funds which may be applied to the payment of interest on Canal loans and School Funds, for the year 1836, composed of the following items, to wit:

Balance of Canal Fund in the Treasury Nov. 15, 1835, - - - - - - -			$94,493 53 3
Amount of tolls and donations, - - - -			270,000 00 0
"	Ohio Canal Lands, - - - -		40,000 00 0
"	School Lands, - - - -		100,000 00 0
	Total, : : : : :		$504,493 53 3

Deduct amount of interest on foreign

   loans, - - $260,000 00 0

 "   domestic,   do 41,000 00 0

             301,000 00 0

Balance applicable to the Sinking Fund, - - $203,493 53 3

 The foregoing exhibits the transactions of this department of the State Government, for the year just closed. The recommendation which accompanied my two former Reports, for dispensing with a return to this office, of the several items of personal property embraced in the county duplicates, has been carried into effect under a law of the last winter session of the Legislature; and the aggregate of the personal property, *only*, is hereafter to be incorporated in the several County Auditor's returns. This salutary measure will prove a saving of some expense to the State, and essentially obviate many of the inconveniences arising from the former practice in this particular.

 At a prior Session of the Legislature, provision was made for taking A REVALUATION OF THE REAL PROPERTY OF THE STATE. This important measure, which the increasing wealth and prosperity of the State seemed to demand, has been carried into successful operation, under the law in question; and the additional amount of taxable property, which has, in consequence, been brought into the service of the State, on the *Grand Levy*, since the revaluation of 1825, is $45,730 07 0. *The aggregate* of the taxable property of the State, for the year ending Nov. 15, 1834, was $75,593,212, shewing an increase in one year, of $19,750,665.

 If we go back still further, we will find that this increase has arisen, mainly, if not exclusively, from the unprecedented rapidity of our settlements, and the important changes effected through the instrumentality of our admirable system of internal improvements;—and the contrast cannot fail to appear the more palpable and striking, when we extend our view to the early history of the State, and see from what small beginnings, in a short period, we have arisen to a powerful State—to that condition of agricultural and commercial wealth which places us almost by the side of New York and Pennsylvania, and which, for rapidity of growth, and enlarged resources, is without its parallel in the history of any other member of the confederacy.

 We have arrived at that period in the progress of OUR SYSTEM, when a short, comparative view of the *past* with the *present*, may be deemed of some public importance. Hitherto, this office has confined its ANNUAL REPORT to the actual condition of the revenue, and the public disbursements. But in this, many interesting facts and particulars will be found embodied, shewing the great changes which the hand of industry has effected, and the rapidity with which we are moving forward in the march of prosperity and internal wealth.

So far back as 1809, the number of acres of land returned for taxation, was 9,924,033. The amount of taxation, on this return, for the same year, was $63,991 87 1.

In 1810, the quantity of land, taxable for State purposes, was 10,479,029 acres, and the taxes paid into the Treasury for the same year, were $67,501 60 5.

In 1811, the acres of land returned, were 12,134,777, and the taxes for that year, were $170,546 74 5, shewing an increase from 1809, of upwards of one hundred thousand dollars. But our public resources were even then in their infancy.

From 1811 to 1816, the average increase of the taxes, paid by the several counties, was $59,351.

This latter period may be considered as the commencement of our rapid advancement to our present condition of prosperity. Although the amount of taxes received, are always more or less fluctuating from year to year, the receipts into the Treasury should always, nevertheless, bear some relative proportion to the actual improvements of the country. By Legislative anactment, the *per centum* to be levied is often reduced, so as to materially lessen the amount of the revenue collected.

For several years following 1816, the quantity of lands returned as taxable, did not materially vary; nor was the aggregate of taxation greatly increased. In 1820, the number of acres thus returned, was something rising of 13,000,000, while the aggregate of taxes, as reported to the Legislature, was only $205,-346 95 5. But in 1826, 1827, 1828, 1829 and 1830, a material change was effected; a change in the amount of property taxable, from a few hundred thousands, to rising of FIFTY MILLIONS. By the returns of the past year, the total value of the taxable property of the State, exclusive of three or four counties from which returns have not been received, amounts to the sum of NINETY FOUR MILLIONS, FOUR HUNDRED and THIRTY SEVEN THOUSAND, NINE HUNDRED and FIFTY ONE DOLLARS.

The successful operations of the government, it is well known, depend in a great measure, on the skilful and economical management of the public finances, and the important charge confided to this office, is, consequently, felt to be one of deep and abiding interest to the people. The support of the public credit, and the protection of the revenue, are intimately interwoven with the duties of the public servant, in whatever situation he may be placed; and this great essential has ever been regarded by the citizens of Ohio, as one of the foundation pillars of true independence and freedom.

With this object in view, the amount annually drawn from the Treasury, has been, except in a very few instances of pressing public importance, barely sufficient to meet the ordinary demands of the government, and to provide for such improvements as our actual facilities seemed to justify. But no system of public economy will warrant an entire forbearance of all public expenditure. Our means of internal improvement are extensive and commanding. Canals, Rail Roads, and other great sources of industry and enterprise, are constantly multiplying around us; and in almost every portion of our State and country, they form the very centre point of attraction. These improvements, when successfully carried into execution, form the grand arteries of our internal commerce and trade; and it should be the policy, as it is the obvious interest of the people, to encourage and sustain them. Indeed, the public welfare demands that all the great works now in progress and in contemplation, should be regulated by an enlightened *system* of public economy; and that when guided and supported by the *public voice*, they should always bring back a *public benefit*, in at least an equal ratio with the expenditure made. A diversity of individual interests, it is true, will be found to mingle, more or less, in all these projects; but it is the great purpose of the government to look to the general good, and to the advancement of the common interests of the *whole people*, rather than that which gives to one section, advantages which are withheld from others. The revenue of the State, is the money of its citizens; and that portion of it which remains, after meeting the annual expenses of the government, if drawn from the Treasury for any purpose, should be judiciously applied to the advancement of the common well being of the country.

One item in the disbursements of the financial year, which closed on the 15th of November last, was incurred under the law of the last session, for running and re-marking our Northern Boundary line, and the Legislation consequent upon the prosecution of that great undertaking. This expenditure, when the magnitude of the subject is taken into consideaation, is comparatively small; and, as the amount thus paid, exceeds the ordinary annual expenses of the government, I have thought proper to notice it in this communication. The appropriation by the Legislature, to meet this object, and to prosecute our claim to the territory in dispute, was $300,000. The expenses of the extra session, called to deliberate upon the proper measures to be adopted in reference to the course pursued by the authorities of Michigan, was $6,823 30.

The actual amount paid from the Treasury, on the order of the Governor, including the pay of Commissioners, Officers and individuals connected with the boundary controversy, as it stands upon the books of this Office, is $8,837 58; and, considering the nature of the subject in conflict, and the multiplied embarrassments attending the firm maintenance of the position assumed by the State, this expenditure is but trifling in amount—and it should form a subject of mutual felicitation with the people of Ohio, that, by a judicious course of proceeding, so light a call has been made upon our finances; and that, through a commendable forbearance on our part, an open rupture was so far avoided, as to preserve, unimpaired, the interest and credit of the State.

A REVENUE SYSTEM, in which so many important public principles are involved, should never be fluctuating or uncertain. It is impossible, it is true, to foresee every emergency which may make a call upon the public Treasury: and the graduation of the receipts of the revenue, with the actual expenditures of the government, is consequently attended with some difficulty. This arises from the necessity of the *annual estimates* required to be made for the current expenses and disbursements of the ensuing year.

By a reference to the first part of this report, in which the general disbursements of the year are recapitulated, a deficit of $33,599 07 9, will be found in the general revenue. But this amount of deficiency is principally balanced by the monies drawn from the Treasury, for the expenses of the extra session of the Legislature—the amount paid the State Printer—the appropriation made for clearing and improving the Muskingum river;—the appropriation for running and remarking the northern boundary line, and the payment of troops, &c. The deficit in the revenue, as set forth in my last annual report, was $16,622 72 3, which makes a part of the sum now due that fund. The whole amount of these expenditures is nearly $40,000, which would have left in the Treasury, if unexpended, a *surplus* of more than the *five thousand and ninety six dollars*, as estimated in my report of 1834. This deficiency in the estimated revenue of last year, is thus accounted for, but such provision should be hereafter made, as will avoid the possibility of all future contingencies on the subject.

The reduction of the *per centum* on our *canal tax*, from one and a half to the fourth of mill on the dollar, has fallen short of

3 A. R.

meeting the interest on our domestic loans. By an act of the Legislature, of last winter, it was made the duty of the Auditor of State, to *fund* so much of the interest as had accrued on the Connecticut Western Reserve School Fund, prior to the 1st day of January, 1835, amounting to $15,055 86 3; also, the interest arising on the whole of said fund for distribution, after the 1st day of June, 1836, which makes, unprovided for, the sum of $22,293 64 2.

The estimate of tolls on our Canals for 1835, was $260,000. When that estimate was made, it was thought amply moderate, but the actual returns from the different Collector's Offices for the year ending Nov. 1, 1835, are twenty-two thousand. three hundred and forty two dollars, less than this estimate. In Pennsylvania, which was behind Ohio in her great works of internal improvement, (though greatly our superior in her present resources,) the revenue derived from her Canals, for the year ending Oct. 16th, 1835, as I have recently learned, was $1,231,566, or more than five times the amount received into our Treasury from the like source.

In New York, where this policy was first introduced, and where the system has met with astonishing success, the amount of tolls received, is still much greater. By information recently received from that State, the tolls of the present fiscal year, ending Oct. 15, are $2,212,600, or more than nine times the amount of our receipts for the like period. From whatever cause the public expectation has failed to be realized in the receipts of our Canal Tolls for the current year, it may be found upon proper examination of the subject, that some essential facilities may be hereafter given to this important branch of the public revenue.

In looking into the condition of the Treasury of the United States, whose economical example it may be well for every State in the confederacy to follow, we find, at this time, a *surplus* of about SIXTEEN MILLIONS, notwithstanding the recent heavy drafts upon it for the payment of the national debt. The receipts into that department of the General Government, from the sales of the public lands alone, for the current year, amount to the unprecedented sum of SIX MILLIONS OF DOLLARS. This is rising of two millions and a half over the receipts of any former year, demonstrating most clearly, that our public resources are in a state of advancement and success unknown to any prior period in our history.

The Secretary of the Treasury of the United States, in remarking upon the receipts from these sales, for the year, 1831, which were then $3,000,000, observed, "that they had *gone beyond all former example:*" and as a component part of the monies from these sales, have flowed from the Land Offices in this State, Ohio is a participator in the benefits, and must share in the public advantages to be derived from them.

Some of these important facts are alluded to in this communition, to sustain my position as to the rapid settlement and growth of the State, and the promise we have of its future advancement. The sales of these lands, while giving an *impetus* to the enterprise and industry of the country, are also adding to the means of internal communication among the people. Two very important public works are now in progress through the very heart of our north-western counties, where most of the unsold lands are situate; and as it is to be expected that all that part of them belonging to the State, will be speedily brought into market, (from which an increase of revenue will be derived,) the rapid settlement and improvement of all that desirable portion of country must necessarily follow.

The THREE PER CENT. FUND, which is set apart and designed exclusively for the improvement of roads and bridges, is greatly enhanced by the progress of these sales;—and in a new and thriving country like ours, where the soil is rich and productive, nothing is found more welcome with the people; the early emigrant, than the application of a portion of this fund, to the improvement and repair of roads. Small as is the apportionment made to the several counties, when contrasted with the general revenue of the State, it is, nevertheless, an item of value,—an item, conveying relief to many who suffer,—to numbers of that class of our worthy fellow-citizens, who, from their very location, are excluded from the convenient means of intercourse with the world.

The poor man of the country, the early western settler, bears up under the privations incident to his condition, without a murmur; and he contents himself as a citizen, with the guaranty of that principle of our free constitution, which provides that equal rights and equal privileges shall be extended to every class of the community.

The better to bring in all the objects of taxation, many important laws have been passed, and great changes have taken place, from time to time, in the amount of the *per centum* to be levied for State and Canal purposes. One important alteration which I have to recommend in the existing law, relative to the plan of paying taxes, is to require all the payments, as well from non-residents, as resident land holders, to be made in the county where the property is situate. This subject, which has ever been viewed as one of some public importance, has been previously brought to the notice of the Legislature, and I repeat it in this place, in the hope of its meeting with the deliberate consideration and definitive action of the present General Assembly, should they deem the change suggested, invited by the public interest.

It may not be out of place in this communication, to advert to our existing foreign debt, the present aggregate amount of which, is $4,400,000.

The legal annual interest on this sum, is $260,000. Our domestic debt, which arises from the different school funds of the State, is $579,287 09, and the interest upon the latter sum, per annum, is $34,757 22. Our Canal tolls, for the year just *closed,* amount to $242,357 20 7, and the receipts from the sale of *Ohio* Canal lands for the past year, amount to $64,549 84 7; so that these two items of revenue, as may readily be seen, are more than sufficient to pay the interest accruing upon our canal loans. The amount of sales of these lands, at the State Land Offices, will necessarily diminish, from year to year; but not, probably, in an equal ratio with the actual receipts into the Treasury, from the increase of transportation and business upon our Canals. It was a wise provision in the law of this State, requiring the levy of an annual tax, to meet the interest upon the *canal loans;* and by the salutary operation of this important measure, OHIO STOCKS now command a high character abroad, and the credit of the State is placed upon a permanent foundation.

The amount of money, annually received into, and disbursed from the Treasury, varies from two hundred thousand to two hundred and fifty thousand dollars. This is exclusive of the several drafts, made through this office, upon the Canal fund, which amount annually to about five hundred thousand dollars; making in all, rising of SEVEN HUNDRED THOUSAND DOLLARS.

The tabular statement, appended to this report, (marked A,) exhibits the total amount of the monthly receipts from tolls and collections, made upon the Ohio and Miami canals, from Nov. 1st, 1834, to the 31st of October, 1835; also, monies paid for water rents, &c., during the same period.

The tabular statement, (B,) shews the number of acres of land, and the value thereof, in the several counties, including houses, mills, &c., together with the amount of the State and Canal tax, upon lawyers, physicians, school houses, &c., and the aggregate amount of the taxes of the State for 1835.

The sources of the public revenue are not numerous in Ohio. The several school funds afford the greatest amount of productive capital to the State of any of our available means, the interest upon which yield a large annual income. This fund stands

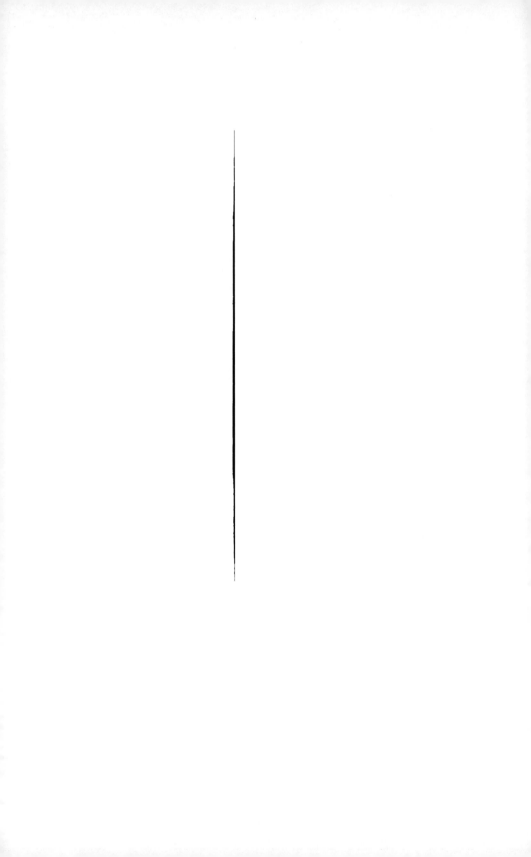

ANNUAL REPORT

OF

THE TREASURER OF STATE,

TO THE

General Assembly of the State of Ohio;

BEGUN AND HELD IN THE CITY OF COLUMBUS,

MONDAY, DECEMBER 7, 1835.

Columbus:

JAMES B, GARDINER, PRINTER TO THE STATE.

ANNUAL REPORT.

TREASURY OFFICE,

Columbus, Dec. 9th, 1835.

The Treasurer of State, in compliance with the duties assigned him by law, submits to the Honorable, the General Assembly of the State of Ohio, the following statement of the receipts and disbursements of public money, from the 15th Nov. 1834, to the 15th Nov. 1835, to wit:

The amount received for taxes, &c. between the 15th
Nov. 1834, and the 15th Nov. 1835,   -   -   201,766 50 4

From which deduct the following payments, viz:

Deficiency in the general revenue, for the year ending Nov. 15, 1834,	16,622 72 3	
The amount of audited bills redeemed between the 15th Nov. 1834, and 15th Nov. 1835, - -	182,905 55 0	
The amount of interest paid on the School Fund arising from the sale of section 16, - - -	22,331 61 0	
The amount of interest paid on the U. S. Military School Fund, -	4,743 14 1	
The amount of interest paid on the Virginia Military School Fund, -	6,026 94 0	
The amount collected for Canal purposes, and transferred to the Canal Fund, - - - -	2,735 61 9	
Total, - - - -		235,365 58 3

Making a deficiency in the general revenue, which
has been paid out of the other funds, of   - $33,599 07 9

The amount of Virginia Military School Fund, remaining in the Treasury, Nov. 15th, 1834, was   5,196 95 2

The amount received for rent of said land, between Nov. 15th, 1834, and Nov. 15th, 1835,   -   4,157 92 0

The amount of interest on the Irreducible Fund, for the year ending January 1st, 1835,   -   -   -   6,026 94 0

         Total,   -   -   15,381 81 2

From which deduct the amount paid on drafts drawn by the Auditor of State, on said Fund, between the 15th Nov. 1834, and the 15th Nov. 1835,   -   -   -   -   11,091 77 0

Balance of said Fund in the Treasury,   -   -   -   4,290 04 2

The amount of the United States Military School Fund, remaining in the Treasury, Nov. 15th, 1834,   16,259 43 9

The amount of interest on the Irreducible Fund, for the year ending 1st January, 1835, is   -   -   4,743 14 1

         Total,   -   -   21,002 58 0

From which deduct the amount paid on drafts drawn by the Auditor of State, on said Fund, between the 15th Nov. 1834, and the 15th Nov. 1835,   -   -   -   -   11,367 26 0

Balance of said Fund in the Treasury,   -   -   9,635 32 0

The amount of interest on the fund arising from the sale of School section 16, for the year ending January 1st, 1835,   -   -   -   -   -   -   22,331 61 0

From which deduct the amount paid on drafts drawn on said Fund, for the year ending Nov. 15th, 1835,   22,162 91 6

Balance of said Fund remaining in the Treasury, $168 69 4

The amount of the Miami Canal Fund remaining in the Treasury, Nov. 15th, 1834, was   -   -   -   20,016 47 0

The amount received from the sale of lands granted by Congress for the extension of said Canal, from the 15th Nov. 1834, to the 15th Nov. 1835. - - - - - 146,953 07 0

Total, - - - - 166,969 54 0

From which deduct the amount paid on drafts drawn by the Auditor of State on said Fund, for the year ending Nov. 15th, 1835, - - 166,933 54 0

Balance of said Fund in the Treasury, - - $36 00 0

OHIO CANAL FUND.

The amount of said Fund remaining in the Treasury, Nov. 15, 1834, was 101,052 59 4

The amount of tolls, &c. received between the 15th Nov. 1834, and the 15th Nov. 1835, was - - 242,357 21 2

The amount of revenue collected for Canal purposes, for the year 1835, after deducting the interest on the Irreducible School Funds, is - - 2,735 61 9

The amount received from the sale of lands granted by Congress to aid the State in the construction of the Ohio Canals, for the year ending Nov. 15th, 1835, - - - - 64,549 84 7

The amount received for the sale of School section 16, from the 15th Nov. 1834, to the 15th Nov. 1835, - - 73,654 90 9

The amount received for the sale of Virginia Military School Land, for the year ending Nov. 15th, 1835, - 3,684 85 3

The amount received for the sale of U. S. Military School Lands, for the year ending Nov. 15th, 1835, . - 7,173 16 8

The amount received for the sale of Salt Reserve Lands, for the use of Common Schools, for the year ending Nov. 15th, 1835, - - - - - 1,068 27 0

The amount received for the sale of Connecticut West. Reserve School

Lands, during the year ending Nov.
15th, 1835, - - - - - - - 13,045 90 5

        Total, - - - - - - - - , 509,322 37 5

From which deduct the amount paid on drafts drawn
by the Auditor of State on said Fund, for the year
ending Nov. 15th, 1835, - - - - - - - 414,828 84 2

Balance of said Fund in the Treasury, - - - - $94,493 53 3

The amount of the Literary Fund remaining in the Treasury, Nov. 15th,
1834, was - - - - 221 95 2
The amount received into the Treasury on account of said Fund, for the
year ending Nov. 15th, 1835, 2,101 96 0

        Total, - - 2,323 91 2

From which deduct the amount paid
on draft drawn by the Auditor of
State on said Fund, between the 15th
Nov. 1834, and 15th Nov. 1835, - - 1,858 72 0

Balance of said Fund in the Treasury, 965 19 2

The amount of the Miami and Western
Reserve Road Fund remaining in the
Treasury Nov. 15th, 1834, 10,934 12
The amount received of the Superin-
tendant of said Road for the year
ending Nov. 15th, 1835, - - 3,951 66

Amount of said Fund in the Treasury, - - - 14,885 78

The amount of the United States Road
Fund remaining in the Treasury,
Nov. 15th, 1834, - - - 4,313 71
The amount of tolls collected and paid
into the Treasury for the year end-
ing Nov. 15th, 1835, - - - 16,442 26

        Total, - - - 20,755 97

From which deduct the amount paid on
drafts drawn by the Auditor of State

on said Fund, between the 5th Nov.
1834, and 15th Nov. 1835, - 18,702 45

Balance of said Fund in the Treasury, - - 2,053 52
The amount of the Three per cent. Fund
  remaining in the Treasury Nov.
  15th, 1834, - - - - 11,468 51 8
The amount received of the General
  Government on account of said Fund
  between the 15th Nov. 1834, and the
  15th Nov. 1835, - - - 17,243 89 0

    Total, - - $28,712 40 8

From which deduct the amount paid on
  County Auditor's drafts between the
  15th Nov. 1834, and 15th Nov. 1835, 10,064 00

Balance of said Fund in the Treasury, - - 18,648 40 8

Aggregate balance in the Treasury, - - $111,577 41 0

RECAPITULATION.

The amount of the Virginia Military School Fund
    remaining in the Treasury Nov. 15th,
    1835, - - - - - $4,290 04 2
" United States Military School Fund, 9,635 32 0
" School Section 16, - - - 168 69 4
" Miami Canal Fund, - - - 36 00 0
" Ohio Canal Fund, - - - 94,493 53 3
" Literary Fund, - - - 965 19 2
" Miami and Western Reserve Road Fund, 14,885 78 0
" United States Road Fund, - - 2,053 52 0
" Three per cent. Fund, - - 18,648 40 8

    Total, - - - - $145,176 48 9

From which deduct the amount of deficiency in the
    general revenue account, - - 33,599 07 9

Aggregate balance in the Treasury, - - $111,577 41 0

From the above report, it will be seen that there is a deficiency in the general revenue, of thirty-three thousand five hundred and ninety-nine dollars seven cents nine mills, which sum has been paid out of other funds.

It was deemed proper to pursue such a course as there were funds in the Treasury, that most probably would not be drawn for, until they could be replaced from the receipt of taxes for the ensuing year, thereby saving to the State, the interest that would have accrued on the deficiency above stated.

In the funds counted as general revenue, there is rising nine thousand dollars of unavailable funds, which, added to the above would make the present deficiency in the general revenue rising forty-two thousand dollars.

Respectfully submitted,

J. WHITEHILL,
Treasurer of State.

Lightning Source UK Ltd.
Milton Keynes UK
UKHW020624120219
337137UK00005B/531/P